THE 1917 OR PIO-BENEDICTINE CODE OF CANON LAW

THE
1917 OR PIO-BENEDICTINE CODE OF CANON LAW

in
English Translation

with
Extensive Scholarly Apparatus

Foreword by
Most Rev. John J. Myers, S. T. L., J. D., J. C. D.

Dr. Edward N. Peters
Curator

IGNATIUS PRESS SAN FRANCISCO

Latin edition: Codex Iuris Canonici, Pii X Pontificis Maximi, iussu digestus; Benedicti Papae XV, auctoritate promulgatus. Praefatione, fontium annotatione et indice analytico-alphabetico ab emo Petro Card. Gasparri, auctus. Published by P.J. Kennedy & Sons, New York, 1918

Cover design by Roxanne Mei Lum

ISBN 978–0–89870–831–8
Library of Congress control number 00–109336
Printed in the United States of America ♾

CONTENTS

THE CODE OF CANON LAW

First Book
General Norms
Canons 1–86

Second Book
On Persons
Canons 87–725

Third Book
On Things
Canons 726–1551

Fourth Book
On Procedures
Canons 1552–2194

Documents

FOREWORD

It has not been uncommon in the course of Church history to refer to the "sacred canons". In an age when even loyal Catholics sometimes consider canon law as a necessary evil this may appear strange. Yet, Pope John Paul II when promulgating the 1983 Code of Canon Law did not hesitate to include that older tradition which considered canon law to be a sacred discipline. Its roots are found in Sacred Scripture, in both the Old Testament and the New Testament. The synods and councils which characterized Church life from the beginning invariably included disciplinary provisions rooted in the teaching and faith of the Church. Over the centuries a great body of law grew out of the Spirit-led life of the Church in the most diverse cultural settings.

The law was drawn together in various collections, perhaps the greatest being the multi-volume *Corpus Iuris Canonici* upon which people relied well into the twentieth century. Cardinal Gasparri, acting under the mandate of Pope St. Pius X and then Pope Benedict XV, worked to codify the canon law following a pattern that extended from Justinian through Napoleon to modern European States.

Cardinal Gasparri and his collaborators succeeded brilliantly, as can be ascertained from the study of the Pio-Benedictine Code which served the life of the Church for over sixty years. Codification in this form was a new feature for the Church. It brought order and also focused Church discipline for the realities of the twentieth century.

I can remember Fr. Henry J. Hahn, a priest of the Peoria Diocese who was my pastor for many years. He was ordained a priest in 1911 and died in February 1983. Thus, he served as a priest during the time of the *Corpus Iuris Canonici*, under the 1917 Code, and was alive when the 1983 Code was promulgated. He always had a sense of how deeply rooted the law is in the life of the Church.

This sense of continuity in faith, teaching, and discipline is critical for today. Some claim that the Second Vatican Council introduced discontinuity even in matters of faith. An associated strain of thought seems to hold that canon law began with the 1983 Code. As a result, they often take a shortsighted and even positivist view of the canons. They consider words and phrases and "tease" their meaning in an attempt to change the life and teaching of the Church inappropriately. Such should never be the case.

Dr. Edward Peters has rendered scholars and students of the law a major service in this volume. Acknowledging that facility with Latin may be in short supply among canonists and pastoral personnel today, he provides a fine translation of the 1917 Code. He facilitates a much broader and deeper acquaintance with canon law by references to doctoral dissertations, official interpretations, and associated documents. Those who wish to teach and work within the long and living canonical tradition of our Church will find Dr. Peters' work very helpful indeed. He is to be congratulated for perceiving this need and meeting it with diligence and expertise.

✠ Most Reverend John J. Myers, S.T.L., J.C.D.
Peoria, August 1999

CURATOR'S INTRODUCTION

Since almost no one is left alive today who remembers the Roman Catholic Church when she was *not* governed by a single code of canon law, the monumental significance of the Pio-Benedictine Code of Canon Law[1] (promulgated in 1917 and in force until 1983) and the inestimable contribution made by its chief architect, Pietro Cardinal Gasparri (1852–1934), regrettably escape all but a few specialists in the history of ecclesiastical discipline.

When Giuseppe Sarto assumed the papacy in 1903, canon law had functioned as an independent ecclesiastical discipline for nearly one thousand years, and, as an adjunct to theology, it traced its roots back at least an additional five hundred years.[2] But the distillation of what, over those fifteen hundred years, had become a vast and confusing collection of canonical materials into a single authoritative reference known as a code had patiently to await the coincidence of a genius like Gasparri and an administrator like Pope St. Pius X.[3]

---

[1] *Codex Iuris Canonici Pii X Pontificis Maximi iussu digestus, Benedicti Papae XV auctoritate promulgatus* (Typis Polyglottis Vaticanis, 1917) [hereafter, 1917 CIC]. The entire work is called the 1917 Code of Canon Law, commemorating the year it was promulgated (although it did not take full effect until 1918), or the Pio-Benedictine Code of Canon Law, after Popes St. Pius X, who inaugurated the project, and Benedict XV, who saw it through to completion. Either appellation is correct. All extant versions of the 1917 Code are textually reliable, even though there are slight variations from printing to printing. These discrepancies are of the simple typographical error sort, and there is no need to note them as variants.

[2] Histories of canon law in English are regrettably few, but, besides Cardinal Gasparri's preface to the 1917 Code available herein, see R. C. Mortimer, *Western Canon Law* (Berkeley: University of California Press,1953), Constant van de Wiel, *History of Canon Law* (Louvain: Peeters Press, 1991), and J. Alesandro, "General Introduction", *The Code of Canon Law: A Text and Commentary*, ed. J. Coriden, T. Green, and D. Heintschel (New York: Paulist Press, 1985), esp. pp. 1–8.

[3] Besides being an accomplished professor of canon law and a highly respected Vatican official, Gasparri was also a recognized expert in the history of western civil law in general and of Roman law in particular. Pope St. Pius X, besides his personal holiness, was also, as it turned out, the only pope of the twentieth century to assume the papal throne after many years (some

During its sixty-five-year enforcement period, the 2,414 canons of the 1917 Code were never translated from the original Latin and published in English as an entire work. Indeed, translations of the 1917 Code were forbidden, at least in part to assure that disputes about the application of what was, for the Church, a revolutionary legal structure would be resolved within the language of the Legislator, and not according to the scores of languages amid which the 1917 Code operated. Moreover, since a comfortably high percentage of the ecclesiastical administrators con-sulting the code were conversant with Latin, such a restriction raised few problems.

Notwithstanding the restriction on translations, of course, vernacular versions of the canons appeared over the years in various articles, reviews, and monographs. For example, Archbishop Amleto Cicognani, one-time Apostolic Delegate to the United States, translated into English the eighty-six canons of Book I of the code (or about 3 percent of the text) for use in his historical commentary.[4] More ambitiously, Msgr. John Abbo (an Italian who taught in the United States) and Fr. Jerome Hannan, later bishop of Scranton, gave English renderings of most of the canons of Books I–III of the code (representing some 60 percent of the total text) in the course of their two-volume commentary.[5] Finally, Fr. Stanislaus Woywod, a Franciscan canon and civil lawyer, paraphrased in English nearly every canon of the code in the course of his own two-volume commentary.[6] None of these authors, however, claimed to be translating the 1917 Code (nor did any claim permission for their renderings), and in fact, an examination of their work indicates that what they produced was more akin to

---

seventeen) of experience as a parish priest, from which vantage point he knew well the difficulties pastors confronted when trying to apply canon law, as it then existed, in the concrete circumstances of grass-roots ecclesiastical life. See generally J. Noonan, *Power to Dissolve: Lawyers and Marriages in the Courts of the Roman Curia* (Cambridge: Harvard University Press, 1972), esp. pp. 159–65. For a brief description of Pope Benedict XV's personal contribution to the 1917 Code, see Walter Peters, *The Life of Benedict XV* (Milwaukee: Bruce Pub. Co., 1959), pp. 202–12.

[4] Amleto Cicognani, *Canon Law*, 2d rev. English ed. (Philadelphia: Dolphin Press, 1935), esp. pp. 444–860.

[5] John Abbo and Jerome Hannan, *The Sacred Canons: A Concise Presentation of the Current Disciplinary Norms of the Church*, 2 vols. (St. Louis: Herder, 1952). Abbo-Hannan is often, but mistakenly, thought of as a pantextual commentary. Actually, only about one hundred pages out of some 1,700 are devoted to a survey of penal law, and hardly twenty-five pages are spent on procedural law.

[6] Stanislaus Woywod, *A Practical Commentary on the Code of Canon Law*, 2 vols. (New York: Wagner, 1925). This work was later revised by Rev. Callistus Smith, O. F. M.

a paraphrase, however graceful, for the convenience of those administrators whose Latin was too rusty to admit of utility in applying the law.

Today, the Pio-Benedictine Code is no longer the law of the Roman Catholic Church, having been replaced by the 1983 Code of Canon Law promulgated by Pope John Paul II.[7] In startling contrast to Pio-Benedictine discipline, however, numerous vernacular translations of the 1983 Code have been readily approved by Vatican authorities. These translations, while not supplanting the binding Latin text of the law, make the application of modern canon law much easier for Church leaders and render its content much more accessible to researchers from a variety of fields. Meanwhile, though, the yellowing pages of the 1917 Code seem more than ever to envelop some mysterious religious discipline; at present, the 1917 Code exists only in the shrouded domain of clerical academe.

This situation requires immediate repair.

Consider: the 1983 Code of Canon Law, governing the ecclesiastical life of nearly one billion Roman Catholics, did not drop whole and entire as if some gift from heaven; it did not emerge fully formed, or even nearly so, from the final sessions of the Second Vatican Council. Rather, it was the fruit of sixteen years of painstaking drafting, during which time those charged with producing the new law had the documents of Vatican II (conveniently translated) on one hand and the 1917 Code of Canon Law on the other. It is impossible to understand and appreciate the accomplishments or the failings of the 1983 Code without a thorough grasp of the accomplishments and the failings of the 1917 Code. One might as well try to assess the 1983 Code without reference to the Ecumenical Council that inspired it. It simply cannot be done.

Additionally, the Church never wholly discards anything of value, even if she goes on to make use of things more valuable still. Beyond all dispute, the Pio-Benedictine Code was a work of great administrative and pastoral value. It should come as no surprise, then, that the old law has not been wholly discarded. The Legislator, while abrogating the 1917 Code in favor of the 1983 Code (see 1983 CIC 6), nevertheless expressly calls upon the former law for help in understanding and applying the newer: "In case of doubt", he declares in Canon 23 of the 1983 Code, "the revocation of

[7] *Codex Iuris Canonici auctoritate Ioannis Pauli PP. II promulgatus* (Typis Polyglottis Vaticanis, 1983) [hereafter, 1983 CIC]. The document is referred to as the 1983, or revised, Code of Canon Law.

pre-existing law is not presumed, but later laws are to be related to earlier ones and, insofar as it is possible, harmonized with them."[8] Common sense impels an understanding of what preceded as part of understanding what is.

Of course, few ecclesiastical administrators come to their tasks with a facile grasp of Latin any more, a fact which makes their consultation of the original text of the Pio-Benedictine law very difficult. As a result, the administrative and pastoral insights gained over a millennium and a half and epitomized in the 1917 Code lie essentially untapped in our day, hardly three generations after their first confection and barely one generation after their juridic conclusion. At the same time, greatly increased numbers of lay persons who are otherwise uninitiated into pastoral and theological sciences, or at least into canon law, find themselves personally or professionally interested in the past and present enunciation of ecclesiastical rights and obligations. Ironically, the very Council which spelled the end of the 1917 Code also launched a veritable tidal wave of active lay people with a serious need—although they often do not appreciate this fact—to understand the legal history made by, and summarized within, the 1917 Code. With rare exceptions, though, these people have no Latin whatever. As a result of such factors, most of what little research is currently being done into the 1917 Code is limited to locating paraphrases of individual canons scattered throughout the commentaries on the old law (which are themselves increasingly hard to find as the years since their final publication continue to accumulate), rather than in directly accessing and discussing the text of the law itself, albeit in translation. Hardly a satisfactory situation.

This translation seeks, therefore, to serve two ends: first, obviously, to present in one place a reliable English translation of the entire text of the Pio-Benedictine Code, including its famous preface, its enabling legislation, and the most important of the supplemental documents originally incorporated therein;[9] second, insofar as the 1917 Code was a living doc-

[8] "In dubio revocatio legis praeexistentis non praesumitur, sed leges posteriores ad priores trahendae sunt et his, quantum fieri potest, conciliandae." (1983 CIC 21). Canons 6, 17, and 19 of the 1983 Code provide additional support for consulting the provisions of the older law in attempting to determine what precisely is the modern discipline.

[9] Gasparri had included as supplements to the 1917 Code all or part of eight legislative documents, each designed to flesh-out various canons of the old code. Document 1, Pope Pius X Constitution, *Vacante Sede Apostolica* of 25 December 1904, dealing with the governance of the Church during a vacancy in the Apostolic See, was referenced in 1917 CIC 160, 241, 262, and

ument subjected to official interpretations, emendations, and scholarly reflections, to identify where such pronouncements on and major studies of the text can be found in English, allowing researchers to determine the extent to which such additional information might be relevant to their own studies.

This second goal is achieved easily enough. Immediately following the text of each Pio-Benedictine canon there are citations to the places, if any, where official information on that canon was reported in the ten volumes (nearly 8,500 pages) of *Canon Law Digest*.[10] Because virtually all the materials in *Canon Law Digest* are already translated into English, those using this translation of the 1917 Code will find it very easy to trace the subsequent official development of any individual canons. Moreover, thanks to those faculties of canon law who made their canonical dissertation lists available, I have footnoted nearly one thousand scholarly English works under the specific canon, or at times set of canons, to which their topics referred.[11] Finally, next to each Pio-Benedictine canon number, there fol-

---

2330. Document 2, Pope Pius X Constitution, *Commissum Nobis* of 20 January 1904, also dealt with pontifical elections. Document 3, Pope Leo XIII Constitution, *Praedecessores Nostri* of 24 May 1882, likewise dealt with pontifical elections. Since, however, these documents were replaced not once but several times by later popes during the enforcement period of the Pio-Benedictine Code, their translation was omitted in this work. See, however, John Griffiths, *Apostolic Constitutions of the 20th Century Regulating the Election of the Supreme Pontiff and Their Historical Foundations* (diss. 1665, 12 January 1997). Document 4, Pope Benedict XIV Constitution *Cum illud* of 14 December 1742, dealt with appointment to office by concursus and was referenced in 1917 CIC 459, and Document 5, Pope Benedict XIV Constitution *Sacramentum Poenitentiae* of 1 June 1741, dealing with the sacrament of penance, was referenced in 1917 CIC 884 and 904. These two documents also had only limited impact on the development of future provisions, and they were omitted from this work for reasons of space. Documents 6, 7, and 8, however, referenced in 1917 CIC 1125, which dealt with special marriage situations, because they contributed notably to the development of Church law in this area, are included in English translation following Canon 2414 of the 1917 Code, which is where Gasparri also placed his documents.

[10] The first six volumes of *Canon Law Digest* were brought out by Bruce Publishing of Milwaukee. The last four volumes were published by the Chicago Province of the Society of Jesus. The series, which now numbers eleven volumes, is currently under the care of the Canon Law Society of America, with editorial offices at Caldwell Hall, The Catholic University of America, Washington, D.C., U.S.A., 20064.

[11] Canonical dissertation lists for the Catholic University of America (Washington, D.C., with 487 reported dissertations in English) and the University of Ottawa/University of St. Paul (Ottawa, Canada, with 33 reported dissertations in English) were published in *The Jurist* 50/2 (1990) at pp. 684–719, and *Studia Canonica* 22/2 (1988) at pp. 431–47, respectively. That for the Pontifical University of St. Thomas Aquinas (Rome, with 154 reported dissertations in English

lows in parentheses a correlation to the place, if any, wherein the same topic is addressed by the 1983 Code.[12]

Regarding the first goal, however, the translation itself, only those who have translated a lengthy work can know the innumerable crises of conscience that such a project imposes. To misappropriate some words of St. Bernadette, for this small group, no explanation of translation choices is necessary; for all the others, no explanation will impress.

---

after 1929) is found in Angelo Urru, *La Facoltà di Diritto Canonico della Pontificà Università di San Tommaso d'Aquino in Roma: Cento Anni di Storia* (Tipolitografia Pioda sas: Rome, 1998), which work was provided by its author. That for the Pontifical Gregorian University (with some 138 dissertations in English after 1934) was derived variously from its *Elencho Tesi Stampate dal 1934 al 1983, nn. 1–3121*, and other partial lists. That for the Pontifical Lateran University (with 51 dissertations in English reported between 1941 and 1968) was kindly supplied by Dr. Philip Milligan. A private dissertation list from the University of Maynooth (Ireland, with 13 reported dissertations in English after 1934) was kindly provided by Ms. Patricia Hearn. That for the Royal and Pontifical University of St. Thomas (Manila, with 7 dissertations in English reported after 1936) was kindly provided by Rev. Javier González. That for the Pontifical University "Antonianum" (Rome, with 2 reported dissertations in English after 1934) was kindly provided by Dr. Nikolaus Schöch. That for the Pontifical University Comillas (Madrid, with 3 reported dissertations in English after 1938) was kindly provided by Fdo. Luis Vela Sánchez. That of the University of Laval (Quebec, with 7 dissertations in English reported after 1940) was kindly provided by Ms. Diane Poirer. That for the Pontifical Salesian University (1 dissertation in English after 1940) was kindly conveyed by Rev. Prof. Piero Giorgio Marcuzzi. Mr. Kurt Martens of the Catholic University of Louvain located 7 dissertations in English in various years. Sr. José Enériz kindly confirmed that there were no English language dissertations from the University of Navarra (Spain), going back to 1960. Abbé Bernard David did likewise for the Catholic Institute of Toulouse going back to 1925. Other pontifical and ecclesiastical faculties of canon law did not respond to my requests for copies of their dissertation lists. From these faculties, only those dissertations consequently, of which I was aware from other sources are listed herein, along with some of the more notable English-language monographs on canon law. Some dissertations, however, could not reliably be assigned to a specific canon or group of canons. These works are listed by category in Appendix I: Non-assigned Dissertations. Due to space and time limitations, no consistent attempt was made herein to distinguish between those dissertations available only in manuscript form versus those later published in book or other forms. Such information, to the extent needed, would be available from the above institutions.

[12] Several nearly identical sets of correlations between the 1917 Code and the 1983 Code have been published by various groups, chiefly the Canon Law Society of America, the Canon Law Society of Great Britain and Ireland, and the Canadian Canon Law Society. My correlation, somewhat simplified, draws on all three of these, though with a few personal modifications. Following the correlation to the 1983 Code, I have also listed as a cross-reference any Pio-Benedictine canons which made reference to the subject canon. There are over 500 such cross-references in the 1917 Code; curiously, these were never collected and set out clearly. Cross-references which included six or more canons are listed in Appendix 2: Multiple Express References within Canons.

As an Anglo-American degreed and licensed in the common law before I came to canon law, I have a reverence for the actual text of the law. Thus, despite the fact that it is not clear to me that Continental law, or at least curial canon law, shares the same devotion to precision and concision in legal drafting with which I was originally trained, I have chosen, for the most part, to render a more literal translation of the Latin text than others would perhaps have done. I do this because I believe *how* the law says what it says is second only in importance to *what* the law says. In any event, it seems better to allow others to assess the significance of the manner of expression used by the Legislator in each canon rather than to impose the conventions of American English, or my own preferences, on his text.

In one other respect, this translation of canonical materials differs from others in that I have not permitted any so-called "untranslatable" Latin words or expressions to appear herein. With due respect for the canonical translations that attempt no English renderings of terms such as *latae sententiae*, *restitutio in integrum*, *fatalia legis*, *ad beneplacitum nostrum*, and so on, I believe that such canonical concepts can be and ought to be conveyed in English through the use of English words invested with the same special meanings as developed over time for each of these Latin expressions. To hold otherwise would not demonstrate the obvious, namely, that Latin is not English, but rather imply that some ecclesiastical, specifically juridical, concepts can never quite be explained to the mass of Catholics not privileged to know Latin.

As for other matters of translation, I generally tried to respect the voice of verbs, though I at times moderated Gasparri's heavy use of the passive to help the law avoid coming across as "sterile" or "heavy". There also seemed to me little consistency in the original text in presenting concepts in the singular or in the plural. I freely chose whichever number seemed more functional in context. On the other hand, with rare exception, capitalizations, italicizations, use of parentheses, and abbreviations follow that of the original Latin (even where it was inconsistent), and not conventional English.[13] I respected the Latin sentence unit as well as most clauses

[13] The abbreviations used in the 1917 Code are chiefly the following: "const." stands for "constitution"; "H." stands for "Holy"; "H. R. C." stands for "Holy Roman Church"; "Prop." stands for "Propagation"; "S." stands for "Sacred". References to the "City" mean Rome. I chose to spell out and capitalize the word "canon" whenever the 1917 Code made reference to a specific provision thereof. I also chose to capitalize the words "Christian", "Catholic", and "Marian" to conform with long-standing English usage, although these terms are lower-cased in Latin.

set off by semicolons. The 1917 Code's infrequent use of colons, however, was too inconsistent to retain, and I freely placed and dropped commas in this translation for ease of reading and sense. I hope I chose wisely in these matters, but, despite these and other precautions, doubtless I am guilty in this translation of many of the same sins (chiefly, inconsistency of expression) that I attribute to the original text. For that I apologize.

It is a maxim of political science that no revolution is reckoned successful until it peacefully hands over power to its successors. The 1917 Code, which took ecclesiastical discipline from the unwieldy realm of disparate collections and placed it within the sure confines of a single code, was the greatest revolution in canon law since the time of Gratian. The peaceful advent of the 1983 Code, which obviously retains the theory, structure, and even much of the content of the Pio-Benedictine Code, shows that the canonical revolution that Cardinal Gasparri and Popes St. Pius X and Benedict XV worked was a success.

But let there be no mistake: even as I write, here on the threshold of the third millennium, codified ecclesiastical law is still in its infancy. To date, less than 5 percent of Church history has been spent under an integrated code. The presence of the 1983 Code shows that the first steps that the Church took toward bringing its legal system under control were worth following up on, and there remains very much to be learned from that initial attempt. This pantextual translation of the Pio-Benedictine Code, and the scholarly apparatus which supports it, is nothing but an aid for those finer minds and purer hearts who, coming after, will conduct those studies.

Edward N. Peters, JD/JCD
Ann Arbor, Michigan

RESEARCHING THE 1917 CODE IN ENGLISH

There is more research material on the 1917 Code of Canon Law available in English than in any other language except Latin. Although many factors contributed to this surprising situation, chief among them must be that North America was spared, not one, but two Continental wars (with the concomitant social and political chaos) during the sixty-five-year enforcement period of the Pio-Benedictine Code, and it did not suffer the loss of large parts of its territory and resources to Communist domination for nearly half a century. Thus English-speaking ecclesiastical life in general, and American Catholicism in particular, was conducted during the period of the 1917 Code amid great political stability, by superabundant ecclesiastical personnel, amid relatively extensive financial resources, all of which factors fostered the formidable intellectual gifts of English-speaking scholars and canonists. It was a confluence of factors, alas, not likely to be repeated for some time.

All canonical research into the Pio-Benedictine Code begins, of course, with the text of the law itself. This English translation of the 1917 Code now makes accessing the law by those without a ready grasp of Latin an easy matter. As directed by Canon 18 of the first code, however, researchers must consider not only the text of the law, but its context as well, along with other places in the Code which treat of the same or similar topics. The answer to a canonical question, or at least the complete answer, seldom lies within a single canon. This is why the internal correlations of the 1917 Code are useful.

Having examined the text of the law, a researcher must then study any official pronouncements on or applications of the canons. Simply finding these pronouncements in any language other than English is, to put it bluntly, a most tedious task. But thanks to the work of Jesuit scholars Lincoln Bouscaren (a theologian and civil lawyer) and James O'Connor (theologian and canon lawyer) this research has been greatly simplified for readers of English. Beginning in 1934 and concluding in the last days of the Pio-

Benedictine law (1983), these men collected and, where necessary, translated thousands of official interpretations of, pronouncements on, and applications of the 1917 code and then assigned each resulting document to at least one specific canon of the old code. Their work, known as the *Canon Law Digest*, spanned ten volumes during the life of the 1917 Code. The only deficiency in this Herculean project, namely, the lack of a comprehensive index, has been remedied by this translation of the 1917 Code, which obviates the need for an index by listing, after each translation, exactly where, if at all, each canon was subjected to digest by Bouscaren and O'Connor.

At this point, one's canonical research shifts from the examination of original sources (albeit in translation) to the study of private, scholarly works on the law. For sheer erudition and depth of commentary, one must recognize canonical doctoral dissertations (sometimes called theses) as having pride of place. Most such dissertations or theses not only present coherently the various opinions of the commentators on various canons (discussed in more detail below) but they usually offer a historical background for the debate over various canons and some suggestions for resolution of such disputes in the practical order. At a minimum, no scholarly contribution to the understanding of a canon of the 1917 Code is possible without taking into consideration the dissertation(s) that might have been produced on it.

The Catholic University of America in Washington, D.C., produced nearly five hundred doctoral dissertations on canon law in English during the period of the 1917 Code, more than the combined English-language output of all other canonical faculties in the world. Lists of CUA dissertations are accessible to researchers, and nearly all of the works themselves can be obtained, in one form or another, with relatively little effort. Note, however, that many dissertations treated of matters separated by some distance in the 1917 Code, and to keep the footnotes from becoming unwieldy, each dissertation is listed only once, generally under the canon which most closely, or which first, corresponded to the general topic of the dissertation.

After taking into account the words of the law in text and context, and how the law was evaluated by leading scholars, one will turn next to standard commentaries on the law. There are several multi-volume, pantextual commentaries on the 1917 Code of Canon Law in English. In order of author, the major ones are as follows:

John Abbo (an Italian canonist and papal diplomat with various duties in North America) and Jerome Hannan (vice-rector of Catholic University of America and later bishop of Scranton) wrote *The Sacred Canons*, a highly regarded two-volume work. It appeared in various editions, being first published in 1952 by Herder of St. Louis. Although considered by many as pan-textual in scope, the work actually concentrates on Books I–III of the 1917 Code (comprising over 1,600 pages), while summarizing sanctions (Book V) in just over one hundred pages and treating of procedures (Book IV) in hardly twenty-five pages. The commentary is consistently insightful and reliable. Most of the canons discussed by Abbo and Hannan in Books I–III are also paraphrased or practically translated.

Dom Augustine (né Charles Bachofen), a Benedictine monk writing from Missouri, penned his eight-volume *Commentary on the New Code of Canon Law* over several years. This work appeared in various editions by Herder of St. Louis. Paraphrases of some canons are worked into the text, but generally Augustine assumes the reader's facility with the Latin original. Besides the high level of scholarship expected in a comprehensive work, Augustine, more than any other author in English, attempted to explain the 1917 Code in light of pre-code law, citing such authorities as Reiffenstuel and Schmalzgrüber with some frequency.

Stanislaus Woywod was a Franciscan priest trained in civil law. His two-volume *Practical Commentary on the Code of Canon Law* was first published by Wagner of New York in 1925 and went through numerous editions, the later ones revised under the direction of fellow Franciscan Callistus Smith. The work is considerably more scholarly than its "hand-bookish" title would indicate. Virtually every canon is carefully discussed and, although Woywod only claimed to be paraphrasing the text of the old code, many of his renditions of canons read more like thoughtful translations than mere paraphrases. There are frequent allusions to civil law counterparts of various canonical institutions, some of which comparisons are rather dated by this point but which are always illustrative of their subjects.

Each of these works should be consulted for a thorough grounding in English-language positions on Pio-Benedictine canonical issues. A few one-volume works should, however, also be listed for their utility in general research.

Lincoln Bouscaren (referenced above) and fellow Jesuit Adam Ellis produced in one volume what quickly became the standard seminary textbook on canon law, *The Canon Law: Text and Commentary*, published by

Bruce of Milwaukee. The book appeared in numerous editions, the last of which was supervised by Francis Korth, S.J. The commentary, while geared to student needs, is generally reliable. It omits discussion of most procedural issues. Also, Patrick Lydon, a priest of the Diocese of Duluth in Minnesota, authored a large, one-volume handbook of canonical terms and institutions, much like a dictionary. Called *Ready Answers in Canon Law*, it appeared in various editions by Benziger beginning in 1934 and would serve well as an general orientation to canonical topics, especially for those encountering unfamiliar issues in the course of their research.

Numerous academic journals serve the English-speaking researcher of Pio-Benedictine canon law.

The Jurist, published quarterly (and more recently, semi-annually) by Catholic University of America since 1940, is the flagship of professional academic journals of canon law in English. *The Jurist Seminar*, also from Catholic University of America, appeared from 1941 to 1953 and was geared more to historical topics. The *American Ecclesiastical Review*, published almost entirely in English, appeared more or less monthly from 1890 until the mid-1970s. This multi-disciplinary journal contained a wealth of canonical studies and many full-length articles on canon law. It is an undervalued resource for canon law.

Studia Canonica was first published in 1966 and has appeared under the auspices of St. Paul's College/University of Ottawa semi-annually since then. Approximately half of the articles therein are in English, and the French articles have an English synopsis available for consultation. *Canon Law Abstracts* is published semi-annually by the Canon Law Society of Great Britain and Ireland. For many years, this small but invaluable journal has abstracted into English canonical articles from a wide range of publications appearing in numerous languages. Complete citations are offered, of course, for those who wish to consult the original works. The *Newsletter* of this Society often runs short studies of scholarly (as opposed to more practical) substance on various topics.

Finally, one should not hesitate to consult general theological dictionaries and encyclopedias, as they frequently contain entries on canon law by respected authors.

ACKNOWLEDGMENTS

My wife, Angela, my oldest son, Thomas, and my good friend James Akin spent uncounted hours typing hundreds of canonical translations as I dictated them at odd hours of the day and night, and along the way each of them asked questions and made observations that helped me refine the final version in many places. These three, along with my second son, Charles, and daughter Catherine, helped me assemble multitudinous correlations, and my other children always made sure I had plenty of tea and crackers, spiced with enthusiastic love, when I most needed it. Without the help and support of all of these people, I simply could not have finished what I started.

I am also grateful to all of my Latin teachers and friends over the years, notably Dr. Joseph Koterski, S.J., Dr. John Petrucione, Dr. Frank Mantello, Dr. Elizabeth McDonough, O.P., Fr. Suitbertus Seidel, O. Carm., and Jan Halisky, Esq.

The translation of *Providentissima Mater* I took, with slight modifications, from A. Cicognani, *Canon Law*, 2d revised edition, authorized English translation by J. O'Hara and F. Brennen (Philadelphia: Dolphin Press, 1935) at pp. 441–43, who in turn, however, took it from *The American Ecclesiastical Review* 57 (October 1917): 357–60.

The translation of *Cum iuris canonici* I took, with slight modifications, from the *Canon Law Digest*, 1:55–57.

The translation of the brief quotation from the Council of Trent that Gasparri included in Canon 2214 I took, with slight modifications, from H. Schroeder, *Canons and Decrees of the Council of Trent* (Rockville, Ill.: Tan Books, 1978).

The translations of Document 6, Pope Paul III Constitution, *Altitudo*; Document 7, Pope Saint Pius V Constitution, *Romani Pontificis*; and Document 8, Pope Gregory XIII Constitution, *Populis*, I took, with slight modifications, from Francis Burton, *A Commentary on Canon 1125*, Canon Law Studies, no. 121 (Washington, D.C.: Catholic University of America Press, 1940).

Pope Saint Pius X

Launched the first codification of the Church's legal system.

Pope Benedict XV

Oversaw completion of and promulgated the 1917 Code after the death of Pope Saint Pius X.
(© Bettman/CORBIS)

Pietro Cardinal Gasparri

Architect of the Pio-Benedictine Code of Canon Law.

Charles Bachofen, O.S.B.

Swiss-born canonist who came to the United States and was better known by his religious name, Dom Augustine. Author of an eight-volume pan-textual study, *Commentary on the New Code of Canon Law.*

(Photo used with permission of Conception Abbey, Conception, Missouri.)

T. Lincoln Bouscaren, S.J.

Canon and civil lawyer, founder of the *Canon Law Digest* and co-author of the widely used textbook *Canon Law*.
(Photo used with the permission of the Midwest Jesuit Archives, St. Louis, Missouri.)

Adam Ellis, S.J.

Co-author of the very influential two-volume work, *Canon Law: A Text and Commentary.*
(Photo used with the permission of the Midwest Jesuit Archives, St. Louis, Missouri.)

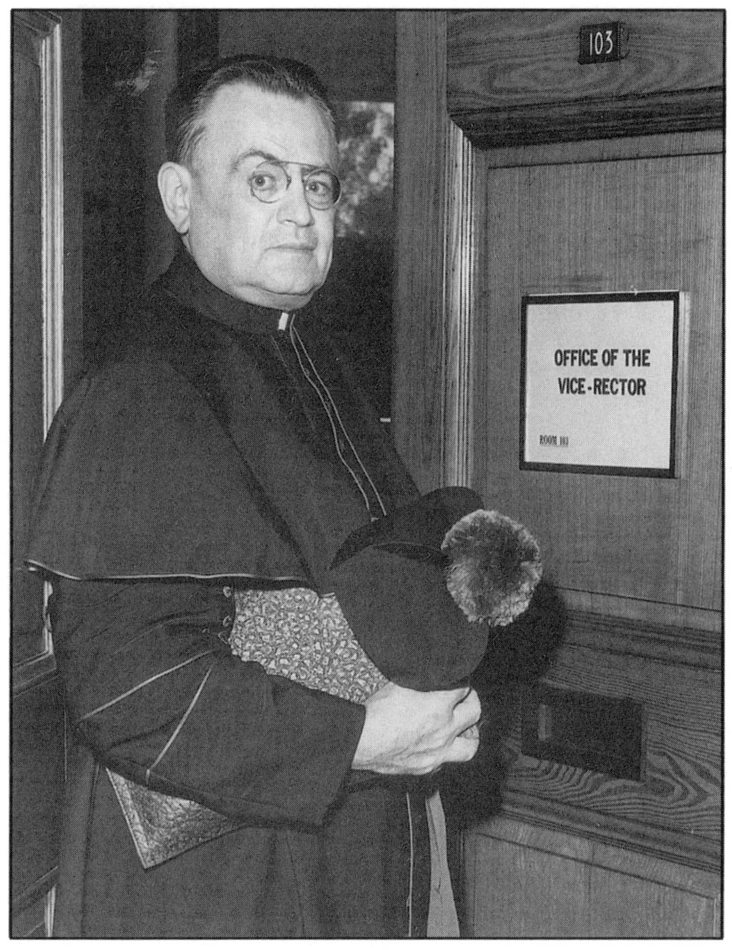

Jerome D. Hannon

Professor of canon law and later bishop of Scranton, co-author of the very influential two-volume work, *The Sacred Canons.*
(Photo used with permission of the Diocese of Scranton.)

James I. O'Connor, S.J.

Continued the *Canon Law Digest*.
(Photo used with the permission of the Midwest Jesuit Archives, St. Louis, Missouri.)

Callistus Smith, O.F.M.

Revised Woywod's influential *Practical Commentary on the Code of Canon Law.*
(Photo used with permission of the Holy Name Province, O.F.M.)

Stanislaus Woywod, O.F.M.

A canon and civil lawyer, author of the widely used two-volume *Practical Commentary on the Code of Canon Law.* (Photo used with permission of the Holy Name Province, O.F.M.)

PREFACE

[to the 1917 Code by Pietro Cardinal Gasparri]

It had long been a proposal of the Catholic Church that, just as, at an opportune time, the laws of imperial Rome were redacted into a Body of law, so the sacred canons would likewise be gathered into one, in order that knowledge of them, and their use and observance, would become easier for all. For this reason, no one should be surprised that this syllabus of ecclesiastical law should, after quite a sufficient passage of time, now be produced and published.

Generally speaking, lest anyone remain ignorant, those laws that were laid down before Gratian (between the years 1140–1150) are called, even in our day, the *old law*; those appearing from the time of Gratian until the Council of Trent (1545–1563) are styled the *new law*, even though they seem to us quite old; and those that came out after the Tridentine Synod are called the *newest law*. It is hardly necessary to add regarding the collections of new law treated below that they contain still more ancient laws, that is to say, laws that were promulgated before the time of Gratian.

It is likewise clear that collections of ancient law, without any mandate of the Apostolic See, were compiled by private efforts. In earlier ages, canonical collections were nothing other than the laws themselves, especially those laid down by Councils, arranged in chronological order; among these, one ancient collection of canons from the oriental Councils, especially Nicaea, stands out and is considered the source or font of nearly all the collections of ancient laws that appeared. DIONYSIUS EXIGUUS translated this into the Latin language and additionally collected those outstanding decretal letters of the Roman Pontiffs that were drafted in the 4th and 5th centuries. Truly, the work of Dionysius Exiguus, when it came into use by the Roman Church, carried great weight, and eventually, as it was augmented by additions, the text was given as a gift by Pope Hadrian to Charles, King of the Franks, and, as it were, of the Roman Church; and upon its reception by the Franks, it came to be called by its proper name, *The Book of Canons*.

Among the chronologies that are called collections, there was admittedly in use, until rather recent times, albeit privately, a noteworthy compilation published in the middle of the 9th century, supposedly brought out by Isidore Mercator. This unknown author added to the ample collection received by the Spanish many letters falsely attributed to Roman popes of earlier ages. Nevertheless, there are none today who assert, as contended by enemies of the Catholic name, that the discipline of the Church was even slightly affected internally by the pseudo-Isidorian decretal subterfuge.

And now, beginning about this time, collections that might be called systematic appeared; for in them, canons culled from all parts were, according to their sense and the various matters treated, arranged under various titles, following a certain logic. Throughout the 11th century, not a few of these works were elaborated as an aid to the outstanding men who, being led by the holy Pope Gregory VII, were struggling to protect the rights and liberty of the Church; but the Decree of Gratian virtually eclipsed these.

Before the middle of the 12th century, Gratian, a monk and man of outstanding ingenuity, as he came so well to understand how much it would redound to the common good if all the canons that were then scattered about, and that not infrequently clashed with each other, could be rightly gathered into one place, set about to organize a single new compendium of ecclesiastical law: at first it was called the *Concordance of discordant canons*, but after Gratian himself had departed life, it was known as *Gratian's Decree*. But as it turned out, not only did he produce such a [great] collection, but also, when assessed in the light of its day, he treated the matters so wisely and eruditely that the study of canon law, whether one was concerned with fundamentals or with initial studies, developed with an outstanding utility for the future.

The materials that Gratian took most abundantly for his Decretum came from all of the collections that had come before; innumerable canons of Synods and Decretals of the Pontiffs, and more than enough rescripts, to which he added excerpts of sacred Scripture and works of the holy Fathers [of the Church] and ecclesiastical writers; he even culled things taken from books by the Roman Church and other particular Churches, including the *Roman Ordo*, the *Daily Book of the Roman Pontiffs*, and likewise some things from the [Irish] penitential books; finally he took not a few citations from Roman and Germanic law.

Gratian's Decree at no time received public authority, and, even though the Apostolic See amended and published it, it did not take responsibility for it and never declared it authentic or conferred the force of law on the canons as a whole or on the individual [provisions] that comprised it: everyone can easily see why it would not do so, since so many of these canons depended on highly specific situations. The canons placed in Gratian's Decree are thus shown never to have received any authority beyond what they had from their source, and it need hardly be added that these various collections, especially Pseudo-Isidore, merited no [official binding authority].

After the appearance of the decree of Gratian, two Ecumenical Councils were celebrated, namely, Lateran III and Lateran IV; the pontiffs who, in that age, guided the Church, especially Alexander III and Innocent III, [both of] whom one would rightly number as being among the most outstanding legislators, not only helped the Church with the wisest of laws, but also established some principles of discipline concerning, and this was most important, those things that were until then uncertain or that from use did not have a correct interpretation.

When therefore new collections seemed necessary, or it appeared opportune to complete or supplement the decree of Gratian, some collections were composed one after the other, the most important of which, being five in number, were called *First Collection*, *Second Collection*, and so on. The *First Collection* or *Compilation* (in 1190), whose name was *Breviarium Extravagantium*, was produced by Bernard Papiensis, and it included canons that had escaped Gratian as well as laws laid down later; this work followed an order of subjects and their subdivisions, and through this compendium was presented what the first omitted. That which is called the *Third Collection* or *Compilation* came out under the command and care of Innocent III, it being the work of his companion Pietro Beneventano, sub-deacon and notary of this Pontiff. It consisted of all the decretals laid down from the first to the twelfth year of his pontificate (1198–1210). This work Innocent III promulgated by the apostolic constitution *Devotioni vestrae* on 12 December 1210 [addressed] to the professors and auditors of the University of Bologna, ". . . *so that these may be used free of any scruple of doubt insofar as necessary both in trials and in class.*" Soon thereafter John Gallensis or Wallensis, although charged with no mandate of the Apostolic See, collected into one those laws laid down from the time of Gratian until Innocent III, especially the decretals of Clement III and Celestine III; and for this reason, this *Compilation*, although it was produced after the third, is nevertheless called the *Second*. The *Fourth Compilation* incorporates the decretals of Innocent given up to the year 1215 and the canons of the Fourth Lateran Council, which was held in the meantime, and was produced by an unknown author: several authors, among whom was Pope Benedict XIV under the direction of the same Innocent, could be considered to have produced it. Finally, the *Fifth Compilation* or *Collection*, in which are contained the decretals of HONORIUS III, was composed at the command of this Pontiff, who, in the bull of promulgation *Novae causarum* given on 31 January 1226 [and delivered] to the Bologna archidiaconal professor Tancredum, indicated his intention as follows: "*Thus, for your discretion, We order through apostolic writings that, insofar as these are solemnly published and are free of any scruple of doubt, you shall make use of them and [in order] that they be accepted by others, you shall do this both in trials and in class.*" To sum up, it can be shown with sufficient clarity that of these collections, the third and fifth certainly, and the fourth probably, were authentic; but the first [two] lacked public authority, even though the canons that had been gathered into one retained their original legal force.

With the collections in such a jumbled state, not even trials could be conducted without becoming embroiled in difficulties, whereupon the Apostolic See took it upon itself to produce publicly a new and unified compendium; thus GREGORY IX produced, with the able assistance of ST. RAYMOND of PENAFORT, O. P., the five Books of Decretals, bringing them out in the year 1234. The same Pontiff, in the bull of promulgation *Rex Pacificus* issued on the 5th of September of the same year, set forth most distinctly the reasons why he had taken up such a serious work in these words: "*Obviously the diverse Constitutions and Decretal letters of Our Predecessors, scattered throughout various volumes, some of which are very similar, while others are contrary and some simply so long-winded, seem to lead to confusion; others are wandering around outside the above-mentioned volumes, [a fact] that frequently redounds to confusion in trials, such that We have ordered a reorganization, at the service of common utility and especially for students, through Our beloved son brother Raymond, Our Chaplain and Confessor, of these into one volume, eliminating the superfluous and adding Our Constitutions and Decretal Letters through which some [matters] that were in doubt earlier are declared.*" With all the collections published after the Decrees of Gratian up to that day having been abrogated, he forbade others from being prepared in the future without a special mandate of the Apostolic See: "*Desirous therefore that only this universal compilation be used in trials and in courses, we most strictly prohibit lest anyone presume to produce another in the absence of special authorization of the Apostolic See.*" By this constitution, as is obvious, even the authentic Compilations of Innocent III and Honorius III were stripped of all public authority.

But, with the passage of sixty-four years, when so many laws had been laid down outside of the five Books of Decretals, Boniface VIII added a sixth book to the five, organized under his authority, which supplemented the Decretals of Gregory IX. Boniface outlined his reasons in the bull of promulgation *Holy Roman Church* on 3 May 1298: "*Through such an unfathomable and most high divine providence over the universe, with an unchanging will, he placed Us ruling over the churches, and he wished moreover to bring about a desirable leadership, and so We are consumed with earnest and continuous care, and We are urged by assiduous meditation, so that, in accord with the office of dispensing [authority] accorded to Us, insofar as it has been granted to Us from on high, for the convenience of Our subjects, in whose prosperity We also prosper, We intend to bind Ourselves to careful efforts. We embrace this labor wholeheartedly, for their peace of mind, and We pass sleepless nights in order to remove scandal from their midst. And human nature (always suggesting new ways of doing these things) strives on a daily basis to litigate, now using a declaration from the ancients, now relying on a new version of the law, and insofar as possible, all of this We reprobate. Of course, since [the appearance] of the volume of Decretals of Pope Gregory IX of happy memory, Our Predecessor, that which was so providently and usefully compiled, some others from him and from other successive Roman Pontiffs, on a variety of matters [outside] of these Decretals, have appeared: and so people [are left wondering] whether a given Decretal exists, and there are doubts about their authority appearing both in trials and schools. We are desirous that ambiguity and uncertainty of this type, affecting so many things, be utterly removed and explained, so that [one knows] what should be held according to the Decretals, and what should be rejected in the future—We order that, most diligently, these sorts of Decretals be reviewed and that many be thoroughly excised (since they are of temporary value, or are in conflict with themselves or with other laws, or are simply superfluous), and that those remaining undergo abbreviation and be completely or partly changed, with numerous corrections, subtractions, additions, and finally [that they should be] worked into one Book, and thus We order that Our Constitutions be redacted and collected under the appropriate titles. This Book is to be added to the other five volumes of Decretals, and We order that it be called the Sixth, so that this book, now comprising a sextet with the others, will be henceforth counted along with the others, thus completing their treatment of things and the manner of acting.*" He also addressed those who wanted the five Books of Decretals, with additions being added, to be republished rather than a new book made, speaking thus to them: "*Not without cause have We failed to observe the path of Our Predecessors, lest untold books be destroyed and others could not be made without a great expenditure of effort and money.*" Finally he abrogated all Decretals of his Predecessors that were contained in the *Sexto*, unless they were expressly reserved: "*Therefore We order, by Apostolic words, your Universities [to honor] a Book of this sort, produced with such grave maturity, and which We send under Our Bull to you, taking effect promptly, so that you will make use of it in classes and trials: and no other, besides these, shall be added except those that are specially reserved therein, [even if] they are Decretals or Constitutions from any of our Predecessor Roman Pontiffs, after the promulgation and publication of this aforesaid volume, nor can they be received or considered as Decretals.*"

Moved by nothing but good motives, John XXII added to the six Books of Decretals the Constitutions of his Predecessor Clement V, and taking their name, *Clementinae*, from their author, he promulgated them by the bull *Quoniam nulla*, on 25 October 1317, at Avignon.

When finally at Paris in the year 1500, the *Corpus Iuris Canonici* was ordered to be reprinted, JOHN CHAPPUIS, who oversaw the edition, added both twenty Decretals *Extravagantes* of John XXII that had been attached earlier to the *Clementines* in the form of an appendix since the year 1325 and seventy Decretals *Extravagantes* of other Pontiffs and called therefore the *Extravagantes Communes*, because they were commingled in the *Corpus Iuris Canonici* rather like an appendix; these really ought to have been there [in the first place]. It is clear that neither compendium of *Extravagantes*, insofar as it was a compendium, ever received the approval of the Apostolic See; but it is also clear that the Decretals collected in both, because they were authentic and given for the universal Church, had the force of law in the Catholic world, unless they could be shown to have been abrogated.

These therefore were the principal compendia of the *new law* that [taken together] constituted that work called the *Corpus Iuris Canonici*, although no one can deny that the *Extravagantes* of John XXII and the *Extravagantes Communes* were included therein, since they had been added to the *Corpus Iuris Canonici*, albeit by private counsel. It was this *Corpus Iuris Canonici* that Gregory XIII in the year 1582 ordered to be most accurately republished in its entirety.

From the year 1500 until the convocation of the Council of Trent, no compendium of canons was produced, by either private or public authority. The Tridentine Synod, to which the Catholic Church owes the emendation of the Christian discipline taken from the middle ages, inaugurates the *newest law*; its very Acts could rightly be considered an outstanding compendium of canons on faith and morals.

Gregory XIII, whom we mentioned above, also took care of a new publication of the *Corporis Iuris Canonici* and ordered that a fuller compendium be developed that would include pontifical canons laid down before Trent but not incorporated into the *Corpus*; this eventually resulted in the *Clementinae* or at length the *Extravagantes* of John XXII and the *Extravagantes Communes* that appeared in a Parisian volume in 1500. The death of the Pontiff in the year 1585, after the completion of the twenty-second Tridentine Synod, interrupted the matter that had been entrusted to a Committee of three Cardinals. Sixtus V took up the completion of his predecessor's work, one that he desired to pursue quickly, and assigned the responsibility to Cardinal Pinellio, giving him a group of highly educated men as co-workers in the task; and when, with the task still incomplete, Sixtus himself died, Clement VIII took it up in order to bring the work to conclusion. In August 1598, Cardinal Pinellio handed the same Pontiff a volume that was inscribed *The Decretals of Our Most Holy Lord Pope Clement VIII*; but this new compendium, which stood under such study and labor, for reasons that escape us, went without approval or promulgation. But Book Seven of the Decretals was published under private authority by the legal scholar Peter Matthew of London in the year 1590, and even though it was placed as an Appendix in many editions of the *Corporis Iuris Canonici*, it was nevertheless not approved by the Apostolic See and indeed was listed on the *Index* of prohibited books.

And there the matter rested until our own age; except that Benedict XIV, following in the footsteps of his predecessors, published the constitutions from the first six years of his Pontificate and ordered these collected, promulgating them by letters given to the faculty and students at the University of Bologna; no one can doubt, therefore, that this part of the Benedictine Bulls is considered quite authentic.

Of what remains of the *newest law*, it is contained in the Roman Bullaria that, being a published work of several private men, concluded with the acts of Gregory XVI. Add to this, however, the laws of the following pontificates, the rules of the apostolic chancery, and the decrees and responses of the Sacred Congregations and the Tribunals of the Roman Curia, and in this regard it is recognized by all that the responses of the Congregation of Sacred Rites and Indulgences have been compiled into an authentic compendium of positions.

Under these conditions, until the most recent years, canon law was conducted. From what we have said it should be clear that it was by the wisest counsel of Innocent III, Honorius III, Gregory IX, Boniface VIII, and John XXII that the sacred canons of the Church were collected into one in order that the Christian people would both know them more easily and follow them more surely, but with the additions of following ages, although it remained just as important to follow them, this [goal] was actually weakened over time. Indeed, before our own day, if one really wanted to discover what Church discipline demanded under such-and-such a circumstance, it would require consultation with all of the sources that we have just listed. And one scarcely appreciates how much work the study of canon law had heretofore required: it would be very evident if one took note of the following: (1) one order of time is observed in the Bullaria, in the collections that contain the decrees and responses of the Sacred Congregation and Ecclesiastical Tribunals, in the Acts of the Council of Trent, [and] in the Acts of the Roman Pontiffs who succeeded Gregory XVI; scarcely any [order of time is observed] in the Decree of Gratian; finally, a defective and imperfect [order of time is employed] in other parts of the *Corpus Iuris Canonci*; for example, concerning those things that impede holy orders, which is a convoluted enough subject already, [the topic] is treated in books I, III, and IV, at some points fully and completely, while at other points without any context. (2) Among the documents that are presented in the sources of canon law, several lack all usefulness, and often they amount to an obstacle for the study of canon law, inasmuch as they either repeat the same points made many times before or contain no relevant statute. (3) Some documents offer a response given with respect to a particular case, from which it would be necessary that a universal or general precept be gathered together or extracted; therefore, in documents of this sort, many things [are] superfluous, this [being] the greater number by far, and often the same difficulties [are simply left] for [one's] own effort. (4) Canon law was entirely silent concerning certain [topics]; and therefore, one turned either to Roman law (such as for example to determine the amount of time by which custom was prescribed) or to jurisprudence, or to custom, or to the thinking of the doctors (such as for example in defining the notion of quasi-domicile). (5) Many laws, even though contrary to custom or abrogated by laws laid down later, still existed throughout the Catholic world or in a large part of it, as particular laws in various sources, offering the greatest mental confusion in studies. As an example to confirm this, in common law it was determined that Bishops should be selected from the rank of canons, and almost all chapters of the title *On Elections* pertain to this way of selecting them, even though this [practice] is not in force today except in a few dioceses of Germany and Switzerland; legitimate rites that were to have been preserved in ecclesiastical judgments for the prescripts of the second book of Gregory IX's Decretals, as well as the sixth, have to a great extent fallen into disuse; the concordats into which the Apostolic See entered with the rulers of state, after the *Corpus Iuris Canonici* was completed, alter the common law in a certain respect.

Things being as they were, it was scarcely possible to see canon law any differently from how Livy saw Roman law, "*an immense accumulation of laws on top of laws*" (l. III, c. 34); nor could anyone wonder that those directly affected by laws were often ignorant as to whether a law on this topic or that even existed, or they were left in doubt as to whether the law was still in force, or as to exactly what it meant, even if it concerned an important matter or applied to practice. Thus, in order to make any progress in canon law, to explore not just a sprinkling of sources, but rather to plumb its full teaching, there were only a few clerics up to the task, namely those who were by nature inclined to such studies and who had the time to wade through great piles of books, and all of this, despite the advice of Pope Celestine, which we read in Gratian, in writing to the Bishops of Apulos and Calabros: "*It is not acceptable that any priests be ignorant of the sacred canons, nor indeed to do anything that deviates from the rules of the Fathers*"; and Gregory IX, 1, tit. 2, *On Constitutions*: "*The statutes of the canons are to be observed by all, and no one, in conduct or in ecclesiastical trials, shall side-step their sense or authority.*" Even in our own day, the Apostolic See has not ceased to recommend studies of this sort, and one [ironic] result of this is that precepts given on this matter by several dioceses are neglected. Whatever the factors that have contributed to this situation, whether ignorance or negligence, this for the most part, as we have said, accurately describes canon law [at the beginning of the twentieth century.]

Even to this, finally, one adds another consideration of no small moment, namely, that some ecclesiastical laws initially laid down most prudently, because of a change in the conditions of time and subject matter, had been rendered either difficult to enforce or at least less conducive to the salvation of souls: therefore, it seemed necessary that these be emended in the same way as is the Church, so that this society constituted for men would act consistently in cases not dissimilar. Consider, for example, that in the Fourth Lateran Council the impediment of consanguinity in the collateral line would be contracted [only] up to the fourth degree because "*in further degrees it is not possible without grave expense to observe a wider prohibition*", and yet, for the same reason, many [experts] in later times were of the opinion that an impediment of this sort should be contracted [only to] the third degree. It was similarly suggested on all sides, and rightly so, that in our age some accommodation should temper both the laws that were contained in the decree *Tametsi* and those in force concerning fast and abstinence, and so on.

Weighing all these things together, it is hardly to be wondered why those working in canon law, and so many Bishops throughout the Catholic world, were already persuaded that canon law should be reorganized according to some rationale.

This position suggested itself to the Fathers at the Vatican Council; indeed the Bishops from the year 1865, when they responded to the letters given by the Apostolic See about the Ecumenical Council to be held in Rome, asked the Great Pontiff [about reforming canon law] and even urged consideration of something so clearly to the benefit of the Church; once they were gathered in Council, it was not possible to put off the proposal.

The Neapolitan Bishops spoke first about reorganizing appropriately the sacred canons into one work: "*It seems necessary to produce a new Body of canon law; or at least to begin with a new process for cases that could be more and more expeditious.*"

Many Bishops of France put it this way: "*It is obvious and already known by everyone and proclaimed everywhere that some revision or reform of canon law is necessary and even urgent; indeed under such serious circumstances and in light of the changes within human society, many laws, including useless ones, are impossible to observe or [are possible to observe, but only with] great difficulty. There is ambiguity about countless canons as to whether or not they are still in force. And finally with the passage of the ages, the number of ecclesiastical laws has increased, and more laws are still being added to various Collections of law, so that we can say in a certain sense:* WE ARE WEIGHED DOWN BY LAW. *All of this results in inextricable difficulties in determining the limits of the study of canon law and allows controversies and protracted procedures to occur; this gives rise to a thousand crises of conscience and drives one toward contempt for law.*

"*The Council therefore is most desirous that the great and necessary work of reforming canon law be attended to forthwith; and that this might be more conveniently done:*

"*1) The Council itself should decide upon the most principal and urgent articles of reform and at the same time indicate the mentality and general conception by which the legal reforms should be pursued.*

2) A Congregation should be instituted, made up of the best-educated theologians and canonists, together with practical men taken from all the nations who can devote themselves most attentively to the revision of universal canon law and, rejecting what ought to be rejected, modifying what ought to be modified, and adding what seems should be added, produce a new Body of law that is accommodated to the present state of the Church and organized under titles, chapters, and articles according to the order of the materials, and then propose it for the review and affirmation of this Council or another to be convoked."

The Bishops of Germany put it this way: "*Whereas there are so many prescriptions found in the* Corpus Iuris Canonici *that at present no longer have force of law, it is greatly to be desired that a new collection be made of these canons that are still in force, eliminating those others that are recognized as already being abrogated.*"

The Bishops of Belgium sounded a similar note: "*The Vatican Council having been completed, let His Holiness commit to men well-versed in the sacred canons the task of completely reorganizing the complex of ecclesiastical law into a new Code accommodated to the practice of today and distribute it in various titles, chapters, and so on, according to the variety of the material.*"

And then the Archbishops and Bishops from the ecclesiastical province of Quebec and Halifax stated: "*Let it be proposed that the whole of ecclesiastical law, under the care of the Supreme Pontiff, now that the Vatican Council is completed, be worked into a Codification with the addition of those enactments on subjects that seem more useful and applicable. Our reasons are as follows: (1) knowledge of the law that now consists of innumerable constitutions and canons will emerge more easily and widely; (2) many of these have already fallen into desuetude or have been rendered impossible or can be changed to the great benefit of the Church.*"

Several Bishops from central Italy added: "*Given their concerns that studies of canonical science cannot progress along such a cluttered way as a result of the jumble of laws that presently obtains, they asked that the* Corpus Iuris Canonici *be reorganized most diligently.*"

Thereupon, thirty-three Bishops from various parts of the world signed this proposal: "*In order that ecclesiastical laws gain efficacy in morals, in life, and in the formation of the Christian people, nothing is more suitable and nothing is more opportune than to have [the laws] collected into a single code and arranged in a wise order according to the norm of sacred law and that it be used in trials and taught in schools and applied to daily religious use. Certainly the Roman Pontiffs, when they wisely perceived this, at no time failed to commit efforts in this behalf, in accord with their vigilance and prudence. Innocent III saw this clearly enough, as did Honorius III, in whose edition of the Collection of Decretals further outstanding proofs of special care are sufficiently evident. Further, who can fail to see how well Gregory IX served sacred jurisprudence, under whose auspices, resources, and authority the most complete code of pontifical law was published? Nor is less gratitude due to Boniface VIII, who enriched [and] completed Gregory's work with a very valuable and particularly useful appendix.*

"*But these provident cares by the high pontiffs, although they were quite enough for the standards of earlier days, still leave something to be desired in our own day. There should be no surprise to anyone if he, but for a little while, considers that the disciplinary laws thus need to be accommodated to the diverse conditions of the age, so that they are changed as years pass and increase as new cases occur. Therefore several Constitutions of the Roman Pontiffs and Decrees of Councils have not yet been incorporated into the* Corpus Iuris Canonici, *and yet it is of great importance not only for judgments but also for the science of law that these various things not get lost for a long time. For as long as they are circulated scattered about in numerous documents, as if they were limbs of some body that had been torn apart, it is difficult, given the broad reach of the Christian world, to be properly distinguished by all; even if they are distinguished, there is still need for a carefully worked out awareness of the contexts (a rare achievement) so as to avoid a misunderstanding of times and circumstances in their interpretation.*

"*Having maturely considered all these things, it is now time to entreat earnestly Our Most Holy Lord Pius IX, that, applying the works and genius of the best-educated men of this time, he direct a new codification of canon law and not delay releasing it under Apostolic authority. It is a most difficult task; but the more difficult it is, the more it befits the dignity of such a Pontiff.*"

The Apostolic See certainly saw the necessity of the project and was unable to do otherwise than to grant the request of the Pastors of the Church, at least regarding those things that pertain to correct discipline and that seemed most important to urge. By the counsel of Pius IX, through the constitution *Apostolicae Sedis*, the number of automatic censures was reduced; Leo XIII issued the constitutions named *Officiorum* and *Conditae a Christo*, the first of which provided equitable and accurate regulations on books, the other of which made regulations concerning laws in religious Congregations dealing with simple vows; finally the Sacred Congregation [for Bishops and Regulars], on 11 June 1880, issued an *Instruction* "On the required manner of proceeding expeditiously in ecclesiastical Curias in the disciplinary and criminal cases of clerics." Although the other prescriptions of canon law remained in the state that they had enjoyed up to that time, many Bishops and other Purpled Fathers asked the Apostolic See that [it act] in order to reform canon law and bring it into a more useful order, following the recent example of all the nations, [noting that] they did not doubt that the example of Gregory IX and [the Emperor] Justinian could be followed.

Pope Pius X of happy memory, who, before he entered his pontificate, prudently saw what an outstanding improvement to the Church this kind of reform promised, had already estimated how much time such a work would require, and hardly was the convocation [of his election] concluded at the beginning of the month of March in the year 1904 than he did inquire of the Cardinals of the [Holy Roman Church] who were present in the City what they thought about the proposition, and with the approving counsel of these most Eminent men, he issued to the Catholic world the letter *Arduum sane munus* on the 19th of the same month and announced what had been hoped by many for a long time, [namely,] that he also desired "*that the laws of the universal Church published up to this time, arranged in a clear order, could be collected into one, removing from there those that were abrogated or obsolete, and with the others, where this is necessary, being accommodated to the conditions of our own times.*" In order that this be brought about correctly, by his own motion, with sure knowledge and mature deliberation, he ordered the following:

"*I. We will constitute a Council, or as they say, Pontifical Commission, that will have complete supervision and care of the whole matter and that will consist of some Cardinals of the H. R. C. designated by name by the Pontiff.*

"*II. The Pontiff will preside over this Council, and, in the absence of the Pontiff, the Cardinal Dean will stand over it.*

"*III. There will also be a just number of Consultors whom the Cardinal Fathers will select from among men in canon law and highly expert theologians, with the approval of the Pontiff.*

"*IV. We also desire that the universal Episcopate, according to opportune norms to be given, will contribute to and concur in this most grave work.*

"V. While a precise method for conducting these process is to be developed, the Consultors shall prepare their materials and publish them, being presided over by him whom the Pontiff designates from the Council of Cardinals. The Cardinal Fathers shall deliberate over these things maturely in developing the studies and opinions. Finally, everything will be turned over to the Pontiff, who will make decisions regarding final approval."

Meanwhile, since he had decreed in regard to the aforementioned letter that all bishops should collaborate in so great and so difficult a work as was then being prepared for the good of the whole Church, the Pontiff first of all saw to it that the Cardinal in charge of the public affairs of the Church, by a letter sent to each and every Archbishop of the Catholic world on March 25th of that year, should [in turn] direct them that, having notified their Suffragans and, if there are any, the Ordinaries who ought to participate in a provincial synod, they should, as soon as possible, that is, not more than four months from having received the letter, send back to the Holy See in a brief report their own opinions and those of others as to whether and what sorts of things are needed, especially by way of some change or emendation. Furthermore, to the Bishops of individual nations, the duty was assigned to send to Rome one or another man, outstanding in knowledge of the sacred canons and of theology, selected by common consent, and to be supported by the resources of the bishops themselves, for assignment to the Council of Consultors. But if they should prefer, the Bishops could also designate one of their own who would then be numbered among the consultors by the Cardinal Fathers and could transmit to him what they want to be communicated to the Council of Consultors; or they could even name someone from their own nation who, although remaining outside the City, would offer helpful service to the Consultors by letter. Further, whatever counsel on this matter in a cooperative spirit they may have received, the Bishops of individual nations should send to the Holy See through one regarded as especially worthy or senior among them.

Whereupon the Pontiff established the Council or *Commission* described in the letter *Arduum sane munus*, naming to it the following Cardinal Fathers: Serafino Vannutelli, Antonio Agliardi, Vincenzo Vannutelli, Francesco Satolli, Mariano Rampolla del Tindaro, Hieronimus M. Gotti, Domenico Ferrata, Francesco di Paola Cassetta, François-Désiré Mathieu, Casimiro Gennari, Beniamino Cavicchioni, Andreas Steinhuber, Francesco Segna, José Calasanz Vives y Tuto, Felice Cavagnis, and Raphael Merry del Val. Not long after, in order that the project proceed more quickly and expeditiously, the Pontiff decided to establish another special Council in which he placed the Cardinal Fathers Domenico Ferrata, Felice Cavagnis, Beniamino Cavicchioni, Casimiro Gennari, and José Calasanz Vives y Tuto; as death carried these off, he replaced them with Cardinals Sebastiano Martinelli, Gaetano de Lai, Basil Pompili, Gaetano Bisleti, Wilelm van Rossum, Vincenzo Vannutelli, Michele Lega, and Filippo Giustini.

The Pontiff delegated Cardinal Pietro Gasparri, then Archbishop of Caesarea and Secretary of the Sacred Congregation for extraordinary affairs of the Church, to which Council the acts [of the canonical reform process would] belong: and the actual work, what they called chancery, [took place] in that same Sacred Congregation. He directed, though, that the care of whatever came up in publishing [would be seen to] by the Vatican printing office.

The Pontifical Council addressed things in the beginning so that it could secure for itself, with the approval of the Roman Pontiff, worthy Consultors; it selected members from among the most expert Prelates of the Roman Curia, and from outstanding regular clerical members, as well as other authorities in sacred disciplines, so that all of these, both Italians and foreigners, could be frequently gathered in a short time to make up a complete College over which, at the mandate of the Pontiff, the same Cardinal Gasparri ruled.

Now, again in order that the task might be carried out the more expeditiously, two members of the staff of that College were chosen and formed a committee, or what is called a *Commission*, to accomplish the delicate and scholarly work of suitably considering and editing the canons so as to satisfy every expectation. Now, since there had not been complete agreement, there was need to send the suggested texts to all the Consultors whenever some part of the Code was as ready as possible to be brought to conclusion, so that if any of them found anything that needed to be changed, he could indicate that in writing. Further, besides the Consultors, as many canonists as possible, Italian and foreign, under the title "Collaborators", even if they lived outside the City, provided outstanding assistance.

The various Committees or *Commissions* having been established thus, a specific law was laid down and approved by the Supreme Pontiff on April 11th of the same year, which set forth norms to guide this most serious work and direct the progress of the Committees. By this same law, it was provided that ecclesiastical Institutes, [specifically] those of religious men, as well as their libraries and archives, should, if books were requested of them, supply them without delay, giving interdicts and censures under Pontifical authority for the sake of this project; it also established that Consultors who were bound by choir service, lest by the performance of their duties they suffer any losses, should be absent from choir for the time necessary for meetings, though they nevertheless should enjoy the distributions made to those considered *present.*

When gradually the desires and preferences of the Bishops, complying with the will of the Pope, were sent to the Apostolic See, and those points, after careful examination at a suitable time by the Consultors, had been brought into harmony, it was then discussed whether a vote about the whole matter should be taken, and it was decided that a vote should be called that could, nevertheless, in accord with this law, be rightly considered in a general way, within canon law, a [major preliminary draft], and all this [was done] so that a vote of this type could be held in a timely way, so that a certain anticipation of this work might make more clear how these matters touching on the Code as a whole would at long last be brought to a conclusion, even if, insofar as necessity should require, it [later had to] be amended.

Without further delay, there were selected from among the Consultors and Collaborators those who were to consider and prepare specific parts of the Code about which there still needed to be discussion in particular committees. Those on whom the choice fell complied with a very generous spirit, a fact that we are pleased to remember here. Each heading for a given schema, for example, *on baptism*, *on church burial*, and so on, was entrusted to a pair of Consultors or Collaborators, or, if at times the seriousness of the subject matter so required, even to three or four [of them], but in such a way that one would not know the name of the other or others who were writing about the same subject. Now, these [individuals] rightfully belonged to either the committee or the commission to which the texts that needed to be examined were referred; but when all had been bound by pontifical secrecy, a day was fixed by which they were bound to turn in their *vote* to His Eminence Cardinal Gasparri.

So as to the law discussed above, the Consultors and Collaborators gave the following general directions:

"I. That only those laws should be included in the Code that concern discipline. Nothing prohibits, however, that certain principles can and ought to be worked into the Code that refer to natural justice or to the Faith itself.

"II. That the Consultor or other supervisor of operations diligently shall search out laws for the discipline of the Church, omitting those obsolete or abrogated from the *Corpus Iuris [Canonici]*, the Tridentine Council, from the Acts of the Roman Pontiffs, and from the decrees of the Sacred Roman Congregations or Ecclesiastical Tribunals; these should be distilled into canons and contain only the dispositive part of the law, and that, if it seems expedient, should be subdivided into paragraphs.

"III. The Consultor or other supervisor of operations, in drafting the canons taken from the words of documents, insofar as practical, shall duly note these documents and briefly and clearly reference the other parts of these documents discussing these matters, carefully adding the page and volume and edition, and so forth.

"IV. The Consultor or other supervisor of operations, in serious matters pertaining to practice, where there are various opinions among the doctors, shall propose one and establish it definitely.

"V. But if the Consultor or other supervisor of operations thinks it opportune or necessary to change something from the current law, he shall recast the canon, advising about the subject of the change and briefly giving reasons for it. He could do the same if he thought something new ought to be interjected.

"VI. The Latin language should be used consistent with its dignity insofar as it reflected the majesty of sacred law and was so happily used in Roman law."

Following this rationale of studies, the work of each Committee was undertaken on November 13, 1904. One [Committee] met on Thursday and the other on Sunday each week, various things being assigned to each Committee for discussion. The President sought the thinking of the Consultors, one after another, on individual canons, in whatever manner they were proposed, and these, when they had been freely expressed, he most diligently had entered into the acts. Obviously, if the matter was the same, with no changes being introduced, the following week it would be sent to the individual committees, to be readied for discussion, both to clear up any unclear points and so that more progress could be made. For this reason, in order to avoid all delays, the President himself, from the various schemata of the canons, in light of the *votes* and thinking of each Consultor, would add or remove things that seemed to him should be added or removed, developing thus a more mature schema so that, when typeset, it could be immediately reviewed by the Consultors in their residences and jointly discussed the following week. And thus things went until the Consultors reached agreement among themselves as to how the canon should read. For this reason, nothing is read in the new Code that was not discussed four or five times in the manner outlined above, and sometimes ten or twelve times if difficulties were found. But if perchance, in a certain canon to be worked out, there was lacking common consensus, it was left to the thinking of the majority just how the canon was [to be] constituted according to the norm of law, with concern, however, for the thinking of the minority or what law established in another area. The schemata, developed thus by the particular Committees, was sent to the College of Consultors, so that each could make written reply, and within a certain set period of time, they undertook to refer it all to his Eminence Card. Gasparri. Finally, with regard to the schemata and all of the observations made by the College of Consultors, which was under the care of Card. Gasparri, the most reverend Fathers of the particular Council spoken of above reviewed it at least twice and rendered one more vote.

At the same time, as the parts of the new Code gradually came together, the Supreme Pontiff Pius X ordered that the judgment of the Bishops of the whole Catholic world be sought, and likewise all Prelates of regular Orders who were among those typically called to an Ecumenical Council, and their thinking requested. And so there were sent to all these sorts both the first and second books of the Code, the third and the fourth, and finally the fifth, advising them to return them to the Apostolic See at a given time, adding to them any written observations that they judged opportune. In turn, after his Excellency Card. Gasparri had duly examined and organized them, they were forwarded to the specific Councils who investigated whether, with regard to the desires expressed by the Bishops, the canons should be amended.

While the Code was the object of such intense labor, a terrible event arose, namely, the eruption of the world war in which all of Europe was engaged, and his Holiness, the Supreme Pontiff Pius X, by whose authority and great presence the work of producing the Code had begun to take form, departed this life with the mourning and grief of the whole Catholic world. Despite the death of this Pontiff and the horrors of war that erupted in Italy itself, ten months later there was enough of a [lull] that Pope Benedict XV could happily reach the Chair of Peter, and he was full of hope that the work could be completed quickly. This most Holy Father from the very beginning of his Pontificate made it clear that this was his desire and wish. And so under the patronage and moderation of this same Pontiff, it was continually pursued so that, near the beginning of the third year of his Pontificate, he could foresee and bring about the finishing touches on the new Code.

It was this that the most Holy Father, with mature judgment, set out and approved in the [apostolic] constitution *Providentissima Mater Ecclesia*, given on the feast of Pentecost (27 May) in the year 1917, and he promulgated [the Code] and decreed that it would have force of law for the whole Church beginning on the feast of Pentecost (19 May) of the following year 1918.

And thus the new Code of canon law was published by the Vatican press, and with regard to those things needed for a splendid publication, clearly nothing is lacking. Notes have been added to the canons at the bottom of each page that indicate the various sources from which they were taken: it is scarcely necessary to add that the canons are not always consistent with all of their sources in the parts used, and this is especially true for the penal canons of Book V, where the ancient penal laws are set out, which, although they have penalties attached to them, often differ with the penalties in the new canons. The sources in this edition of the Code—especially those that have been lifted from the ancient *Corpus Iuris Canonici* and the Ecumenical Councils with authority and that have been arranged in temporal order marked with a semicolon (;)—are distinguished unless they treat of something that was raised in the same case before the same Sacred Congregation. Indeed their sources are to be published just as soon as this can be done, in a *Collectaea*, in order to facilitate study; but even this will not contain prescriptions from liturgical books, the Acts of the Tridentine Synod, or the *Corpus Iuris Canonici*.

And so at last by God's help, this first Code of ecclesiastical law, a work perfected by such learned men over twelve solid years, is auspiciously given to all of Catholic name. The Supreme Pontiff Benedict XV, whom God has so carefully protected, issued the promulgation by which this religious discipline is made a permanent fixture. May the most benign God make it so by the prayers of the Blessed Virgin Mary, her holy spouse, Joseph, patron of the universal Church, and with the prayers of the holy apostles Peter and Paul.

APOSTOLIC CONSTITUTION

Providentissima Mater Ecclesia
By Pope Benedict XV
27 May 1917

TO THE VENERABLE BRETHREN AND BELOVED SONS, THE PATRIARCHS, PRIMATES, ARCHBISHOPS, BISHOPS, AND OTHER ORDINARIES, AND ALSO TO PROFESSORS AND STUDENTS OF CATHOLIC UNIVERSITIES AND SEMINARIES

BENEDICT BISHOP
SERVANT OF THE SERVANTS OF GOD

FOR A PERPETUAL REMEMBRANCE

That most provident Mother, the Church, endowed by her Divine Founder with all the requisites of a perfect society, when, in obedience to the Lord's mandate, she commenced in the very beginning of her existence to teach and govern all nations, undertook by promulgating laws the task of guiding and safeguarding the discipline of the clergy and the faithful.

As time elapsed, particularly after she had gained her liberty and, daily waxing stronger, had extended her kingdom, she never ceased to set forth and to define her own inherent right of making laws. Witness in proof of this the many and various decrees of the Roman Pontiffs and Ecumenical Councils which were published as the times and circumstances suggested. By these laws and enactments not only did she make wise provision for the direction of the clergy and people, but, as history bears witness, she promoted also most effectively the development of civilization. For not only did she abolish the laws of barbarous nations and remodel on more humane lines their savage customs, but likewise, with God's assistance, she reformed and brought to Christian perfection the very law of the Romans, that wonderful monument of ancient wisdom which is deservedly styled written reason, so as to have at hand, as the rule of public and private life improved, abundant material both for medieval and modern legislation.

With inevitable changes nevertheless in the conditions of the times and in the needs of men, as Our predecessor, Pius X of happy memory pointed out in the Motu Proprio *Arduum sane* [*munus*], issued 17 March 1904, it became apparent that Canon Law could no longer readily attain the fullness of its aims. Indeed in the passing of centuries many, many laws had been published, of which some had been abrogated by the supreme authority of the Church or had fallen into desuetude, while others, owing to changed conditions, had become difficult of execution, or less useful and expedient for the common good. Moreover, these laws had so increased in number and were so separated one from another and scattered about that many of them were unknown not merely to the people at large, but even to the most learned.

For these reasons Our predecessor, [Pope St.] Pius X of happy memory, immediately on his accession to the Pontificate, realizing how helpful it would be for the stable restoration of ecclesiastical discipline to put an end to the serious inconveniences above referred to, resolved to arrange in a clear and orderly collection all the laws of the Church which had been proclaimed down to our day, abolishing those already abrogated or obsolete, adapting others to present needs, and making new ones as necessity or expediency should require.

Setting about this most difficult task after mature deliberation, he considered it necessary to consult the bishops whom the Holy Ghost had placed to rule the Church of God, so as to know fully their mind on this matter; and first of all he caused the Cardinal Secretary of State to write letters to all the archbishops of the Catholic world, charging them to interrogate their suffragans, and other Ordinaries, who are obliged to assist at provincial synods, if there were any such, and to inform the Holy See with as little delay as possible and briefly concerning the modifications and corrections which in their opinion might be especially necessary in the present laws of the Church.

Then, having summoned several canonists of note, resident in Rome and elsewhere, to lend their aid, he committed to Our beloved son Cardinal Gasparri, who was at that time Archbishop of Caesarea, the office of directing, perfecting, and, if need be, supplementing the work of the Consultors. He, moreover, formed a committee or, as it is called, a Commission of Cardinals of the Holy Roman Church, appointing as its members

Cardinals Domenico Ferrata, Casimiro Gennari, Beniamino Cavicchioni, José Calasanz Vives y Tuto, and Felice Cavagnis, who, with Cardinal Gasparri as reporter, were to examine diligently the proposed canons and modify, correct, or perfect them as their judgment might suggest.

On the death, one after another, of these five, their places were taken by Our beloved sons, Cardinals Vincenzo Vannutelli, Gaetano de Lai, Sebastiano Martinelli, Basil Pompili, Gaetano Bisleti, Wilelm van Rossum, Filippo Giustini, and Michele Lega, who have admirably completed the work imposed on them.

Lastly, seeking once more the prudence and authority of all the brethren of the Episcopate, he directed that to each of them and to all superiors of Religious Orders who are legitimately invited to an ecumenical council, a copy of the new Code, compiled and corrected, should be sent before its promulgation, in order that they might freely express their views in regard to the canons as prepared.

In the meantime, however, to the sorrow of the whole Catholic world, Our predecessor of immortal memory passed from this life, and it devolved on Us, as by the secret council of God We entered on the Pontificate, to receive with due honor the opinions, coming from every quarter of the world, of those who with us constitute the teaching Church. Finally We ratified, approved, and sanctioned in all its parts the new Code of the whole of Canon Law, which was asked for by many bishops in the Vatican Council and which was begun over twelve years ago.

Therefore, having sought the aid of Divine grace, trusting in the authority of the Blessed Apostles Peter and Paul, moved Ourselves, of Our certain knowledge and in the fullness of the Apostolic power with which we are invested, by this Our constitution, which We wish to be binding for all time; We promulgate, and We decree and order that the present Code, just as it is drawn up, have in future the force of law for the universal Church, and We entrust it for safekeeping to your custody and vigilance.

That all concerned, however, may have full knowledge of the prescripts of this Code before they become effective, We decree and ordain that they shall not have the force of law until Pentecost of next year, that is, on the nineteenth day of May, 1918.

All enactments, constitutions and privileges whatsoever, even those worthy of special mention, and customs, even immemorial, and all other things whatsoever to the contrary notwithstanding.

Wherefore let no one violate or rashly oppose in any way this document of Our constitution, ordinance, limitation, suppression, derogation, and expressed will. And if anyone shall presume to attempt to do so, let him know that he will incur the wrath of Almighty God and of his Blessed Apostles Peter and Paul.

Given at Rome, at St. Peter's, on the Feast of Pentecost, in the year nineteen hundred and seventeen, the third of Our Pontificate.

PETRUS CARD. GASPARRI
Secretary of State

O. CARD. CAGIANO DE AZEVEDO
Chancellor of the H. R. C.

MOTU PROPRIO OF BENEDICT XV

Cum Iuris Canonici
15 September 1917

By Our Own Motion

THE COMMISSION IS INSTITUTED FOR THE AUTHENTIC INTERPRETATION OF THE CANONS OF THE CODE

As We, a short time ago, fulfilled the expectations of the whole Catholic world by promulgating the Code of Canon Law which had been drawn up by order of Our Predecessor, Pius X, of happy memory, the welfare of the Church and the very nature of the matter certainly require that We should take precautions as far as We can to insure that the stability of so great a work be not at any time endangered either by the uncertain opinions and conjectures of private persons regarding the true meaning of the canons, or by the frequent enactment of various new laws. We have therefore determined to guard against both of these dangers; and in order to do so We now, upon Our own motion, from certain knowledge and after mature deliberation, do ordain and decree as follows:

I. Following the example of Our Predecessors, who entrusted the interpretation of the decrees of the Council of Trent to a special Commission of Cardinals, We hereby establish a Committee or *Commission* which shall have the exclusive right of authentically interpreting the canons of the Code, upon consultation, however, in matters of greater moment, with that Sacred Congregation within whose peculiar province the matter which is proposed for decision to the Commission lies. This Commission We desire to consist of a number of Cardinals of the Holy Roman Church, of whom one shall be designated President, all to be chosen by Our authority and that of Our successors; to these shall be added some distinguished man to act as Secretary, and also a number of canonists from both branches of the clergy to act as Consultors; the Commission may also ask the opinions of the Consultors of the various Sacred Congregations on matters within their competency.

II. The Sacred Roman Congregations shall hereafter enact no *new General Decrees*, unless some grave necessity of the universal Church require it. Their ordinary function in this matter will therefore be not only to see that the prescriptions of the Code are religiously observed, but also to issue *Instructions*, as need arises, whereby those prescriptions may be more fully explained and appropriately enforced. These documents are to be drawn up in such a manner that they shall not only be in reality explanations of and complements to the canons, but also that they may be clearly seen to be such; and therefore it will be very helpful to cite the canons themselves in the text of these documents.

III. If ever in the course of time the welfare of the universal Church shall require that a new general decree be issued by any of the Sacred Congregations, the Sacred Congregation itself shall draw up the decree and, if it is not in agreement with the laws of the Code, shall inform the Supreme Pontiff of that fact. After the decree shall have been approved by the Supreme Pontiff, the same Sacred Congregation shall present it to the Commission, whose office it shall then be to draw up a canon or canons according to the decree. If the decree is not in harmony with the law of the Code, the Commission shall indicate which law of the Code is to be supplanted by the new law; if the decree concerns a matter which is not mentioned in the Code, the Commission shall decide at what point the new canon or canons shall be inserted in the Code; but it (or they) shall be designated by repeating the number of the canon immediately preceding, with the addition *bis*, or *ter*, etc., so that no canon of the Code shall ever lose its place, nor the series of numbered canons be in any way confused. And immediately after the decree of the Sacred Congregation, let the whole matter be reported in the *Acta Apostolicae Sedis [Acts of the Apostolic See]*. It is Our will and command that all and each of these provisions which We have appropriately decreed in this matter shall be and remain valid and effective; all things to the contrary not withstanding.

Given from St. Peter's at Rome on the 15th day of September, 1917, the fourth year of Our Pontificate.

PROFESSION OF CATHOLIC FAITH

[used in accord with 1917 CIC 1406]

I, *N.*, with firm faith, believe and profess every and each thing contained in the symbol of Faith, which is used by the holy Roman Church, namely: I believe in one God, the Father almighty, maker of heaven and earth, of everything visible and invisible. And in one Lord Jesus Christ, Only Son of God. And he was born of the Father, before all ages. God from God, light from light, true God from true God. Generated not made, consubstantial to the Father: through whom all things were made. Who for us men, and for our salvation, came down from heaven. And he was incarnated by the Holy Spirit from the Virgin Mary and was made Man. He was crucified for us, under Pontius Pilate: he suffered, and was buried. And he rose on the third day, according to Scriptures. And he ascended into heaven: he sits at the right hand of the Father. And he will come again with glory to judge the living and the dead: of whose reign there will be no end. And in the Holy Spirit, Lord and vivifier: who proceeds from the Father and the Son. Who with the Father and the Son is together adored and glorified: who has spoken through the prophets. And in One, Holy, Catholic and Apostolic Church. I confess one Baptism in remission of sins. And I look for the resurrection of the dead. And for life in the coming world. Amen.

I admit and embrace most firmly the apostolic and ecclesiastical traditions and relics of that Church and its observances and constitutions. Likewise I admit sacred Scripture according to its sense which Mother Church held and holds and to whom it belongs to judge the true sense and interpretation of the Scriptures; I will accept and will interpret nothing except according to the unanimous consent of the Fathers.

I profess also there to be seven true and proper Sacraments of the new law instituted by our Lord Jesus Christ and for the salvation of the human race even though not each individually, namely Baptism, Confirmation, Eucharist, Penance, Last Anointing, Order[s], and Matrimony; and that they confer grace and that of these, Baptism, Confirmation, and Order[s], cannot be repeated without sacrilege.—I receive and admit the received and approved rights of the Catholic Church's solemn administration of all the above-said Sacraments.—I embrace and receive each and everything that was defined and declared about original sin and about justification in the sacrosanct Tridentine Synod.—I profess likewise that in the Mass true God is offered, a proper and fitting Sacrifice for the living and the dead; and that in the most holy Sacrament of the Eucharist there is truly, really, and substantially the Body and Blood, together with soul and divinity, of our Lord Jesus Christ, and that a conversion is made of the whole substance of the bread into the Body, and the whole substance of the wine into the Blood, which conversion the Catholic Church calls Transubstantiation. I acknowledge also that under only one species the whole of Christ, integrally and true Sacrament, is taken.—I constantly hold Purgatory to exist where the souls of the faithful are detained [and] are helped by prayers, similarly that the Saints, reigning together with Christ, are to be venerated and invoked that they may offer their prayers to God for us, and [that] their Relics are to be venerated. I firmly assert that the images of Christ and the God-Bearer ever Virgin, as well as other saints, should be had and retained, and that due honor and veneration should be imparted to them.—I affirm that the power of indulgences was left by Christ to the Church and that the use of these by the Christian people is most healthy.—I acknowledge a Holy, Catholic, and Apostolic Roman Church, mother and teacher of all the Churches, and I give and swear true obedience to the Roman Pontiff, successor of blessed Peter, Prince of Apostles, and Vicar of Jesus Christ.

I undoubtedly receive and profess likewise all those things given, defined, and declared by the Sacred Canons and Ecumenical Councils, and especially by the Sacrosanct Tridentine Synod and by the Ecumenical Vatican Council, especially concerning the primacy of the Roman Pontiff and the infallible magisterium, and at the same time I equally damn, reject, and anathematize against all those things and heresies of whatever sort damned and rejected and anathematized by the Church. I, the same N., promise, pledge, and swear this true Catholic Faith outside of which no one can be saved, which I now freely profess and truly hold, complete and inviolate, until the last breath of life, most constantly, God helping, and which I keep and confess and which I will hold, teach and preach to those subject to me, that is, those whose care falls to my responsibility for so long as I have such care. So help me God, and this holy Gospel of God.

FIRST BOOK
GENERAL NORMS

Canon 1[1] (1983 CIC 1)

Although in the Code of canon law the discipline of the Oriental Church is frequently referenced, nevertheless, this [Code] applies only to the Latin Church and does not bind the Oriental, unless it treats of things that, by their nature, apply to the Oriental.

Canon Law Digest
I: 3–42; II: 3–8; III: 27–34; IV: 13–24; V: 7–17; VI: 3–30;
VII: 3–25; VIII: 3–57; IX: 11–27; X: 3

Canon 2[2] (1983 CIC 2)

The Code, for the most part, determines nothing concerning the rites and ceremonies that the liturgical books approved by the Latin Church determine are to be observed in the celebration of the most holy sacrifice of the Mass, in the administration of the Sacraments, and in conducting other holy Sacramentals. Therefore, all of these liturgical laws retain their force, unless something about them is expressly corrected in this Code.

Canon Law Digest
I: 42–47; II: 8–10; III: 34–38; IV: 25–67; V: 17–157; VI: 30–141;
VII: 25–62; VIII: 57–99; IX: 27–35; X: 4–5

[1] John Duskie, "The Canonical Status of the Orientals in the United States", Canon Law Studies, no. 48 (J.C.D. thesis, Catholic University of America, 1928); Michael Diederichs, "The Jurisdiction of the Latin Ordinaries over Their Oriental Subjects", Canon Law Studies, no. 229 (thesis, Catholic University of America, 1946). Consult also the section entitled "Eastern Canon Law" in appendix 1: "Non-assigned Dissertations".

[2] Charles Augustine, *Liturgical Law: A Handbook of the Roman Liturgy* (St. Louis, Mo.: Herder Book Co., 1931); Gerald Sigler, "The Roman Ritual: The History of a Canonical Source Book" (MS no. 3462, Gregorian University, 1963); George Schembri, "The Role of the Competent Authority in Liturgy according to *Sacrosanctum concilium*" (diss. no. 9, Pontifical University of St. Thomas [Rome], 1970–1971).

Canon 3[3] (1983 CIC 3)

The canons of this Code in no way abrogate from or in any way obrogate treaties entered into by the Apostolic See with various Nations; these treaties, therefore, maintain their present force, notwithstanding any contrary prescriptions of this Code.

Canon Law Digest
I: 47–49; II: 11–24; III: 38; IV: 68; V: 158; VI: 141;
VII: 62–63; VIII: 99; IX: 35–36; X: 5

Canon 4 (1983 CIC 4)

Other acquired rights, and likewise privileges and indults, granted by the Apostolic See to physical or moral persons up to this time, that are still in use and not revoked, remain intact, unless they are expressly revoked by the canons of this Code.

Canon Law Digest
I: 49–50; II: 24–25; V: 158

Canon 5 (1983 CIC 5) Cross-Ref.: 1917 CIC 30

Customs presently in force, whether universal or particular, but against the prescriptions of these canons, if they are indeed expressly *reprobated*, are to be corrected as a corruption of the law, even if they are immemorial, nor are they permitted to revive in the future; other customs, clearly centenary or immemorial, can be tolerated if Ordinaries determine that, due to circumstances of person or place, they cannot be prudently re-

[3]Joseph Prunskis, "Comparative Law, Ecclesiastical and Civil, in Lithuanian Concordat", Canon Law Studies, no. 222 (J.C.D. thesis, Catholic University of America, 1945); Andrea MacDonald, "The Vatican and the United States of America" (Pontifical Lateran University, 1951); Joseph Madurga, "The Negotiations Leading to the Restoration of the Hierarchy in England" (diss. no. 13, Pontifical University of St. Thomas [Rome], 1953–1954); Salvatore Micallef, "A Survey of the Diplomatic Relations between the British Sovereigns and the Vatican" (Pontifical Lateran University, 1955); Richard Rieman, "The Nature of the Diplomatic Relations between the Holy See and the United States of America" (diss. no. 39, Pontifical University of St. Thomas [Rome], 1956–1957); William Nessel, "First Amendment Freedoms, Papal Pronouncements, and Concordat Practice: A Comparative Study in American Law and Public Ecclesiastical Law", Canon Law Studies, no. 412 (J.C.D. thesis, Catholic University of America, 1961); John Loftus, "English Catholic Emancipation: A Study in State-Church Relations in Great Britain 1778–1829" (MS no. 3385, Gregorian University, 1962). Consult also the section entitled "Christian Political Issues" in appendix 1: "Non-assigned Dissertations".

moved; other customs are considered suppressed, unless the Code expressly provides otherwise.

Canon Law Digest
I: 50; II: 25

Canon 6[4] (1983 CIC 6) Cross-Ref.: 1917 CIC 22

The Code for the most part retains the discipline now in force, although it brings about opportune changes. Therefore:

1.° Any laws, whether universal or particular, opposed to the prescriptions of this Code are abrogated, unless something else is expressly provided regarding particular laws;
2.° Canons that refer to the old law as an entirety are to be assessed according to the old authorities and similarly according to the received interpretations of the approved authors;
3.° Canons that are only partly congruent with the old law, insofar as they are congruent, should be assessed according to the old law; to the extent they are discrepant, they are to be assessed according to their own wording;
4.° In cases of doubt as to whether a canonical prescription differs from the old law, it is not considered as differing from the old law;
5.° As applying to penalties, if no mention is made of them in the Code, whether they are spiritual or temporal, medicinal or, as they say, vindicative, automatic or formally imposed, [such] are considered abrogated;
6.° Among the other disciplinary laws now in force, if they are contained neither explicitly nor implicitly in the Code, they should be said to have lost their force, unless they are repeated in liturgical books, or unless the law is of divine law, whether positive or natural.

Canon Law Digest
I: 50–52; II: 25; III: 38; V: 158

[4] George Leech, "A Comparative Study of the Constitution *Apostolicae Sedis* and the *Codex Juris Canonici*", Canon Law Studies, no. 15 (J.C.D. thesis, Catholic University of America, 1922); Nicolas Neuberger, "Canon 6; or, The Relation of the *Codex Juris Canonici* [Code of Canon Law] to Preceding Legislation", Canon Law Studies, no. 44 (J.C.D. thesis, Catholic University of America, 1927).

Canon 7 (1983 CIC 361)

Under the name Apostolic See or Holy See in this Code come not just the Roman Pontiff, but also, unless by the nature of the thing or from the context of the words something else appears, the Congregations, Tribunals, and Offices through which the same Roman Pontiff is wont to expedite the affairs of the universal Church.

TITLE 1
On ecclesiastical laws[5]

Canon 8[6] (1983 CIC 7, 13)

§ 1. Laws are instituted when they are promulgated.

§ 2. A law is not presumed personal, but territorial, unless something else is established.

Canon Law Digest
V: 158; VI: 141–46; VII: 63–72; VIII: 100–111; IX: 36–41; X: 5–6

Canon 9[7] (1983 CIC 8)

Laws laid down by the Apostolic See are promulgated by publication in the official commentary *Acta Apostolicae Sedis* [Acts of the Apostolic See], unless in particular cases another mode of promulgation has been prescribed; and they take their force only upon the completion of three months from the day on which the number of the *Acta* [Acts] comes out, unless by the nature of the thing they bind immediately, or in the law itself a longer or shorter pre-enforcement period is specially and expressly established.

Canon Law Digest
III: 38; V: 158–59

---

[5] Basil Malone, "The Function and Limited Extension of Ecclesiastical Laws" (doctoral diss. 29, University of Ottawa, 1949); William Lee, "Legislator and Subject: A Study in St. Thomas" (D.C.L. thesis, Librarian's Office 698, Maynooth [Ireland], 1969); Roger Kenyon, "A Concept of Ecclesial Law" (doctoral diss. 64, St. Paul University [Ottawa, Canada], 1981).

[6] Martin Lohmuller, "The Promulgation of Law", Canon Law Studies, no. 241 (J.C.D. thesis, Catholic University of America, 1947).

[7] James Gavit, "*Vacatio Legis* [pre-enforcement period] in Canon Law" (thesis no. 160, Pontifical Lateran University, 1960).

Canon 10[8] (1983 CIC 9)

Laws look to the future, not the past, unless the past is provided for in them by name.

Canon Law Digest
I: 52–53; II: 25; V: 159

Canon 11[9] (1983 CIC 10)

Only those laws are considered invalidating or incapacitating that expressly or equivalently establish that an act is null or that a person is incapable [of acting].

Canon 12[10] (1983 CIC 11)

Those who have not received baptism are not bound by merely ecclesiastical laws, nor are those baptized who do not enjoy sufficient use of reason, nor are those who, although they have attained the use of reason, have not yet completed seven years of age, unless the law expressly provides otherwise.

Canon Law Digest
I: 53–54; III: 38

Canon 13 (1983 CIC 12)

§ 1. General laws bind all over the earth those for whom such laws were laid down.

---

[8] Basil Frison, "The Retroactivity of Law", Canon Law Studies, no. 231 (J.C.D. thesis, Catholic University of America, 1946).

[9] D. Morrison, *"Leges Irritantes* [invalidating laws]" (D.C.L. thesis, Librarian's Office 538, Maynooth [Ireland], 1955); Edward Roelker, *Invalidating Laws* (Paterson, N.J.: St. Anthony Guild Press, 1955).

[10] Joseph McCloskey, "The Subject of Ecclesiastical Law according to Canon 12", Canon Law Studies, no. 165 (J.C.D. thesis, Catholic University of America, 1942); Colin Pickett, "The Insane and the Laws of the Church: An Historical Synopsis of Roman and Ecclesiastical Law and a Canonical Commentary" (doctoral diss. 30, University of Ottawa, 1949); Andreas Flores y Reines, "The Subjection of Persons to Merely Ecclesiastical Laws" (diss. no. 26, Pontifical University of St. Thomas [Rome], 1958–1959); Henry Bowen, "The Juridic Authority of the Church over the Non-baptized", Canon Law Studies, no. 431 (J.C.D. thesis, Catholic University of America, 1963).

§ 2. Laws established for a specific territory bind those for whom they were laid down and who have a domicile or quasi-domicile there and are actually present there, though observing the prescription of Canon 14.

Canon Law Digest
VI: 146

Canon 14[11] (1983 CIC 13) Cross-Ref.: 1917 CIC 13

§ 1. [Regarding] travelers:

1.° They are not bound by the particular laws of their own territory for so long as they are absent from it, unless the transgression of those laws would cause harm in their own territories or the laws are personal;

2.° Neither are they bound by the laws of the territory in which they are present, with the exception of those laws that apply to public order or that determine the formalities of acts;

3.° But they are bound by general laws, even if those laws have no force in their own territory, but by no means if they do not bind in the territory in which they are present.

§ 2. Wanderers are bound by the general and particular laws that have force in the place in which they are present.

Canon Law Digest
I: 54–55

Canon 15[12] (1983 CIC 14)

Laws, even invalidating and incapacitating ones, do not bind when there is a doubt of law; when there is a doubt of fact, the Ordinary can dispense from them, provided it concerns a law from which the Roman Pontiff is wont to dispense.

Canon Law Digest
I: 55

[11] George Childs, "Who Are Obligated by Ecclesiastical Law: A Commentary on Canon 14" (diss. no. 9, Pontifical University of St. Thomas [Rome], 1938–1939); John Hammill, "The Obligations of the Traveler according to Canon 14", Canon Law Studies, no. 160 (J.C.D. thesis, Catholic University of America, 1942); Thomas Larkin, "Exempt Religious and Episcopal Laws which Protect Public Order" (diss. no. 4, Pontifical University of St. Thomas [Rome], 1949–1950); John Hackett, "The Concept of Public Order", Canon Law Studies, no. 399 (thesis, Catholic University of America, 1959).

[12] Roger Viau, "Doubt in Canon Law", Canon Law Studies, no. 346 (thesis, Catholic University of America, 1954).

Canon 16[13] (1983 CIC 15)

§ 1. Ignorance of an invalidating or incapacitating law does not excuse, unless the law expressly says otherwise.

§ 2. Ignorance or error concerning a law or a penalty or concerning a personal fact or a notorious fact about another is generally not presumed; concerning a non-notorious fact about another, it is presumed, until the contrary is proven.

Canon 17[14] (1983 CIC 16)

§ 1. Laws are authentically interpreted by the legislator or his successor and by those to whom the power of interpretation has been committed by [the legislator or his successors].

§ 2. An authentic interpretation, given out in the manner of law, has the same force as does the law itself; and if it merely declares what is certain from the words of the law, it does not require promulgation and is effective retroactively; but if it narrows or extends the law or resolves a doubt, it is not retroactive and must be promulgated.

§ 3. That [interpretation] given by means of a judicial sentence or by a rescript in a specific matter does not have the force of law and binds only those persons and affects only those matters for which it was given.

Canon Law Digest
I: 55–57; III: 38; IV: 68; V: 159–60

Canon 18[15] (1983 CIC 17)

Ecclesiastical laws are to be understood according to the meaning of their own words considered in their text and context; as for those things that remain unclear or in doubt, reference should be made to parallel pro-

---

[13] Francis Herlihy, "When Does Ignorance Excuse" (MS no. 714, Gregorian University, 1939); Michael Regan, "Canon 16", Canon Law Studies, no. 307 (thesis, Catholic University of America, 1959).

[14] John Schmidt, "The Principles of Authentic Interpretation in Canon 17 of the Code of Canon Law", Canon Law Studies, no. 141 (J.C.L. thesis, Catholic University of America, 1940).

[15] Andrew Quinn, "Doctrinal Interpretation of Law according to the Canonical Tradition and according to Canon 18 of the Code of Canon Law" (MS no. 588, Gregorian University, 1938; printed version, no. 145, 1938); Matthew Shekleton, "Doctrinal Interpretation of Law", Canon Law Studies, no. 345 (thesis, Catholic University of America, 1961).

visions in the Code, if there are any, to the purposes and circumstances of the law and to the mind of the legislator.

Canon Law Digest
I: 57

Canon 19[16] (1983 CIC 18)

Laws that establish a penalty, or that restrict the free exercise of a right, or that contain an exception to the law, are subject to strict interpretation.

Canon Law Digest
I: 58

Canon 20[17] (1983 CIC 19)

If on a given matter there is lacking an express prescription of law, whether general or particular, the rule is to be surmised, unless it concerns the application of a penalty, from laws laid down in similar cases; [then] from the general principles of law observed with canonical equity; [then] from the style and practice of the Roman Curia; and [finally] from the common and constant opinions of the doctors.

Canon Law Digest
I: 58; II: 25; III: 38

Canon 21 (NA)

Laws laid down for the prevention of general dangers oblige, even if in particular circumstances there is no danger.

Canon 22 (1983 CIC 20)

A later law, laid down by the competent authority, [abrogates] a prior law if it expressly says so, or if it is directly contrary to it, or if it com-

---

[16] Porter White, "The Evolution of the Canonical Concept of Strict Interpretation of Law" (MS no. 1836, Gregorian University, 1951; printed version, no. 743, 1951); Gregory Cocuzzi, "The Concept of the Favorable and Odious at Law" (MS no. 2218, Gregorian University, 1954); John Calhoun, "The Restraint of the Exercise of One's Rights", Canon Law Studies, no. 432 (J.C.D. thesis, Catholic University of America, 1965).

[17] Augustine Mater Dolorosa, "The Historical Development of Canonical Equity" (MS no. 3175, Gregorian University, 1961; printed version, no. 1380, 1961).

pletely reorders the matter treated in the earlier law; but, and though observing Canon 6, n. 1, general laws in no way derogate from the special [laws] of places and from the statutes of [inferior authorities], unless expressly established otherwise in the law.

Canon Law Digest
I: 58; II: 25

Canon 23[18] (1983 CIC 21)

In cases of doubt, the revocation of a preexisting law is not presumed, but later laws are to be brought in line with older laws and, to the extent possible, reconciled with them.

Canon 24[19] (1983 CIC 54, 58)

Precepts, given individually, bind recipients everywhere, but they cannot be judicially enforced and cease upon the cessation of the authority of their author, unless they were imposed by legitimate document or in the presence of two witnesses.

TITLE 2
On custom[20]

Canon 25 (1983 CIC 23)

Custom in the Church obtains the force of law only by the consent of the competent ecclesiastical Superior.

Canon Law Digest
I: 59; VIII: 111

---

[18] Alphonse Thomas, "The Juridic Effect of Doubtful Cessation of Law according to the Code of Canon Law" (University of Laval, 1948).

[19] Gerard Sugden, "Precepts that Come under Canon 24" (diss. no. 17, Pontifical University of St. Thomas [Rome], 1949–1950).

[20] Merlin Guilfoyle, "Custom", Canon Law Studies, no. 105 (J.C.D. thesis, Catholic University of America, 1937).

Canon 26[21] (1983 CIC 25)

A community that is capable at least of receiving an ecclesiastical law can introduce a custom that could obtain the force of law.

Canon 27 (1983 CIC 26)

§ 1. No custom can derogate from divine law, whether natural or positive; neither can it prejudice ecclesiastical law, unless the custom was reasonable and has been observed for forty continuous and complete years; but against an ecclesiastical law that contains a clause prohibiting future customs, only a reasonable custom can be prescriptive if it is centenary or immemorial.

§ 2. A custom that is expressly reprobated in law is not reasonable.

Canon Law Digest
I: 59

Canon 28[22] (1983 CIC 28)

A custom beyond the law, if it has been knowingly observed by a community with the intention of obliging itself, leads to law, if the custom was equally reasonable and legitimately observed for forty continuous and complete years.

Canon 29[23] (1983 CIC 27)

Custom is the best interpreter of laws.

Canon Law Digest
V: 160

Canon 30 (1983 CIC 28)

While observing Canon 5, custom against the law or beyond the law is revoked by a contrary custom or law; but, unless express mention of them is made, a law does not revoke centenary or immemorial customs, nor does a general law [revoke] particular customs.

---

[21] John Cook, "Ecclesiastical Communities and Their Ability to Induce Legal Customs", Canon Law Studies, no. 300 (thesis, Catholic University of America, 1950).

[22] John Ahern, "The Animus Required for the Introduction of a Custom in Canon Law" (D.C.L. thesis, Librarian's Office 505, Maynooth [Ireland], 1946).

[23] John Cavanaugh, "Custom Is the Best Interpreter of Law" (Pontifical Lateran University, 1961).

TITLE 3
On computation of time[24]

Canon 31 (1983 CIC 200)

With due regard for liturgical law, time, unless otherwise expressly established, is calculated according to the norms of the canons that follow.

Canon 32 (1983 CIC 202)

§ 1. A day consists of 24 continuous hours, calculated from midnight; a week is 7 days.

§ 2. In law, a month covers a period of 30 days, and a year is a period of 365 days, unless the month and year are said to be reckoned as they are in the calendar.

Canon 33 (NA)

§ 1. In calculating the hours of the day, the standard usage common to the place should be used; but in the private celebration of the Mass, in the private recitation of the canonical hours, in receiving holy communion, and in observing the laws of fast and abstinence, it is permitted to follow the time of place or the true or mean time, or the legal time, whether regional or extraordinary, even if it is calculated by other than the local usage.

§ 2. As for what applies to the time for fulfilling contractual obligations, there should be observed, unless the contract has expressly agreed otherwise, the prescriptions of law in force in that territory.

Canon Law Digest
I: 59; III: 38–39

Canon 34 (1983 CIC 202–3)

§ 1. If a month or a year is designated by its own name or its equivalent, for example, the *month of February, the next year in the future*, it is to be reckoned as it is in the calendar.

---

[24] Arthur Dubé, "The General Principles for the Reckoning of Time in Canon Law", Canon Law Studies, no. 144 (J.C.D. thesis, Catholic University of America, 1941); John Finnegan, "Selected Questions on the Computation of Time in Canon Law" (Pontifical Lateran University, 1965).

§ 2. If the time *from which* is neither explicitly nor implicitly assigned, for example, *suspension from the celebration of Mass for a month or two years, vacation for three months per year,* etc., time is calculated from moment to moment; and if the time is continuous, as in the above example, the months and the years are calculated as they are in the calendar; if interrupted, the week is understood as 7 days, a month as 30 [days], and a year as 365 [days].

§ 3. If the time consists of one or more months or years, one or more weeks, or several days, the time *from which* is explicitly or implicitly assigned thus:

1.° Months and years are taken as they are in the calendar;

2.° If the time *from which* coincides with the initial day, for example, *two months of vacation from August 15*[th], the first day is counted in the calculation and the time is ended at the beginning of the last day with the same number;

3.° If the time *from which* does not coincide with an initial day, for example, *age fourteen, novitiate year, eight days from the vacancy of an episcopal see, ten days for appeal,* etc., the first day is not counted and the time is ended with the completion of the day of the same number;

4.° But if a month lacks a day of the same number, for example, *one month from the 30*[th] *day of January*, then for various cases, the time ends at the beginning or the end of the last day of the month;

5.° If it concerns actions of the same sort that are to be renewed at established times, for example, *the three years toward perpetual profession after temporary [profession], three years or some other period before the renewal of an election,* etc., the time is ended upon the reoccurrence of the day on which it started, but the new act can be placed throughout the entire day.

Canon Law Digest
I: 59–60

Canon 35 (1983 CIC 201)

Useful time is understood as that [time] during which one may exercise or defend a right, so that [the time] does not run if one is ignorant of the right or unable to use it; *continuous* time suffers no interruption.

TITLE 4
On rescripts[25]

Canon 36 (1983 CIC 60)

§ 1. Rescripts, whether from the Apostolic See or from other Ordinaries, can be petitioned freely by anyone who is not expressly prohibited from doing so.

§ 2. Favors and dispensations of any sort can be granted by the Apostolic See and are valid even for those afflicted by a censure, with due regard for the prescription of Canons 2265, § 2, 2275, n. 3, and 2283.

Canon Law Digest
IV: 68; VI: 146

Canon 37 (1983 CIC 61)

A rescript can be petitioned on behalf of another even without his assent; and even though he can use the favor granted by rescript or not use it, the rescript is still valid before his acceptance, unless something else appears in a contrary clause.

Canon 38 (1983 CIC 62)

Rescripts by which a favor is granted without executive action take effect from the moment at which the letters are issued; others from the time of execution.

Canon Law Digest
II: 25; VII: 72

Canon 39 (1983 CIC 39)

Conditions in rescripts are considered essential for validity only when they appear with the particles *si* [if], *dummodo* [so long as], or are expressed in other ways with the same meaning.

Canon Law Digest
IX: 41

---

[25] William O'Neill, "Papal Rescripts of Favor", Canon Law Studies, no. 57 (diss., Catholic University of America, 1930); Bernard Havlik, "The Cessation of Rescripts", Canon Law Studies, no. 370 (Catholic University of America, not published).

Canon 40[26] (1983 CIC 62)

In every rescript there should be understood, even if not expressed, the condition: *If the requests are in truth*, though observing the prescriptions of Canons 45 and 1054.

Canon Law Digest
III: 39; IX: 42

Canon 41 (1983 CIC 63)

In rescripts for which there is no executor, the requests should be in truth at the time the rescript is given; in others, [they should be in truth] at the time of execution.

Canon Law Digest
I: 60; II: 25

Canon 42 (1983 CIC 63)

§ 1. Withholding of the truth, that is, subreption, in a request does not for that reason prevent the rescript from having force, so long as there was expressed whatever is required for validity according to the style of the Curia.

§ 2. Nor does the presentation of a falsehood, that is, obreption, [prevent a rescript from having force,] provided one proposed motive or at least one of several motives is true.

§ 3. The fault of obreption or subreption in just one part of a rescript does not render another part infirm if there were several favors granted together with it in the rescript.

Canon Law Digest
III: 39

Canon 43 (1983 CIC 64)

A favor denied by one Sacred Congregation or Office of the Roman Curia is invalidly granted from another Sacred Congregation or Office or local Ordinary, even if it has power, if it was granted without the assent of the Sacred Congregation or Office that was originally approached, with due regard for the authority of the S. Penitentiary for the internal forum.

---

[26] Donald Adams, "The Truth Required in the Preces for Rescripts", Canon Law Studies, no. 392 (J.C.D. thesis, Catholic University of America, 1960).

Canon 44 (1983 CIC 65) Cross-Ref.: 1917 CIC 369

§ 1. No one denied a favor by one Ordinary can ask for it from another without mentioning the fact of the denial; mention having been made, however, the Ordinary is not to grant the favor without first knowing the reasons for the denial by the prior Ordinary.

§ 2. A favor denied by a Vicar General and later sought from a Bishop, without mention of the earlier denial, is invalid; moreover, a favor denied by a Bishop cannot be validly sought from a Vicar General, even if mention is made of the earlier denial, without the consent of the Bishop.

Canon 45 (1983 CIC 63) Cross-Refs.: 1917 CIC 40, 2361

When a rescript to a request [made] by a petitioner has attached to it the clause: *Motu proprio* [self-moved; by one's own initiative], it is valid even if there is withheld whatever truth is necessary to have been expressed, but not, however, if the only motivating cause is false, though observing the prescription of Canon 1054.

Canon 46 (1983 CIC 38)

A rescript, even if granted *Motu proprio* [self-moved], to a person who by common law is incapable of pursuing the favor that it concerns, and likewise one given contrary to the legitimate custom of the place or special statute, or against the already acquired right of another, cannot be sustained, unless there is attached to the rescript an express clause derogating from these [obstacles].

Canon 47 (1983 CIC 66)

Rescripts are not made invalid by an error in the name of the person to whom or by whom they [were or] are issued, or [by errors] in the place in which they are found, or [by errors] in the subject matter, so long as, in the judgment of the Ordinary, there is no doubt concerning the person or the subject matter it concerns.

Canon 48 (1983 CIC 53, 67)

§ 1. If it happens that two rescripts contrary to each other have been requested, a specific [provision], regarding those things that are specifically expressed, prevails over a general [provision].

§ 2. If the specific and the general [provisions] are equal, the one prior in time prevails over the later, unless in the second [provision] there is express mention of the first, or unless the petitioner of the first, through fault or notable negligence, has not made use of his rescript.

§ 3. But if they were granted on the same day and it is not clear which of them was issued first, they are both invalid, and, if circumstances require, recourse should be had again to the one who granted the rescripts.

Canon 49[27] (1983 CIC 36)

Rescripts are to be understood according to the meaning of their own words and the common usage of speech, and they must not be extended to cases other than those expressed.

Canon Law Digest
I: 60

Canon 50 (1983 CIC 36) Cross-Refs.: 1917 CIC 68, 85

In doubt, rescripts that refer to litigation, or that injure the acquired rights of others, or that go against the law in accommodation of private persons, or that, finally, are a reply to a request for ecclesiastical benefice, receive a strict interpretation; all others [receive] a wide [interpretation].

Canon Law Digest
I: 60–61

Canon 51 (1983 CIC 68)

A rescript of the Apostolic See in which no executor is given need only be presented to the Ordinary of the petitioner when the letter itself so indicates, or if it concerns public matters, or [if] it is necessary to prove certain conditions.

Canon Law Digest
I: 61.

Canon 52 (1983 CIC 69)

Rescripts whose presentation is not limited to a certain time may be presented at any time, [though] in a manner free of fraud or dolus.

---

[27] Bernard Gerhardt, "Interpretation of Rescripts", Canon Law Studies, no. 398 (thesis, Catholic University of America, 1959).

Canon 53 (1983 CIC 40)

The executor of a rescript invalidly performs his functions before he receives the letters and has verified their integrity and authenticity, unless previous notice of them had been transmitted to him by the rescripting authority.

Canon Law Digest
IV: 68–69

Canon 54 (1983 CIC 41, 70)

§ 1. If in a rescript there is committed the mere task of execution, the execution of the rescript cannot be denied, unless it is manifestly obvious that the rescript is void to the point of nullity by subreption or obreption, or if in the rescript there are attached conditions that appear not to have been fulfilled, or if the one asking for the rescript, in the judgment of the executor, seems so unworthy that to grant the favor would be offensive to others; if the last scenario occurs, the executor, withholding execution, shall immediately make this known to the rescriptor.

§ 2. But if in the rescript there is granted the favor of execution, it is for the executor to decide according to his own prudent judgment and conscience whether to grant or deny the favor.

Canon 55 (1983 CIC 42)

An executor must proceed in accord with the norm of the mandate, and, unless he fulfills the essential conditions listed in the letters and substantially observes the form of procedure, the execution is invalid.

Canon 56 (1983 CIC 37)

The execution of rescripts that pertain to the external forum is to be made in writing.

Canon Law Digest
I: 61

Canon 57 (1983 CIC 43)

§ 1. The executor of rescripts can substitute another for himself in accord with his own prudent judgment, unless substitution is prohibited or a designated substitute is given.

§ 2. But if [the executor] was selected because of personal skills, he is not permitted to commit the execution to another, aside from preparatory acts.

Canon 58 (1983 CIC 44)

Rescripts of any sort can be entrusted to successors of the executor in that office or dignity, unless he had been selected because of personal skills.

Canon 59 (1983 CIC 45)

§ 1. It is fundamental for the executor that, if he has erred in the execution of a rescript in any way, he can order its execution again.

§ 2. As to what applies to the fees attached to execution of a rescript, the prescription of Canon 1507, § 1, is to be followed.

Canon 60 (1983 CIC 47, 73) Cross-Ref.: 1917 CIC 71

§ 1. A rescript revoked by special act of the Superior remains in effect until the revocation is made known to him who obtained it.

§ 2. No rescript is revoked by a contrary law, unless the law provides otherwise or the law was issued by the Superior of the one who issued the rescript.

Canon Law Digest
I: 61

Canon 61 (NA) Cross-Ref.: 1917 CIC 207

A vacancy in the Apostolic See or in a diocese does not bring about the end of a rescript issued by the Apostolic See or the Ordinary, unless it appears otherwise from attached clauses, or the rescript contains the power given to someone for granting favors to certain persons named therein, and the matter is still in the preliminary stages.

Canon 62 (1983 CIC 75)

If the rescript contains not simply a favor, but a privilege or dispensation, the prescriptions of the canons that follow should also be observed.

TITLE 5
On privileges[28]

Canon 63 (1983 CIC 76)

§ 1. Privileges can be acquired not only by direct grant of the competent authority and by communication, but also by legitimate custom and prescription.

§ 2. Centenary or immemorial possession leads to a [favorable] presumption about the concession of the privilege.

Canon Law Digest
I: 61; II: 25

Canon 64[29] (NA)

Through communication of a privilege, even if it was granted in principal form, only that privilege that is direct, perpetual, and without relation to a certain place, thing, or person is considered as extended as it was to the first recipient of the privilege, taking into consideration the capacity of the subject to whom the communication is being made.

Canon 65 (NA)

Privileges that are acquired in accessory form are increased, decreased, or lost by fact, insofar as those of the principal privilege are increased, diminished, or cease; it is otherwise with regard to those acquired in principal form.

Canon 66[30] (1983 CIC 132) Cross-Ref.: 1917 CIC 368

§ 1. Habitual faculties that are granted either in perpetuity or for a definite time, or for a definite number of cases, are considered privileges outside the law.

---

[28] Edward Roelker, "Principles of Privilege according to the Code of Canon Law", Canon Law Studies, no. 35 (J.C.D. thesis, Catholic University of America, 1926); Patrick Lopez y Maqui, "Some Privileges and Indults in the Philippines" (diss. no. 26, Pontifical University of St. Thomas [Rome], 1957–1958).

[29] Raymond Matulenas, "Communication, a Source of Privileges", Canon Law Studies, no. 183 (J.C.D. thesis, Catholic University of America, 1943).

[30] Hubert Motry, "Diocesan Faculties according to the Code of Canon Law", Canon Law Studies, no. 16 (J.C.D. thesis, Catholic University of America, 1922); George Eagleton, "The Diocesan Quinquennial Faculties, Formula IV", Canon Law Studies, no. 248 (thesis, Catholic University of America, 1948); Peter Chyang, "Decennial Faculties for Ordinaries in Quasi-Dioceses", Canon Law Studies, no. 402 (J.C.D. thesis, Catholic University of America, 1961).

§ 2. Unless in their granting a recipient was chosen because of special qualities or it is otherwise expressly provided, habitual faculties granted by the Apostolic See to a Bishop or someone else mentioned in Canon 198, § 1, do not disappear upon the cessation of the recipient from office, even if they had begun to be used, but they transfer to the Ordinaries who succeed him in office; likewise those granted to the Bishop are granted to the Vicar General.

§ 3. The grant of faculties also carries with it other powers that are necessary for their use; for that reason, there is included the faculty of dispensing and also the power of absolving from ecclesiastical penalties if perchance these obstruct matters, but only to the degree [needed] to bring about the effect of the dispensation.

Canon Law Digest
I: 61–77; II: 26–42; III: 39–55; IV: 69–82; V: 160–91;
VI: 146–57; VII: 72–87; VIII: 112–15; IX: 42–46

Canon 67 (1983 CIC 77)

A privilege is to be evaluated according to its own tenor, and it is not licit to extend or restrict it.

Canon Law Digest
I: 77

Canon 68[31] (1983 CIC 77)

In doubt, privileges are to be interpreted according to the norm of Canon 50, but that interpretation is always to be followed by which some benefit of the privilege accrues to a person by the good will of the grantor.

Canon Law Digest
I: 77–78

Canon 69 (1983 CIC 71)

No one is compelled to use a privilege granted in his own favor, unless this obligation arises from some other source.

---

[31] John Ruef, "The Development of the Principles for the Broad and Strict Interpretation of Privileges" (diss. no. 17, Pontifical University of St. Thomas [Rome], 1953-1954).

Canon 70 (1983 CIC 78)

A privilege, unless it appears otherwise, is considered perpetual.

Canon Law Digest
I: 78; II: 42

Canon 71[32] (1983 CIC 79)

Privileges contained in this Code are revoked by general law; as to what applies to others, the prescription of Canon 60 is observed.

Canon 72 (1983 CIC 80)

§ 1. Privileges cease by a renunciation accepted by the competent Superior.

§ 2. Privileges constituted in one's own favor can be renounced by a private person.

§ 3. A concession granted to a community, a dignity, or place is not to be renounced by a private person.

§ 4. Nor is a community or group as a whole to renounce a privilege granted to it by law, or if the renunciation [would] work to the detriment of the Church or others.

Canon Law Digest
II: 43

Canon 73 (1983 CIC 81)

A privilege is not extinguished upon the cessation of the grantor from office, unless it was granted with the clause: *at our good pleasure*, or some equivalent [phrase].

Canon 74 (1983 CIC 78)

A personal privilege follows the person and expires with him.

Canon 75 (1983 CIC 78) Cross-Ref.: 1917 CIC 924

Real privileges cease upon the complete destruction of the thing or place; local privileges, however, revive if the place is restored within fifty years.

[32] Jeremiah Kelliher, "Loss of Privileges", Canon Law Studies, no. 364 (J.C.D. thesis, Catholic University of American, 1964).

Canon 76 (1983 CIC 82)

Privileges that are not a burden to others do not cease through non-use or through contrary use; but if this brings about harm to others, they can be lost if legitimate prescription or tacit renunciation occurs.

Canon 77 (1983 CIC 83)

A privilege also ceases if, in the progress of time, circumstances are such that, in the judgment of the Superior, they have changed to the point where harm can arise or use [of the privilege] becomes illicit; it likewise ceases with the lapse of the time or the completion of the number of cases for which the privilege was granted, with due regard for Canon 207, § 2.

Canon Law Digest
I: 78

Canon 78 (1983 CIC 84)

Whoever abuses a power allowed to him by privilege deserves to be deprived of that privilege; the Ordinary shall not fail to notify the Holy See if one is gravely abusing a privilege granted by it.

Canon 79 (1983 CIC 74)

Although a privilege obtained orally from the Holy See can be applied in the forum of conscience by the one asking for it, nevertheless, no one may use a privilege against another in the external forum unless he can legitimately demonstrate that the privilege was granted to him.

TITLE 6
On dispensations[33]

Canon 80 (1983 CIC 85)

A dispensation, that is, the relaxation of the law in a particular case, can be granted by the author of the law, by his successor or Superior, as well as by him to whom the power of dispensing has been granted.

Canon Law Digest
VI: 157; IX: 47

---

[33] Edward Reilly, "The General Norms of Dispensation", Canon Law Studies, no. 119 (J.C.D. thesis, Catholic University of America, 1939).

Canon 81 (1983 CIC 87) Cross-Refs.: 1917 CIC 82, 336

Ordinaries below the Roman Pontiff cannot dispense from the general laws of the Church, even in a specific case, unless this power has been explicitly or implicitly granted them, or unless recourse to the Holy See is difficult and there is also grave danger of harm in delay and the dispensation concerns a matter from which the Apostolic See is wont to dispense.

Canon Law Digest
I: 78; II: 43–45; III: 56; IV: 82–83; VI: 157; VII: 87; IX: 47

Canon 82[34] (1983 CIC 88)

Bishops and other local Ordinaries are able to dispense from diocesan laws and from laws of provincial or plenary Councils in accord with Canon 291, § 2, but not from laws specially handed down by the Roman Pontiff for a particular territory, except in accord with Canon 81.

Canon 83[35] (1983 CIC 89)

Pastors cannot dispense from either general or particular law unless this power has been expressly granted them.

Canon 84[36] (1983 CIC 90)

§ 1. Ecclesiastical law is not to be dispensed except for just and reasonable cause, taking into consideration the importance of the law from which dispensation [is sought]; in other cases, dispensation given by an inferior is illicit and invalid.

§ 2. In doubt about the sufficiency of the cause, dispensation can licitly be sought and can be licitly and validly granted.

Canon Law Digest
I: 79; II: 45–46; IV: 83–86; VI: 157

[34] Richard Ryan, "The Authority of the Residential Bishop in the Latin Rite to Dispense from the General Laws of the Church", Canon Law Studies, no. 482 (Catholic University of America, 1973).

[35] John Huhmann, "The Pastor's Power of Dispensing" (diss. no. 32, Pontifical University of St. Thomas [Rome], 1955–1956).

[36] Stanislaus Kubik, "Invalidity of Dispensations according to Canon 84 § 1", Canon Law Studies, no. 340 (thesis, Catholic University of America, 1953); Maurice Fitzgerald, "The Doubtfully Existing Cause for a Dispensation" (diss. no. 26, Pontifical University of St. Thomas [Rome], 1953–1954).

Canon 85 (1983 CIC 92)

Not only is dispensation subject to strict interpretation in accord with the norm of Canon 50, but so too is the faculty of dispensing that is granted for a certain case.

Canon Law Digest
I: 79

Canon 86 (1983 CIC 93)

A dispensation that has successive applicability ceases in the same way as does a privilege, as well as with the certain and complete cessation of the motivating cause.

SECOND BOOK
ON PERSONS

Canon 87[1] (1983 CIC 96)

By baptism a man is constituted a person in the Church of Christ with all of the rights and duties of Christians unless, in what applies to rights, some bar obstructs, impeding the bond of ecclesiastical communion, or there is a censure laid down by the Church.

Canon Law Digest
I: 83; II: 49; III: 59; V: 195; VI: 161; VII: 91

Canon 88 (1983 CIC 97, 99) Cross-Ref.: 1917 CIC 745

§ 1. A person who has completed the twenty-first year of life is an adult; below this age, a minor.

§ 2. A minor, if a boy, is considered pubescent upon completing fourteen years, and if a girl, upon twelve.

§ 3. A prepubescent, before reaching seven, is called an infant or a boy [or a girl] or a little one and is not considered mentally competent; having completed seven years, he [or she] is presumed to have the use of reason. Those who habitually lack the use of reason are treated as children.

Canon 89[2] (1983 CIC 98)

An adult person has the full exercise of his rights; a minor remains under the authority of parents or guardians in the exercise of his rights, ex-

---

[1] Albert Reed, "The Juridical Aspect of Incorporation into the Church of Christ (Canon 87)" (diss. no. 30, Pontifical University of St. Thomas [Rome], 1957-1958); Paul Purta, "Status of Physical Persons in Code of Canon Law" (Pontifical Lateran University, 1959); David Morrison, "The Juridic Status of Women in Canonical Law and in United States Law: A Comparative Socio-Juridical Study" (Pontifical Lateran University, 1965); Michael Hughes, "The Act of Membership of the Catholic Church and the Nature of Ecclesial Juridicity" (thesis, Gregorian University; printed version, no. 2594, Ottawa, 1974); Katherine Meagher, "The Status of Women in the Post-conciliar Church" (Ph. D. diss., St. Paul University [Ottawa, Canada], 1976).

[2] Bertram Ryan, "The Exemption of Minors from Parental Control" (diss. no. 8, Pontifical University of St. Thomas [Rome], 1950–1951).

cept in those things in which the law exempts minors from the authority of parents.

Canon 90 (1983 CIC 101)

§ 1. The place of origin for a child, as well as for a neophyte, is that in which, when the child was born, the father had a domicile or, in defect of a domicile, a quasi-domicile; if the child was illegitimate, or was born posthumously, it is the mother's place [that counts].

§ 2. If the matter concerns the child of transients, the place of origin is that very place of birth; if the child was abandoned, it is the place in which he was found.

Canon 91 (1983 CIC 100) Cross-Ref.: 1917 CIC 1032

A person is called: a *resident* in the place where he has a domicile; a *tenant* in the place where he has a quasi-domicile; a *traveler* if he is outside of the place of domicile or quasi-domicile that he retains; a *wanderer*, if he has a domicile or quasi-domicile nowhere.

Canon Law Digest
I: 83; II: 49; III: 59

Canon 92[3] (1983 CIC 102)

§ 1. Domicile is acquired by being in a given parish or quasi-parish, or at least in a diocese, apostolic vicariate, or apostolic prefecture; which presence is either joined with the intention of remaining there perpetually, unless one is called away from there, or is protracted for ten complete years.

§ 2. Quasi-domicile is acquired by staying as above, and is joined with the intention of remaining there for the greater part of a year, unless one is called away from there, or if it is actually protracted for the greater part of a year.

§ 3. Domicile or quasi-domicile in a parish or quasi-parish is called *parochial*; in a diocese, vicariate, [or] prefecture, though not in a parish or quasi-parish, [it is called] *diocesan*.

Canon Law Digest
VIII: 119

---

[3] Neil Farren, "Domicile and Quasi-Domicile: An Historical and Practical Study in Canon Law" (D. C. L. thesis, St. Patrick's College, Maynooth [Ireland]; Dublin: M. H. Gill, 1920); John Costello, "Domicile and Quasi-Domicile", Canon Law Studies, no. 60 (J. C. D. thesis, Catholic University of America, 1930); William Thompson, "Quasi-Domicile" (thesis, Catholic University of Louvain, 1952; St. Meinrad, Ind.: Abbey Press, 1956).

Canon 93[4] (1983 CIC 104–5) Cross-Ref.: 1917 CIC 95

§ 1. A wife, not legitimately separated from her husband, necessarily retains the domicile of her husband; the incompetent [have the domicile] of their guardian; a minor [has the domicile] of the one to whose power he is subject.

§ 2. A minor past infancy can obtain his own quasi-domicile; likewise a wife not legitimately separated from her husband [can obtain quasi-domicile], and once legitimately separated, [she can obtain] a domicile as well.

Canon Law Digest
I: 83–84

Canon 94 (1983 CIC 107)

§ 1. Through one's domicile or quasi-domicile, ones pastor and Ordinary are determined.

§ 2. The proper pastor or Ordinary of a transient is the pastor or Ordinary of the place in which the transient is actually present.

§ 3. As for those who have nothing more than a diocesan domicile or quasi-domicile, the proper pastor is the pastor of the place in which they are actually present.

Canon Law Digest
I: 84; II: 49; VI: 161

Canon 95 (1983 CIC 106)

Domicile and quasi-domicile are lost by leaving a place with the intention of not returning, though observing the prescription of Canon 93.

Canon 96 (1983 CIC 108)

§ 1. Consanguinity is calculated by lines and degrees.

§ 2. In the direct line, there are as many degrees as there are generations, that is, persons, omitting the common ancestor.

[4] Marion Gibbons, "Domicile of Wife Unlawfully Separated from Her Husband", Canon Law Studies, no. 249 (thesis, Catholic University of America, 1947).

§ 3. In the collateral line, if treating of cases of equal length, there are as many degrees as there are generations in one line; if treating of unequal cases, there are as many degrees as there are generations in the longer line.

Canon 97 (1983 CIC 109)

§ 1. Affinity arises from a valid marriage, whether merely ratified or ratified and consummated.

§ 2. It applies between a man and the blood-relatives of the woman, and likewise between the woman and the blood-relatives of the man.

§ 3. It is calculated so that the blood-relatives of the man are affines in the same line and degree to the woman as they are to the man, and vice versa.

Canon Law Digest
I: 84; IV: 89

Canon 98[5] (1983 CIC 111–12)

§ 1. Among the various Catholic rites, one belongs to that one according to whose ceremonies one was baptized, unless perhaps baptism by a minister of an alien rite was brought about fraudulently, or in case of grave necessity when it was not possible to have a priest of one's own rite present, or if it came about by apostolic dispensation whereby the faculty was given to baptize one in a certain rite while remaining ascribed to the other rite.

§ 2. Clerics shall not presume in any manner to induce latin-rite faithful to transfer to an oriental [rite], or oriental-rite faithful to transfer to the latin [rite].

§ 3. It is not lawful for anyone, without coming to the Apostolic See, to transfer to another rite, or, after legitimate transfer, to return to the former.

§ 4. It is the right of a woman of rite different from the rite of the man, either going into marriage or during it, to transfer [rites]; when the marriage is ended, she has the power of returning freely to her former rite, unless by particular law it is provided otherwise.

---

[5] Bernard Shimkus, "The Determination and Transfer of Rite", Canon Law Studies, no. 244 (Catholic University of America, not published); William Bassett, "The Determination of Rite" (MS no. 3729, Gregorian University, 1965; printed version, no. 1910, Rome: Gregorian University Press, 1967).

§ 5. The practice, however long in duration, of receiving the sacred Synax in a foreign rite does not bring about a change of rite.

Canon Law Digest
I: 84–87; II: 49–50; III: 59; V: 195; VI: 161–62; IX: 51

Canon 99[6] (1983 CIC 113)

In the Church, besides physical persons, there are also moral persons, established by public authority, that are distinguished as collegial moral persons and non-collegial ones, such as churches, Seminaries, benefices, and so on.

Canon 100[7] (1983 CIC 113–15) Cross-Refs.: 1917 CIC 687, 1649

§ 1. The Catholic Church and the Apostolic See have moral personality by reason of divine ordinance; other inferior moral persons in the Church arise in her either by prescription of the law itself or by special concession of the competent ecclesiastical Superior granted by formal decree for a religious or charitable purpose.

§ 2. Collegial moral persons cannot be constituted unless they consist of at least three physical persons.

§ 3. Moral persons, whether collegial or non-collegial, are considered minors.

Canon Law Digest
I: 87; III: 59; IV: 89

Canon 101[8] (1983 CIC 119) Cross-Refs.: 1917 CIC 174, 1460

§ 1. Concerning acts of a collegial moral person:

1.° Unless it has been expressly established otherwise by common or particular law, that [act] has the force of law that, apart from null votes, has the approval of the absolute majority of those who cast votes or, after two inconclusive ballots, has a relative

[6] Brendan Brown, "The Canonical Juristic Personality with Special Reference to Its Status in the United States of America", Canon Law Studies, no. 39 (J. U. D.. thesis, Catholic University of America, 1927); James Granville, "Moral Personality in Canon Law and in the Law of Canada" (University of Laval, 1949).

[7] Thomas White, "The International Juridic Personality of the Holy See in Civil and Canon Legal Doctrine" (Pontifical Lateran University, 1960); Robert Stern, "The Catholic Church as a Moral Person by Divine Ordinance" (Pontifical Lateran University, 1965).

[8] John King, "Non-collegiate Acts of Moral Persons" (Pontifical Lateran University, 1951).

majority in the third ballot; but if the votes were equal, the presider can cast his vote after a third ballot to break a tie or, if it concerns an election and the president does not wish to cast his vote to break a tie, he is considered elected who is senior in ordination, first profession, or age.

2.° Whatever touches all as individuals must be approved by all.

§ 2. If it concerns the acts of a non-collegial moral person, the particular statutes and the norm of common law that govern such persons are to be followed.

Canon Law Digest
I: 87; VIII: 119

Canon 102 (1983 CIC 120)

§ 1. A moral person is by its nature perpetual; it can, nevertheless, be extinguished if it is suppressed by legitimate authority or if it has ceased to act for a period of one hundred years.

§ 2. If even [only] one of the members of a collegial moral person survives, all of the rights [of the moral person] fall to that individual.

Canon Law Digest
II: 50

Canon 103 (1983 CIC 125)

§ 1. Acts placed by physical or moral persons in virtue of extrinsic force that cannot be resisted are considered invalid.

§ 2. Acts placed under grave and unjustly incurred fear or by dolus are valid unless the law states otherwise; but they can, according to Canons 1684–89, be rescinded by judicial sentence, sought either by the injured party or by office.

Canon Law Digest
II: 50

Canon 104 (1983 CIC 126)

Error renders an act invalid if it concerns something that constitutes the substance of the act or if it amounts to a condition *that without which*; otherwise the act is valid unless otherwise provided in law; but in contracts, error gives rise to a rescissory action according to the norm of law.

Canon 105[9] (1983 CIC 127)

When the law requires that a Superior, in order to act, needs the consent or advice of various persons:

1.° If consent is required, the Superior invalidly acts against their vote; if only advice [is required] through such words as, for example, *from the advice of the consultors*, or *having heard the Chapter, pastor*, and so on, it is sufficient to act validly that the Superior shall hear those persons; although he is bound by no obligation of acceding to their vote, even if it is unanimous, still, great [care should be taken] when there are many persons to be heard, to deferring to their united opinions, nor from them, without prevailing reasons, in his judgment, [should he] depart;
2.° If there is required the consent or advice of not just one or two persons, but several together, these persons are to be legitimately convened, with due regard for the prescription of Canon 162, § 4, and their minds made known; the Superior can, in his prudent judgment about the gravity of the matter, apply to these [people] an oath of preserving secrecy;
3.° All those whose consent or advice is requested shall offer their opinion with reverence, fidelity, and sincerity.

Canon 106[10] (NA) Cross-Refs.: 1917 CIC 347, 478, 491, 701

Concerning precedence among various persons, whether physical or moral, the norms that follow are to be observed, with due regard for the special provisions that are given in their respective places:

1.° One who acts for another enjoys the precedence of that one; but in councils and similar meetings, a proxy yields precedence to those of the rank of his principal who are personally present;
2.° One who has authority over other persons, whether physical or moral, has the right of precedence over them;

[9] Gerard McKay, "Counsel and Consent: The Governance of the Diocesan Church according to the *Commentaria in Quinque Libros Decretalium* of Sinibaldo de'Freschi" (thesis, Gregorian University; printed version, no. 3091, Glasgow, 1982).

[10] Paul Schreiber, "Canonical Precedence", Canon Law Studies, no. 408 (J. C. D. thesis, Catholic University of America, 1961).

3.° Among various ecclesiastical persons, none of whom has authority over the others: those who pertain to a higher rank precede those of a lower; among those of the same rank, but not of the same order, those in a higher order precede those in a lower; if, finally, among those of the same rank and the same order, precedence is given to him who was the earlier advanced to that rank; if they were promoted at the same time, precedence goes to him senior in ordination, unless the junior was ordained by the Roman Pontiff; and if they received ordination at the same time, the one senior in age [has precedence];

4.° In precedence diversity of rite is not regarded;

5.° Among various moral persons of the same class and rank, that moral person takes precedence that is in uncontested quasi-possession of it; and if there is no evidence of this quasi-possession of precedence, precedence is given that moral person that was first established in the place where the issue arose. Among the members of the college, the right of precedence is determined by its legitimate constitutions, otherwise by legitimate custom, and, in the absence of both, by the norms of common law;

6.° It is for the local Ordinary in his own diocese to determine precedence among his subjects, taking into consideration the principles of common law, legitimate diocesan customs, and the offices held by those concerned. In pressingly urgent cases he may decide disputes concerning precedence even among exempt religious, if the latter are to participate with others in a public function; from such a decision there lies no suspensive appeal, but without prejudice to anyone's rights.

7.° Concerning persons belonging to the pontifical Household, precedence is fixed according to the particular privileges, rules, and traditions of that pontifical Household.

Canon Law Digest
I: 88; II: 50

Canon 107 (1983 CIC 207)

By divine institution there are in the Church *clerics* distinct from *laity*, although not all clerics [possess orders that] are of divine institution; either of them can be *religious*.

FIRST PART
ON CLERICS

SECTION 1
ON CLERICS IN GENERAL

Canon 108 (1983 CIC 266)

§ 1. Those who are taken into divine ministries at least by the reception of first tonsure are called clerics.

§ 2. [Clerics] are not all of the same rank, but among them there is a sacred hierarchy in which some are subordinated to others.

§ 3. By divine institution, the sacred hierarchy in respect of orders consists of Bishops, priests, and ministers; by reason of jurisdiction, [it consists of] the supreme pontificate and the subordinate episcopate; by institution of the Church other grades can also be added.

Canon Law Digest
VI: 162; VII: 91; IX: 51

Canon 109 (NA)

Those who are taken into the ecclesiastical hierarchy are not bound thereto by the consent or call of the people or secular power, but are constituted in the grades of the power of orders by sacred ordination; into the supreme pontificate, by divine law itself upon the completion of the conditions of legitimate election and acceptance; in the remanding grades of jurisdiction, by canonical mission.

Canon 110 (NA)

Although the title of Prelate is, for the sake of honor, given without jurisdiction to some clerics by the Apostolic See, nevertheless, properly speaking, Prelates in law are those clerics, whether secular or religious, who obtain ordinary jurisdiction in the external forum.

Canon Law Digest
II: 51

TITLE 1
On the ascription of clerics to a given diocese[1]

Canon 111 (1983 CIC 265–66)

§ 1. Every cleric whatsoever must be ascribed to a given diocese or religious [institute], so that wandering clerics are in no way admitted.

§ 2. Through the reception of first tonsure a cleric is ascribed, or, as they say, *incardinated*, into that diocese for whose service he was promoted.

Canon Law Digest
I: 89–91; II: 51–52; VI: 162; VII: 91

Canon 112 (1983 CIC 267)

Beyond those cases mentioned in Canons 114 and 641, § 2, in order for a cleric from another diocese to be validly incardinated, he must obtain from his own Ordinary letters of perpetual and absolute excardination written by him, as well as letters of similar perpetual and absolute incardination written by the Ordinary of the other diocese.

Canon Law Digest
IX: 52–60

Canon 113 (1983 CIC 272)

Excardination and incardination cannot be granted by the Vicar General without a special mandate, or by the Vicar Capitulary, except when the episcopal see has been vacant for one year and [then] with the consent of the Chapter.

Canon 114 (NA) Cross-Ref.: 1917 CIC 112

Excardination and incardination are considered [to take place] when a cleric has received a residential benefice from the Ordinary of another diocese with the consent of his own Ordinary given in writing, or when

[1] James McBride, "Incardination and Excardination of Seculars", Canon Law Studies, no. 145 (J. C. D. thesis, Catholic University of America, 1941).

[a cleric] receives permission in writing from him to be gone from the diocese forever.

Canon Law Digest
VI: 162; VII: 91

Canon 115 (1983 CIC 268)

One is likewise excardinated from his own diocese by religious profession in accord with Canon 585.

Canon Law Digest
II: 52

Canon 116 (1983 CIC 267)

Excardination is not to be granted except for just causes, and does not take effect until incardination in another diocese is secured, the Ordinary of which is to inform the prior Ordinary as quickly as possible.

Canon Law Digest
I: 93–97; III: 60

Canon 117 (1983 CIC 269)

The Ordinary shall not allow the incardination of outside clerics except:

1.° When the necessity or utility of the diocese require it, and with due regard for the prescriptions of law concerning canonical title of ordination;

2.° When he has learned from a legitimate document shown to him about the obtaining of legitimate excardination, and also has from the [excardinating] Curia, under secrecy if necessary, useful information about the [cleric's] birth, life, morals, and studies, especially when it concerns the incardination of clerics from different nations and language groups; the [excardinating] Ordinary moreover is gravely burdened in his conscience to be vigilant that the information be in conformity with the truth;

3.° The cleric has declared under oath in the presence of the Ordinary or his delegate that he wishes to be added forever to the service of the new diocese according to the norms of the sacred canons.

Canon Law Digest
III: 60

TITLE 2
On the rights and privileges of clerics

Canon 118[2] (1983 CIC 129, 274)

Only clerics can obtain powers, whether of orders or of ecclesiastical jurisdiction, and benefices or ecclesiastical pensions.

Canon Law Digest
I: 97–98; VII: 91

Canon 119 (1983 CIC 1370) Cross-Refs.: 1917 CIC 614, 680

All of the faithful should show reverence toward clerics according to the diversity of their grades and responsibilities, and they are struck by the crime of sacrilege if they ever inflict real damage on a cleric.

Canon 120[3] (NA) Cross-Refs.: 1917 CIC 614, 680, 1553, 2198, 2341

§ 1. Clerics shall in all cases, whether contentious or criminal, be brought before an ecclesiastical judge, unless it has been legitimately provided otherwise in certain places.

§ 2. Cardinal Fathers, Legates of the Apostolic See, Bishops, even titular ones, Abbots or Prelates *of no one*, supreme Superiors of religious [institutes] of pontifical right, and major Officials of the Roman Curia may not be summoned before lay judges for matters pertaining to their duties without coming to the Apostolic See; [the same is true for] others enjoying the privilege of the forum, without coming to the Ordinary of the place where the matter will be tried; the Ordinary, however, especially when a lay person is the petitioner, will not deny this permission except for just and grave causes, all the more so when he was unable to bring about a resolution of the controversy between the parties.

§ 3. If [clerics] nevertheless have been sued by one without the requisite permission, they can comply by reason of necessity in order to avoid greater dangers, notifying, however, the Superior who should have been contacted.

Canon Law Digest
III: 60

---

[2] Alexander Sigur, "Lay Cooperation with Ecclesiastical Jurisdiction" (diss. no. 7, Pontifical University of St. Thomas [Rome], 1949–1950).

[3] Annetto Depasquale, "Ecclesiastical Immunity and the Powers of the Inquisitor in Malta (1777–1785)" (Pontifical Lateran University, 1968).

Canon 121[4] (1983 CIC 289) Cross-Refs.: 1917 CIC 614, 680

All clerics are immune from military service and from other public civil offices that are alien to the clerical state.

Canon Law Digest

I: 98–109; II: 52–53; III: 61; IV: 90–93; VI: 163

Canon 122 (NA) Cross-Refs.: 1917 CIC 614, 680, 1923

Those clerics who are required to pay their creditors ought to be secure in regard to those things that are necessary for their honest upkeep, according to the prudent decision of the ecclesiastical judge, retaining, however, the obligation of paying their creditors as soon as possible.

Canon 123 (NA) Cross-Refs.: 1917 CIC 614, 680

A cleric cannot renounce the privileges [just] named; but he can lose them if he is reduced to the lay state or is struck by the perpetual privation of the right to wear religious garb, according to the norm of Canons 213, §1, and 2304; but he recovers them if this penalty is remitted or he is again admitted among clerics.

TITLE 3
On the obligations of clerics

Canon 124 (1983 CIC 276)

Clerics must lead an interior and exterior life holier than that of laity and should excel in rendering them an example of virtue and good deeds.

Canon Law Digest

II: 53; III: 61; IV: 93–96; VII: 91; VIII: 119–23; IX: 60–86; X: 9

[4] John Downs, "The Concept of Clerical Immunity", Canon Law Studies, no. 126 (J. C. D. thesis, Catholic University of America, 1941); James McGrath, "The Privilege of the Canon", Canon Law Studies, no. 242 (J. C. D. thesis, Catholic University of America, 1946); Richard Mulcahy, "The Exemption of the Clerics from Military Service" (diss. no. 27, Pontifical University of St. Thomas [Rome], 1957–1958); Arnold Simonse, "The Exemption of Clerics from Military Service" (diss. no. 2, Pontifical University of St. Thomas [Rome], 1968–1969).

Canon 125 (1983 CIC 276)

Local Ordinaries shall take care:

1.° That all clerics wash the stains of conscience by frequent sacramental penance;

2.° That [clerics] devote some part of every day to mental prayer, visitation of the most holy Sacrament, cultivation of the Marian rosary of the Virgin Mother of God, and strict examination of conscience.

Canon Law Digest
I: 109; II: 53; VII: 91

Canon 126[5] (1983 CIC 276) Cross-Refs.: 1917 CIC 420, 465

All secular priests must, at least every three years, perform spiritual exercises, for a time determined by the proper Ordinary, in a pious or other religious house designated by him; no one is exempt from this, except in particular cases, for a just cause and with the express permission of his Ordinary.

Canon Law Digest
I: 110–14; II: 53; V: 195; VI: 163; VII: 91–92

Canon 127[6] (1983 CIC 273)

All clerics, but especially presbyters, are bound by a special obligation to show reverence and obedience to their own Ordinary.

Canon Law Digest
I: 114; V: 195; VII: 92

Canon 128 (1983 CIC 274)

Whenever and as often as, in the judgment of the proper Ordinary, the necessity of the Church requires it, clerics are to take and faithfully fulfill the responsibilities that have been committed to them by the Bishop, unless a legitimate impediment excuses.

Canon Law Digest
IX: 86; X: 9–10

---

[5] Charles Patterson, "The Obligation of Spiritual Retreats for the Secular Clergy according to Canon 126" (diss. no. 42, Pontifical University of St. Thomas [Rome], 1956–1957).

[6] Joseph Sheehan, "The Obligation of Respect and Obedience of Clerics toward Their Ordinary (Canon 127)", Canon Law Studies, no. 344 (thesis, Catholic University of America, 1954).

Canon 129 (1983 CIC 279)

Upon ordination to the priesthood, clerics shall not interrupt their studies, especially sacred ones; in sacred disciplines, the solid and traditional doctrine that has been commonly received by the Church shall be followed, avoiding profane verbal novelties and what falsely passes for science.

Canon Law Digest
I: 115–19; III: 61–63; V: 196; VI: 163; VII: 92

Canon 130 (NA) Cross-Refs.: 1917 CIC 389, 404, 459, 2376

§ 1. The course of studies having been completed, all priests, even if they hold a parochial or canonical benefice, unless they have been exempted by the local Ordinary for just cause, shall submit each year for at least three years to an examination in the various disciplines in the sacred sciences, opportunely indicated beforehand, according to the manner determined by the same Ordinary.

§ 2. All things being equal, in the conferral of offices and benefices, preference should be given to those who did well in the above-mentioned trials.

Canon Law Digest
I: 119–20; VII: 92

Canon 131[7] (1983 CIC 279) Cross-Refs.: 1917 CIC 448, 2377

§ 1. In the episcopal city and in each vicariate several times per year, on days determined by the local Ordinary, meetings are to be held, called conferrals or conferences, on morals and liturgy; to which can be added other exercises that the Ordinary judges to be useful toward promoting the knowledge and piety of clerics.

§ 2. If meetings are difficult to have, written answers to questions should be sent in according to norms established by the Ordinary.

§ 3. All secular priests, even exempt religious if they have care of souls, are to attend the conference or, there being no conference, are to send in written answers to the cases, unless they have obtained express exemption

[7] Lawrence Hoffman, "Clergy Conferences: Canon 131", Canon Law Studies, no. 383 (thesis, Catholic University of America, 1957).

from the Ordinary beforehand; the same applies to other religious if they have obtained from the Ordinary the faculty of hearing confessions [and] if they do not have conferences in their houses.

Canon Law Digest
II: 53; VII: 92

Canon 132 (1983 CIC 277)

§ 1. Clerics constituted in major orders are prohibited from marriage and are bound by the obligation of observing chastity, so that those sinning against this are sacrilegious, with due regard for the prescription of Canon 214, § 1.

§ 2. Minor clerics can enter marriage, but, unless the marriage was null because of inflicted force and fear, they drop from the clerical state by the law itself.

§ 3. A married man who, even in good faith, takes up major orders without apostolic dispensation is prohibited from exercising those orders.

Canon Law Digest
I: 120–21; III: 63; V: 197; VI: 163; VII: 92–101;
VIII: 123; IX: 86

Canon 133 (1983 CIC 277) Cross-Ref.: 1917 CIC 2176

§ 1. Clerics should take care not to retain or in other ways to frequent women upon whom suspicion can fall.

§ 2. It is permitted to them to cohabit only with the sort of women whose natural bond places them above suspicion, such as a mother, sister, aunt, and others of this kind, or others whose upright way of life in view of maturity of years removes all suspicion.

§ 3. The judgment about retaining or frequenting women, even those who commonly fall under no suspicion, in particular cases where scandal is possible or where there is given a danger of incontinence, belongs to the local Ordinary, who can prohibit clerics from retaining or frequenting [such women].

§ 4. Contumacious [clerics] are presumed [to be living in] concubinage.

Canon Law Digest
VII: 101

Canon 134[8] (1983 CIC 280) Cross-Ref.: 1917 CIC 476

The custom of common life among clerics is praiseworthy and to be favored so that, where it exists, to the degree possible, it should be preserved.

Canon Law Digest
VII: 101

Canon 135[9] (1983 CIC 276)

Clerics constituted in major orders, except those mentioned in Canons 213 and 214, are bound by the obligation of reciting completely the canonical hours according to the proper and approved liturgical books.

Canon Law Digest
I: 121–22; II: 54–55; III: 64–67; IV: 96–97; V:197–99;
VI: 164–66; VII: 101–10; VIII: 123–24; IX: 87–91

Canon 136[10] (1983 CIC 284) Cross-Ref.: 1917 CIC 2379

§ 1. All clerics must wear a decent ecclesiastical habit, according to the legitimate customs of the place or the prescriptions of the local Ordinary, [and] a tonsure or clerical crown, unless the received mores of the people indicate otherwise, [and] they shall cultivate simplicity in the wearing of hair.

§ 2. They shall not wear a ring, unless this right has been conceded them by apostolic privilege or law.

§ 3. Minor clerics who, on their own authority [and] without legitimate cause, leave off the ecclesiastical habit and tonsure, [upon] having been warned by the Ordinary, unless they correct their ways within one month, fall from the clerical state by the law itself.

Canon Law Digest
I: 123–25; VI: 167–68; VII: 110; VIII: 124–27; IX: 91; X: 11–15

---

[8] Mason Borgman, "The Common Life among Clerics in the Writings of St. Augustine of Hippo and Ecclesiastical Legislation", Canon Law Studies, no. 459 (J. C. D. thesis, Catholic University of America, 1968).

[9] Martin Semple, "The Obligation of the Divine Office in the Latin and Oriental Churches", Canon Law Studies, no. 454 (J. C. D. thesis, Catholic University of America, 1967).

[10] Bernard Ganter, "Clerical Attire", Canon Law Studies, no. 361 (thesis, Catholic University of America, 1955).

Canon 137 (1983 CIC 285)

Clerics are prohibited from posting bonds, even out of their own goods, if they have not consulted the local Ordinary.

Canon 138[11] (1983 CIC 285)

Clerics shall entirely abstain from all those things that are indecent to their state; they shall not engage in indecorous arts; they shall abstain from gambling games with risks of money; they shall not carry arms, except when there is just cause for fearing; hunting should not be indulged, and [then] never with clamor; taverns and similar places should not be entered without necessity or another just cause approved by the local Ordinary.

Canon Law Digest
I: 125; II: 55

Canon 139[12] (1983 CIC 285)

§ 1. They should avoid those things that, while not indecent, are still alien to the clerical state.

§ 2. They shall not exercise medicine or surgery without an apostolic indult; they shall not act as public functionaries or notaries, except in the ecclesiastical Curia; they shall not assume public offices that encompass the exercise of lay jurisdiction or administration.

§ 3. Without the permission of their Ordinary, they shall not go into the conduct of goods belonging to lay persons or into secular offices requiring the duty of rendering accounts; they shall not act in the role of procurator or advocate except in ecclesiastical tribunals or in civil [cases] that involve their goods or the goods of their church; in lay criminal trials threatening grave personal penalties [to the defendant], they shall take no part, not even by offering testimony without necessity.

§ 4. They shall not seek the responsibilities of senators or speakers passing laws, which one calls *deputies*, or accept [such offices] without the permission of the Holy See in those places where a pontifical prohibition exists; likewise they should not [be involved] anywhere without the per-

---

[11] John Donovan, "The Clerical Obligations of Canons 138 and 140", Canon Law Studies, no. 272 (thesis, Catholic University of America, 1949).

[12] Joseph Brunini, "The Clerical Obligations of Canons 139 and 142", Canon Law Studies, no. 103 (J. C. D. thesis, Catholic University of America, 1937); Ellsworth Kneal, "Medical Practice by the Clergy: The Limitations of Canons 139 § 2 and 985, n. 6 of the Code of Canon Law" (diss. no. 1, Pontifical University of St. Thomas [Rome], 1965–1966).

mission both of their own Ordinary and of the Ordinary of the place in which the election is being held.

Canon Law Digest
I: 126–37; II: 55–75; IV: 97–103; V: 199–205; VI: 168–69;
VII: 110; VIII: 128–30; X: 15–18

Canon 140[13] (NA)

Where there is danger of scandal, especially in public theaters, clerics should avoid shows, dances, and spectacles.

Canon Law Digest
I: 137–40; III: 67–68

Canon 141 (1983 CIC 289) Cross-Ref.: 1917 CIC 188

§ 1. [Clerics] should not volunteer in secular armies, except with the permission of the local Ordinary, which they might do in order to be free of an earlier draft; nor should they become involved in civil wars or disturbances of the public order in any way.

§ 2. A minor cleric who freely gives his name to the army in violation of the prescription of § 1 falls by law from the clerical state.

Canon 142[14] (1983 CIC 286) Cross-Ref.: 1917 CIC 2380

Clerics are prohibited from exercising, either for themselves or for the advantage of another, business or trades, either in their own name or by using the name of another.

Canon Law Digest
III: 68–69; VI: 169

Canon 143 (1983 CIC 283)

Clerics, even though they do not have a benefice or residential office, shall nevertheless not leave their diocese for a notable period of time without the at least presumed permission of their own Ordinary.

Canon Law Digest
I: 140; II: 75; VIII: 130

[13] Gerard Moverly, "The Theater Law of the First and Fourth Provincial Councils of Westminster" (diss. no. 14, Pontifical University of St. Thomas [Rome], 1953–1954); John Rafferty, "The Theater Law in Irish Plenary Councils" (diss. no. 10, Pontifical University of St. Thomas [Rome], 1962–1963).

[14] Arthur Dwyer, "The Decree *Pluribus ex documentis*" (diss. no. 10, Pontifical University of St. Thomas [Rome], 1951–1952).

Canon 144 (1983 CIC 271)

[A cleric] who goes to another diocese with the permission of his Ordinary remains incardinated in his diocese [and] can be recalled for just cause and observing natural equity; moreover, the Ordinary of the other diocese can for a just cause deny him permission to stay longer in his territory, unless he has conferred on him a benefice.

Canon Law Digest
I: 140; IX: 91

TITLE 4
On ecclesiastical office[15]

Canon 145 (1983 CIC 145)

§ 1. Ecclesiastical office in the wide sense is any responsibility exercised legitimately for a spiritual end; in the strict sense, however, it is a divinely or ecclesiastically ordered responsibility, constituted in a stable manner, conferred according to the norms of the sacred canons, entailing at least some participation in ecclesiastical power, whether of orders or of jurisdiction.

§ 2. In law, ecclesiastical office is taken in the strict sense, unless it appears otherwise from the context of the words.

Canon 146 (NA)

On offices attached to benefices in particular, besides the canons that follow, the prescriptions of Canons 1409 and following are to be kept.

Chapter 1
On the provision of ecclesiastical offices

Canon 147 (1983 CIC 146)

§ 1. No ecclesiastical office can be validly obtained without canonical provision.

[15] Donald Heintschel, "The Mediaeval Concept of an Ecclesiastical Office", Canon Law Studies, no. 363 (thesis, Catholic University of America, 1956).

§ 2. Under the name *canonical provision* comes a grant of ecclesiastical office made by the competent ecclesiastical authority according to the norms of the sacred canons.

Canon Law Digest
III: 69–71; IV: 103–4

Canon 148 (1983 CIC 147)

§ 1. The provision of ecclesiastical office is made either through free conferral by the legitimate Superior, or by his institution if it was preceded by presentation from a patron or by appointment, or by his confirmation or admission if there preceded an election or postulation, or even by simple election and acceptance of the election, if the election does not require confirmation.

§ 2. On the provision of offices by institution, the prescriptions of Canons 1448–71 are observed.

Canon Law Digest
I: 140; II: 75; III: 71

Canon 149 (1983 CIC 15) Cross-Ref.: 1917 CIC 1464

Those elected, postulated, presented, or appointed by anyone to ecclesiastical office are not to be confirmed, admitted, or instituted by a Superior below the Roman Pontiff until they are evaluated as suitable by their own Ordinary, even by examination, if it is required by law or by reason of the office or if the Ordinary deems it opportune.

Canon 150 (1983 CIC 153)

§ 1. The provision of an office that is not vacant by law according to the norm of Canon 183, § 1, is by that fact without force, nor does a subsequent vacancy revive [the attempted appointment].

§ 2. Nor does the promise of an office, whoever might have promised it, give rise to any juridic effect.

Canon 151 (1983 CIC 154)

An office that is vacant by law but that perchance is still held by another illegitimately can be conferred provided that, duly according to the sacred canons, this possession is declared not to be legitimate and that mention of this declaration is made in the letter of conferral.

Article 1—*On free conferral*[16]

Canon 152 (1983 CIC 157)

The local Ordinary has the right of providing for ecclesiastical offices in his own territory, unless it is shown otherwise; the Vicar General lacks this power, however, unless there is a special mandate.

Canon Law Digest
I: 141

Canon 153 (1983 CIC 149)

§ 1. That cleric is to be promoted to a vacant ecclesiastical office who is outstanding with those qualities that are required for that office by common or particular or foundational law.

§ 2. He shall be assumed [into office] who, all things being considered, is better suited, without regard to person.

§ 3. If the one being appointed lacks the requisite qualities, the appointment is null if it is so provided in the common, particular, or foundational law; otherwise it is valid, although it can be invalidated by sentence of the legitimate Superior.

Canon 154 (1983 CIC 150)

Offices that encompass the care of souls either in the external forum or the internal cannot be validly conferred on clerics who are not initiated into priesthood.

Canon 155 (1983 CIC 151) Cross-Ref.: 1917 CIC 458

The provision of an office to which no term is prescribed by special law shall not be deferred beyond six months' available time from the receipt of notice of the vacancy, with due regard for Canon 458.

Canon 156 (1983 CIC 152) Cross-Refs.: 1917 CIC 460, 1439, 2396

§ 1. Two incompatible offices cannot be conferred on anyone.

§ 2. Those offices are incompatible that cannot be fulfilled by the same person at the same time.

§ 3. With due regard for the prescription of Canon 188, n. 3, the grant of a second office made by the Apostolic See is invalid, unless, in the

[16] Joseph Manning, "The Free Conferral of Offices", Canon Law Studies, no. 219 (diss., Catholic University of America, 1945).

petitioning document, mention of the first incompatible office is made or a derogatory clause is attached.

Canon 157 (NA)

An office vacant by resignation or by sentence of privation from an Ordinary who accepted the resignation or who issued the sentence cannot validly be conferred on his or the resigning one's familiars or blood-relatives or affines up the second degree inclusive.

Canon 158 (1983 CIC 155)

Whoever, while supplying for another's negligence or inability, confers an office acquires no power thereby over the one appointed; instead the juridic status thus constituted is the same as if the provision had been made according to the regular norm of law.

Canon 159 (1983 CIC 156) Cross-Ref.: 1917 CIC 364

The provision of any office is to be done in writing.

Article 2—*On election*[17]

Canon 160 (1983 CIC 164)

The election of the Roman Pontiff is guided solely by the const. of [Pope] Pius X *Vacante Sede Apostolica* of 25 Dec. 1904; in other ecclesiastical elections, the prescriptions of the canons that follow are to be observed [as well as] those special ones, if there are any, that are established for individual offices.

Canon Law Digest

I: 141–42; II: 75; III: 71; V: 205–11; VI: 169–70; VIII: 130–69

[17] Daniel Galliher, "Canonical Elections", Canon Law Studies, no. 2 (D. C. L. thesis, Catholic University of America, 1917; Somerset, Ohio: Rosary Press, 1917); Anscar Parsons, "Canonical Elections", Canon Law Studies, no. 118 (thesis, Catholic University of America, 1939); John MacCormack, "The Number and Computation of Votes in a Canonical Election" (Pontifical Lateran University, 1950); Isaac Jacob, "The Meaning of Pars Sanior in the Rule of St. Benedict and Its Use in the Decretal Collection of Pope Gregory IX with a Study of the Electoral Law as Found in the Decretum of Gratian", Canon Law Studies, no. 437 (diss., Catholic University of America, 1964).

Canon 161 (1983 CIC 165)

If a college has the right of electing to a vacant office, the election, unless established otherwise by law, is not to be deferred beyond three available months calculated from having notice of the [vacant] office; if this time runs without action, the ecclesiastical Superior who has the right of confirming the election or of providing successively [for it] can provide for the vacant office freely.

Canon 162 (1983 CIC 166) Cross-Ref.: 1917 CIC 105

§ 1. With due regard for particular constitutions or customs, the president of the college, having determined a manner, place, and time convenient for the electors, shall convoke all of the college; this convocation, when it must be personal, is valid if it is done either in the place of the domicile or quasi-domicile [of the elector] or in the place of actual presence.

§ 2. If one of those to be called was neglected and therefore was absent, the election is valid, but upon his request, his omission and absence being proven, [the election] must be invalidated by the competent Superior even following confirmation, provided it is juridically shown that within three days of having notice of the election, [the objection] was transmitted.

§ 3. But if more than one-third of the electors are neglected, the election is null by law.

§ 4. A defect of convocation does not bar [validity] if the ones overlooked nevertheless were there.

§ 5. If it concerns election to an office that the elected one will hold for life, a convocation of electors before the vacancy of the office has no juridic effect.

Canon Law Digest
I: 142

Canon 163 (1983 CIC 167)

A convocation having legitimately been done, the right of electing belongs to those who are present on the established convocation day, excluding the faculty of casting a vote not only by letter but also by procurator, unless special law provides otherwise.

Canon Law Digest
I: 142

Canon 164 (1983 CIC 168)

Even though one has the right of casting several votes from [multiple] titles in his own name, he can cast only one [ballot].

Canon 165 (1983 CIC 169)

No stranger to the college can be admitted to the vote, with due regard for legitimately acquired privileges; otherwise, the election is null by that fact.

Canon 166 (1983 CIC 170)

If laity in any way involve themselves against the canonical liberty of the ecclesiastical election, the election is invalid by law.

Canon 167[18] (1983 CIC 171)

§ 1. [The following] cannot cast a vote:

1.° Those incapable of a human act;

2.° Those below the age of puberty;

3.° Those affected with a censure or infamy of law, though after a declaratory or condemnatory sentence;

4.° Those who have given their name to a heretical or schismatic sect or [who] publicly adhere [to same];

5.° Those lacking an active voice either from a legitimate sentence of a judge or by common or particular law.

§ 2. If one of the above-mentioned is admitted, his vote is null but the election is valid, unless it is shown that without his vote the one elected would not have gathered the required number of votes or unless he was knowingly admitted [while] excommunicated by a declaratory or condemnatory sentence.

Canon Law Digest
VI: 170–71; VIII: 169–70

[18] Timothy Mock, "Disqualification of Electors in Ecclesiastical Elections", Canon Law Studies, no. 365 (thesis, Catholic University of America, 1958).

Canon 168 (1983 CIC 167)

If one of the electors is present in the house in which the election takes place but cannot be at the election because of infirmity, his written vote can be requested by the teller, unless established otherwise by particular law or legitimate custom.

Canon 169 (1983 CIC 172)

§ 1. A vote is null unless it was:

1.° Free; and therefore the vote is invalid if the electors, directly or indirectly, were subjected to grave fear or dolus in order to vote for a certain person or for several together;

2.° Secret, certain, absolute, and determinate.

§ 2. Conditions attached to a vote before the election are considered as not having been attached.

Canon Law Digest
VIII: 170

Canon 170 (NA)

No one can validly give a vote for his own self.

Canon 171 (1983 CIC 173)

§ 1. Before an election by secret ballot, there should be appointed, unless they are already appointed by their own statutes, at least two tellers from the membership of the college, who together with the president, if he is a member of the college, shall take an oath that they will faithfully fulfill their duties and maintain secrecy concerning the acts of the sessions, even after the election is completed.

§ 2. The tellers will take care that the election be conducted secretly, diligently, individually, and according to the order of precedence among the electors; the final votes having been collected, in the presence of the presider of the election, according to the form prescribed by their own constitutions or legitimate customs, they shall determine whether the number of votes matches the number of electors, [and] they shall examine the votes and make public how many votes were gained by each [candidate].

§ 3. If the number of votes exceeds the number of eligible ones, the acts are null.

§ 4. Once the counting is completed, or after the session, if there were several votes in the same session, the ballots are burned immediately.

§ 5. All of the acts of the election are to be accurately recorded by him who acted as notary and signed at least by him who was notary, [as well as] by the president and the tellers, and diligently preserved in the tabulary of the college.

Canon 172 (1983 CIC 174)

§ 1. The election, unless otherwise provided by law, can also be accomplished by compromise if indeed the electors, by unanimous and written consent, transfer the right of electing from themselves to one or several suitable [persons], either members of the college or outsiders, who in the name of all elect in virtue of the received faculty.

§ 2. If it concerns a clerical college, the compromisors must be priests, otherwise the election is invalid.

§ 3. The compromisors must observe, for the validity of the election, the conditions applied to them that are not contrary to common law; if no conditions were attached, the common law on elections applies to them; but conditions contrary to law are considered not to have been applied.

§ 4. If only one person was named by the electors as a compromisor, this one cannot elect himself; if several were designated as compromisors, none of them can add his own consent to the remaining ones in order to bring about his own election.

Canon 173 (1983 CIC 175)

The compromise ceases and the right of electing returns to the [members] if:

1.° The college revokes its authority [the process not having started];
2.° One of the conditions imposed on the compromisors has not been observed or followed;
3.° There was an absolute election, [but] it was null.

Canon 174 (1983 CIC 176)

That one is considered elected and should be proclaimed by the president of the college who has gotten the required number of votes according to the norm of Canon 101, § 1, n. 1.

Canon 175 (1983 CIC 177) Cross-Ref.: 1917 CIC 182

The election should be communicated quickly to the one elected, who must within at [most] eight useful days from the reception of the information make known whether he consents to the election or whether he refuses it; otherwise he loses all rights acquired from the election.

Canon Law Digest
III: 71–72

Canon 176 (1983 CIC 177–79)

§ 1. If an elected one refuses [to accept office], he loses all acquired rights from the election, even if afterward he repents of the refusal; but he can be elected again; the college must proceed to a new election within one month of having notice of the refusal.

§ 2. If the elected one accepts the election and confirmation is not required, he obtains full rights immediately; otherwise he acquires only a right to office.

§ 3. Before accepting confirmation, [the elected one] shall not involve himself on pretext of the election in any administrative offices, whether spiritual or temporal, and any acts he might place then are null.

Canon 177 (1983 CIC 179)

§ 1. The elected one, if the election requires confirmation, must at least within eight days from the date of the election seek confirmation personally or through another from the competent Superior; otherwise he is deprived of all rights, unless he can prove that he was legitimately detained by a just impediment from petitioning confirmation.

§ 2. The Superior, if the elected one is suitable and the election was conducted in accord with the norm of law, cannot refuse confirmation.

§ 3. This confirmation must be given in writing.

§ 4. Upon receipt of confirmation, the elected one obtains full rights in the office, unless otherwise provided by law.

Canon Law Digest
III: 72

Canon 178 (NA)

If the election is not conducted within the prescribed period, or if the college is deprived of the right of electing by penalty, free provision of the office devolves on the Superior who would have been the one to confirm the election, or to whomever the right of provision belongs successively.

Article 3—*On postulation*[19]

Canon 179 (1983 CIC 180)

§ 1. If an impediment bars the election of one whom the electors think is, and prefer as, the more suitable, and it is possible and usual for this impediment to be dispensed, they can cast their vote for him, unless otherwise provided by law, and postulate him to the competent Superior, even if it concerns an office for which the elected one requires no confirmation.

§ 2. Compromisors cannot postulate [a candidate] unless they are expressly authorized to do so in the mandate.

Canon Law Digest
I: 142; VIII: 170

Canon 180 (1983 CIC 181)

§ 1. In order that the postulation have force, it must have the majority of the votes; moreover, if it coincides with election, at least two-thirds are required.

§ 2. A vote for postulation must be expressed by the words "*I postulate*" or its equivalent; a formula "*I vote for or postulate*" or its equivalent is valid for election if an impediment does not exist, otherwise [it suffices] for postulation.

Canon Law Digest
I: 142–43

Canon 181 (1983 CIC 182)

§ 1. A postulation must be sent at least within eight days to the Superior to whom it pertains to confirm the election, if he has the faculty of dispensing from the impediment; otherwise to the Roman Pontiff or to another [Superior] having the faculty [of dispensation].

§ 2. If within the prescribed time the postulation is not sent, by that fact it falls into nullity and the electors are deprived of the right of electing or postulating for that time, unless they prove they were impeded by a just obstacle from sending the postulation.

§ 3. Through postulation the one postulated acquires no rights, and the Superior is permitted to reject him.

---

[19] Charles Schettler, "Postulation by Ecclesiastical Bodies", Canon Law Studies, no. 453 (Catholic University of America, 1967).

§ 4. The electors cannot revoke the presentation postulated to the Superior unless the Superior consents.

Canon Law Digest
III: 73

Canon 182 (1983 CIC 183)

§ 1. If the postulation is rejected by the Superior, the right of electing returns to the college, unless the electors postulated one whom they knew to be detained by an impediment from which one could not be or usually is not dispensed; in that case the provision pertains to the Superior.

§ 2. If the postulation is accepted, it is signified to the one postulated, who must respond according to the norms of Canon 175.

§ 3. If he accepts it, he immediately acquires full rights in the office.

Chapter 2
On the loss of ecclesiastical offices[20]

Canon 183 (1983 CIC 184) Cross-Refs.: 1917 CIC 150, 208, 873

§ 1. Ecclesiastical office is lost by resignation, privation, removal, transfer, or lapse of a predetermined time.

§ 2. Ecclesiastical office is not lost by the termination of the authority of the Superior by whom the grant was made, unless the law provides otherwise or in the grant [of office] the clause *at our good pleasure* or its equivalent is present.

Canon Law Digest
VI: 171

Canon 184[21] (1983 CIC 187)

Anyone of sound mind can resign ecclesiastical office for a just cause, unless resignation is specifically forbidden to him by a special prohibition.

Canon Law Digest
VIII: 170

---

[20] Gary Gresko, "Stability in the Pastoral Office" (diss. no. 1, Pontifical University of St. Thomas [Rome], 1982–1983).

[21] Gerald McDevitt, "The Renunciation of an Ecclesiastical Office", Canon Law Studies, no. 218 (J. C. D. thesis, Catholic University of America, 1945).

Canon 185 (1983 CIC 188)

Resignation is invalid by law if it was made out of grave fear unjustly inflicted, [or from] fraud, substantial error, or simony.

Canon 186 (1983 CIC 189) Cross-Refs.: 1917 CIC 1487, 2150

Resignation, in order to be valid, must be made by the one resigning either in writing or orally in the presence of two witnesses or even by a procurator who is endowed by a special mandate; the written document of resignation is placed in the Curia.

Canon 187 (1983 CIC 189) Cross-Ref.: 1917 CIC 2314

§ 1. Generally, in order that resignation be valid, it must be submitted to him by whom it must be accepted, or if acceptance is not required, [it must be submitted to the Superior] from whom the cleric took the office or who holds his place.

§ 2. Therefore, if office was conferred by confirmation, admission, or institution, resignation must be made to the Superior who by law makes the confirmation, admission, or institution.

Canon 188 (1983 CIC 194) Cross-Refs.: 1917 CIC 156, 1444, 2168, 2314, 2379, 2388

Any office becomes vacant upon the fact and without any declaration by tacit resignation recognized by the law itself if a cleric:

1.° Makes religious profession with due regard for the prescription of Canon 584 concerning benefices;
2.° Within the useful time established by law or, legal provision lacking, as determined by the Ordinary, fails to take possession of the office;
3.° Accepts another ecclesiastical office incompatible with the prior, and has obtained peaceful possession of [the other office];
4.° Publicly defects from the Catholic faith;
5.° Contracts marriage even, as they say, merely civilly;
6.° Against the prescription of Canon 141, § 1, freely gives his name to a secular army;
7.° Disposes of ecclesiastical habit on his own authority and without just cause, unless, having been warned by the Ordinary, he

resumes [wearing it] within a month of having received the warning;

8.° Deserts illegitimately the residence to which he is bound and, having received a warning from the Ordinary and not being detained by a legitimate impediment, neither appears nor answers within an appropriate time as determined by the Ordinary.

Canon 189 (1983 CIC 189)

§ 1. Superiors, without just or proportionate cause, should not accept resignations.

§ 2. The local Ordinary shall accept or reject a resignation within one month.

Canon Law Digest
I: 143

Canon 190 (1983 CIC 189)

§ 1. Once a resignation has been legitimately made and accepted, the office becomes vacant as soon as the acceptance is made known to the one resigning.

§ 2. One resigning remains in office until he has received certain notice of acceptance from the Superior.

Canon 191 (1983 CIC 189)

§ 1. Once resignation has been legitimately done, there is given no more place for reconsideration, although the one resigning can obtain the [same] office by another title.

§ 2. Upon acceptance of the resignation, notice should be promptly given to those who have any right in the provision of the office.

Canon Law Digest
I: 143

Canon 192[22] (1983 CIC 193, 196)

§ 1. Privation of office is incurred either by law or by deed of the legitimate Superior.

[22] Chester Thompson, "The Simple Removal from Office", Canon Law Studies, no. 285 (diss., Catholic University of America, 1951).

§ 2. If it concerns an irremovable office, the Ordinary cannot deprive a cleric of it except by means of a process according to the norm of law.

§ 3. If [it concerns] a removable [office], privation can be decided by the Ordinary for any just cause, in his prudent judgment, even without a delict, observing natural equity, though [he is] scarcely bound to follow any certain manner of proceeding, [though] with due regard for the prescription of the canons concerning removable parishes; but privation does not take effect until after it has been communicated by the Superior; and recourse is given against the decree of the Ordinary to the Apostolic See, but only in devolution.

Canon 193 (1983 CIC 190)

§ 1. Transfer from one ecclesiastical office to another can be done only by one who has the right both of accepting resignation and of removing [one] from the first office and of promoting him to another.

§ 2. For transfer, if it is done with the consent of the cleric, any just cause suffices; if the cleric refuses, there is required nearly the same cause as in the manner of proceeding to privation, with due regard for the prescriptions of Canons 2162–67 that apply to the transfer of pastors.

Canon Law Digest
I: 143

Canon 194 (1983 CIC 191) Cross-Ref.: 1917 CIC 430

§ 1. In transfer, the first office becomes vacant when the cleric takes canonical possession of the second [office], unless otherwise indicated by law or prescript of the legitimate Superior.

§ 2. The one transferred receives the revenues of the first office until he occupies the second.

Canon 195 (NA)

Those who elect or postulate or present a cleric to office are not able to deprive him of office or recall him or remove him or transfer him to another.

TITLE 5
On ordinary and delegated power[23]

Canon 196 (1983 CIC 129–30)

The power of jurisdiction or governance, which exists in the Church by divine institution, is for the external forum and for the internal forum or conscience, whether sacramental or extra-sacramental.

Canon Law Digest
III: 73

Canon 197 (1983 CIC 131)

§ 1. Ordinary power of jurisdiction is that which is attached to an office by law; delegated [power is that which] is committed to a person.

§ 2. Ordinary power can be either proper or vicarious.

Canon Law Digest
II: 75; III: 73

Canon 198[24] (1983 CIC 134) Cross-Ref.: 1917 CIC 66

§ 1. In law by the name of *Ordinaries* are understood, unless they are expressly excepted, in addition to the Roman Pontiff, a residential Bishop in his own territory, an Abbot or Prelate *of no one* and their Vicar General, Administrator, Vicar or Prefect Apostolic, and likewise those who, in the absence of the above-mentioned, temporarily take their place in governance by prescript of law or by approved constitution, and, for their subjects, major Superiors of exempt clerical religious [institutes].

§ 2. By the name of *Local Ordinaries* come all those just mentioned with the exception of religious Superiors.

Canon Law Digest
I: 144; II: 75–76; III: 73–75

[23] Raymond Kearney, "The Principles of Delegation", Canon Law Studies, no. 55 (J. C. D. thesis, Catholic University of America, 1929); James Tobin, "The Necessity of Knowledge and Acceptation of Delegated Jurisdiction for Its Validity" (diss. no. 18, Pontifical University of St. Thomas [Rome], 1949–1950); James Cuneo, "Concepts in Ecclesiastical Power in Recent Studies Edited by the Canon Law Society of America: Reflections toward Understanding Jurisdiction for Functioning in the Church" (Gregorian University; printed version, no. 2576, 1975).

[24] Michael Keene, "Religious Ordinaries and Canon 198", Canon Law Studies, no. 135 (J. C. D. thesis, Catholic University of America, 1942).

Canon 199 (1983 CIC 137) Cross-Ref.: 1917 CIC 1606

§ 1. Whoever has ordinary power of jurisdiction can delegate it to another in whole or in part, unless it is expressly provided otherwise by law.

§ 2. Even the power of jurisdiction delegated by the Apostolic See can be subdelegated either for an act or even habitually, unless [the one with the power] was chosen because of personal characteristics or subdelegation is prohibited.

§ 3. Power delegated for a universe of causes by one below the Roman Pontiff who has ordinary power can be subdelegated for individual cases.

§ 4. In other cases, delegated power of jurisidiction can only be subdelegated by a concession expressly made, although delegated judges can delegate the non-jurisdictional elements [of their work] without express commission.

§ 5. No subdelegated power can be subdelegated again, unless this was expressly granted.

Canon Law Digest
I: 145; III: 75

Canon 200 (1983 CIC 131, 138) Cross-Ref.: 1917 CIC 1606

§ 1. Ordinary power of jurisdiction delegated for a universe of causes is to be widely interpreted; any others are to be strictly [interpreted]; the one to whom power is delegated is also understood as having all that power that, if lacking, would render him unable to exercise power.

§ 2. On him who asserts delegated power falls the burden of proving the delegation.

Canon 201[25] (1983 CIC 91, 136) Cross-Ref.: 1917 CIC 1606

§ 1. The power of jurisdiction can be exercised directly only over subjects.

§ 2. Judicial power, whether ordinary or delegated, cannot be exercised on one's own behalf or outside of [one's own] territory, with due regard for the prescriptions of Canons 401, § 1, 881, § 2, and 1637.

§ 3. Unless it is established otherwise by the nature of the things or by law, voluntary power of jurisdiction, that is, non-judicial [power], can be

[25] David Thomas, "The Extra-Territorial Powers of the Local Ordinary" (thesis, Gregorian University; printed version, no. 1138, 1958).

exercised on one's own behalf or while outside of [one's own] territory and over subjects absent from [one's] territory.

Canon Law Digest
I: 145; II: 76; III: 75

Canon 202 (NA) Cross-Ref.: 1917 CIC 1606

§ 1. An act of jurisdictional power, whether ordinary or delegated, placed for the external forum applies as well in the internal [forum], but not conversely.

§ 2. Power placed for the internal forum can be exercised also in the internal forum extra-sacramentally, unless a sacrament is required.

§ 3. If the forum for which the power is given is not expressed, the power is to be understood as [being] granted for both fora, unless it appears otherwise from the nature of the thing.

Canon Law Digest
I: 145

Canon 203 (1983 CIC 133) Cross-Ref.: 1917 CIC 1606

§ 1. A delegate who exceeds the limits of his mandate either in regard to subject matter or persons accomplishes nothing.

§ 2. A delegate is not considered to have acted excessively, however, if he acts in a manner other than one that would have pleased the one delegating, unless the manner of acting was prescribed as a condition by the one delegating.

Canon 204 (1983 CIC 139) Cross-Ref.: 1917 CIC 1048, 1606

§ 1. But if someone goes to the Superior, skipping the inferior, the power of the inferior is not therefore suspended, whether this was ordinary or delegated.

§ 2. Nevertheless, the inferior should not involve himself in things brought to the Superior except for grave and urgent cause; in this case he should notify the Superior immediately.

Canon 205 (1983 CIC 140) Cross-Ref.: 1917 CIC 1606

§ 1. If several obtain delegated jurisdiction for the same matter, and it is unclear whether the delegation was made in solidarity or collegially, it is presumed made in solidarity regarding voluntary matters and collegially regarding judicial ones.

§ 2. If several are delegated in solidarity, whoever first sees to the matter excludes the others from it, unless afterward he is impeded or wishes to proceed no further in the matter.

§ 3. If several are delegated collegially, all of them must proceed together for the validity of their acts in treating the matter, unless provided otherwise in the mandate.

Canon 206 (1983 CIC 141) Cross-Ref.: 1917 CIC 1606

Several having been delegated successively, that one must see to the matter whose mandate was earliest and was not abrogated later by express rescript.

Canon Law Digest
III: 76

Canon 207[26] (1983 CIC 142) Cross-Ref.: 1917 CIC 77, 1606

§ 1. Delegated power is extinguished by completion of the mandate; [likewise] by the elapse of time; [likewise] by exhaustion of the number of cases for which it was granted, by the cessation of the final cause of the delegation, by revocation of the one delegating directly communicated to the delegate, or by resignation of the one delegated communicated directly to the one delegating and accepted by him, but not by the loss of authority on the part of the one delegating, except for the two cases mentioned in Canon 61.

§ 2. But for power granted for the internal forum, an act placed inadvertently after the elapse of time or exhaustion of the number of cases is valid.

§ 3. When there are several delegated collegially, if one ceases [to have power], the delegation of the others also ceases, unless something else is shown by the tenor of the delegation.

Canon Law Digest
III: 76

Canon 208 (1983 CIC 143)

According to the norm of Canon 183, § 2, ordinary power is not extinguished by the loss of authority by the one granting the office to which

[26] Max De Witt, "The Cessation of Delegated Power", Canon Law Studies, no. 330 (thesis, Catholic University of America, 1954).

the power is attached; but it ceases with the loss of office; and it is silent with legitimate appeal having been placed, unless perhaps the appeal is only in devolution, with due regard for the prescription of Canons 2264 and 2284.

Canon Law Digest
III: 76

Canon 209[27] (1983 CIC 144) Cross-Ref.: 1917 CIC 1606

In common error or in positive or probable doubt about either law or fact, the Church supplies jurisdiction for both the external and internal forum.

Canon Law Digest
II: 76–77; III: 76; VII: 110; VIII: 170–74; IX: 91

Canon 210 (NA)

Power of orders committed to a person or attached to office by a legitimate ecclesiastical Superior cannot be passed on to others, unless this is expressly allowed by law or by the indult of grant.

TITLE 6
On the reduction of clerics to the lay state[28]

Canon 211 (1983 CIC 290)

§ 1. Although sacred ordination, once validly received, can never be invalidated, nevertheless, a major cleric can be returned to the lay state by a rescript of the Holy See, by a decree or sentence according to the norm of Canon 214, or finally as a penalty of degradation.

[27] Francis Miaskiewicz, "Supplied Jurisdiction according to Canon 209", Canon Law Studies, no. 122 (diss., Catholic University of America, 1940); Laurence Carr, "A Study of the Power Supplied by the Church in Common Error according to Canon 209" (D. C. L. thesis, Librarian's Office 693, Maynooth [Ireland], 1947); John Finn, "Applicability of Canon 209 to Assistance at Marriage" (diss. no. 23, Pontifical University of St. Thomas [Rome], 1949–1950).

[28] Stephen Findlay, "Canonical Norms Governing the Deposition and Degradation of Clerics", Canon Law Studies, no. 130 (J. C. D. thesis, Catholic University of America, 1941); John Lennon, "The Non-penal Reduction of Secular Clergy to the Lay State" (MS no. 880, Gregorian University, 1941); Francis Sweeney, "The Reduction of Clerics to the Lay State", Canon Law Studies, no. 223 (J. C. D. thesis, Catholic University of America, 1945); Matthew Forman, "The Laicization of Priests" (diss. no. 7, Pontifical University of St. Thomas [Rome], 1971–1972).

§ 2. A minor cleric can be returned to the lay state not only automatically as a result of the causes described in law but also upon his own will, having informed the local Ordinary, or by a decree of the same Ordinary given for a just cause, if namely the Ordinary, all things considered, prudently judges that the cleric is not [sufficiently] consistent with the decorum of the clerical state to be promoted to sacred orders.

Canon Law Digest
II: 77; III: 76–77; IV: 104–6; VII: 110

Canon 212 (1983 CIC 293)

§ 1. One who was constituted in minor orders and who for any reason returned to the lay state, in order that he be readmitted to the clergy, requires the permission of the Ordinary of the diocese in which he was incardinated by ordination, [which permission] is not to be granted except after a diligent examination of the life and morals and an appropriate trial, according to the judgment of that Ordinary.

§ 2. A cleric in major orders who returned to the lay state, in order that he be admitted again to the clergy, requires the permission of the Holy See.

Canon 213 (1983 CIC 291–92) Cross-Refs.: 1917 CIC 123, 135

§ 1. All those who are legitimately removed or who return from the clerical state to the lay state by that fact lose all offices, benefices, clerical rights, and privileges and are prohibited from going around in ecclesiastical garb and wearing the tonsure.

§ 2. A major cleric, however, is bound by the obligation of celibacy, with due regard for the prescription of Canon 214.

Canon Law Digest
VI: 171

Canon 214 (1983 CIC 290, 1708–12)
Cross-Refs.: 1917 CIC 132, 135, 211, 213

§ 1. A cleric who, coerced by grave fear, receives sacred ordination, and does not later, once the fear has passed, ratify that ordination at least tacitly by the exercise of orders, [and] wanting by such an act to subject himself to clerical obligations, is returned to the lay state by sentence of a judge, upon legitimate proof of coercion and lack of ratification, [by which sentence] all obligations of celibacy and canonical hours cease.

§ 2. The coercion and lack of ratification must be proved according to the norm of Canons 1993–98.

Canon Law Digest
I: 146; II: 78; IV: 106–7; V: 211–12; VI: 171;
VII: 110–24; VIII: 174–79; IX: 92–101

SECTION 2
ON CLERICS IN SPECIFIC

Canon 215[29] (1983 CIC 368, 373, 381)

§ 1. It is for the supreme power of the Church alone to erect or otherwise circumscribe, divide, unite, [or] suppress ecclesiastical provinces, dioceses, abbeys and prelatures *of no one*, apostolic vicariates, [or] apostolic prefectures.

§ 2. Under the name of dioceses in law come also abbeys and prelatures *of no one*; [likewise under the name of] Bishop come Abbots and Prelates *of no one*, unless from the nature of the thing or the context of words something else appears.

Canon Law Digest
I: 146; II: 78; III: 77–80; IV: 107; VI: 171; VII: 124–25;
VIII: 179–81; IX: 102–3; X: 18–19

Canon 216[30] (1983 CIC 374) Cross-Ref.: 1917 CIC 451

§ 1. The territory of every diocese is to be divided up into distinct territorial parts; to each part a specific church and determined population are assigned, with its own rector as its pastor, who is over it for the necessary care of souls.

§ 2. In an equivalent manner, an apostolic vicariate and an apostolic prelature should be divided where this can be done conveniently.

[29] Bernard Prusak, "The Canonical Concept of Particular Church before and after Vatican II" (Pontifical Lateran University, 1967).

[30] Nicholas Connolly, "The Canonical Erection of Parishes", Canon Law Studies, no. 114 (J. C. D. thesis, Catholic University of America, 1938); Joseph Ciesluk, "National Parishes in the United States", Canon Law Studies, no. 190 (thesis, Catholic University of America, 1944); Anthony Mickells, "The Constitutive Elements of Parishes", Canon Law Studies, no. 296 (thesis, Catholic University of America, 1950); John Kelly, "The Legal Status of Mission Stations" (doctoral diss. 39, University of Ottawa, 1953); Paul O'Connell, "The Concept of the Parish in the Light of the Second Vatican Council", Canon Law Studies, no. 470 (Catholic University of America, 1969).

§ 3. The parts of the diocese mentioned in § 1 are *parishes*; the parts of the apostolic vicariate and apostolic prelature, if a specific rector has been assigned, are called *quasi-parishes*.

§ 4. Parishes based on diversity of the language or nationality of the faithful found in the same city or territory cannot be constituted without special apostolic indult, nor can familial or personal parishes; as to those already constituted, nothing is to be modified without consulting the Apostolic See.

Canon Law Digest
I: 146–54; II: 78–80; III: 80; IV: 108; V: 212–14;
VI: 171–72; VII: 125; X: 19–21

Canon 217 (1983 CIC 374) Cross-Ref.: 1917 CIC 445

§ 1. The Bishop shall distribute his territory into regions, that is, districts, consisting of several parishes, that come under the name of *vicariates forane*, *deaneries*, *archpresbyteries*, and so on.

§ 2. If this distribution, by reason of circumstances, seems impossible or inopportune, the Bishop shall consult the Holy See, unless provision has already been made by the [Holy See].

Canon Law Digest
I: 154

TITLE 7
On supreme power and those who by ecclesiastical law are participants therein

Chapter 1
On the Roman Pontiff[31]

Canon 218 (1983 CIC 331, 333)

§ 1. The Roman Pontiff, the Successor in primacy to Blessed Peter, has not only a primacy of honor, but supreme and full power of jurisdiction

[31] James Moynihan, "Papal Immunity and Liability in the Writings of the Medical Canonists" (MS no. 3182, Gregorian University, 1961; printed version, no. 1435, 1961); Thomas Pazhayampallil, "The Indirect Power of the Pope in Temporal Matters according to William Barclay" (thesis no. 71, Pontifical Salesian University; Madras, 1966).

over the universal Church both in those things that pertain to faith and morals, and in those things that affect the discipline and government of the Church spread throughout the whole world.

§ 2. This power is truly episcopal, ordinary, and immediate both over each and every church and over each and every pastor and faithful independent from any human authority.

Canon Law Digest
I: 154; II: 80–95; III: 80; IV: 108–11; V: 214–38; VI: 172–224;
VII: 125–31; VIII: 182–91; IX: 104–16; X: 21–25

Canon 219 (1983 CIC 332)

The Roman Pontiff, legitimately elected, immediately upon accepting the election, obtains by divine law the full power of supreme jurisdiction.

Canon Law Digest
VIII: 191

Canon 220 (NA)

Matters of greater importance that are reserved only to the Roman Pontiff either by their nature or by positive law are called *great cases*.

Canon 221 (1983 CIC 332)

If it happens that the Roman Pontiff resigns, for the validity of this resignation, acceptance by a Cardinal or another is not necessary.

Chapter 2
On an Ecumenical Council

Canon 222 (1983 CIC 338)

§ 1. An Ecumenical Council cannot be held that was not convoked by the Roman Pontiff.

§ 2. It is for this same Roman Pontiff to preside himself or through another over the Ecumenical Council, to establish and designate the matters that are to be treated and the order to be observed, and to transfer, suspend, dissolve, and confirm the Council and its decrees.

Canon Law Digest
V: 238–69; VI: 224–309; VII: 131–37; VIII: 191; IX: 116–18

Canon 223 (1983 CIC 339) Cross-Ref.: 1917 CIC 224

§ 1. The following are called to a Council and have the right of a deliberative vote:

1.° Cardinals of the H. R. C., even if they are not Bishops;

2.° Patriarchs, Primates, Archbishops, [and] residential Bishops, even if they are not yet consecrated;

3.° Abbots and Prelates *of no one*;

4.° Abbots Primate, Abbots Superior of monastic Congregations, and supreme Moderators of clerical exempt religious [institutes], but not other religious [institutes], unless it is decreed otherwise in the convocation;

§ 2. Also, titular Bishops called to the Council obtain a deliberative vote, unless it is expressly determined otherwise in the convocation.

§ 3. Theologians and experts in the sacred canons might be invited to the Council, but they have no vote, unless consultative.

Canon Law Digest
VI: 310

Canon 224 (NA)

§ 1. If one of those called to a Council according to the norm of Canon 223, § 1, is detained by a just impediment and cannot be present, he shall send a procurator and prove the impediment.

§ 2. If the procurator is one of the Council Fathers, he does not enjoy a double vote; if he is not [a Council Father], he may be present only for public sessions, but without a vote; at the conclusion of the Council he has the right of subscribing the acts.

Canon 225 (NA)

None of those who must be present at a Council may leave before the Council is rightly concluded except with the permission of the president of the Council, to whom has been made known and who has approved the reason for seeking departure and has sought permission for leaving.

Canon 226 (1983 CIC 338)

The Fathers can add to the questions proposed by the Roman Pontiff other [questions] approved beforehand, however, by the president of the Council.

Canon 227 (1983 CIC 341)

The decrees of a Council do not have definitive obliging force unless they are confirmed by the Roman Pontiff and promulgated by his command.

Canon 228 (1983 CIC 333)

§ 1. An Ecumenical Council enjoys supreme power over the universal Church.

§ 2. Appeal from a sentence of the Roman Pontiff to an Ecumenical Council is not given.

Canon 229 (1983 CIC 340)

If it happens that the Roman Pontiff, during the celebration of a Council, leaves life, [the Council] by law is interrupted until a new Pontiff resumes it and orders it to be continued.

Chapter 3
On the Cardinals of the Holy Roman Church

Canon 230 (1983 CIC 349)

The Cardinals of the H. R. C. constitute a Senate of the Roman Pontiff and are the principal counselors to him in governing the Church and are helpers who assist [him].

Canon Law Digest
II: 95; III: 80–81; IV: 111; V: 269; VI: 310; VII: 137–45; VIII: 191

Canon 231 (1983 CIC 350)

§ 1. The Sacred College [of Cardinals] is divided into three orders: episcopal, to which belong only those six Cardinals over the various suburbicarian dioceses; presbyteral, which consists of fifty Cardinals; and diaconal, which [consists of] fourteen [Cardinals].

§ 2. Every Cardinal priest and Cardinal deacon has his own title or diaconate assigned in the City by the Roman Pontiff.

Canon Law Digest
V: 270–75; VI: 310–12

Canon 232 (1983 CIC 351)

§ 1. Cardinals are men freely selected by the Roman Pontiff from throughout the whole world who are at least constituted in the presbyteral order [and who] are notably outstanding for their doctrine, piety, and prudence in conducting affairs.

§ 2. Prohibited from the dignity of the cardinalate are:

1.° Illegitimates, even if they were legitimized by a later marriage; likewise all those irregular for or impeded from sacred orders in accord with canonical sanction, even if they were ordained [or placed in ecclesiastical] dignities with apostolic authority, including dispensation [necessary for] the episcopate;

2.° Those who have received children even from a legitimate marriage or grandchildren from same;

3.° Those who are related in the first or second degree of consanguinity to a living Cardinal.

Canon 233 (1983 CIC 351)

§ 1. Cardinals are created and published by the Roman Pontiff in a Consistory, and those so created and published obtain the right of electing the Roman Pontiff and the privileges described in Canon 239.

§ 2. If, however, the Roman Pontiff announces the creation of some [Cardinal] in Consistory [but] keeps his name reserved in his heart, one so promoted in the meantime enjoys no rights or privileges of a Cardinal, but, when the Roman Pontiff later makes his name known, he enjoys these from the date of publication, but with right of precedence from [the time of] the reservation in the heart.

Canon Law Digest
V: 275; VII: 145; VIII: 191–93; IX: 118; X: 25–26

Canon 234 (NA) Cross-Ref.: 1917 CIC 2397

If one promoted is absent from the [Roman] Curia, he must, upon receiving the red biretta, swear that within one year, unless detained by a legitimate impediment, he will present himself to the Supreme Pontiff.

Canon 235 (NA)

Unless provided otherwise in particular cases by the Holy See, upon promotion to the sacred purple, the one being promoted loses by that fact not only all dignities, churches, and benefices that he already possessed, but also all ecclesiastical pensions are lost.

Canon 236 (1983 CIC 350)

§ 1. By an option made in Consistory and approved by the Supreme Pontiff, Cardinals in the presbyteral order can transfer to another title, observing priority of ordination and precedence, and Cardinal Deacons [can move] to another diaconate and, having passed ten years in the diaconal order, can also go to the presbyteral order.

§ 2. A Cardinal in the diaconal order who transfers to the presbyteral order takes a place before all those other Cardinal priests who took up the honor of the sacred purple after he did.

§ 3. If a suburbicarian see goes vacant, Cardinals in the presbyteral order who at the moment of the vacancy were present in the Curia or who were absent from it at that time due to a commission they had from the Roman Pontiff can opt for the vacancy in Consistory, observing the priority of promotion.

§ 4. Cardinals assigned to one of the suburbicarian churches cannot opt for another; but when a Cardinal attains the rank of Dean, he adds to his diocese Ostia, which from then on, in the person of the Cardinal Dean, is joined with his other suburbicarian diocese.

Canon Law Digest
II: 95; V: 275–76; VI: 312

Canon 237 (1983 CIC 352)

§ 1. The Dean, that is, he who first was promoted to a suburbicarian see, presides over the Sacred College of Cardinals, [but] over the other Cardinals [he] has no jurisdiction, [although] he is considered a first among equals.

§ 2. When the deanship falls vacant, the Subdean succeeds by law, whether at the time of the vacancy he is present in the Curia, or whether he is in his suburbicarian diocese, or whether he is absent for a time on a task committed to him by the Roman Pontiff.

Canon Law Digest
VI: 312–13; VIII: 193

Canon 238 (1983 CIC 356) Cross-Ref.: 1917 CIC 333

§ 1. Cardinals are bound by the obligation of residing in the Curia, and it is fundamental that they not leave from there without the permission of the Roman Pontiff, with due regard for the prescriptions of §§ 2 and 3 of this canon.

§ 2. This obligation binds even suburbicarian Cardinal Bishops, but they do not require this permission to go to dioceses committed to them whenever they judge it opportune.

§ 3. Cardinals who are bishops in non-suburbicarian dioceses are exempt from the law of residence; but when they come to the City they shall present themselves to the Supreme Pontiff, nor shall they leave from the City until they have sought from him permission for leaving.

Canon Law Digest
VI: 313

Canon 239[32] (1983 CIC 355) Cross-Refs.: 1917 CIC 233, 349, 628, 782, 876, 1008, 1473

§ 1. Beyond the other privileges that are enumerated in this Code under various titles, all Cardinals from their promotion in Consistory enjoy the following faculties:

1.° Of hearing confessions throughout the world, even those of religious, of either sex, and of absolving from all sins and censures, even reserved ones, excepting only censures reserved most specially to the Apostolic See, and those attached to the revelation of secrets of the H. Office;
2.° Of selecting a priest confessor for his confession and that of his attendants who, if he lacks jurisdiction, obtains it by law, even in regard to sins and censures including those reserved, excepting only those censures described in n. 1;
3.° Of preaching the word of God everywhere;
4.° Of celebrating or permitting others to celebrate in his presence one Mass on [Friday] of the great week and three Masses on the night of the Birth of the Lord;
5.° Of blessing anywhere, only with the sign of the cross, with all the indulgences that the Holy See is accustomed to grant, rosaries and other precatory crowns, crosses, medals, statues, [and] scapulars approved by the Apostolic See, and of imposing them without the requirement of enrollment;
6.° Of erecting with a single blessing in churches or oratories, even private ones, and other pious places, the *Way of the Cross*

[32] Harry Hynes, "The Privileges of Cardinals", Canon Law Studies, no. 217 (J. C. D. thesis, Catholic University of America, 1945).

with all the indulgences that are granted to those performing a pious exercise of this sort; and also of blessing, for the faithful who, because of infirmity or another legitimate impediment, cannot visit the sacred *Way of the Cross*, icons of Crucifixes, with the application of all indulgences attached by the Roman Pontiff to a devotional exercise of this same *Way of the Cross*;

7.° Of celebrating on a portable altar not only in their own house of residence, but wherever they are; and of letting others with them celebrate another Mass;

8.° Of celebrating on the seas, observing due precautions;

9.° In all churches and oratories, of celebrating Mass in conformity with their own calendar;

10.° Of enjoying a personally privileged altar daily;

11.° Of gaining indulgences in their own chapels, for whose acquisition there is prescribed a visit to a temple or public building in the city or place in which the Cardinal is actually present, in which privilege those in his household may also partake;

12.° Of blessing people everywhere as would a Bishop; but in the City only in those churches and pious or faith-filled places so allowed;

13.° Of, just like Bishops, wearing a cross over the chest and even on the mozetta and of using the miter and pastoral staff;

14.° Of celebrating Sacred [rites] in any private chapel without prejudice to those who enjoy an indult;

15.° Of conducting pontificals with the throne and baldachin in all churches outside the City, having notified the Ordinary in advance if it is a cathedral church;

16.° Of enjoying the honors wherever they are conferred that are typically given to local Ordinaries;

17.° Of vouching in the external forum as witnesses of pontifical utterances;

18.° Of enjoying a chapel exempt from visitation of the Ordinary;

19.° Of freely disposing of the income of a benefice even by will, with due regard for the prescription of Canon 1298;

20.° Of performing consecrations and blessings of churches, altars, sacred furnishings, abbeys, and so forth, with the exception of the consecration of holy oils if the Cardinal lacks episcopal character, in any place, observing those things that ought to be observed, with due regard for the prescription of Canon 1157;

21.° Of taking precedence over all Prelates, even Patriarchs, even Pontifical Legates, unless the Legate is a Cardinal residing in his own territory; but a Cardinal Legate from the side takes precedence outside the City over all;

22.° Of conferring first tonsure and minor orders, provided the one to be promoted has dimissorial letters from his own Ordinary;

23.° Of ministering the sacrament of confirmation, with due regard for the burden of forwarding the names of the ones confirmed according to the norm of law;

24.° Of granting indulgences of two hundred days, as often as they can be earned, in places and institutes and persons under their jurisdiction and protection; likewise indulgences in other places, but only to be earned by those present, on an individual basis.

§ 2. The Cardinal Dean enjoys the privilege of ordaining and consecrating the Pontiff-elect, if he lacks ordination and episcopal consecration, and then of using the pallium; to which privilege, in the absence of the Cardinal Dean, accedes the Subdeacon, and in his absence, the oldest of the suburbicarian Cardinal Bishops.

§ 3. Finally, the Cardinal proto-Deacon places the pallium on Archbishops and Bishops enjoying the privilege or on their procurators, in place of the Roman Pontiff; and he announces to the people the name of the newly elected Pontiff.

Canon Law Digest

I: 154; II: 95–96; III: 82; IX: 118

Canon 240 (1983 CIC 357)

§ 1. A Cardinal promoted to a suburbicarian see and placed in possession of it canonically is a true Bishop in his diocese and partakes of that power in it that a residential Bishop has in his own diocese.

§ 2. Other Cardinals in their title or diaconate, after they have taken up canonical possession in same, can do all those things that local Ordinaries can do in their churches except in the judicial order and in jurisdiction over the faithful but with due regard for power over those things that pertain to discipline, the correction of morals, and service of the church.

§ 3. Cardinals in the presbyteral order can in their own title conduct pontificals with the throne and baldachin, and Cardinals in the diaconal order can assist pontifically in their own deaconship, and no other one can do this without the assent of the Cardinal there; but in other churches of the City, Cardinals cannot use the throne and baldachin without the permission of the Roman Pontiff.

Canon Law Digest
V: 276; VII: 146–47

Canon 241 (1983 CIC 359)

During the vacancy of the Apostolic See, the Sacred College of Cardinals and Roman Curia have no power beyond that which is defined in the const. of [Pope] Pius X, *Vacante Sede Apostolica* of 25 Dec. 1904.

Canon Law Digest
I: 154; VIII: 193

Chapter 4
On the Roman Curia

Canon 242 (1983 CIC 360)

The Roman Curia consists of the Sacred Congregations, Tribunals, and Offices that are enumerated and described below.

Canon Law Digest
II: 96; IV: 111; VI: 313–57; VII: 147–80;
VIII: 193–205; IX: 119–20; X: 26–31

Canon 243 (NA)

§ 1. In each Congregation, Tribunal, and Office, discipline is to be observed and matters treated according to the norms, whether general or particular, that the Roman Pontiff has set out for them.

§ 2. All of those who belong to Congregations, Tribunals, and Offices of the Roman Curia are bound to observe secrecy within their limits and according to the manner determined by the discipline proper to each [dicastery].

Canon Law Digest
I: 154; VIII: 205–10; IX: 120–21

Canon 244 (NA)

§ 1. Nothing grave or extraordinary is treated in these Congregations, Tribunals, [or] Offices, unless their significance has been communicated to the Roman Pontiff by the Moderator.

§ 2. Favors and resolutions of all sorts require pontifical approval, except for those things for which special pontifical faculties have been given to the Moderators of Offices, Tribunals, [and] Congregations, with the exception of sentences from the Tribunal of the Sacred Roman Rota and the Apostolic Signatura.

Canon Law Digest
I: 155; VIII: 210

Canon 245 (NA)

Controversy that might arise regarding competence between Sacred Congregations, Tribunals, and Offices of the Roman Curia are decided by a committee of Cardinals of the H. R. C. that is designated by the Roman Pontiff on a case-by-case basis.

Canon Law Digest
I: 155; II: 96

Article 1 — *On Sacred Congregations*

Canon 246 (NA)

A Cardinal Prefect presides over each Congregation or, if the Roman Pontiff presides over it himself, a Cardinal Secretary directs it; to these are added other Cardinals whom the Pontiff thinks should be added, along with other necessary ministers.

Canon Law Digest
VIII: 210

Canon 247[33] (NA) Cross-Refs.: 1917 CIC 249, 251, 257

§ 1. The Congregation of the H. Office, over which the Supreme Pontiff presides, protects the doctrine of faith and morals.

---

[33] Robert Miller, "The Congregation for the Doctrine of the Faith: Its Origin, Concept, and the Development of Its Competency", Canon Law Studies, no. 484 (Catholic University of America, 1975).

§ 2. It judges those delicts that are reserved to itself by proper law, with power in these criminal cases of hearing not only in the appellate grade from tribunal of the local Ordinary, but also in first instance, if they were directly communicated to it.

§ 3. It alone considers those [matters] that, whether directly or indirectly, in law or in fact, concern the privilege that is called Pauline and that concern dispensation from the matrimonial impediment of disparity of cult and mixed religion; and likewise to it belongs the faculty for dispensing from these impediments. For that reason, every question of this sort is to be referred to this Congregation, which can, however, if it so thinks in a case, refer the question to another Congregation or to the Tribunal of the Sacred Roman Rota.

§ 4. To this same [Congregation] pertains not only the diligent examination of books referred to it and, if it thinks it opportune, their prohibition; but also, by office, [it may] inquire, by whatever manner seems in order, about writings being published of any sort that ought to be condemned, and so informing Ordinaries, who are likewise bound religiously to keep check on pernicious writings and denounce them to the Holy See, according to the norm of Canon 1397.

§ 5. It alone is competent concerning all those things respecting the eucharistic fast for priests celebrating Mass.

Canon Law Digest
I: 155–59; II: 96–100; III: 82–84; V: 277; VI: 358–60;
VII: 180–88; VIII: 210–11; IX: 121; X: 31–34

Canon 248 (NA)

§ 1. The Prefect of the Congregation of the Consistory is the Roman Pontiff. Besides others who belong to it, there are [included] by office the Cardinal Secretary of the H. Office, the Prefect of the Congregation for Seminaries and University, and the Secretariat of State. Among the Consultors there are always the Assessor of the H. Office, the Secretary for the Congregation for extraordinary ecclesiastical affairs, and the Secretary for the Congregation for Seminaries and University.

§ 2. This Congregation not only prepares the agenda for Consistories, but also, in places not subject to the Congregation for the Prop. of the Faith, constitutes new dioceses, provinces, and chapters, whether cathedral or collegial; it divides dioceses already constituted; it proposes the constitution of Bishops, Apostolic Administrators, Coadjutors, and Auxiliary Bishops, and diligently performs canonical inquiries or processes regarding those to be promoted and indicates matters that might be of importance to the faith, with due regard for the prescription of Canon 255.

§ 3. On this Congregation depend all those things that pertain to the constitution, preservation, and status of dioceses. Therefore it is watchful about those obligations being fulfilled, or less than so, to which Ordinaries are bound; it examines those writings from Bishops about the state of their dioceses; it directs apostolic visitations and examines those things that transpired, transmitting in either case those things to individual Congregations for treatment that especially pertain to them.

Canon Law Digest
I: 159; II: 100–105; III: 84–98; IV: 111–23; V: 277–89; VI: 360; VII: 188–224; VIII: 211–23; IX: 122–50; X: 34–38

Canon 249[34] (NA)

§ 1. The Congregation of the discipline of the Sacraments supervises universal legislation concerning the seven Sacraments, without prejudice to the rights of the Congregation of the H. Office concerning matters treated in Canon 247, and of the Congregation of Sacred Rites concerning the rites and ceremonies that in the confection of the Sacraments must be observed by ministers and recipients.

§ 2. This [Congregation] has charge of all those things that are customary in the examination for and granting of [dispensations] in matrimonial discipline, as well as in the discipline of other Sacraments, not excluding the Eucharistic Sacrifice, excepting only those things that are reserved to other Congregations.

§ 3. It also takes exclusive cognizance of fact in matrimonial nonconsummation cases and on the existence of causes for granting dispensations, as well as all things that are connected to it. It can treat these things itself, or, if it judges it to be expedient, it can remit them to the Sacred Roman Rota. Likewise to it are deferred questions about the validity of marriage, which however, if a more accurate examination or investigation is required, it can remit to the competent tribunal. Similarly, to it belongs the supervision of all things connected to obligations of major

[34] Robert Sheehy, "The Sacred Congregation of the Sacraments: Its Competence in the Roman Curia", Canon Law Studies, no. 333 (thesis, Catholic University of America, 1954).

orders and examination of questions about the validity of sacred ordination itself, or it can send these to the competent tribunal. It can do this with the other Sacraments.

Canon Law Digest

I: 159–60; II: 105–7; VI: 360; VII: 224–25; VIII: 223–27; X: 39

Canon 250[35] (NA)

§ 1. To the Congregation of the Council are committed all those things that pertain to the universal discipline of secular clergy and the Christian people.

§ 2. For this reason, it is to take care that the precepts of Christian life are observed, with the opportune faculty of dispensing the faithful from same; it also supervises pastors and canons; and it sees to pious sodalities, pious unions (even if they are dependent on a religious [institute] or are erected in its churches or houses), pious legacies, pious works, Mass stipends, benefices and offices, ecclesiastical goods both mobile and immobile, diocesan tributes, taxes of episcopal Curias, and other things of this sort. To it is reserved the faculty of exempting the required conditions for placement in a benefice, as often as their conferral belongs to Ordinaries; of admitting to settlements those who occupy ecclesiastical goods, even if they belong to religious; of permitting that the faithful acquire ecclesiastical goods that have been usurped by civil powers.

§ 3. It sees also to all those things that pertain to the immunity of the Church, and likewise controversies about precedence, with due regard for the rights of the Congregation of religious members and the Congregation for Ceremonies.

§ 4. To it pertain all those things that refer to the celebration and recognition of Councils and committees or conferences of Bishops, outside of those matters that are under the Congregation for the Prop. of the Faith.

[35] Bernard Prince, "Episcopal Conferences and the Canadian Catholic Conference" (diss. no. 7, Pontifical University of St. Thomas [Rome], 1965–1966); Michael Sheehan, "The State Catholic Conference: A New Development in Interecclesial Cooperation in the United States of America" (Pontifical Lateran University, 1971); Raymond Kutner, "The Development, Structure and Competence of the Episcopal Conference", Canon Law Studies, no. 480 (Catholic University of America, 1972); Benedict Etafo, "National Episcopal Conference of Nigeria: Its Legal Functionality" (Pontifical University Urbaniana, 1983).

§ 5. This Congregation is competent in all controversial matters committed to its supervision that, in a disciplinary line, it thinks should be treated; the others are deferred to the competent tribunal.

Canon Law Digest
I:160–61; II: 107; III: 98–100; VI: 360; VII: 225

Canon 251 (NA)

§ 1. The Congregation for matters of religious members is exclusively competent concerning governance, discipline, studies, goods, and privileges of religious members of either sex, whether in solemn or simple vows, and those who, although not in vows, conduct a life in common as religious, such as third Order seculars, without prejudice to the rights of the Congregation for the Prop. of the Faith.

§ 2. Therefore, [while] questions to be treated in the judicial order are transmitted to the competent tribunal, always without prejudice to the rights of the Congregation of the H. Office and the Congregation of the Council concerning matters under their jurisdiction, this Congregation determines all questions of its competence in disciplinary lines; but if a question arises between a religious member and a person not in a religious [institute], it can, especially at the request of a party, also send the matter to another Congregation or tribunal.

§ 3. To this Congregation finally is reserved the concession of dispensations that by law are common to religious members, with due regard for the prescription of Canon 247, § 5.

Canon Law Digest
I: 161–62; III: 100–101; IV: 123–26; VI: 360; VIII: 227–28; IX: 151–55

Canon 252[36] (NA)

§ 1. The Congregation for the Propagation of the Faith presides over Catholic doctrine and the preaching of the Gospel in the missions, constitutes and arranges necessary ministers, and has the faculty of treating,

[36] Demetrio Valeza, "The Canonicity of Foreign Missions" (diss. no. 7, University of St. Thomas [Manila], 1950); Bernard Welling, "Episcopal Hierarchy: A Study of Its Erection in Mission Countries (1946–1956)" (Gregorian University; printed version, no. 1154, Tilburg, 1958); Raphael Song, "The Sacred Congregation for the Propagation of the Faith", Canon Law Studies, no. 420 (thesis, Catholic University of America, 1961); Francis Morrisey, "The Juridical Status of the Catholic Church in Canada (1534–1840)" (Ph. D. diss. 53, St. Paul University [Ottawa, Canada], 1972).

working, and following through on all those things that are necessary and opportune.

§ 2. It takes care of all those things involved in the celebration and recognition of Councils in territories subject to it.

§ 3. Its jurisdiction is circumscribed to those regions where the sacred hierarchy is not yet constituted and the status of missions remains. Also subject to this Congregation are those regions where the hierarchy was constituted but now is not functioning. Also societies of ecclesiastics and Seminaries founded exclusively for the [missions], so that in them are trained missionaries for outside missions, are likewise subject to it, especially in what regards rules, administration, and opportune grants of requests for the sacred ordination of students.

§ 4. This Congregation is bound to defer to the competent Congregation matters that touch the faith, marriage cases, and the treatment or interpretation of general norms on the discipline of sacred rites.

§ 5. But as to what applies to religious members, the Congregation supervises all that touches religious as missionaries, whether individually or in groups. But whatever touches religious as such, whether individually or in groups, it leaves or sends to the Congregation for religious affairs.

Canon Law Digest
I: 163–65; II: 107–9; III: 101; VI: 361; VII: 225–38;
VIII: 228–29; IX: 156–59; X: 40

Canon 253[37] (NA) Cross-Ref.: 1917 CIC 1999

§ 1. The Congregation for Sacred Rites has authority to see and establish all those things that proximately involve the sacred rites and ceremonies of the Latin Church, but not which refer to sacred rites in the wide sense, things like the right of precedence and others of this sort, which are treated either in the judicial order or in the disciplinary line.

§ 2. It is for it especially to be vigilant that the sacred rites and ceremonies are diligently observed in celebrating the Sacred [Synax], in the administration of Sacraments, in conducting divine offices, and in all those things that respect cult in the Latin Church; [it can] grant opportune dispensations; it can give out insignia and privileges of honor whether per-

[37] Frederick McManus, "The Congregation of Sacred Rites", Canon Law Studies, no. 352 (thesis, Catholic University of America, 1954).

sonal or for a time, whether to places or perpetually, in matters affecting sacred rites and ceremonies, and shall take care lest these fall into abuse.

§ 3. Finally all those things that pertain to the beatification and canonization of the Servants of God or to sacred relics in any way are referred to it.

Canon Law Digest
I: 166–67; VI: 361; VII: 238–45; VIII: 229

Canon 254 (NA)

It belongs to the Congregation for Ceremonies to moderate the ceremonies to be observed in the Pontifical Chapel and Hall and those sacred functions that Cardinal Fathers conduct outside of the pontifical chapel; likewise this same Congregation takes cognizance of questions concerning precedence among the Cardinal Fathers and Legates whom the various Nations send to the Holy See.

Canon Law Digest
I: 167–68; V: 289; VI: 361

Canon 255 (NA) Cross-Refs.: 1917 CIC 248, 263

It is for the Congregation for extraordinary ecclesiastical affairs to constitute or divide dioceses and to promote suitable men to vacant dioceses, as often as these matters involve civil Governments; moreover to this Congregation fall those matters that are subjected to its examination by the Supreme Pontiff through the Cardinal Secretary of State, especially concerning those things connected by civil law whenever there are treaties with the various Nations.

Canon Law Digest
I:168–69; VI: 361

Canon 256[38] (NA)

§ 1. The Congregation for Seminaries and Universities watches over all those things pertaining to the governance, discipline, administration of

[38]James Markham, "The Sacred Congregation of Seminaries and Universities of Studies", Canon Law Studies, no. 384 (thesis, Catholic University of America, 1957).

property, and studies of Seminaries, without harm to the right of the Congregation for the Prop. of the Faith. Likewise committed to it is the moderation of the governance and studies that must be done in those athenaea or what are called Universities or Faculties that are dependent on the authority of the Church, including those that are directed by the members of some religious family. It assesses and approves new institutions; it grants the faculty of conferring academic degrees and gives the norms by which they are to be conferred, and when it concerns an individual man commended for doctrine, it can confer the degrees on him.

§ 2. In this Sacred Congregation there are numbered, among others, the Cardinal Secretary of the Consistorial Congregation, and among the Consultors, the Assessor of this same Congregation.

Canon Law Digest

I: 169–72; II: 109–10; III: 102–4; IV: 126; V: 289–90;
VI: 361–62; IX: 159; X: 40

Canon 257[39] (NA)

§ 1. The Congregation for the Oriental Church is presided over by the Roman Pontiff. To this Congregation is reserved all those sorts of things that refer to persons or to the discipline or to the rites of the oriental Churches, even if they are mixed, that is, if either by reason of matter or of persons they also affect latins.

§ 2. Therefore this Congregation enjoys all faculties for the oriental rites of the Church that other Congregations obtain for the latin rites of the Church, without harm, nevertheless, to the rights of the Congregation of the H. Office, according to the norm of Canon 247.

§ 3. This Congregation decides controversies by the disciplinary manner; whatever it determines should be decided in the judicial order, it remits to whatever tribunal it designates.

Canon Law Digest

I: 172–74; II: 110–14; VI: 363

[39] Michael Dziob, "The Sacred Congregation for the Oriental Church", Canon Law Studies, no. 214 (thesis, Catholic University of America, 1945); Michael Moran, "The Sacred Congregation for the Oriental Church" (diss. excerpt, Pontificium Institutum Orientalium Studiorum, 1971).

Article 2—*On the Tribunals of the Roman Curia*

Canon 258[40] (NA)

§ 1. The Major Cardinal Penitentiary presides over the Sacred Penitentiary. The jurisdiction of this tribunal is limited to those things respecting the internal forum, even if it is not sacramental; therefore this tribunal grants favors, absolutions, dispensations, commutations, sanations, and condonations only for the internal forum; it also addresses matters of conscience directed to it.

§ 2. It also, moreover, judges those things attached to the use and granting of indulgences, with due regard for the right of the H. Office to see to those things that affect doctrinal dogma in indulgences, and new prayers and devotions.

Canon Law Digest
I: 174; II: 114; III: 104; VI: 363; VIII: 229

Canon 259 (NA)

Cases requiring treatment in the judicial order are heard in Sacred Roman Rota or the Supreme Tribunal of the Apostolic Signatura, within the limits and according to the norms given in Canons 1598–1605, with due regard for the law in cases proper to the Congregation of the H. Office and the Congregation of Sacred Rites.

Canon Law Digest
II: 114–15; VI: 363; VII: 246–77; VIII: 229; IX: 159–69

Article 3—*On the Offices of the Roman Curia*

Canon 260 (NA)

§ 1. The Apostolic Chancery, over which presides the Cardinal Chancellor of the Holy Roman Church, has as its proper task the preparation of letters or bulls, for the provision of benefices and consistorial offices, the institution of new provinces and dioceses and chapters, and the confection of other major ecclesiastical affairs.

---

[40] William Kubelbeck, "The Sacred Penitentiaria and Its Relations to Faculties of Ordinaries and Priests", Canon Law Studies, no. 5 (thesis, Catholic University of America, 1918; Somerset, Ohio: Rosary Press, 1918).

§ 2. These letters or bulls are not to be sent except by mandate of the Consistorial Congregation concerning matters within its competence, or by mandate of the Supreme Pontiff concerning other matters, observing in individual cases the limits of the mandate.

Canon Law Digest
I: 175; III: 104; VI: 363; VIII: 229–33; IX: 169–71

Canon 261 (NA)

The Apostolic Datary, which is moderated by the Datary Cardinal of the Holy Roman Church, assesses the suitability of those to be promoted to benefices reserved to the Apostolic See outside of consistories; it produces and sends the apostolic letters for their conferral; it exempts from required conditions in the conferral of benefices, as often as their conferral does not belong to an Ordinary; it takes care of the pensions and obligations that the Supreme Pontiff imposes in conferring these referenced benefices.

Canon Law Digest
VI: 363

Canon 262 (NA)

The Apostolic Camera, over which presides the Cardinal Chamberlain of the Holy Roman Church, takes care of the administration of goods and temporal rights of the Holy See, especially when there is a vacancy there, and then the norms established in the const. of [Pope] Pius X *Vacante Sede Apostolica* of 25 Dec. 1904 are to be most assiduously observed.

Canon Law Digest
VI: 363

Canon 263 (NA)

The Office of the Secretary of State, whose moderator is the Cardinal Secretary of State, consists of three parts in this order:

1.° The first part, over which presides the Secretary of the Congregation for extraordinary ecclesiastical affairs, deals in matters that must be subject to the examination of this same Congregation according to the norm of Canon 255, and other matters that due to their nature are sent to it by specific Congregations;

2.° The second part, over which there is a Substitute, deals with ordinary affairs;

3.° The third part is directed by the Chancellor for Apostolic Briefs, who oversees the expedition of Briefs.

Canon Law Digest
VI: 363; VIII: 234; IX: 171

Canon 264 (NA)

To the Secretary for Briefs to Princes and latin Letters belongs the task of writing in latin the acts of the Supreme Pontiff that are committed to the Secretary.

Canon Law Digest
VI: 363; VIII: 234

Chapter 5
On Legates of the Roman Pontiff[41]

Canon 265 (1983 CIC 362)

It is the right of the Roman Pontiff, independent of civil power, to send into any part of the world Legates, with or without ecclesiastical jurisdiction.

Canon Law Digest
II: 115; VII: 277–85; VIII: 234–35; IX: 171; X: 40

Canon 266 (1983 CIC 358)

They are called *Legates from the side*, those Cardinals who like *another self* are sent by the Roman Pontiff with this title, and such a one can only do what was committed to him by the Roman Pontiff.

[41] Gino Paro, "The Right of Papal Legation", Canon Law Studies, no. 211 (thesis, Catholic University of America, 1947); William Carew, "The Apostolic Delegate" (Ph. D. diss. 32, University of Ottawa, 1950); Edward Cassidy, "The Apostolic Delegate" (Pontifical Lateran University, 1955).

Canon 267[42] (1983 CIC 364–65)

§ 1. Legates who are sent with the title of Nuncio or Internuncio:

1.° Foster, according to the norms received from the Holy See, relations between the Apostolic See and the civil Governments within which the legation functions in a stable manner;

2.° In the territories assigned to them, they must be vigilant about the state of the Church and inform the Roman Pontiff about it;

3.° Beyond these two ordinary powers, they obtain other faculties that, however, are all delegated.

§ 2. But those who are sent with the title *Apostolic Delegate* have only that ordinary power described in § 1, n. 2, besides those other faculties committed to them by the Holy See.

Canon Law Digest
I: 175–87; II: 115–18; III: 104–7; IV: 126–27; V: 290–306;
VI: 364; VII: 285–89; VIII: 235; IX: 172–92

Canon 268 (1983 CIC 367)

§ 1. The duties of Legates with all faculties committed to them do not expire with the vacancy of the Apostolic See, unless stated otherwise in the pontifical letters [appointing them].

§ 2. They do cease, however, upon completion of the mandate, upon their revocation once communicated, or upon resignation and acceptance by the Roman Pontiff.

Canon 269 (1983 CIC 364)

§ 1. Legates shall leave to local Ordinaries the free exercise of their jurisdiction.

§ 2. Even if by chance they lack episcopal character, they take precedence over all Ordinaries who are not signed with cardinalitial dignity.

§ 3. If they are possessed of episcopal character they can, without the permission of the Ordinary, in all their churches, except the cathedral,

[42] Antonio Gauci, "The Nunciature of Msgr. Lambruschini in France" (Pontifical Lateran University, 1954); Joseph Herres, "The Activity of Lodovico Taverna, Apostolic Nuncio in Spain (1582–1586)" (thesis, Gregorian University; printed version, no. 2936, Canberra, Australia, 1980).

bless the people and conduct divine offices, even in pontifical manner using also the throne and staff.

Canon 270 (NA)

Bishops who, by reason of their see, are decorated with the title of Apostolic Legate derive thereby no special rights.

Chapter 6
On Patriarchs, Primates, and Metropolitans

Canon 271[43] (1983 CIC 438)

The title of Patriarch or Primate, beyond being a prerogative of honor and [having] the right of precedence according to the norm of Canon 280, imparts no special jurisdiction, unless by particular law on some matter it appears otherwise.

Canon Law Digest
IV: 127; VI: 364; VII: 289; VIII: 235

Canon 272[44] (1983 CIC 435)

A Metropolitan, that is, an Archbishop, presides over an ecclesiastical province; that dignity is joined to an episcopal see [as] determined and approved by the Roman Pontiff.

Canon Law Digest
II: 119; V: 306; VI: 364

Canon 273[45] (NA)

With due regard for the prescription of Canons 275–80, a Metropolitan in his own diocese has the same obligations and rights that a Bishop has in his [diocese].

---

[43] Thomas Kane, "The Jurisdiction of the Patriarchs of the Major Sees in Antiquity and in the Middle Ages", Canon Law Studies, no. 276 (thesis, Catholic University of America, 1949).

[44] Alexander McDonald, "The Rights and Obligations of the Metropolitan as Such according to the Code of Canon Law" (doctoral diss. 24, University of Ottawa, 1948); Augustine Bennett, "The Jurisdiction of the Archbishop of Canterbury" (thesis, Gregorian University; printed version, no. 1155, 1958).

[45] Alphonse Popek, "The Rights and Obligations of Metropolitans", Canon Law Studies, no. 260 (thesis, Catholic University of America, 1947).

Canon 274 (1983 CIC 436) Cross-Refs.: 1917 CIC 338, 343, 785

In his suffragan dioceses, a Metropolitan can only [do the following]:

1.° Install those presented to a benefice by a patron if the Suffragan, within the time determined by law and not detained by a just impediment, fails to do so;
2.° Grant an indulgence of one hundred days just as in his own diocese;
3.° Depute a Vicar Capitulary according to the norm of Canon 432, § 2;
4.° Be vigilant that faith and ecclesiastical discipline are accurately observed and inform the Roman Pontiff about abuses;
5.° Conduct canonical visitation for reasons approved in advance by the Apostolic See, if the Suffragan neglects it; at the time of this visitation, he can preach, hear confessions, and also absolve from cases reserved to the Bishop, investigate the life and conduct of clerics, making those clearly [unworthy] known to their Ordinaries that they might punish them, denounce notorious crimes and manifest and notorious offenses committed against him or against those attached to him, and punish [same] with just penalties, not excluding censures;
6.° In all churches, even exempt ones, having notified the local Ordinary if it is a cathedral church, [he may] conduct pontificals, as [would] a Bishop in his own territory, bless the people, and have his cross carried in front of him, but not otherwise do those things implying jurisdiction;
7.° Accept appeals from definitive sentences or interlocutory sentences having definitive force given in the Curias of the suffragans according to the norm of Canon 1594, § 1;
8.° Determine in first instance the controversies described in Canon 1572, § 2.

Canon Law Digest
II: 119

Canon 275 (1983 CIC 437)

A Metropolitan is bound by the obligation, within three months of consecration or, if he is already consecrated, from his canonical provision in Consistory, of seeking from the Roman Pontiff the pallium, either personally or through a procurator, that signifies archiepiscopal power.

Canon Law Digest
V: 306; IX: 192–94

Canon 276 (NA)

Wherefore, before the imposition of the pallium, outside of a special apostolic indult, he illicitly places any acts, whether of metropolitan jurisdiction or of episcopal orders, that, in accord with liturgical law, require the use of the pallium.

Canon Law Digest
IV: 127

Canon 277 (1983 CIC 437)

A Metropolitan can use the pallium in any church, even exempt ones, within his province in solemn Mass, on days that are designated in the Roman Pontifical or perhaps otherwise granted to him; but in no case [may he use it] outside of his province, even with the consent of the local Ordinary.

Canon 278 (1983 CIC 437)

If a Metropolitan loses his pallium or is transferred to another archiepiscopal see, he needs a new pallium.

Canon 279 (NA)

A pallium cannot be lent or given away or left after death to anyone, but instead all the palliums that a Metropolitan has obtained are to be buried with him.

Canon 280 (NA) Cross-Ref.: 1917 CIC 271

Patriarchs precede Primates, Primates [precede] Archbishops, and these [are] over Bishops, with due regard for the prescription of Canon 347.

Canon Law Digest
II: 119

CHAPTER 7
On plenary and provincial Councils[46]

Canon 281 (1983 CIC 439)

Several Ordinaries of ecclesiastical provinces can convene a plenary Council, having come with a petition to the Roman Pontiff, who will designate his Legate to convoke and preside over the Council.

Canon Law Digest
I: 187–88; II: 119

Canon 282 (1983 CIC 443) Cross-Ref.: 1917 CIC 286

§ 1. At a plenary Council, there must be present with a deliberative vote, besides the Apostolic Legate, Metropolitans, residential Bishops who in their place can send Coadjutors and Auxiliaries, Apostolic Administrators of dioceses, Abbots and Prelates *of no one*, Apostolic Vicars, Apostolic Prefects, and Vicars Capitulary.

§ 2. Titular Bishops, [being then] present in the territory, if according to instructions received from the Pontifical Legate, also may be called to the Council and must have a deliberative vote, unless in the convocation something else is expressly provided.

---

[46] John Barrett, "A Comparative Study of the Councils of Baltimore and the Code of Canon Law", Canon Law Studies, no. 83 (J. C. D. thesis, Catholic University of America, 1932); Robert Duggan, "Plenary and Provincial Councils" (diss. no. 4, Pontifical University of St. Thomas [Rome], 1937–1938); Francis Murphy, "Legislative Powers of the Provincial Council", Canon Law Studies, no. 257 (thesis, Catholic University of America, 1947); James Kondrath, "The Laws of the Third Plenary Council of Baltimore concerning the Temporalities of the Church in the United States of America" (MS no. 2492, Gregorian University, 1956; printed version, no. 1174, 1956); Pedro Bantigue, "The Provincial Council of Manila of 1771; Its Text Followed by a Commentary on Actio II, *De Episcopis*", Canon Law Studies, no. 376 (thesis, Catholic University of America, 1957); Elias Olarte Poblete, "The Plenary Council", Canon Law Studies, no. 372 (thesis, Catholic University of America, 1958); Robert Sampon, "A Comparative Study of the First Provincial Council of Milwaukee and the Code of Canon Law", Canon Law Studies, no. 407 (Catholic University of America, not published); Bertram Griffin, "The Provincial Councils of Portland in Oregon" (Pontifical Lateran University, 1964); John Cannon, "Irish Episcopal Meetings, 1778–1882" (diss. no. 4, Pontifical University of St. Thomas [Rome], 1974–1975); Raphael Magno Sison, "The First Philippine Council (1771): Its Controversies as Reflected in the Unpublished Documents of Its Preparatory Congregations" (diss. no. 4, Pontifical University of St. Thomas [Rome], 1977–1978).

§ 3. Other men of either [secular or religious] clergy, [though] perhaps invited to the Council, do not enjoy a vote except consultative.

Canon 283 (1983 CIC 440)

In each ecclesiastical province, a provincial Council is to be celebrated at least every twenty years.

Canon Law Digest
I: 188

Canon 284 (1983 CIC 442) Cross-Ref.: 1917 CIC 292

If the Metropolitan is legitimately impeded or if there is a vacancy in the archiepiscopal see, the Suffragan senior in promotion to the suffragan church:

1.° Chooses the place for the celebration of the Council within the provincial territory, having heard all of those who must assist with a deliberative vote; if, however, just impediments cease, the metropolitan church should not be neglected;
2.° Convokes the Council and presides over it.

Canon 285 (NA) Cross-Refs.: 1917 CIC 286, 292, 429, 432, 1594

Bishops who are under no Metropolitan, Abbots and Prelates *of no one*, and Archbishops lacking Suffragans should choose a neighboring Metropolitan, unless they already have chosen one, once for always, with the prior approval of the Apostolic See, in whose provincial Councils they should be present with others, and whatever is ordained there they shall take care to observe and see that such things are observed.

Canon Law Digest
I: 188; II: 119

Canon 286 (1983 CIC 443)

§ 1. Besides the Bishops, Abbots and Prelates *of no one,* and Archbishops mentioned in Canon 285, all those Suffragans who are mentioned in Canon 282, § 1, shall be called and must be convened to a provincial Council with a deliberative vote.

§ 2. Titular Bishops who are in the province, with the consent of the major part of those who are present with a deliberative vote, can be convoked by the president, and if they are convoked, they have a deliberative vote, unless provided otherwise in the convocation.

§ 3. Cathedral chapters and diocesan consultors of any diocese with an Ordinary mentioned in § 1 must be called, and when they are invited they must send two of the chapter [members] or consultors collegially designated, who nevertheless obtain only a consultative vote.

§ 4. Major Superiors of clerical exempt religious or monastic Congregations, if they reside in the province, are to be invited, and those invited must be there, unless an impediment that detains them is communicated to the Council; but these and whoever else of either clergy of men who might be called have only a consultative vote.

Canon 287 (1983 CIC 444)

§ 1. Whoever must be present for a plenary or provincial Council with a deliberative vote, if detained by a just impediment, shall send a procurator and prove the impediment.

§ 2. The procurator, if he is one of the Fathers who has a deliberative vote, does not enjoy a double vote; if he does not have a vote, the vote he has is only consultative.

Canon 288 (1983 CIC 442)

In a Council, whether plenary or provincial, the president, having the consent of the Fathers if it concerns a provincial Council, determines the order to be observed in examining questions and opens, transfers, prorogues, and concludes the Council.

Canon 289 (NA)

Once a plenary or provincial Council starts, none of those required to be there may leave, unless with a just cause approved by the Pontifical Legate or by the provincial Council Fathers.

Canon 290 (1983 CIC 445)

The Fathers gathered in a plenary or provincial Council shall studiously investigate and discern what things will increase the faith, moderate morals, correct abuses, resolve controversies, and preserve and lead to united discipline, insofar as these things seem opportune in each of their territories.

Canon Law Digest
I: 188

Canon 291 (1983 CIC 446) Cross-Ref.: 1917 CIC 82

§ 1. At the conclusion of a plenary or provincial Council, the president shall transmit all the acts and decrees to the Holy See, and he shall not promulgate them beforehand until they have been [reviewed] and recognized by the Sacred Congregation of the Council; these same Council Fathers shall designate the manner of promulgation of the decrees and the time at which the promulgated decrees shall begin to oblige.

§ 2. The promulgated decrees of a plenary or provincial Council oblige throughout all the territory, nor shall local Ordinaries dispense from them except in particular cases for just cause.

Canon Law Digest
I: 188–89

Canon 292 (NA)

§ 1. Unless otherwise provided by the Apostolic See for particular places, the Metropolitan, or in his absence the senior among the Suffragans according to Canon 284, shall take care that local Ordinaries, at least every five years, at a set time, come together at the place of the Metropolitan or of one of the other Bishops, so that, gathered together in council, they may examine those things that ought to be done in the dioceses so that the good of religion is promoted, and so that they can prepare what things ought to be treated in a future provincial Council.

§ 2. Also, those Bishops mentioned in Canon 285, together with other Ordinaries, shall be convoked and must come.

§ 3. These same Ordinaries gathered together shall designate the site of the next meeting.

Canon Law Digest
I: 189–90; IV: 127; VI: 364–66; VII: 289–314;
VIII: 235–36; IX: 195–203; X: 40

Chapter 8
On Vicars and Prefects Apostolic[47]

Canon 293 (1983 CIC 371)

§ 1. Territories that are not erected into dioceses are ruled by Vicars or Prefects Apostolic; all of these are appointed only by the Apostolic See.

§ 2. A Vicar or Prefect Apostolic takes up possession of his territory by showing his apostolic letters, a decree, or patent letters from the Sacred Congregation for the Prop. of the Faith, personally or through a procurator, to him who governs the territory according to the norm of Canon 309.

Canon Law Digest
II: 119; VII: 314

Canon 294 (1983 CIC 381) Cross-Refs.: 1917 CIC 310, 323

§ 1. Vicars and Prefects Apostolic enjoy the same rights and faculties in their territories that residential Bishops have in their [territories], unless some [of these] have been reserved by the Apostolic See.

§ 2. Even those who lack episcopal character can, within the limits of their territory and for the duration of their responsibility, impart all blessings reserved to Bishops, excepting only pontifical ones; consecrate chalices, patens, and portable altars with holy oils blessed by a Bishop; grant

[47] Francis Winslow, "Vicars and Prefects Apostolic", Canon Law Studies, no. 24 (J. C. D. thesis, Catholic University of America, 1924); Roger Pelow, "The Vicar Delegate of Mission Ordinaries" (doctoral diss. 12, University of Ottawa, 1943); Matthew Grehan, "The Relations between a Superior of a Foreign Missionary Society of Priests without Vows and the Ecclesiastical Superior on the Mission" (diss. no. 13, Pontifical University of St. Thomas [Rome], 1949–1950); Melencio de Vera y Santiago, "The Peaceful Method of the Mission Theory and Its Application in the Philippines" (diss. no. 4, Pontifical University of St. Thomas [Rome], 1950–1951); Michael Hely, "Interim Mission Government" (MS no. 2058, Gregorian University, 1953); Maurice Leary, "The Missionaries of Emigrants" (diss. no. 2, Pontifical University of St. Thomas [Rome], 1954–1955); Joseph McNamara, "The Holy See and the Place of Religious Missionaries: The Law and Its Evolution (1600 to the Present Day)" (diss. no. 20, Pontifical University of St. Thomas [Rome], 1958–1959); Paul Golden, "The Relationship between the Congregation of the Mission and the Local Ordinary in the Apostolate of the Diocese" (diss. no. 7, Pontifical University of St. Thomas [Rome], 1970–1971); Emmanuel Akpan, "Canon Law and Missionary Apostolate in Nigeria: The Orientation of the Ecclesial Legal System to Evangelization" (Pontifical University Urbaniana, 1982).

indulgences of fifty days; and confer confirmation, first tonsure, and minor orders according to the norm of Canons 782, § 3, and 957, § 2.

Canon Law Digest
I: 190–91; II: 119; III: 107; VI: 366

Canon 295 (NA)

§ 1. Vicars and Prefects Apostolic can and must require all missionaries, even religious, to show their patents or other [documents] about their mission, destination, constitution, and deputation and, regarding those refusing to show them, prohibit the exercise of any ecclesiastical ministry.

§ 2. All missionaries, even regulars, shall seek from Vicars and Prefects Apostolic permission for the exercise of sacred ministry, who in turn shall not deny same except regarding individuals for grave reason.

Canon 296 (NA)

§ 1. Even regular missionaries are subject to the jurisdiction, visitation, and correction of Vicars and Prefects Apostolic in those things that pertain to governance of the mission, care of souls, administration of the Sacraments, direction of schools, donations made in support of the missions, and the fulfillment of pious wills made in favor of the mission.

§ 2. Although Vicars and Prefects Apostolic are permitted in no way, beyond those cases envisioned in law, to involve themselves in religious discipline that depends on a religious Superior, if, nevertheless, a conflict arises concerning those things in the above paragraph, [then as] between the mandates of the Vicars or Prefects Apostolic and the mandate of a [religious] Superior, the prior must prevail, with due regard for the right of recourse in devolution to the Holy See, and observing the special statutes approved by the Apostolic See.

Canon Law Digest
I: 191–92; II: 119

Canon 297 (NA)

If there is a deficit of secular [priests], Vicars and Prefects Apostolic can compel religious, even exempt ones, attached to the vicariate or prefecture, having heard their Superior, to exercise care of souls, with due regard for particular statutes approved by the Apostolic See.

Canon 298 (NA)

If there happens to arise any conflict in those things pertaining to the care of souls, whether between individual missionaries or between different religious [institutes], or between missionaries and others, Vicars and Prefects Apostolic shall take care as soon as possible to address these sorts of questions and, where necessary, to decide them, there remaining, nevertheless, recourse to the Apostolic See that does not suspend the effect of the decree.

Canon 299 (1983 CIC 400)

Vicars Apostolic are bound by the obligation of visiting the Sacred Threshold of the Blessed Apostles Peter and Paul by quite the same law as are residential Bishops according to the norm of Canon 341; this responsibility, if something gravely prevents them from fulfilling it themselves, can be satisfied by a procurator, even one living in the City.

Canon 300 (NA)

§ 1. According to the norm of Canon 340, Vicars and Prefects Apostolic are bound by the obligation of showing to the Apostolic See a full and accurate report on their own pastoral office, on everything about whatever pertains to the state of the vicariate or prefecture, missionaries, religious, discipline of the people, attendance at schools, and finally about the welfare of the faithful committed to their care under any rationale; this report is to be in writing, signed by the Vicar or Prefect himself, or by at least one of the councilors mentioned in Canon 302.

§ 2. Moreover immediately upon the completion of a year they will send to the Holy See a list or accounting of the numbers of conversions, baptisms, and administrations of the Sacraments that year, together with any worthy notations.

Canon Law Digest
I: 192–93; II: 120

Canon 301 (NA)

§ 1. They shall be present in the regions committed to them, and it is not permitted that they be absent from there for a notable time without grave and urgent cause, [and] without consulting the Apostolic See.

§ 2. They must themselves, or, if they are legitimately impeded, through another, visit the regions entrusted to them, whenever it seems necessary, and examine all those things that refer to faith, good morals, administration of the Sacraments, preaching of the word of God, observance of feasts, divine cult, instruction of the young, and ecclesiastical discipline.

Canon 302 (1983 CIC 495) Cross-Refs.: 1917 CIC 300, 457

They shall constitute a Council of at least three of the more senior and more prudent missionaries, whose opinion, at least through letter, they shall hear in more grave and difficult affairs.

Canon Law Digest
I: 193; II: 120–21

Canon 303 (NA)

Whenever the opportunity arises, they shall gather at least the principal missionaries, whether religious or secular, at least once a year, so that from the experience and counsel of them as individuals, they can arrive at those things that will perfect order.

Canon Law Digest
I: 193.

Canon 304 (NA)

§ 1. Vicars and Prefects Apostolic are equally bound by the laws concerning the constitution of archives that bind Bishops, taking into consideration factors of locations and persons.

§ 2. Equivalently, those things regarding plenary and provincial Councils prescribed in Canons 281–91 must be applied, due adaptation being made, in plenary or provincial or regional Councils in regions subject to the authority of the Sacred Congregation for the Prop. of the Faith; those things [prescribed] for a diocesan Synod in Canons 356–62 [apply in a similar manner] to the Synod of a vicariate apostolic; but there is no predetermined time for the celebration of a provincial Council or Synod, and the canons of the Council, before they are promulgated, must be recognized by the Sacred Congregation for the Prop. of the Faith.

Canon 305[48] (NA)

They must studiously take care, their conscience being gravely burdened, that, from among the indigenous Christians or inhabitants of their region, suitable clerics be formed and initiated into priesthood.

Canon Law Digest
III: 107

Canon 306 (NA) Cross-Ref.: 1917 CIC 466

They must apply the sacrifice of the Mass for the people committed to their care on at least the solemnities of the Birth of the Lord, Epiphany, Easter, Ascension, Pentecost, the most holy Body of Christ, Immaculate Conception, and Assumption of the Blessed Virgin Mary, Saint Joseph her spouse, the Holy Apostles Peter and Paul, and All Saints, with due regard for the prescription of Canon 339, §§ 2, and foll[owing].

Canon Law Digest
I: 193; II: 121–22; IV: 128

Canon 307 (NA)

§ 1. It is not permitted for them, without consulting the Apostolic See, to allow missionaries sent by it to leave the vicariate or prefecture perpetually or transfer to another [institute or territory] or in any manner to expel them.

§ 2. But in the case of public scandal, they can, having heard the Council, and if it concerns a religious, having notified in advance the Superior if possible, remove a missionary immediately, sending immediate notice to the Apostolic See.

Canon 308 (NA) Cross-Ref.: 1917 CIC 315

Vicars and Prefects, augmented with episcopal character, enjoy those honorific privileges that the law grants to titular Bishops; but if they lack this character, they have, for the duration of their responsibilities and in

[48] William Beentjes, "The Canonical Requisites in Candidates for the Indigenous Clergy in Mission Countries" (thesis, Gregorian University; printed version, no. 916, Beverwijk, The Netherlands, 1955); Charles de Melo, "The Recruitment and Formation of Native Clergy in India" (thesis, Gregorian University; printed version, no. 920, Lisbon, 1955).

their own territory, only the insignia and privileges of Protonotaries Apostolic participating in that number.

Canon Law Digest
I: 193

Canon 309 (1983 CIC 420) Cross-Refs.: 1917 CIC 293, 310

§ 1. Vicars and Prefects, when they first come into their territory, shall depute from one clergy or the other a suitable Pro-vicar or Pro-prefect, unless a Coadjutor with right of succession has been given by the Holy See.

§ 2. A Pro-vicar or Pro-prefect has no power while the Vicar or Prefect lives, unless it was committed to him by the latter; but in the absence of the Vicar or Prefect, or if his jurisdiction is impeded according to the norm of Canon 429, § 1, he must assume complete governance and remain in this responsibility until the Holy See provides otherwise.

§ 3. In a similar way, the Pro-vicar or Pro-prefect who succeeds the titular must immediately depute an ecclesiastical man who, as above, succeeds him in responsibility.

§ 4. If it happens that no one either by the titular or pro-titular has been designated, then the senior one in the vicariate or prefecture, namely, the one who being present in the territory first presented to him his letters of destination, is considered as delegated by the Holy See for purposes of assuming governance, and among several equally senior, that priest who is older [in orders is so considered].

Canon Law Digest
I: 193

Canon 310 (1983 CIC 420)

§ 1. They to whom the care of a vicariate and prefecture apostolic comes according to the norm of Canon 309 must as soon as possible notify the Apostolic See.

§ 2. In the meantime, they have all of the faculties, whether ordinary, according to the norm of Canon 294, or delegated, that a Vicar or Prefect had, unless they were committed in virtue of the qualities of the person.

Canon Law Digest
I: 194

Canon 311 (NA)

Whoever is placed in a vicariate and prefecture apostolic for a certain time must remain there with all the faculties granted to him, even though the definite time has already lapsed, until the canonical successor takes up possession of his duties.

Chapter 9
On Apostolic Administrators[49]

Canon 312 (1983 CIC 371)

Sometimes the Supreme Pontiff for grave and special causes commits to an Apostolic Administrator, either perpetually or for a time, the governance of a canonically erected diocese, whether the see is occupied or vacant.

Canon Law Digest
II: 122; V: 306–7; VII: 314; IX: 203

Canon 313 (NA)

§ 1. Any Apostolic Administrator, if he is given to a diocese when the see is occupied, enters into his canonical possession of administration by showing his letters of appointment both to the Bishop, if he is mentally alert and present in the diocese, and to the Chapter, according to the norm of Canon 334, § 3.

§ 2. But if the see is vacant, or if the Bishop is not in command of his mental powers or is no longer in the diocese, the Apostolic Administrator assumes possession as would a Bishop according to the above-cited Canon 334, § 3.

Canon 314 (NA)

The rights, duties, and privileges of the Apostolic Administrator are contained in his letters of deputation or, unless otherwise expressly provided therein, in the prescriptions of the canons that follow.

[49] Thomas McDonough, "Apostolic Administrators", Canon Law Studies, no. 139 (J. C. D. thesis, Catholic University of America, 1941).

Canon 315 (NA)

§ 1. An Apostolic Administrator permanently constituted enjoys the same rights and honors, and is bound by the same obligations, as a residential Bishop.

§ 2. If he is given for a time:

1.° He has the same rights and duties as Vicar Capitulary; but, when the see is occupied, he can visit the diocese to apply justice; but he is not bound by the obligation that weighs on a Bishop of applying Mass for the people;

2.° As to what applies to honorific privileges, the prescription of Canon 308 binds; but as for the Bishop who is transferred to another see, if he retains the administration of the prior, then he is competent for all of the honorific privileges of residential Bishops.

Canon Law Digest
VI: 366

Canon 316 (NA)

§ 1. If an Apostolic Administrator is appointed for a diocese while the see is occupied, the jurisdiction of the Bishop and the Vicar General is suspended.

§ 2. Although the Apostolic Administrator is not under the authority of the Bishop, he must not involve himself in matters concerning the Bishop or instruct or take due notice in a trial or process of the Vicar General for acts done during his administration.

Canon 317 (NA)

If the jurisdiction of the Apostolic Administrator is impeded, or if he fails in same, the Apostolic See is to be notified immediately; and in the meantime, if the diocese is vacant or if the Bishop is not of sound mind, the prescriptions of Canons 429 and foll[owing] are in force; otherwise the Bishop rules the diocese, unless otherwise provided by the Apostolic See.

Canon 318 (NA)

§ 1. The jurisdiction of an Apostolic Administrator does not cease with the death of the Roman Pontiff or the Bishop.

§ 2. But it does cease when the Bishop takes up legitimate possession of the diocese according to the norm of Canon 334, § 3.

Chapter 10
On inferior Prelates[50]

Canon 319 (1983 CIC 370)

§ 1. Prelates who are over their own territory, separated from every diocese, with clergy and people, are called Abbots or Prelates *of no one*, namely [of no] diocese, insofar as their church enjoys abbatial or simple prelature dignity.

§ 2. An abbacy or prelature *of no one* not consisting of at least three parishes is governed by a singular law and to it are not applied the canons established for abbacies and prelatures *of no one*.

Canon Law Digest
VII: 314; VIII: 236–39

Canon 320 (NA)

§ 1. Abbots or Prelates *of no one* are appointed and instituted by the Roman Pontiff, with due regard for the rights of election or presentation, if those are legitimately applicable; in which case they must be confirmed or installed by the Roman Pontiff.

§ 2. For the assumption of an abbey or prelature *of no one*, they must be endowed with the same qualities that the law requires for a Bishop.

Canon 321 (NA) Cross-Ref.: 1917 CIC 329

If a college has the right of electing an Abbot or Prelate *of no one*, for the validity of the election there is required an absolute majority of the number of votes, not counting null votes, with due regard for any particular law that requires a greater number of votes.

Canon 322 (NA) Cross-Ref.: 1917 CIC 2402

§ 1. Abbots or Prelates *of no one* shall not under any title, either personally or through others, involve themselves in the governance of the abbey or prelature before they take up canonical possession, according to the norm of Canon 334, § 3.

---

[50] Matthew Benko, "The Abbot Nullius [of no one]", Canon Law Studies, no. 173 (J. C. D. thesis, Catholic University of America, 1943); Pio Morales, "The Powers of Prelates Nullius [of no one]" (diss. no. 18, University of St. Thomas [Manila], 1960).

§ 2. Abbots or Prelates *of no one* who must be blessed by apostolic prescription or their own religious constitutions must take this blessing from any Bishop they choose within three months from the receipt of apostolic letters, any legitimate impediment ceasing.

Canon Law Digest
I: 194; VII: 314

Canon 323 (NA)

§ 1. An Abbot or Prelate *of no one* has the same ordinary powers and the same obligations with the same sanctions that a residential Bishop has in his own diocese.

§ 2. If he is not endowed with episcopal character and he receives the blessing that he must receive, he can, in addition to those things described in Canon 294, § 2, consecrate churches and immovable altars.

§ 3. As to what applies to the constitution of the Vicar General, the prescriptions of Canons 366–71 are observed.

Canon Law Digest
I: 194; II: 122; VI: 366; VIII: 239

Canon 324 (NA)

A religious Chapter of an abbey or prelature *of no one* is governed by its own laws and constitutions; [and] a secular Chapter [is governed] by common law.

Canon 325 (NA) Cross-Ref.: 1917 CIC 625

Abbots or Prelates *of no one*, even though they lack episcopal character, can nevertheless use in their own territory pontifical insignia with the throne and baldachin and by law can celebrate therein with pontifical rites the divine offices; they can also wear the pectoral cross and a ring with a stone, and a purple skullcap outside of their territory.

Canon 326 (NA)

If a secular prelature lacks a Chapter, the consultors are elected according to the norm of Canons 423–28.

Canon 327 (NA)

§ 1. When a vacancy occurs in an abbacy or prelature *of no one*, if it concerns an abbacy or prelature of religious, the Chapter of religious succeeds, unless the constitution determines otherwise; if of seculars, the Chapter of canons [succeeds]; in either case, the Chapter must, within eight days, depute a Vicar Capitulary according to the norm of Canons 432 and foll[owing], who rules the abbey or prelature until the election of the new Abbot or Prelate.

§ 2. If the abbey or prelature is impeded, the prescription of Canon 429 is observed.

Canon 328 (NA)

Concerning Householders of the Roman Pontiff, whether they enjoy the title of prelate or whether [they do] not, the privileges, rules, and traditions of the pontifical House stand.

Canon Law Digest
II: 122; VI: 367–70; VII: 314–22; VIII: 239

TITLE 8
On episcopal power and those who participate in it

Chapter 1
On Bishops[51]

Canon 329[52] (1983 CIC 375, 377)

§ 1. Bishops are successors of the Apostles and by divine institution are placed over specific churches that they govern with ordinary power under the authority of the Roman Pontiff.

§ 2. The Roman Pontiff freely appoints them.

---

[51] Carlos Warnholtz, "The Nature of the Episcopal Office according to the Second Vatican Council", Canon Law Studies, no. 455 (Catholic University of America, 1967).

[52] Joseph George, "The Principle of Subsidiarity with Special Reference to Its Role in Papal and Episcopal Relations in the Light of *Lumen Gentium*", Canon Law Studies, no. 463 (J. C. D. thesis, Catholic University of America, 1968); Otto Luis Garcia, "*Sacramentalitas Episcopatus*: Evolution of the Text of *Lumen Gentium*, n. 21b" (thesis, Gregorian University; printed version, no. 2846, 1979); John Tutone, "Constitutive Law in *De Episcoporum Muneribus*" (diss. no. 8, Pontifical University of St. Thomas [Rome], 1980–1981).

§ 3. If the right of electing a Bishop has been granted to a college, the prescriptions of Canon 321 are observed.

Canon Law Digest
II: 122; VI: 370–412; VII: 322–66; VIII: 240–46;
IX: 204–13; X: 40–41

Canon 330 (NA)

Before anyone is assumed into the [episcopate], it must be demonstrated, according to the manner determined by the Apostolic See, that he is suitable.

Canon Law Digest
I: 194–99; VI: 412; VII: 366–73

Canon 331 (1983 CIC 378) Cross-Ref.: 1917 CIC 974

§ 1. In order that one be considered suitable, he must:

1.° Be born of a legitimate marriage, but not be legitimated even by a subsequent marriage;

2.° Be at least thirty years of age;

3.° Be constituted in the sacred order of the presbyterate for at least five years;

4.° Be of good morals, pious, zealous for souls, prudent, and outstanding in those other qualities that will make him apt for the governance of a diocese and the things that concern it;

5.° Have a doctoral degree or at least a licentiate [degree] in sacred theology or canon law, preferably from an athenaeum or Institute of studies approved by the Holy See, or at least be truly expert in these disciplines; but if he belongs to a religious [institute], he shall have testimony from his major Superior about [this] title or at least [about] his true expertise.

§ 2. Even regarding one who is elected, presented, or in any other way designated by those who have been granted the privilege of electing, presenting, or otherwise designating [one] by grant of the Holy See, he must be mindful to partake of these qualities.

§ 3. It pertains solely to the Apostolic See to judge whether one is suitable.

Canon Law Digest
VII: 373

Canon 332[53] (1983 CIC 377, 380)

§ 1. Whoever is to be promoted to the episcopate, even if he is elected, presented, or designated even by a civil Government, needs canonical provision or institution by which the Bishop is constituted in a vacant diocese, which only the Roman Pontiff can give.

§ 2. Before canonical institution or provision, a candidate, beyond the profession of faith mentioned in Canons 1406–8, shall make an oath of fidelity to the Holy See according to a formula approved by the Apostolic See.

Canon Law Digest
I: 199; III: 108

Canon 333 (1983 CIC 379, 382) Cross-Refs.: 1917 CIC 430, 2398

Unless prohibited by a legitimate impediment, one promoted to the episcopate, even if he is a Cardinal of the H. R. C., must within three months of receipt of the apostolic letters take up consecration and within four [months] go to his diocese, with due regard for the prescription of Canon 238, § 2.

Canon 334 (1983 CIC 381–82) Cross-Refs.: 1917 CIC 313, 318, 322, 353, 430, 443, 958, 1095

§ 1. Residential Bishops are ordinary and immediate pastors in the dioceses committed to them.

§ 2. In the government of the diocese, however, neither personally nor through others nor under any title can they involve themselves before they have first taken up possession canonically of the diocese; but if, before being designated for the episcopate, they have been appointed Vicars Capitulary, officials, or economes, these offices they may retain and exercise after designation [as Bishop].

§ 3. Residential Bishops take up canonical possession of a diocese immediately upon showing the apostolic letters personally or through a procu-

[53] John Eidenschink, "The Election of Bishops in the Letters of Pope Gregory the Great", Canon Law Studies, no. 215 (J. C. D. thesis, Catholic University of America, 1945); Herculano Izquierdo, "Nomination of Bishops in Present Day Concordats", Canon Law Studies, no. 439 (Catholic University of America, not published); James Harvey, "The Jurisdiction of the Episcopal College according to Gianvincenzo Bolegni: An Exposition in Light of the Teaching of *Lumen Gentium* of the Second Vatican Council" (thesis, Gregorian University; printed version, no. 2890, 1980).

rator to the Chapter of the cathedral church in that diocese in the presence of the secretary of the Chapter or chancellor of the Curia, who records the matter in the acts.

Canon Law Digest
I: 199; II: 122; VI: 413; IX: 213

Canon 335[54] (1983 CIC 8, 391)

§ 1. To them belongs the right and duty of governing the dioceses both in spiritualities and temporalities with legislative, judicial, and coercive power to be exercised according to the norm of sacred canons.

§ 2. Episcopal laws begin to oblige immediately upon promulgation, unless provided otherwise in the laws themselves; the manner of promulgation is determined by the Bishop himself.

Canon Law Digest
I: 199–200; II: 123–30; III: 108; VII: 373; IX: 213; X: 41

Canon 336[55] (1983 CIC 392)

§ 1. Bishops shall urge the observance of ecclesiastical laws; nor shall they dispense from common law except according to the norm of Canon 81.

§ 2. They shall be vigilant lest abuse appear in ecclesiastical discipline, especially concerning the administration of Sacraments and Sacramentals, the cult of God and of the Saints, preaching of the word of God, sacred indulgences, and the implementation of pious wills; they shall take care that the purity of faith and morals among the clergy and people is preserved, and that the faithful, especially children and the unlettered, are offered the pabulum of Christian teaching, and that in schools of children and young people instruction is handed on according to principles of the Catholic religion.

§ 3. Concerning the task of preaching, the prescription of Canon 1327 is observed.

Canon Law Digest
I: 200; II: 131; IV: 129–51; V: 307; VI: 413

---

[54] Gerald Ryan, "Principles of Episcopal Jurisdiction", Canon Law Studies, no. 120 (J. C. D. thesis, Catholic University of America, 1939).

[55] Donald Hellmann, "The Concept and Exercise of Episcopal Vigilance" (MS no. 2811, Gregorian University, 1957); Joseph Tobin, "The Teaching Office of the Diocesan Bishop" (Ph. D. diss. 70, St. Paul University [Ottawa, Canada], 1983).

Canon 337 (1983 CIC 390) Cross-Ref.: 1917 CIC 2279

§ 1. A Bishop throughout his diocese, not excluding exempt places, can exercise pontificals; but not outside the diocese without the express or at least reasonably presumed consent of the local Ordinary and, if it concerns an exempt church, the consent of the religious Superior.

§ 2. It is [for him] to exercise pontificals in law and to perform sacred functions which by liturgical law require pontifical insignia or the pastoral staff and miter.

§ 3. A Bishop, in granting permission for the exercise of pontificals in his territory, can permit the use of the throne and baldachin.

Canon Law Digest
I: 200; II: 131; V: 307; VII: 373–82

Canon 338 (1983 CIC 395) Cross-Refs.: 1917 CIC 354, 418, 440

§ 1. Even Bishops who have Coadjutors are bound by the law of personally residing in the diocese.

§ 2. Except for the cases of visiting the Sacred Threshold, Councils that they must attend, or civil duties attached legitimately to their churches, they can be absent for good causes not beyond two or three months within a year, whether continuously or with interruptions, provided that they have taken precautions that their absence occasions no detriment to their diocese: but this time cannot be added either to the time they have to take possession of their promotion, or for the visitation to the Sacred Threshold, or for assistance at a Council, or with the time of vacation in a subsequent year.

§ 3. They shall not be absent from cathedral churches during Advent and Lent, [nor on] the day of the Nativity, Resurrection of the Lord, Pentecost, and the Body of Christ, except for grave and urgent cause.

§ 4. If they are absent from the diocese illegitimately for more than six months, the Metropolitan shall denounce the Bishop to the Apostolic See, according to the norm of Canon 274, n. 4, and the senior resident Suffragan [shall similarly denounce] the Metropolitan.

Canon 339 (1983 CIC 388) Cross-Refs.: 1917 CIC 306, 440, 466

§ 1. They must also, after taking possession of the see, to the exclusion of all excuse based on income and removed from any other exception, apply Mass for the people committed to them on all [Sundays] and other feast days of precept, even if suppressed.

§ 2. On the feast of the Nativity of the Lord, if this feast of precept falls on a [Sunday], it is sufficient that they apply one Mass for the people.

§ 3. If a feast is so transferred that the day *to which* not only has the office with the Mass of the feast transferred, but there is also the obligation of hearing Mass and of abstaining from servile works, the Mass for the people is to be applied on the day *to which*; otherwise, [it shall be applied] on the day *from which*.

§ 4. The Bishop must personally apply Mass for the people on the above-indicated days; if he is legitimately impeded from celebration, he shall apply it on the stated day through another; if he can do neither, he shall apply it personally or through another on another day as soon as possible.

§ 5. Even though a Bishop has two or more dioceses and rules them principally as one, or if, besides his own diocese, he has the administration of another or others, he nevertheless satisfies the obligation by the celebration and application of one Mass for all the people committed to him.

§ 6. A Bishop who does not satisfy the obligations mentioned in the above paragraphs shall promptly apply as many Masses for the people as he omitted.

Canon Law Digest
I: 201; III: 108; IV: 151–52; V: 307

Canon 340[56] (1983 CIC 399) Cross-Ref.: 1917 CIC 300

§ 1. All Bishops are bound every five years to make a report to the Supreme Pontiff on the status of the diocese committed to them according to the formula given by the Apostolic See.

§ 2. The five years are fixed and common and are computed from 1 January 1911; in the first year of the five, the Bishops of Italy and of the islands of Corsica, Sardinia, Sicily, Melitia and the other adjoining little islands must make a report; [likewise] in the next [year], the Bishops of Spain, Portugal, France, Belgium, Holland, England, Scotland, and Ireland, with the adjoining islands; [likewise] in the third [year], the other Bishops of Europe, with the adjoining islands; [likewise] in the fourth [year], the Bishops of all America and the adjoining islands; [likewise] in the fifth [year], the Bishops of Africa, Asia, Australia, and the islands adjacent to this part of the world.

[56] James Carroll, "The Bishop's Quinquennial Report", Canon Law Studies, no. 359 (thesis, Catholic University of America, 1956).

§ 3. If the year assigned for giving the report falls either completely or in part within the first two years from the start of his diocesan governance, the Bishop for this time can abstain from making and showing a report.

Canon Law Digest
I: 202; II: 131; VIII: 246–52; IX: 214–41; X: 41–43

Canon 341 (1983 CIC 400) Cross-Ref.: 1917 CIC 299

§ 1. All and every Bishop, in the year in which they are bound to present a report, shall come to the City to venerate the tombs of the Blessed Apostles Peter and Paul and present themselves to the Roman Pontiff.

§ 2. But Bishops who are outside of Europe are allowed to seek the City in alternate quinquennial periods, that is, every ten [years].

Canon Law Digest
I: 202; V: 307; VIII: 252

Canon 342 (1983 CIC 400)

A Bishop must satisfy the aforesaid obligation personally or through a Coadjutor, if he has one, or, for just cause demonstrated to the Holy See, through a suitable priest who resides in the diocese of the Bishop.

Canon Law Digest
VIII: 252

Canon 343[57] (1983 CIC 396)

§ 1. For the preservation of healthy and orthodox doctrine, the protection of good morals, the correction of the depraved, and the promotion of peace, innocence, piety, and discipline among the people and clergy, and for the establishment of those other things which by reason of circumstance will advance the cause of religion, Bishops are bound by the obligation of visiting the diocese each year completely or in part so that, at least every five years, personally or, if he is legitimately impeded, through the Vicar General or another, it is all inspected.

§ 2. It is fundamental that the Bishop may take two clerics, even from the cathedral or collegial Chapter, together with him as assistants; he may choose whomever he wants, reprobating any contrary privilege or custom whatever.

---

[57] Andrew Slafkosky, "The Canonical Episcopal Visitation of the Diocese", Canon Law Studies, no. 142 (J. C. D. thesis, Catholic University of America, 1941).

§ 3. If a Bishop gravely neglects the obligation mentioned in § 1, the prescription of Canon 274, nn. 4 and 5, is observed.

Canon Law Digest
II: 131; VI: 413

Canon 344 (1983 CIC 397)

§ 1. Subject to ordinary episcopal visitation are persons, things, and pious places, even though exempt, that are contained within the ambit of the diocese, unless it can be proven that there was a special exemption from visitation granted to them by the Apostolic See.

§ 2. The Bishop can visit exempt religious only in those cases expressed in law.

Canon 345 (NA)

The Visitator, in those things that respect the object and purpose of his visit, must proceed in a paternal manner, and recourse against his precepts or decree is given only in devolution; but in other cases, even at the time of the visit, the Bishop must proceed in accord with the norm of law.

Canon 346 (1983 CIC 398)

Bishops shall attentively complete the pastoral visitation with due diligence and without useless delay: they shall take care lest superfluous consumption be a grave burden to anyone or that, on the occasion of their visit, they or any of their [assistants] seek or receive gifts for themselves, reprobating any contrary custom whatsoever; but concerning the food and supplies to be given them and their [assistants] and expenses of the trip, legitimate local custom is followed.

Canon Law Digest
I: 203

Canon 347 (NA) Cross-Ref.: 1917 CIC 280

In his own territory, a Bishop takes precedence over all Archbishops and Bishops, except for Cardinals, Pontifical Legates, and his own Metropolitan; outside of this territory the norms given in Canon 106 are observed.

Canon Law Digest
II: 131

Canon 348 (NA)

§ 1. Titular Bishops exercise no power in their diocese nor do they take possession of it.

§ 2. It is becoming out of charity, though outside of any obligation, that they apply some sacrifice of the Mass for their diocese.

Canon 349[58] (NA)

§ 1. From the acceptance of authentic notice of a completed canonical provision, Bishops, whether residential or titular:

1.° Enjoy, besides those recited in their title, the privileges mentioned in Canon 239, § 1, nn. 7–12; those also in n. 2, even though it concerns cases reserved to the local Ordinary; [likewise] in n. 3, with at least the presumed consent of the local Ordinary; [likewise] in n. 4, although he is not bound to celebrate in the cathedral; [and likewise] in nn. 5 and 6, albeit by rites prescribed by the Church;

2.° Have the right of wearing episcopal insignia according to the norm of liturgical law.

§ 2. But from taking possession of leadership, residential Bishops also have the right:

1.° Of receiving income from the episcopal table;

2.° Of granting indulgences of fifty days in their place of jurisdiction;

3.° Of erecting in all churches in their dioceses a throne with a baldachin.

Canon Law Digest
I: 203–11; II: 131; III: 108–9; VI: 413–14

Chapter 2
On Coadjutors and Auxiliaries of Bishops[59]

Canon 350 (1983 CIC 403)

§ 1. It is for the Roman Pontiff alone to constitute Coadjutor Bishops.

§ 2. Usually a Coadjutor is given for the person of the Bishop with a right of succession; but one can also be given to the see.

[58] Francis McElroy, "The Privileges of Bishops", Canon Law Studies, no. 282 (thesis, Catholic University of America, 1951).

[59] George Lynch, "Coadjutors and Auxiliaries of Bishops", Canon Law Studies, no. 238 (J. C. D. thesis, Catholic University of America, 1947).

§ 3. A Coadjutor given for the person of the Bishop without a right of succession is called by the special name of *Auxiliary*.

Canon Law Digest
VI: 414; VII: 382; VIII: 252–53

Canon 351 (1983 CIC 405, 408)

§ 1. The rights of a Coadjutor given to the person of Bishops are contained in the apostolic letters by which they are constituted.

§ 2. Unless provided otherwise in these letters, a Coadjutor who is given to a Bishop who is entirely incapacitated has all episcopal rights and duties; otherwise, [he has] only those that the Bishop commits to him.

§ 3. Those things that the Coadjutor can and wants to do, the Bishop shall not habitually delegate to others.

§ 4. A Coadjutor, not detained by just impediment, must, as often as he is requested by the Bishop, [perform] pontifical and other functions to which the Bishop himself is attached.

Canon 352 (NA)

A Coadjutor given to a see can in that territory exercise all episcopal orders except for sacred ordination; in other matters, he can [do] only those things committed to him by the Holy See or by the Bishop.

Canon Law Digest
I: 211

Canon 353 (1983 CIC 404) Cross-Ref.: 1917 CIC 355

§ 1. Every Coadjutor, in order that he take up canonical possession of his office, needs to show his apostolic letters to the Bishop.

§ 2. A Coadjutor with future succession and a Coadjutor given to a see also need to show these [documents] to the Chapter according to the norm of Canon 334, § 3.

§ 3. If the Bishop has fallen into a state wherein he cannot place human acts, the prescription of § 1 is omitted and only the prescription of § 2 need be observed by all Coadjutors.

Canon 354 (1983 CIC 410)

Every Coadjutor is bound by the obligation, as is a Bishop, of residing in the diocese, from which, outside of vacation time according to the norm of Canon 338, he is not permitted to leave except for brief time, the [Bishop of the] Coadjutor permitting.

Canon 355 (1983 CIC 409)

§ 1. A Coadjutor with right of succession, upon the vacancy of the see, becomes the Ordinary of the diocese for which he was constituted, provided he has taken up canonical possession of it according to the norm of Canon 353.

§ 2. The office of Auxiliary expires with the responsibility of the Bishop, unless provided otherwise in the apostolic letters.

§ 3. If a Coadjutor was given to a see, his office perdures even with the vacancy of the see.

Canon Law Digest
I: 211; VI: 414; VIII: 253–54

Chapter 3
On the diocesan Synod[60]

Canon 356 (1983 CIC 460–61)

§ 1. In each diocese at least every ten years, there is to be celebrated a diocesan Synod, in which only those things are treated that refer to the needs or utility of the clergy and people of the particular diocese.

§ 2. If a Bishop has several dioceses and rules them principally as one, or he has one [diocese] in title and another in perpetual administration, he can convoke just one diocesan Synod for all of the dioceses.

Canon Law Digest
V: 307–8

[60] Francis Donnelly, "The Diocesan Synod", Canon Law Studies, no. 74 (J. C. D. thesis, Catholic University of America, 1932); Jonas Thaliath, "The Synod of Diamper" (MS no. 2006, Gregorian University, 1951; printed version, no. 1166, 1958); Patrick Barry, "The Irish National Synod of Thuries (1850)" (MS no. 2220, Gregorian University, 1954); Ernest Fontinell, "A Study of the Legislation concerning the Sacraments in the First Synod of Scranton" (Pontifical Lateran University, 1956); Robert Ammann, "The Magisterium of the Church as Related to the Catholic Schools according to the Fifth Synod of Archdiocese of Cincinnati" (Pontifical Lateran University [Rome], 1956); Seamus O'Connor, "The Structure of a Post-Conciliar Diocesan Synod in the United States of America", Canon Law Studies, no. 473 (Catholic University of America, 1970); Higino Candame Velarde, "The Fourth Synod of Manila of 1979 (an Historico-Juridical Study of Its Structures)" (diss. no. 2, Pontifical University of St. Thomas [Rome], 1981–1982).

Canon 357 (1983 CIC 462)

§ 1. The Bishop convokes and presides over the diocesan Synod, but not the Vicar General without a special mandate or a Vicar Capitulary.

§ 2. It is to be celebrated in the cathedral church, unless reasonable cause persuades otherwise.

Canon 358 (1983 CIC 463)

§ 1. [The following] are to be called to the Synod and must attend:

1.° The Vicar General;

2.° The canons of cathedral churches or diocesan consultors;

3.° The rector of a diocesan Seminary, at least the major one;

4.° The vicars forane;

5.° The deputies of any collegial church chosen from the membership by the Chapter of the same church;

6.° The pastors in the city in which the Synod is celebrated;

7.° At least one pastor from each vicariate forane, to be chosen from among all those who have actually entered into the care of souls; the pastor chosen must, for the time of his absence, secure a substitute for himself according to the norm of Canon 465, § 4;

8.° The abbots of governance and one of the Superiors of each clerical religious [institute] present in the diocese, designated by the provincial Superior, unless the provincial house is in the diocese and the provincial Superior wishes to attend himself.

§ 2. The Bishop, if he judges it opportune, can call others to the Synod, or even all of the canons, pastors, religious Superiors, and, indeed, each secular diocesan priest, excepting only those who are necessary lest the care of souls in parishes suffer; those invited have the right of voting in all things just as the others, unless the Bishop expressly notes otherwise in the invitation.

Canon 359 (1983 CIC 464)

§ 1. Those who must come to the Synod, if they are detained by a legitimate impediment, are not permitted to send a procurator who takes part in their name at the Synod; but they shall inform the Bishop about the impediment.

§ 2. The Bishop can compel and punish negligent ones with just penalties, unless it concerns exempt religious who are not pastors.

Canon 360 (NA)

§ 1. The Bishop, if it seems expedient to him, at an opportune time before the Synod, shall appoint one or several *commissions* from the clergy of the city and of the diocese, that is, a committee of men who will prepare the things to be treated in the Synod.

§ 2. Before the sessions of the Synod, the Bishop shall take care that a schema of the [proposed] decrees is given to all who are convoked and attend.

Canon 361 (1983 CIC 465)

All proposed questions, under the presidency of the Bishop, either personally or through another, are subject to the free discussion of all present in the preparatory sessions.

Canon 362 (1983 CIC 466)

Only the Bishop is a legislator in a Synod, the others having only a consultative vote; only he signs the synodal constitutions; these begin to oblige immediately if they are promulgated in the Synod, unless expressly determined otherwise.

Canon Law Digest
I: 211

Chapter 4
On the diocesan Curia

Canon 363 (1983 CIC 469)

§ 1. The diocesan Curia consists of those persons who render assistance in the governance of the whole diocese to the Bishop or others who govern the diocese in the place of the Bishop.

§ 2. Belonging to it, therefore, are the Vicar General, officialis, chancellor, promoter of justice, defender of the bond, synodal judges and examiners, pastor consultors, auditors, notaries, couriers, and citation servers.

Canon Law Digest
I: 212–14; VI: 414–16; VIII: 254–67

Canon 364 (1983 CIC 470–71)

§ 1. The appointment of those who exercise the aforesaid offices or responsibilities shall be made in writing according to the norm of Canon 159.

§ 2. Those appointed must:

1.° Give an oath in the hands of the Bishop of exercising their responsibility faithfully beyond any acceptance of persons;
2.° Conduct affairs that look to them under the authority of the Bishop in accord with the norm of law;
3.° Maintain secrecy within the limits and according to the manner determined by the Bishop or by law.

Canon 365 (1983 CIC 472)

The prescriptions of Canons 1573–93 are to be observed concerning the officialis, promoter of justice, defender of the bond, synodal judges, auditors, couriers, and citation servers; concerning the Vicar General, chancellor and other notaries, synodal examiners, and pastor consultors, the prescriptions of the canons that follow [are to be observed].

Article 1—*On the Vicar General*[61]

Canon 366 (1983 CIC 475, 477)

§ 1. As often as the correct governance of the diocese requires it, the Bishop is to constitute a Vicar General, who helps him by ordinary power in the whole territory.

§ 2. The Vicar General is designated freely by the Bishop, who can remove him at his discretion.

§ 3. Only one shall be constituted, unless either a diversity of rites or the size of the diocese requires otherwise; but, the Vicar General being absent or impeded, the Bishop can constitute another who supplies his place.

Canon Law Digest
VI: 416; VIII: 267–79

[61] A. Joaquin, "The Power of the Vicar General Acting with a Special Mandate of the Bishop" (MS no. 2543, Gregorian University, 1956); Joseph Penna, "The Episcopal Vicar", Canon Law Studies, no. 475 (J. C. D. thesis, Catholic University of America, 1971); Thomas Dougherty, "The Vicar General of the Episcopal Ordinary", Canon Law Studies, no. 447 (J. C. D. thesis, Catholic University of America, 1966).

Canon 367 (1983 CIC 478)

§ 1. The Vicar General must be a priest of the secular clergy, not less than thirty years of age, having a doctorate or licentiate in theology and canon law, or at least being truly expert in these disciplines, of healthy doctrine, probity, prudence, and commended with experience in conducting affairs.

§ 2. If the diocese has been committed to a religious [institute], the Vicar General can be a member of the same religious [institute].

§ 3. The task of Vicar General cannot be committed to a canon penitentiary or to a blood-relative of the Bishop, especially in the first degree or in the second mixed with the first, or, excluding necessity, to a pastor or another having the care of souls; but it is not prohibited for the Bishop to take a Vicar General from his own diocese.

Canon Law Digest
I: 214

Canon 368 (1983 CIC 479) Cross-Ref.: 1917 CIC 435

§ 1. The Vicar General, in virtue of his office, is competent in the universal jurisdiction of the diocese for spiritual and temporal [things] that pertain to the Bishop by ordinary law, excepting those things that the Bishop reserves to himself or that by law require a special mandate of the Bishop.

§ 2. Unless otherwise expressly provided, the Vicar General can execute apostolic rescripts that have been sent to the Bishop or to the preceding rector of the diocese, and generally [he enjoys] those habitual faculties granted by the Holy See that pertain to the local Ordinary, according to the norm of Canon 66.

Canon Law Digest
I: 215; II: 131

Canon 369 (1983 CIC 480)

§ 1. The Vicar General refers the principal acts of the Curia to the Bishop and will inform him of those things done or that ought to be done for the protection of clerical and lay discipline.

§ 2. He shall take care lest his powers be used against the mind and will of his Bishop, with due regard for the prescription of Canon 44, § 2.

Canon 370 (NA) Cross-Ref.: 1917 CIC 439

§ 1. In the presence of the Bishop, the Vicar General has the right of precedence both publicly and privately over all diocesan clerics, not excluding those in dignities and the canons of the cathedral churches, even in choir and chapter acts, unless there is a cleric shining with episcopal character and the Vicar General lacks this.

§ 2. If the Vicar General is a Bishop, he obtains all of the privileges of titular Bishops; otherwise, during his duties he has only those privileges and insignia of a titular Protonotary apostolic.

Canon Law Digest
I: 215–16

Canon 371 (1983 CIC 481)

The jurisdiction of the Vicar General expires with his resignation according to the norm of Canons 183–91, or with its revocation communicated to him by the Bishop, or with the vacancy of the episcopal see; but it is suspended along with the suspension of the episcopal jurisdiction.

Article 2—*On the chancellor and other notaries and the episcopal archive*

Canon 372[62] (1983 CIC 482)

§ 1. In every Curia the Bishop shall constitute a chancellor, who must be a priest, whose principal responsibility is to maintain the acts of the Curia in the archive, to arrange them in chronological order, and to make an index chart of them.

§ 2. Necessity obtaining, he can be given a helper, whose name is vice-chancellor or vice-tabulary.

§ 3. A chancellor is by that fact a notary.

Canon Law Digest
VI: 416; VIII: 280

[62] John Prince, "The Diocesan Chancellor", Canon Law Studies, no. 167 (J. C. D. thesis, Catholic University of America, 1942).

Canon 373 (1983 CIC 483, 485) Cross-Ref.: 1917 CIC 1592

§ 1. Besides the chancellor, the Bishop can constitute other notaries whose writing or signature confers public credibility.

§ 2. These can be constituted either for all acts, or only for judicial acts, or only for the acts of certain causes, or for the confection of certain transactions.

§ 3. If clerics are lacking, they can be taken from among the laity; but the notary in criminal cases of clerics must be a priest.

§ 4. The chancellor and other notaries must be of good reputation and above any suspicion.

§ 5. All of them can be removed or suspended by him who constituted them or by his successor or Superior, but not by the Vicar Capitulary without the consent of the Chapter.

Canon 374[63] (1983 CIC 484)

§ 1. The duties of notaries are [as follows]:

1.° To produce the acts or instruments, concerning dispositions, obligations, citations, and judicial communications, decrees, sentences, and other works of this sort as required;

2.° Faithfully to reduce to writing those things done with an indication of the place, day, month, and year, and to sign them;

3.° To show acts and instruments legitimately sought from the files, observing those things that ought to be observed and declaring copies to be in conformance [with the originals] by their signatures.

4.° A notary cannot compose acts outside the territory of the Bishop by whom he was appointed or concerning matters other than those for which he was legitimately constituted.

Canon 375[64] (1983 CIC 486) Cross-Ref.: 1917 CIC 379

§ 1. Bishops shall erect in a safe and convenient place a diocesan archive or tabulary in which instruments and writings that concern the spiritual or temporal affairs of the diocese are suitably disposed and kept diligently secure.

[63] Robert Spaight, "Ecclesiastical Public Documents: Authorship and Solemnities" (diss. no. 17, Pontifical University of St. Thomas [Rome], 1959–1960).

[64] William Louis, "Diocesan Archives", Canon Law Studies, no. 137 (J. C. D. thesis, Catholic University of America, 1941).

§ 2. An inventory or catalogue of documents contained in the archive will be produced with all diligence and care, [along with] a brief synopsis of each writing.

Canon Law Digest
II: 131; IV: 152; V: 308–9; VI: 416

Canon 376 (NA)

§ 1. Each year, during the first two months, an inventory or catalogue of writings will be added concerning those things that were done or others [that were] neglected during the preceding year.

§ 2. Ordinaries shall sedulously inquire after papers and writings that by chance are separated or dispersed elsewhere; and they shall apply every necessary remedy in order that these writings be restored to the archives.

Canon 377 (1983 CIC 487)

§ 1. The archive must be [locked], and no one is allowed to enter without the permission of the Bishop or the Vicar General and chancellor.

§ 2. Only the chancellor shall have the key to [the archive].

Canon 378 (1983 CIC 488) Cross-Ref.: 1917 CIC 383

§ 1. It is not permitted to carry writings from the archives without the consent of the Bishop or Vicar General, and they are to be returned to their place within three days. The Ordinary has, however, the faculty of extending this time, which extension should not be granted except moderately.

§ 2. Whoever takes a writing from the archives shall leave a signed receipt signifying this fact with the chancellor.

Canon 379[65] (1983 CIC 489–90) Cross-Refs.: 1917 CIC 1047, 1107

§ 1. Bishops shall also have another secret archive or at least a safe or box, entirely closed and covered, in the common archive, from which place it cannot be moved. In it secret writings are to be most cautiously preserved; but promptly once a year, documents in criminal cases are to be burned in morals cases, [or] in which the defendant has died or ten years have passed from the condemnatory sentence, retaining only a brief summary of the facts, with the text of the definitive sentence.

[65] Charles Kekumano, "The Secret Archives of the Diocesan Curia", Canon Law Studies, no. 350 (thesis, Catholic University of America, 1954).

§ 2. An inventory or catalogue of the secret archives or safe shall be made according to the norm of Canon 375, § 2.

§ 3. This archive or safe shall be opened with two keys different from each other, one of which stays with the Bishop or Apostolic Administrator, the other [of which stays] with the Vicar General or, in his absence, the chancellor of the Curia.

§ 4. The Bishop or Apostolic Administrator, having taken back the other key, by himself, with no one around, if he deems it necessary, can open and inspect the secret archive or safe, which thereupon is closed with both keys once again.

Canon Law Digest
II: 132

Canon 380 (NA) Cross-Ref.: 1917 CIC 1301

Immediately upon taking possession [of the diocese], the Bishop shall designate a priest who, if the see is vacant or impeded, shall take up the key of the secret tabulary or box that the Bishop had.

Canon 381 (NA)

§ 1. Unless an Apostolic Administrator has been given to the diocese:

1.° When the see is impeded according to the norm of Canon 429, § 1, the priest designated by the Bishop, if indeed the governance of the diocese has been given to an ecclesiastical man designated by the Bishop, shall give the key to him; but if it has been given to a Vicar General, he shall retain it;

2.° But if the see is vacant or impeded according to the norm of the cited Canon 429, § 3, that same priest shall remit the key to the Vicar Capitulary or to the chancellor immediately after his designation; but the Vicar General or chancellor must give the key retained by him at the same time to the first Chapter dignitary or to the diocesan consultor senior in office.

§ 2. Before the keys that must be handed over according to the norm of § 1 are sent, the Vicar General or chancellor and the priest, as designated by the Bishop above, shall seal the tabulary or safe with the seal of the Curia.

Canon 382 (1983 CIC 490)

§ 1. The tabulary or safe shall not be opened or the seal removed from it except in urgent necessity and [then] by the Vicar Capitulary himself in the presence of two canons or diocesan consultors, who shall be vigilant lest any writings be carried out of the tabulary; only the Vicar Capitulary can inspect documents that must be preserved in the tabulary, with these same canons or consultors standing by, and never can he carry any [materials] off. The archive, however, after this inspection, must be sealed again.

§ 2. Upon the arrival of the new Bishop, if the seal has been removed from the tabulary or the safe opened, the Vicar Capitulary shall give the reason that in urgent necessity caused his action.

Canon 383 (1983 CIC 491)

§ 1. Bishops shall take care that an inventory or catalogue of archives, whether of cathedral, collegial, or parochial churches, as well as confraternities and pious places, is made in two copies, one of which remains in its own archive, the other in the episcopal archive, with due regard for the prescription of Canons 470, § 3, 1522, nn. 2 and 3, and 1523, n. 6.

§ 2. Original documents shall not be removed from the archives except according to the norm of Canon 378.

Canon 384 (1983 CIC 487, 491)

§ 1. Documents in a parochial or Curial archive that need not be preserved under secrecy can be inspected by anyone interested in them; likewise it can be requested that copies be made and handed over at their own expense.

§ 2. Chancellors of Curias, pastors, and others who take care of archives, in communicating documents and preparing and sending copies, shall observe the rules given by legitimate ecclesiastical authority and in cases of doubt shall consult the local Ordinary.

Article 3—*On synodal examiners and pastor consultors*[66]

Canon 385 (NA) Cross-Ref.: 1917 CIC 1574

§ 1. In every diocese there shall be synodal examiners and pastor consultors, all of whom are constituted in the Synod, proposed by the Bishop, approved by the Synod.

[66] John Connolly, "Synodal Examiners and Parish Priest Consultors", Canon Law Studies, no. 177 (J. C. D. thesis, Catholic University of America, 1943).

§ 2. As many are elected as the Bishop in his prudent judgment deems necessary, but not, however, fewer than four or more than twelve.

Canon 386 (NA) Cross-Ref.: 1917 CIC 1574

§ 1. For those examiners and pastor consultors who cease from their duties because of death or other reasons in the time between one Synod and another, the Bishop can substitute other pro-synodal [examiners and pastor consultors] with the advice of the cathedral Chapter.

§ 2. This rule is also followed in constituting examiners and pastor consultors whenever a Synod is not held.

Canon 387 (NA) Cross-Ref.: 1917 CIC 1574

§ 1. Examiners and pastor consultors, whether constituted in the Synod or outside of it, lose office ten years after taking up their duties, or sooner, if a new Synod occurs; but they can continue tasks already taken up and, with due regard for those things that ought to be observed in law, can be constituted again.

§ 2. Those constituted for the place of absent examiners or pastor consultors remain in office only for so long as they for whom they substitute [would have remained].

Canon 388 (NA) Cross-Ref.: 1917 CIC 1574

They cannot be removed by the Bishop, except for grave cause and with the advice of the cathedral Chapter.

Canon 389 (NA)

§ 1. Synodal examiners shall diligently give their cooperation especially in the tests for the provision of parishes as well as for the procedures mentioned in Canons 2147 and foll[owing].

§ 2. But for those tests required for the ordination of clerics and for the approval of priests who seek the faculty of sacramental confessions and for [giving] sacred sermons, and for the examinations mentioned in Canon 130, it is the right of the Bishop to make use of synodal examiners and others.

Canon 390 (NA)

The same one can be an examiner and pastor consultor, but not in the same case.

Chapter 5
On the Chapter of canons

Canon 391 (1983 CIC 503)

§ 1. A Chapter of canons, whether cathedral or collegial, that is, gathered together, is a college of clerics so instituted that it does the more solemn acts of cult to God in a church and, if it concerns a cathedral Chapter, serves, as it were, as a senate for the Bishop according to the norm of the sacred canons, and, the see being vacant, supplies his place in the governance of the diocese.

§ 2. A collegial Chapter is called distinguished or quite distinguished if it enjoys this title by apostolic privilege or from time immemorial.

Canon Law Digest
VI: 416; VII: 382

Canon 392 (1983 CIC 504)

The institution or erection of a Chapter, whether cathedral or collegial, or its modification or suppression, is reserved to the Apostolic See.

Canon 393 (1983 CIC 507) Cross-Ref.: 1917 CIC 411

§ 1. In every church, chapters are the dignitaries and canons among whom various offices are distributed; there can also be minor benefices in one or several grades.

§ 2. The chapter consists of dignitaries and canons, unless, in what applies to dignitaries, something else is expressly given in the chapter constitutions; inferior beneficiaries and officeholders who render assistance to the canons [are excluded].

§ 3. A canonry without income attached shall not be instituted without special concession from the Apostolic See.

Canon Law Digest
I: 216; II: 132

Canon 394 (NA) Cross-Ref.: 1917 CIC 1414

§ 1. In enumerated Chapters there are as many [canons benefiting] from prebends as there are prebends; in non-enumerated [Chapters], there are as many as the income can decently support, in the Bishop's judgment, having heard the Chapter.

§ 2. The erection of a dignity is reserved to the Apostolic See; but it is within the power of the Bishop, with the consent of the Chapter, to restore prebends perhaps extinct and to add to the prebends already existing in the Chapter others, whether canonical or beneficial.

§ 3. In cathedral churches and distinguished collegial churches where the receipts of the prebends, together with the daily distributions, are plainly impaired in their ability to sustain the canons decorously, Bishops, having heard the Chapter, and having obtained permission of the Holy See, can unite simple prebends or benefices, or if this manner of provision is not available, they can suppress other prebends, with the consent of the patrons, if they are under a lay right of patronage, so that the fruits and income of the remaining prebends can be applied to the daily distributions, reducing these to a smaller number so that those that survive can respond conveniently to the celebration of divine cult and the dignity of the church.

Canon 395 (NA)

§ 1. In churches, whether cathedral or collegial, in which there are no daily distributions, or where the support seems truly neglected, Bishops shall separate a third-part of the fruits, incomes, and receipts, in which dignitaries, canons, and other officers and beneficiaries of the church participate, and convert them to daily distributions.

§ 2. If distributions cannot be introduced for any reason, the Bishop is bound to answer with distributions from fines imposed on dignitaries, canons, and beneficiaries who take their place.

§ 3. Distributions are granted to the diligent, excluding all sorts of remission or collusion;but if the dignitaries have an income from assets or goods of separate or diverse sources, the distributions lost by these are granted to the present dignitaries, if there are any, otherwise to the upkeep of the church, insofar as it is needy, or to a pious place, [chosen] by the Bishop.

§ 4. From each Chapter, according to its own statutes, one or more censors or *punctators* shall be appointed, who will note those absent from divine offices daily, having first taken, in the presence of the Chapter or its president, an oath of faithfully fulfilling his office; to which the Bishop can add another punctator, and if the punctators are absent, the senior among the canons who is present shall fill their places.

Canon Law Digest
I: 217; II: 132–33; IX: 241

Canon 396 (NA) Cross-Ref.: 1917 CIC 1435

§ 1. The conferral of dignities, whether in a cathedral or collegial Chapter, is reserved to the Apostolic See.

§ 2. Option is prohibited, reprobating any contrary custom, with due regard for the law of foundation.

§ 3. The first dignity in a cathedral Chapter, insofar as possible and all things being equal, shall go to one with a doctoral degree in sacred theology or canon law.

Canon Law Digest
I: 218–22; II: 134–37; III: 109–11; IX: 241

Canon 397 (NA) Cross-Refs.: 1917 CIC 462, 850, 938, 1230

Unless otherwise provided in chapter statutes, it is the right and duty of the dignitaries and canons, in the order of their precedence:

1.° To take the place of the Bishop in performing sacred functions in the more solemn feasts of the year;
2.° To offer a Bishop celebrating pontificals the sprinkler at the entrance to the church and to be the one who fulfills the office of assisting priest.
3.° To administer the Sacraments to him while [he is] abed; and to conduct his funeral once [he is] dead;
4.° To convoke the Chapter and to preside over it and to prescribe and order those things referring to the direction of the choir, provided the one with such a dignity is a member of the Chapter.

Canon Law Digest
I: 222–23

Canon 398 (NA)

§ 1. In no cathedral church shall there be lacking the office of canon theologian and, to the extent it can be done, canon penitentiary.

§ 2. Even in collegial churches, especially the more noteworthy, the office of canon theologian and penitentiary can be constituted.

Canon 399 (NA)

§ 1. The canon theologian and penitentiary are to be selected from those who appear more suitable regarding those qualities [that are required] to fulfill their responsibility; but, other things being equal, doctors in sacred theology are to be preferred, if it concerns the canon theologian, and sacred theology or canon law [is to be preferred] if [it concerns] the penitentiary; it is expedient, moreover, that the canon penitentiary have completed thirty years of age.

§ 2. The theological and penitentiary prebends are not to be conferred unless there is first full proof concerning the life, morals, and doctrine of the candidates, with due regard for the law of concursus, when such has been constituted.

§ 3. The canon penitentiary is prohibited from taking or exercising at the same time any office in the diocese to which there is attached jurisdiction in the external forum.

Canon Law Digest
I: 223; II: 137–38; IX: 241

Canon 400 (NA)

§ 1. It belongs to the canon theologian, on days and times designated by the Bishop, with the advice of the Chapter, to explain publicly sacred Scripture in church; but the Bishop, if he judges it useful, can commit to him other arguments of Catholic doctrine to be explained in church.

§ 2. The canon theologian shall complete his duties personally or through another, or, if he is impeded beyond six months, at his own expense through another priest deputed by the Bishop.

§ 3. For grave cause the Bishop can instruct the canon theologian, in place of lectures in the church, to teach sacred disciplines in the Seminary.

Canon Law Digest
I: 223

Canon 401 (1983 CIC 508) Cross-Refs.: 1917 CIC 201, 873, 899

§ 1. A canon penitentiary, whether of the cathedral church or of a collegial church, obtains by law the ordinary power, which, however, he cannot delegate to others, of absolving, even from sins and censures reserved to the Bishop, even strangers in the diocese and also diocesan [faithful] outside the territory of the diocese.

§ 2. He must be seated in a seat reserved to him for the hearing of confessions in the chapter church at a determined time that is convenient for the faithful in the judgment of the Bishop, and even more opportunely must he be available for those coming for the confession of their sins even during the time of divine offices.

Canon 402 (1983 CIC 510)

If the Chapter is connected with the care of souls, this shall be exercised by a parochial vicar according to the norm of Canon 471.

Canon 403 (1983 CIC 509)

With the exception of dignities, it pertains to the Bishop, having heard the Chapter, to confer all and every benefice and canonry in churches, whether cathedral or collegial, reprobating every contrary custom and revoking every contrary privilege, but respecting any contrary laws of the foundation and with due regard for the prescription of Canon 1435.

Canon Law Digest
I: 223–25; II: 138–40

Canon 404 (1983 CIC 509)

§ 1. The Bishop shall confer a canonry on priests outstanding for doctrine and integrity of life.

§ 2. In conferring a canonry, all things being equal, consideration shall be given to those who have earned doctorates in sacred theology or canon law in some athenaeum, or who have laudably exercised ecclesiastical ministry or teaching, with due regard for the prescription of Canon 130, § 2.

Canon Law Digest
I: 225–26

Canon 405 (NA)

§ 1. Dignitaries, canons, and beneficiaries, upon taking legitimate possession of their benefices according to the norm of Canons 1443–45, immediately acquire for their grade, besides insignia and proper privileges, a stall in the choir, the right of participating in the fruits and distributions, and a voice in the chapter according to the norm of Canon 411, § 3.

§ 2. They are bound by the prescription of Canons 1406–8 concerning the giving of a profession of faith by them before their taking possession.

Canon 406 (NA) Cross-Ref.: 1917 CIC 405

§ 1. It belongs to the Bishop, but not the Vicar General or the Vicar Capitulary, to appoint honorary canons, whether diocesan or extra-diocesan, with the advice of the Chapter to which the canon is to be ascribed, but the Bishop should rarely and cautiously use this right.

§ 2. Regarding a priest of another diocese who is to be named an honorary canon, the Bishop, besides getting the advice of the Chapter, shall seek the consent of the Ordinary to whom the one to be appointed is subject, under pain of nullity of the appointment, and shall inform this Ordinary about the insignia and privileges that the one to be appointed will henceforth enjoy.

§ 3. Honorary canons who are outside the diocese in which they are appointed shall comprise less than one-third of the titular canons.

Canon 407 (NA) Cross-Ref.: 1917 CIC 405

§ 1. Honorary canons of some basilica or collegial sustaining church in the City can use their privileges and insignia only within that basilica or collegial church and the vicinity of its filial [churches]; but the honorary canons of churches outside the City can use their privileges and insignia only in the diocese in which they are appointed, but not outside the diocese except in accord with the norm of Canon 409, § 2.

§ 2. Honorary canons, besides insignia and privileges or honorific rights, also obtain a stall in the choir.

Canon 408 (NA) Cross-Ref.: 1917 CIC 405

§ 1. A cathedral Chapter takes precedence over a collegial one, even a distinguished one, even in its own church; a distinguished Chapter takes precedence over a non-distinguished one; in the same Chapter, with due regard for particular statutes or legitimate custom, dignitaries, preserving the order of precedence among themselves, precede canons; older canons, namely those who took possession earlier, [are] over later ones; titular canons [are] over honorary ones; honorary ones [are] over beneficiaries; but dignitaries or chapters marked with episcopal character precede all dignitaries and canons constituted only in presbyteral orders.

§ 2. In Chapters in which there are distinct presbyteral, diaconal, and subdiaconal prebends, there is observed precedence based on order; and in the same order, precedence [is based] on reception into orders, but not into the Chapter.

Canon Law Digest
I: 226–27; V: 309

Canon 409 (NA) Cross-Ref.: 1917 CIC 407

§ 1. In every church, whether cathedral or collegial, those constituted in episcopal dignity wear episcopal vestments in choir; all of the others, dignitaries, canons, and beneficiaries, [wear] the vestments assigned to them in the bull of erection or granted in apostolic indult; otherwise they are considered absent.

§ 2. They can wear choral vestments and special chapter insignia throughout the diocese in which the Chapter is [located], but, reprobating every contrary custom, not outside the diocese, unless they are with the Bishop or represent the Bishop or Chapter in a Council or other solemnity.

Canon Law Digest
I: 227–28; III: 111; VII: 382–83

Canon 410 (1983 CIC 505)

§ 1. Each Chapter shall not be without its own statutes, which are to be religiously observed by all dignitaries, canons, and beneficiaries.

§ 2. The capitular statutes, established by legitimate chapter act, are subject to the Bishop's approval, without whose authority they cannot later be abrogated or changed.

§ 3. If, the Bishop having directed that the statutes be prepared, the Chapter neglects to offer any, six months having run from this communication, the Bishop shall produce them and impose them on the Chapter.

Canon Law Digest
I: 229

Canon 411 (NA) Cross-Ref.: 1917 CIC 405

§ 1. At an established time and place, a committee of canons of its church shall gather and conduct Chapter affairs; other meetings can be held as often as it seems expedient to the Bishop or Chapter president or to a majority of the canons.

§ 2. In order to hold this ordinary committee, no special convocation is required; but for an extraordinary one, however, it should be made according to the chapter statutes.

§ 3. The canons have a voice in chapter, exclusive of honorary ones, [as do] dignitaries if they are constituted together with the Chapter canons according to the norm of Canon 393, § 2.

Canon Law Digest
I: 229

Canon 412 (NA) Cross-Ref.: 1917 CIC 421

§ 1. Canons invited by him, whether of the cathedral or collegial church, must assist and serve the Bishop in solemnly celebrating Mass or in exercising other pontificals, even in the other churches of the city or its suburbs, provided there remain in the judgment of the Bishop sufficient numbers of canons and ministers in the church: and [these two shall] go with him to the cathedral church and be of assistance according to the norm of the Ceremonial of Bishops.

§ 2. The Bishop can take two [canons] from the Chapter, whether cathedral or collegial, and keep them in order that they might assist him in ecclesiastical ministry or service to the diocese.

Canon Law Digest
I: 229–30

Canon 413 (NA)

§ 1. Every Chapter is bound by the obligation of performing correctly the daily divine office in choir, with due regard for the laws of the foundation.

§ 2. The divine office includes the psalms of the canonical hours along with the celebration of a sung conventual Mass, besides other Masses to be celebrated either according to the rubrics of the Missal or [because of] the pious foundation.

§ 3. It is permitted to celebrate weekly a conventual Mass without singing when, in a church, by pontifical rites, the Bishop or someone in the place of the Bishop celebrates.

Canon Law Digest
I: 230–31; VI: 417

Canon 414 (NA)

Each and every [ecclesiastical man] who obtains a choral benefice is bound to perform in that choir the divine office each day, unless service by *turns* has been indulted by the Apostolic See or by the laws of the foundation.

Canon Law Digest
I: 231–32; V: 310

Canon 415 (1983 CIC 510) Cross-Ref.: 1917 CIC 609

§ 1. If a cathedral or collegial church is at the same time a parish, the juridic relations between the Chapter and the pastor are governed by the norms that follow, unless otherwise determined by indult of the Apostolic

See or by particular agreement entered into upon erection of the parish and legitimately approved by the local Ordinary.

§ 2. To the pastor it belongs:

1.° To apply the Mass for the people and, at required times, to preach and to educate the faithful in Christian doctrine;

2.° To take care of the parish books and to draw attestations from them;

3.° To conduct the parish functions mentioned in Canon 462. It pertains to the Chapter only to perform funerals that according to the norms of law are to be conducted in the church, not excluding funeral Masses, in case of the funeral of some dignitary or canon, even if only honorary, or of a beneficiary;

4.° To conduct other functions not strictly parochial [but] that are usually conducted in parishes, but not in a manner so as to impede choral service, unless the Chapter performs these functions;

5.° To collect alms for the good of the parish and to receive offerings directly or indirectly, and to administer and, according to the will of the donors, to distribute them.

§ 3. To the Chapter it belongs:

1.° To keep custody of the most holy Sacrament of the Eucharist; but the other key of the sacred ciborium must be kept by the pastor;

2.° To be vigilant that the laws on conducting liturgies are observed by the pastor in the chapter church;

3.° To have care of the church and to administer its goods along with pious legacies.

§ 4. Neither the pastor shall interfere with chapter functions and duties, nor [shall] the Chapter [interfere] with parochial; if conflict arises, the local Ordinary shall determine the question, who in the first place must take care that catechetical instruction and the explanation of the Gospels always be had at a time more convenient to the faithful.

§ 5. Not only shall the Chapter not interfere with the pastor in the exercise of his care of the parish, but chapters shall also know that they are bound in charity, especially if designated assistants are lacking, to render him all assistance possible, according to the manner determined by the local Ordinary.

Canon Law Digest
II: 141; IX: 242

Canon 416 (NA)

In the chapter statutes a just norm shall be designated under which the canons and beneficiaries perform service at the altar by turns, whether it is the office of the celebrant or the ministry of deacon or subdeacon, excluding, however, from this ministry dignitaries, the canon theologian, the penitentiary, and, if these are considered distinct in the prebend, canons in the presbyteral order.

Canon Law Digest
I: 232–33

Canon 417 (NA)

§ 1. The conventual Mass is to be applied for all benefactors generally.

§ 2. A chapter [member] detained by infirmity is not required to offer the stipend to the chapter priest who supplies his place in the celebration and application of the conventual Mass, unless chapter statutes or particular custom determine otherwise.

§ 3. The custom can be preserved whereby the stipend of the celebrating prebend can be made from the total distribution or from the income of all the prebends by contribution.

Canon Law Digest
I: 233

Canon 418 (NA)

§ 1. Reprobating any contrary custom, canons and beneficiaries are bound to daily attendance in choir; they can be individually absent for three months in a year, whether continuous or interrupted, provided the statutes of their own church or legitimate custom do not require longer service.

§ 2. Without legitimate cause and special permission of the Bishop, they shall not have holidays during the times of Lent and Advent, or on the principal solemnities mentioned in Canon 338, § 3; nor is it permitted that more than a third part of the chapter be absent at the same time.

§ 3. During vacation time all sorts of distributions are to be omitted, notwithstanding any remissions made by others in chapters; but they do participate in the fruits of the prebend and receive a two-thirds part distribution if all of the fruits of the prebends consist of distributions.

Canon Law Digest
I: 233–35; II: 141

Canon 419 (NA)

§ 1. In those churches in which not all need be present for choir, those who are so bound cannot satisfy this obligation through another, except in particular cases, for a just and reasonable cause, [provided] that the one who satisfies choir [duty] is not bound to be there at the same time and that he be a canon in the same church if it concerns supplying for a vice-canon, [and be a] beneficiary if it is a beneficiary [institute]; but those who are not bound by choir are not bound by the law of residence in the place of the benefice for the days they are absent from choir.

§ 2. If anyone is required on the same day to [offer] Mass both for the people and the conventual [Mass], this he can offer and apply himself, while the other [is said by] another [priest] or by himself on a subsequent day.

Canon Law Digest
I: 235–36

Canon 420 (NA)

§ 1. The following are excused from choir in such a way that they still partake of the fruits of the prebend and daily distributions:

1.° *Jubilary* chapters according to the norm of Canon 422, § 2;
2.° A canon theologian on each day that he performs his functions;
3.° A canon penitentiary for the time he is absent from choir hearing confessions;
4.° A parochial vicar or other deputed by the Bishop or the pastor for so long as he fulfills parochial offices;
5.° Those who because of infirmity or other physical impediment are prohibited from assisting at choir;
6.° Those who are elsewhere acting in a pontifical legation or are in actual service to the person of the Roman Pontiff;
7.° Those absent for pious exercises according to the norm of Canon 126; by which indult, however, only once per year are they liberated from choir service;
8.° Those going with the Bishop or in his place to visit the Threshold of the Apostles;
9.° Those who are sent by the Bishop or Chapter to an Ecumenical, plenary, or provincial Council, or to a diocesan Synod;
10.° Those who, with the consent of the Chapter, and the Bishop not objecting, are absent from choir for the utility of the Chapter or their own church;

11.° Those who assist the Bishop in performing sacred [functions] according to the norm of Canon 412, § 1;
12.° Those who accompany the Bishop on the diocesan visitation or who conduct this visitation in his name and mandate;
13.° Those who assist in the task of conducting processes in those cases mentioned in Canons 1999 and foll[owing], or who are called as witnesses, for the days and times at which they must be present for this duty;
14.° Pastor consultors, examiners, and synodal judges, while they perform their function.

§ 2. But only those enumerated in § 1, nn. 1, 7, 11, and 13, participate in distributions that are called *among those present*, unless the express will of the foundation obstructs.

Canon Law Digest
I: 237–39; II: 141; III: 111–12

Canon 421 (NA)

§ 1. The following are excused from choir, but they participate in the fruits of the prebends, although not in the distributions:
1.° Those who publicly teach, with the permission of the local Ordinary, sacred theology or canon law, in schools recognized by the Church;
2.° Those who are studying, with the permission of the local Ordinary, sacred theology or canon law, in public schools approved by the Church;
3.° The Vicar Capitulary, Vicar General, officialis, and chancellor, if they happen to be members, for so long as they are away for their duties;
4.° The canons who serve the Bishop according to the norm of Canon 412, § 2.

§ 2. But if all of the fruit of the prebend consists of [daily] distributions, and these incomes do not amount to one-third of the distribution, then all of the above-mentioned shall enjoy only a two-thirds distribution obtained from the fruits of the prebend and the distributions.

Canon Law Digest
I: 240–41; II: 141; V: 310–11; VI: 417

Canon 422 (NA) Cross-Ref.: 1917 CIC 420

§ 1. Those enjoying prebends can seek only from the Apostolic See an indult of emeritus, that is, as they say, *jubilarian*, [status] after forty continuous and laudable years of choir service in the same or distinct churches in the same city or at least diocese.

§ 2. A jubilarian, even if he is not resident in the place of the benefice, partakes both of the fruits of the prebend and in the distributions among those present, unless the express will of the founder or donor, or the statutes of the church, or custom, prevents.

§ 3. The right of option, if the laws of the foundation provide [for such], does not belong to a jubilarian chapter.

Canon Law Digest
I: 241; III: 113

Chapter 6
On diocesan consultors[67]

Canon 423[68] (1983 CIC 502)

In any diocese in which there cannot yet be established or restored a cathedral Chapter of canons, there shall be instituted by the Bishop, with due regard for the special prescriptions of the Apostolic See, diocesan consultors, [consisting of] priests commended for their piety, morals, learning, and prudence.

Canon Law Digest
I: 241–42; VI: 417; VII: 383–91; VIII: 280–88

Canon 424 (1983 CIC 502)

The Bishop appoints the consultors with due regard for the prescription of Canon 426.

Canon Law Digest
VII: 391

[67] Peter Klekotka, "Diocesan Consultors", Canon Law Studies, no. 8 (J. C. D. thesis, Catholic University of America, 1920).

[68] Michael Jamail, "The Senates of Priests in the Province of San Antonio, Texas: A Descriptive Study", Canon Law Studies, no. 467 (Catholic University of America, 1969); Bernard Rossi, "Priests' Senate: Canadian Experiences" (thesis, Gregorian University; printed version, no. 2821, 1979).

Canon 425 (1983 CIC 502)

§ 1. The diocesan consultors shall be at least six in number; but in a diocese where there are not many priests, at least four; and they shall live in the cathedral city or in a nearby place.

§ 2. Before they take up their duties, they are to take an oath faithfully to fulfill their duties without regard to persons.

Canon Law Digest
I: 242

Canon 426 (1983 CIC 502) Cross-Ref.: 1917 CIC 424

§ 1. The office of the consultors is for three years.

§ 2. At the end of three years, the Bishop replaces them with others or confirms the same ones for another three years, which shall be done every three years.

§ 3. But if a consultor for any reason fails to finish three years, the Bishop shall replace him with another for the remaining period of the three years, with the advice of the other consultors.

§ 4. But if it happens that the three years expire during the vacancy of the episcopal see, the consultors remain in office until the arrival of the new Bishop, who within six months of beginning his possession [of the diocese] must see [to the matter] according to the norm of this canon.

§ 5. But if, during a vacancy in the see, a consultor dies or resigns, the Vicar Capitulary, with the consent of the other consultors, appoints another, who, nevertheless, in order to perform his function, requires confirmation by the new Bishop when the see is filled.

Canon 427 (1983 CIC 502)

The committee of diocesan consultors, like a senate of the Bishop, takes the place of the cathedral Chapter; therefore, all those canons on the governance of the diocese, whether the seat is occupied, impeded, or vacant, in reference to the cathedral Chapter are to be understood as applying also to the committee of diocesan consultors.

Canon Law Digest
I: 242–43; VII: 391; VIII: 288; IX: 243–46

Canon 428 (NA)

For the duration of their appointment, consultors cannot be removed except for a just cause and with the advice of the other consultors.

Chapter 7
On the impeded or vacant see and on the Vicar Capitulary[69]

Canon 429 (1983 CIC 412–13, 415) Cross-Refs.: 1917 CIC 309, 317, 327, 381, 455

§ 1. If a see is impeded by the captivity, imprisonment, exile, or incapacity of the Bishop, so that he is not able to communicate with his diocese even by letters, the governance of the diocese, unless the Holy See provides otherwise, falls to the Vicar General of the Bishop or to another ecclesiastical man delegated by the Bishop for this.

§ 2. The Bishop can in such case, for serious cause, delegate several [successors] who will succeed each other in responsibility.

§ 3. These being absent, or, as mentioned above, impeded, the Chapter of the cathedral church will constitute its Vicar, who will assume governance with the power of a Vicar Capitulary.

§ 4. Whoever takes up the governance of the diocese as above will as soon as possible advise the Holy See about the impeded see and the assumption of duties.

§ 5. If the Bishop incurs excommunication, interdict, or suspension, the Metropolitan, or in his absence, or if it concerns him, the senior among the Suffragans, will confer promptly with the Apostolic See in order that it might provide [for the matter]; but if it concerns a diocese or prelature mentioned in Canon 285, the Metropolitan who was legitimately chosen for it is bound by the obligation of conferring.

Canon Law Digest
I: 244; VII: 391

Canon 430 (1983 CIC 416–18)

§ 1. The episcopal see empties by the death of the Bishop, by resignation accepted by the Roman Pontiff, by transfer, or by privation communicated to the Bishop.

§ 2. Nevertheless, except for the conferral of benefices and ecclesiastical offices, all those things that are done by the Vicar General have force until he has received certain notice of the death of the Bishop, and by the

[69] Leo Jaeger, "The Administration of Vacant and Quasi-Vacant Dioceses in the United States", Canon Law Studies, no. 81 (J. C. D. thesis, Catholic University of America, 1932).

Bishop and the Vicar General until certain notice of the above-mentioned pontifical actions come to them.

§ 3. Upon certain notice of transfer, the Bishop must seek to assume canonical possession of the diocese *to which* within four months according to the norm of Canons 333 and 334, and from the day of [that] possession the diocese *from which* becomes fully vacant; but in the meantime the Bishop in that [former] diocese:

1.° Obtains the powers of the Vicar Capitulary and is bound by the same obligations; any Vicar General ceases from power;
2.° Preserves the honorific privileges of residential Bishops;
3.° Participates fully in the fruits of the episcopal table according to the norm of Canon 194, § 2.

Canon 431 (1983 CIC 419)

§ 1. With the see vacant, unless there is present an Apostolic Administrator or the Holy See has made other provision, the governance of the diocese falls to the Chapter of the cathedral church.

§ 2. If anywhere, by special disposition of the Holy See, an Archbishop or other Bishop designates the Administrator of a vacant diocese, this one has all and only those faculties that belong to a Vicar Capitulary, [as well as] being liable to the same obligations and penalties.

Canon Law Digest
I: 244; IV: 152; VI: 417

Canon 432 (1983 CIC 421–22) Cross-Refs.: 1917 CIC 274, 327, 443

§ 1. The Chapter of the cathedral church, upon the vacancy of the see, within eight days of having accepted notification of the vacancy, must constitute a Vicar Capitulary who governs the diocese in its place, and if the duties include receiving income, [it must also constitute] one or more economes who are faithful and diligent.

§ 2. If the Chapter, within the prescribed time, for any reason, has not deputed a Vicar or an econome, the deputation falls to the Metropolitan; but if it is the metropolitan church that is vacant or if it is vacant at the same time as the suffragan [see], then [the decision] goes to the senior suffragan Bishop.

§ 3. If it is a diocese or abbey or prelature mentioned in Canon 285 that is vacant, and the Chapter has not appointed within eight days a Vicar or econome, then the Metropolitan who is legitimately selected according to the above-cited canons shall constitute [one], unless in the abbey or religious prelature *of no one* something else is provided in the constitution.

§ 4. The Chapter shall with alacrity inform the Apostolic See about the death of the Bishop, and then the one elected as Vicar Capitulary [shall give notice] about his election.

Canon Law Digest
I: 244

Canon 433 (1983 CIC 423–24)

§ 1. [Only] one shall be elected Vicar Capitulary, reprobating every contrary custom; otherwise the election is invalid.

§ 2. The constitution of the Vicar Capitulary and the econome must be made by a chapter act according to the norm of Canons 160–82, with due regard for particular Chapter norms, and for validity there is required an absolute major number of votes, not counting null votes.

§ 3. The same one can be deputed Vicar Capitulary and econome.

Canon 434 (1983 CIC 425)

§ 1. For the duty of Vicar Capitulary a cleric cannot be validly deputed who has not already been promoted to the sacred order of presbyterate, and who has not completed thirty years of age, and who has [not] been elected, appointed, or presented for that same vacant see.

§ 2. The Vicar Capitulary should, moreover, have a doctorate or licentiate in theology or canon law, or at least be truly expert in these disciplines, and be of intact morals, piety, sound doctrine, and effusive of praiseworthy prudence.

§ 3. If the prescriptions of § 1 were overlooked, the Metropolitan, or if it is the metropolitan church that is vacant or if it concerns the metropolitan Chapter itself, the senior Bishop of the province, having learned the truth of the matter, shall depute a Vicar in his place; the acts of the one selected by the Chapter are null by the law itself.

Canon 435 (1983 CIC 426–28)

§ 1. Just as before the deputation of the Vicar Capitulary, the ordinary jurisdiction of the Bishop is transferred to the Chapter in matters spiritual and temporal, so from [the Chapter] do they go to the Vicar Capitulary, except for those things that are expressly prohibited to them in law.

§ 2. Therefore the Chapter, and afterward the Vicar Capitulary, can [do] all those things enumerated in Canon 368, § 2; likewise, they enjoy the faculty of permitting the exercise of pontificals in the diocese to any Bishop, indeed, if the Vicar Capitulary is a Bishop, he can even exercise them himself, exclusive, however, of the use of the throne with a baldachin.

§ 3. It is not permitted for the Vicar Capitulary and the Chapter to act in a way that would be prejudicial to the rights of the diocese or the bishop; most particularly, neither the Vicar Capitulary nor the Chapter nor anyone inside or outside of it, whether cleric or lay, personally or through another, can remove documents from the episcopal Curia or destroy, conceal, or alter them.

Canon 436 (1983 CIC 428)

With the see vacant, nothing is to be innovated.

Canon 437 (NA)

In establishing a Vicar, the Chapter can retain for itself no part of his jurisdiction, or define the period of exercising power, or set out any other restrictions.

Canon 438 (1983 CIC 427)

A Vicar Capitulary, having given the profession of faith mentioned in Canons 1406–8, immediately obtains jurisdiction, which scarcely needs other confirmation.

Canon 439 (NA)

Those things prescribed in Canon 370 about the Vicar General are understood as being said about the Vicar Capitulary as well.

Canon 440 (1983 CIC 429)

The Vicar Capitulary is bound by the obligation of residing in the diocese and of applying the Mass for the people according to the norm of Canons 338 and 339.

Canon 441 (NA)

Unless it has been otherwise legitimately provided:

1.° A Vicar Capitulary and an econome have the right to a congruent payment, designated by the provincial Council or granted by received custom, [that is] taken from the episcopal table income or from other emoluments;

2.° The other emoluments, for the time the episcopal see is vacant, if they would apply to the Bishop when the see is not vacant, are reserved for the future Bishop [who will use them] for diocesan necessities.

Canon 442 (NA) Cross-Ref.: 1917 CIC 420

The econome conducts matters for the care and provision of ecclesiastical affairs, under the authority, however, of the Vicar Capitulary.

Canon 443 (1983 CIC 430)

§ 1. The removal of the Vicar Capitulary and the econome is reserved to the Holy See; resignation in authentic form is to be shown to the Chapter, acceptance by whom, however, is not required for validity; the constitution of the new Vicar Capitulary or econome after the resignation, death, or removal of the earlier one belongs to the Chapter, which will conduct things according to the norm of Canon 432.

§ 2. Moreover, this office ceases with the inauguration of possession by the new Bishop according to the norm of Canon 334, § 3.

Canon 444 (NA)

§ 1. The new Bishop shall require an accounting from the Chapter, the Vicar Capitulary, the econome, and other officials who, during the vacancy of the see, were constituted, concerning their offices, jurisdiction, and administrations of any sort, and he will take due note of those who were delinquent in their office or administration, even if upon rendering their accounts they were absolved by or sought release from the Chapter or deputies of the Chapter.

§ 2. In the same way they shall give to the new Bishop an accounting of writings pertaining to the Church, if any came to them.

Chapter 8
On vicars forane

Canon 445 (1983 CIC 553)

A vicar forane is that priest, established by the Bishop, who governs a vicariate described in Canon 217.

Canon 446 (1983 CIC 553–54)

§ 1. A Bishop is to select for the duties of vicar forane that priest whom he judges to be worthy, especially from among the rectors of parish churches.

§ 2. A vicar forane can be removed at the discretion of the Bishop.

Canon 447 (1983 CIC 555)

§ 1. Beyond those faculties given him by the diocesan Synod, and according to norms legitimately established by the Synod or by the Bishop, it is the right and duty of the vicar forane to be most vigilant:

1.° That ecclesiastical men within the boundaries of his territory lead a life according to the norms of the sacred canons and diligently satisfy their offices, especially concerning the law of residence, preaching the divine word, imparting catechism to children and adults, and the obligation of assisting the infirm;

2.° That the decrees given by the Bishop in his sacred visit have been subject to execution;

3.° That the due precautions regarding the material of the Eucharistic Sacrifice are being applied;

4.° That the decor and neatness of churches and sacred furnishings, especially in the custody of the most holy Sacrament and the celebration of Mass, are being observed; whether sacred functions are being celebrated according to the prescriptions of sacred liturgy; [whether] ecclesiastical goods are being diligently administered and that obligations attached thereto, in the first place Mass, are being rightly fulfilled; and [whether] the parochial books are being rightly drafted and preserved.

§ 2. In order that he may be assured of these things, the vicar forane must visit the parishes of his district at times established by the Bishop.

§ 3. It also pertains to the vicar forane, immediately upon hearing that some pastor in his district is gravely ill, to render all spiritual and material aid and [to make sure] that he does not lack decent burial if he dies; and to take care, while he is sick or when he dies, that the books, documents, and sacred furnishings or other things belonging to the church do not disappear or are not carried off.

Canon 448 (1983 CIC 555)

§ 1. The vicar forane must, on days designated by the Bishop, convoke the presbyters of his own district to the meeting or convention mentioned in Canon 131 and preside over it; but where there are several such meetings in various locations throughout the area, he shall be vigilant that they are rightly celebrated.

§ 2. If he is not a pastor, he must reside in the territory of the vicariate or in another place not too distant according to the norms defined by the Bishop.

Canon 449 (NA)

At least once a year the vicar forane shall give a report on his own vicariate to the local Ordinary, expounding not only those things that went well during the year but also those things that came out badly, what scandals arose, what remedies for their repair were applied, and what he thinks ought to be done for their eradication.

Canon 450 (NA)

§ 1. The vicar forane shall have the seal of his own vicariate.

§ 2. He takes precedence over all the other pastors and other priests of his district.

Canon Law Digest
I: 244

Chapter 9
On pastors[70]

Canon 451[71] (1983 CIC 516, 519, 569)

§ 1. A pastor is a priest or moral person upon whom a parish is conferred in title along with the care of souls to be exercised under the authority of the local Ordinary.

---

[70] Charles Koudelka, "Pastors, Their Rights and Duties according to the New Code of Canon Law", Canon Law Studies, no. 11 (J. C. D. thesis, Catholic University of America, 1921); Peter Kinlin, "Canonical and Civil Status of Parishes in Canada (outside the Civil Province of Quebec)" (doctoral diss. 28, University of Ottawa, 1949); Angel Acerra, "The Jurisdiction of the Pastor" (diss. no. 23, Pontifical University of St. Thomas [Rome], 1953–1954).

[71] George Subotich, "The Juridic Status of Chaplain in the Army of the United States of America according to the Norms of American Military Law and the Prescriptions of the Holy See" (Pontifical Lateran University, 1953); Michael Barry, "The Juridical Status of the Military Vicariate, Military Vicar, and Military Chaplains of Canada" (diss. no. 11, Pontifical University of St. Thomas [Rome], 1954–1955); Robert Ogle, "The Faculties of Canadian Military Chaplains: A Commentary on the Faculty Sheet of December, 1955, and the Directives for Holy Week Promulgated March 14, 1956" (doctoral diss. 41, University of Ottawa, 1956); Bernard

§ 2. Equal to pastors, with all the parochial rights and obligations of pastors in law, [are those who] come under the following names:

1.° Quasi-pastors who govern quasi-parishes mentioned in Canon 216, § 3;

2.° Parochial vicars, if they enjoy the complete power over a parish.

§ 3. The particular prescripts of the Holy See stand concerning military chaplains, whether major or minor.

Canon Law Digest
I: 245; II: 141–46 & 587–628; III: 113–18; IV: 152–61;
V: 311–35; VI: 417–22; VII: 391–92; VIII: 289–98;
IX: 247–51

Canon 452 (1983 CIC 520)

§ 1. Without an indult of the Apostolic See, parishes cannot be fully united to moral persons such that the moral person would be the pastor according to the norm of Canon 1423, § 2.

§ 2. A moral person to which a parish is united by full right can retain only the habitual care of souls, with due regard for the prescription of Canon 471 as to what applies to the actual [care of souls].

Canon Law Digest
II: 146; VI: 422; IX: 252

Canon 453 (1983 CIC 521)

§ 1. In order that one validly assume a parish, he must be constituted in the sacred presbyteral order.

§ 2. He should, moreover, be outstanding for good morals, doctrine, zeal for souls, prudence, and those other virtues and qualities that are required for the praiseworthy governance of the vacant parish in both common and particular law.

Canon Law Digest
I: 246

Deutsch, "Jurisdiction of Pastors in the External Forum", Canon Law Studies, no. 378 (thesis, Catholic University of America, 1957); Renatus Schatteman, "The Present Special Faculties of the Military Chaplains of the United States" (diss. no. 44, Pontifical University of St. Thomas [Rome], 1957–1958); Jeremias Rebanal, "Ecclesiastical Jurisdiction in the Armed Forces of the Philippines" (diss. no. 13, University of St. Thomas [Manila], 1958); John Smith, "The Military Ordinariate in the USA", Canon Law Studies, no. 443 (Catholic University of America, 1966).

Canon 454 (1983 CIC 522, 538) Cross-Refs.: 1917 CIC 471, 477, 486, 631, 2157

§ 1. Those who are placed in parochial administration as proper rectors should be in it with stability; but this does not prevent, nevertheless, that all of them could be removed from it according to the norm of law.

§ 2. But not all pastors obtain stability; those who enjoy more [are] irremovable; those [who enjoy] less are usually called removable.

§ 3. Irremovable parishes cannot be turned into removable ones without apostolic pleasure; removable ones can be declared irremovable by the Bishop, but not by a Vicar Capitulary, with the advice of the cathedral Chapter; new ones erected are irremovable, unless the Bishop, in his prudent judgment, attentive to the particular circumstances of places and persons, having heard the Chapter, decrees that removable is more expedient.

§ 4. Quasi-parishes are all removable.

§ 5. But pastors belonging to a religious family are always, by reason of person, removable at the discretion of the local Ordinary, the Superior having been advised, or, with equal right, by the Superior, having advised the Ordinary, and not requiring the consent of the other: and in neither case need the cause of this judgment be explained, and even less does it have to be proved, with due regard for recourse in devolution to the Apostolic See.

Canon Law Digest
I: 246; VI: 422–23; VIII: 298

Canon 455[72] (1983 CIC 523, 525) Cross-Ref.: 1917 CIC 1432

§ 1. The right of appointing and instituting pastors belongs to the local Ordinary, except for parishes reserved to the Holy See, reprobating any contrary custom, but with due regard for the privilege of election or presentation, where this legitimately applies.

§ 2. During the vacancy of the see or its impedance according to the norm of Canon 429, it pertains to the Vicar Capitulary or another who rules the diocese to:

1.° Constitute parochial vicars according to the norm of Canons 472–76;

[72] John Coady, "The Appointment of Pastors", Canon Law Studies, no. 52 (J. U. D.. thesis, Catholic University of America, 1929).

2.° Confirm the election or accept the presentation to a vacant parish and to grant institution to the one elected or presented;

3.° Confer parishes by free grant, if the see has been vacant for at least a year.

§ 3. The Vicar General is competent for none of these things without a special mandate with due regard for the prescription of [above-]cited Canon 429, § 1.

Canon Law Digest
I: 246; VI: 423

Canon 456 (NA)

It belongs to the Superior under the constitutions to present to the local Ordinary a priest of that religious [institute] for parishes entrusted to religious; who in turn, with due regard for the prescription of Canon 459, § 2, shall grant the institution.

Canon Law Digest
I: 246

Canon 457 (NA)

The local Ordinary appoints quasi-pastors from his own secular clergy, having heard the Council mentioned in Canon 302.

Canon 458 (NA) Cross-Refs.: 1917 CIC 155, 1432

The local Ordinary shall take care to provide for vacant parishes according to the norm of Canon 155, unless peculiar circumstances of places and persons, in the prudent judgment of the Ordinary, persuade that the conferral of a parochial title should be deferred.

Canon Law Digest
III: 118

Canon 459 (1983 CIC 521, 524) Cross-Refs.: 1917 CIC 456, 471

§ 1. The local Ordinary, gravely burdened in his conscience, is bound by the obligation of conferring a vacant parish on him who is the most suitable for its governance, without any regard to persons.

§ 2. In this decision, account must be taken not only of doctrine, but also of all those other qualities that are required for the right governance of a vacant parish.

§ 3. Thus, the local Ordinary:

1.° Shall not omit obtaining those documents, if there are any, from the tabulary of the Curia that refer to the cleric to be nominated, examining them, and he will seek out information, even secret, if he judges it opportune, even from outside the diocese;

2.° Keep before his eyes the prescription of Canon 130, § 2;

3.° Subject the cleric to examination on doctrine in his presence and that of synodal examiners; from which, with the consent of the examiners, he can dispense, if it concerns a priest of commendable theological doctrine;

4.° In those places in which the provision of a parish is made by concursus, whether a special one according to the norm of the const. of [Pope] Benedict XIV, *Cum illud*, 14 Dec. 1742, or a general one, this form is to be retained until the Apostolic See decrees otherwise.

Canon Law Digest
I: 247–50; II: 147; VI: 423; VII: 393

Canon 460 (1983 CIC 526)

§ 1. A pastor, according to the norm of Canon 156, can have title to only one parish, unless it concerns a parish to which it is in principle equally united.

§ 2. In one parish there shall be only one pastor who has the care of souls, reprobating every contrary custom and revoking every contrary privilege whatsoever.

Canon Law Digest
I: 250–51

Canon 461 (1983 CIC 527)

The pastor obtains the care of souls from the moment of taking possession according to the norm of Canons 1443–45; and before possession, or in taking possession, he must give the profession of faith mentioned in Canon 1406, § 1, n. 7.

Canon Law Digest
I: 251

Canon 462[73] (1983 CIC 530) Cross-Ref.: 1917 CIC 415

The functions reserved to the pastor are, unless otherwise provided by law:

1.° To confer baptism solemnly;

2.° To carry the most holy Eucharist publicly to the infirm of his own parish;

3.° To carry the most holy Eucharist publicly or privately as Viaticum to the infirm and those constituted in danger of death, to strengthen those by extreme unction, with due regard for the prescription of Canons 397, n. 3, 514, 848, § 2, and 938, § 2;

4.° To announce holy ordinations and those going into marriage; to assist at marriage, to impart nuptial blessings;

5.° To conduct due funerals according to the norm of Canon 1216;

6.° To bless homes according to the norms of liturgical books on Holy [Saturday] and other days according to local custom;

7.° To bless the baptismal fount on Holy [Saturday], to lead a public procession outside of church, to impart blessings outside of church with pomp and solemnity, unless it concerns a chapter church and the Chapter performs these functions.

Canon Law Digest
I: 251–53

Canon 463 (1983 CIC 531) Cross-Ref.: 1917 CIC 2349

§ 1. The pastor has a right to the fees that are owed to him by approved custom or by legitimate taxation according to the norm of Canon 1507, § 1.

§ 2. Those demanding more are bound to restitution.

§ 3. Although the pastor's office was fulfilled by someone else, the fees are nevertheless granted to the pastor, unless the contrary is shown by the will of donors concerning the amount that exceeds the fee.

§ 4. The pastor shall not deny free ministry to those not equal to paying.

Canon 464 (NA) Cross-Ref.: 1917 CIC 514

§ 1. The pastor is bound by office to exercise the care of souls for all those in his parish, unless they are legitimately exempt.

[73] Bernard Kelly, "The Functions Reserved to Pastors", Canon Law Studies, no. 250 (thesis, Catholic University of America, 1947).

§ 2. The Bishop can for a just and grave cause remove from parochial care religious families and pious houses that are in his territory and [that are] not [already] exempt by law.

Canon Law Digest
I: 253; III: 118

Canon 465[74] (1983 CIC 533) Cross-Refs.: 1917 CIC 358, 465, 474

§ 1. The pastor is bound by the obligation of residing in a parochial house near his own church; the local Ordinary, nevertheless, for a just cause can permit that he stay elsewhere, provided the house is not so distant from the parish church that it causes any detriment to the performance of parochial duties from there.

§ 2. He is permitted to be absent for at most two months within a year, whether continuous or interrupted, unless for grave cause, in the judgment of his own Ordinary, he requires a longer absence or [the Ordinary] will only permit him a briefer one.

§ 3. The days on which the pastor is gone for the pious exercises according to the norm of Canon 126 are not counted, once per year, in the two vacation months mentioned in § 2.

§ 4. If the vacation time, whether continuous or interrupted, includes an absence that goes longer than a week, the pastor, besides [needing] legitimate cause, must have the permission of the Ordinary in writing and leave a substitute vicar in his place to be approved by the same Ordinary; but if the pastor is a religious, he also requires the consent of the Superior and a substitute to be approved by both the Ordinary and the Superior.

§ 5. If the pastor suddenly and for grave reason leaves [the parish] and is compelled to be gone for more than a week, he shall alert the Ordinary as soon as possible by letters, indicating the cause why he left and supplying a priest, and obey his directions.

§ 6. A pastor must provide for the necessities of the faithful even for a briefer time of absence, especially when special circumstances of things suggest it.

Canon Law Digest
I: 253

[74] Peter Reilly, "Residence of Pastors", Canon Law Studies, no. 97 (J. C. D. thesis, Catholic University of America, 1935).

Canon 466 (1983 CIC 534)

§ 1. The pastor is bound by the obligation of applying Mass for the people according to the norm of Canon 339; a quasi-pastor [is bound] according to the norm of Canon 306.

§ 2. A pastor who might perhaps govern several parishes principally united or, besides [having] his own parish, has the administration of one or more others need only apply one Mass for the people committed to him on the prescribed days.

§ 3. The local Ordinary can permit for a just cause the pastor to apply the Mass for the people on a day other than that on which he is bound by law.

§ 4. The pastor celebrates the Mass to be applied for the people in the parish church, unless circumstances of things require or suggest the celebration of the Mass elsewhere.

§ 5. A pastor legitimately absent can apply the Mass for the people himself or through another in the place in which he is, or through a priest who acts in his place in the parish.

Canon Law Digest
I: 253–57; II: 147; III: 118; IV: 162; V: 335–37; VII: 393

Canon 467 (1983 CIC 528) Cross-Ref.: 1917 CIC 2182

§ 1. The pastor must celebrate divine offices, administer Sacraments to the faithful as often as they legitimately ask, know his sheep and prudently correct the erring, assist with paternal charity the poor and destitute, and apply the utmost care in the Catholic instruction of the young.

§ 2. The faithful are to be so admonished that frequently, where this can be done conveniently, they attend their parochial churches and are present there for divine offices, and hear the word of God.

Canon Law Digest
II: 147; VII: 394–418; IX: 252

Canon 468[75] (1983 CIC 529-530) Cross-Ref.: 1917 CIC 2182

§ 1. The pastor must help the sick in his parish with sedulous care and unrestrained charity, but especially those close to death, affording them the Sacraments solicitously and commending their souls to God.

---

[75] William Drumm, "Hospital Chaplains", Canon Law Studies, no. 178 (J. C. D. thesis, Catholic University of America, 1943).

§ 2. To the pastor and other priests who assist the infirm, the faculty is given them of granting the apostolic blessing with a plenary indulgence at the time of death, according to the form given in the approved liturgical books, which benediction [they] shall not omit to impart.

Canon 469 (1983 CIC 528)

The pastor shall be diligently vigilant lest anything that is contrary to faith or morals be given in his parish, especially in public and private schools, and he shall foster or start works of charity, faith, and piety.

Canon Law Digest
I: 258; IV: 162–66; VI: 423

Canon 470[76] (1983 CIC 535) Cross-Refs.: 1917 CIC 383, 576, 798, 1011, 1103

§ 1. The pastor shall have parochial books, namely, a book of baptisms, confirmations, marriages, and deaths; he shall also take care as far as possible to produce a book on the status of souls; and all of these books, according to the approved use of the Church and the prescriptions of his own Ordinary, he shall complete and diligently preserve.

§ 2. In the books of baptisms there shall also be noted whether the baptized has received confirmation, contracted marriage, with due regard for the prescription of Canon 1107, or whether he has taken up the sacred order of the subdiaconate or given solemn profession, and these annotations shall always be recorded in documents [issued] about the reception of baptism.

§ 3. At the end of any year the pastor shall transmit an authentic copy of the parish books to the episcopal Curia, except for the book on the status of souls.

§ 4. He shall use a parish seal and keep a tabulary, that is, archives, in which the above-mentioned books are kept together with letters from the Bishops, and other documents, which it seems necessary or useful to keep; all these things are [to be available] for inspection by the Ordinary or his

[76] James O'Rourke, "Parish Registers", Canon Law Studies, no. 88 (J. C. D. thesis, Catholic University of America, 1934); Eugene Sullivan, "Proof of the Reception of the Sacraments", Canon Law Studies, no. 209 (J. C. D. thesis, Catholic University of America, 1944); Andrew Kennedy, "The Annual Pastoral Report to the Local Ordinary", Canon Law Studies, no. 277 (Catholic University of America, not published); William Fitzgerald, "The Parish Census and the *Liber Status Animarum*", Canon Law Studies, no. 339 (thesis, Catholic University of America, 1954).

delegate [at the time] of visitation or another opportune time, and he shall religiously be on guard lest they come into the hands of strangers.

Canon Law Digest

I: 258–59; II: 147–50; III: 118; VII: 418; VIII: 298

Chapter 10
On parochial vicars[77]

Canon 471 (NA) Cross-Refs.: 1917 CIC 402, 452

§ 1. If a parish has been united in full law to a religious house, capitular church, or other moral person, a vicar must be constituted who actually conducts the care of souls [and to whom there is] assigned an appropriate share of its proceeds, in the judgment of the Bishop.

§ 2. Except in the case of legitimate privilege or custom, or of endowment made by the Bishop to the vicariate, reserving to himself free conferral, the religious Superior or chapter or other moral person presents the vicar; it is for the local Ordinary, if [the candidate] is suitable, with due regard for the prescription of Canon 459, to examine and install him.

§ 3. If the vicar is a religious he is removable just as is a religious pastor mentioned in Canon 454, § 5; all other vicars are perpetual on the part of the presenter, but they can be removed by the Bishop, after the manner of pastors, giving notice to him who presented him.

§ 4. The complete care of souls pertains exclusively to the vicar, [who has] all the rights and obligations of pastors according to the norm of common law and according to approved diocesan statutes and praiseworthy customs.

Canon Law Digest

I: 259–61; II: 150–52; III: 118–19

Canon 472 (1983 CIC 539) Cross-Refs.: 1917 CIC 477, 1481

When a parish is vacant:

1.° The local Ordinary shall constitute therein, as soon as possible, a suitable vicar econome, with the consent of the Superior if it

---

[77] Clement Bastnagel, "The Appointment of Parochial Adjutants and Assistants", Canon Law Studies, no. 58 (J. U. D.. thesis, Catholic University of America, 1930); Urban Wagner, "Parochial Substitute Vicars and Supplying Priests", Canon Law Studies, no. 265 (thesis, Catholic University of America, 1947).

concerns a religious, who will govern it during the time of vacancy [and] to whom is assigned a part of the proceeds for his decent sustenance;

2.° Before the constitution of the econome, unless other provision has been made, a vicar cooperator shall assume in the meantime the governance of the parish; if there are several vicars, the first among them [shall act]; if they are all equal, the one oldest in duty [shall act]; if vicars are lacking, the nearest pastor [shall act]; and if it concerns a parish entrusted to religious, the Superior of the house [shall act]; the local Ordinary, in the Synod or outside the Synod, shall determine in good time which parish is considered closer to a given parish;

3.° Whoever takes up the governance of a parish according to the norm of n. 2 must immediately inform the local Ordinary about the vacancy of the parish.

Canon Law Digest
I: 261

Canon 473 (1983 CIC 540) Cross-Ref.: 1917 CIC 477

§ 1. A vicar econome enjoys the same rights and is bound by the same duties as is a pastor in those things that look to the care of souls; it is not permitted for him, however, to do anything in the parish that can bring about prejudice to the rights of the pastor or of the parochial benefice.

§ 2. The econome shall hand over the key of the archive and the inventory of books and other documents that pertain to parish matters to the new pastor or successor econome in the presence of the vicar forane or another priest designated by the Ordinary and shall give an accounting of income and expenses during the time of administration.

Canon Law Digest
I: 261

Canon 474 (NA) Cross-Ref.: 1917 CIC 477

A vicar substitute who is constituted according to the norm of Canons 465, §§ 4 and 5, and Canon 1923, § 2, holds the place of a pastor in everything that looks to the care of souls, unless the local Ordinary or the pastor excepts something.

Canon Law Digest
I: 261

Canon 475 (NA) Cross-Refs.: 1917 CIC 477, 1433, 2147

§ 1. If a pastor because of old age, mental weakness, inexpertness, blindness, or other permanent cause becomes impaired with regard to fulfilling his duties rightly, the Ordinary can give him a vicar assistant, presented by the Superior if it deals with a parish entrusted to religious, who fills his place and to whom is assigned an appropriate share of the proceeds, unless other provision has been made.

§ 2. An assistant, who [is so assigned that] in all regards he supplies the place of the pastor, enjoys all rights and offices proper to pastors with the exception of the Mass for the people that binds the pastor; but if [the assistant] supplies for him only in part, then he assumes only those rights and obligations [listed] in the letter of deputation.

§ 3. If the pastor is in control of his [mental faculties], the assistant must remain in his task under the authority of [the pastor] according to the [appointment] letters of the Ordinary.

§ 4. But if it is not possible to provide for the good of souls through an assistant vicar, the pastor shall be removed according to the norm of Canons 2147–61.

Canon Law Digest
I: 261

Canon 476 (1983 CIC 545, 547–48, 550) Cross-Refs.: 1917 CIC 477, 1427, 1433

§ 1. If a pastor because of a multitude of people or from other causes is unable, in the judgment of the Ordinary, alone conveniently to conduct the care of the parish, one or several vicar cooperators shall be given him, to whom is assigned a decent remuneration.

§ 2. Vicar cooperators can be constituted for the whole parish or for a determined part of the parish.

§ 3. It belongs not to the pastor but to the local Ordinary, having heard the pastor, to appoint vicar cooperators from the secular clergy.

§ 4. The Superior to whom this [is entrusted] by the constitutions presents religious vicar cooperators to the Ordinary, [the Superior] having heard the pastor, and it is for the Ordinary to approve them.

§ 5. A vicar cooperator is bound by the obligation of residing in the parish according to the diocesan statutes or praiseworthy customs or as prescribed by the Bishop; indeed, the Ordinary shall prudently take care that, according to the norm of Canon 134, he live in the same parish house.

§ 6. His rights and obligations are contained in the diocesan statutes, the letter of [appointment from] the Ordinary, and from the commission of the pastor; but, unless otherwise expressly provided, he must by reason of office supply the place of the pastor and help him in the ministry of the whole parish, except for the application of the Mass for the people.

§ 7. He is under the pastor, who shall instruct him paternally and direct him in the care of souls, and keep watch over him and at least once per year report on him to his Ordinary.

§ 8. If not even through vicar cooperators can the spiritual welfare of the faithful be achieved, the Bishop shall provide [for the matter] according to the norm of Canon 1427.

Canon Law Digest
I: 262–63; II: 152

Canon 477 (1983 CIC 552)

§ 1. Parochial vicars mentioned in Canons 472–76, if they are religious, can be removed according to the norm of Canon 454, § 5; otherwise [they can be removed] at the discretion of the Bishop or Vicar Capitulary, but not by the Vicar General without a special mandate.

§ 2. But if the vicariate is a benefice, the vicar cooperator can be removed in a process according to the norm of law not only for the reasons for which a pastor can be removed, but also if he gravely fails to show required deference to the pastor in the exercise of his functions.

Canon 478 (NA)

§ 1. Just like the pastor of a cathedral church, so the parochial vicar of the cathedral Chapter takes precedence over all other pastors and vicars of the diocese; but the econome has the right of precedence as governed by the norms established in Canon 106.

§ 2. Substitute vicars and assistants precede, for the duration of their duties, vicar cooperators; and these [are over] other priests attached to the parish church.

Canon Law Digest
I: 263–64

Chapter 11
On rectors of churches

Canon 479 (1983 CIC 556)

§ 1. By the name of rectors of churches there come those priests to whom care of some church is mandated that is neither a parish nor a chapter nor attached to the house of a religious community, in which he celebrates offices.

§ 2. Regarding chaplains of women religious, of lay sodalities of male religious, [and] of confraternities and other legitimate associations, the prescripts of particular canons are to be observed.

Canon Law Digest
I: 264; III: 119

Canon 480 (1983 CIC 557)

§ 1. Rectors of churches are freely appointed by the local Ordinary, with due regard for the right of election and presentation, if it applies to someone; in which case, it is for the Ordinary to approve the rector.

§ 2. Even if a church belongs to some exempt religious [institute], the rector nevertheless must be appointed by the Superior and approved by the local Ordinary.

§ 3. If a church is joined with a Seminary or other college that is governed by clerics, the Superior of the Seminary or college is at once the rector of the church, unless the Ordinary constitutes otherwise.

Canon 481 (1983 CIC 558)

In a church committed to him, the rector cannot perform any parochial functions.

Canon 482 (1983 CIC 559)

The rector of a church can celebrate even the solemn divine offices there, with due regard for the legitimate laws of the foundation and provided they do not injure parochial ministry; in doubt about whether or not there is harm of this sort involved, it is for the local Ordinary to decide and to prescribe opportune norms to avoid such things.

Canon Law Digest
I: 264

Canon 483 (1983 CIC 560)

If a church, in the judgment of the Ordinary, is so distant from the parish that parishioners cannot without grave inconvenience be present at the parochial church where divine offices are available:

1.° The local Ordinary, even with grave penalties being established, can order the rector that, at times more convenient to the people, he celebrate offices, announce days of feast or fast to the faithful, and give catechetical instruction and explanation of the Gospels;

2.° The pastor can take the most holy Sacrament, which may be reserved there in accord with Canon 1265, for the infirm.

Canon 484 (1983 CIC 561)

§ 1. Without the at least presumed permission of the rector or other legitimate Superior, no one is permitted to celebrate Mass in a church or to minister the Sacraments or perform other sacred functions; but this permission shall not be given or denied except in accord with the norm of law.

§ 2. As to what applies to sermons to be held in the church, the prescriptions of Canons 1337–42 are to be observed.

Canon 485 (1983 CIC 562)

The rector of the church, under the authority of the local Ordinary and observing legitimate statutes and acquired rights, must take care or be vigilant that divine offices and the prescriptions of the sacred canons be correctly done in the church, that duties are faithfully fulfilled, goods rightly administered, that sacred furnishings and buildings be maintained and decorated, and that nothing happens that is repugnant to the sanctity of the place and the reverence due to the house of God.

Canon Law Digest
III: 119

Canon 486 (1983 CIC 563)

The rector of a church, even if he is elected or presented by others, can be removed by the Bishop at his discretion for any just reason; but if the rector is a religious, the prescription of Canon 454, § 5, shall be observed concerning his removal.

SECOND PART
ON RELIGIOUS

Canon 487[1] (1983 CIC 573, 598, 607, 710, 731)

The religious state is a stable manner of living in common, by which the faithful take up, besides common precepts, also the evangelical counsels of observing by vow obedience, chastity, and poverty, [and it] must be held in honor by all.

Canon Law Digest
I: 265–66; III: 119–35; IV: 166–83; V: 337–56; VI: 423–40;
VII: 418–54; VIII: 299–313; IX: 252–82; X: 43–82

Canon 488[2] (1983 CIC 573, 588–89, 591, 593, 607–8, 613, 620–21)
Cross-Ref.: 1917 CIC 673

In the canons that follow [the following definitions apply]:

1.° *Religious* [institute] is a society approved by legitimate ecclesiastical authority in which the members, according to the laws of their own institute, pronounce public vows, perpetual or tem-

---

[1] Sidney Turner, "The Vow of Poverty", Canon Law Studies, no. 54 (J. U. D.. thesis, Catholic University of America, 1929); Norman McFarland, "Religious Vocation-Its Juridic Concept", Canon Law Studies, no. 328 (thesis, Catholic University of America, 1953); James King, "The Juridical Nature of the Religious State" (diss. no. 6, Pontifical University of St. Thomas [Rome], 1958–1959); Stephen Naidoo, "The Juridical Significance of the Vow and Oath of Perseverance in the Congregation of the Most Holy Redeemer" (diss. no. 12, Pontifical University of St. Thomas [Rome], 1963–1964); Joseph Collins Seosamh, "The Notion of Religious State in the Documents of Vatican II" (diss. no. 3, Pontifical University of St. Thomas [Rome], 1967–1968); Joseph Rehage, "The Private Ownership of Property by Individual Religious before 1917: A Historical Study of Canonical Legislation prior to the Code of Canon Law", Canon Law Studies, no. 478 (Catholic University of America, 1971); Vincent Grogan, "The Canonical Implementation of the Renewal of Religious Formation, Government, and Internal Discipline since the Second Vatican Council in the Order of Friars Minor in the United States", Canon Law Studies, no. 483 (J. C. D. thesis, Catholic University of America, 1974).

[2] Thomas Brockhaus, "Religious Who Are Known as Conversi", Canon Law Studies, no. 225 (J. C. D. thesis, Catholic University of America, 1945); Francis Callahan, "The Centralization of Government in Pontifical Institutes of Women with Simple Vows (from Their Beginnings till the Legislation of Leo XIII)" (thesis, Gregorian University; printed version, no. 560, 1948); Donnell Walsh, "The New Law on Secular Institutes", Canon Law Studies, no. 347 (thesis, Catholic University of America, 1953); D. Meade, "The Constitutional Element of the Monastic Congregation of Vallambrosa from 1035–1448" (Pontifical Lateran University, 1960); Dismas Bonner, "Extern Sisters in Monasteries of Nuns", Canon Law Studies, no. 430 (J. C. D.

porary, to be renewed upon the elapse of time, and who tend to evangelical perfection;

2.° An *order* is a religious [institute] in which solemn vows are pronounced; *monastic Congregation* is a joining of several independent monasteries among themselves under the same Superior; *exempt religious* is a religious [institute], whether of solemn or simple vows, removed from the jurisdiction of the local Ordinary; *religious Congregation* or simple *Congregation* is a religious [institute] in which only simple vows, whether perpetual or temporary, are given out;

3.° *Religious [institute] of pontifical right* is a religious [institute] that has secured approval or at least a decree of praise from the Apostolic See; *of diocesan right*, refers to a religious [institute] erected by the Ordinary that has not yet obtained a decree of praise;

4.° *Clerical religious [institute]* is a religious [institute] in which most of the members are priests; otherwise it is *lay*;

5.° A *religious house* is the house of any religious in general; a *regular house* is a house of Orders; a *formal house* is a religious house in which at least six professed religious are present, of whom, if it concerns clerical religious, at least four must be priests;

6.° A *province* is a joining of several religious houses among themselves under the same Superior, constituting a part of the same religious [institute];

7.° *Religious* refers to those whose vows are pronounced in any religious [institute]; *religious of simple vows*, when they are in a religious Congregation; *regulars*, when they are in Orders; *sisters*, when they are religious women of simple vows; *nuns*, when they are religious women of solemn vows or, unless it is established by the nature of the thing or the context of the words, religious women whose vows are solemn in the institute but in certain places are simple by prescription of the Apostolic See;

---

thesis, Catholic University of America, 1963); Enid Williamson, "The Nature of the Congregation of Servite Sisters according to Its Constitutions" (thesis, Gregorian University; printed version, no. 2831, 1979); Sharon Holland, "The Concept of Consecration in Secular Institutes" (thesis, Gregorian University; printed version, no. 2961, 1981); Thomas Olmsted, "The Secularity of Secular Institutes" (thesis, Gregorian University; printed version, no. 2977, 1981).

8.° *Major Superiors* [are] Abbots Primate, Abbots Superior of monastic Congregations, and Abbots of independent monasteries, even though they belong to a monastic Congregation, the supreme Moderator of a religious [institute], a provincial Superior, and their vicars having power like that of a provincial.

Canon Law Digest

I: 266–70; II: 153; III: 135–57; IV: 183–90; V: 357–62;
VI: 440–42; VII: 454–57; VIII: 313–20;
IX: 282–92; X: 82–87

Canon 489[3] (1983 CIC 587)

Rules and particular constitutions of individual religious [institutes] not contrary to the canons of this Code retain their force; but those that are opposed are abrogated.

Canon Law Digest

I: 270–72; II: 153–56; III: 158; IV: 190–91; VI: 442–45

Canon 490 (1983 CIC 606)

What is established concerning religious, even if expressed in masculine vocabulary, applies by equal law to women, unless it is shown otherwise by the context of the words or the nature of the thing.

Canon 491 (NA)

§ 1. Religious precede laity; clerical religious [precede] lay religious; canons regular [precede] monks; monks [precede] other regulars; regulars [precede] religious Congregations; Congregations of pontifical rite [precede] Congregations of diocesan rite; among those of the same sort, the prescription of Canon 106, n. 5 is observed.

§ 2. But a secular cleric precedes both laity and religious outside of their churches and even in their churches if it concerns lay religious; but a Chapter, whether cathedral or collegial, takes precedence over these in any place.

---

[3] Chrysostom Rafter, "The Juridical Nature of the Dominican Constitutions" (diss. no. 6, Pontifical University of St. Thomas [Rome], 1959–1960); D. O'Friel, "Dispensation from the General Constitutions of the Orders of Friar Minor" (diss. no. 97, Pontifical University "Antonianum", discussed June 18, 1959); Thomas Glover, "The Juridical Nature of the Oratory and Oratorians Today" (diss. no. 5, Pontifical University of St. Thomas [Rome], 1971–1972).

TITLE 9

On the erection and suppression of religious [institutes], provinces, and houses

Canon 492[4] (1983 CIC 579, 594) Cross-Ref.: 1917 CIC 495

§ 1. Bishops, but not the Vicar Capitulary or the Vicar General, can found religious Congregations; but they shall not found them or allow them to be founded without consulting the Apostolic See; but if it concerns tertiaries living in common, it is also required that they be aggregated by the supreme Moderator to the first Order of that religious [institute].

§ 2. A Congregation of diocesan right, even though over the course of time it becomes spread over several dioceses, nevertheless, remains diocesan for so long as it lacks pontifical approbation or testament of praise, and it is fully subject to the jurisdiction of the Ordinary according to the norm of law.

§ 3. Neither a name nor a religious habit already constituted can be assumed by anyone who does not belong to it or by a new religious [institute].

Canon Law Digest
I: 272; II: 156–60; III: 158; VI: 445; VII: 457–59;
VIII: 320–23; IX: 292

Canon 493 (1983 CIC 584) Cross-Ref.: 1917 CIC 498

Any religious [institute], even one of only diocesan right, once it is legitimately founded, even if it consists of only one house, can be suppressed by no one except the Holy See, to which is reserved in such case [the disposal] of the goods, always with due regard for the will of the donors.

Canon Law Digest
I: 273; II: 160; VI: 445–46; VII: 459–61;
VIII: 324–25; IX: 292–95

[4] Clement Orth, "The Approbation of Religious Institutes", Canon Law Studies, no. 71 (J. C. D. thesis, Catholic University of America, 1931); Stephen Quinn, "Relation of the Local Ordinary to Religious of Diocesan Approval", Canon Law Studies, no. 283 (thesis, Catholic University of America, 1949); Theodore Baa, "The Ecclesiastical Approbation of a Religious Institute" (diss. no. 21, Pontifical University of St. Thomas [Rome], 1960–1961).

Canon 494 (1983 CIC 580–82, 585, 593)

§ 1. It pertains solely to the Apostolic See to divide the provinces of a religious [institute] of pontifical right, to unite a province already founded or otherwise to circumscribe them, to found new ones or suppress others, and to separate monasteries of their own right from monastic Congregations and to unite others.

§ 2. Upon extinction of a province, unless the constitutions provide otherwise, and with due regard for the law of justice and wills of the donors, the disposition of its goods belongs to the general Chapter or, if it is outside of the times of the Chapter, to the Moderator general with his Council.

Canon Law Digest
VI: 446; VII: 461; VIII: 325

Canon 495[5] (1983 CIC 583, 594–95)

§ 1. A religious Congregation of diocesan right cannot constitute houses in another diocese, except with the consent of both Ordinaries, both of the place where there is the principal house and of the place where it wishes to go; the local Ordinary from which it leaves, however, shall not deny this consent except for grave cause.

§ 2. If it happens that [other houses] are propagated in other dioceses, nothing can be changed regarding its laws, except with the consent of each of the Ordinaries of the dioceses in which it has a building, with due regard for those things that, according to the norm of Canon 492, § 1, are subject to the Apostolic See.

Canon Law Digest
III: 158; VI: 447

Canon 496 (1983 CIC 610)

No religious house can be erected unless it can be prudently judged that either from its own income or from customary donations or in some other way an appropriate living and sustenance can be provided.

Canon Law Digest
VIII: 325–28

---

[5] Bernard Flanagan, "The Canonical Erection of Religious Houses", Canon Law Studies, no. 179 (J. C. D. thesis, Catholic University of America, 1943); Peter Miles, "The Juridic Status of Dominican Non-priorial Houses and Their Superiors" (diss. no. 8, Pontifical University of St. Thomas [Rome], 1961–1962).

Canon 497[6] (1983 CIC 609, 611–12)

§ 1. For the erection of an exempt religious house, whether formal or not formal, or a monastery of nuns or of any religious house whatsoever in any place subject to the Sacred Congregation for the Prop. of the Faith, there is required the good pleasure of the Apostolic See and the consent of the local Ordinary given in writing; otherwise it is sufficient that the Ordinary approves.

§ 2. Permission for the constitution of a new house includes the faculty for clerical religious to have a church or public oratory attached to the house, with due regard for the prescription of Canon 1162, § 4, and to conduct sacred ministry, observing those things that in law ought to be observed; for all religious, [it includes the right] of exercising pious works proper to the religious [institute] with due regard for conditions laid down in this permission.

§ 3. In order that a school be built and opened, or [likewise] a hospital or a similar building separated even from an exempt house, it is necessary and sufficient that the special permission of the Ordinary [be had] in writing.

§ 4. In order that a constituted house be converted to another use, those formalities required in § 1 [shall be observed], unless it concerns the conversion, with due regard for the law of foundation, of something that only refers to the internal governance and discipline of the religious [institute].

Canon Law Digest

I: 273; IV: 191–92; V: 362–65; VI: 447; VII: 461–62; X: 88–90

Canon 498[7] (1983 CIC 616)

A religious house, whether formal or not formal, if it pertains to an exempt religious [institute], cannot be suppressed without apostolic good pleasure; if [it pertains] to a non-exempt Congregation of pontifical rite, it can be suppressed by the supreme Moderator, the local Ordinary consenting; if [it pertains] to a Congregation of diocesan rite, [it can be suppressed] with only the authority of the local Ordinary, having heard the Moderator of the Congregation, with due regard for the prescription of

---

[6] Francis Spence, "The Juridical Nature and Relationship with the Local Ordinary of Schools, Hospices, and Similar Edifices Separate from Religious Houses" (diss. no. 23, Pontifical University of St. Thomas [Rome], 1954–1955).

[7] Thomas Cunningham, "The Canonical Suppression of Religious Houses", Canon Law Studies, no. 416 (Catholic University of America, not published).

Canon 493, and if it concerns the only house [of the institute], then with due regard for the right of recourse in suspension to the Apostolic See.

Canon Law Digest
VI: 447; VII: 462

TITLE 10
On the governance of religious [institutes]

CHAPTER 1
On Superiors and on Chapters[8]

Canon 499 (1983 CIC 590)

§ 1. All religious, as to a supreme Superior, are subject to the Roman Pontiff, whom they are bound to obey even in virtue of the vow of obedience.

§ 2. The Cardinal Protector of any religious [institute], unless expressly provided otherwise in particular cases, enjoys no jurisdiction over the re-

[8] Dunwald Carroll, "Rights and Duties of Local Ordinaries over the Ecclesiastical Goods of Religious Women" (MS no. 356, Gregorian University, 1937); John Jones, "The Power of the Local Ordinary over Pontifical Congregations of Sisters" (diss. no. 6, Pontifical University of St. Thomas [Rome], 1937–1938); George Gallik, "The Rights and Duties of Bishops regarding Diocesan Sisterhoods" (diss. no. 11, Pontifical University of St. Thomas [Rome], 1938–1939); Joseph O'Brien, "The Exemption of Regulars" (MS no. 500, Gregorian University, 1938; printed version, no. 448, 1938, and Milwaukee, 1943); Benjamin Farrell, "The Rights and Duties of the Local Ordinary regarding Congregations of Women Religious of Pontifical Approval", Canon Law Studies, no. 128 (J. C. D. thesis, Catholic University of America, 1941); William Conway, "The Organization of the Early Irish Church and Its Influence on the Growth of Religious Exemption in the Merovingian Period" (MS no. 895, Gregorian University, 1941); Patrick Clancy, "The Local Religious Superior", Canon Law Studies, no. 175 (J. C. D. thesis, Catholic University of America, 1943); Gordian Lewis, "Chapters in Religious Institutes", Canon Law Studies, no. 181 (J. C. D. thesis, Catholic University of America, 1943); Timothy Lynch, "Contracts between Bishops and Religious Congregations", Canon Law Studies, no. 239 (J. C. D. thesis, Catholic University of America, 1946); Romaeus O'Brien, "The Provincial Religious Superior: A Historical Conspectus and a Commentary on the Rights and Duties of the Provincial Religious Superior in Religious Orders of Men", Canon Law Studies, no. 258 (thesis, Catholic University of America, 1947); Thomas Bowe, "Religious Superioresses", Canon Law Studies, no. 228 (thesis, Catholic University of America, 1946); Robert McGrath, "The Local Superior in Non-exempt Clerical Congregations", Canon Law Studies, no. 351 (thesis, Catholic University of America, 1954); Charles Henry, "Canonical Relations between Bishops and Abbots at the Beginning of the Tenth Century", Canon Law Studies, no. 382 (J. C. D. thesis,

ligious [institute] or the individual members, nor can he immerse himself in the interior discipline and the administration of goods, but he is only to promote by his counsel and patronage the good of the religious [institute].

Canon Law Digest

III: 158; V: 365–74; VI: 447; VIII: 328; IX: 295; X: 91

Canon 500 (1983 CIC 595, 614)

§ 1. Religious are likewise subject to the local Ordinary, except in regard to those things for which there is a privilege of exemption from the Apostolic See, always with due regard for the power that law also grants over them to local Ordinaries.

§ 2. Nuns who by prescript of their constitution are under the jurisdiction of the Superior of regulars are subject to the local Ordinary only in cases expressed in law.

§ 3. No religious [institute] of men, without a special apostolic indult, can have subject to it religious Congregations of women or the care of women religious, or specially retain for itself any entrustment [of same].

Canon Law Digest

I: 273–75; II: 160; III: 158; IV: 192–93; VI: 448;
VIII: 328–29; IX: 296–341; X: 91–98

Canon 501 (1983 CIC 596, 601, 608, 620, 631)

§ 1. Superiors and Chapters, according to the norm of constitutions and common law, have dominative power over subjects; in clerical exempt religious [institutes], they have ecclesiastical jurisdiction both for the internal forum and for the external.

§ 2. It is, nevertheless, strictly prohibited for any Superiors whatsoever to interfere in cases concerning the H. Office.

§ 3. Abbots Primate and the Superiors of monastic Congregations do not have all power and jurisdiction that the common law grants to major

---

Catholic University of America, 1957); Francis Mitchelstown, "The Capuchin Local Superior" (MS no. 3000, Gregorian University, 1959; printed version, no. 1305, 1960); Dominic McKenna, "The Local Superior and His Government in the Congregation of the Most Holy Redeemer 1732–1764" (diss. no. 11, Pontifical University of St. Thomas [Rome], 1963–1964); Edward Gilbert, "Redemptorist Exemption", Canon Law Studies, no. 464 (J. C. D. thesis, Catholic University of America, 1968); David Hynous, "The Relationship between Religious and the Hierarchy since the Second Vatican Council" (diss. no. 6, Pontifical University of St. Thomas [Rome], 1968–1969); Albert Verbrugghe, "A Canonical Investigation of the Episcopal Vicar for Religious" (Pontifical Lateran University, 1982).

Superiors, but [rather] their power and jurisdiction is assumed by the proper constitutions and particular decrees of the Holy See, with due regard for the prescriptions of Canons 655 and 1594, § 4.

Canon Law Digest
III: 158; V: 374–75; VI: 448–78; VII: 462–84;
VIII: 329–52; IX: 342–63; X: 98–112

Canon 502[9] (1983 CIC 617)

The supreme Moderator of a religious [institute] obtains power over all provinces, houses, [and] members of the religious [institute], exercising this according to the constitutions; other Superiors enjoy it within the limits of their responsibility.

Canon Law Digest
I: 275; IV: 193–202; VII: 484; VIII: 352

Canon 503 (NA)

Major Superiors in clerical exempt religious [institutes] can constitute notaries, but only for the ecclesiastical affairs of their religious [institute].

Canon 504 (1983 CIC 623)

With due regard for the constitutions of religious [institutes] that require a more advanced age or other qualities, they are incapable of the office of major Superior who have not been professed in that same institute for at least ten years calculated from first profession, or who were not born from a legitimate marriage, or who have not completed forty years of age if it concerns the supreme Moderator of a religious [institute] of women or Superioress in a monastery of nuns; or [who are not yet] thirty years [of age] for other major Superiors.

Canon Law Digest
VI: 478; VII: 484; VIII: 353

Canon 505 (1983 CIC 624)

Major Superiors are temporary, unless the constitutions indicate otherwise; local minor Superiors are not to be constituted for a term in excess

[9] Maurice Grajewski, "The Supreme Moderator of Clerical Exempt Religious Institutes", Canon Law Studies, no. 369 (thesis, Catholic University of America, 1957); Robert Gavotto, "The Prior General: The Principle of Unity in the Order of St. Augustine" (thesis, Gregorian University; printed version, no. 2442, 1973).

of three years; but which [term] having been completed, they can assume the same responsibility again if the constitutions so provide, but not a third time immediately in the same religious house.

Canon Law Digest
I: 275–79; IV: 202; V: 375–76; VI: 479;
VIII: 353–54; IX: 363

Canon 506 (1983 CIC 625–26)

§ 1. Before coming to the election of the major Superior in religious [institutes] of men, each and every [member] of the Chapter will promise by oath to elect those whom they feel according to God ought to be elected.

§ 2. In monasteries of nuns, the local Ordinary or his delegate presides over the election committee of the Superioress, though without entering the cloister, along with two priest tellers if the nuns are subject to him; otherwise, the regular Superior [presides]; but even in this case, the Ordinary must be advised in good time about the day and hour of election so that, together with the regular Superior, he can assist personally or through another and, if he assists, preside.

§ 3. The ordinary confessors of nuns shall not act as tellers.

§ 4. The Ordinary of the place in which the election is conducted presides, personally or through another, over the general election of the Superioress in Congregations of women if it concerns a Congregation of diocesan right, [and it is for him] to confirm the election results or to rescind it as an action of conscience.

Canon Law Digest
I: 279–80; II: 160; VIII: 354–57; IX: 364–65

Canon 507 (1983 CIC 626)

§ 1. In elections that are done by Chapters, the common law mentioned in Canons 160–82 is observed, besides the other constitutions of the religious [institute] that are not contrary [to the common law].

§ 2. Let all take care to avoid procuring votes directly or indirectly for themselves or for others.

§ 3. Postulation can be admitted only in an extraordinary case and provided it is not prohibited in the constitutions.

Canon Law Digest
I: 280; VI: 479; VIII: 358; IX: 365–66

Canon 508 (1983 CIC 629)

Superiors shall stay in their own house and shall not leave it except according to the norm of the constitutions.

Canon Law Digest
VIII: 358

Canon 509 (1983 CIC 592)

§ 1. Every Superior must promote notice and execution of the decrees of the Holy See that concern religious among their subjects.

§ 2. Let local Superiors take care:

1.° That at least once a year on stated days their own constitutions are publicly read, and likewise the decrees that the Holy See prescribes be publicly read;

2.° That at least twice a month, with due regard for the prescription of Canon 565, § 2, instruction on Christian catechesis be offered for lay brothers and familiars accommodated to the condition of the listeners and, especially in lay religious [institutes, that there be offered] a pious exhortation to the whole group.

Canon Law Digest
I: 280–82

Canon 510[10] (1983 CIC 592)

Abbots Primate, the Superiors of monastic Congregations, and the supreme Moderators of each religious [institute] of pontifical right must send by document to the Holy See a report on the status of the religious [institute] every five years, or more often if the constitutions so direct, signed by themselves with their Council and, if it concerns a Congregation of women, [signed] also by the Ordinary of the place in which the supreme Superioress with her Council resides.

Canon Law Digest
I: 282–93; III: 158–212; VI: 479–80

Canon 511 (1983 CIC 628)

The major Superiors of a religious [institute] whom the constitutions designate for this task shall visit personally or through others, if they are

---

[10] Mel Brady, "The Quinquennial Report of Religious Institutes to the Holy See", Canon Law Studies, no. 422 (J. C. D. thesis, Catholic University of America, 1963).

legitimately impeded, at times designated in the [constitutions], each house subject to them.

Canon 512[11] (1983 CIC 595, 628)

§ 1. The local Ordinary personally or through another must visit every five years:

1.° Each monastery of nuns that is immediately subject to him or to the Apostolic See;

2.° Each house of Congregations, whether of men or of women, of diocesan right.

§ 2. He must at the same time visit:

1.° Monasteries of nuns that are under regulars, concerning those things that look to the law of cloister; indeed, concerning all things if the regular Superior has not visited it for five years;

2.° Each house of a clerical Congregation of pontifical right, even exempt ones, regarding those things that pertain to the church, sacristy, public oratory, and seat of sacramental confession;

3.° Each house of a lay Congregation of pontifical right, not only concerning those things included in the above numbers, but in other things that look to internal discipline, according to the norm, however, of Canon 618, § 2, n. 2.

§ 3. In what applies to the administration of goods, the prescriptions of Canons 532–35 are observed.

Canon Law Digest
I: 293–94; V: 376

Canon 513 (1983 CIC 628)

§ 1. A Visitator has the right and duty of questioning those religious whom he judges [should be questioned] and of learning from them those matters pertaining to the visitation; and all religious are bound by the obligation of answering according to the truth, and it is reprehensible that

[11] Thomas Reilly, "Visitation of Religious", Canon Law Studies, no. 112 (J. C. D. thesis, Catholic University of America, 1938); Carthach MacCarthy, "Competency as Regards Monastic Visitation in Pre-Tridentine Legislation" (D. C. L. thesis, Librarian's Office 524, Maynooth [Ireland], 1948); William Roach, "The Local Ordinary and Visitation of Women Religious" (diss. no. 22, Pontifical University of St. Thomas [Rome], 1954–1955).

a Superior in any way should steer them away from such obligations or otherwise impede the scope of the visitation.

§ 2. Recourse is given against the decree of a Visitator, [but] only in devolution, unless the Visitator proceeded in a judicial manner.

Canon Law Digest
I: 294; IX: 366

Canon 514 (NA) Cross-Refs.: 1917 CIC 462, 850, 875, 938, 1245, 1313, 1338

§ 1. In every clerical religious [institute], it is the right and duty of the Superior, personally or through another, to administer Holy Viaticum and last anointing to the sick, whether professed, novice, or to others staying in the religious house day and night, or [to those] who are there for the sake of [service], education, hospitality, or recovery from infirmity.

§ 2. In a house of nuns, the ordinary confessor, or one who takes his place, has the same right and duty.

§ 3. In other lay religious [institutes], this right and duty belongs to the pastor of the place or to the chaplain whom the Ordinary names to take the place of the pastor according to the norm of Canon 464, § 2.

§ 4. In funerals, the prescriptions of Canons 1221 and 1230, § 5, are observed.

Canon Law Digest
I: 294; VI: 480

Canon 515 (NA)

Merely honorific titles of dignity or of office are prohibited; the only [honorific] titles permitted, in accord with the constitutions, are those of major offices that the religious in his own religious [institute] might have actually held [previously].

Canon 516 (1983 CIC 627, 636)

§ 1. The Supreme Moderator of a religious [institute] or monastic Congregation, the provincial or local Superior, or at least [the Superior] of a house of formation, shall have counselors, whose consent or advice is necessary according to the norm of the constitutions and the sacred canons.

§ 2. There shall also be economes for the administration of temporal goods: they shall generally administer all the goods of the religious [institute, and it is called] a provincial [council if it is] over a province, and a local [council if it is] over individual houses; all those who serve in this function are under the direction of the Superior.

§ 3. The Superior cannot perform the duties of general or provincial econome; but he can be a local econome, [and] although it is better if it is distinguished from the Superior, he can function thus together if necessity requires it.

§ 4. If the constitutions are silent on the selection of the econome, the major Superior with the consent of the Council makes the selection.

Canon Law Digest
VI: 480; VII: 484–85; VIII: 358–59; IX: 366–67

Canon 517 (NA)

§ 1. Each religious [institute] of pontifical right of men shall have a procurator general designated according to the constitutions who conducts the affairs of his religious [institute] before the Holy See.

§ 2. Before the time prescribed in the constitutions expires, he shall not be removed without consulting the Apostolic See.

Canon Law Digest
I: 294–95

Chapter 2
On confessors and chaplains[12]

Canon 518 (1983 CIC 630) Cross-Ref.: 1917 CIC 896

§ 1. In each religious clerical house there shall be appointed several, given the number of members, legitimately approved confessors with the power, if it concerns exempt religious, of absolving even in cases reserved in the religious [institute].

§ 2. Religious Superiors having the power of hearing confessions can, those things being observed that in law ought to be observed, hear the

[12] Robert McCormick, "Confessors of Religious", Canon Law Studies, no. 33 (J. C. D. thesis, Catholic University of America, 1926); Raymond Daley, "The Confessors of Men Religious" (diss. no. 11, Pontifical University of St. Thomas [Rome], 1955–1956).

confessions of subjects who ask for it from them by their own decision and act accordingly, but without grave cause they shall not do this in the manner of a habit.

§ 3. Superiors shall be cautious lest one of their subjects be induced either by them or through another, or by force, fear, or inappropriate suggestion, or other reason to confess his sins to them.

Canon Law Digest
II: 160; IV: 202–3

Canon 519 (NA) Cross-Refs.: 1917 CIC 566, 874, 896

With due regard to the constitutions that establish times for confession and even suggest that it be made to determinate confessors, if a religious, even an exempt one, for the quieting of his conscience, goes to a confessor approved by the local Ordinary, even if he is not listed among the ones designated [by the institute], the confession, revoking any contrary privilege whatsoever, is valid and licit; and the confessor can even absolve the religious from sins and censures reserved in the religious [institute].

Canon Law Digest
II: 160; VII: 486

Canon 520 (1983 CIC 630) Cross-Ref.: 1917 CIC 522

§ 1. In each religious house of women there shall be only one ordinary confessor, who shall hear the sacramental confessions of the whole community, unless, because of their great number or other just cause, there ought to be a second or several [others].

§ 2. But if a religious woman, for the quieting of her spirit and for better progress in the way of God, asks for a special confessor or spiritual moderator, the Ordinary shall grant it easily; [the Ordinary] nevertheless shall remain vigilant lest abuse arises from this concession; and if it does arise, he shall cautiously and prudently eliminate it with due regard for the liberty of conscience.

Canon Law Digest
I: 295; II: 160; VII: 486

Canon 521 (1983 CIC 630) Cross-Refs.: 1917 CIC 522, 2414

§ 1. In each religious community of women there shall be given an extraordinary confessor who at least four times a year will go to the religious house and to whom all the religious must appear at least to receive a blessing.

§ 2. Where religious communities of women exist, local Ordinaries shall designate some priests for each house to whom there is easy recourse for sacramental penances in particular cases whenever necessary so that it is scarcely necessary to go to the Ordinary each time.

§ 3. If a religious woman asks for one of these confessors, no Superioress is permitted, herself or through others, directly or indirectly, to inquire about the reason for the request or with words or deeds to decline the request or by any other means to show herself to be upset.

Canon Law Digest
II: 160; VII: 486

Canon 522 (1983 CIC 630) Cross-Refs.: 1917 CIC 876, 2414

If, notwithstanding the prescription of Canons 520 and 521, any religious, for the tranquillity of her conscience, goes to a confessor approved by the local Ordinary for women, and the confession is performed in any church or oratory, even in a semi-public one, it is valid and licit, revoking any contrary privilege whatsoever; nor shall the Superioress prohibit or inquire about it of her, not even indirectly; and the religious woman is bound to refer nothing to the Superioress.

Canon Law Digest
I: 295–97; II: 161

Canon 523 (1983 CIC 630) Cross-Refs.: 1917 CIC 876, 2414

All religious women, when they are gravely sick, even if danger of death is absent, can approach any priest approved for the hearing of the confessions of women, even if he is not assigned to religious, for so long as the grave infirmity perdures, as often as they wish to be confessed, nor can the Superioress directly or indirectly prohibit them.

Canon Law Digest
I: 297; II: 161

Canon 524 (1983 CIC 630)

§ 1. Priests who are outstanding for moral integrity and prudence, whether from the secular clergy or religious, with the permission of their

Superiors, can be deputed for the task of ordinary and extraordinary confessors of religious women; moreover, they shall be forty years of age, unless for a just cause in the judgment of the Ordinary something else is required, and they shall have no power in the external forum over the same religious women.

§ 2. The ordinary confessor cannot be reappointed as the extraordinary [confessor] except for the case considered in Canon 526, nor can the ordinary [confessor] be deputed again for the same community until one year from the completion of duty; but the extraordinary [confessor] can be immediately renamed as the ordinary confessor.

§ 3. Ordinary and extraordinary confessors of religious women shall in no way immerse themselves in the internal or external governance of the community.

Canon Law Digest
VII: 486

Canon 525 (1983 CIC 630) Cross-Ref.: 1917 CIC 876

If a house of religious women is immediately subject to the Apostolic See or to the local Ordinary, this one shall select priests for both ordinary and extraordinary confession; if there is a regular Superior, this one presents confessors to the Ordinary, and it is for him to approve them for hearing the confession of the nuns and to supply for the negligence of the Superior if necessary.

Canon 526 (1983 CIC 630) Cross-Ref.: 1917 CIC 524

The ordinary confessor of religious women shall not exercise his office beyond three years; but the Ordinary, however, can confirm him for a second and indeed for a third three-year [period] if he is not able to provide otherwise because of a shortage of priests suitable for this office or because the major part of the religious who, even in other matters, do not have the right of casting a vote come together by secret vote for the confirmation of the same confessor; but the dissenters, if they wish, must be provided for otherwise.

Canon Law Digest
VI: 481

Canon 527 (1983 CIC 630)

The local Ordinary, according to the norm of Canon 880, can for a grave cause remove an ordinary as well as an extraordinary confessor of religious women even if a monastery is under regulars and the same priest confessor is a regular, nor is he bound to give any reason for the removal except to the Apostolic See if required of him; but he must advise the regular Superior about the removal if the nuns are subject to regulars.

Canon 528 (1983 CIC 630)

Even in lay religious [institutes] of men, there shall be deputed according to the norm of Canon 874, § 1, and 875, § 2, an ordinary and extraordinary confessor; and if a religious asks for a special confessor, the Superior shall grant one, in no way inquiring as to the reasons for the petition, or showing himself to be upset about it.

Canon Law Digest
VII: 487

Canon 529 (1983 CIC 567)

If it concerns non-exempt lay religious [institutes], it is for the local Ordinary to designate a priest for sacred [ministry] and to approve one for preaching; if it is an exempt one, the regular Superior will designate some priests for it, the Ordinary supplying for negligence.

Canon 530[13] (1983 CIC 630)

§ 1. All religious Superiors are strictly forbidden to induce in any manner persons subject to them to make a manifestation of conscience to them.

§ 2. But subjects are nevertheless not prohibited from freely and voluntarily opening their [hearts] to their Superiors; indeed, it is expedient that with filial trust they go to Superiors and before them, if they are priests, even set forth their anxieties of conscience.

[13] Francis Korth, "The Evolution of 'Manifestation of Conscience' in Religious Rules [in the] III–XVI Centuries" (thesis, Gregorian University; printed version, no. 588, 1949); Dacian Dee, "The Manifestation of Conscience", Canon Law Studies, no. 410 (J. C. D. thesis, Catholic University of America, 1960).

Chapter 3
On temporal goods and their administration[14]

Canon 531 (1983 CIC 634)

Not [only] religious [institutes], but also provinces and houses are capable of acquiring and possessing temporal goods with stable incomes or foundations, unless their capacity for these is excluded or restricted in the rules and constitutions.

Canon 532 (1983 CIC 635, 638) Cross-Refs.: 1917 CIC 512, 533

§ 1. The goods of a religious [institute] or province or house are to be administered according to the norm of the constitution.

§ 2. Besides Superiors, other officials who in the constitutions are designated for this within the limits of their duties [can] incur expenses and validly [perform] juridic acts of ordinary administration.

Canon 533 (1983 CIC 638) Cross-Refs.: 1917 CIC 512, 535, 618, 631

§ 1. The prescription of Canon 532, § 1, is observed for investments of money; but the previous consent of the local Ordinary must be obtained by:

1.° Superiors of nuns and religious [institutes] of diocesan right for any sort of investment; indeed, if the monastery of nuns is subject to a regular Superior, his consent is also necessary;

2.° The Superioress in a religious Congregation of pontifical right, if the investment consists of the dowry of a professed, according to the norm of Canon 549;

3.° The Superior and Superioress of a religious Congregation's house if the funds have been left to the house by will or for the support of the cult of God taking place there;

[14] James McManus, "The Administration of Temporal Goods in Religious Institutes", Canon Law Studies, no 109 (J. C. D. thesis, Catholic University of America, 1937); Romuald Kowalski, "Sustenance of Religious Houses of Regulars", Canon Law Studies, no. 199 (J. C. D. thesis, Catholic University of America, 1944); Francis Demers, "The Temporal Administration of the Religious House of a Non-exempt, Clerical, Pontifical Institute", Canon Law Studies, no. 396 (J. C. D. thesis, Catholic University of America, 1961).

4.° Any religious, even though a [member] of a regular Order, if the money has been given to a parish or mission or to a religious on behalf of a parish or mission.

§ 2. These likewise must be observed for any change in investment.

Canon Law Digest
I: 297

Canon 534 (1983 CIC 638) Cross-Refs.: 1917 CIC 512, 618, 2347

§ 1. With due regard for the prescription of Canon 1531, if it concerns the alienation of precious goods or those [goods] whose value exceeds the sum of thirty-thousand francs or lire, or contracting debts and obligations beyond this indicated sum, the contract lacks force unless apostolic good pleasure has preceded it; otherwise, the permission of the Superiors according to the norm of the constitution, with the consent of the Chapter or the Council manifested by secret vote given in writing, is required and suffices; but if it concerns nuns or sisters of diocesan right, consent is additionally necessary from the local Ordinary given in writing and [that of] the regular Superior if the monastery of nuns is subject to him.

§ 2. In the request to obtain consent to contract debts or obligations, there must be expressed those other debts and obligations by which the moral person or religious [institute] or province or house is bound at that time; otherwise the consent obtained is invalid.

Canon Law Digest
II: 161–66; III: 212; IV: 203–6; V: 376–77; VI: 481;
VII: 487; VIII: 359; IX: 367–71

Canon 535 (1983 CIC 637) Cross-Refs.: 1917 CIC 512, 618, 631

§ 1. In every monastery of nuns, even exempt ones:

1.° An account of administration, demanded without charge, shall be given at least once a year, or more often if so prescribed in the constitutions, by the Superioress to the local Ordinary, and likewise to the regular Superior if the monastery is subject to him;

2.° If the account of administration is not approved by the Ordinary, he can apply opportune remedies, even removing, if he thinks it warranted, the econome or other administrators; but if the monastery is subject to a regular Superior, the Ordinary shall advise him about how things look; but if [the Superior] neglects things, [the Ordinary] can see to matters himself.

§ 2. In other religious [institutes] of women, an account of the administration of goods that make up the endowment is given the local Ordinary on the occasion of his visit and even more often if the Ordinary concludes it is necessary.

§ 3. The local Ordinary moreover can always take cognizance of:

1.° The economic situation of a religious house of diocesan right;

2.° The administration of foundations or legacies mentioned in Canon 533, § 1, nn. 3 and 4.

Canon Law Digest
I: 297–98

Canon 536 (1983 CIC 639)

§ 1. If a moral person (whether a religious [institute], province, or house) contracts debts and obligations, even with the permission of the Superiors, it is bound to answer for them.

§ 2. If a regular contracts such with the permission of the Superiors, the moral person must answer whose Superior gave the permission; if [it is] a religious of simple vows, he must answer, unless he acted with permission of the Superior on business of the religious [institute].

§ 3. If a religious contracts without the permission of any Superior, he must answer, but not the religious [institute] or province or house.

§ 4. It always remains clear that an action can at any time be instituted against him to whom some benefit flowed from entering the contract.

§ 5. Let religious Superiors be cautious lest they permit that debts be contracted, unless it can be clearly shown that the expenses can be paid out of normal income and that within not too long a time the capital sum can be repaid through legitimate *amortization*.

Canon Law Digest
II: 166

Canon 537 (1983 CIC 640)

Gifts from the goods of the house, province, or religious [institute] are not permitted except by reason of almsgiving or another just cause, having come to the Superiors and according to the norm of the constitution.

TITLE 11
On admission into a religious [institute]

Canon 538 (1983 CIC 597)

Any Catholic who is not prevented by a legitimate impediment, and who is moved by right intention, and who is suitable for the burdens imposed by religious [life] can be admitted into a religious [institute].

Canon Law Digest
V: 377; VI: 481–88; VII: 487–509; IX: 371; X: 112

Chapter 1
On postulancy[15]

Canon 539 (1983 CIC 597) Cross-Ref.: 1917 CIC 542

§ 1. All women in religious [institutes] of perpetual vows and, if it concerns religious [institutes] of men, lay brothers, before being admitted to the novitiate, must perform a postulancy of at least six integral months; but in religious [institutes] of temporary vows, as to what applies to the necessity and time of the postulancy, the constitutions stand.

§ 2. The major Superior can extend the prescribed time of postulancy, but not beyond another six months.

Canon Law Digest
III: 213; VI: 489; VIII: 359

Canon 540 (NA) Cross-Ref.: 1917 CIC 542

§ 1. The postulancy must be performed either in the novitiate house or in another house of the religious [institute] in which discipline according to the constitutions is accurately observed under the special care of approved religious.

§ 2. Postulants will wear modest attire, different from the clothes of novices.

[15] Joseph Waters, "The Probation in Societies of Quasi-Religious", Canon Law Studies, no. 306 (thesis, Catholic University of America, 1951); James McGuire, "The Postulancy", Canon Law Studies, no. 386 (thesis, Catholic University of America, 1959).

§ 3. Aspirants in monasteries of nuns while they perform postulancy are bound by the law of cloister.

Canon Law Digest
I: 298

Canon 541 (NA) Cross-Ref.: 1917 CIC 542

Postulants before they begin the novitiate shall undergo spiritual exercises for at least eight integral days; and, according to the prudent judgment of the confessor, they shall set forth a general confession of their prior life.

Canon Law Digest
VII: 509; VIII: 359

Chapter 2
On the novitiate[16]

Article 1—*On the requirements for one to be admitted to the novitiate*

Canon 542[17] (1983 CIC 597, 642–45) Cross-Refs.: 1917 CIC 555, 677, 2411

With due regard for the prescription of Canons 539–41 and those others [found] in the constitutions of each religious [institute]:

1.° They are invalidly admitted to the novitiate:
   [a] Who adhere to non-Catholic sects;
   [b] Who do not have the age required for novitiate;
   [c] Who enter religious [life] induced by force, grave fear, or dolus, or whom a Superior receives having been induced in the same manner;

[16] Lucy Vazquez, "The Common Law on the Novitiate in the Western Church from the Council of Trent to the Present", Canon Law Studies, no. 486 (J. C. D. thesis, Catholic University of America, 1975).

[17] Donald Stewart, "Force, Fear, and Deceit in Relation to Validity of Entrance into Religion and Religious Profession" (diss. no. 16, Pontifical University of St. Thomas [Rome], 1949–1950); James Brown, "The Invalidating Effects of Force, Fear, and Fraud upon the Canonical Novitiate", Canon Law Studies, no. 311 (thesis, Catholic University of America, 1951).

[d] A spouse while the marriage perdures;
[e] Who are obstructed or have been obstructed by the bond of [prior] religious profession;
[f] Those targeted by a penalty for a committed grave delict of which they are accused or can be accused;
[g] A Bishop, whether residential or titular, even if he has only been designated by the Roman Pontiff;
[h] Clerics who by institution of the Holy See are bound by the sworn obligation thoroughly to dedicate themselves for the good of their diocese or mission, for so long as the obligation of the oath perdures.

2.° Illicitly but validly admitted are:
[a] Clerics constituted in sacred [orders] without consulting the local Ordinary or contradicting him, where their departure would result in grave harm to souls that can otherwise not be avoided;
[b] Ones bound by grave debts that they are not equal to repaying;
[c] Those legally liable for rendering accounts or who are implicated in other secular transactions from which litigation and troubles can disturb the religious [institute];
[d] Children whose parents, that is, mother or father or grandfather or grandmother, are constituted in grave necessity and must be helped, and parents who must provide upkeep and necessary education to children;
[e] Those destined for priesthood in a religious [institute] from which, however, they are removed by irregularity or other canonical impediment;
[f] Orientals in latin religious [institutes] without receiving permission in writing from the Sacred Congregation for the Oriental Church.

Canon Law Digest
I: 298; II: 166; V: 377–78; VI: 489; VII: 509–10;
VIII: 359; IX: 371–72; X: 112–14

Canon 543 (1983 CIC 641, 656, 658)

The right of admitting to the novitiate and to subsequent religious profession, whether temporary or perpetual, pertains to Superiors with the vote of the Council or Chapter, according to the special constitutions of each religious [institute].

Canon 544[18] (1983 CIC 645, 684) Cross-Ref.: 1917 CIC 2411

§ 1. In any religious [institute], all aspirants, before they are admitted, must present testimony of the reception of baptism and confirmation.

§ 2. Male aspirants must also secure testimonial letters from the Ordinary of the place of origin and from those places in which, after completion of the fourteenth year, they were present for at least one morally continuous year, notwithstanding any contrary privilege.

§ 3. If it concerns admitting those who were in a Seminary, college, or other postulancy or novitiate of another religious [institute], they are also required to secure testimonial letters given accordingly in these various cases by the rector of the Seminary or college, having heard the local Ordinary, or by the major religious Superior.

§ 4. For the admission of clerics, beyond testimony of ordination, testimonial letters from Ordinaries in whose diocese after ordination they were present for one morally continuous year suffice, with due regard for the prescription of § 3.

§ 5. For professed religious, for transfer to another religious [institute] by apostolic indult, the testimony of the major Superior in the previous religious [institute] is satisfactory.

§ 6. Beyond this testimony required by law, Superiors who have the right of taking persons into the religious [institute] can require other [testimony] that appears to them necessary and opportune for this purpose.

§ 7. Women, finally, should not be received unless there has been an accurate investigation of their character and morals, with due regard for the prescription of § 3.

Canon Law Digest
I: 298–99; VII: 510

---

[18] Leo Koesler, "Entrance into the Novitiate by Clerics in Major Orders", Canon Law Studies, no. 327 (thesis, Catholic University of America, 1953); Ignatius Foley, "Testimonial Letters Required for Admission into a Religio[us Institute]" (diss. no. 12, Pontifical University of St. Thomas [Rome], 1953–1954); William Hogan, "The Testimonies and Testimonials Required for the Admission of Aspirants to the Novitiate" (MS no. 3015, Gregorian University, 1960; printed version, no. 1365, 1961).

Canon 545 (NA)

§ 1. Those who are required to give testimonial letters by prescription of law shall give them not to the aspirants but to the religious Superiors, without charge, within a period of three months from the request, sealed shut, if it concerns those in the Seminary, college, religious postulancy, or novitiate, and confirmed by oath of the Superior.

§ 2. If for grave reason they decide they cannot give a response, they shall explain the matter to the Apostolic See within the same period.

§ 3. If they answer that the aspirant is not sufficiently known to them, the religious Superior shall make up for that by another accurate investigation and worthy report on faith; but if they respond with nothing, the inquiring Superior shall make known to the Apostolic See the fact of not receiving a report.

§ 4. In their testimonial letters, following diligent examination, even by secret information, they must report, gravely burdened in the conscience to expose the truth, concerning the birth of the aspirant, morals, character, life, reputation, condition, and knowledge; and whether the one for whom inquiries are being made is under any censure, irregularity, or other canonical impediment, or whether his own family needs his assistance, and finally, if it concerns those who have already been in a Seminary, college, or religious postulancy, or novitiate, whether they were dismissed for cause or left on their own.

Canon Law Digest
I: 299; VII: 510

Canon 546 (NA)

All those who receive the aforesaid information are bound by the strict obligation of maintaining secrecy concerning the notices received and the persons who gave them.

Canon 547[19] (NA)

§ 1. In monasteries of nuns, a postulant shall provide a dowry established in the constitutions or determined by legitimate custom.

---

[19] Thomas Kealy, "Dowry of Women Religious", Canon Law Studies, no. 134 (J. C. D. thesis, Catholic University of America, 1941); Hugh MacHugh, "The Thirteenth Century Period of the Evolution of the Dowry of Today: An Historical-Legal Study of the Origins of a Custom" (D. C. L. thesis, Librarian's Office 528/1–2, Maynooth [Ireland], 1947).

§ 2. This dowry shall be handed over to the monastery before receiving the habit, or at least its transfer shall be assured in a form valid under civil law.

§ 3. In religious [institutes] of simple vows, as to what pertains to the dowry of religious women, the constitutions stand.

§ 4. The prescribed dowry cannot be waived in whole or in part without an indult of the Holy See if it concerns a religious [institute] of pontifical right; likewise, without coming to the local Ordinary if it is a religious [institute] of diocesan right.

Canon Law Digest
VI: 489

Canon 548 (NA)

A dowry is irrevocably acquired by a monastery or a religious [institute] by the death of the religious even though she had pronounced nothing but temporary vows.

Canon 549 (NA) Cross-Refs.: 1917 CIC 533, 2412

After the first profession of the religious, the dowry shall be placed in a safe, lawful, and fruitful [investment] by the Superioress with her Council and the consent of the local Ordinary and the regular Superior if the house is dependent on one; it is entirely prohibited that in any manner before the death of the religious it be spent, not even on the building of the house or other alienations for debt.

Canon 550 (NA)

§ 1. Dowries shall be cautiously and completely administered in a monastery or habitual residence house of the supreme Moderator or provincial Superioress.

§ 2. Local Ordinaries shall be sedulously vigilant about the preservation of the dowries of religious women, and especially they shall require accountings about them in the sacred visitation.

Canon 551 (NA) Cross-Refs.: 1917 CIC 635, 2412

§ 1. The dowry of a professed religious, whether of solemn or simple vows, who leaves for any reason must be restored without the income already earned.

§ 2. But if a professed religious by apostolic indult transfers to another religious [institute] during the novitiate, the income, with due regard for the prescription of Canon 570, § 1, [goes to the religious institute]; but upon giving the new profession, the dowry is owed to the religious [institute]; but if [one transfers] to another monastery of the same Order, the dowry is owed to this [monastery] from the day of transfer.

Canon Law Digest
I: 300

Canon 552 (NA) Cross-Ref.: 1917 CIC 2412

§ 1. The Superioress, even of exempt religious, must inform the local Ordinary at least two months in advance about the coming admission to the novitiate and to temporary or perpetual profession, whether solemn or simple.

§ 2. The local Ordinary or, if he is absent or impeded, a priest deputed by him shall diligently and without charge explore, at least thirty days before novitiate or profession as above, but not entering the cloister, whether she has been coerced or pressured and whether she knows what she is doing; and if he concludes that [she is acting] with fully free will and for pious [motives], then the aspirant can be admitted to the novitiate or the novice to profession.

Canon Law Digest
I: 300; VII: 510–11

Article 2—*On the formation of novices*

Canon 553 (NA)

The novitiate starts by taking up the habit or in another manner prescribed in the constitutions.

Canon Law Digest
I: 300; VI: 489; VII: 511–12

Canon 554 (1983 CIC 647, 651) Cross-Ref.: 1917 CIC 587

§ 1. A novitiate house is erected according to the norm of the constitution; but if it concerns a religious [institute] of pontifical right, the permission of the Apostolic See is necessary to erect it.

§ 2. Several novitiate houses in the same province, if the religious [institute] is divided into provinces, cannot be designated except for grave cause and with a special apostolic indult.

§ 3. Superiors shall not assign to the novitiate or house of studies any religious except those who are studious in their example of observance of the rule.

Canon Law Digest
III: 213; VI: 489; VIII: 359

Canon 555[20] (1983 CIC 643, 648) Cross-Ref.: 1917 CIC 572

§ 1. Beyond the other things that are enumerated in Canon 542 for the validity of the novitiate, the novitiate must, for validity, be conducted as follows:

1.° [It must not begin] before the completion of at least the fifteenth year of age;
2.° [It must] last for one integral and continuous year;
3.° [It must] be in the novitiate house.

§ 2. If a longer time for novitiate is prescribed in the constitutions, it is not necessary for validity of the novitiate, unless the contrary is expressly stated in the constitutions.

Canon Law Digest
I: 301; II: 166–67; VI: 489; VII: 512–14

Canon 556 (1983 CIC 647, 649)

§ 1. The novitiate is interrupted such that it must be begun anew and be completed if the novice, dismissed by the Superior, leaves the house, or if he deserts the house without permission, not [intending] to return, or [stays] outside the house, even if he will return, beyond thirty days, whether continuous or interrupted, for any reason, even with the permission of the Superior.

§ 2. If a novice, for more than fifteen days but not more than thirty days, even if interrupted, with the permission of the Superior, or [having been] coerced [while outside], stays outside the walls of house under obedience to the Superior, it is necessary for validity of the novitiate to make up for those days; if [the absence] is not beyond fifteen days, its replacement can [still] be prescribed by the Superior, but it is not necessary for validity.

§ 3. Superiors shall not give permission for staying outside the walls of the novitiate except for a just and grave cause.

[20] Ralph Balzer, "The Computation of Time in a Canonical Novitiate", Canon Law Studies, no. 212 (J. C. D. thesis, Catholic University of America, 1945).

§ 4. If a novice is transferred by a Superior to another novitiate house of the same religious [institute], the novitiate is not interrupted.

Canon Law Digest
I: 301; VI: 489; VII: 514

Canon 557 (NA)

The complete novitiate is to be conducted in the habit prescribed for novices by the constitutions, unless special circumstances of place require otherwise.

Canon Law Digest
VIII: 359

Canon 558 (NA)

In religious [institutes] in which there are two classes of members, a novitiate prescribed for one class is not valid for the other.

Canon Law Digest
I: 301; VI: 490

Canon 559[21] (1983 CIC 650–51) Cross-Ref.: 1917 CIC 588

§ 1. The Master who is to be over the instruction of novices shall be at least five and thirty years of age, at least ten years from first profession, conspicuous for prudence, charity, piety, and religious observance, and if it concerns a religious [institute] of clerics, one constituted in the priesthood.

§ 2. If it seems expedient because of the number of novices or for some other reason, an associate Master of novices shall be added subject immediately to him in those things that look to the governance of the novitiate, [and who is] at least thirty years of age, at least five years from first profession, and [being possessed of] other necessary and opportune qualities.

§ 3. Both shall be freed of all other offices and burdens that could impede the care and governance of the novices.

Canon Law Digest
I: 302; IV: 206; VII: 514; VIII: 360

Canon 560 (1983 CIC 651)

The Master of novices and his associate are selected according to the norms of the constitutions, and this task is for a prescribed time, [and]

[21] James Lover, "The Master of Novices", Canon Law Studies, no. 254 (thesis, Catholic University of America, 1947).

while it obtains, they shall not be removed without just and grave cause; but they can be selected again.

Canon 561 (1983 CIC 650, 652)

§ 1. The office of supervising the formation of novices belongs to the Master alone, and to him alone the governance of the novitiate looks, therefore it is not permitted to anyone, under any pretext, to immerse themselves in same, except Superiors who are so permitted in the constitutions and Visitators; but in what pertains to the discipline of the whole house, the Master, and indeed the novices, are liable to the Superior.

§ 2. A novice is under the authority of the Master and the religious Superior and is bound to obey them.

Canon 562 (1983 CIC 652)

The Master is bound by the grave obligation of conducting everything carefully so that the students, according to the constitutions, are sedulously brought along in religious discipline, according to the norm of Canon 565.

Canon 563 (1983 CIC 652)

During the novitiate year, the Master, according to the norm of the constitutions, shall offer and report on the progress of each student to the Chapter or major Superior.

Canon 564 (1983 CIC 652)

§ 1. The novitiate should be in a separate part of the house, if this is possible, from where the professed live, so that, without special cause and permission of the Superior or Master, the novices will have no communication with the professed, nor these with the novices.

§ 2. Lay brothers should be assigned a separate space in the novitiate.

Canon Law Digest
I: 302; VI: 490; VIII: 360

Canon 565 (1983 CIC 652) Cross-Refs.: 1917 CIC 509, 562

§ 1. The novitiate year must be passed under the discipline of the Master [and be] so designed that the soul of the student is informed by study of the rule and constitution, by pious meditations and assiduous prayer, learning deeply those things that pertain to vows and virtue, by opportune exercises ridding himself of the roots and seeds of vice, [learning] to control emotions, and acquiring virtue.

§ 2. Lay brothers should be diligently instructed in Christian doctrine by special conferences had for them at least once a week.

§ 3. The novitiate year is not to be burdened with having [to give] sermons, hearing confessions, or [doing] external works of religion, nor [should it] be dedicated to studying works of literature, science, or the arts; lay brothers in a religious house may perform those duties of lay brothers (but not as the primary officials thereof) insofar as they do not interfere with the exercises constituted during novitiate for them.

Canon Law Digest
I: 302–4; VI: 490

Canon 566 (NA)

§ 1. Concerning the priest [who serves] as a confessor in a novitiate of women, the prescriptions of Canons 520–27 are observed.

§ 2. In religious [institutes] of men, with due regard for the prescription of Canon 519:

1.° There shall be one or several ordinary confessors given the number of novices, with due regard for the prescription of Canon 891;

2.° Ordinary confessors, if it concerns a clerical religious [institute], shall stay in the novitiate house itself; if [it concerns] laity, they shall at least frequently go to the novitiate house in order to hear the confession of the novices;

3.° Besides ordinary confessors there shall be designated other confessors to whom the novices can freely go in particular cases, nor shall the Master show himself to be upset by this;

4.° At least four times a year an extraordinary confessor will be given to the novices to whom all must appear at least to receive a blessing.

Canon 567 (NA)

§ 1. Novices enjoy all of the privileges and spiritual favors granted to the religious [institute]; and if death intervenes, they have the right to those suffrages that are prescribed for the professed.

§ 2. During the novitiate they shall not be promoted to orders.

Canon Law Digest
I: 304

Canon 568 (NA)

In the course of the novitiate, if a novice renounces his benefices or goods in any manner or encumbers [them], the renunciation or obligation is not only illicit, but by the law it is invalid.

Canon 569[22] (NA) Cross-Refs.: 1917 CIC 580, 583

§ 1. Before profession of simple vows, whether temporary or perpetual, a novice must for the whole time in which he is bound by simple vows cede the administration of his goods to whomever he wishes, and, unless the constitutions provide otherwise, he freely disposes of their use and fruit.

§ 2. If this cession or disposition was omitted because of a lack of goods and later [the novice] comes into property, or if it was done and [the novice] later obtained goods by another title, [the cession or disposition] shall be repeated according to the norm established in § 1 notwithstanding having given simple profession.

§ 3. A novice in a religious Congregation before profession of temporary vows shall freely produce a will concerning present goods and those perhaps to be acquired.

Canon Law Digest

I: 304–5; II: 167; III: 213; V: 378–80; VII: 514; VIII: 360; IX: 372–73

Canon 570 (NA) Cross-Refs.: 1917 CIC 551, 635

§ 1. Nothing for the expenses of postulancy or novitiate can be required except for food and the religious habit that in the constitutions or in express contract has been indicated will be owed upon entering postulancy or the novitiate.

§ 2. Whatever the aspirant brought and has not consumed by use shall be restored to him if he leaves the religious [institute] without having given profession.

Canon 571 (1983 CIC 653) Cross-Ref.: 1917 CIC 2411

§ 1. A novice can freely leave a religious [institute] or be dismissed for just cause by the Superiors or by the Chapter according to the constitutions, but the Superior or Chapter is not bound to disclose to the one dismissed the reason for dismissal.

---

[22] Kevin Rourke, "The Cession of Administration of Property and the Disposition of Use and Usufruct of Property" (diss. no. 13, Pontifical University of St. Thomas [Rome], 1957–1958).

§ 2. The novitiate being completed, if he is judged suitable, a novice is admitted to profession; otherwise he is dismissed; if doubt remains about whether he is suitable, the major Superior can extend the time of probation, but not beyond six months.

§ 3. The novice shall undergo for at least eight solid days spiritual exercises [concerning] the vows to be pronounced.

Canon Law Digest
I: 305; VII: 514; VIII: 360

Chapter 3
On religious profession

Canon 572[23] (1983 CIC 656, 658)

§ 1. For the validity of any religious profession it is required that:

1.° The one who is to give it must have the legitimate age according to the norm of Canon 573;

2.° The legitimate Superior according to the constitutions admits him to profession;

3.° A valid novitiate according to the norm of Canon 555 will have preceded;

4.° The profession be given without force or grave fear or dolus;

5.° It be express;

6.° It be received by the legitimate Superior according to the constitutions personally or through another.

§ 2. But for the validity of perpetual profession, whether solemn or simple, there is also required that a simple temporary profession according to the norm of Canon 574 will have preceded.

Canon Law Digest
I: 305–8; VII: 514–15; VIII: 361–64; IX: 373–74

[23] Wolfgang Frey, "The Act of Religious Profession", Canon Law Studies, no. 63 (J. C. D. thesis, Catholic University of America, 1931); Christopher Yeo, "The Structure and Content of Monastic Profession: A Juridical Study, with Particular Regard to the Practice of the English Benedictine Congregation since the French Revolution" (thesis, Gregorian University; printed version, no. 3046, 1982).

Canon 573 (1983 CIC 656, 658) Cross-Ref.: 1917 CIC 572

Whoever will give a religious profession must have completed sixteen years of age if it concerns temporary profession; twenty-one years [of age] if [it concerns] perpetual [vows].

Canon Law Digest
I: 308

Canon 574 (1983 CIC 655, 657) Cross-Refs.: 1917 CIC 572, 578, 634, 964

§ 1. In any Order, whether of men or of women, and in any Congregation that has perpetual vows, after completion of the novitiate, a novice must in the same novitiate house give perpetual vows, whether solemn or simple, with due regard for the prescription of Canon 634, [after] three years of experiencing the profession of simple vows, or for a longer time if the required age for perpetual profession is further off, unless the constitutions require annual profession.

§ 2. The legitimate Superior can extend this time, with the temporary profession having been renewed by the religious, but not beyond another three years.

Canon Law Digest
I: 308–10; III: 213–15; V: 381–82; VI: 490–91; VIII: 364–65; IX: 374

Canon 575[24] (1983 CIC 656–58, 688)

§ 1. Upon completion of the time for temporary profession, a religious, according to the norm of Canon 637, either gives perpetual profession, whether solemn or simple, according to the constitutions, or returns to the world; but even during the time of temporary profession, he can, if he is not considered worthy of pronouncing perpetual vows, be dismissed by the legitimate Superior according to the norm of Canon 647.

§ 2. The vote of the Council or Chapter for the time of first profession is deliberative; for subsequent perpetual profession, whether solemn or simple, it is only consultative.

Canon Law Digest
I: 310; VII: 515; VIII: 365; IX: 375

[24] Leonard Voegtle, "Canonical Reasons for the Rejection of Candidates to Final Vows", Canon Law Studies, no. 435 (J. C. D. thesis, Catholic University of America, 1963).

Canon 576 (NA)

§ 1. In giving religious profession, the rite prescribed in the constitutions is observed.

§ 2. The document of profession [being] given, it is signed by the one professed and at least by him in whose presence the profession was given out, [and] it is preserved in the archives of the religious [institute]; and moreover if it concerns solemn profession, the Superior accepting it must notify the pastor of baptism about it according to the norm of Canon 470, § 2.

Canon Law Digest

I: 310; III: 215; VII: 515–26; VIII: 365–66; IX: 376

Canon 577 (1983 CIC 657)

§ 1. The time having elapsed for the giving of vows, their renovation must suffer no delay.

§ 2. Nevertheless, Superiors have the faculty for a just cause of permitting that the renewal of temporary vows for a specific time be anticipated, but not beyond one month.

Canon 578 (NA)

Those professed with the temporary vows mentioned in Canon 574:

1.° Enjoy those indulgences, privileges, and spiritual favors that those professed by solemn vows or professed by simple perpetual vows enjoy; and if death intervenes they have the same right to suffrages;

2.° They are bound by the same obligation of observing the rules and constitutions, but where the obligation of choir is in force, they are not bound by the law of privately reciting the divine offices, unless they are constituted in sacred [orders] or the constitutions expressly prescribe otherwise;

3.° They lack active and passive voice, unless something else is expressly provided in the constitutions; but the time prescribed to participate with an active and passive voice, with the constitutions being silent, is counted from first profession.

Canon Law Digest

I: 310; VII: 526–27; VIII: 367–69; IX: 376

Canon 579 (1983 CIC 1088)

Simple profession, whether it is temporary or perpetual, renders illicit, but not invalid, acts that are contrary to the vows, unless something else is expressly provided; [but with] solemn profession, if they are subject to invalidity, they are also invalid.

Canon Law Digest
VIII: 369–70

Canon 580[25] (NA) Cross-Ref.: 1917 CIC 594

§ 1. Anyone professed by simple vows, whether perpetual or temporary, unless otherwise provided in the constitutions, maintains proprietary rights over his goods and the capacity of acquiring other goods, except for those that are prescribed in Canon 569.

§ 2. Whatever he acquires by effort or by reason of the religious [institute], he acquires for the religious [institute].

§ 3. A professed can change the cession or disposition [of goods] mentioned in Canon 569, § 2, but not by his own judgment, unless the constitutions allow it, but with the permission of the supreme Moderator or, if it concerns nuns, with the permission of the local Ordinary and, if a monastery is subject to regulars, [of] the regular Superior, providing the change of at least a notable part of the goods is not done in favor of the religious [institute]; and upon leaving the religious [institute], a cession or disposition of this sort has no force.

Canon Law Digest
I: 311; II: 167; VII: 527; VIII: 371–72; IX: 377–78

Canon 581 (NA)

§ 1. One professed by simple vows cannot validly before, but within sixty days before solemn profession must, renounce all goods that he actually has, in favor of whomever he wants, subject to the condition of profession [actually] following, with due regard for any particular indults granted by the Holy See.

---

[25] Adalbertus Mayr, "Peculium in Ecclesiastical Legislation as Applied to Congregations with Simple Vows" (diss. no. 28, Pontifical University of St. Thomas [Rome], 1956–1957).

§ 2. Upon profession, everything that is necessary for the renunciation to have effect in civil law must be done immediately.

Canon Law Digest
VI: 491; VIII: 372; IX: 378

Canon 582 (NA) Cross-Refs.: 1917 CIC 594, 628

After solemn profession, and with equal regard for specific indults of the Apostolic See, [regarding] all goods that regulars receive in any way:

1.° In Orders capable of possessing, [regulars] shall cede it to the Order or the province, or to the house according to the constitutions;
2.° In Orders not capable [of possessing], property is acquired by the Holy See.

Canon Law Digest
I: 311–12

Canon 583 (NA)

Those professed by simple vows in religious Congregations are not permitted:

1.° To abdicate by an act between living persons ownership of their goods gratuitously;
2.° To alter the testament designed according to the norm of Canon 569, § 3, without permission of the Holy See or, if the matter is urgent and there is not time for recourse there, without the permission of the major Superior or, if he cannot be reached, [that of the] local [Superior].

Canon Law Digest
III: 215; V: 382; VI: 491; VIII: 373

Canon 584 (NA) Cross-Refs.: 1917 CIC 188, 1484

After one year from making any religious profession, parochial benefices vacate; after three years, the others [vacate].

Canon Law Digest
II: 167–70

Canon 585 (NA) Cross-Refs.: 1917 CIC 115, 641

One professed by perpetual vows, whether solemn or simple, loses by law his own diocese that he had as a secular.

Canon 586 (NA)

§ 1. A religious profession null because of an external impediment does not become valid through a subsequent act, but it is for the Apostolic See to sanate it or it be legitimately given again upon awareness of the nullity and the removal of the impediment.

§ 2. But if it was null because of a merely internal defect of consent, it becomes valid by giving it, provided consent has not been revoked on the part of the religious.

§ 3. If there are grave arguments against the validity of religious profession and the religious refuses as a precaution either to renew profession or to seek sanation of it, the matter is to be referred to the Apostolic See.

TITLE 12
On the course of studies in clerical religious [institutes]

Canon 587 (1983 CIC 659)

§ 1. Every clerical religious [institute] shall have a seat of studies approved by the general Chapter or by the Superiors with due regard for the prescription of Canon 554, § 3.

§ 2. In the house of studies, the common life applies without exception; otherwise the students cannot be promoted to orders.

§ 3. If a religious [institute] or a province cannot have a house of studies duly instructed or, if it has one, if it is difficult in the judgment of the Superiors to go there, the religious students are sent either to a house of studies correctly arranged of another province or religious [institute], or to the schools of the episcopal Seminary, or to a public Catholic athenaeum.

§ 4. Religious who, for the sake of studies, are sent a long way from their own places are not permitted to live in private houses, but must be received in some religious house of their institute or, if this is not possible, [that of] some religious institute of men, or in another Seminary or pious house in which men in sacred orders are present and which has been approved by ecclesiastical authority.

Canon Law Digest
I: 312–13; V: 383; VI: 491; VII: 527

Canon 588[26] (1983 CIC 659)

§ 1. For the entire course of studies, religious [students] are to be entrusted to the special care of a spiritual Prefect or Master who will inform their souls about the religious life through opportune admonitions, instructions, and exhortations.

§ 2. The spiritual Prefect or Master must be endowed with those qualities that are required of the Master of novices according to the norm of Canon 559, §§ 2 and 3.

§ 3. Superiors will be sedulously vigilant that all those things that are prescribed for religious under Canon 595 are most perfectly observed in the house of studies.

Canon Law Digest
I: 313

Canon 589 (1983 CIC 659)

§ 1. Religious correctly instructed in lower disciplines shall diligently pursue philosophical studies for at least two years and sacred theology for at least four years, adhering to the teachings of D[om] Thomas according to the norm of Canon 1366, § 2, according to the instructions of the Apostolic See.

§ 2. During the time of studies, offices shall not be imposed on teachers or students that would call them [away] from studies or in any manner impede them; but the supreme Moderator and in particular cases other Superiors can, in their own prudent judgment, exempt them from some community activities, even from choir, especially during the nighttime hours, as often as this seems necessary to the pursuit of studies.

Canon Law Digest
I: 313; III: 215; VIII: 374; IX: 379

Canon 590 (1983 CIC 659, 661)

Religious priests, excepting only those who are exempt for a grave cause by the major Superiors, or who teach sacred theology, canon law, or scholastic philosophy, after the completion of their course of studies each year,

---

[26] Nicholas Gill, "The Spiritual Prefect in Clerical Religious Houses of Study", Canon Law Studies, no. 216 (J. C. D. thesis, Catholic University of America, 1945); Cornelius Breed, "The Juridical Figure of the Spiritual Director in Ecclesiastical Seminaries" (thesis, Gregorian University; printed version, no. 910, Tilburg, The Netherlands, 1955).

for at least five years, are to be examined by grave teaching fathers in the various disciplines of sacred doctrine opportunely indicated beforehand.

Canon Law Digest
I: 314

Canon 591 (1983 CIC 659, 661)

At least in every formal house, a minimum of once a month, there shall be the resolution of a moral or a liturgical case to which, if the Superior thinks it opportune, there can be added a lecture on a related dogmatic doctrine; and all professed clerics who are then in sacred theology studies or who have completed them and are in the house are bound to attend, unless the constitutions provide otherwise.

TITLE 13
On the obligations and privileges of religious

Chapter 1
On obligations

Canon 592 (1983 CIC 672, 699)

All religious are also bound by the common obligations of clerics mentioned in Canons 124–42, unless from the context of the words or the nature of the thing something else is established.

Canon Law Digest
III: 216; V: 383; VIII: 374; IX: 379–410

Canon 593 (1983 CIC 662)

Each and every religious Superior as well as subjects must not only preserve the vows that they pronounced faithfully and completely, but also arrange their life according to the rules and constitutions of their own religious [institute] and strive for perfection in their state.

Canon Law Digest
III: 217–19; VI: 491–94; VII: 528; VIII: 374–85;
IX: 410–31; X: 114–18

Canon 594 (1983 CIC 668)

§ 1. In the common life of each religious [institute] there shall be accurately observed by all those things that pertain to food, dress, and furnishings.

§ 2. Whatever is acquired by a religious, even by a Superior according to the norm of Canons 580, § 2, and 582, n. 1, is mixed with the goods of the house, province, or religious [institute], and every sort of money under *title* is to be deposited in the common safe.

§ 3. The furniture of religious must be consistent with the poverty they have professed.

Canon Law Digest
IV: 206–10; VI: 494; VII: 529–31; VIII: 385; IX: 431

Canon 595 (1983 CIC 663) Cross-Ref.: 1917 CIC 588

§ 1. Let Superiors take care that all religious:

1.° Undergo spiritual exercises each year;

2.° Be present for Sacred [rites] each day, [if] they are not legitimately impeded, leave room for mental prayer, and apply themselves diligently in other offices of piety that are prescribed by the rule and constitutions;

3.° Approach the sacrament of penance at least once a week.

§ 2. Superiors shall promote among their subjects frequent and even daily reception of the most holy Body of Christ; rightly disposed religious shall be freely [allowed] frequent and indeed even daily access to the most holy Eucharist.

§ 3. But if after the last sacramental confession a religious of the community gravely scandalizes [it] or commits a grave and external fault, then until he can approach the sacrament of penance again the Superior can prohibit him lest he approach holy communion.

§ 4. If there are any religious [institutes], whether of solemn or simple vows, that have certain days fixed in the rule or constitutions or even in the community calendar [for reception of the Eucharist], these norms have only directive force.

Canon Law Digest
I: 314; VI: 494; VII: 531–33; VIII: 385; IX: 431–32

Canon 596 (1983 CIC 669)

All religious must wear the habit of their religious [institute] both inside and outside of the house, unless grave cause excuses, [to be assessed] in urgent necessity according to the judgment of the Superior, even a local one.

Canon Law Digest
IV: 210; V: 383; VI: 494; VII: 534–35;
VIII: 385–89; IX: 432–37; X: 118

Canon 597[27] (1983 CIC 667)

§ 1. In canonically erected houses of regulars, whether of men or women, even if not formal [houses], papal cloister is observed.

§ 2. The law of papal cloister affects the entire house that the community of regulars inhabit, with gardens and green areas reserved for the exclusive access of the religious; excluding however, a public [church] with its contained sacristy, and also a hospice for travelers, if there is one, or a conversation room that, if possible, must be established near the entrance to the house.

§ 3. Parts of the cloister subject to law should be clearly indicated; but the major Superior or general Chapter, according to the constitutions, or if it concerns a monastery of nuns, the Bishop, shall define the limits of the cloister and for just cause can change them.

Canon Law Digest
I: 314; VII: 535–36; IX: 437

Canon 598 (1983 CIC 667) Cross-Ref.: 1917 CIC 604

§ 1. Women of any age, sort, or condition are not to be admitted into the cloister of regular men on any pretext.

§ 2. Exempted from this law are the wives of those who hold the supreme place of governance over a people, along with their entourage.

Canon Law Digest
III: 220

Canon 599 (1983 CIC 667) Cross-Ref.: 1917 CIC 604

§ 1. If a house of regular men has attached to it a residence for internal students or for other works of religion, if it is possible, there should be a separate part of the building reserved habitually for the religious, subject to the law of cloister.

[27] Valentine Schaaf, "The Cloister", Canon Law Studies, no. 13 (J. C. D. thesis, Catholic University of America, 1921); R. Cain, "The Influence of the Cloister on the Apostolate of Congregations of Religious Women" (Pontifical Lateran University, 1965).

§ 2. Persons of the opposite sex are not to be admitted without adequate cause and permission of the Superior, even to a place outside of cloister or one reserved for external and internal students or for other religious works of that [institute].

Canon 600 (1983 CIC 667) Cross-Ref.: 1917 CIC 604

No one, of any sort, condition, sex, or age can be admitted into the cloister of nuns without the permission of the Holy See, except the following persons:

1.° The local Ordinary or regular Superior visiting a monastery of nuns or other Visitators delegated by them [who] may go in only for the sake of inspection, being cautious that at least one cleric or male religious of mature age come along with him;

2.° A confessor or one who acts in his place, with due precautions about entering the cloister, to minister the Sacraments to the infirm or to assist the dying;

3.° They can enter the cloister who hold the supreme place of governance over a people and their wives with their entourage; likewise Cardinals of the H. R. C.;

4.° Superioresses can permit, due precautions being taken, physicians, surgeons, and others who are necessary to enter the cloister, having sought at least the habitual permission of the local Ordinary beforehand; but if necessity urges and there is not time for such requests, it is presumed in the law.

Canon Law Digest
I: 314–20; II: 170–72; III: 220–53; IV: 210–37; V: 383–93; VI: 495–500; VII: 536–45; VIII: 390–409; IX: 437–45

Canon 601 (1983 CIC 667) Cross-Ref.: 1917 CIC 2342

§ 1. No nun is permitted to leave the monastery after profession, even for a brief time, on any pretext, without a special indult of the Holy See, except in case of imminent danger of death or some other evil of the worst sort.

§ 2. This danger, if there is time, should be recognized in writing by the local Ordinary.

Canon Law Digest
VI: 501; VIII: 409

Canon 602 (1983 CIC 667)

The cloister of monasteries of nuns must be closed so that, to the extent possible, no one in it or from it [has] an external view of persons.

Canon Law Digest
V: 393; VII: 545–46

Canon 603 (1983 CIC 667)

§ 1. The cloister of nuns, even those subject to regulars, is under the vigilance of the local Ordinary, who can correct and coerce offenders, male regulars not excepted, with penalties and even censures.

§ 2. Care of the cloister of nuns subject to him is committed also to the regular Superior, who can punish nuns and others of his subjects if they offend in that regard, even with penalties.

Canon Law Digest
I: 320

Canon 604 (1983 CIC 667)

§ 1. Cloister shall be observed in the houses even of religious Congregations, whether of pontifical or diocesan [right], into which no one of the other sex shall be admitted except those mentioned in Canon 598, § 2, and Canon 600 and those others who for a just and reasonable cause the Superiors think can be admitted.

§ 2. The prescription of Canon 599 is applied even in the house of a Congregation of religious, whether of men or of women.

§ 3. The Bishop in particular circumstances, grave causes appearing, can enforce this cloister with censures, unless it concerns exempt clerical religious; he shall always take care that it is rightly observed and will correct anything that tends to weaken it.

Canon Law Digest
VII: 546; VIII: 409; IX: 446

Canon 605 (1983 CIC 667)

All those who have care of the cloister shall be sedulously vigilant lest outside visitors, by useless conversation, disturb the discipline and bring about harm to the religious spirit.

Canon 606 (NA)

§ 1. Let religious Superiors accurately observe [matters] prescribed in their own constitutions regarding the departure of their subjects from the cloister and about the receiving and admitting of strangers.

§ 2. It is nefarious for Superiors, with due regard for the prescriptions of Canons 621–24, to permit subjects to spend time outside their own religious house except for grave and just cause and for a period that must be brief according to the constitutions; but for an absence that exceeds six months, except for the case of studies, the permission of the Apostolic See is required.

Canon Law Digest
IV: 237–38; VI: 501; VIII: 410–14; IX: 446–52

Canon 607[28] (1983 CIC 665)

Superioresses and local Ordinaries shall be very vigilant lest religious, outside of the case of necessity, be present individually outside the house.

Canon Law Digest
VII: 546

Canon 608[29] (1983 CIC 675)

§ 1. Let Superiors take care that religious subjects, designated by them, especially in the diocese in which they are present, freely offer themselves whenever they are required for ministry by the local Ordinary and their pastor for the necessary care of the people, whether within or outside of their own churches or public oratories, with due regard for religious discipline.

§ 2. Local Ordinaries and pastors, in return, may freely make use of the works of religious, especially those present in the diocese, in sacred ministry and especially in the administration of sacramental penance.

Canon Law Digest
VI: 501

---

[28] Aloysius Gaffigan, "Residence of Religious", Canon Law Studies, no. 322 (Catholic University of America, not published); Francis Orsini, "The Common Life in Religious Institutes, in Societies of the Common Life, and in Secular Institutes" (Pontifical Lateran University, 1950).

[29] David O'Connor, "Parochial Relations and Co-operation of the Religious and the Secular Clergy", Canon Law Studies, no. 401 (thesis, Catholic University of America, 1958).

Canon 609 (NA) Cross-Ref.: 1917 CIC 1171

§ 1. If a church within which a religious community resides is also parochial, there shall be observed, due adaptation being made, the prescription of Canon 415.

§ 2. A parochial [church] cannot be erected into a church of religious women, whether of simple or solemn vows.

§ 3. Superiors shall be vigilant lest the celebration of divine offices in their own churches offer harm to catechetical instruction or to the explanation of the Gospels given in parochial churches; it pertains to the local Ordinary to decide whether there is harm or not.

Canon Law Digest
VIII: 414

Canon 610[30] (1983 CIC 663)

§ 1. In religious [institutes], whether of men or of women, in which there is an obligation of choir and in which there are at least four religious obligated to choir and who are not impeded from legitimately acting, or even fewer if the constitutions so direct, the divine office must be performed daily in community according to the norm of the constitutions.

§ 2. Also the Mass corresponding to the office of the day must be celebrated according to the rubrics of the day in religious [institutes] of men and even, where it is possible, in religious [institutes] of women.

§ 3. In the same religious [institutes], whether of men or of women, those who are solemnly professed who are absent from choir must, except for lay brothers, privately recite the canonical hours.

Canon Law Digest
I: 320–21; III: 253; V: 394; VI: 501–5; VII: 546–52

Canon 611 (NA)

All religious, whether men or women, can send letters, subject to no inspection, to the Holy See and to its Legate in each nation, to the Cardinal Protector, to their own major Superiors, and to the Superior of a house perhaps absent, to the local Ordinary to whom they are subject, if it concerns nuns who are under the jurisdiction of regulars, and even to

[30] Bernard Siegle, "Choral Obligation of Religious" (diss. no. 15, Pontifical University of St. Thomas [Rome], 1951–1952).

the major Superior of Orders; and from all of these the aforesaid religious, men and women, can receive letters, which can be inspected by no one.

Canon Law Digest
II: 172; III: 253; VIII: 414

Canon 612 (1983 CIC 678)

Beyond the prescription of Canon 1345, if the local Ordinary for some public cause orders the ringing of bells, certain prayers, or sacred solemnities, all religious, even exempt, are bound to obey, with due regard for the constitutions and privileges of each religious [institute].

Chapter 2
On privileges

Canon 613 (NA)

§ 1. Every religious [institute] enjoys only those privileges that are contained in this Code, or that have been directly granted to it by the Apostolic See, exclusive of any communication in the future.

§ 2. The privileges that are enjoyed by an Order of regulars apply also to nuns of the same Order, insofar as they are capable of them.

Canon Law Digest
II: 172–73; VI: 505

Canon 614 (NA) Cross-Ref.: 1917 CIC 1553

Religious, even laity and novices, enjoy the clerical privileges mentioned in Canons 119–23.

Canon Law Digest
I: 321

Canon 615 (1983 CIC 591)

Religious, not excluding novices, whether men or women, with their houses and churches, excepting those nuns who are not subject to regular Superiors, are exempt from the jurisdiction of the local Ordinary, except in those cases expressed in law.

Canon Law Digest
I: 321–22; III: 253; V: 394; VI: 505; VII: 552; VIII: 415; IX: 452

Canon 616 (NA)

§ 1. Regulars illegitimately present outside the house, even under pretext of approaching Superiors, do not enjoy the privilege of exemption.

§ 2. If they commit a delict outside the house but are not punished by a Superior with notice of it, they can be punished by the local Ordinary even if they left the house legitimately and returned to it.

Canon 617 (1983 CIC 679, 683)

§ 1. If abuses occur in the houses or churches of exempt religious or other regulars, and the Superiors with notice fail to look into it, the local Ordinary is bound by the obligation of deferring the matter immediately to the Apostolic See.

§ 2. A non-formal house remains under the special vigilance of the local Ordinary [who], if abuses occur and give scandal to the faithful, can provide for the matter himself in the meantime.

Canon 618 (1983 CIC 583, 586) Cross-Ref.: 1917 CIC 512

§ 1. Religious in simple vows do not enjoy the privilege of exemption, unless it has been specially granted them.

§ 2. The local Ordinary is not permitted, in regard to religious [institutes] of pontifical right:

1.° To change in any way their constitutions or to act in economic affairs, with due regard for the prescription of Canons 533–35;

2.° To involve himself in the internal governance and discipline, except in those cases provided by law; nevertheless, in regard to lay religious [institutes], he can and must inquire as to whether discipline is in force according to the constitutions, or whether anything detrimental to sound doctrine and approved morals has started, whether there have been any sins against cloister, whether the Sacraments are duly and frequently taken; and if Superiors, advised about perhaps grave abuses, do not provide [for the matter] opportunely, he shall deal with it himself; but if, however, something of greater moment occurs that will allow no delay, he shall decide it immediately; and he shall send a decree to the Holy See immediately.

Canon Law Digest
II: 173; V: 394; IX: 453

Canon 619[31] (1983 CIC 1320)

In all things in which religious are subject to the local Ordinary, they can be coerced by him even with penalties.

Canon 620 (NA)

By indult legitimately granted by the local Ordinary, the obligation of common law ceases also for all religious living in the diocese, with due regard for vows and constitutions proper to each religious [institute].

Canon 621 (NA) Cross-Refs.: 1917 CIC 606, 1503

§ 1. Regulars who by institute are called and are mendicants can make requests for alms in a diocese where their religious house is constituted with only the permission of their Superior; but outside the diocese, they need the permission given in writing of the local Ordinary where they desire to take up the alms.

§ 2. Local Ordinaries, especially of bordering dioceses, shall not deny or revoke this permission, except for grave and urgent cause, if the religious house in the one diocese in which it is constituted cannot survive any other way.

Canon Law Digest
I: 323; VII: 553–54; VIII: 415–21

Canon 622 (NA) Cross-Refs.: 1917 CIC 606, 1503

§ 1. All other religious of Congregations of pontifical right, without a special privilege of the Holy See, are prohibited from seeking stipends; and for which, if they seek this privilege, they are also required to seek the permission of the local Ordinary in writing, unless otherwise provided in the [pontifical] privilege itself.

§ 2. Religious of Congregations of diocesan right may never seek stipends without the written permission given by the Ordinary of the place in which the house is situated and [from] the Ordinary of the place where they desire to seek the stipends.

[31] Mariner Smith, "The Penal Law for Religious", Canon Law Studies, no. 98 (J. C. D. thesis, Catholic University of America, 1935).

§ 3. To those religious mentioned in §§ 1 and 2 of this canon, the local Ordinary shall not grant permission for requesting stipends especially in places where there are convents of regulars who go by the name of and are mendicants, unless it has been shown that there is true need in the house or for pious works, which cannot be satisfied in any other way; and if this necessity can be provided by requesting stipends within a place or district or diocese in which they are [already located], this permission shall not be expanded.

§ 4. Without an authentic and recent rescript of the Sacred Congregation for the Oriental Church, latin Ordinaries shall not allow orientals of any order or dignity to collect money in their diocese or send their subjects for this purpose into an oriental diocese.

Canon Law Digest
I: 323; II: 173; III: 254–56; VI: 505

Canon 623 (NA) Cross-Refs.: 1917 CIC 606, 1503

It is not permitted for a religious Superior to commit the collection of [offerings] to anyone other than a professed [member of the institute who is] of mature age and spirit, especially in the case of women, and never to those who are in studies.

Canon 624 (NA) Cross-Refs.: 1917 CIC 606, 1503

As to what applies to the manner of seeking [offerings] and the manner of keeping those [offerings] collected, religious of either sex must stand by the instructions given by the Apostolic See concerning this.

Canon 625 (NA)

Regular abbots of government, legitimately elected, must within three months of the election take a blessing from the Bishop of the diocese in which the monastery is located; after they have received the blessing, besides the power of conferring orders according to the norm of Canon 964, n. 1, they enjoy those privileges mentioned in Canon 325, except for [wearing] the violet cap.

Canon Law Digest
I: 323; VII: 554–55

Chapter 3

On the obligations and privileges of religious promoted to ecclesiastical dignity or governance of a parish

Canon 626 (1983 CIC 671)

§ 1. A religious cannot, without the authority of the Apostolic See, be promoted to dignities, offices, or benefices that are not compatible with the religious state.

§ 2. One legitimately elected by a college cannot assent to the election without the permission of the Superior.

§ 3. If by vow he is bound not to accept dignities, special dispensation from the Roman Pontiff is necessary.

Canon 627[32] (1983 CIC 705)

§ 1. A religious named as a Cardinal or Bishop, whether residential or titular, remains a religious participating in the privileges of his religious [institute] and is bound by the vows and other obligations of his profession, except for those things that he prudently judges to be incompatible with his dignity, with due regard for the prescription of Canon 628.

§ 2. He is exempt, nevertheless, from the power of the Superior and, in virtue of his vow of obedience, remains subject only to the Roman Pontiff.

Canon Law Digest
III: 256

Canon 628 (1983 CIC 706) Cross-Ref.: 1917 CIC 627

[Regarding] a religious raised to episcopal dignity or to another [dignity] outside his own religious [institute]:

1.° If by profession he lost the ownership of goods, for those goods that come to him, he has the use and the income and the administration of them; but a residential Bishop, Vicar Apostolic, or Prefect Apostolic acquires property for the diocese, vicariate or prefecture; otherwise it goes to the order or to the Holy See according to the norm of Canon 582 with due regard for the prescription of Canon 239, § 1, n. 19;

[32]Joseph Marositz, "Obligations and Privileges of Religious Promoted to the Episcopal or Cardinalitial Dignities", Canon Law Studies, no. 256 (thesis, Catholic University of America, 1948).

2.° If by profession he has not lost ownership of goods, the goods that he has he recovers in regard to their use, income, and administration; those that he obtains later he acquires fully for himself;

3.° In either case, those goods that come to him not by reason of his person must be disposed of as voluntary offerings.

Canon 629 (1983 CIC 707)

§ 1. Once dismissed from the cardinalate or episcopate, or having completed his duties outside the religious [institute] that were committed to him by the Apostolic See, a religious is bound to return to his religious [institute].

§ 2. A religious Bishop or Cardinal, however, can choose whatever religious house for himself to stay in; but he lacks active and passive voice.

Canon Law Digest
IX: 453

Canon 630[33] (NA)

§ 1. A religious who governs a parish, whether under the title of pastor or the title of vicar, remains obligated to the observance of vows and constitution insofar as this observation can be done consistently with the responsibilities of his office.

§ 2. Therefore, in those things that pertain to religious discipline, he is under the Superior to whom belongs, indeed, without regard to the local Ordinary, [the authority] to inquire of him about his manner of acting in all things and, if the case requires, to correct him.

§ 3. Goods that come to him by reason of the parish that he governs are acquired by the parish; the others he acquires in the manner of other religious.

§ 4. Notwithstanding the vow of poverty, he may accept and collect donations for parish goods or for Catholic schools or for pious places attached to the parish offered in whatever manner and administer the collected receipts, and likewise, observing the will of the donors, according to his prudent judgment, distribute them always with regard for the vigilance of his Superior; but with regard to donations for building, conserving, repairing, and decoration of the parish church, it belongs to Superiors to retain them-

[33] Benedict Velikkathu, "The Administration of Temporal Goods of Parishes Governed by Religious" (Pontifical Oriental Institute, 1966).

selves and collect or administer [such funds] if the church belongs to a religious community; otherwise [it belongs to] the local Ordinary.

Canon Law Digest
I: 324; IX: 453

Canon 631 (1983 CIC 681–82) Cross-Ref.: 1917 CIC 1425

§ 1. Likewise a religious pastor or vicar, even though he exercises ministry in the house or place where the major religious Superiors have their ordinary seat, remains immediately and in every way under the jurisdiction, visitation, and correction of the local Ordinary, not unlike secular pastors, excepting only the observance of the rule.

§ 2. The local Ordinary, when he finds him deficient in his duty, can apply opportune decrees and can establish deserved penalties on him; in which, nevertheless, the faculties of the Ordinary are not lost, but rather they are cumulative with the right of the Superior over him so that, if it requires discernment either by the Superior or by the Ordinary, the decree of the Ordinary must prevail.

§ 3. In what pertains to the removal of a religious pastor or vicar from a parish, the prescription of Canon 454, § 5, is observed; and for what [pertains] to temporal goods, the prescription of Canons 533, § 1, n. 4, and 535, § 3, n. 2 [are observed].

Canon Law Digest
I: 324

TITLE 14
On transfer to another religious [institute][34]

Canon 632 (1983 CIC 684) Cross-Ref.: 1917 CIC 681

A religious cannot transfer to another religious [institute], even a stricter one, or to a monastery of its own right without the authority of the Apostolic See.

Canon Law Digest
I: 324–25; III: 256–57; VI: 506; IX: 454–55; X: 119–20

[34] Joseph Konrad, "The Transfer of Religious to Another Community", Canon Law Studies, no. 278 (thesis, Catholic University of America, 1949).

Canon 633 (1983 CIC 684–85) Cross-Ref.: 1917 CIC 681

§ 1. One transferring to another religious [institute] must perform the novitiate; during which his vows remain, [but] special rights and obligations that he had in the former religious [institute] remain suspended, and he is bound by the obligation of complying with the Superiors of the new religious [institute] and their Master of novices also in virtue of the vow of obedience.

§ 2. If he does not make profession in the religious [institute] to which he is transferring, he is bound to return to the first religious [institute], unless in the meantime temporary vows expired.

§ 3. One transferring to another monastery of the same Order does not undergo novitiate or make a new profession.

Canon Law Digest
I: 325; VII: 555–56; IX: 455

Canon 634 (1983 CIC 684) Cross-Refs.: 1917 CIC 574, 681

One professed solemnly or professed by simple, perpetual vows, if he transfers to another religious [institute] with solemn vows or simple, perpetual vows, is either admitted, after novitiate and the completion of temporary profession mentioned in Canon 574, to solemn profession or to simple, perpetual profession, or returns to the prior religious [institute]; it is, nevertheless, the right of the Superior to prolong this probation, but not more than one year from the completion of novitiate.

Canon Law Digest
I: 325; VIII: 421–22

Canon 635 (1983 CIC 684) Cross-Ref.: 1917 CIC 681

One transferring to another monastery of the same religious [institute], from the day of transfer, or to another religious [institute], from having given the new profession:

1.° Loses all the rights and obligations of the prior religious [institute] or monastery and takes up the rights and duties of the other;

2.° The goods remain with the religious [institute] or monastery *from which*, that had already been acquired by him by reason of the religious [institute]; for what pertains to the dowry and the income and other personal goods if the religious had any, the prescription of Canon 551, § 2, is observed; as for the rest, the new religious [institute] has the right for the time of novitiate to a just repayment if this is in order according to the norm of Canon 570, § 1.

Canon 636 (1983 CIC 685)

The solemnity of vows in him who legitimately pronounced simple vows in a religious Congregation according to the above canons is extinguished, unless something else is expressly provided in the apostolic indult.

TITLE 15
On departure from a religious [institute][35]

Canon 637 (1983 CIC 688–89) Cross-Ref.: 1917 CIC 575

One professed by temporary vows, upon the completion of the time of the vows, is able freely to [leave] a religious [institute]; likewise the religious [institute] for just and reasonable causes can exclude one from the renewal of temporary vows or from giving perpetual profession, but not, however, because of infirmity, unless it has been certainly proved that this was intentionally withheld or simulated prior to profession.

Canon Law Digest
I: 325; VII: 556; IX: 455

Canon 638[36] (1983 CIC 686, 691)

An indult of staying outside the cloister, whether temporary, in which case it is an indult of *exclaustration*, or perpetual, in which case it is an indult of *secularization*, can only be given by the Apostolic See in a reli-

[35] John Madigan, "The Juridical Position of Religious Dispersed by Civil Governments" (MS no. 2333, Gregorian University, 1955; printed version, no. 955, 1955).

[36] Edelhard Schneider, "The Status of Secularized Ex-Religious Clerics", Canon Law Studies, no. 284 (thesis, Catholic University of America, 1948); Joseph Corbett, "The Juridical Status of the Exclaustrated Religious Priest" (diss. no. 5, Pontifical University of St. Thomas [Rome], 1958–1959).

gious [institute] of pontifical right; in a religious [institute] of diocesan right [it can also be given by] the local Ordinary.

Canon Law Digest

I: 326; II: 173; III: 257; IV: 238–40; VI: 506; VII: 556–59; VIII: 423; X: 121

Canon 639 (1983 CIC 687)

Whoever seeks an indult of exclaustration from the Apostolic See remains bound by the vows and other obligations of his profession that can be reconciled with his state; nevertheless, he must not wear outside [the institute] the habit or style of the religious [institute]; during the period of the indult, one lacks active and passive voice but enjoys the merely spiritual privileges of his religious [institute], and is under the Ordinary of the place where he is by reason of the vow of obedience, in place of the Superior of his own religious [institute].

Canon Law Digest

I: 326; III: 257; IV: 240–44; IX: 455–69

Canon 640 (1983 CIC 690, 692–93)

§ 1. One who has obtained an indult of secularization and leaves the religious [institute]:

1.° Is separated from the religious [institute], must put off the exterior habit or style, and in Mass and in the canonical hours and in the use and dispensation of Sacraments is considered a secular;

2.° He remains freed from vows, [but not from] the burdens attached to major orders if he was in sacred [orders]; he is not bound by the obligation of reciting the canonical hours in view of profession, nor is he bound by the other rules and constitutions.

§ 2. If by apostolic indult he is once again received into a religious [institute], he shall undergo novitiate and profession and obtain a place among the professed from the day of the new profession.

Canon Law Digest

I: 326–27; III: 257–58; VI: 506; VII: 559; VIII: 423; IX: 469–80

Canon 641 (1983 CIC 693) Cross-Refs.: 1917 CIC 112, 642, 648

§ 1. If a religious constituted in sacred [orders] has not lost his own diocese according to the norm of Canon 585, he must, not having renewed his vows or having obtained an indult of secularization, return to his own diocese and be received by his own Ordinary; if he has lost it, he cannot exercise sacred orders outside the religious [institute] until he finds reception by a benevolent Bishop or until the Apostolic See provides otherwise.

§ 2. A Bishop can receive a religious either purely and simply or for an experimental [period] of three years: in the first case the religious is by that [fact] incardinated into the diocese; in the second the Bishop can demand a time of probation but not beyond another three years; the which [time] having passed, the religious, unless he has been dismissed beforehand, is by that fact incardinated into the diocese.

Canon Law Digest
II: 173–75; IV: 244–45; VIII: 423–24; X: 121–23

Canon 642 (NA) Cross-Refs.: 1917 CIC 648, 672

§ 1. Any professed having returned to the world is still able according to the norm of Canon 641 to exercise sacred orders, but they are nevertheless prohibited without a new and special indult of the Holy See [from having]:

1.° Any benefice in a major or minor basilica and in a cathedral church;
2.° Any teaching [post] and office in a major or minor Seminary or college in which clerics are educated and likewise in Universities and Institutes that enjoy the conferral of academic degrees by apostolic privilege;
3.° Any office or duty in an episcopal Curia and in religious houses of men or women even if it concerns a diocesan Congregation.

§ 2. These things apply even for those who gave temporary vows or an oath of perseverance or certain special promises according to the norm of the constitutions and were dispensed from them if for six complete years they were bound by them.

Canon Law Digest
I: 327; V: 394–95; VII: 559

Canon 643 (1983 CIC 702) Cross-Refs.: 1917 CIC 647, 652

§ 1. Whoever leaves a religious [institute] at the completion of temporary vows or who has obtained an indult of secularization or who was dismissed from it can seek nothing for any works done on behalf of the religious [institute].

§ 2. If, however, a religious woman was received without a dowry [and] she is not able to provide for herself out of her own goods, the religious[institute] out of charity must give to her what is required for a safe and becoming return home and so provide [for her] for a period of time observing natural equity by mutual consent or in the case of disagreement to be determined by the local Ordinary so that she can live honestly.

Canon Law Digest
I: 327; VII: 560–62; VIII: 424–27; IX: 480

Canon 644[37] (NA)

§ 1. One professed by perpetual vows, whether solemn or simple, who has illegitimately left from the religious house without the intention of returning or who has legitimately left but has ceased his religious obedience and who is not returning, is called an apostate from a religious [institute].

§ 2. This evil will mentioned in § 1 is presumed in law if a religious has not returned within one month or manifested to the Superior the intention of returning.

§ 3. A fugitive is one who without the permission of the Superiors leaves the religious house with the intention of returning to the religious [institute].

Canon 645 (1983 CIC 665) Cross-Ref.: 1917 CIC 681

§ 1. An apostate and a fugitive are not absolved of the obligation of the rule and vows and must return without delay to the religious [institute].

§ 2. Superiors must inquire after them solicitously and receive them if they return with an act of true penitence; the local Ordinary shall take care cautiously for the return of apostate or fugitive nuns, and, if it concerns an exempt monastery, the regular Superior [shall do so also].

Canon Law Digest
VIII: 428

[37] Albert Riesner, "Apostates and Fugitives from Religious Institutes", Canon Law Studies, no. 168 (J. C. D. thesis, Catholic University of America, 1942).

TITLE 16
On the dismissal of religious[38]

Canon 646 (1983 CIC 694–95) Cross-Refs.: 1917 CIC 654, 670, 2385

§ 1. Upon the fact, they are considered as legitimately dismissed religious:

1.° [Those who are] public apostates from the Catholic faith;

2.° [A] religious man who has run off with a woman or a religious woman [who has run off] with a man;

3.° Those attempting or contracting marriage even if the bond is, as they say, civil.

§ 2. In these cases, it suffices that the major Superior with his Chapter or Council issue a declaration of fact according to the norm of the constitution; he shall take care that the collected evidence of the fact is preserved in the records of the house.

Canon Law Digest
I: 327–28; II: 175; VIII: 428

Chapter 1
On the dismissal of religious who have pronounced temporary vows

Canon 647[39] (1983 CIC 696, 698, 700, 702)
Cross-Refs.: 1917 CIC 575, 648, 650

§ 1. The supreme Moderator of a religious [institute] or the abbot of a monastery of its own right can dismiss one professed by temporary vows, whether in an Order or in a Congregation of pontifical right, with the

---

[38] Wenceslas Michalicka, "Judicial Procedure in Dismissal of Clerical Exempt Religious", Canon Law Studies, no. 19 (thesis, Catholic University of America, 1923); Benedict Pfaller, "The Ipso Facto Effected Dismissal of Religious", Canon Law Studies, no. 259 (thesis, Catholic University of America, 1948); Ludowickj Hiegel, "The Juridical Bond of Dismissed Religious in the Light of the Origin and Development of the Juridical Bond Itself" (thesis, Gregorian University; printed version, no. 904, New Orleans, 1954).

[39] Francis O'Neill, "The Dismissal of Religious in Temporary Vows", Canon Law Studies, no. 166 (J. C. D. thesis, Catholic University of America, 1942); Edward Stokes, "The Decree *Quicumque regularis* of the Council of Trent and the Religious Profession" (MS no. 2484, Gregorian University; printed version, no. 1212, 1959).

consent of his Council manifested by secret ballot or if it concerns nuns the local Ordinary, and if the monastery is under regulars, of the regular Superior, after sworn reasons for the case in writing have been given to the Superioress of the monastery with her Council; but in Congregations of diocesan right, the Ordinary of the place in which the religious house is located [acts] who, nevertheless, shall not use his right if the Moderators are unaware [of the matter] or if they justly dissent.

§ 2. All of these gravely burdened in their conscience shall not dismiss religious unless the following things are observed:

1.° The causes for dismissal must be grave;

2.° These must have arisen either on the part of the religious [institute] or on the part of the religious. A lack of religious spirit that is giving scandal to others is sufficient cause for dismissal if a repeated warning, together with a salutary penance, was imposed without effect, but not sickness, unless it is certain that this was culpably hidden or dissimulated prior to profession;

3.° Even though they must be obvious to the dismissing Superior, it is nevertheless not necessary that they be proved by a formal trial. But they must always be disclosed to the religious giving permission for a full response to them; and the responses must be faithfully communicated to the dismissing Superior;

4.° Against a decree of dismissal the religious has the faculty of taking recourse to the Apostolic See; and while the recourse is pending the dismissal has no juridic effect;

5.° If it concerns a woman, the prescription of Canon 643, § 2, must be observed.

Canon Law Digest
I: 328–29; VIII: 428–29

Canon 648 (1983 CIC 693, 701)

A religious dismissed according to the norm of Canon 647 is by that fact absolved from all religious vows except for the burdens attached to major orders if he was in sacred [orders] and with due regard for the prescription of Canons 641, § 1, and 642; but a cleric constituted in minor orders is automatically returned to the lay state.

Canon Law Digest
I: 329

CHAPTER 2

On the dismissal of religious who pronounce perpetual vows in a non-exempt clerical religious [institute] or in a lay religious [institute]

Canon 649 (1983 CIC 696–97)

In order that one professed by perpetual vows be dismissed from a non-exempt clerical religious [institute] of men or of laity, there must first precede three delicts with the double warning and the failure of emendation according to the norm of Canons 656–62.

Canon Law Digest
I: 329; VIII: 430

Canon 650 (1983 CIC 698–700) Cross-Ref.: 1917 CIC 651

§ 1. These things being proved, the supreme Moderator of the religious [institute] with his Council, having weighed all the circumstances of fact, shall decide whether dismissal is in order.

§ 2. If the major number of votes is for dismissal:

1.° In a religious [institute] of diocesan right, the whole thing is deferred to the Ordinary of the place in which the religious house of the professed is located, to whom it belongs to decide on the dismissal according to his prudent judgment according to the norm of Canon 647;

2.° In a religious [institute] of pontifical right, the supreme Moderator of the religious [institute] will issue the decree of dismissal; but in order for any effect to arise, it must be confirmed by the Apostolic See.

§ 3. The religious has the right of explaining freely his reasons; and his responses must be recorded faithfully in the acts.

Canon Law Digest
IV: 245–46

Canon 651 (1983 CIC 696, 698)

§ 1. Grave external reasons together with incorrigibility in the judgment of the Superioress, indicating by prior experience that there is no hope of one's returning to one's senses, is required also for the dismissal of religious women professed by perpetual vows, whether solemn or simple.

§ 2. The prescription of Canon 650, § 3, must also be observed in the dismissal of religious women.

Canon Law Digest
VIII: 430–52; IX: 480–86; X: 123–27

Canon 652 (1983 CIC 699–700)

§ 1. If it concerns religious of diocesan right, the Ordinary of the place in which the house of the professed sister is located must examine the causes for dismissal and issue the decree of dismissal.

§ 2. If it concerns nuns, the local Ordinary shall transmit all the acts and documents to the Sacred Congregation [for Religious] with his opinion and that of the regular Superior, if the monastery was subject to regulars.

§ 3. If it [concerns] other religious [institutes] of pontifical right, the supreme Moderator of the religious [institute] will also send the complete case to the Sacred Congregation [for Religious] along with all the acts and documents; this Sacred Congregation in this case and in the preceding case will consider what it thinks best to do and decide on it with due regard for the prescription of Canon 643, § 2.

Canon Law Digest
VIII: 452

Canon 653 (1983 CIC 703) Cross-Ref.: 1917 CIC 668

In cases of grave exterior scandal and of imminent harm of the worst sort to the community, a religious can be returned to the world immediately by the major Superior with the consent of his Council or even, if there is danger in delay and there is no time for hearing the major Superior, by the local Superior with the consent of his Council and the local Ordinary, the religious habit immediately being shed, and notwithstanding this, the matter without delay shall be subjected to the judgment of the Holy See by the Ordinary or by the major Superior, if there was one [involved].

Canon Law Digest
VI: 506

Chapter 3

On the judicial process for the dismissal of religious who pronounce perpetual vows, whether solemn or simple, in a clerical exempt religious [institute]

Canon 654 (NA)

A man professed by solemn or simple perpetual vows in an exempt clerical religious [institute] shall not be dismissed except by a process undertaken with due regard for the prescription of Canons 646 and 668 and revoking every contrary privilege.

Canon Law Digest
I: 329; II: 258; VII: 563–69; VIII: 452–55

Canon 655 (1983 CIC 699) Cross-Ref.: 1917 CIC 501

§ 1. The supreme Moderator of a religious or monastic Congregation with his Council or Chapter, which will consist of at least four religious, is competent to pass a sentence of dismissal; if there is a deficiency [in the number], the president will choose a religious for his place with the consent of the others, who then constitutes the collegial tribunal.

§ 2. The president will appoint a promoter of justice with the consent of the others according to the norm of Canon 1589, § 2.

Canon 656 (NA)

A process may not come to be instructed unless there precedes:

1.° External grave delicts either against common law or against the special law of religious [institutes];
2.° Admonitions;
3.° Failure of emendation.

Canon Law Digest
VIII: 455

Canon 657 (NA)

The delicts must be at least three of the same species or, if different, such that taken together they manifest a perverse will lingering in evil or, if it is only one on-going [offense], such that from the repeated warnings it becomes virtually triple.

Canon 658 (NA) Cross-Ref.: 1917 CIC 659

§ 1. In order to conduct a warning, it is necessary that the delict be notorious or that it be shown either by the extrajudicial confession of the offender or from other sufficient evidence that a previous investigation supplies.

§ 2. In conducting the inquisition, there shall be observed, due adaptation being made, the prescriptions of Canons 1939 and foll[owing].

Canon 659 (1983 CIC 697)

The warning must be made by the immediate major Superior personally or through another by his mandate; but the Superior shall not give a mandate except upon previous information about the facts according to the norm of Canon 658, § 1; a mandate given for the first warning is also valid for the second.

Canon Law Digest
III: 258; VIII: 455

Canon 660 (1983 CIC 697)

There must be two warnings, namely, one for each of the first two delicts; in continuous or permanent delicts, it is necessary that there pass between the first and the second warning a space of at least three integral days.

Canon Law Digest
VIII: 455

Canon 661 (1983 CIC 697)

§ 1. The Superior shall add to the warnings opportune exhortations and correction and prescribe penances and, moreover, other penal remedies that he considers suitable for the emendation of the offender and the repair of scandal.

§ 2. Moreover, the Superior is bound to remove the offender from the occasion of relapse even by transfer, if it is necessary, to another house where vigilance is easier and the occasion of delinquency more remote.

§ 3. A specific warning about dismissal shall be added to the individual warnings.

Canon 662 (1983 CIC 697)

A religious is considered not to have emended himself if after the second warning he commits a new delict or remains in the old one; after the last warning six days must be awaited before progressing onward.

Canon Law Digest
VIII: 455

Canon 663 (1983 CIC 697) Cross-Ref.: 1917 CIC 667

The immediate major Superior, after the warnings and corrections cease without effect, shall diligently collect all of the acts and documents and transmit them to the supreme Moderator; he [in turn] will hand them to the promoter of justice, who examines them and proposes his own conclusions.

Canon 664 (NA) Cross-Refs.: 1917 CIC 665, 667

§ 1. If the promoter of justice, to whom it is fundamental that he be able to conduct further investigations that he feels are opportune, proposes accusation, the process is instructed, observing the prescriptions of canons of the First Part of the Fourth Book [of this Code], due adaptation being made.

§ 2. In this process there must be shown the perpetration of the delict, that the two prior warnings were given, and the failure of emendation.

Canon 665 (NA) Cross-Ref.: 1917 CIC 667

The tribunal, diligently weighing the allegations both of the promoter of justice and of the defendant, if indeed it judges that those things mentioned in Canon 664, § 2, are sufficiently proven, shall pronounce the sentence of dismissal.

Canon 666 (1983 CIC 700) Cross-Ref.: 1917 CIC 667

Execution of the sentence cannot be mandated unless it was confirmed by the Sacred Congregation [of Religious]; to which the president of the tribunal will take care to send both the sentence and all of the acts of the process as soon as possible.

Canon Law Digest
VIII: 455

Canon 667 (NA)

For distant regions, even in ordinary cases, supreme Moderators, with the consent of their Councils or Chapters, can bestow the faculty of dismissal on sober and prudent religious, who must be at least three in number, with due regard for the prescription of Canons 663–66.

Canon 668 (1983 CIC 703) Cross-Ref.: 1917 CIC 654

In the case described in Canon 653, a religious can be immediately returned to the lay state by a major Superior or, if there is danger in delay and there is no time for recourse to the major Superior, even by a local Superior, with the consent of the Council, immediately entailing loss of religious habit; but the religious having been dismissed, a process should immediately be instituted, if it has not yet been instituted, according to the norms of the canons that follow.

Canon Law Digest
VI: 506

Chapter 4
On dismissed religious who have pronounced perpetual vows[40]

Canon 669 (1983 CIC 701)

§ 1. A professed [religious] who has given perpetual vows and who is dismissed from the religious [institute] remains bound by religious vows, with due regard for the constitutions and indults of the Apostolic See that determine otherwise.

§ 2. If a cleric is constituted in minor orders, he is by that [fact] reduced to the lay state.

Canon 670 (NA) Cross-Ref.: 1917 CIC 671

A cleric in sacred [orders] who commits any offense mentioned in Canon 646, or who is dismissed for a delict that in common law is punished with infamy of law or deposition or degradation, is perpetually prohibited from wearing ecclesiastical habit.

[40] Charles O'Leary, "Religious Dismissed after Perpetual Profession", Canon Law Studies, no. 184 (J. C. D. thesis, Catholic University of America, 1943).

Canon 671 (NA)

But if one is dismissed for the minor delicts listed in Canon 670:

1.° He remains automatically suspended until he obtains absolution from the Holy See;

2.° The Sacred Congregation [of Religious], if it judges it expedient, can order that the one dismissed, dressed in the clothes of a secular cleric, shall stay in a certain diocese, indicating to the Ordinary the reason for which he was dismissed;

3.° If a dismissed does not abide by the precept in n. 2, the religious [institute] is not bound to [do] anything, and the one dismissed is deprived of the right of wearing the ecclesiastical habit;

4.° The Ordinary of the diocese in which his stay is designated shall send the religious to a house of penitence, or commit him to the care and vigilance of a pious and prudent priest; and if the religious does not comply, there shall be observed the prescriptions of n. 3 [of this canon];

5.° The religious [institute], through the hands of the Ordinary of the place of his staying, shall supply the one dismissed with a charitable subsidy [suitable for] the necessities of sustaining life, unless he is able otherwise to provide for himself;

6.° If one dismissed, by reason of his life, does not conduct himself in a manner worthy of an ecclesiastical man, upon the completion of a year, or sooner in the judgment of the Ordinary, he shall be deprived of the charitable subsidy, and ejected from the house of penitence, and stripped of the right of wearing ecclesiastical habit by the same Ordinary, who shall immediately take care to send an opportune report both to the Apostolic See and to the religious [institute];

7.° But if the one dismissed in the aforesaid time conducts himself laudably, so that he can be rightly said to have amended, the Ordinary can commend his request to the Holy See for absolution from the censure of suspension, and, that obtained, permit him, in his own diocese [and] observing due precautions and limitations, the celebration of Mass and even, in his own prudence and judgment, other sacred ministry, from which he can derive an honest living; in which case the charitable subsidy of the religious [institute] can be interrupted. But if it concerns a deacon or subdeacon, the matter is deferred to the Holy See.

Canon 672 (1983 CIC 701)

§ 1. One dismissed [but] not absolved of the religious vows given is bound to return to the cloister; and if one has given indications of full emendation for three years, the religious [institute] is bound to accept him back; but if there are grave reasons preventing [this] on the part of either the religious [institute] or the religious, the matter is subjected to the Apostolic See.

§ 2. Whenever the religious vows given cease, [and] if the dismissed has found a benevolent Bishop who will accept him, he remains under [his] special vigilance and his jurisdiction, [with] the prescription of Canon 642 remaining; otherwise the matter is deferred to the Holy See.

Canon Law Digest
II: 175; VIII: 456

TITLE 17
On societies, whether of men or of women, living in common without vows[41]

Canon 673 (1983 CIC 731–32, 740, 588)

§ 1. A society, whether of men or of women, in which the members live in common imitating a religious rule under the government of a Superior according to an approved constitution, yet not obligated by the three usual public vows, is not properly religious, nor are its members properly designated by the term religious.

§ 2. A society of this sort is clerical or religious, [and] of pontifical or diocesan right, according to the norm of Canon 488, nn. 3 and 4.

Canon Law Digest
I: 330; II: 175; V: 395; IX: 486–87

---

[41] Bernard Ristuccia, "Quasi-Religious Societies", Canon Law Studies, no. 261 (thesis, Catholic University of America, 1949); Richard Hochawalt, "The Concept: '*In Communi Viventium Sine Votis*'" (diss. no. 21, Pontifical University of St. Thomas [Rome], 1953–1954); John Nugent, "Ordination in Societies of the Common Life", Canon Law Studies, no. 341 (J. C. D. thesis, Catholic University of America, 1958); Judith Barnhiser, "A Study of the Authority Structures of Three Nineteenth-Century Apostolic Communities of Religious Women in the United States", Canon Law Studies, no. 487 (J. C. D. thesis, Catholic University of America, 1975).

Canon 674 (1983 CIC 579, 584–85, 732–33)

Concerning the erection or suppression of a society and its provinces or houses, those things established for religious Congregations are equally applicable.

Canon 675 (1983 CIC 734, 738)

Governance is determined in each society by its constitutions; but in all things, Canons 499–530 are to be observed, due adaptation being made.

Canon Law Digest
I: 330; VI: 506

Canon 676 (1983 CIC 741)

§ 1. A society and its provinces and houses are capable of acquiring and possessing temporal goods.

§ 2. The administration of goods is governed by the prescription of Canons 532–37.

§ 3. Whatever the members come into by reason of the society is acquired by it; members retain, acquire, and administer other goods according to the constitutions.

Canon 677 (1983 CIC 735)

In admitting candidates the constitutions are observed, with due regard for the prescription of Canon 542.

Canon 678[42] (1983 CIC 735–36)

In those things that pertain to the course of studies and the taking up of orders, the members are bound by the same laws as are secular clerics, with due regard for special prescriptions given by the Holy See.

Canon Law Digest
I: 330; II: 175

Canon 679 (1983 CIC 737, 739)

§ 1. Members of societies, beyond those obligations that as members they are subject to according to the constitutions, are [also] bound by the common obligations of clerics, unless by the nature of the thing or the context of the words it appears otherwise, and likewise they must stand by the prescriptions of Canons 595–612, unless the constitutions state otherwise.

---

[42] Kevin Scanlan, "Ordination and the Canonical Status of Clerics in Societies without Vows" (diss. no. 14, Pontifical University of St. Thomas [Rome], 1957–1958).

§ 2. Cloister must be observed in accord with the constitutions under the vigilance of the local Ordinary.

Canon Law Digest
II: 175

Canon 680 (1983 CIC 737) Cross-Ref.: 1917 CIC 1553

[Members], even laity, enjoy those clerical privileges that are mentioned in Canons 119–23 and those others directly granted to the society, but not the privileges of religious without special indult.

Canon 681 (1983 CIC 742–46)

Concerning transfer from one society to another religious [institute] or concerning the departure of a member from a society even of pontifical right, besides the proper constitutions of each society, there shall be observed, insofar as they are applicable, the prescriptions of Canons 632–35, and 645; concerning their dismissal, [see] Canons 646–72.

Canon Law Digest
I: 331

THIRD PART
ON LAITY[1]

Canon 682 (1983 CIC 213)

Laity have the right of receiving from the clergy, according to the norm of ecclesiastical discipline, spiritual goods and especially that aid necessary for salvation.

Canon Law Digest
VI: 506–7

[1] Timothy Champoux, "The Juridical Position of the Laity in the Church" (MS no. 499, Gregorian University, 1938; printed version, no. 172, 1939); Ronald Cox, "A Study of the Juridic Status of Laymen in the Writing of the Medieval Canonists", Canon Law Studies, no. 395 (J. C. D. thesis, Catholic University of America, 1959); James Hertel, "The Laity, Luther and Trent", Canon Law Studies, no. 465 (Catholic University of America, 1968); Henry Bretena Perez, "The Appraisal of the Juridical Personality of the Laity in the Post Conciliar Era" (diss. no. 2, Pontifical University of St. Thomas [Rome], 1967–1968); Thomas Green, "Principle and Practice of Lay Consultation in the Church" (thesis, Gregorian University; printed version, no. 2025, 1968); John Louis, "The Evolution of the Juridical Concept of the Laity between Vatican I and Vatican II" (thesis, Gregorian University; printed version, no. 2133, 1969).

Canon 683 (NA)

It is not permitted for laity to wear clerical habit, unless it concerns either a student in a Seminary or others aspiring to orders as described in Canon 972, § 2, or those laity legitimately dedicated to the service of a church while they are in the church or are outside of it taking part in some ecclesiastical ministry.

Canon Law Digest
IV: 246

TITLE 18
On associations of the faithful in general

Canon 684[2] (1983 CIC 298)

Those faithful are worthy of praise if they give their name to associations erected or commended by the Church; but they should be cautious about joining secret, damned, seditious, or suspect associations or those that seek to distance themselves from the legitimate vigilance of the Church.

Canon Law Digest
I: 333; III: 259–91; IV: 246; V: 395–96; VI: 507–11;
VII: 569–79; VIII: 456–62; IX: 487–95; X: 127

Canon 685[3] (1983 CIC 298)

Associations distinct from religious [institutes] or societies mentioned in Canons 487–681 can be constituted by the Church for the promotion of the perfection of Christian life among members, or for the exercise of other pious or charitable works, or finally for the increase of public cult.

Canon Law Digest
VI: 511; VII: 579; IX: 495; X: 128–35

---

[2] Thomas Clarke, "Parish Societies", Canon Law Studies, no. 176 (J. C. D. thesis, Catholic University of America, 1943); Leo McDougall, "The Young Men's Christian Association in the Light of Canon Law" (diss., no. 10, Pontifical University of St. Thomas [Rome], 1952–1953); Hugo Mulvenna, "The Society of St. Vincent de Paul and Its Legal Status in the Church" (diss. no. 39, Pontifical University of St. Thomas [Rome], 1954–1955); Lionel Morand, "The Character of the Legion of Mary in the Law of the Church" (diss. no. 9, Pontifical University of St. Thomas [Rome], 1954–1955).

[3] Joseph Sasaki, "Juridical Relationship between the Lay Apostolate and the Hierarchy" (doctoral diss. 48, St. Paul University [Ottawa, Canada], 1966).

Canon 686[4] (1983 CIC 299, 312) Cross-Ref.: 1917 CIC 703

§ 1. No association is recognized in the Church that has not been erected or at least approved by legitimate ecclesiastical authority.

§ 2. Besides the Roman Pontiff, it pertains to local Ordinaries to erect or approve associations, except in those cases wherein the right of their erection or approval is reserved to others.

§ 3. Even though the concession of the privilege is proven, nevertheless, there is always required for the validity of the erection, unless otherwise provided by privilege itself, the consent of the local Ordinary given in writing; the consent, however, of the Ordinary that was given for the erection of a religious house is valid also for the erection in that same house or church of an association attached to it, which is not constituted as an organic body [but] belongs to the religious house itself.

§ 4. A Vicar General with only a general mandate and a Vicar Capitulary cannot erect associations or give consent for their erection or aggregation.

§ 5. Letters of erection that are given by those who erect an association in virtue of an apostolic privilege are granted without charge, excepting only a fee for necessary expenses.

Canon Law Digest
I: 333; VII: 580; IX: 495

Canon 687 (1983 CIC 313)

According to the norm of Canon 100, associations of the faithful acquire juridic personality in the Church only when they have obtained from a legitimate ecclesiastical Superior a formal decree of erection.

Canon Law Digest
I: 334

Canon 688 (1983 CIC 300)

The title or name of an association shall not assume [an air] of levity or one that smacks of novelty or that expresses a devotion not approved by the Apostolic See.

[4] Richard Schendt, "Commendation, Approbation, and Erection of the Associations of the Faithful" (diss. no. 33, Pontifical University of St. Thomas [Rome], 1959–1960).

Canon 689 (1983 CIC 304, 314)

§ 1. Each association shall have its statutes examined and approved by the Apostolic See or the local Ordinary.

§ 2. Statutes that are not confirmed by the Apostolic See are always subject to the moderation and correction of the local Ordinary.

Canon 690 (1983 CIC 305)

§ 1. All associations, even if erected by the Apostolic See, unless there is a special privilege in the way, are subject to the jurisdiction and vigilance of local Ordinaries, who have the right and duty of inspecting them according to the norms of the sacred canons.

§ 2. It is fundamental, however, that local Ordinaries cannot visit associations that in virtue of apostolic privilege belong to churches of exempt religious in what pertains to internal discipline or that look to the spiritual direction of the association.

Canon 691 (1983 CIC 319)

§ 1. An association legitimately erected, unless it is expressly provided otherwise, can possess and administer temporal goods under the authority of the local Ordinary, to whom at least once per year an accounting of the administration must be given, according to the norm of Canon 1525, but by no means to the pastor, unless it is erected in his territory, or unless the Ordinary himself establishes otherwise.

§ 2. It can, according to the norm of the statutes, receive offerings and apply the receipts only to the pious association itself, with due regard for the will of the donors.

§ 3. No association is allowed to collect alms, unless permitted by the statutes or necessity suggests it, and then with the consent of the Ordinary and following the form prescribed by him.

§ 4. For the collection of alms outside of [its] territory, there is required the approval of each Ordinary, given in writing.

§ 5. The association shall give to the local Ordinary an accounting of the offerings and alms from the faithful.

Canon Law Digest
II: 177; III: 291; VIII: 462

Canon 692 (1983 CIC 306)

In order to enjoy the rights, privileges, indulgences, and other spiritual favors of an association, it is necessary and sufficient that one be validly received into it according to the statutes of the association, and not be legitimately expelled from it.

Canon Law Digest
III: 291–92

Canon 693 (1983 CIC 307, 316) Cross-Ref.: 1917 CIC 696

§ 1. Non-Catholics and those who belong to condemned sects, or those notoriously under censure, or general public sinners, cannot be validly received.

§ 2. The same person can belong to several associations, with due regard for the prescription of Canon 705.

§ 3. Absent persons are not to be enrolled in associations constituted as organic bodies; those present, however, [cannot be enrolled] unless they are knowing and willing.

§ 4. With due regard for the prescription of Canon 704, religious can give their name to pious associations, except in those whose laws, in the judgment of their Superiors, cannot be reconciled with the observance of [their own religious] rules and constitution.

Canon Law Digest
V: 397; VIII: 462

Canon 694 (1983 CIC 307)

§ 1. Reception shall be done according to the norm of law and the statutes of each association.

§ 2. In order that reception be proven, an inscription must always be made in the album of the association; indeed, this inscription, if the association has been erected as a moral person, is necessary for validity.

Canon Law Digest
III: 292

Canon 695 (NA)

On the occasion of reception into an association, nothing, directly or indirectly, shall be required beyond what is designated in legitimately approved statutes or that the local Ordinary, by reason of special circumstances, expressly permits in favor of the association.

Canon 696 (1983 CIC 308, 316)

§ 1. No one legitimately enrolled shall be dismissed from an institute except for just cause according to the norm of the statutes.

§ 2. Whoever falls into the case mentioned in Canon 693, § 1, shall be expelled, having been previously warned, observing the proper statutes, and with due regard for the right of recourse to the Ordinary.

§ 3. Even if there is nothing expressly mentioned in the statutes, the local Ordinary for all associations, and the religious Superior for associations erected by the religious by apostolic indult, can dismiss members.

Canon 697 (1983 CIC 309)

§ 1. Legitimately erected associations have the right, according to the norm of their statutes and the sacred canons, of holding meetings, of giving out particular norms that concern their members, [and] of choosing administrators of goods, officers, and ministers, with due regard for the prescription of Canon 715.

§ 2. In those things that concern the holding of meetings and elections, the common law is observed, [namely] that which is given in Canons [160]–182 and the statutes [of the association] that are not contrary to common law.

Canon Law Digest
VII: 580

Canon 698 (1983 CIC 317–18)

§ 1. Unless apostolic privilege expressly provides otherwise, appointment of the moderator or chaplain pertains to the local Ordinary for associations erected or approved by him or the Apostolic See and for associations erected by religious in virtue of apostolic privilege outside their own churches; in cases involving their own churches, the consent of only the local Ordinary is necessary if the Superior names a moderator or chaplain from among the secular clergy.

§ 2. The moderator or chaplain can, for the duration of his office, bless the habits or insignia, of the association, scapulars, and so on, and invest them on members; but as to what applies to sermons, the prescriptions of Canons 1337–42 are to be observed.

§ 3. Moderators and chaplains can be recalled by the one who appointed them or by the Superiors or successors for just cause.

§ 4. The same person can be both moderator and chaplain.

Canon 699 (1983 CIC 320)

§ 1. For grave causes, and with due regard for the right of recourse to the Apostolic See, the local Ordinary can suppress not only an association erected by himself or his predecessor, but also an association erected by religious by apostolic indult with the consent of the local Ordinary.

§ 2. Associations erected by the Apostolic See itself can be suppressed by no one else.

TITLE 19
On associations of the faithful in specific

Canon 700 (NA)

Three kinds of associations are distinguished in the Church: third Order seculars, Confraternities, [and] pious unions.

Canon 701 (NA)

§ 1. Among pious associations of laity, the order of precedence is that which follows, with due regard for the prescription of Canon 106, nn. 5–6:

1.° Third Orders;
2.° Archconfraternities;
3.° Confraternities;
4.° Primary pious unions;
5.° Other pious unions.

§ 2. Confraternities of the most holy Sacrament, when in procession with the most holy Sacrament, take precedence over archconfraternities.

§ 3. All of these only have the right of precedence when they are marching together under their own cross or standard and in the habit that is the insignia of the association.

Canon Law Digest
II: 177–78; III: 292–93

Chapter 1
On third Order seculars[5]

Canon 702 (NA)

§ 1. Third Order seculars are those in the world, under the moderation of a certain Order, according to its spirit, working to attain Christian per-

[5] Gerald Reinmann, "The Third Order Secular of St. Francis", Canon Law Studies, no. 50 (D. C. L. thesis, Catholic University of America, 1928).

fection in a secular way of life according to rules approved for them by the Apostolic See.

§ 2. If a secular third Order is divided into several associations, each of them legitimately constituted is called a *sodality of tertiaries*.

Canon Law Digest
VII: 580; IX: 496

Canon 703 (NA)

§ 1. With due regard for the privilege granted to some Orders, no religious can join a third Order.

§ 2. The Apostolic privilege having been given, religious Superiors can add various particular members to a third Order, but they cannot validly erect a sodality of tertiaries without the consent of the local Ordinary according to the norm of Canon 686, § 3.

§ 3. Neither can they grant to sodalities erected by them the use of a particular garb to be worn in sacred public functions without the special permission of that Ordinary.

Canon 704 (NA) Cross-Ref.: 1917 CIC 693

§ 1. Whoever has taken up vows, whether perpetual or for a time, in any religious [institute] cannot at the same time belong to any third Order, even if he had enrolled in it before.

§ 2. If [one is] absolved from vows and returns to the world, the earlier enrollment revives.

Canon Law Digest
IX: 497

Canon 705 (NA) Cross-Ref.: 1917 CIC 693

No sodality of tertiaries, without Apostolic indult, can enroll the members of another Order while remaining in the other; individual members, however, for a just cause, can transfer from one third Order to another, or from one sodality of that third Order to another [sodality of that Order].

Canon 706 (NA)

Tertiaries can, but are not bound to do so, collegially participate in public processions, funerals, and other ecclesiastical functions; if they do so in a group they must march with their own insignia under their own cross.

Canon Law Digest
III: 293

Chapter 2
Of confraternities and pious unions

Canon 707 (NA)

§ 1. Associations of the faithful that are erected for the exercise of some pious or charitable work come by the name *pious union*; those that are constituted in the manner of an organic body are called *sodalities*.

§ 2. Sodalities erected for the increase of public cult are called by the special name *confraternity*.

Canon Law Digest
VI: 511–13; VII: 580; X: 135

Canon 708 (NA)

Confraternities can be constituted only through a formal decree of erection; for pious unions, the approval of the Ordinary suffices, which, having been obtained, makes them capable of obtaining spiritual favors and especially indulgences, though they are not moral persons.

Canon Law Digest
VIII: 462

Canon 709 (NA)

§ 1. Male members of confraternities cannot participate in sacred functions unless they are wearing the habit or insignia of the confraternity.

§ 2. Female members of confraternities can be enrolled only for the gaining of indulgences and spiritual favors granted to the male members.

Canon 710 (NA)

The title or name of the confraternity or pious union should be taken either from an attribute of God, or from the mysteries of Christian religion, or from a feast of the Lord or the Blessed Virgin Mary, or from the Saints, or from a pious work of the sodality.

Canon 711 (NA)

§ 1. Several confraternities or pious unions of the same title or institute are not to be erected or approved in the same place, unless there has been a special concession to them or [other] legal provision; but if it concerns large cities, it is permitted, provided in the judgment of the local Ordinary an appropriate distance separates them.

§ 2. Local Ordinaries shall take care that in every parish there are instituted confraternities of the most holy Sacrament and of Christian doctrine; these once legitimately erected are by law aggregated to the same archconfraternities erected in the City by the Cardinal Vicar of the City.

Canon Law Digest
I: 334; II: 178; IV: 246–47; VI: 513

Canon 712 (NA)

§ 1. Confraternities or pious unions shall not be erected except in a church or public oratory, or at least a semi-public [oratory].

§ 2. They should not be instituted in cathedral or collegial churches without the consent of the Chapter.

§ 3. In the churches or oratories of women religious, the local Ordinary can permit the erection of associations of women only, or of a pious union devoted only to prayer and enjoying only the communication of spiritual favors.

Canon 713 (NA)

§ 1. Religious in confraternities or pious unions erected by them can and must communicate all and only those spiritual favors that are specifically recorded in the faculties from the Apostolic See and expressly declared communicable, and they shall be manifested in the act of erection to everyone, with due regard for the prescription of Canon 919.

§ 2. It is not permitted to confraternities erected by them to put on their proper habit or insignia that is to be worn in public processions in other sacred functions without the special permission of the local Ordinary.

Canon 714 (NA)

A confraternity shall not discard or change its own habit or insignia without the permission of the local Ordinary.

Canon Law Digest
II: 178

Canon 715 (NA) Cross-Ref.: 1917 CIC 697

§ 1. It belongs to the local Ordinary to preside over meetings of the confraternity, even if they are celebrated in the churches or oratories of regulars, whether himself or through a delegate, but without, however, the right of voting, [and] to confirm worthy and suitable officials and elected ministers, to reprove or remove those unworthy or unsuitable, and to correct and approve statutes or other norms, unless they were approved by the Apostolic See.

§ 2. The confraternity will notify in a timely manner the local Ordinary or his delegate about the celebration of extraordinary meetings; otherwise the Ordinary has the right of preventing the meeting or of declaring its decrees infirm.

Canon 716 (NA) Cross-Ref.: 1917 CIC 717

§ 1. Confraternities and pious unions erected in their own churches, observing those things that ought to be observed, can exercise non-parochial functions, provided it is not injurious to parochial functions in parochial churches.

§ 2. The same is true even in the case of a parish being erected in the church of a confraternity.

§ 3. In doubt as to whether the functions of the confraternity or pious union are injurious or not to parochial ministry, the right of deciding belongs to the local Ordinary and likewise [it is for him to] establish practical norms to be observed.

Canon 717 (NA)

§ 1. If [they are] in churches not erected by them, they can perform their own ecclesiastical functions only in a chapel or at an altar in which they are erected according to the norm of Canon 716 and particular statutes.

§ 2. The patrimony of a confraternity [or] pious union that is not erected in its own church, or [if] the church is also a parish church, must be separated from the upkeep funds or [those of the] community.

Canon 718 (NA)

Confraternities are bound [to march] together in the usual processions and others that the local Ordinary indicates with their own insignia and under their own banner, unless the Ordinary prescribes otherwise.

Canon 719 (NA)

§ 1. With the consent of the local Ordinary, a confraternity or pious union can be transferred from one see to another, unless transfer is prohibited by law or by statutes approved by the Apostolic See.

§ 2. As often as it concerns the transfer of a confraternity or pious union that is reserved to a religious [institute], the consent of the Superior is to be required.

Chapter 3
On archconfraternities and primary unions[6]

Canon 720 (NA)

Sodalities that by law are able to be aggregated to others or with associations of the same kind are called *archsodalities* or *archconfraternities* or pious unions, congregations, [or] *primary* societies.

Canon Law Digest
IV: 247; V: 397

Canon 721 (NA)

§ 1. No association can validly aggregate itself to another without apostolic indult.

§ 2. Archconfraternities and primary unions can only aggregate themselves to archconfraternities and pious unions that are of the same title or end, unless apostolic indult arranges otherwise.

Canon Law Digest
III: 293–95

Canon 722 (NA)

§ 1. Through aggregation there are communicated all those indulgences, privileges, and other spiritual favors that have been or in the future will be granted to the aggregated association directly and by name by the Apostolic See, unless provided otherwise in the apostolic indult.

§ 2. From this communication, the aggregating association acquires no rights over the aggregated one.

Canon 723 (NA)

For the validity of the aggregation it is required that:

1.° The association must already be canonically erected and not be aggregated to another archconfraternity or primary union;

2.° There must be written consent from the local Ordinary together with his testimonial letters;

[6] Edmund Quinn, "Archconfraternities, Archsodalities, and Primary Unions, with a Supplement on the Archconfraternity of Christian Mothers", Canon Law Studies, no. 421 (J. C. D. thesis, Catholic University of America, 1962).

3.° The indulgences, privileges, and other spiritual favors that are to be communicated by the aggregation should be enumerated in a list, inspected by the Ordinary of the place in which the archconfraternity is located, and sent to the aggregated society;
4.° The aggregation must be made in perpetuity [according to] a formula prescribed in the statutes;
5.° The letters of aggregation are to be processed free of all charges and no offering, even one freely made, can be accepted except for necessary expenses.

Canon 724 (NA)

An archconfraternity or primary union can be transferred from one see to another only by the Apostolic See.

Canon 725 (NA)

The title *archsodality* or *archconfraternity* or *primary union*, even if it is merely honorary, can be granted to an association only by the Apostolic See.

THIRD BOOK
ON THINGS

Canon 726 (NA)

The things treated in this book are just those means that are necessary for the Church to pursue her end, some of which are spiritual, others temporal, [and] others mixed.

Canon 727[1] (NA)

§ 1. By divine law, simony is the studied will to buy or sell for a temporal price an intrinsically spiritual thing, for example, Sacraments, ecclesiastical jurisdiction, consecration, indulgences, and so forth, or temporal things so connected with spiritual things that without the spiritual they cannot exist, for example, ecclesiastical benefices, and so on, or a spiritual thing that is, even in part, the object of a contract, for example, the consecration of a chalice consecrated in sale.

§ 2. By ecclesiastical law, simony is to give temporal things that are attached to spiritual ones for other temporal things that are attached to spiritual, or spiritual things for spiritual things, or even temporal for temporal if, in so doing, there is a danger of that irreverence toward spiritual things that is prohibited by the Church.

Canon Law Digest
VIII: 465; IX: 501

Canon 728 (NA)

When dealing with simony, buying-selling, bartering, and so on, are understood as involving any kind of agreement, even if it did not take effect, [and] even if it was tacit, in which simoniacal intent is not expressly manifest but is gleaned from circumstances.

---

[1] Raymond Ryder, "Simony", Canon Law Studies, no. 65 (J. C. D. thesis, Catholic University of America, 1931); James Toppo, "The Doctrine of Simony in the Works of Suarez" (MS no 3680, Gregorian University, 1964).

Canon 729 (NA) Cross-Ref.: 1917 CIC 2392

In addition to the penalties against simoniacs established by law, a simoniacal contract and simony committed in regard to benefices, offices, dignities, and subsequent provisions lacks all force, even if the simony was committed by a third person, even if unknowingly, provided this was not done in fraud of such a one or over his objections. Therefore:

1.° Even before judicial sentence, those things given or received in simony must be restored if restitution is possible and not prevented by the reverence owed to a spiritual thing, and a benefice, office, or dignity is lost;

2.° Simoniacal provision does not yield fruit; but if the fruits are received in good faith, it is left to the prudence of the judge or the Ordinary to permit the condonation of the fruits provided in whole or in part.

Canon 730[2] (NA)

It is not considered simony when a temporal thing is not given for a spiritual thing but rather on the occasion [of a spiritual event] and it is owed by a just title in the sacred canons or by legitimate recognized custom; the same is true when a temporal thing is given for a temporal thing, even though the temporal thing might be attached to a spiritual, for example, a consecrated chalice, although the price may not be increased because of its connection to the spiritual thing.

FIRST PART
ON SACRAMENTS

Canon 731[1] (1983 CIC 840, 844)

§ 1. As all the Sacraments of the New Law, instituted by Christ our Lord, are the principal means of sanctification and salvation, the greatest

---

[2] James Richardson, "The Just Title in Canon 730 for Giving Something Temporal on the Occasion of the Sacred Ministry" (diss. no. 3, Pontifical University of St. Thomas [Rome], 1934–1935).

[1] James King, "The Administration of the Sacraments to Dying Non-Catholics", Canon Law Studies, no. 23 (J. C. D. thesis, Catholic University of America, 1924); John Behen, "The Administration of the Sacraments to Unconscious Non-Catholics in Danger of Death" (diss. no. 16, Pontifical University of St. Thomas [Rome], 1955–1956); Leo Vanyo, "Requisites of Intention

diligence and reverence is to be observed in opportunely and correctly administering them and receiving them.

§ 2. It is forbidden that the Sacraments of the Church be ministered to heretics and schismatics, even if they ask for them and are in good faith, unless beforehand, rejecting their errors, they are reconciled with the Church.

Canon Law Digest

III: 299–300; VI: 517; VII: 583–90; VIII: 465–72; IX: 501–8; X: 139–40

Canon 732 (1983 CIC 845)

§ 1. The Sacraments of baptism, confirmation, and orders, which imprint a character, cannot be repeated.

§ 2. But if a prudent doubt exists about whether really and validly these [Sacraments] were conferred, they are to be conferred again under condition.

Canon Law Digest

VI: 517

Canon 733 (1983 CIC 845)

§ 1. In confecting, administering, and receiving the Sacraments, the rites and ceremonies that are prescribed in the approved ritual books of the Church are to be accurately observed.

§ 2. Each individual shall follow his own rite, with due regard for the prescription of Canons 851, § 2, and 866.

Canon Law Digest

III: 301; IV: 251–53; V: 401

Canon 734 (1983 CIC 847)

§ 1. The holy oils that are used in the administration of certain Sacraments must be blessed by the Bishop on the [Holy Thursday] immediately before; older [oils] shall not be used unless necessity urges.

§ 2. In case of an insufficient supply of blessed oil, the non-blessed oil of olives can be added, [and] even [added] again, though in an amount less than [was] the original.

Canon Law Digest

III: 301; VII: 590–91; VIII: 472–73

Canon 735 (1983 CIC 847, 1003) Cross-Ref.: 1917 CIC 946

Pastors must request holy oils from their own Ordinary and diligently preserve them under key in the church in careful and decent protection;

---

in the Reception of the Sacraments", Canon Law Studies, no. 391 (J. C. D. thesis, Catholic University of America, 1965).

they shall not keep them in their house except because of necessity or other reasonable cause, [and] with the permission of the Ordinary.

Canon Law Digest
VI: 517

Canon 736[2] (1983 CIC 848)

For the administration of Sacraments, the minister shall not for any reason or occasion, directly or indirectly, require or request [anything] beyond the offerings mentioned in Canon 1507, § 1.

TITLE 1
On baptism

Canon 737 (1983 CIC 849)

§ 1. Baptism, the gateway and foundation of the Sacraments, actually or at least in desire is necessary for all for salvation and is not validly conferred except by washing with true and natural water along with the prescribed formula of words.

§ 2. When it is administered in accord with all of the rites and ceremonies that are prescribed in the ritual books, it is called *solemn*; otherwise, [it is called] *non-solemn* or *private*.

Canon Law Digest
IV: 253; VI: 517; VII: 591; VIII: 473

Chapter 1
On the minister of baptism[3]

Canon 738 (1983 CIC 857, 861)

§ 1. The ordinary minister of solemn baptism is a priest; but its conferral is reserved to the pastor or other priests with the permission of the

[2] Michael Fitzpatrick, "The Gratuity of the Sacraments: An Historical Study and Interpretation of Canon 736" (MS no. 3431, Gregorian University, 1962).

[3] Joseph Waldron, "The Minister of Baptism", Canon Law Studies, no. 170 (J. C. D. thesis, Catholic University of America, 1942).

local Ordinary or of the same pastor, which in case of necessity is legitimately presumed.

§ 2. Even a traveler may be solemnly baptized by his own pastor in his own parish, if this can be done easily and without delay; otherwise any pastor can solemnly baptize a traveler in his territory.

Canon 739 (1983 CIC 862)

In another's territory it is not permitted to anyone, without the required permission, to confer solemn baptism even on his own residents of [his own] place.

Canon 740 (NA)

Where parishes or quasi-parishes have not been constituted, reference should be made to particular statutes and received custom in order to determine which priest, besides the Ordinary, has the right of baptizing in the whole territory or part of it.

Canon 741 (1983 CIC 61)

The extraordinary minister of solemn baptism is a deacon; who, however, shall not use his power without the permission of the local Ordinary or the pastor, granted for a just cause that, when necessity urges, is legitimately presumed.

Canon Law Digest
VII: 591–92; X: 140

Canon 742 (1983 CIC 861)

§ 1. Non-solemn baptism, discussed in Canon 759, § 1, can be administered by anyone, preserving the required matter, form, and intention; when it can be done this way, two witnesses, or at least one, should be used, by which the conferral of the baptism can be proved.

§ 2. If there is a priest present, he is preferred to a deacon, a deacon to a subdeacon, a cleric to layman, and a man to a woman, unless for the sake of modesty it is more becoming that a woman baptize instead of a man, or unless a woman knows the form and manner of baptism better than does a man.

§ 3. It is not permitted that the father or mother baptize their own child, except in danger of death, when there is no one else who can baptize.

Canon 743 (1983 CIC 861)

The pastor shall take care that the faithful, especially obstetricians, doctors, and surgeons, are carefully taught the correct manner of baptizing in case of necessity.

Canon 744 (1983 CIC 863)

The baptism of adults, where this can be done conveniently, should be deferred to the local Ordinary, so that, if he wishes, [baptism] can be solemnly conferred by him or one delegated by him.

Canon Law Digest
V: 401–6

Chapter 2
On the subject of baptism

Canon 745 (1983 CIC 852, 864)

§ 1. That subject capable of baptism is every and only a living human [being] not yet baptized.

§ 2. When it concerns a baptism:

1.° They are considered a child or infant under Canon 88, § 3, who have not attained the use of reason or who have been without reason since infancy regardless of their age;

2.° They are considered adults who exercise the use of reason, likewise those who sufficiently ask for baptism on their own and can be admitted to it.

Canon Law Digest
VIII: 473; IX: 508–27; X: 141–44

Canon 746 (NA)

§ 1. No one should be baptized in the mother's womb so long as there is a hope that he can be baptized correctly outside of it.

§ 2. If the head of an infant is exposed and there is imminent danger of death, let him be baptized on the head; later, if he is delivered alive, he should not be baptized again under condition.

§ 3. If another part of the body is exposed, and if danger [of death] is imminent, let him be baptized under condition thereupon, and then, if he survives birth, he should be once again baptized under condition.

§ 4. If a pregnant mother dies, and if the fetus is delivered by those who do such things, and if he is certainly alive, he should be baptized absolutely; if there is doubt, [he should be baptized] under condition.

§ 5. A fetus baptized in the womb should be baptized again under condition after [being born].

Canon 747 (1983 CIC 871)

Care should be taken that aborted fetuses, at whatever time they are born, if they are certainly alive, be baptized absolutely; if there is doubt, under condition after [being born].

Canon 748 (NA)

Deformed or abnormal fetuses should be baptized at least under condition; if there is doubt as to whether there is one or several humans, one should be baptized absolutely, the others under condition.

Canon 749 (1983 CIC 870)

Exposed and discovered infants, the matter having been thoroughly investigated, should be baptized under condition, absent proof of their [earlier] baptism.

Canon 750[4] (1983 CIC 868)

§ 1. The infant of infidels, even over the objections of the parents, is licitly baptized when life is so threatened that it is prudently foreseen that death will result before the infant attains the use of reason.

§ 2. Outside of danger of death, provided provision is made for Catholic education, [an infant] is licitly baptized if:

1.° If the parents or guardians, or at least one of them, consents;

[4] Paul Wachtrle, "The Baptism of the Children of Non Catholics", Canon Law Studies, no. 246 (Catholic University of America, not published); Ralf Wiatrowski, "The Responsibility of Parents in Presenting a Child for Baptism: The General Development of Church Law and Recent Particular Applications of Various Dioceses in the United States of America" (diss. no. 4, Pontifical University of St. Thomas [Rome], 1980–1981).

2.° If the parents, that is, father, mother, grandfather, grandmother, or guardians are no more, or have lost their rights over [the infant] or cannot in any way exercise it.

Canon Law Digest
I: 337; II: 181–82; III: 301; V: 406–7; VII: 592–94

Canon 751 (1983 CIC 868)

Generally the norms specified in the above canons are to be observed whenever it is a case of the baptism of the infant of two heretics or schismatics, or of two Catholics who have fallen into apostasy, heresy, or schism.

Canon Law Digest
III: 302

Canon 752[5] (1983 CIC 851, 865)

§ 1. An adult should not be baptized unless he knowingly and with desire has been rightly instructed; moreover, he should be admonished to be sorry for sins.

§ 2. But in danger of death, if the adult is not able to be diligently instructed in the principal mysteries of the faith, it is sufficient for the conferral of baptism that he shows by some sign that he agrees with them and seriously commits himself to the observance of the mandates of the Christian religion.

§ 3. But if he is not able to ask for baptism, [yet] either before or during the present state he manifested in some probable way the intention of receiving it, he should be baptized under condition; if he later recovers and there is doubt about the validity of the baptism conferred, he should be baptized again under condition.

Canon Law Digest
II: 182–84; V: 407–8; VII: 594

Canon 753 (1983 CIC 866)

§ 1. It is becoming that both the priest who is going to baptize adults and the adults themselves, if they are healthy, observe a fast.

[5] Hugo Amico, "Adult Catechetical Instruction" (diss. no. 27, Pontifical University of St. Thomas [Rome], 1954–1955).

§ 2. Unless grave and urgent causes obstruct, baptized adults should immediately assist at Mass and receive holy communion.

Canon 754 (1983 CIC 852)

§ 1. The insane or mad should not be baptized unless they were such from birth or from before they attained the use of reason; and then they are to be baptized as if infants.

§ 2. If they have lucid intervals, while they are in possession of their senses, they can be baptized if they wish.

§ 3. If in imminent danger of death, they can likewise be baptized if before they were insane, they showed the desire of taking baptism.

§ 4. If they are in a coma or delirium, they can be baptized only when awake and desirous [of baptism]; but if danger of death occurs, the prescript of § 3 is to be observed.

Chapter 3
On the rites and ceremonies of baptism

Canon 755 (NA)

§ 1. Baptism is to be conferred solemnly, with due regard for the prescription of Canon 759.

§ 2. The local Ordinary can for a grave and reasonable cause permit the ceremonies prescribed for the baptism of an infant to be applied in the baptism of an adult.

Canon Law Digest
V: 409; VII: 594–96; VIII: 473

Canon 756 (1983 CIC 111)

§ 1. Children must be baptized according to the rite of the parents.

§ 2. If one parent belongs to the latin rite, and the other to an oriental [rite], the children are baptized according to the rite of the father, unless provided otherwise by special law.

§ 3. If only one [parent] is Catholic, the children are to be baptized in that rite.

Canon Law Digest
I: 337–38; III: 302

Canon 757 (1983 CIC 853)

§ 1. In solemn baptism water blessed for this purpose is to be used.

§ 2. If the blessed water in the baptistery is so depleted that it seems insufficient, it can be mixed with other non-blessed water, even again, nevertheless remaining less than the original amount.

§ 3. But if it has become corrupt or evaporated, or is in any other way deficient, the pastor shall pour new water into the fount, cleaned well and polished, and bless it according to the proper prescribed rites in his liturgical books.

Canon 758 (1983 CIC 854)

Although baptism can be validly conferred by infusion, or by immersion, or by aspersion, the first or the second manner, or a mixture of both, whichever is in greater use, shall be retained, according to the approved ritual books of the various Churches.

Canon 759 (NA) Cross-Refs.: 1917 CIC 742, 755, 760

§ 1. In case of danger of death, baptism is licitly conferred privately; and if it is conferred by a minister who is neither a priest nor a deacon, he should do only those things necessary for the validity of baptism; if a priest or deacon is available, they should apply, if time allows, the baptismal norms that follow.

§ 2. Outside of danger of death, the local Ordinary should not permit private baptism, unless it is a case of heretics who are being baptized under condition at an adult age.

§ 3. The ceremonies that were omitted in the conferral of the baptism, for whatever reason, should be supplied in a church as soon as possible, except in cases described in § 2.

Canon Law Digest
I: 338; III: 302–3

Canon 760 (NA)

Whenever baptism is repeated under condition, the ceremonies, if indeed they were omitted in the first baptism, are supplied, with due regard for the prescription of Canon 759, § 3; but if they were applied in the first baptism, their repetition can be omitted in the second.

Canon 761 (1983 CIC 855)

Pastors should take care that a Christian name is given to those whom they baptize; but if they are not able to bring this about, they will add to the name given by the parents the name of some Saint and record both names in the book of baptisms.

Canon Law Digest
VII: 597

CHAPTER 4
On sponsors[6]

Canon 762 (1983 CIC 872)

§ 1. Out of the most ancient practice of the Church, no one should be solemnly baptized unless he has, insofar as possible, a sponsor.

§ 2. Even in private baptism, a sponsor, if he can be had readily, should be used; if he is not available, let him be used in the supplemental ceremonies of baptism, although in this case he does not contract a spiritual relationship.

Canon 763 (NA)

§ 1. When baptism is repeated under condition, the same sponsor, insofar as this is possible, as might have been present the first time should be used; outside of this case a sponsor is not necessary in conditional baptism.

§ 2. In a baptism repeated under condition, neither the sponsor who was present for the first baptism, nor the one used for the second, contracts a spiritual relationship, unless the same sponsor was used in both baptisms.

Canon 764 (1983 CIC 873)

Only one patron, even if of a different sex from the one to be baptized, or a pair consisting of one male and one female, is to be admitted.

---

[6] Richard Kearney, "Sponsors at Baptism according to the Code of Canon Law", Canon Law Studies, no. 30 (J. C. D. thesis, Catholic University of America, 1925).

Canon 765 (1983 CIC 874) Cross-Ref.: 1917 CIC 795

In order to be a patron, one must:

1.° Be baptized, have attained the use of reason, and have the intention of performing the office;

2.° Belong to no heretical or schismatic sect, not be under a condemnatory sentence or declaration of excommunication or be infamous by infamy of law or excluded from legitimate acts, or be a deposed or degraded cleric;

3.° Be neither the father, mother, or spouse of the one to be baptized;

4.° Be designated by the one to be baptized, or the parents, or guardians or, these being absent, the minister;

5.° Himself or through another physically hold or touch the one to be baptized in the act of baptism or immediately lift him up or receive him from the sacred font or from the hands of the one baptizing.

Canon Law Digest
I: 338–44; V: 409; VII: 597–99; VIII: 474

Canon 766 (1983 CIC 874) Cross-Ref.: 1917 CIC 796

In order that one be licitly admitted as sponsor, he ought:

1.° To have attained the age of fourteen, unless it seems otherwise to the minister for a just cause;

2.° Not be excommunicated because of a notorious delict or excluded from legitimate acts or infamous by infamy of law, although not without a sentence, or be interdicted or otherwise publicly a criminal or infamous by infamy of fact;

3.° To know the rudiments of the faith;

4.° Not be a novice or professed as a religious, unless necessity urges and then with the express approval of the Superior at least of that place;

5.° Not be constituted in sacred orders, unless he has received the express permission of his own Ordinary.

Canon Law Digest
I: 344

Canon 767 (NA)

In doubt as to whether or not one can be validly or licitly admitted to the role of sponsor, the pastor, if time allows, shall consult the Ordinary.

Canon 768 (NA) Cross-Ref.: 1917 CIC 1079

From baptism a spiritual relationship is contracted only between the one baptizing, the one being baptized, and the sponsor.

Canon Law Digest
I: 344; V: 409

Canon 769 (1983 CIC 872)

It is for sponsors, having taken up their duties, to regard as a spiritual son the one committed to them, and in those things that look to Christian upbringing, to take diligent care that he acts throughout life in the way that they promised him to be in the future by solemn ceremony.

Canon Law Digest
I: 344; VIII: 474

Chapter 5
On the time and place for conferring baptism[7]

Canon 770[8] (1983 CIC 867)

Infants should be baptized as soon as possible; pastors and preachers should frequently stress with the faithful the gravity of their obligation.

Canon Law Digest
V: 409

Canon 771 (NA)

Private baptism, in urgent necessity, is to be administered at any time and in any place.

Canon 772 (1983 CIC 856)

Of course solemn baptism can be administered on any day; it is fitting, however, that the baptism of adults, according to the most ancient rites of

[7] Thomas Horton, "The Time and Place of Baptism" (doctoral diss. 18, University of Ottawa, 1947); Walter Conway, "The Time and Place of Baptism", Canon Law Studies, no. 324 (thesis, Catholic University of America, 1954).

[8] Dennis Schnurr, "The Quamprimum of Infant Baptism in the Western Church", Canon Law Studies, no. 501 (J. C. D. thesis, Catholic University of America, 1981).

the Church, be conferred, if this can be conveniently done, during the vigil of Easter and Pentecost, especially in metropolitan or cathedral churches.

Canon 773 (1983 CIC 857)

The proper place for the administration of solemn baptism is the baptistery of a church or public oratory.

Canon Law Digest
I: 345

Canon 774 (1983 CIC 858)

§ 1. Every parish church whatsoever, all contrary statutes, privileges, or customs being revoked and reprobated, shall have a baptismal fount, with due regard for the legitimate and cumulative acquired rights of other churches.

§ 2. For the convenience of the faithful, the local Ordinary can permit or order that a baptismal fount be placed also in another church or public oratory within the parish boundaries.

Canon Law Digest
I: 345–46; II: 184

Canon 775 (1983 CIC 859)

If because of distance or other matters, one to be baptized cannot, without grave inconvenience or danger, approach or be brought to the parish church or another church that enjoys the right of having a [baptismal] fount, solemn baptism can and must be conferred by the pastor in a nearby church or public oratory within the parish boundaries, even though it lacks a baptismal fount.

Canon Law Digest
I: 346

Canon 776 (1983 CIC 860)

§ 1. Solemn baptism must not be administered in private houses, except under these circumstances:

1.° If the ones to be baptized are the children or grandchildren of those who have the supreme governing power over a people or have the right to ascend to the throne, as often as they legitimately request it;

2.° If the local Ordinary, according to his own prudent judgment and conscience, for a just and reasonable cause, thinks it should be allowed in certain extraordinary cases.

§ 2. In the above cases, baptism is to be conferred in a domestic chapel or at least in some other decent place, and blessed baptismal water [should be used] per practice.

Canon Law Digest
I: 346–47; VII: 599–603

Chapter 6
On recording and proving the conferral of baptism

Canon 777 (1983 CIC 877)

§ 1. Pastors must carefully record without any delay in the baptismal book the names of persons baptized, making mention of the minister, parents and sponsors, and the place and day of the conferral of baptism.

§ 2. Where it concerns illegitimate children, the name of the mother is to be inserted, if her maternity is proven publicly, or if she asks for it on her own in writing or in the presence of two witnesses; likewise the name of the father if he asks for it of his pastor on his own in writing or in the presence of two witnesses, or if he is known [to be the father] from an authentic public document; in other cases, let only the name of the child be inscribed and [“]father unknown[”] or [“]parents unknown[”].

Canon Law Digest
I: 347; II: 184; V: 409

Canon 778 (1983 CIC 878)

If the baptism was administered neither by the pastor nor in his presence, the minister of that conferral [of baptism] shall as soon as possible make the baptism known to the pastor of the place of domicile of the one baptized.

Canon Law Digest
I: 348; II: 184; V: 410

Canon 779 (1983 CIC 876)

In order to prove the conferral of baptism, if it is not prejudicial to anyone, one witness entirely above suspicion is sufficient, or the oath of the baptized person himself if he received baptism as an adult.

TITLE 2
On confirmation

Canon 780 (1983 CIC 880)

The Sacrament of confirmation must be conferred by the imposition of hands together with anointing by chrism on the forehead and with the words prescribed in the pontifical books approved by the Church.

Canon Law Digest
VII: 604–11; VIII: 474–75

Canon 781 (1983 CIC 880)

§ 1. The chrism that is to be used in the sacrament of confirmation must be consecrated by the bishop even if the sacrament, by law or apostolic indult, is being administered by a priest.

§ 2. Anointing is not to be made by an instrument, but by the very hand of the minister duly imposed on the forehead of the one to be confirmed.

Canon Law Digest
II: 185; VI: 518; VII: 611

Chapter 1
On the minister of confirmation[9]

Canon 782 (1983 CIC 882–83) Cross-Ref.: 1917 CIC 294

§ 1. The ordinary minister of confirmation is only a Bishop.

[9] John Coleman, "The Minister of Confirmation", Canon Law Studies, no. 125 (thesis, Catholic University of America, 1941); John Quinn, "The Extraordinary Minister of Confirmation according to the Most Recent Decrees of the Sacred Congregations" (MS no. 1520, Gregorian University, 1949; printed version, no. 678, 1949); Henry Dziadosz, "The Provisions of the Decree *Spiritus Sancti Munera*: The Law for the Extraordinary Minister of Confirmation", Canon Law Studies, no. 397 (J. C. D. thesis, Catholic University of America, 1958).

§ 2. The extraordinary minister is a priest to whom the faculty has been granted, either by common law or special indult of the Apostolic See.

§ 3. Besides Cardinals of the H. R. C. according to Canon 239, § 1, n. 23, Abbots or Prelates *of no one* and Apostolic Vicars and Prefects enjoy this faculty by law, although they cannot act validly except within the limits of their territory and for so long as they hold their posts.

§ 4. Priests of the latin rite who have this faculty in virtue of an indult confer confirmation validly only on the faithful of their own rite, unless it is expressly provided otherwise in the indult.

§ 5. It is nefarious for priests of the oriental rites who enjoy the privilege or faculty of confirming infants of their own rite at the time of their baptism to administer [confirmation] to latin rite infants.

Canon Law Digest
II: 185–89; III: 303–14; IV: 253–56; V: 410–13; VI: 518;
VIII: 475–77; IX: 527–28; X: 144–45

Canon 783 (1983 CIC 886)

§ 1. A Bishop in his own diocese legitimately administers this sacrament even to outsiders, unless there is an express prohibition from their own Ordinary.

§ 2. In another diocese [a Bishop] requires the permission of the local Ordinary, at least reasonably presumed, unless it concerns his own subjects whom he will confirm privately without a crosier and miter.

Canon 784 (1983 CIC 887)

A priest also, who has an apostolic indult for a local privilege, confirms even outsiders in his designated territory, unless they are expressly prohibited from this by their own Ordinary.

Canon 785 (1983 CIC 885)

§ 1. A Bishop is bound by the obligation of conferring this sacrament on his subjects who rightly and reasonably petition it, especially at the time of his diocesan visit.

§ 2. A priest is bound by the same obligation, having an apostolic privilege, [to confirm] those on whose behalf the favor was granted.

§ 3. An Ordinary, impeded by legitimate cause or lacking the power of confirming, must, insofar as possible, see that this sacrament is administered to his subjects at least every five years.

§ 4. If [the Ordinary] gravely neglects to administer the sacrament of confirmation either himself or through another, the prescription of Canon 274, n.4 is followed.

Chapter 2
On the subject of confirmation[10]

Canon 786 (1983 CIC 889)

One not washed by the water of baptism cannot be validly confirmed; moreover, in order that one be fruitfully and licitly confirmed, he must be constituted in the state of grace and, if he has obtained the use of reason, be sufficiently instructed.

Canon Law Digest
II: 189

Canon 787 (1983 CIC 890)

Although this sacrament is not necessary as a means of salvation, it is not permitted for anyone, when occasion arises, to neglect it; indeed, pastors shall take care that the faithful approach it at an opportune time.

Canon 788 (1983 CIC 891)

Although the administration of the sacrament of confirmation in the Latin Church is conveniently deferred until about the age of seven years, nevertheless, it can be conferred earlier if an infant is constituted in danger of death or there appear to the minister grave and just causes to expedite it.

Canon Law Digest
I: 348–49; II: 189; III: 314–15; VII: 611; IX: 528–29

Canon 789 (NA)

If there are many to be confirmed, they should be present for the first imposition or extension of the hands and should not leave until the rite has been completed.

---

[10] James Bennington, "The Recipient of Confirmation", Canon Law Studies, no. 267 (thesis, Catholic University of America, 1952).

Chapter 3

On the time and place for conferring confirmation

Canon 790 (1983 CIC 881)

This sacrament can be conferred at any time; it is most becoming that it be administered during Pentecost week.

Canon 791 (1983 CIC 881)

Although the proper place for the administration of confirmation is a church, for causes that the minister judges to be just and reasonable, the sacrament can be conferred in any decent place.

Canon 792 (1983 CIC 888)

The right belongs to the Bishop of administering confirmation within the limits of his diocese even in exempt places.

Chapter 4

On sponsors

Canon 793 (1983 CIC 892)

From the oldest practice of the Church, just as in baptism, so also in confirmation a sponsor is to be used, if this can be done.

Canon Law Digest
I: 349

Canon 794 (NA)

§ 1. A sponsor presents only one person to be confirmed, or two, unless it seems otherwise to the minister for just cause.

§ 2. There is also only one sponsor for each person to be confirmed.

Canon 795 (1983 CIC 893)

In order to be a sponsor it is required that one:

1.° Also be confirmed, having obtained the use of reason, and having the intention of fulfilling the role;

2.° Not belong to any heretical or schismatic sect, or be under any penalty mentioned in Canon 765, n. 2, or be under a declaratory or condemnatory sentence;

3.° Not be the father, mother, or spouse of the one to be confirmed;

4.° Be designated by the one being confirmed or the parents or the guardians or, if these are absent or refuse [to name a sponsor], by the minister or the pastor;

5.° Physically touch personally or through a procurator the one being confirmed in the very act of confirmation.

Canon Law Digest
VII: 612

Canon 796 (1983 CIC 893)

In order to be licitly admitted to the role of sponsor it is required:

1.° That he be different from the sponsor at baptism unless for reasonable cause in the judgment of the minister it argues otherwise, or if confirmation is legitimately conferred immediately after baptism;

2.° That he [or she] be of the same sex as the one being confirmed unless in particular cases it seems to the minister there are reasonable causes to do otherwise;

3.° That the additional prescriptions of Canon 766 be observed.

Canon Law Digest
I: 350; II: 189; VII: 612

Canon 797 (1983 CIC 892)

From a valid confirmation there arises between the one confirmed and the sponsor a spiritual relationship by which the sponsor is bound by the obligation of perpetual concern toward the one confirmed and of taking care for his Christian education.

Canon Law Digest
I: 350

Chapter 5
On recording and proving the conferral of confirmation

Canon 798 (1983 CIC 895)

The pastor will inscribe the name of the minister, the ones confirmed, the parents and sponsors, and the day and place of the confirmation in a special book, beyond the annotation [he needs to make] in the book of the baptized mentioned in Canon 470, § 2.

Canon Law Digest
I: 350

Canon 799 (1983 CIC 896)

If the proper pastor of the one confirmed was not present, the minister himself or through another shall inform the pastor about the conferral as soon as possible.

Canon 800 (1983 CIC 894)

In order to prove the conferral of confirmation, if it is not prejudicial to anyone, it suffices that there be one witness above all exception, or the oath of the one confirmed [suffices], unless confirmation was received while an infant.

TITLE 3
On the most holy Eucharist[11]

Canon 801 (1983 CIC 897–99)

In the most holy Eucharist under the species of bread and wine Christ the Lord himself is contained, offered, and received.

Canon Law Digest
VI: 518–49; VII: 612; VIII: 477–516; IX: 529–74; X: 145

Chapter 1
On the sacrosanct sacrifice of the Mass

Article 1—*On the priest celebrating the sacrifice of the Mass*

Canon 802 (1983 CIC 900)

Only priests have the power of offering the sacrifice of the Mass.

Canon Law Digest
IV: 256

[11] Thomas Donnellan, "The Obligation of the *Missa pro Populo*", Canon Law Studies, no. 155 (J. C. D. thesis, Catholic University of America, 1942).

Canon 803[12] (1983 CIC 902)

It is not licit that several priests concelebrate, beyond the Mass of ordination of priests and in the Mass of consecration of Bishops according to the Roman Pontifical.

Canon Law Digest
IV: 256–57; VII: 612–14; VIII: 516; IX: 574–75

Canon 804[13] (1983 CIC 903)

§ 1. A priest from outside the church in which he wishes to celebrate, showing an authentic and currently valid letter of commendation from his own Ordinary if he is secular, or from his Superior if he is religious, or from the Sacred Congregation for the Oriental Church if he is of an oriental rite, is to be admitted to the celebration of Mass unless in the meantime it is shown that he committed some deed that would require him to be prevented from the celebration of Mass.

§ 2. If he lacks these letters but the rector of the church is quite convinced of his worthiness, he can be admitted to celebrate; but if he is unknown to the rector he can be admitted once or twice, provided though, that he is dressed in ecclesiastical garb, and he receives no title in virtue of celebrating in the church, and he signs his name, office, and diocese in a special book.

§ 3. Special rules on this matter, consistent with the prescriptions of these canons, that are given by the local Ordinary are to be observed by all, even exempt religious, unless it concerns permitting a religious to celebrate in the church of his religious [institute].

Canon Law Digest
I: 350; II: 189; III: 315–16; IX: 575–77

Canon 805 (1983 CIC 904)

Priests are bound by the obligation of offering Mass several times per year; the Bishop or religious Superior shall take care that they perform divine [actions] at least on [Sundays] and other feasts of precept.

---

[12] Harmon Skillin, "Concelebration", Canon Law Studies, no. 450 (Catholic University of America, 1966).

[13] George Schorr, "The Law of the Celebret", Canon Law Studies, no. 332 (thesis, Catholic University of America, 1952).

Canon 806[14] (1983 CIC 905) Cross-Ref.: 1917 CIC 2321

§ 1. Except on the day of the Nativity of the Lord and the day of commemoration of all the faithful departed, for which there is the faculty of offering the Eucharistic Sacrifice three times, it is not licit that priests celebrate Mass several times a day except by apostolic indult or power granted by the local Ordinary.

§ 2. The Ordinary is not to grant this faculty except when, in his own prudent judgment, because of a shortage of priests a notable part of the faithful will be without Mass on a day of precept; it is not within his power to permit the same priest to say more than two Masses.

Canon Law Digest
I: 350–51; II: 189–93; IV: 257–58; V: 413–17; VI: 549–50;
VII: 614–16; VIII: 516–17; X: 145–46

Canon 807 (1983 CIC 916)

Priests conscious of grave sin, no matter how contrite they believe themselves to be, shall not dare to celebrate Mass without prior sacramental confession; but if because there is lacking a sufficient supply of confessors and there is urgent necessity, he shall make an act of perfect contrition, celebrate, and as soon as possible confess.

Canon 808 (1983 CIC 919) Cross-Ref.: 1917 CIC 2321

It is not licit for priests to celebrate without having observed a natural fast from midnight.

Canon Law Digest
I: 351–52; II: 193; III: 316–18; IV: 259;
VI: 550; IX: 577

[14] Joseph Gray, "Two Obligations of Justice by Bination" (diss. no. 4, Pontifical University of St. Thomas [Rome], 1959–1960); Lawrence Beeson, "The Number of Masses that May Be Celebrated in One Day according to the Motu Proprio *Pastorale munus* Faculty Number Two" (diss. no. 9, Pontifical University of St. Thomas [Rome], 1964–1965).

Canon 809 (1983 CIC 901)

It is basic that Mass can be applied for the living and for the dead undergoing expiation by fire in purgatory, with due regard for the prescription of Canon 2262, § 2, n. 2.

Canon Law Digest
VIII: 517

Canon 810 (1983 CIC 909)

Priests shall not fail to dispose themselves by pious prayers to offer the Eucharistic Sacrifice, and when it is finished, to give thanks to God for such a gift.

Canon 811 (1983 CIC 929)

§ 1. A priest about to celebrate Mass shall wear an appropriate garb that reaches the ankles and those sacred ornaments that are prescribed in the rubrics of his rite.

§ 2. He shall also abstain from a cap and ring unless he is a Cardinal of the H. R. C., or a Bishop or blessed Abbot, or unless by apostolic indult the use of these is permitted him in celebrating Mass.

Canon Law Digest
I: 352

Canon 812 (NA)

No celebrating [priest], other than the Bishop and other prelates enjoying pontifical use prerogatives, may, solely for the sake of honor or solemnity, have an assisting presbyter.

Canon 813[15] (1983 CIC 906)

§ 1. A priest should not celebrate Mass without a minister who assists him and responds.

§ 2. The minister serving at Mass should not be a woman unless, in the absence of a man, for a just cause, it is so arranged that the woman respond from afar and by no means approach the altar.

Canon Law Digest
III: 318–40; X: 146–47

---

[15] Anselm Regan, "The Law Requiring a Server at Mass: A Study of Its Origin, and of the Development of Its Interpretation" (doctoral diss. 37, University of Ottawa, 1952).

Article 2—*On the rites and ceremonies of Mass*

Canon 814 (1983 CIC 924)

The sacrosanct sacrifice of the Mass must be offered with bread and wine, to which the smallest amount of water is mixed.

Canon Law Digest
V: 417–18

Canon 815 (1983 CIC 924)

§ 1. The bread must be pure wheat and recently made so that there is no danger of corruption.

§ 2. The wine must be a natural product of the vine and not corrupt.

Canon Law Digest
I: 352–67; II: 193–95; V: 418–19; VI: 551;
VII: 617; VIII: 517–20; IX: 577–85

Canon 816 (1983 CIC 926)

A priest in the celebration of the Mass, according to his own rite, must use unleavened or leavened bread whenever he says the Holy [Mass].

Canon 817 (1983 CIC 927)

It is nefarious, even if urged by extreme necessity, to consecrate one matter without the other, or even both outside of the celebration of Mass.

Canon 818 (1983 CIC 846)

Reprobating every contrary custom, celebrating priests are to observe accurately and devoutly the rubrics of their own ritual books, taking care lest they add other ceremonies or prayers on their own authority.

Canon Law Digest
I: 367–82; II: 195–202; III: 340–61; IV: 260–62; V: 419–30;
VI: 551–52; VII: 617–36; VIII: 520–29;
IX: 585–88; X: 147–48

Canon 819 (1983 CIC 928)

The sacrifice of the Mass is to be celebrated in the liturgical language approved by the Church for that rite.

Canon Law Digest
VI: 552–53

Article 3—*On the time and place for the celebration of Mass*[16]

Canon 820 (1983 CIC 931)

The sacrifice of the Mass can be celebrated on any day, except on those that are excluded by the priest's own rite.

Canon 821 (1983 CIC 931)

§ 1. The beginning of the celebration of Mass shall not occur earlier than one hour before first light or later than one hour after noon.

§ 2. On the night of Birth of the Lord only a conventual or parochial Mass can be held at midnight, and no other without apostolic indult.

§ 3. Nevertheless, in all religious or pious houses having an oratory with the faculty of habitually keeping the most holy Eucharist, on the night of the Birth of the Lord, one priest can say three ritual Masses or, those things being observed that ought to be observed, only one [Mass] which counts for the satisfaction of the precept for all who are there, and can minister sacred communion to all requesting it.

Canon Law Digest

I: 382–84; II: 202–3; IV: 263–64; V: 430–31; VI: 553–54; VIII: 529

Canon 822[17] (1983 CIC 932)

§ 1. Mass is to be celebrated on a consecrated altar and in a church or oratory consecrated or blessed according to the norm of law with due regard for the prescription of Canon 1196.

§ 2. The privilege of a *portable altar* can only be granted by law or by indult of the Apostolic See.

§ 3. This privilege is to be understood as encompassing the faculty of celebrating everywhere, provided the place is upright and decent and upon a sacred rock, but not on the seas.

---

[16] Vincent Nowak, "When to Say Mass" (thesis, Gregorian University; printed version, no. 197, 1939); Paul Leibold, "The Time of Mass" (diss. no. 4, Pontifical University of St. Thomas [Rome], 1948–1949); James Godley, "Time and Place for the Celebration of Mass", Canon Law Studies, no. 275 (thesis, Catholic University of America, 1948).

[17] Joseph Buckley, "The Celebration of Mass in 'Extraordinary' Places" (thesis, Gregorian University; printed version, no. 521, Bristol, England, 1947); Joseph Gallagher, "The Celebration of Mass outside of Churches and Oratories" (University of Laval, 1948); G. Izzo, "An Inter-Ritual Study concerning the Christian Altar in Canon Law: The Portable Altar, and in particular the Antimension, in the Canonical Tradition of Both Byzantine and Latin Churches" (diss. no. 125, Pontifical University "Antonianum", discussed June 24, 1968).

§ 4. The local Ordinary or, if it concerns the house of exempt religious, the major Superior can grant permission for celebrating outside a church [or] oratory [but] on a sacred rock and in a decent place, but never in a bedroom, only for a just and reasonable cause, in some extraordinary case, and one case at a time.

Canon Law Digest
I: 384–93; II: 203–4; III: 361–63; IV: 264–68; V: 432–33;
VI: 554–55; VII: 637–42; VIII: 529

Canon 823 (1983 CIC 933)

§ 1. It is not permitted to celebrate Mass in the temples of heretics or schismatics, even if at one time [they were] duly consecrated or blessed.

§ 2. In the absence of an altar of his own rite, it is fundamental that a priest can celebrate his own rite on an altar consecrated in another Catholic rite, but not on the *antimensiis* [altar cloths] of the Greeks.

§ 3. No one shall celebrate on papal altars without apostolic indult.

Canon Law Digest
VI: 555–57

Article 4—*On offerings or stipends for Mass*[18]

Canon 824 (1983 CIC 945, 951)

§ 1. According to the received and approved manner and institution of the Church it is permitted to every priest celebrating and applying a Mass to receive an offering, that is, a stipend.

§ 2. As often as a priest celebrates on a day, if he applies one Mass by a title of justice, except on the day of the Nativity of the Lord, he cannot receive another offering, except by some payment based on an extrinsic title.

Canon Law Digest
I: 393–95; II: 204–6; V: 433–34; VI: 557–58;
VII: 642–43; VIII: 530–36; IX: 588–89

[18] Charles Keller, "Mass Stipends", Canon Law Studies, no. 27 (J. C. D. thesis, Catholic University of America, 1925); Francis Keogh, "The Development of the Law on Gifts for Masses in England and Ireland" (ref. no. 30, Pontifical University Comillas [Madrid], 1961).

Canon 825 (NA)

It is never permitted:

1.° To apply a Mass for the intention of one who, upon offering the offering, will ask for the application [of a Mass], but has not yet done it, and later to retain the offering for the Mass applied before;

2.° To receive an offering for a Mass that by another title must be [offered] and applied;

3.° To accept two offerings for the application of the same Mass;

4.° To receive one offering only for the celebration and another for the application of the same Mass, unless it was certainly shown that one stipend was made for the application without celebration.

Canon Law Digest
III: 363–65; VI: 558–59

Canon 826 (NA)

§ 1. Stipends that the faithful offer for a Mass either out of their own devotion, as it were by hand, or by an obligation, even perpetual, made by a testator on his heirs, are called *manual.*

§ 2. Stipends for foundation Masses are called *similar to manual,* which cannot be offered in their own place or by those who are to offer them according to the records of the foundation, and likewise those that by law or indult of the Holy See are given to other priests for their satisfaction.

§ 3. Other stipends that are received from the assets of a foundation are called *founded* or *foundation Masses.*

Canon 827 (1983 CIC 947) Cross-Ref.: 1917 CIC 2324

From any kind of Mass stipend every hint of business or commercialism should be avoided.

Canon Law Digest
I: 395

Canon 828 (1983 CIC 948) Cross-Ref.: 1917 CIC 2324

There should be as many Masses applied and celebrated as there are stipends given and accepted.

Canon Law Digest
I: 395; III: 365–66; VI: 559; VII: 643–45; IX: 590

Canon 829 (1983 CIC 949)

Even though a Mass offering, given and accepted, might be lost without any fault of the one who is gravely bound to celebrate it, the obligation does not cease.

Canon 830 (1983 CIC 950)

If someone puts down a sum of money for the application of Masses, not indicating their number, it should be calculated according to the offerings customarily given in that place, unless his intention must be legitimately presumed otherwise.

Canon Law Digest
II: 206–7

Canon 831 (1983 CIC 952)

§ 1. It is for the local Ordinary to determine by decree the stipend for manual Masses in his diocese, [and this decree] as far as possible [is to be] laid down in a diocesan Synod; nor is it permitted for a priest to demand one higher.

§ 2. Where there is lacking a decree of the Ordinary, the custom of the diocese is observed.

§ 3. Religious, too, even exempt ones, must stand by the decree of the local Ordinary concerning manual stipends, or by diocesan custom.

Canon Law Digest
I: 395–96

Canon 832 (1983 CIC 952)

It is fundamental that a priest can accept a stipend for the celebration of Mass larger than [established in that area]; and, unless the local Ordinary prohibits it, [likewise to accept] one smaller.

Canon Law Digest
I: 396

Canon 833 (NA)

It is presumed that an offering is solely for the application of Mass; if, however, the offeror expressly determines other circumstances to be observed in the celebration of the Mass, the priest who accepts the offering must stand by those wishes.

Canon Law Digest
I: 396

Canon 834 (NA)

§ 1. Masses for which celebration a time is expressly prescribed by the offeror [of the stipend] must in every event be celebrated at that time.

§ 2. If the offeror does not prescribe a time for the celebration of manual Masses:

1.° Masses [requested] for urgent causes must be celebrated as soon as possible [and while the cause exists];

2.° In other cases Masses are to be celebrated within the least amount of time given the higher or lower number of Masses.

§ 3. But if the offeror expressly leaves the time of celebration to the decision of the priest, the priest can pick a time most convenient to himself, with due regard for the prescription of Canon 835.

Canon Law Digest
VI: 559

Canon 835 (1983 CIC 953) Cross-Ref.: 1917 CIC 834

It is not permitted to anyone to accept more responsibilities for the celebration of Masses than he can satisfy within one year.

Canon Law Digest
I: 396

Canon 836 (1983 CIC 954)

In churches in which, because of a special devotion of the faithful, Mass offerings are abundant, such that all of the Masses cannot be celebrated there in the required time, the faithful should be advised, by a posting in an obvious and accessible spot, that Masses with offerings are celebrated there when this can be done conveniently, or elsewhere.

Canon Law Digest
I: 396–99

Canon 837 (1983 CIC 955)

Whoever has Masses to be celebrated through others shall distribute them as soon as possible with due regard for the prescription of Canon 841; but the legitimate time for their celebration begins on the day the priest who will celebrate them receives them, unless otherwise demonstrated.

Canon 838 (1983 CIC 955)

Those who have a number of Masses that they are freely permitted to pass on [to others] can give them to any priest acceptable to them provided they are thoroughly convinced that he is above major exception or he has the testimonial commendation of his own Ordinary.

Canon Law Digest
I: 399–400

Canon 839 (1983 CIC 955)

Those who transfer Masses received from the faithful or committed to them in any other manner remain bound by the obligation until the obligation is accepted by these others and they obtain evidence of the receipt of the stipend.

Canon Law Digest
I: 400

Canon 840 (1983 CIC 955) Cross-Ref.: 1917 CIC 2324

§ 1. One who transmits to others Masses of the manual sort must transmit the entire receipts, unless the offeror expressly permits him to retain a portion or it is certainly shown that the excess given above the diocesan rate was intended personally.

§ 2. In Masses like manual [Masses], unless the intention of the founder prevents, the excess is legitimately retained, and it is sufficient to send only the offering for which Masses are celebrated in the diocese if the pledged offering represents in part the income of the benefice or the pious cause.

Canon Law Digest
I: 400–404; II: 207

Canon 841 (1983 CIC 956) Cross-Ref.: 1917 CIC 837

§ 1. Each and every administrator of pious causes or those who are bound in any way to fulfill Mass obligations, whether ecclesiastical or lay, at the end of each year, shall send to his Ordinary in a manner determined by [the latter] Mass obligations that have not yet been satisfied.

§ 2. This time is thus considered as running, for the obligation of sending Masses like manual [Masses], from the end of that year in which the obligation must be fulfilled; but for manual stipends, it is one year from the date of acceptance of the obligation, with due regard for a different desire on the part of the offeror.

Canon Law Digest
X: 149–51

Canon 842 (1983 CIC 957)

The right and duty of seeing to it that Mass obligations are fulfilled pertains in secular churches to the local Ordinary; in the churches of religious, [it pertains] to their Superiors.

Canon 843 (1983 CIC 958) Cross-Ref.: 1917 CIC 1549

§ 1. Rectors of churches or other pious places, whether secular or religious, that are wont to receive Mass offerings shall have a special book in which are accurately noted the number of received Masses, the intention, the offering, and the celebration.

§ 2. Ordinaries are bound by the obligation at least once a year of inspecting these kinds of books, whether personally or through others.

Canon 844 (1983 CIC 955)

§ 1. Also, local Ordinaries as well as religious Superiors who commit Masses to be celebrated either to their subjects or to others shall take care to record in their order the offerings they have received and the amounts and shall take care that they are celebrated as soon as possible.

§ 2. Likewise all priests, whether secular or religious, must accurately note whatever Mass intentions they receive and which ones are satisfied.

Chapter 2
On the most holy sacrament of the Eucharist

Article 1—*On the minister of holy communion*[19]

Canon 845 (1983 CIC 910) Cross-Ref.: 1917 CIC 1274

§ 1. The ordinary minister of holy communion is only a priest.

§ 2. A deacon is an extraordinary [minister], authorized by the local Ordinary or a pastor, granted for grave cause, which in case of legitimate necessity is presumed.

Canon Law Digest

I: 404; II: 207; VI: 560–61; VII: 645–52; VIII: 536–47; IX: 591; X: 151–58

---

[19] Daniel Sheehan, "The Minister of Holy Communion", Canon Law Studies, no. 298 (thesis, Catholic University of America, 1950).

Canon 846 (NA)

§ 1. Any priest whatsoever, during Mass and, if he celebrates privately, even just before and immediately after, can administer holy communion, though observing the prescription of Canon 869.

§ 2. Even outside of Mass any priest whatsoever, if he is a stranger, partakes of the same faculty with the at least presumed permission of the rector of the church.

Canon 847 (NA)

Holy communion is to be brought to the sick publicly, unless a just and reasonable cause persuades otherwise.

Canon Law Digest
I: 404–7

Canon 848 (NA) Cross-Refs.: 1917 CIC 462, 850

§ 1. The right and duty of bringing holy communion publicly to the infirm, even non-parishioners outside the church, belongs to the pastor within his territory.

§ 2. Other priests may do this only in case of necessity or with the at least presumed permission of their pastor or the Ordinary.

Canon Law Digest
I: 407

Canon 849 (NA)

§ 1. Any priest can bring private communion to the infirm with at least the presumed permission of the priest to whom custody of the most holy Sacrament is committed.

§ 2. Whenever holy communion is privately administered to the infirm, the reverence and decency that is due to such a holy sacrament is to be carefully observed, according to the prescriptive norms of the Apostolic See.

Canon Law Digest
I: 407–8; VI: 561

Canon 850 (1983 CIC 911)

It belongs to the pastor in accord with Canon 848, with due regard for the prescription of Canons 397, n. 3, and 514, §§ 1–3, to bring holy communion in the form of Viaticum to the sick, whether publicly or privately.

Canon 851[20] (1983 CIC 926) Cross-Ref.: 1917 CIC 733

§ 1. Priests will distribute holy communion [made from] leavened or unleavened bread, according to the proper rites.

§ 2. Where necessity urges and there is not present a priest of a different rite, it is permitted to an oriental priest who uses fermented bread to minister the Eucharist in unleavened [form], and likewise to a latin or oriental priest who uses unleavened [bread] to use leavened [bread]; each must observe his own rites of administration.

Canon Law Digest
I: 408; VII: 652–58; VIII: 548–49

Canon 852[21] (1983 CIC 925)

The most holy Eucharist is to be given only under the form of bread.

Canon Law Digest
V: 434; VI: 562–65; VII: 659–63; IX: 591–92; X: 158–59

Article 2—*On the subject of holy communion*

Canon 853 (1983 CIC 912)

Any baptized person who is not prohibited by law can and must be admitted to holy communion.

Canon Law Digest
II: 208; VII: 663

Canon 854[22] (1983 CIC 913–14)

§ 1. The Eucharist should not be administered to children who, because of a deficiency of age, do not have knowledge of or desire for this sacrament.

---

[20] Joseph Henry, "The Mass and Holy Communion: Interritual Law", Canon Law Studies, no. 235 (J. C. D. thesis, Catholic University of America, 1946).

[21] John Huels, "The Interpretation of the Law on Communion under Both Kinds", Canon Law Studies, no. 505 (J. C. D. thesis, Catholic University of America, 1982).

[22] Matthew Crotty, "The Recipient of First Holy Communion", Canon Law Studies, no. 247 (thesis, Catholic University of America, 1947).

§ 2. In danger of death, in order that the most holy Eucharist can and must be administered, it suffices that they know how to discern the Body of Christ from common bread and reverently adore it.

§ 3. Outside of danger of death a fuller knowledge of Christian doctrine and more accurate preparation is correctly required, namely, that they perceive according to their capacities at least those mysteries of the faith necessary as a means to salvation and devoutly according to the manner of their age approach the most holy Eucharist.

§ 4. Judgment about the sufficiency of the disposition of children for first communion is left to the priest who is their confessor and to the parents or those who take their place.

§ 5. To the pastor belongs the duty of being vigilant, even by examination if he prudently judges it opportune, lest children approach the sacred Synax before attaining the use of reason or without sufficient disposition; likewise, of taking care that those who have attained reason and are sufficiently disposed receive the divine food as soon as possible.

Canon Law Digest
I: 408; IV: 268; VII: 664; VIII: 550

Canon 855 (1983 CIC 915)

§ 1. All those publicly unworthy are to be barred from the Eucharist, such as excommunicates, those interdicted, and those manifestly infamous, unless their penitence and emendation are shown and they have satisfied beforehand the public scandal [they caused].

§ 2. But occult sinners, if they ask secretly and the minister knows they are unrepentant, should be refused; but not, however, if they ask publicly and they cannot be passed over without scandal.

Canon Law Digest
I: 408–9

Canon 856 (1983 CIC 916)

No one burdened by mortal sin on his conscience, no matter how contrite he believes he is, shall approach holy communion without prior sacramental confession; but if there is urgent necessity and a supply of ministers of confession is lacking, he shall first elicit an act of perfect contrition.

Canon Law Digest
II: 208–15; VII: 664; IX: 592

Canon 857 (1983 CIC 917)

It is not licit for anyone to receive the most holy Eucharist who has received it already on the same day, except for the cases mentioned in Canon 858, § 1.

Canon Law Digest
VI: 565; VII: 664–65; VIII: 550

Canon 858[23] (1983 CIC 919) Cross-Ref.: 1917 CIC 857

§ 1. Whoever has not observed a natural fast from midnight cannot be admitted to the most holy Eucharist, unless danger of death urges, or it is necessary to avoid irreverence toward the sacrament.

§ 2. Those who have been sick lying down for a month, however, without a certain hope of a speedy recovery, with the prudent advice of a confessor, can take the most holy Eucharist once or twice in a week even if beforehand they have taken some medicine or some liquid as a drink.

Canon Law Digest
I: 409; II: 215–16; III: 366–73; IV: 268–90; V: 434–39;
VI: 566; VII: 665–66; VIII: 550

Canon 859[24] (1983 CIC 920)

§ 1. All the faithful of either sex after they have arrived at the years of discretion, that is, the use of reason, must once a year, at least at Easter, receive the sacrament of the Eucharist, unless perchance with the advice of their own priest, for some reasonable cause, they are led to abstain from this reception for awhile.

§ 2. Easter communion should be made from Palm [Sunday] to [Low Sunday]; but it is fundamental to the local Ordinary that, if conditions of persons or place require, this time can be anticipated for all the faithful,

---

[23] Thomas Anglin, "The Eucharistic Fast", Canon Law Studies, no. 124 (J. C. D. thesis, Catholic University of America, 1941); James Ruddy, "The Apostolic Constitution *Christus Dominus*: Text, Translation, and Commentary, with Short Annotations on the Motu Proprio *Sacram Communionem*", Canon Law Studies, no. 390 (thesis, Catholic University of America, 1957).

[24] Connell Clinton, "The Paschal Precept", Canon Law Studies, no. 73 (J. C. D. thesis, Catholic University of America, 1932).

but not before the fourth [Sunday] of Lent, or extended, but not beyond the feast of the most Holy Trinity.

§ 3. The faithful are to be persuaded to satisfy this precept in their own parishes; those who satisfy it in another parish should take care to let their own pastor know about their fulfilling the precept.

§ 4. The precept of paschal communion continues to bind if, for any reason, it is not fulfilled by one during the prescribed time.

Canon Law Digest
I: 409; II: 216; IV: 291; VIII: 550

Canon 860 (NA)

The obligation of the precept of receiving communion that binds those below the age of puberty falls especially on those who are bound to have their care, that is, parents, guardians, confessors, teachers, and pastors.

Canon 861 (NA)

The precept of receiving communion is not satisfied by a sacrilegious communion.

Canon 862 (NA)

It is expedient that on [Thursday] of the great week all clerics, even priests who abstain from celebrating Sacred [Rites] that day, be refreshed by the Body of Christ in Mass, whether solemn or conventual.

Canon Law Digest
IV: 291–93

Canon 863[25] (NA)

Let the faithful be excited so that frequently, even daily, they be refreshed by the Eucharistic bread according to the norms given in the decrees of the Apostolic See; therefore those at Mass, rightly disposed, should

[25] Joseph Stadler, "Frequent Holy Communion", Canon Law Studies, no. 263 (thesis, Catholic University of America, 1947).

communicate not only spiritually but also sacramentally by reception of the most holy Eucharist.

Canon Law Digest
II: 216; VI: 566

Canon 864[26] (1983 CIC 921)

§ 1. In danger of death, from whatever cause it arises, the faithful are bound by the precept of receiving holy communion.

§ 2. Even if on that same day they have already partaken of holy communion, it is nevertheless greatly to be recommended that they be led to communicate again in a life crisis.

§ 3. For as long as danger of death remains, it is licit and decent that holy Viaticum be administered many times on distinct days according to the prudent counsel of the confessor.

Canon 865 (1983 CIC 922)

Holy Viaticum for the infirm is not to be deferred too much; those who take care of souls should be sedulously watchful that the infirm in full command of their senses partake in it.

Canon 866 (1983 CIC 923) Cross-Ref.: 1917 CIC 733

§ 1. To all the faithful of whatever rite, the faculty is given, for the sake of piety, to take communion in whatever rite it is confected.

§ 2. It is to be urged that the faithful satisfy their Easter communion in their own rite.

§ 3. Holy Viaticum should be taken by those who belong [to that] rite; but in urgent necessity, it is fundamental that it can be taken in any rite.

Canon Law Digest
I: 410; III: 374

Article 3—*On the time and place in which holy communion can be distributed*

Canon 867 (1983 CIC 918, 931)

§ 1. The most holy Eucharist is licitly distributed on any day.

[26] James Hannon, "Holy Viaticum", Canon Law Studies, no. 314 (thesis, Catholic University of America, 1951).

§ 2. On [Friday] of the great week it is permitted only to bring holy Viaticum to the sick.

§ 3. On Holy [Saturday], holy communion cannot be administered to the faithful except during solemn Mass or immediately after and continuously with it.

§ 4. Holy communion can be distributed at any hour at which Mass could be celebrated, unless a reasonable cause persuades otherwise.

§ 5. But holy Viaticum can be administered at whatever hour of the day or night.

Canon Law Digest
I: 410; II: 216–17; III: 374–75; IV: 293;
V: 440–42; VI: 566

Canon 868 (1983 CIC 932)

A celebrating priest is not allowed to distribute the Eucharist during Mass to those faithful who are so distant from him that he loses sight of the altar.

Canon 869 (1983 CIC 932) Cross-Ref.: 1917 CIC 846

Holy communion can be distributed wherever it is permitted to celebrate Mass, even in a private oratory, unless the local Ordinary, for just cause, prohibits it in particular cases.

Canon Law Digest
I: 410; II: 217

TITLE 4
On penance

Canon 870 (1983 CIC 959)

In the sacrament of penance, through judicial absolution imparted by a legitimate minister, those sins committed after baptism are remitted from the rightly disposed faithful.

Canon Law Digest
VI: 567; VIII: 550–52; IX: 592–97

Chapter 1

On the minister of the sacrament of penance[27]

Canon 871 (1983 CIC 965)

The minister of this sacrament is only a priest.

Canon 872 (1983 CIC 966)

Besides the power of orders, for the valid absolution of sins there is required in the minister the power of jurisdiction, whether ordinary or delegated, over the penitent.

Canon Law Digest
I: 410; III: 375–76

Canon 873 (1983 CIC 967–68)

§ 1. Ordinary jurisdiction for taking confessions throughout the universal Church belongs to, besides the Roman Pontiff, Cardinals of the H. R. C.; for their own territory, [likewise] local Ordinaries and pastors and those who have the place of pastors.

§ 2. This same jurisdiction is enjoyed by canons penitentiary even in collegiate churches, according to the norm of Canon 401, § 1, and exempt religious Superiors for their subjects, according to the norm of the constitution.

§ 3. This jurisdiction ceases upon loss of office according to the norm of Canon 183, and after a condemnatory or declaratory sentence, excommunication, suspension from office, and interdict.

Canon Law Digest
V: 442

Canon 874[28] (1983 CIC 969) Cross-Ref.: 1917 CIC 528

§ 1. Where confessions are heard, the local Ordinary confers delegated jurisdiction on secular or religious priests to receive confessions of anyone,

[27] James Kelly, "The Jurisdiction of the Simple Confessor", Canon Law Studies, no. 43 (J. C. D. thesis, Catholic University of America, 1927); Ralph Shuhler, "Privileges of Regulars to Absolve and Dispense", Canon Law Studies, no. 186 (J. C. D. thesis, Catholic University of America, 1943); John Walsh, "The Jurisdiction of the Interritual Confessor in the United States and Canada", Canon Law Studies, no. 320 (thesis, Catholic University of America, 1950).

[28] Marcellus McCartney, "Faculties of Regular Confessors", Canon Law Studies, no. 280 (thesis, Catholic University of America, 1949).

whether secular or religious; religious priests are not to use this without the at least presumed permission of their Superior with due regard for the prescription of Canon 519.

§ 2. Local Ordinaries shall not grant jurisdiction for the hearing of confessions habitually to religious who are not presented by their own Superior; but for those who are presented by their own Superior, it shall not be denied except for grave cause, with due regard for the prescription of Canon 877.

Canon Law Digest
I: 410–11; II: 217–18; III: 376; VI: 567–68;
VII: 666–67; VIII: 552–54; IX: 598

Canon 875 (1983 CIC 969) Cross-Ref.: 1917 CIC 528

§ 1. In exempt clerical religious [institutes] their own Superior confers delegated jurisdiction for receiving the confessions of professed [members], novices, and others mentioned in Canon 514, § 1, according to the norm of their constitution; to whom it is fundamental that they can also grant [jurisdiction] to priests of the secular clergy or other religious.

§ 2. In exempt lay religious [institutes] the Superior proposes a confessor who, nevertheless, must obtain jurisdiction from the local Ordinary where the religious house is located.

Canon Law Digest
VI: 568

Canon 876 (NA)

§ 1. Revoking any contrary privilege or particular law, priests, whether secular or religious, of any grade or office, for the valid and licit receiving of confession of female professed [members] or novices of religious [institutes], require particular jurisdiction, with due regard for the prescription of Canons 239, § 1, n. 1, 522, and 523.

§ 2. The local Ordinary where the house of the religious is located confers this jurisdiction according to the norm of Canon 525.

Canon Law Digest
I: 411; VII: 667

Canon 877 (1983 CIC 970) Cross-Refs.: 1917 CIC 874, 1340

§ 1. Neither local Ordinaries or religious Superiors are to grant permission or jurisdiction for the hearing of confessions except to those who are shown to be suitable by examination, unless it concerns a priest whose theological learning is demonstrated in another way.

§ 2. If, after the granting of jurisdiction, they prudently doubt whether the one approved by them continues to be a suitable priest, [the latter] can be put through a new test of doctrine, even if it concerns a pastor or canon penitentiary.

Canon 878 (1983 CIC 972)

§ 1. Delegated jurisdiction or permission for hearing confessions can be granted within certain established bounds.

§ 2. Nevertheless, local Ordinaries and religious Superiors should take care lest jurisidiction or permission be unduly limited without reasonable cause.

Canon Law Digest
I: 411

Canon 879 (1983 CIC 973)

§ 1. To hear confessions validly it is required that jurisdiction be expressly granted in writing or orally.

§ 2. For the granting of jurisdiction nothing can be required.

Canon 880 (1983 CIC 974) Cross-Ref.: 1917 CIC 527

§ 1. The local Ordinary or a religious Superior shall not revoke or suspend jurisdiction or permission for hearing confessions without grave cause.

§ 2. But for grave cause the Ordinary can interdict the task of confession to a pastor or [canon] penitentiary, with due regard for the right of recourse in devolution to the Apostolic See.

§ 3. It is not permitted for a Bishop, however, without consulting the Apostolic See, if it concerns a formation house, to take away at one time the jurisdiction of all religious confessors in the house.

Canon 881 (NA) Cross-Ref.: 1917 CIC 201

§ 1. All priests of either type of clergy who are approved for the hearing of confessions in a place, whether so enabled by ordinary or delegated jurisdiction, can also validly and licitly absolve wanderers and travelers from another diocese or parish coming to them, and likewise Catholics of any oriental rite.

§ 2. Those who have ordinary power of absolving can absolve their subjects anywhere in the world.

Canon 882 (1983 CIC 976) Cross-Ref.: 1917 CIC 2261

In danger of death all priests and bishops, even those not approved for confessions, validly and licitly absolve all penitents whatsoever of all sins and censures whatsoever, no matter how reserved or notorious, even if there is present an approved priest, with due regard for the prescription of Canons 884 and 2252.

Canon Law Digest
I: 411–12

Canon 883[29] (NA)

§ 1. All priests who are making a sea trip, provided they had duly taken the faculty of hearing confessions either from their own Ordinary or from the Ordinary of a port in which the ship will visit, can, throughout the trip, hear the confessions of the faithful aboard the ship during the trip wherever the ship goes and even if sometimes they will be in various places with subjects under the jurisdiction of diverse Ordinaries.

§ 2. As often as it occurs on the ship during the trip, they can also hear the confessions of the faithful who for whatever reason come aboard the ship as well as those who happen to approach them on land seeking confession, and they can validly and licitly absolve them even from cases reserved to the local Ordinary.

Canon Law Digest
I: 412–13; II: 218–19; III: 376–77

Canon 884 (1983 CIC 977) Cross-Ref.: 1917 CIC 882

The absolution of an accomplice in a sin of turpitude is invalid, except in danger of death; even in case of danger of death, outside of a case of necessity, it is illicit on the part of the confessor according to the norm of the apostolic constitutions, specifically the constitution of [Pope] Benedict XIV *Sacramentum Poenitentiae* of 1 Jun. 1741.

Canon Law Digest
I: 413

[29] Richard McCullen, "The Jurisdictional Power of a Confessor on a Sea Voyage" (diss. no. 6, Pontifical University of St. Thomas [Rome], 1955–1956).

Canon 885 (NA)

Although the prayers added by the Church to the formula of absolution are not necessary in order to obtain absolution, nevertheless, they should not be omitted without just cause.

Canon 886[30] (1983 CIC 980)

If the confessor has no doubt about the disposition of the penitent and he seeks absolution, absolution should not be denied or deferred.

Canon Law Digest
III: 377–79; VII: 667–73; VIII: 554–61; IX: 598–99

Canon 887 (1983 CIC 981)

According to the quality and number of sins and the condition of the penitent a confessor should enjoin salvific and appropriate [penances]; which the penitent should accept willingly and must perform personally.

Canon 888 (1983 CIC 978–79)

§ 1. Priests, in hearing confessions, shall remember that they sustain in their person equally judges and physicians, constituted by God, to look after the divine honor and the welfare of souls.

§ 2. Let them in all respects avoid inquiring about the names of accomplices as well as useless or curious questions, particularly about the sixth commandment of the Decalogue, and particularly when they inquire about such things with young people ignorant of them.

Canon Law Digest
III: 379–83

Canon 889[31] (1983 CIC 983) Cross-Refs.: 1917 CIC 903, 2369

§ 1. The sacramental seal is inviolable; therefore a confessor will diligently take care that neither by word nor by sign nor in any other way or for any reason will he betray in the slightest anyone's sin.

[30] Edward Mitchell, "The Obligation to Absolve according to Canon 886" (Pontifical Lateran University, 1965).

[31] John Roos, "The Seal of Confession", Canon Law Studies, no. 413 (J. C. D. thesis, Catholic University of America, 1960).

§ 2. Interpreters are likewise bound by the obligation of preserving the sacramental seal, as well as all those who in any way come into knowledge of the confession.

Canon Law Digest
I: 413–14; II: 219; VIII: 561

Canon 890 (1983 CIC 984)

§ 1. Any use to the detriment of the penitent of knowledge acquired by confession is entirely prohibited to the confessor, even excluding all danger of revelation.

§ 2. Both Superiors at the time and confessors who become Superiors after they resign, who have notice concerning sins from confession, cannot use this [knowledge] in any way for external governance.

Canon Law Digest
VIII: 561

Canon 891 (1983 CIC 985) Cross-Refs.: 1917 CIC 566, 1360, 1368, 1383

The master of novices and his associate and the Superior of a Seminary or college shall not hear the sacramental confessions of the students living with them in the same house unless the students for a grave and urgent cause seek it of their own accord.

Canon 892 (1983 CIC 986)

§ 1. Pastors and others to whom in virtue of their task is granted the care of souls are bound by the grave obligation in justice of hearing, themselves or through others, the confessions of the faithful committed to them, as long as they reasonably ask for them to be heard.

§ 2. In urgent necessity, all confessors are bound by the obligation of charity to hear the confessions of the faithful, and in danger of death all priests [are so bound].

Chapter 2
On the reservation of sins

Canon 893 (NA)

§ 1. Whoever by ordinary law can grant the power to hear confessions or to pass censures can also, excepting the Vicar Capitulary and the Vicar

General without a special mandate, call other cases to himself for judgment, limiting for inferiors the power of absolving.

§ 2. This calling [of cases to oneself] is called *reservation* of cases.

§ 3. As for what applies to the reservation of censures, the prescription of Canons 2246–47 is observed.

Canon Law Digest
I: 415

Canon 894 (1983 CIC 982) Cross-Ref.: 1917 CIC 2363

The only sin reserved to the Holy See by reason of being what it is, is false denunciation by which an innocent priest is accused of the crime of solicitation before ecclesiastical judges.

Canon Law Digest
I: 415

Canon 895 (NA)

Local Ordinaries are not to reserve sins to themselves unless, having discussed the matter in the diocesan Synod, or outside of Synod having heard the cathedral Chapter and some of the more prudent and proven [ones] among those in the diocese having care of souls, the reservation seems truly necessary or is shown to be useful.

Canon Law Digest
VIII: 562–63

Canon 896 (NA)

Among religious Superiors of clerical exempt [institutes] only the Superior general or, in monasteries of their own right, the Abbot, with the [support] of his own Council, can reserve the sins of his subjects as above, with due regard for the prescription of Canon 518, § 1, and 519.

Canon 897 (NA)

Cases of reservation should be very few, namely three, or at most four, of the gravest and most atrocious external crimes specially determined; and the reservation should remain in force for no more than is necessary for the public extraction of some ingrown evil and the restoration of a perhaps collapsed Christian discipline.

Canon 898 (NA)

Everyone should entirely stay away from reserving sins to himself that are already reserved to the Apostolic See by reason of censure, and [likewise] normally from [reserving] those to which a censure, even though not reserved, is imposed by law.

Canon 899 (NA)

§ 1. When they have decided on reservations that truly seem necessary or useful, local Ordinaries shall take care to give notice of these to their subjects in whatever way seems best to them, and conduct things so that the faculty of absolving from reserved [sins] is not given out everywhere.

§ 2. But the faculty of absolving from this sort [of matter] belongs by law to a canon penitentiary according to the norm of Canon 401, § 1, and it should be given habitually to vicars forane, adding, especially in places of the diocese more remote from the episcopal see, the faculty of subdelegating confessors in their area as often as it is needed for some of the more urgent determined cases that come to them.

§ 3. By the law itself, pastors and others who are included in law under the name of pastors can absolve from whatever [sins] are reserved to the Ordinary for the entire time given for the satisfaction of the paschal precept, as [can] individual missionaries for the entire time they are in touch with people for a mission.

Canon 900 (NA)

Any kind of reservation lacks all force:

1.° When it occurs in the confessions of the sick who cannot leave their houses and spouses for the sake of entering marriage;

2.° Whenever a legitimate Superior denies a faculty petitioned for a specific case of absolving or, in the prudent judgment of the confessor, the faculty of absolving cannot be sought from the Superior without grave inconvenience to the penitent or without danger of violation of the sacramental seal;

3.° Outside the territory of the one reserving, even if the penitent has gone out of it only to obtain the absolution.

Canon Law Digest
I: 415–16; III: 383

CHAPTER 3
On the subject of sacramental penance[32]

Canon 901 (1983 CIC 988)

Whoever perpetrates a mortal [sin] that has not yet been directly remitted through the keys of the Church must after a thorough in all respects discussion of conscience confess and explain in confession the circumstances that change the species of the sin.

Canon Law Digest
I: 416; VI: 568; IX: 599

Canon 902 (1983 CIC 988)

Sins committed after baptism, whether mortal and already directly remitted by the power of the keys or whether venial, are sufficient but not necessary material for the sacrament of penance.

Canon 903 (1983 CIC 990)

Whoever cannot otherwise confess is not prohibited if they want from confessing through an interpreter, taking care against abuse and scandal with due regard for the prescription of Canon 889, § 2.

Canon 904 (NA) Cross-Ref.: 1917 CIC 2368

In accord with the norm of the apostolic constitutions and specifically the constitution of [Pope] Benedict XIV *Sacramentum Poenitentiae* of 1 Jun. 1741, a penitent must within one month denounce to the local Ordinary or to the Sacred Congregation of the H. Office a priest [accused] of the delict of solicitation in confession; the confessor must, under grave obligation of his conscience, advise the penitent of this duty.

Canon Law Digest
VI: 568; IX: 599

Canon 905 (1983 CIC 991)

It is fundamental to each member of the faithful [to be allowed] to confess his sins, if he wishes, to a legitimately approved confessor even of another rite.

---

[32]John Paul, "The Recipient of the Sacrament of Penance", Canon Law Studies, no. 425 (J. C. D. thesis, Catholic University of America, 1962).

Canon 906[33] (1983 CIC 989)

All members of the faithful of either sex after attaining the years of discretion, that is, the use of reason, are bound faithfully to confess all their sins at least once a year.

Canon Law Digest
I: 417; IV: 293; VII: 673; VIII: 563–608

Canon 907 (NA)

The precept of confessing sins is not satisfied by one who makes a sacrilegious confession or one that is intentionally null.

Chapter 4
On the place of hearing confessions[34]

Canon 908 (1983 CIC 964)

The proper place for hearing confessions is a church or public or semi-public oratory.

Canon 909 (1983 CIC 964)

§ 1. The confessional seat for hearing the confessions of women must always be placed in an obvious and conspicuous spot and generally [be located] in a church or public or semi-public oratory assigned to women.

§ 2. The confessional seat must have inserted a thin, fixed perforated screen between the penitent and the confessor.

Canon Law Digest
I: 417; IX: 599

Canon 910 (1983 CIC 964)

§ 1. The confessions of women should not be heard outside of a confessional seat except in cases of illness or other true necessity, and following the precautions that the local Ordinary decides are opportune.

---

[33] Gerald Kelly, "The Years of Discretion for Confession", Canon Law Studies, no. 466 (Catholic University of America, 1968).

[34] Francis Fazzalaro, "The Place for the Hearing of Confessions", Canon Law Studies, no. 301 (thesis, Catholic University of America, 1950).

§ 2. The confessions of men may be heard licitly even in any private building.

Canon Law Digest
I: 417; II: 220

Chapter 5
On indulgences[35]

Article 1—*On the granting of indulgences*

Canon 911 (1983 CIC 992, 994)

Everyone should greatly value indulgences, that is, a remission in the presence of God of the temporal punishment owed because of sins, the fault attached to which is already forgiven, that ecclesiastical authority grants from the treasury of the Church by mode of absolution to the living and through the mode of suffrages for the dead.

Canon 912 (1983 CIC 995)

Besides the Roman Pontiff, to whom the dispensation of the whole spiritual treasury of the Church has been committed by Christ the Lord, only those to whom express grant has been made by law can grant indulgences by ordinary power.

Canon Law Digest
I: 417–19; II: 220–22; III: 384; V: 442; VI: 568–69; IX: 599

Canon 913[36] (1983 CIC 995)

Those below the Roman Pontiff cannot:

1.° Commit to others the faculty of granting indulgences, unless this has been expressly granted to them by indult of the Apostolic See;

---

[35] Francis Hagedorn, "General Legislation on Indulgences", Canon Law Studies, no. 22 (J. C. D. thesis, Catholic University of America, 1924).

[36] Joseph Campbell, "The Ordinary Power of Prelates Inferior to the Pope to Grant Indulgences" (doctoral diss. 20, University of Ottawa, 1948).

2.° Grant indulgences applicable to the dead;

3.° Add other indulgences to the same thing or act of piety or sodality to which indulgences have already been granted by the Apostolic See or by someone else, unless new conditions are prescribed that must be fulfilled.

Canon Law Digest
II: 222

Canon 914 (NA)

Bishops are able to grant a papal blessing with a plenary indulgence according to the prescribed formula in their own dioceses twice a year, this, on the solemn day of the Paschal Resurrection and on another solemn feast day designated by them, even if they are only there for solemn Mass; Abbots and Prelates *of no one*, and Apostolic Vicars and Prefects, even if they lack episcopal dignity, are able [to do this] in their own territories, [though] on only one of the more solemn days of the year.

Canon Law Digest
I: 419; II: 222; III: 384–85; VI: 569–70; IX: 599

Canon 915 (NA)

Regulars who have the privilege of imparting papal blessing are not only bound by the obligation of observing the prescribed formula, but cannot use this privilege except in their own churches or in the churches of monks or tertiaries legitimately attached to their own Order; [they shall not do so] on the same day and place on which the same Bishop imparts it.

Canon Law Digest
II: 222; VII: 673

Canon 916 (NA)

Bishops, Abbots and Prelates *of no one*, and Apostolic Vicars and Prefects and major Superiors of exempt clerical religious can designate and declare one altar privileged daily [and] forever, provided there is not one in cathedral, abbatial, collegial, conventual, parochial, and quasi-parochial churches, but not in public or semi-public oratories, unless a parochial church is united with or subsidiary to it.

Canon 917 (NA)

§ 1. On the day of the Commemoration of all the faithful departed, all Masses enjoy the privilege just as if they were celebrated at a privileged altar.

§ 2. All the altars of churches, on those days in which there is conducted therein the devotion of the Forty Hours, are privileged.

Canon Law Digest
I: 420; II: 223–24; III: 385

Canon 918 (NA)

§ 1. In order to indicate that an altar is privileged nothing else need be inscribed except: *privileged altar* and, according to the words of grant, perpetual or for a time, daily or not.

§ 2. For the celebration of Masses on a privileged altar, no greater offering for the Mass can be required on the basis of the privilege.

Canon 919[37] (NA) Cross-Ref.: 1917 CIC 713

§ 1. New indulgences, even those granted to the churches of regulars, that have not been promulgated in Rome should not be published without consulting the local Ordinary.

§ 2. In publishing books, pamphlets, and so on, in which are collected indulgences that have been granted for various prayers and pious works, the prescription of Canon 1388 is observed.

Canon Law Digest
I: 420

Canon 920 (NA)

Whoever seeks from the Supreme Pontiff grants of indulgences for all the faithful is bound by the obligation under pain of nullity of the granted favor to present an authentic copy of his grant to the Sacred Penitentiary.

Canon Law Digest
I: 420

[37] J. Christopher, C. Spence, and J. Rowan, eds., *Enchiridion Indulgentiarum: Preces et Pia Opera, The Raccolta or a Manual of Indulgences*, authorized English ed. (New York: Benziger Brothers, 1957).

Canon 921 (NA)

§ 1. Plenary indulgences that are granted for feasts of our Lord Jesus Christ or for feasts of the Blessed Virgin Mary are understood as being granted only for those feasts that are represented in the universal calendar.

§ 2. Full or partial indulgences granted for the feasts of the Apostles are understood as being granted only for their birthday [into eternal life] feast.

§ 3. A plenary indulgence granted as *perpetual, daily,* or *for a time* to those visiting a church or a public oratory are so understood that they can be acquired by any of the faithful on any day, but only once in a year unless it is expressly said otherwise in the decree.

Canon 922 (NA)

Indulgences attached to feasts or sacred supplications or novena prayers or seven-day [exercises] or three-day [exercises] or before or after a feast or even while its octave is going on are understood as being translated to that day to which a feast of this sort is legitimately transferred if the translated feast has an office with Mass, [albeit] without solemnity and external celebration, and if the transfer is made in perpetuity, or if it is transferred either for a time or in perpetuity, with the external celebration and solemnities.

Canon Law Digest
I: 420–21

Canon 923 (NA) Cross-Ref.: 1917 CIC 1246

In order to gain an indulgence attached to a certain day, if the visitation of a church or oratory is required, this can be done from noon of the preceding day up to midnight of the established day on which it closes.

Canon Law Digest
I: 421; II: 224

Canon 924 (NA)

§ 1. According to the norm of Canon 75, indulgences attached to a church do not cease if the church is completely destroyed but within fifty years is once again rebuilt in the same or almost the same place and under the same title.

§ 2. Indulgences attached to rosaries and other things only cease when the rosaries or other things completely cease to be or are sold.

Canon Law Digest

I: 421–23; II: 224–25; V: 442–46; VI: 570

Article 2—*On acquiring indulgences*

Canon 925 (1983 CIC 996)

§ 1. In order that one be capable of gaining an indulgence for himself, he must be baptized, not excommunicated, in the state of grace at least at the end of the prescribed works, [and] a subject of the granter.

§ 2. In order that a capable subject truly receive [the indulgence], he must have at least the general intention of acquiring it and fulfill the enjoined works within the established time and in the required manner according to the tenor of the grant.

Canon Law Digest

I: 423–49 & 863–78; II: 225–36; III: 385–91; IV: 293–97; V: 446–52; VI: 570–76; VII: 673–82; VIII: 608–18; X: 159

Canon 926 (NA)

A plenary indulgence is so granted that it is understood that one who is not able to gain it in full nevertheless can gain it partially according to the disposition that he has.

Canon 927 (NA)

Unless it appears otherwise from the tenor of the grant, indulgences granted by the Bishop can be gained by subjects outside the territory, [and] by travelers, by wanderers, and by exempt ones actually in the territory.

Canon 928 (NA)

§ 1. Plenary indulgences, unless it is otherwise expressly established, can be gained only once a day, even if the same prescribed work is placed several times.

§ 2. A partial indulgence, unless the contrary is expressly noted, can be gained as often in a day as the work is repeated.

Canon 929 (NA)

The faithful of either sex, in the pursuit of perfection or training or education or even for health, leading a common life in a house lacking a church or public chapel, with the consent of the constituted Ordinaries, as well as of those persons who live there to minister to them, whenever a visit to a non-determined church or to an indeterminate public oratory is prescribed to gain an indulgence, can visit the chapel in their own house in which they are able by law to satisfy the obligation of hearing the Sacred [Rites], provided the other enjoined works have been duly done.

Canon Law Digest
III: 391

Canon 930 (1983 CIC 994)

No one gaining indulgences can apply them to other people [still] in life; unless otherwise established, all indulgences granted by the Roman Pontiff are applicable to the souls detained in purgatory.

Canon Law Digest
I: 449

Canon 931[38] (NA)

§ 1. If confession is per chance required for the gaining of any indulgence, it can be done within the eight days immediately preceding the day to which the indulgence is attached; communion can be done on the day before it; both can be completed within eight days following.

§ 2. Likewise for the gaining of indulgences attached to pious exercises over three days, or a week, and so on, as the grant goes, confession and communion can be done within the eight days that immediately follow the completion of the exercise.

§ 3. The Christian faithful who are accustomed, unless legitimately impeded, to approach the sacrament of confession at least twice a month, or

[38] George Carton, "The Time Factor in the Gaining of Indulgences", Canon Law Studies, no. 319 (Catholic University of America, not published).

to receive communion daily in the state of grace and with a correct mental piety, even though they miss once or twice a week, can obtain all indulgences even without the actual confession that is perhaps otherwise necessary for gaining the indulgence, with the exception of indulgences for an ordinary jubilee or for an extraordinary jubilee or for [something] like a jubilee.

Canon Law Digest
I: 450; III: 391–92

Canon 932 (NA)

A work to which one is already obligated by law or precept does not gain an indulgence unless the contrary is expressly stated in its grant; one who, however, performs a work enjoined as sacramental penance that by chance is also endowed with an indulgence can at the same time satisfy the penance and gain the indulgence.

Canon 933 (NA)

To one thing or one place several indulgences can be attached under various titles; but a single work to which several indulgences are attached by various titles cannot acquire several indulgences, unless the required work is confession or communion, or unless it is otherwise expressly provided.

Canon Law Digest
I: 450–51

Canon 934 (NA)

§ 1. If to gain an indulgence a general prayer for the intention of the Supreme Pontiff is prescribed merely mental prayer does not suffice; a vocal prayer at the option of the faithful is acceptable, unless a particular one is assigned.

§ 2. If a particular prayer is assigned, indulgences can be acquired in whatever language it is recited, provided the fidelity of the version [used] is apparent from a declaration either of the Sacred Penitentiary or of one of the local Ordinaries where the language is used [and] in which the prayer has been translated; but indulgences cease entirely as a result of any addition, detraction, or interpolation.

§ 3. For the acquisition of indulgences, it suffices that one alternately recite the prayer with a companion or mentally follow it while it is recited by the other.

Canon Law Digest
I: 451–58; II: 236

Canon 935 (NA)

Confessors can commute the pious works enjoined for the gaining of indulgences into other [works] for those who, detained by a legitimate impediment, cannot perform them.

Canon Law Digest
II: 237; VI: 576

Canon 936 (NA)

The mute can gain indulgences attached to public prayers if together with the other faithful praying in that same place they attend God mentally with pious sentiments; and if it concerns private prayers, it suffices that they recall these mentally or by giving signs or even only following with their eyes.

Canon Law Digest
I: 458

TITLE 5
On extreme unction[39]

Canon 937 (1983 CIC 998)

The sacrament of extreme unction must be conferred by holy anointings, using olive oil duly blessed, and the words prescribed by the ritual books approved by the Church.

Canon Law Digest
I: 459–60; VII: 682–86; VIII: 618–19

---

[39] Adrian Kilker, "Extreme Unction", Canon Law Studies, no. 32 (J. C. D. thesis, Catholic University of America, 1926); Michael Higgins, "The Anointing of the Sick: The Historical Evolution of the Discipline of the Sacrament" (thesis, Gregorian University; printed version, no. 2687, San Diego, 1975).

Chapter 1
On the minister of extreme unction[40]

Canon 938 (1983 CIC 1003) Cross-Ref.: 1917 CIC 462

§ 1. This sacrament is validly administered by every and only a priest.

§ 2. Though observing Canons 397, n. 3, and 514, §§ 1–3, the ordinary minister is the pastor of the place in which the infirm one is found; in case of necessity, however, with the at least reasonably presumed permission of the pastor or the local Ordinary, any other priest can administer this sacrament.

Canon 939 (NA)

The ordinary minister is bound in justice to administer this sacrament personally or through another; in case of necessity, any priest is bound in charity.

Chapter 2
On the subject of extreme unction

Canon 940[41] (1983 CIC 1004)

§ 1. Extreme unction is not to be extended except to the faithful who, having obtained the use of reason, come into danger of death from infirmity or old age.

§ 2. This sacrament is not to be repeated for the same infirmity unless the infirm one, after having received the anointing, recovered and fell into another danger for his life.

Canon Law Digest
VII: 686; VIII: 619–20

[40] Francis Statkus, "The Minister of the Last Sacraments", Canon Law Studies, no. 299 (thesis, Catholic University of America, 1951).

[41] Henry Olislagers, "The Meaning of the Term 'Danger of Death' in the Code of Canon Law" (MS no. 2010, Gregorian University, 1952; printed version, no. 1204, 1952); Charles Renati, "The Recipient of Extreme Unction", Canon Law Studies, no. 419 (J. C. D. thesis, Catholic University of America, 1961).

Canon 941 (1983 CIC 1005)

Whenever there is doubt about whether the infirm one has attained the use of reason, whether he is truly in danger of death, or whether he is dead, the sacrament should be administered under condition.

Canon Law Digest
IV: 297–303

Canon 942 (1983 CIC 1007)

This sacrament is not to be conferred on those who are impenitent, persevering contumaciously in manifest mortal sin; if there is doubt about this, it should be conferred under condition.

Canon 943 (1983 CIC 1006)

Nevertheless, [the sacrament] should be absolutely conferred on those infirm who, when they were in possession of their faculties, had at least implicitly asked [for it] or who seemed to ask [for it], even if later they lost their senses or the use of reason.

Canon 944 (1983 CIC 1001)

Although this sacrament of itself is not necessary as a means to salvation, it is not licit for any one to neglect it; and every care and precaution should be taken that the infirm, while still in possession of their faculties, should receive it.

Chapter 3
On the rites and ceremonies of extreme unction

Canon 945 (1983 CIC 999)

The oil of olives, that is to be used in the sacrament of extreme unction, must be blessed for this purpose by the Bishop, or by a priest who has obtained from the Apostolic See the faculty of blessing it.

Canon Law Digest
VII: 686; VIII: 620

Canon 946 (NA)

The pastor shall diligently keep the oil of the infirm in a clean and becomingly decorated container of silver or nickel, but shall not retain it in a house except according to the norm of Canon 735.

Canon Law Digest
VI: 576–77

Canon 947 (1983 CIC 1000)

§ 1. Anointings are to be accurately done in accord with the words, order, and manner prescribed in the ritual books; in case of necessity, it suffices that there be only the anointing of one sense, more correctly, on the forehead, with the prescribed briefer form, with the obligation of supplying the individual anointings, the danger having passed.

§ 2. Anointing of [the loins] is always omitted.

§ 3. Anointing of the feet can be omitted for any reasonable cause.

§ 4. Outside of cases of grave necessity, anointings are to be made by the hand of the minister, and without the use of any instrument.

Canon Law Digest
I: 460–61; VII: 686–87

TITLE 6
On orders[42]

Canon 948[43] (1983 CIC 1008)

Ordination, by the institution of Christ, distinguishes clerics from laity for the governance of the faithful and the ministry of divine cult.

Canon Law Digest
VII: 688

[42] Aidan Carr, "Vocation to the Priesthood: Its Canonical Concept", Canon Law Studies, no. 293 (thesis, Catholic University of America, 1950); Anthony Viegas y Vales, "Distinction between the Episcopate and the Presbyterate in the Decretals" (MS no. 2848, Gregorian University, 1957; printed version, no. 1543, 1957); Owen Swindlehurist, "Archidiaconate in Medieval England" (MS no. 2790, Gregorian University, 1958); José Casa Medina, "The Law for the Restoration of the Permanent Diaconate", Canon Law Studies, no. 460 (Catholic University of America, 1968); Joseph Pokusa, "A Canonical-Historical Study of the Diaconate in the Western Church", Canon Law Studies, no. 495 (J. C. D. thesis, Catholic University of America, 1979); Alex Menez, "The Restoration of the Permanent Diaconate" (diss. no. 22, University of St. Thomas [Manila], 1981).

[43] Lincoln Knox, "The Ecclesial Dimension of Valid Orders", Canon Law Studies, no. 477 (Catholic University of America, 1971); Emil Labbe, "A Canonical Study of Pastoral Prepara-

Canon 949[44] (1983 CIC 1009) Cross-Ref.: 1917 CIC 950

In the canons that follow, by the name of *major* orders or *sacred* orders are understood presbyterate, diaconate, and subdiaconate; while *minor* orders are acolyte, exorcist, lector, and doorkeeper.

Canon Law Digest
VII: 688; IX: 600–601

Canon 950 (NA)

In law the words: *to ordain, order, ordination,* [and] *sacred ordination* encompass, besides episcopal consecration, those orders enumerated in Canon 949 and first tonsure, unless it can be established otherwise by the nature of the thing or the context of the words.

Chapter 1
On the minister of sacred ordination

Canon 951 (1983 CIC 1012)

The ordinary minister of sacred ordination is a consecrated Bishop; the extraordinary [minister is one who], although lacking episcopal character, either by law or by special indult of the Apostolic See takes up the power of conferring certain orders.

Canon Law Digest
V: 452; VII: 688; VIII: 620–24; IX: 601–2

Canon 952 (NA)

It is not permitted to promote to a higher order anyone who was ordained by the Roman Pontiff without a faculty from the Apostolic See.

---

tion for Priestly Ministry, with Special Reference to the United States", Canon Law Studies, no. 497 (J. C. D. thesis, Catholic University of America, 1978); John Oosterman, "Peter Damiani's Doctrine on the Sacerdotal Office: A Canonical Study of the Validity of Orders and the Worthy Exercise of Ordained Ministry", Canon Law Studies, no. 500 (J. C. D. thesis, Catholic University of America, 1980).

[44] Ladislas Orsy, "The Difference between the Order of Episcopate and the Order of Presbyterate in Gratian's Decree" (thesis, Gregorian University; printed version, no. 1493, 1962); Richard Zenk, "The Office of the Deacon in Ecclesiastical Law" (thesis, Gregorian University; printed version, no. 2205, 1969).

Canon 953 (1983 CIC 1013) Cross-Ref.: 1917 CIC 2370

The consecration of a Bishop is reserved to the Roman Pontiff so that it is not permitted to any Bishop to consecrate another as Bishop without first having gotten a pontifical mandate.

Canon Law Digest
VIII: 625

Canon 954 (1983 CIC 1014)

The consecrating Bishop must use two other Bishops who assist him in the consecration, unless a dispensation from [this] requirement has been obtained from the Apostolic See.

Canon Law Digest
II: 237; III: 392–93

Canon 955 (1983 CIC 1015) Cross-Ref.: 1917 CIC 2373

§ 1. Everyone is to be ordained by his own Bishop or with legitimate dimissorial letters from him.

§ 2. The proper Bishop, not impeded by a just cause, should ordain his subjects himself; but it is not licit to ordain a subject of an oriental rite without an apostolic indult.

Canon Law Digest
I: 461; II: 237–38; III: 393–94; VIII: 625

Canon 956[45] (1983 CIC 1016) Cross-Refs.: 1917 CIC 957, 2410

In regard to the ordination of seculars, the proper Bishop is only the Bishop of the diocese in which the one to be promoted has a domicile together with an origin [there] or a simple domicile without origin; but in the second case, the one to be promoted must have the intention of remaining in the diocese perpetually, this to be confirmed by oath, unless it concerns the promotion to orders of a cleric who is already incardinated in the diocese by first tonsure or the promotion of a student who is destined for the service of another diocese according to the norm of Canon 969, § 2, or the promotion of a professed religious, treated in Canon 964, n. 4.

Canon Law Digest
I: 461–62; II: 238; VII: 688

---

[45] John Moeder, "The Proper Bishop for Ordination and Dimissorial Letters" Canon Law Studies, no. 95 (J. C. D. thesis, Catholic University of America, 1935).

Canon 957[46] (NA) Cross-Refs.: 1917 CIC 294, 2410

§ 1. A Vicar and Prefect Apostolic, [and] an Abbot or Prelate *of no one*, if they have episcopal character, are considered equivalent to a diocesan Bishop in what pertains to ordination.

§ 2. If they lack episcopal character, they can nevertheless in their own territory for so long as their duties perdure, confer first tonsure and minor orders on their own secular subjects according to the norm of Canon 956, and on others who produce the dimissorial letters required by law; ordination conducted beyond these limits is without effect.

Canon Law Digest
VIII: 625

Canon 958 (1983 CIC 1018) Cross-Ref.: 1917 CIC 2409

§ 1. For so long as they retain jurisdiction in their territories, the following can give dimissorial letters for seculars:

1.° The proper Bishop, after he takes possession of his diocese according to the norm of Canon 334, § 3, even if he is not yet consecrated;

2.° The Vicar General, [only] if he has a special mandate of the Bishop;

3.° The Vicar Capitulary with the consent of the Chapter after the see has been vacant for one year; but within one year, only if forced to [do so] in order [for one] to retain or receive a benefice, or by reason of a certain office that because of diocesan necessity must be provided for without delay;

4.° A Vicar and Prefect Apostolic, an Abbot or Prelate *of no one*, even if they lack episcopal character, can [also act thus] with regard to major orders.

§ 2. A Vicar Capitulary is not to grant dimissorial letters to those who were rejected by the Bishop.

Canon Law Digest
I: 462

[46] Roman Galiardi, "The Monastic Abbot as Minister of Orders and the Ministries" (diss. no. 22, Pontifical University of St. Thomas [Rome], 1960–1961).

Canon 959 (1983 CIC 1015)

One who can grant dimissorial letters for the reception of orders can confer those orders personally, if he has the necessary power of ordination.

Canon Law Digest
VII: 688

Canon 960 (1983 CIC 1020)

§ 1. Dimissorial letters are not to be granted unless there have been collected all of the testimonials that are required according to the norm of Canons 993–1000.

§ 2. If new testimonial letters are necessary according to the norm of Canon 994, § 3, after the ones given by the Ordinary, the other Bishop shall not ordain before he receives them.

§ 3. But if the one to be promoted has spent enough time in the diocese of the ordaining Bishop to incur an impediment according to the norm of the [above-mentioned] Canon 994, [the latter] shall gather these testimonials directly.

Canon 961 (1983 CIC 1021)

Dimissorial letters can be sent by the proper Bishop, even by a suburbicarian Cardinal Bishop, to any Bishop having communion with the Apostolic See, excepting, however, unless there is an apostolic indult, to a Bishop of a rite different from the rite of the one to be promoted.

Canon 962 (1983 CIC 1022)

Any Bishop, having received legitimate dimissorial letters, can ordain a foreign subject, provided there is no doubt about the genuineness of the letters, with due regard for the prescription of Canon 994, § 3.

Canon 963 (1983 CIC 1023)

Dimissorial letters can be limited or revoked by the one granting them or by his successor, but once granted they are not extinguished by the loss of authority of the one granting [them].

Canon 964[47] (1983 CIC 1019) Cross-Refs.: 1917 CIC 625, 956

In what applies to the ordination of religious:

1.° Regular abbots of government, even without a territory *of no one*, can confer first tonsure and minor orders, provided the one to be promoted is subject to him at least by force of simple profession, if he himself is a priest and has legitimately accepted abbatial blessing. Outside of these limits, ordination conferred by him, revoking any contrary privilege, is invalid, unless the one ordaining partakes of episcopal character;

2.° Exempt religious can be licitly ordained by no Bishop without dimissorial letters from their own major Superior;

3.° Superiors [can grant] to those professed of simple vows, as described in Canon 574, dimissorial letters only for first tonsure and minor orders;

4.° The ordination of all other students of any religious [institute] is governed by secular law, revoking any contrary indult by which Superiors can grant dimissorial letters for those professed in temporary vows to [go on to] major orders.

Canon Law Digest
I: 462; VI: 577; VII: 688

Canon 965 (NA) Cross-Ref.: 1917 CIC 2410

The Bishop to whom the religious Superior must send the dimissorial letters is the Bishop of the diocese in which is situated the religious house to which family the one to be ordained belongs.

Canon Law Digest
I: 462

Canon 966 (NA) Cross-Refs.: 1917 CIC 2373, 2410

§ 1. The religious Superior can send dimissorial letters to another Bishop only when the diocesan Bishop gives his permission, or when he is of another rite, or is absent, or is not available at the next time for ordination

[47] Maur Dlougy, "The Ordination of Exempt Religious", Canon Law Studies, no. 271 (thesis, Catholic University of America, 1955).

according to the norm of Canon 1006, § 2, or finally if the diocese is vacant and he who governs it does not partake of episcopal character.

§ 2. It is necessary that in each case the Bishop who will ordain is shown this documentation from the authentic episcopal Curia.

Canon 967 (NA) Cross-Ref.: 1917 CIC 2410

Let religious Superiors avoid fraud against diocesan Bishops in sending a subject to be ordained to another religious house, or working it so that dimissorial letters are granted so as to put off the time [for ordination] to when the Bishop will be away or cannot conduct the ordinations.

Chapter 2
On the subject of sacred ordination[48]

Canon 968 (1983 CIC 1024)

§ 1. Only a baptized male validly receives sacred ordination; for liceity, however, he should be outstanding in the qualities according to the norm of the sacred canons, in the judgment of the proper Ordinary, and not detained by any irregularity or other impediment.

§ 2. Those who are detained by an irregularity or other impediment, even if it arises without their fault after ordination, are prohibited from exercising the orders received.

Canon Law Digest
I: 462–63; II: 238; VIII: 625–29

Canon 969 (1983 CIC 1025) Cross-Ref.: 1917 CIC 956

§ 1. No secular [cleric] is to be ordained who in the judgment of the proper Bishop is not necessary or useful for the diocese.

[48] Thomas Gallagher, "The Examination of the Qualities of the Ordinand", Canon Law Studies, no. 195 (J. C. D. thesis, Catholic University of America, 1944); Joseph Christensen, "Character Requisites for Reception of Holy Orders", Canon Law Studies, no. 424 (Catholic University of America, 1962).

§ 2. A Bishop is not prohibited, however, from promoting a subject who in the future, with previous excardination and incardination, is destined for service in another diocese.

Canon Law Digest
I: 463; II: 238; IX: 602–4

Canon 970 (1983 CIC 1030)

The proper Bishop or religious major Superior can prevent one of his clerics, for any canonical cause, even an occult one, even extrajudicially, from going on to orders, with due regard for the right of recourse to the Holy See or even to the Moderator general, if it concerns a religious whose ascent is prevented by a provincial Superior.

Canon Law Digest
I: 463

Canon 971 (1983 CIC 1026)

It is nefarious, by any method, for any reason, to coerce anyone into the clerical state, or to block one canonically suitable from it.

Canon 972 (1983 CIC 235) Cross-Refs.: 1917 CIC 683, 1370

§ 1. Care should be taken that those aspiring to sacred orders be received into the Seminary at a tender age; but all those [so aspiring] are bound to be there at least for all of the sacred theology curriculum, unless the Ordinary in particular cases, for grave cause, his conscience being burdened, dispenses.

§ 2. One who aspires to orders and legitimately lives outside of the Seminary is to be entrusted to a pious and suitable priest, who will be vigilant over him and instruct him in piety.

Canon Law Digest
II: 238

Article 1—*On requirements in the subject of sacred ordination*

Canon 973 (1983 CIC 1038)

§ 1. First tonsure and orders are to be conferred only on those who are proposed for ascending to the presbyterate and who seem correctly understood as, at some point in the future, being worthy priests.

§ 2. One ordained who, however, refuses to receive higher orders cannot be coerced into receiving them by the Bishop or prohibited from the exercise of those orders already received, unless a canonical impediment detains them or another grave cause, in the judgment of the Bishop, so bars.

§ 3. A Bishop shall confer sacred orders on no one unless from positive arguments he is certain that [the recipient] is canonically suitable; otherwise not only does he sin most gravely, but he also places himself in danger of sharing in the sin of the other.

Canon Law Digest
I: 463–82; II: 239; IV: 303–15; V: 452–88; VI: 577–84;
VII: 689–99; VIII: 629–30; IX: 604–5

Canon 974[49] (1983 CIC 1029, 1033) Cross-Ref.: 1917 CIC 2373

§ 1. In order to be licitly ordained, there is required:

1.° Reception of the sacrament of confirmation;
2.° Morals congruent with the order being received;
3.° Canonical age;
4.° Due knowledge;
5.° Taking up the lower orders;
6.° Observation of the interstices;
7.° Canonical title, if it concerns major orders.

§ 2. As to what pertains to episcopal consecration, the prescription of Canon 331 is to be observed.

Canon Law Digest
III: 394; VI: 585; VIII: 630

Canon 975 (1983 CIC 1031) Cross-Ref.: 1917 CIC 976

Subdiaconate is not to be conferred before the completion of the twenty-first year of age; diaconate, before the completion of the twenty-second year; presbyterate, before the completion of the twenty-fifth year.

Canon Law Digest
I: 482–83; II: 239; V: 488; VI: 585; IX: 605–7

[49] Elliott McGuigan, "Meaning and Consequences of Canon 974 § 1, n. 2" (doctoral diss. 10, University of Ottawa, 1941).

Canon 976 (1983 CIC 1032) Cross-Ref.: 1917 CIC 993

§ 1. No one, whether secular or religious, is to be promoted to first tonsure before the beginning of the theology course.

§ 2. With due regard for the prescription of Canon 975, subdiaconate is not to be conferred until the completion of the third year of the theology course, diaconate [not] until the fourth theology year has begun, and presbyterate [not] until the middle of the fourth [theology] year.

§ 3. The theology course must not be done privately but in a school established for this purpose according to the norm of studies determined in Canon 1365.

Canon Law Digest
I: 483–84; V: 488; VII: 699; VIII: 630; IX: 607–8

Canon 977 (NA)

Orders are to be conferred by steps, so that ordination all at once is prohibited.

Canon 978[50] (NA)

§ 1. Interstitial times are to be observed in ordinations so that those ordained, according to the prescriptions of the Bishop, can exercise them.

§ 2. The intervals between first tonsure and doorkeeper and the other individual minor orders are left to the prudent judgment of the Bishop; but between acolyte and subdeacon, subdeacon and deacon, and deacon to presbyter, there shall be no promotions before acolyte [has been exercised] at least one year, [and for] subdeacon and deacon [there need to be] at least three months in which one so ordained can function therein, unless necessity or utility of the Church in the judgment of the Bishop shows otherwise.

§ 3. Nevertheless, without special permission from the Roman Pontiff, minor orders shall never be conferred along with subdiaconate or two holy orders conferred on the same day, reprobating any contrary custom; nor shall first tonsure be conferred with any of the minor orders, nor all of the minor orders at one time.

Canon Law Digest
I: 484; II: 239; V: 489; VII: 699; VIII: 631

---

[50] John Gannon, "The Interstices Required for the Promotion to Orders", Canon Law Studies, no. 196 (J. C. D. thesis, Catholic University of America, 1944).

Canon 979[51] (NA) Cross-Ref.: 1917 CIC 981

§ 1. For secular clerics the canonical title is the title of the benefice or, lacking that, of the patrimony or pension.

§ 2. This title must be both truly secure for the whole life of the cleric and truly sufficient for his due upkeep according to norms that, in light of the diversity of places and times and necessities and circumstances, are to be given by the Ordinary.

Canon Law Digest
I: 484; VII: 699; IX: 608

Canon 980 (NA)

§ 1. One ordained in sacred [orders], if he loses his title, shall secure for himself another unless, in the judgment of the Bishop, his decent upkeep is otherwise provided.

§ 2. Whoever, outside of an apostolic indult, knowingly ordains his subject into sacred [orders] or permits one to be ordained without a canonical title must provide for him, as must his successors, any necessary support until his decent upkeep can be otherwise provided.

§ 3. If a Bishop ordains anyone without a canonical title [but] with the agreement that the one ordained will not seek support from him, such an agreement entirely lacks force.

Canon 981 (NA)

§ 1. If not even one of the titles mentioned in canon 979, § 1, is available, it can be supplied by the title of service to the diocese, and in those places subject to the Sacred Congregation for the Prop. of the Faith, by the title of mission, so that one to be ordained, with an oath in place, will devote himself perpetually to the service of the diocese or missions, under the authority of the local Ordinary at the time.

---

[51] Kenneth O'Brien, "The Nature of Support of Diocesan Priests in the United States", Canon Law Studies, no. 286 (thesis, Catholic University of America, 1949); Philip Hannan, "The Canonical Concept of *Congrua Sustentatio* for the Secular Clergy", Canon Law Studies, no. 302 (thesis, Catholic University of America, 1950); Carmelus Morelos, "The Canonical Title of Benefice" (diss. no. 36, Pontifical University of St. Thomas [Rome], 1957–1958); Bradley Arturi, "The Titles of Ordination of the Diocesan Clergy" (diss. no. 35, Pontifical University of St. Thomas [Rome], 1959–1960).

§ 2. The Ordinary must confer on the presbyter whom he has promoted with the title of service to the church or missions a benefice or office or subsidy sufficient for his decent upkeep.

Canon 982 (NA)

§ 1. For regulars, the canonical title is solemn religious profession or the title, as it is called, of poverty.

§ 2. For religious of simple perpetual vows, it is the title of *common table*, or *of the Congregation*, or something similar, according to the norm of the constitution.

§ 3. Other religious, as for what also pertains to the title of ordination, are governed by the rules of seculars.

Article 2—*On irregularities and other impediments*[52]

Canon 983 (1983 CIC 1040)

No perpetual impediment that comes by the name of *irregularity*, whether of defect or of delict, is contracted except those that are expressly [listed] in the canons that follow.

Canon Law Digest
I: 484

Canon 984[53] (1983 CIC 1041) Cross-Ref.: 1917 CIC 2294

The following are irregular by defect:

1.° Illegitimate ones, whether the illegitimacy is public or occult, unless they were legitimated or professed solemn vows;
2.° Those impaired in body who cannot safely because of the deformity, or decently because of the deformity, conduct ministry of the altar. To prevent the exercise of an order already legitimately received, however, it is required that the defect be more grave, nor can acts that can be rightly placed be prohibited because of this defect;

[52] John Hickey, "Irregularities and Simple Impediments in the New Code of Canon Law", Canon Law Studies, no. 7 (J. C. D. thesis, Catholic University of America, 1920); John Zimmerman, "Impediments to Holy Orders in General" (diss. no. 10, Pontifical University of St. Thomas [Rome], 1938–1939).

[53] Stephen Churchwell, "Epilepsy and Holy Orders in the Canonical Practice of the Western Church", Canon Law Studies, no. 507 (J. C. D. thesis, Catholic University of America, 1982).

3.° Those who are or were epileptics, insane, or possessed by the devil; but if after reception of orders they fall into these and it is certainly proved that they are free, the Ordinary can permit his subjects to exercise once again the orders already received;
4.° Bigamists, namely, those who have contracted two or more valid marriages successively;
5.° Those who are marked by infamy of law;
6.° A judge who passed a sentence of death;
7.° Those who take up the task of [execution] and their immediate and voluntary assistants in the execution of a capital sentence.

Canon Law Digest
I: 485–86; V: 489–91; VI: 585–86; VII: 699

Canon 985 (1983 CIC 1041) Cross-Refs.: 1917 CIC 986, 990, 2409

The following are irregular by delict:
1.° Apostates from the faith, heretics, and schismatics;
2.° Those who, outside of cases of extreme necessity, allowed themselves to be baptized in any way by non-Catholics;
3.° Those who attempt marriage, even civilly, or who dare to place the act [of consent], while themselves bound by the marriage bond or by sacred orders, or by religious vows, even if simple and temporary, or with a woman bound by the same vows or already joined in valid marriage;
4.° Those who perpetrate voluntary homicide or who procure the abortion of a human fetus that was effective, and all cooperators [in same];
5.° Those who have mutilated themselves or others, or who have attempted to take their own lives;
6.° Clerics exercising the art of medicine or surgery prohibited them, if death arises therefrom;
7.° Those who place an act of orders reserved to clerics constituted in sacred orders, either while they lacked such orders or while they were prohibited from the exercise of same by canonical penalty, whether it was personal or local, medicinal or vindicative.

Canon Law Digest
I: 486–87; II: 239; III: 394; VI: 586;
VIII: 631; IX: 608–10

Canon 986 (NA)

These delicts do not result in irregularity unless they were gravely sinful, committed after baptism, with due regard for the prescription of Canon 985, n. 2, and external, whether public or occult.

Canon 987[54] (1983 CIC 1042) Cross-Ref.: 1917 CIC 2294

The [following] are simply impeded:

1.° Sons of non-Catholics, as long as the parents remain in their error;
2.° Men having wives;
3.° Those holding office or administrative [posts] forbidden to clerics by reason of having to render accounts, until, having resolved the office and administration and having made the accountings, they are freed therefrom;
4.° Those who are strictly speaking slaves before receiving liberty;
5.° Those who are civilly bound to ordinary military service until they have completed it;
6.° Neophytes until, in the judgment of the Ordinary, they have been sufficiently proven;
7.° Those who labor under infamy of fact, for so long as, in the judgment of the Ordinary, it perdures.

Canon Law Digest
I: 487; II: 239; V: 491–94; VI: 586; IX: 611–21

Canon 988 (1983 CIC 1045)

Ignorance of irregularities, whether of delict or of defect, and of the impediments arising therefrom, does not excuse.

Canon 989 (1983 CIC 1046)

Irregularities and impediments are multiplied by reason of diversity of causes, but not by the repetition of the same cause, unless it concerns the irregularity arising from voluntary homicide.

[54] Henry Vogelpohl, "The Simple Impediments to Holy Orders", Canon Law Studies, no. 224 (J. C. D. thesis, Catholic University of America, 1945).

Canon 990[55] (1983 CIC 1047–48) Cross-Ref.: 1917 CIC 991

§ 1. It is permitted for Ordinaries, personally or through another, to dispense their subjects from all irregularities arising from occult crime, with the exception of that in Canon 985, n. 4, and others brought to a judicial forum.

§ 2. Every confessor has this same faculty in urgent occult cases in which the Ordinary cannot be reached and there is imminent danger of grave harm or infamy, but this only allows the lawful exercise of orders already received by the penitent.

Canon Law Digest
I: 488; II: 239; VI: 586

Canon 991 (1983 CIC 1049)

§ 1. In seeking dispensation from irregularities or impediments, all the irregularities or impediments are to be set forth; otherwise, the general dispensation is valid for those that were withheld in good faith, excepting those in Canon 990, § 1, but not for those withheld in bad faith.

§ 2. If it concerns an irregularity arising from voluntary homicide, the number of delicts must be expressed under pain of nullity of the dispensation granted.

§ 3. A general dispensation valid for orders is also [valid] for major orders; and one dispensed can obtain non-consistorial benefices and even curacies, but he cannot be named a Cardinal of the H. R. C., Bishop, Abbot or Prelate *of no one*, [or] major Superior in a clerical exempt religious [institute].

§ 4. A dispensation granted in the internal non-sacramental forum is to be put in writing; and it must be preserved in the secret book of the Curia.

Chapter 3
On those things that must precede sacred ordination

Canon 992 (1983 CIC 1036)

All those, whether secular or religious, to be promoted to orders must, themselves or through others, at an opportune time before ordination,

[55] James O'Connor, "The Power to Dispense from Irregularities to Holy Orders" (thesis, Gregorian University; printed version, no. 644, Chicago, 1950).

make known their intention to the Bishop or those acting in the place of the Bishop in such cases.

Canon Law Digest
VII: 700

Canon 993[56] (1983 CIC 1050–51) Cross-Ref.: 1917 CIC 2373

Seculars or religious to be promoted, who are governed by secular law, shall present for ordination:

1.° Testimony of the last ordination or, if it concerns first tonsure, of the receipt of baptism and confirmation;
2.° Testimony of the completion of studies that for each order, according to the norm of Canon 976, is required;
3.° Testimony of the rector of the Seminary, or of the priest if the candidate was living outside of the Seminary, about the good morals of this same candidate;
4.° Testimonial letters from the Ordinary of the place in which the one to be promoted was [present] for a time long enough to be able to contract a canonical impediment;
5.° Testimony of the religious major Superior if the one to be promoted is inscribed in a religious [institute].

Canon Law Digest
I: 488

Canon 994 (NA) Cross-Refs.: 1917 CIC 960, 962, 2373

§ 1. The time for which one to be promoted could have contracted a canonical impediment is, normally, for soldiers three months, for others half a year after puberty; but the ordaining Bishop can in his own prudence require testimonial letters even for a briefer stay [in an area] and for the time preceding puberty.

§ 2. But if the local Ordinary does not, either himself or through others, know the one to be ordained sufficiently so as to be able to testify for him that during the time he was in his territory he contracted no canon-

[56] Joseph Quinn, "Documents Required for the Reception of Orders", Canon Law Studies, no. 266 (thesis, Catholic University of America, 1948).

ical impediment, or if the one to be promoted has wandered through so many dioceses that it is impossible or very difficult to get all the testimonial letters, the Ordinary shall at least take from the one to be promoted a supplementary oath.

§ 3. If, after obtaining the testimonial letters the one to be promoted once again stays in an area for the aforesaid period of time, new testimonial letters from the local Ordinary are necessary.

Canon 995[57] (1983 CIC 1052)

§ 1. The religious Superior shall also testify in his dimissorial letters that the one to be promoted has made religious profession and is a member of the religious family house subject to him, and also that the studies have been completed as well as other requirements of law.

§ 2. The Bishop, after accepting these dimissorial letters, does not require other testimonial letters.

Canon Law Digest
I: 488

Canon 996 (1983 CIC 1028)

§ 1. Anyone to be promoted, whether secular or religious, must undergo a previous diligent examination about the order to be taken up.

§ 2. But those to be promoted to sacred orders shall also do an examination in the treatises of sacred theology.

§ 3. It is for the Bishop to establish by what method [the examination is conducted], in the presence of which examiners [it shall occur], and what treatises of sacred theology those to be promoted [are to] be examined on.

Canon Law Digest
I: 488

Canon 997 (1983 CIC 1052)

§ 1. The local Ordinary who, by proper law, ordains or grants the dimissorial letters, conducts this examination, whether it is for seculars or

---

[57] Edmund Dunne, "Canonical Fitness for the Religious Priesthood" (diss. no. 5, Pontifical University of St. Thomas [Rome], 1950–1951).

for religious; nevertheless, for just cause, he can commit it to the Bishop who ordains, if he is willing to take up this responsibility.

§ 2. A Bishop ordaining the subject of another, whether secular or religious, with legitimate dimissorial letters, by which it is asserted that the examination in § 1 was done and [that the one to be ordained] was found suitable, can acquiesce in this attestation, but he is not required to do so; and if in his conscience he feels the candidate not to be suitable, he shall not promote him.

Canon Law Digest
I: 488

Canon 998 (NA)

§ 1. The names of those to be promoted to individual sacred orders, excepting those religious in perpetual vows, whether solemn or simple, shall be publicly announced in the parish churches of each candidate; but the Ordinary can in his own prudent judgment dispense from this publication for just cause, or order that they be carried out in other churches, or that for publication there be a substitution by way of affixing [the names] to the doors of the churches for a certain number of days, in which [period] at least one feast day is included.

§ 2. Publication shall be made on a day of precept in a church during solemn Mass or on another day and hour in which a greater number of people are present in the church.

§ 3. If within six months the candidate is not promoted, publication is repeated, unless it seems otherwise to the Ordinary.

Canon Law Digest
I: 488

Canon 999 (1983 CIC 1043)

All the faithful are bound to reveal to the Ordinary or to the pastor any impediments to sacred orders, if they know of any, before sacred ordination.

Canon 1000 (NA)

§ 1. The Ordinary shall commission the pastor who conducts the publication, or others if he judges it expedient, to investigate diligently the morals and life of the one to be ordained from those worthy of trust and to send to the Curia testimonial letters referring to the investigation and publication.

§ 2. The Ordinary shall not fail to make other inquiries, even private ones, if he judges it necessary or opportune.

Canon 1001 (1983 CIC 1039)

§ 1. Whoever is to be promoted to first tonsure and minor orders [shall do] spiritual exercises for at least three full days; but those going on to sacred orders shall spend at least six full days [on same]; but in regard to those who, within half a year, are to be promoted to several major orders, the Ordinary can reduce the number of days for the exercises for ordination to diaconate, but not to less than three full days.

§ 2. If, upon completion of the exercises, sacred ordination for any reason is put off for more than six months, the exercises are to be repeated; otherwise, it is for the Ordinary to decide whether they should be repeated or not.

§ 3. Religious shall conduct these spiritual exercises in their own house or in another under the prudent decision of the Superior; but seculars [shall do so] in the Seminary or in another pious or religious house designated by the Bishop.

§ 4. The Bishop shall be notified about the completion of the spiritual exercises by the Superior of the house in which they were conducted, or if it concerns a religious, by the attestation of his own major Superior.

Canon Law Digest
I: 489–92

Chapter 4
On the rites and ceremonies of sacred ordination[58]

Canon 1002 (1983 CIC 1009) Cross-Ref.: 1917 CIC 1064

In conferring any order, the minister must thoroughly observe the proper rites in the Roman Pontifical and other rites described in the liturgical

[58] Walter Clancy, "The Rites and Ceremonies of Sacred Ordination (Canons 1002–1005)", Canon Law Studies, no. 394 (J. C. D. thesis, Catholic University of America, 1962).

books approved by the Church, and for no reason is he permitted to omit or invert them.

Canon Law Digest
I: 492–94; II: 240–48; III: 394–99; VI: 587–88;
VII: 700–706; IX: 621–22

Canon 1003 (NA)

The Mass of ordination or episcopal consecration must always be celebrated by the minister of ordination or consecration himself.

Canon 1004 (NA)

If anyone already promoted to any order in an oriental rite obtains an indult from the Apostolic See to take up higher orders in the latin rite, he must first receive in the latin rite any [lower] order that he did not receive in the oriental rite.

Canon 1005 (NA)

All those promoted to major orders are bound by the obligation of receiving holy communion at that Mass of ordination.

Canon Law Digest
VI: 589

Chapter 5
On the time and place of sacred ordination[59]

Canon 1006 (1983 CIC 1010) Cross-Ref.: 1917 CIC 966

§ 1. The consecration of a Bishop must be done in solemn Mass on a [Sunday] or [a feast day] of an Apostle.

§ 2. Ordination to sacred [orders] is celebrated within solemn Mass on [Ember Saturdays], the [Saturday] before Passion [Sunday], and Holy Saturday.

§ 3. If grave cause interferes, the Bishop may also have these [celebrated] on any [Sunday] or day of precept.

§ 4. First tonsure can be conferred at any day or hour; minor orders [likewise] on any [Sunday] or doubled feast, but only in the morning.

[59] John Reiss, "The Time and Place of Sacred Ordination", Canon Law Studies, no. 343 (thesis, Catholic University of America, 1953).

§ 5. Reprobated is any contrary custom regarding the prescribed times of ordination in the preceding paragraphs; and these times are also to be observed even if a latin rite Bishop, in virtue of an apostolic indult, ordains a cleric of the oriental rite, and the reverse.

Canon Law Digest
I: 494; II: 248–50; IV: 316; V: 494–95; VI: 589; IX: 622

Canon 1007 (NA)

Whenever ordination is to be repeated or any of the rites supplied, whether absolutely or under condition, this can be done outside the [usual] times and secretly.

Canon Law Digest
II: 250

Canon 1008 (1983 CIC 1017)

A Bishop outside his own territory cannot confer orders in which pontifical [ceremonies] are exercised without the permission of the local Ordinary with due regard for the prescription of Canon 239, § 1, n. 15.

Canon 1009 (1983 CIC 1011)

§ 1. General ordinations are to be celebrated publicly in the cathedral church, having called the canons of the church to be present; but if they are held in another place in the diocese, then in the presence of the local clergy, and as far as possible, a more worthy church shall be used.

§ 2. A Bishop is not prohibited, however, when persuaded by a just cause, to have particular ordinations in other churches or likewise in an episcopal house, oratory, or Seminary or a religious house.

§ 3. First tonsure and minor orders can be conferred even in private oratories.

Canon Law Digest
VI: 589

Chapter 6
On the recording and verification of completed ordinations

Canon 1010 (1983 CIC 1053)

§ 1. Upon completion of ordination, the names of each of the ordained and of the minister of ordination shall be noted [along with] the place and day of ordination in a special book diligently maintained in the Curia of the place of ordination, and all of the documents of each ordination shall be accurately preserved.

§ 2. Each of those ordained shall be given an authentic certificate of the order received; they, if they were promoted by an outside Bishop with dimissorial letters, shall show these to their own Ordinary in order that a notation of the ordination [can be made] in a special book to be preserved in the archives.

Canon 1011 (1983 CIC 1054)

Moreover, the local Ordinary, if it concerns the ordination of secular clergy, or the major Superior if [it concerns] the ordination of religious with his dimissorial letters, shall send notice of the ordination celebrated for each subdeacon to the pastor of [the place of] baptism, who will note it in his book of baptisms according to the norm of Canon 470, § 2.

Canon Law Digest
I: 494

TITLE 7
On marriage[60]

Canon 1012[61] (1983 CIC 1055)

§ 1. Christ the Lord raised the marriage contract itself to the dignity of a sacrament among the baptized.

§ 2. Therefore among the baptized there can be no valid contract of marriage without its also being a sacrament.

Canon Law Digest
I: 495; III: 399–401; V: 496; VII: 706; IX: 622

---

[60] Joseph Petrovits, "The New Church Law on Matrimony", Canon Law Studies, no. 6 (J. C. D. thesis, Catholic University of America, 1919); Richard Delany, "The Teaching of St. Peter Damian on Matrimony" (MS no. 1579, Gregorian University, 1949); John Doggett, "The External Appearance or Figure of Marriage" (MS no. 3401, Gregorian University, 1962).

[61] Francis Mueller, "The Inseparability of the Marriage Contract and the Sacrament according to the 17th Century Authors" (MS no. 2837, Gregorian University, 1958; printed version, no. 1198, 1958); Raymond Finn, "Towards a Reinterpretation of Canon 1012: A Study of Its Theological and Canonical Foundations" (diss. no. 1, Pontifical University of St. Thomas [Rome], 1976–1977).

Canon 1013[62] (1983 CIC 1056)

§ 1. The primary end of marriage is the procreation and education of children; the secondary [end] is mutual support and a remedy for concupiscence.

§ 2. The essential properties of marriage are unity and indissolubility, which in Christian marriage obtain special firmness by reason of the sacrament.

Canon Law Digest
I: 495; II: 250; III: 401–4; V: 496; VI: 589–90;
VII: 706–11; VIII: 631–32; IX: 622

Canon 1014[63] (1983 CIC 1060) Cross-Ref.: 1917 CIC 1070

Marriage enjoys the favor of law; therefore in doubt the validity of marriage is to be upheld until the contrary is proved, with due regard for the prescription of Canon 1127.

Canon Law Digest
II: 250; III: 404–5; V: 496–99

Canon 1015[64] (1983 CIC 1061)

§ 1. The valid marriage of the baptized is called *ratified* if consummation has not yet been completed; [it is called] *ratified and consummated* if between

---

[62] John Mussio, "The Education of Offspring [as] a Primary End of Matrimony" (diss. no. 8, Pontifical University of St. Thomas [Rome], 1938–1939); Nicholas Orville Griese, "The Marriage Contract and the Procreation of Offspring", Canon Law Studies, no. 226 (J. C. D. thesis, Catholic University of America, 1946); Dennis Burns, "Matrimonial Indissolubility: Contrary Conditions", Canon Law Studies, no. 377 (J. C. D. thesis, Catholic University of America, 1963); Vincent Berne, "Development of Thought on Canon 1013 § 1" (diss. no. 7, Pontifical University of St. Thomas [Rome], 1968–1969); Joseph Kavanagh, "The Indissolubility of Christian Marriage and Its Relation to the Pauline Symbolism" (diss. no. 4, Pontifical University of St. Thomas [Rome], 1968–1969); Thomas Doyle, "The Understanding of the Concept of *Bonum Fidei* in the Church's Canonical Tradition", Canon Law Studies, no. 496 (Catholic University of America, 1978).

[63] John Manning, "Presumptions of Law in Marriage Cases", Canon Law Studies, no. 94 (J. C. D. thesis, Catholic University of America, 1935); John Reed, "Presumptions in Theory and Matrimonial Practice" (MS no. 1526, Gregorian University, 1949; printed version, no. 623, 1949); Anthony Frendo, "Indissolubility and Divorce in the Theology of Thirteenth Century Scholastics" (diss. no. 2, Pontifical University of St. Thomas [Rome], 1972–1973); Robert Thrasher, "The Application of Canon 1014 to External Forum and Internal Forum Solutions to Marriage Cases", Canon Law Studies, no. 494 (J. C. D. thesis, Catholic University of America, 1978).

[64] Joseph Muzas, "The Concept of *Matrimonium Ratum* in Gratian and the Early Decretists (1140–1215)", Canon Law Studies, no. 441 (Catholic University of America, 1964); John Alesandro, "Gratian's Notion of Marital Consummation" (thesis, Gregorian University; printed version, no. 2306, 1971); Severinus Anatalio, "Sacramental but Not Consummated Marriage

the spouses there has occurred a conjugal act that by its nature is ordered to the marriage contract and by which the spouses are made one flesh.

§ 2. Marriage having been celebrated, if the spouses cohabit together, consummation is presumed, until the contrary is proven.

§ 3. Marriage between the non-baptized that is validly celebrated is called *legitimate*.

§ 4. Invalid marriage is called *putative* if it has been celebrated in good faith by at least one of the parties, until both parties are convinced of its nullity.

Canon Law Digest
I: 495; III: 405; V: 499–500

Canon 1016[65] (1983 CIC 1059) Cross-Ref.: 1917 CIC 1961

Marriage of the baptized is ruled not only by divine law but also by canon [law], with due regard for the competence of civil power concerning the merely civil effects of said marriage.

Canon Law Digest
II: 250–52; V: 500

Canon 1017[66] (1983 CIC 1062)

§ 1. A promise of marriage, whether unilateral or bilateral, that is, an engagement, is invalid in either forum unless it was made in writing, signed by the parties and by either the pastor or the local Ordinary, or at least by two witnesses.

Cases" (diss. no. 7, Pontifical University of St. Thomas [Rome], 1974–1975); Edward Hudson, "Marital Consummation according to Ecclesiastical Legislation" (doctoral diss. 59, St. Paul University [Ottawa, Canada], 1977).

[65] Robert White, "Canonical Ante-Nuptial Promises and the Civil Law", Canon Law Studies, no. 91 (J. C. D. thesis, Catholic University of America, 1934); William Goldsmith, "The Competence of Church and State over Marriage—Disputed Points", Canon Law Studies, no. 197 (J. C. D. thesis, Catholic University of America, 1944); James Huck, "Civil Competency in Mixed Questions concerning Marriage" (MS no. 1377, Gregorian University, 1947); Paul Miklosovic, "Attempted Marriages and Their Consequent Juridic Effects", Canon Law Studies, no. 203 (Catholic University of America, not published); Bernard Sullivan, "Legislation and Requirements for Permissible Cohabitation in Invalid Marriages", Canon Law Studies, no. 356 (thesis, Catholic University of America, 1954); Edward Dillon, "The Applicability of the Impediments of Consanguinity, Affinity, Nonage, and Prior Bond as Found in Georgia Law to the Summary Process of *Causas Matrimoniales*", Canon Law Studies, no. 489 (J. C. D. thesis, Catholic University of America, 1976). See also the section entitled "Marriage Issues, Church-State", in appendix 1, "Non-assigned Dissertations".

[66] Chester Wrzaszczak, "The Betrothal Contract in the Code of Canon Law (Canon 1017)", Canon Law Studies, no. 326 (thesis, Catholic University of America, 1954).

§ 2. If either or both parties do not know how to write or are unable to [write], for its validity, this fact is to be put in writing, to which is added another witness who with the pastor or local Ordinary and two witnesses, mentioned in § 1, sign the writing.

§ 3. But from the promise of marriage, although it is valid and there is no just reason for not fulfilling it, no action is given for the demand of the celebration of marriage; there is, however, given an action for damages if these are owed.

Canon Law Digest
I: 495–96

Canon 1018[67] (1983 CIC 1063)

The pastor shall not fail prudently to educate the people about the sacrament of marriage and its impediments.

Canon Law Digest
II: 253

Chapter 1

On those things that must be set out before marriage, especially the publication of matrimonial [banns][68]

Canon 1019 (1983 CIC 1066, 1068)

§ 1. Before marriage is celebrated, it must be shown that there is nothing obstructing its valid and licit celebration.

§ 2. In danger of death, if some of this evidence cannot be produced, it suffices, unless there are contrary indications, that the contractants confirm by oath that they are baptized and are not detained by any impediment.

Canon Law Digest
VIII: 632–33

[67] Edmund Way, "Educating to Catholic Marriage: An Historical Development and Canonical Commentary, with Particular Reference to Canada" (doctoral diss. 31, University of Ottawa, 1949); Joseph MacNeil, "The Pastor's Obligation to Give Premarital Instructions" (diss. no. 35, Pontifical University of St. Thomas [Rome], 1957–1958); John McReavey, "Emotional Immaturity and Marriage: A Canonical Analysis of Diocesan Pre-marriage Policies and Ecclesiastical Jurisprudence" (thesis, Gregorian University; printed version, no. 2851, 1979).

[68] James Roberts, "The Banns of Marriage", Canon Law Studies, no. 64 (J. C. D. thesis, Catholic University of America, 1931); Thomas Fulton, "The Prenuptial Investigation", Canon Law Studies, no. 274 (thesis, Catholic University of America, 1948).

Canon 1020[69] (1983 CIC 1064, 1067)

§ 1. The pastor who has the right of assisting at the marriage shall, at an opportune time beforehand, diligently investigate whether anything obstructs the marriage to be contracted.

§ 2. Of both the groom and the bride, and that individually, he shall cautiously inquire whether either is detained by any impediment, and whether consent is being given freely, especially that of the woman, and whether they have been sufficiently instructed in Christian doctrine, unless from the qualities of the persons this final inquiry seems useless.

§ 3. It is for the local Ordinary to give specific norms for this sort of investigation by pastors.

Canon Law Digest
I: 496–99; II: 253–76; V: 500–501

Canon 1021 (1983 CIC 1065)

§ 1. Unless baptism was conferred in his own territory, the pastor shall require proof of baptism from both parties, or from the Catholic party if it concerns a marriage to be contracted with a dispensation from the impediment of disparity of cult.

§ 2. Catholics who have not yet received the sacrament of confirmation should receive it before being admitted to marriage, if this can be done without grave inconvenience.

Canon 1022 (NA)

Those between whom marriage is to be contracted shall be publicly announced by the pastor.

Canon 1023 (1983 CIC 1067)

§ 1. The publication of marriage shall be done by the proper pastor.

§ 2. If a party has been in another place for six months after the age of puberty, the pastor shall notify the Ordinary, who in accord with his own prudence [might] require that publications be made there or prescribe

[69] James Donovan, "The Pastor's Obligation in Pre-nuptial Investigation", Canon Law Studies, no. 115 (J. C. D. thesis, Catholic University of America, 1938); Patrick Rice, "Proof of Death in Pre-nuptial Investigation", Canon Law Studies, no. 123 (J. C. D. thesis, Catholic University of America, 1940).

that other evidence of indications about the free state [of the party] be collected.

§ 3. If there is any suspicion about an impediment being contracted, the pastor shall consult with the Ordinary, even about cases where for a shorter time [than six months a party] lived [elsewhere], who [in turn] shall not permit the marriage until the prior suspicion, according to the norm of § 2, is removed.

Canon Law Digest
I: 499; II: 276–77; IV: 316–17

Canon 1024 (1983 CIC 1067)

Publications shall be made on three consecutive [Sundays] and other feast days of precept in the church with solemn Mass, or between other divine offices that the people frequently attend.

Canon 1025 (1983 CIC 1067)

The local Ordinary can, for his territory, substitute for the [above] publications a publication attached to the doors of the parish or another church, with the names of the contractants, for a space of at least eight days, so that, within this period, there are at least two days of precept contained.

Canon 1026 (1983 CIC 1067)

Publications are not to be done for marriages contracted with a dispensation from the impediment of disparity of cult or mixed religion, unless the local Ordinary in accord with his own prudent judgment, and all scandal being removed, thinks it opportune to permit them, provided apostolic dispensation has been obtained and mention of the religion of the non-Catholic party is omitted.

Canon Law Digest
VII: 711

Canon 1027 (1983 CIC 1069)

All the faithful are bound to reveal to the pastor or local Ordinary any impediments that they know of before the wedding.

Canon 1028 (1983 CIC 1067)

§ 1. The local Ordinary in his own prudent judgment can for legitimate cause dispense from the publications that are to be made even in another diocese.

§ 2. If there are several proper Ordinaries, that one has the right of dispensing in whose diocese the marriage will be celebrated; but if the marriage is going to be entered into outside the diocese [of all of them], any proper Ordinary can dispense.

Canon Law Digest
II: 277

Canon 1029 (1983 CIC 1070)

If another pastor has made the investigations or publications, at the completion of them he shall immediately notify by authentic document the pastor who is to assist at the marriage.

Canon 1030 (NA)

§ 1. The investigations and publication being completed, the pastor will not assist at a marriage before he receives all the necessary documents, and moreover, unless reasonable cause suggests otherwise, until three days have run since the final publication.

§ 2. If marriage is not contracted within six months, the publications are to be repeated, unless it seems otherwise to the local Ordinary.

Canon 1031 (NA)

§ 1. If doubt about the existence of any impediments arises:

1.° The pastor will investigate the matter accurately, questioning under oath at least two witnesses worthy of belief, provided it does not concern an impediment the notice of which would cause infamy to the parties, and if necessary, [he shall question] the parties themselves;

2.° He will conduct or complete the publications if the doubt arose either before they were begun or were completed;

3.° He will not assist at the marriage without consulting the Ordinary, if he judges the doubt to be still operative.

§ 2. If an impediment is discovered with certainty:

1.° If the impediment is occult, the pastor will make or complete the publications, deferring the matter, while withholding the names, to the local Ordinary or to the Sacred Penitentiary;

2.° If it is public and it is detected before the beginning of the publications, the pastor will not proceed further until the impediment is removed, even if he knows dispensation was obtained only in the forum of conscience; if it is detected after the first or second publication, the pastor will complete the publications and refer the matter to the Ordinary.

§ 3. Finally, if no impediment, either doubtful or certain, is detected, the pastor, upon completion of the publications, will admit the parties to the celebration of marriage.

Canon Law Digest
I: 500; II: 277

Canon 1032 (1983 CIC 1071)

The pastor should not assist at the marriage of vagrants described in Canon 91, except in case of necessity, unless he obtains permission to assist thereat from the local Ordinary or from a priest delegated by him.

Canon Law Digest
I: 500; VIII: 633

Canon 1033 (1983 CIC 1063)

A pastor shall not omit, according to the varying conditions of persons, to instruct spouses on the sanctity of the sacrament of marriage and on the mutual obligations of spouses and of parents toward children; likewise he shall strongly exhort them to confess their sins diligently before the celebration of marriage and to receive piously the most holy Eucharist.

Canon Law Digest
VI: 590; VIII: 633; IX: 622

Canon 1034[70] (1983 CIC 1072)

The pastor shall gravely exhort children yet in families not to enter into weddings if the parents are unaware of it or [if they] are reasonably opposed to it; but if they are going to marry, he should not assist without first consulting the local Ordinary.

Canon Law Digest
VIII: 634

[70] Cletus O'Donnell, "The Marriage of Minors", Canon Law Studies, no. 221 (J. C. D. thesis, Catholic University of America, 1945); William Keeler, "Parental Supervision in Matrimonial Law" (MS no. 3195, Gregorian University, 1961; printed version, no. 1399, 1961).

Chapter 2
On impediments in general[71]

Canon 1035 (1983 CIC 1058)

All of those are able to contract marriage who are not prohibited by law.

Canon 1036 (1983 CIC 1073)

§ 1. An *impeding* impediment contains a grave prohibition against contracting marriage; but nevertheless, it does not render it invalid if, notwithstanding the impediment, [marriage] is contracted.

§ 2. A *diriment* impediment both gravely prohibits marriage from being contracted and impedes it so that it is in no way validly contracted.

§ 3. Even though just one party has an impediment, nevertheless, the [whole] marriage is rendered illicit or invalid.

Canon Law Digest
I: 500–501

Canon 1037 (1983 CIC 1074)

That impediment is considered public that can be proven in the external forum; otherwise it is occult.

Canon Law Digest
I: 501; II: 277

Canon 1038 (1983 CIC 1075)

§ 1. Only the supreme authority of the Church declares authentically whenever divine law impedes or invalidates marriage.

§ 2. It also belongs exclusively to the same supreme authority to constitute, through either universal or particular law, other impeding or diriment impediments to marriage for the baptized.

---

[71] Gerald O'Keefe, "Matrimonial Dispensations, Powers of Bishops, Priests, and Confessors", Canon Law Studies, no. 45 (D.C.L. thesis, Catholic University of America, 1927); Victor Flanagan, "Dispensation from Matrimonial Impediments according to the Code of Canon Law" (diss. no. 6, Pontifical University of St. Thomas [Rome], 1933–1934); William O'Mara, "Canonical Causes for Matrimonial Dispensations", Canon Law Studies, no. 96 (J. C. D. thesis, Catholic University of America, 1935).

Canon 1039[72] (1983 CIC 1077)

§ 1. Local Ordinaries can prohibit in particular cases the marriages of all those actually present in their territory and their subjects, even outside of their territory, but only for a time, for so long as the just cause perdures.

§ 2. Only the Apostolic See can add an invalidating clause to the prohibition.

Canon Law Digest
VI: 590–91; VIII: 634

Canon 1040 (1983 CIC 1078)

Besides the Roman Pontiff, no one can abrogate impediments of ecclesiastical law, whether they are impeding or diriment, or derogate from them; likewise, no one can dispense from them unless they have been granted this power either by common law or by special indult of the Apostolic See.

Canon Law Digest
I: 501; II: 277; III: 405–6

Canon 1041 (1983 CIC 1076)

A custom inducing a new impediment or contrary to an existing impediment is reprobated.

Canon Law Digest
VIII: 634

Canon 1042 (NA)

§ 1. Some impediments are of *minor grade*, others are of *major* [grade].

§ 2. Impediments of minor grade are:

1.° Consanguinity in the third degree of the collateral line;
2.° Affinity in the second degree of the collateral line;
3.° Public propriety in the second degree;
4.° Spiritual relationship;

[72] John Waterhouse, "The Power of the Local Ordinary to Impose a Matrimonial Ban", Canon Law Studies, no. 317 (thesis, Catholic University of America, 1952).

5.° The crime of adultery with a promise of marriage or an act of attempted marriage, even if only civilly.

§ 3. All the rest of the impediments are of major grade.

Canon Law Digest
I: 501; VI: 591

Canon 1043 (1983 CIC 1079) Cross-Refs.: 1917 CIC 1044–45

In urgent danger of death, local Ordinaries, for the consolation of consciences and, if there is cause, for the legitimization of children, can dispense their own subjects wherever they are and all those actually in their territory both from the [canonical] form to be observed in the celebration of marriage and from each and every impediment of ecclesiastical law, whether public or occult, even if multiplied, except for those impediments coming from sacred ordination to the presbyterate or affinity in the direct line, the marriage having been consummated, scandal being removed and, if dispensation is granted from disparity of cult or mixed religion, with the usual precautions.

Canon Law Digest
I: 501

Canon 1044 (1983 CIC 1079) Cross-Refs.: 1917 CIC 1045–1046

In the same circumstances of things mentioned in Canon 1043, and only for those cases in which the local Ordinary cannot be [contacted], a pastor enjoys the same faculty of dispensing, as does a priest who assists at the marriage according to the norm of Canon 1098, n. 2, and a confessor, though only for the internal forum in the act of sacramental confession.

Canon Law Digest
I: 502; VIII: 634; IX: 622–23

Canon 1045 (1983 CIC 1080)

§ 1. Local Ordinaries, under the clause established at the end of Canon 1043, can grant dispensation from all the impediments in the above-cit. Canon 1043, as often as the impediment is detected when everything for the wedding is ready and the marriage cannot be put off without a probable danger of grave evil until a dispensation could be obtained from the Holy See.

§ 2. This faculty is valid even for the convalidation of a marriage already contracted, if there is the same danger of delay for the time necessary to go to the Holy See.

§ 3. In the same circumstances of things, all those mentioned in Canon 1044 enjoy the same faculty [of dispensing], but only for occult cases in which the local Ordinary cannot be [reached] or [it cannot otherwise be done] without danger of the violation of a secret.

Canon Law Digest
I: 502–3; II: 277–80

Canon 1046 (1983 CIC 1081)

A pastor or priest mentioned in Canon 1044 shall immediately notify the local Ordinary about the grant of a dispensation for the external forum; this shall be noted in the book of marriages.

Canon 1047 (1983 CIC 1082)

Unless a rescript of the S. Penitentiary arranges otherwise, a dispensation granted in the internal non-sacramental forum from an occult impediment shall be diligently noted in a book preserved in the secret archive of the Curia mentioned in Canon 379, nor is another dispensation necessary for the external forum, even if later the occult impediment becomes public; but it is necessary if the dispensation was granted only for the internal sacramental forum.

Canon Law Digest
I: 503

Canon 1048 (NA)

If a petition of dispensation has been sent to the Holy See, local Ordinaries shall not use their faculties, if they have them, except according to the norm of Canon 204, § 2.

Canon 1049 (NA)

§ 1. Over marriages, whether contracted or about to be contracted, those who enjoy a general indult of dispensing from a certain impediment can, unless in the same indult this is expressly [prohibited], dispense from them even if the impediment is multiplied.

§ 2. Those who have a general indult of dispensing from several different types of impediments, whether diriment or impeding, can dispense from those same impediments, even if they are public, as often as they occur in the same case.

Canon 1050 (NA)

If there occurs, with an impediment or with public impediments over which one can dispense by indult, another impediment that one cannot dispense from, all of them must be referred to the Apostolic See; if, however, the impediment or impediments from which one can dispense are found after contacting the Holy See for dispensation, he can use his faculty.

Canon 1051 (NA)

Through a dispensation granted for a diriment impediment, whether by ordinary power or delegated power by general indult, but not by rescript in a particular case, there is granted also the legitimatization of children if they were already born or conceived by those with the dispensation, except for adulterous or sacrilegious [offspring].

Canon 1052 (NA)

Dispensation from the impediment of consanguinity or affinity granted for any degree of the impediment is valid even though in the petition or grant there was an error about the degree, provided the true degree existing is less [than the one cited], or even though there was withheld an impediment of the same kind in an equal or inferior degree.

Canon Law Digest
I: 504; III: 406

Canon 1053 (NA)

Dispensation given by the Holy See from a ratified and non-consummated marriage or made with permission to go into another marriage because of the presumed death of a spouse includes also a dispensation from the impediment arising from adultery with a promise [of] or attempted marriage, if it is needed, though it by no means [comes] with a dispensation from the impediment mentioned in Canon 1075, nn. 2 and 3.

Canon Law Digest
I: 504; III: 407

Canon 1054 (NA) Cross-Refs.: 1917 CIC 40, 45, 2361

Dispensation granted for a minor impediment is rendered invalid by neither obreption nor subreption, even if the only final cause expressed in the request is false.

Canon 1055 (NA)

Dispensations from public impediments committed to the Ordinary of the requesters are executed by the Ordinary who gave the testimonial letters or who sent the request to the Apostolic See, even if the spouses, during the time that was given for the execution of the dispensation, have left their diocesan domicile or quasi-domicile and have gone into another diocese with no plans of returning, notifying only the local Ordinary, nevertheless, where they wish to contract the marriage.

Canon 1056 (NA) Cross-Ref.: 1917 CIC 1507

Local Ordinaries or other officials cannot, reprobating any contrary custom, require any payment on the occasion of granting a dispensation, except for a small amount charged under the heading of chancery expenses for dispensation in non-pauper cases, unless this faculty has been expressly granted to them by the Holy See; and if they have required any [impermissible payments], they are bound to restitution.

Canon Law Digest
I: 504

Canon 1057 (NA)

Whoever grants a dispensation by power delegated by the Apostolic See will make express mention of the pontifical indult in [the dispensation].

Canon Law Digest
IX: 623

Chapter 3
On impeding impediments

Canon 1058 (NA)

§ 1. A simple vow of virginity, of perfect chastity, of not marrying, or of taking up sacred orders or of embracing the religious state impedes marriage.

§ 2. No simple vow invalidates marriage unless invalidity is established in some cases by special prescription of the Apostolic See.

Canon Law Digest
II: 280

Canon 1059 (NA)

In those regions where under civil law a relationship arising from adoption renders a wedding illicit, by canon law too that marriage is illicit.

Canon Law Digest
VII: 711; VIII: 634–35

Canon 1060[73] (1983 CIC 1124) Cross-Ref.: 1917 CIC 1071

Most severely does the Church prohibit everywhere that marriage be entered into by two baptized persons, one of whom is Catholic, and the other belonging to a heretical or schismatic sect; indeed, if there is a danger of perversion to the Catholic spouse and children, that marriage is forbidden even by divine law.

Canon Law Digest
I: 504–5; II: 280; V: 501; VI: 592; VIII: 635; IX: 623

Canon 1061[74] (1983 CIC 1125) Cross-Ref.: 1917 CIC 1071

§ 1. The Church does not dispense from the impediment of mixed religion, unless:

---

[73] Francis Schenk, "The Matrimonial Impediments of Mixed Religion and Disparity of Cult", Canon Law Studies, no. 51 (D.C.L. thesis, Catholic University of America, 1929); John Morales, "Mixed Marriages and the Second Vatican Ecumenical Council: A Comparative Study in Latin and Oriental Canon Law" (Pontifical Lateran University, 1966); Bernard Konda, "The Changing Attitudes of the Catholic Church toward Mixed Marriages", Canon Law Studies, no. 476 (Catholic University of America, 1971); Philip Hill, "Mixed Marriages and Their Prerequisites in the Light of Ecumenism" (Pontifical Lateran University, 1980); Carol Houghton, "The Evolution of the Canonical Celebration of Mixed Marriages" (diss. no. 3, Pontifical University of St. Thomas [Rome], 1980–1981).

[74] David Boyle, "The Juridic Effects of Moral Certitude on Pre-nuptial Guarantees", Canon Law Studies, no. 150 (J. C. D. thesis, Catholic University of America, 1942); Michael Browne, "The Ante-nuptial Guarantee regarding the Catholic Education of the Children of Mixed Marriages, with Special Reference to the Legal Position in Ireland" (MS no. 1378, Gregorian University, 1947); Vincent Doyle, "The Pre-nuptial Promises in Mixed Marriages", Canon Law Studies, no. 461 (J.C.L. thesis, Catholic University of America, 1968); John Makothakat, "The Sincerity of the Mixed-Marriage Promises according to Recent Legislation" (doctoral diss. 61, St. Paul University [Ottawa, Canada] 1978).

1.° Just and grave causes so urge;
2.° The non-Catholic spouse gives a precaution to remove the danger of perversion from the Catholic spouse, and from both spouses [there is a promise] that all children will be baptized only Catholic and so educated;
3.° There is moral certitude the cautions will be implemented.

§ 2. These cautions are regularly required in writing.

Canon Law Digest
I: 505–6; II: 280–86; III: 407; IV: 317; V: 501–2;
VI: 592–606; VII: 711–41; VIII: 635; IX: 623

Canon 1062 (NA) Cross-Ref.: 1917 CIC 1071

The Catholic spouse is bound by the obligation of prudently taking care for the conversion of the non-Catholic spouse.

Canon 1063 (1983 CIC 1127) Cross-Refs.: 1917 CIC 1071, 2319

§ 1. Although dispensation from the above impediment of mixed religion has been obtained from the Church, the spouses cannot, either before or after the marriage entered into in the presence of the Church, also go, personally or though a procurator, to a non-Catholic minister as [if to] one in ministry, in order to offer or renew matrimonial consent.

§ 2. If the pastor certainly knows that the spouses will violate or have violated this law, he shall not assist at the marriage, except for the most grave causes, having removed scandal, and having consulted the Ordinary first.

§ 3. It is not disallowed, however, civil law so commanding, for the spouses to present themselves to a non-Catholic minister, acting solely in his civil capacity, to fulfill a civil act solely for sake of civil effects.

Canon Law Digest
I: 506–7; VI: 607–10; VII: 741

Canon 1064 (NA) Cross-Ref.: 1917 CIC 1071

Ordinaries and other pastors of souls:

1.° Shall discourage, whenever possible, the faithful from mixed weddings;

2.° If they are unable to impede them, they shall studiously take care that they not be contracted against the laws of God or the Church;

3.° In cases of mixed weddings already celebrated, whether in their own or in another's territory, they shall be sedulously vigilant that the spouses fulfill faithfully the promises made;

4.° In assisting at marriage, they shall observe the prescription of Canon 1102.

Canon Law Digest
V: 502

Canon 1065[75] (1983 CIC 1071)

§ 1. The faithful shall be discouraged from contracting marriage with those who have either notoriously rejected the Catholic faith, even if they have not gone over to a non-Catholic sect, or those who are enrolled in a society damned by the Church.

§ 2. The pastor shall not assist at the aforesaid weddings without consulting the Ordinary, who, having inspected all of the circumstances, can permit that he be present for the marriage, provided there is urgent cause and in his own prudent judgment the Ordinary judges that there is sufficient precaution for the Catholic education of all the children and that the danger of perversion for the other spouse is removed.

Canon Law Digest
II: 286–87; III: 407–8; VI: 610–11; VIII: 635–39

Canon 1066 (1983 CIC 1071)

If a public sinner or one well known to be marked with a censure refuses to approach sacramental confession or to be reconciled with the Church, the pastor should not assist at the marriage, unless grave cause urges, about which, if it can be done, he should consult the Ordinary.

Canon Law Digest
I: 507; III: 408; VI: 611; VII: 741

---

[75] John Heneghan, "The Marriages of Unworthy Catholics: Canons 1065 and 1066" Canon Law Studies, no. 188 (J. C. D. thesis, Catholic University of America, 1944).

Chapter 4
On diriment impediments

Canon 1067[76] (1983 CIC 1072, 1083)

§ 1. A man before completing the sixteenth year of age, and a woman before completing the fourteenth year of age, cannot enter into valid marriage.

§ 2. Although marriage can be validly contracted above these ages, nevertheless, let pastors take care to discourage youths from entering marriage before that age that, according to the accepted manner of the region, they are wont to enter marriage.

Canon Law Digest
I: 508; III: 408–10; V: 502–3; VI: 611–12; VIII: 639–67

Canon 1068[77] (1983 CIC 1084)

§ 1. Antecedent and perpetual impotence, either on the part of the man or on the part of the woman, whether known or not, whether absolute or relative, impedes marriage by natural law itself.

§ 2. If the impediment of impotence is doubtful, whether this be a doubt of law or doubt of fact, marriage should not be impeded.

§ 3. Sterility neither impedes nor [renders illicit] marriage.

Canon Law Digest
II: 287–89; III: 410–20; IV: 317–20; V: 503–7; VI: 612–20;
VIII: 667–77; IX: 624–27; X: 159–65

[76] John O'Dea, "The Matrimonial Impediment of Nonage", Canon Law Studies, no. 205 (J. C. D. thesis, Catholic University of America, 1944).

[77] John McCarthy, "The Matrimonial Impediment of Impotence with Special Reference to the Physical Capacity for Marriage of an 'Excised Woman' and of a '[Doubtfully] Vasectomized Man'" (diss. no. 1, Pontifical University of St. Thomas [Rome], 1945–1947); Arthur McClory, "The Notion of Impotence in Canon Law" (University of Laval, 1951); Peter Frattin, "The Matrimonial Impediment of Impotence: Occlusion of Spermatic Ducts and Vaginismus", Canon Law Studies, no. 381 (thesis, Catholic University of America, 1958); John Brenkle, "The Impediment of Male Impotence with Special Application to Paraplegia", Canon Law Studies, no. 423 (J. C. D. thesis, Catholic University of America, 1963); Aselus Calapre, "Homosexuality and the Impediment of Impotence" (diss. no. 10, Pontifical University of St. Thomas [Rome], 1964–1965); Kenneth Boccafola, "The Requirement of Perpetuity for the Impediment of Impotence" (thesis, Gregorian University; printed version, no. 2600, 1975).

Canon 1069 (1983 CIC 1085) Cross-Ref.: 1917 CIC 1142

§ 1. They invalidly attempt marriage who are bound by a prior bond, even if it is not consummated, with due regard for the privilege of the faith.

§ 2. Although a prior marriage is null or is dissolved for any cause, it is not therefore permitted to contract another before the nullity or dissolution of the first is legitimately and certainly established.

Canon Law Digest
I: 508–11; II: 289–90; III: 420; V: 507–8

Canon 1070[78] (1983 CIC 1086)

§ 1. That marriage is null that is contracted between a non-baptized person and a person baptized in the Catholic Church or converted to her from heresy or schism.

§ 2. If a party at the time of contracting marriage was commonly considered baptized, or there is doubt about the baptism, the validity of the marriage is to be upheld according to the norm of Canon 1014 until it is certainly proved that the one party was baptized and the other was not baptized.

Canon Law Digest
I: 511–12; II: 290–91; III: 420–27; IV: 320–23; V: 508–9;
VI: 621; VIII: 677–78; IX: 627

Canon 1071 (1983 CIC 1129)

Those things that are prescribed for mixed marriages in Canons 1060–64 must also be applied to those marriages that are barred due to the impediment of disparity of cult.

Canon Law Digest
I: 512–13; II: 291–93; III: 427–28; IV: 323–31;
V: 509; VI: 621; VII: 741

Canon 1072[79] (1983 CIC 1087)

Clerics constituted in sacred orders invalidly attempt marriage.

Canon Law Digest
II: 293; V: 510; VI: 621–22; VII: 741; IX: 627

---

[78] Paul Marcinkus, "The Sufficiency of the Protestant Ministers' Intention for Valid Baptism in Matrimonial Cases" (MS no. 2069, Gregorian University, 1953).

[79] Joseph Goracy, "The Diriment Matrimonial Impediment of Major Orders", Canon Law Studies, no. 233 (Catholic University of America, not published).

Canon 1073 (1983 CIC 1088)

Likewise religious who are professed by solemn vows invalidly attempt marriage, [as do those] who are in simple vows to which, by special prescription of the Apostolic See, there is added [a clause] invalidating weddings.

Canon Law Digest
VI: 622

Canon 1074[80] (1983 CIC 1089)

§ 1. Between a kidnapping man and a woman kidnapped with designs of marriage, as long as she remains in the power of the kidnapper, there can exist no marriage.

§ 2. But if she who was kidnapped is set in a safe and free place, separate from the kidnapper, and she consents to have this man, the impediment ceases.

§ 3. As to what applies to the nullity of marriage, the violent retention of a woman is considered the same as kidnapping, namely, when a man violently retains a woman with the intention of entering marriage, while she is in the place where she lives or to which she freely comes.

Canon Law Digest
II: 293

Canon 1075[81] (1983 CIC 1090) Cross-Ref.: 1917 CIC 1053

They cannot validly contract marriage:

1.° Who, during the same legitimate marriage, consummate adultery with each other with the promise of giving each other to marriage or, even only by a civil act, attempt marriage;

2.° Who, also during the same legitimate marriage, commit adultery with each other and one or the other of them perpetrates spousicide;

3.° Who, by mutual physical or moral efforts, even without adultery, bring about the death of a spouse.

Canon Law Digest
II: 293–95; V: 510–11; VI: 622

---

[80] Bartholomew Fair, "The Impediment of Abduction", Canon Law Studies, no. 194 (J. C. D. thesis, Catholic University of America, 1944).

[81] John Donohue, "The Impediment of Crime", Canon Law Studies, no. 69 (J. C. D. thesis, Catholic University of America, 1931).

Canon 1076[82] (1983 CIC 1091)

§ 1. In the direct line, consanguinity renders marriage invalid between all ascendants and descendants, whether legitimate or natural.

§ 2. In the collateral line, [marriage] is invalid up to the third degree inclusive, and the impediment [against] marriage is multiplied as often as the common ancestor is multiplied.

§ 3. Marriage is never permitted if there exists a doubt as to whether the parties are related in any degree of the direct line of consanguinity or in the first grade of the collateral line.

Canon Law Digest
I: 513–16; III: 428; VI: 622; IX: 627–28

Canon 1077 (1983 CIC 1092)

§ 1. Affinity in the direct line is a diriment [impediment] for marriage in any grade; in the collateral line, [it is] up to the second degree inclusive.

§ 2. The impediment of affinity is multiplied:

1.° As often as the impediment of consanguinity from which it comes is multiplied;

2.° By a second marriage with a blood-relative of the deceased spouse.

Canon Law Digest
III: 428; IV: 331; VI: 623

Canon 1078[83] (1983 CIC 1040, 1076)

The impediment of public honesty arises from an invalid marriage, whether consummated or not, and from public or notorious concubinage; it prevents marriage in the first or second degree of the direct line between a man and the blood-relatives of the woman, and vice versa.

Canon Law Digest
I: 516–17; III: 428

---

[82] Francis Wahl, "The Matrimonial Impediments of Consanguinity and Affinity", Canon Law Studies, no. 90 (J. C. D. thesis, Catholic University of America, 1934); Geraldo Hughes, "The Matrimonial Impediments of Consanguinity and Affinity in Canon Law Compared with Various State Legislation in the United States" (Pontifical Lateran University, 1964).

[83] John Gallagher, "The Matrimonial Impediment of Public Propriety", Canon Law Studies, no. 304 (thesis, Catholic University of America, 1952).

Canon 1079 (NA)

Only the spiritual relationship discussed in Canon 768 invalidates marriage.

Canon Law Digest
I: 517; V: 511–12; VII: 741–42; VIII: 678–79

Canon 1080 (1983 CIC 1094)

Those who are considered incapable of entering a wedding between themselves under civil law because of a legal relationship arising due to adoption cannot validly contract marriage between themselves under canon law either.

Canon Law Digest
VII: 743; VIII: 679

Chapter 5
On matrimonial consent[84]

Canon 1081 (1983 CIC 1057)

§ 1. The consent of the parties, legitimately manifested, makes a marriage between persons who are capable in law [of marrying]; no human power is able to supply this consent.

§ 2. Matrimonial consent is an act of the will by which each party gives and accepts perpetual and exclusive rights to the body, for those actions that are of themselves suitable for the generation of children.

Canon Law Digest
I: 517–20; II: 295–96; III: 428–35; IV: 331–32; V: 512–13; VI: 623; VII: 743; VIII: 679–796; IX: 628–34; X: 166–78

[84] Anthony van der Weyden, "The Juridical Value of the Marriage Consent among the Pagan Natives of the Gold-Coast" (MS no. 697, Gregorian University, 1939); Dennis Klemme, "Lucid Intervals and Matrimonial Consent; Historical Background and Jurisprudence of the Sacred Roman Rota" (thesis no. 154, Pontifical Lateran University, 1960); William Van Ommeren, "Mental Illness Affecting Marital Consent", Canon Law Studies, no. 415 (J. C. D. thesis, Catholic University of America, 1961); John Keating, "The Bearing of Mental Impairment on the Validity of Marriage: An Analysis of Rotal Jurisprudence" (MS no. 3481, Gregorian University, 1963; printed version, no. 1634, 1964); Cyriacus Mba, "Matrimonial Consent in Igbo Marriages" (MS no. 3605, Gregorian University, 1964); James Zusy, "Psychic Immaturity and Marriage Nullity" (doctoral diss. 63, St. Paul University [Ottawa, Canada], 1980); Augustine Mendonca, "Antisocial Personality and Nullity of Marriage" (doctoral diss., St. Paul University [Ottawa, Canada], 1982).

Canon 1082[85] (1983 CIC 1096)

§ 1. In order that matrimonial consent be considered [valid], it is necessary that the contractants at least not be ignorant that marriage is a permanent society between a man and woman for the procreation of children.

§ 2. This ignorance is not presumed after puberty.

Canon Law Digest
II: 296–301; III: 435–37; V: 513; VI: 623–27

Canon 1083[86] (1983 CIC 1097)

§ 1. Error concerning the person renders marriage invalid.

§ 2. Error about a quality of the person, even if it gave rise to the contract, renders marriage invalid only:

1.° If the error about quality amounts to an error of the person;

2.° If a free person contracts marriage with a person thought to be free, but he was really a slave in servitude strictly speaking.

Canon Law Digest
I: 520; II: 301; VIII: 796–801; IX: 634–59

Canon 1084 (1983 CIC 1099)

Simple error concerning the unity of marriage or its indissolubility or its sacramental dignity, even if it gave rise to the contract, does not vitiate matrimonial consent.

Canon Law Digest
I: 520; II: 301; V: 513

Canon 1085 (1983 CIC 1100)

Knowledge or opinion of the nullity of marriage does not necessarily exclude matrimonial consent.

Canon Law Digest
II: 301–2

---

[85] Vincent Smith, "Ignorance Affecting Matrimonial Consent", Canon Law Studies, no. 245 (thesis, Catholic University of America, 1950).

[86] Herbert Rimlinger, "Error Invalidating Matrimonial Consent", Canon Law Studies, no. 82 (J.C.D. thesis, Catholic University of America, 1932); Patrick Hennessey, "A Canonico-Historical Study of Error of Person in Marriage" (diss. no. 3, Pontifical University of St. Thomas [Rome], 1977–1978).

Canon 1086[87] (1983 CIC 1101)

§ 1. The internal consent of the mind is always presumed to be in conformity with the words or signs used in celebrating marriage.

§ 2. But if one or the other party, by a positive act of the will, excludes marriage itself, or all rights to the conjugal act, or an essential property of marriage, he contracts invalidly.

Canon Law Digest
I: 521–23; II: 302–20; III: 437–43; IV: 332–34; V: 513–17;
VI: 627; VII: 743–49; VIII: 801–12

Canon 1087[88] (1983 CIC 1103)

§ 1. Also invalid is that marriage entered into under force or grave fear, externally and unjustly imposed, [such that] in order to be free of it, one is coerced into choosing marriage.

§ 2. No other fear, even if it caused the contract, brings about the nullity of the marriage.

Canon Law Digest
I: 523–30; II: 320–25; III: 443–46; IV: 334–38;
V: 517–18; VI: 627; VIII: 813–15

Canon 1088 (1983 CIC 1104)

§ 1. In order to contract marriage validly, it is necessary that the contractants be present themselves or though procurators.

§ 2. The spouses shall express matrimonial consent through words; they may not use equivalent signs if they are able to speak.

Canon Law Digest
I: 530; III: 446–48

---

[87] Basil Courtemanche, "The Total Simulation of Matrimonial Consent", Canon Law Studies, no. 270 (thesis, Catholic University of America, 1948); Ruben Abaya, "Matrimonial Consent: Its External Manifestation and Simulation according to the Doctrine of Thomas Sanchez" (MS no. 3692, Gregorian University, 1964).

[88] Joseph Sangmeister, "Force and Fear as Precluding Matrimonial Consent", Canon Law Studies, no. 80 (J. C. D. thesis, Catholic University of America, 1932); Roch Knopke, "Reverential Fear in Matrimonial Cases in Asiatic Countries: Rota Cases", Canon Law Studies, no. 294 (thesis, Catholic University of America, 1949); Josiah Chatham, "Force and Fear as Invalidating Marriage: The Element of Injustice", Canon Law Studies, no. 310 (thesis, Catholic University of America, 1951); Manuel Monsanto Rey, "Conjugal Love and Fear in the Matrimonial Consent" (thesis, Gregorian University; printed version, no. 2870, 1979).

Canon 1089 (1983 CIC 1105)

§ 1. With due regard for diocesan statutes added to the above, in order that marriage be entered into validly by proxy, there is required a special mandate to contract [marriage] with a certain person, signed by the mandator and either by the pastor or the local Ordinary where the mandator is, or by a priest delegated by either of them, or by at least two witnesses.

§ 2. If the one mandating does not know how to write, this shall be noted in the mandate and another witness added who himself will sign what is to be written; otherwise the mandate is invalid.

§ 3. If, before the procurator contracts [marriage] in the name of the one mandating, the latter revokes this mandate or falls into amentia, the marriage is invalid, even if the procurator and the other contracting party are ignorant of this.

§ 4. In order that the marriage be valid, the procurator must personally perform his function.

Canon Law Digest
III: 448; IV: 338–42; V: 519–20

Canon 1090 (1983 CIC 1106)

Marriage can also be contracted through interpreters.

Canon 1091 (1983 CIC 1071)

Pastors shall not assist at marriages contracted through procurators or interpreters unless there is just cause and there can be no doubt about the authenticity of the mandate or the trustworthiness of the interpreters, and there is had, if time allows, the permission of the Ordinary.

Canon 1092[89] (1983 CIC 1102)

[Regarding] a condition once imposed and not revoked:

1.° If it concerns the future [and is] necessary or impossible, or of turpitude, but not contrary to the substance of marriage, it is considered as not applied;

2.° If it concerns the future [and is] against the substance of marriage, it renders [marriage] invalid;

[89] Bartholomew Timlin, "Conditional Matrimonial Consent", Canon Law Studies, no. 89 (J. C. D. thesis, Catholic University of America, 1934).

3.° If it concerns the future [and is] licit, it suspends the validity of the marriage;
4.° If it is about the past or the present, the marriage will be valid or not insofar as the condition exists or not.

Canon Law Digest
I: 531–39; II: 325–31; III: 448–50; IV: 342; V: 520–21

Canon 1093 (1983 CIC 1107)

Even if marriage is invalid because it was entered into with an impediment, the consent offered is presumed to remain until its revocation is proved.

Chapter 6
On the form of the celebration of marriage[90]

Canon 1094 (1983 CIC 1108)

Only those marriages are valid that are contracted in the presence of the pastor, or the local Ordinary, or a priest delegated by either, and two witnesses, according to the rules expressed in the canons that follow, with due regard for the exceptions mentioned in Canons 1098 and 1099.

Canon Law Digest
II: 332; III: 450; IV: 342; V: 522; VI: 627–30; VII: 749–50;
VIII: 815–20; IX: 659–60; X: 178–83

Canon 1095 (1983 CIC 1109–11)

Cross-Refs.: 1917 CIC 1096, 1098, 1102

§ 1. A pastor and local Ordinary validly assist at marriage:
1.° From that very day they have taken canonical possession of a benefice according to the norm of Canons 334, § 3, [or] 1444,

[90] John Carberry, "The Juridical Form of Marriage", Canon Law Studies, no. 84 (J. C. D. thesis, Catholic University of America, 1934); John Berry, "The Celebration of Catholic Marriage in Scotland, 1560–1908" (MS no. 1553, Gregorian University, 1949); Donald Espen, "The Canonical Form of Marriage—Re-evaluation", Canon Law Studies, no. 462 (Catholic University of America, 1968).

§ 1, or have entered into office, unless by sentence they have been excommunicated, interdicted, or suspended from office, or so declared;

2.° Within the limits of their territory only; they validly assist at the marriages not only of their subjects but also non-subjects;

3.° Provided they are not constrained by force or grave fear [when] they ask for and receive the consent of the contractants.

§ 2. A pastor and local Ordinary who can validly assist at marriage can grant permission to other priests so that within the limits of their territory they validly assist at marriage.

Canon Law Digest

I: 539; II: 333; III: 450; IV: 342–43; VII: 750–51; VIII: 820–21

Canon 1096[91] (1983 CIC 1111, 1113) Cross-Ref.: 1917 CIC 1098

§ 1. Permission granted to assist at a marriage according to the norm of Canon 1095, § 2, must be given expressly to a specific priest for a specific marriage, to the exclusion of any sort of general delegations, unless it concerns a vicar cooperator for the parish to which he is attached; otherwise it is invalid.

§ 2. The pastor or local Ordinary shall not grant this permission unless all of the things that prove the free status in law [of the parties] are completed.

Canon Law Digest

I: 540–41; III: 451–52; V: 522–23; VI: 631;
VII: 752; VIII: 822; IX: 660–73

Canon 1097 (1983 CIC 1114–1115)

§ 1. The pastor or local Ordinary licitly assists at marriage:

1.° When the free state of those contracting is legitimately shown to them in accord with the norm of law;

2.° When there is also demonstrated the domicile or quasi-domicile or month's sojourn [in the territory] or, if it concerns wander-

[91] Paul Cummings, "The Evolution of the Forms of Delegation of the Right to Assist at Matrimony and Canon 1096" (diss. no. 13, Pontifical University of St. Thomas [Rome], 1954–1955); Toribius Villacastin, "Assistant Priest and Faculties for Marriage according to the First Plenary Council of the Philippines" (diss. no. 5, Pontifical University of St. Thomas [Rome], 1963–1964).

ers, the actual presence of at least one of the contractants in the place of the marriage;

3.° When, the conditions mentioned in n. 2 being lacking, he has the permission of the pastor or Ordinary of the domicile or quasi-domicile or month's sojourn of at least one of the contractants, unless it concerns wanderers in the act of traveling, who do not have any see of dwelling, or unless grave cause intervenes that excuses from seeking permission.

§ 2. In any case, as a rule it is held that marriage will be celebrated in the presence of the pastor of the bride, unless just cause excuses; but marriages of Catholics of mixed rite, unless particular law determines otherwise, are celebrated in the rite of the husband and in the presence of his pastor.

§ 3. A pastor who assists at marriage without the permission required by law shall not make his own any stole fees and will remit same to the proper pastor of the contractants.

Canon Law Digest
I: 541; II: 333–34; III: 452–54; IV: 343–44;
VI: 631–33; VII: 752–53

Canon 1098[92] (1983 CIC 1116) Cross-Refs.: 1917 CIC 1044, 1094, 1103

If the pastor or Ordinary or delegated priest who assists at marriage according to the norm of Canons 1095 and 1096 cannot be had or cannot be present without grave inconvenience:

1.° In danger of death marriage is contracted validly and licitly in the presence only of witnesses; and outside of danger of death provided it is prudently foreseen that this condition will perdure for one month;

2.° In either case, if another priest can be present, he shall be called and together with the witnesses must assist at marriage, with due regard for conjugal validity solely in the presence of witnesses.

Canon Law Digest
I: 542–43; II: 335–36; III: 454; V: 523–24;
VII: 753–56; VIII: 822

[92] Edward Fus, "Extraordinary Form of Marriage according to Canon 1098", Canon Law Studies, no. 348 (thesis, Catholic University of America, 1954).

Canon 1099[93] (1983 CIC 1117, 1127) Cross-Ref.: 1917 CIC 1094

§ 1. [The following] are bound to observe the above-stated form:

1.° All those baptized into the Catholic Church or converted to her from heresy or schism, even if these or the others have left her later, as long as they enter marriage among themselves;

2.° All of those mentioned above if they contract marriage with non-Catholics, whether baptized or non-baptized, even after obtaining a dispensation from the impediment of mixed religion or disparity of cult;

3.° Orientals, when they contract with latins bound to this form.

§ 2. With due regard for the prescription of § 1, n. 1, non-Catholics, whether baptized or non-baptized, if they contract among themselves, are not in any way bound to observe the Catholic form of marriage; likewise, those born of non-Catholics, even if they are baptized in the Church, [but] who from infancy grow up in heresy or schism or infidelity or without any religion, as often as they contract marriage with a non-Catholic.

Canon Law Digest
I: 543–45; II: 336–38; III: 454–68; V: 525–27; VI: 633–36; VII: 756–63

Canon 1100 (1983 CIC 1119)

Outside the case of necessity, in the celebration of marriage there are to be observed the prescribed rites in the ritual books approved by the Church, or [those] laudably received [from] custom.

Canon Law Digest
I: 545–46; II: 338; VII: 763; VIII: 823

Canon 1101 (NA)

§ 1. The pastor will take care that the spouses receive a solemn blessing, which he can give to them even after they have lived in marriage for

[93] Warren Boudreaux, "The *Ab Acatholicis Nati* of Canon 1099 § 2", Canon Law Studies, no. 227 (thesis, Catholic University of America, 1946); Ralph Besendorfer, "The Valid and Licit Assistance at Interritual Marriage in the United States of America", Canon Law Studies, no. 458 (Catholic University of America, 1968).

a long time, but only in Mass, observing the special rubrics, and outside of feast times.

§ 2. Only that priest, personally or through another, can give the solemn blessing who can validly and licitly assist at marriage.

Canon Law Digest
VIII: 823–24

Canon 1102 (NA) Cross-Refs.: 1917 CIC 1064, 1109

§ 1. In a marriage between a Catholic party and a non-Catholic party, the inquiries about consent must be done according to the prescription of Canon 1095, § 1, n. 3.

§ 2. But all other sacred rites are prohibited; but if from this prohibition more serious evils will flow, the Ordinary can permit others of the usual ecclesiastical ceremonies [to occur], excluding always the celebration of Mass.

Canon Law Digest
I: 546; II: 338; III: 468–69; IV: 344;
V: 527; VI: 636; VII: 764

Canon 1103 (1983 CIC 1121–22)

§ 1. The marriage having been celebrated, the pastor or one who acts in his place, as soon as possible, will write in the book of marriages the names of the spouses and witnesses, the place and day of the celebrated marriage, and other things according to the manner of the ritual books and by the proper Ordinary so prescribed; this is to be done even though another priest delegated by him or the Ordinary assisted at the marriage.

§ 2. Moreover, according to the norm of Canon 470, § 2, the pastor will note in the book of the baptisms that the spouse on such-and-such a day contracted marriage in his parish. But if a spouse was baptized elsewhere, the pastor of the place where the marriage was entered into will transmit [notice] to the pastor of baptism, whether personally or through the episcopal Curia, so that the marriage can be recorded in the book of baptisms.

§ 3. Whenever marriage is entered into according to the norm of Canon 1098, the priest, if he was present, otherwise the witnesses, are bound together with the contractants to have the entry into marriage recorded in the prescribed books as soon as possible.

Canon Law Digest
I: 547; II: 339; VII: 764; VIII: 824

Chapter 7
On a marriage of conscience[94]

Canon 1104 (1983 CIC 1130)

Only for the gravest and most urgent causes [verified] by the local Ordinary himself, but not the Vicar General without a special mandate, can there be permitted a *marriage of conscience*, that is, a marriage celebrated while omitting all of the announcements and secretly, according to the norm of the canons that follow.

Canon 1105 (1983 CIC 1131)

Permission for the celebration of a marriage of conscience includes the promise and grave obligation of observing secrecy on the part of the assisting priest, the witnesses, the Ordinary and his successors, and even both spouses, as long as one of [the parties] does not consent to divulging it.

Canon 1106 (1983 CIC 1132)

The obligation of this promise on the part of the Ordinary is not extended to a case where some grave scandal or some grave injury to the sanctity of marriage is imminent by observing the secrecy, or where the parents of such a marriage have not taken care that the resulting children be baptized or where they have taken care to have them baptized under false names, unless they give notice to the Ordinary in the meantime within thirty days of when the children are received and baptized, that they are provided with a sincere indication of parentage, nor [does it bind] when they neglect the Christian education of the children.

[94] Vincent Coburn, "Marriages of Conscience", Canon Law Studies, no. 191 (J. C. D. thesis, Catholic University of America, 1944).

Canon 1107 (1983 CIC 1133) Cross-Ref.: 1917 CIC 470

A marriage of conscience is not to be noted in the usual book of marriages and baptisms, but [rather] in a special book preserved in the secret archive of the Curia mentioned in Canon 379.

Chapter 8
On the time and place of the celebration of marriage[95]

Canon 1108 (NA)

§ 1. Marriage can be contracted at any time of the year.

§ 2. The solemn blessing of marriage, however, is prohibited from the first [Sunday] of Advent to the day of the Birth of the Lord, inclusive, and from Ash [Wednesday] until Easter [Sunday], inclusive.

§ 3. Local Ordinaries can, however, with due regard for the liturgical law, also permit [solemn blessings] within the aforesaid times for just cause, having warned the spouses to abstain from too much pomp.

Canon Law Digest
I: 547–48; VI: 636–37

Canon 1109 (1983 CIC 1118)

§ 1. Marriage between Catholics is to be celebrated in the parish church; it cannot be celebrated in another church or oratory, whether public or semi-public, without the permission of the local Ordinary or the pastor.

§ 2. Marriage can be permitted to be celebrated in a private building by the local Ordinary only in some extraordinary case where there must always be a just and reasonable cause; but the Ordinary is not to permit [weddings] in churches or oratories of Seminaries or of women religious unless there is urgent necessity and due precautions are observed.

§ 3. Marriage between a Catholic and a non-Catholic party shall take place outside a church; but if the Ordinary prudently judges that this can-

---

[95] Edward Dodwell, "The Time and Place for the Celebration of Marriage", Canon Law Studies, no. 154 (J. C. D. thesis, Catholic University of America, 1942).

not be done without more serious problems arising, it is left to his prudent judgment to dispense from this, nevertheless, with due regard for the prescription of Canon 1102, § 2.

Canon Law Digest
I: 548; II: 339; III: 469; VI: 637; VII: 764–65; IX: 673

Chapter 9
On the effects of marriage

Canon 1110 (1983 CIC 1134)

From a valid marriage there arises between the spouses a bond that by its nature is perpetual and exclusive; moreover, Christian marriage confers grace on the spouses who do not oppose it.

Canon 1111 (1983 CIC 1135)

To each spouse from the very beginning of the marriage there is an equal right and duty in what pertains to acts proper to the conjugal life.

Canon Law Digest
III: 469–72; IX: 673; X: 184

Canon 1112 (NA)

Unless special law provides otherwise, the wife, as far as canonical effects are concerned, is made a sharer in the status of her husband.

Canon 1113[96] (1983 CIC 1136) Cross-Ref.: 1917 CIC 1372

Parents are bound by the most grave obligation to take care as far as they are able for the education of children, both religious and moral, as well as physical and civil, and of providing them with temporal goods.

Canon Law Digest
I: 548–50; II: 339; III: 472; V: 527–28; VII: 765;
VIII: 825–37; IX: 673; X: 184

[96] Richard Steinhilber, "The Obligations and Rights of Parents in the Code of Canon Law" (MS no. 2511, Gregorian University, 1955).

Canon 1114[97] (1983 CIC 1137)

Those children are legitimate who are conceived or born of a valid or putative marriage unless the parents, because of a solemn religious profession or the taking up of sacred orders, had been, at the time of conception, prohibited from using the marriage contracted earlier.

Canon Law Digest
III: 472; V: 528

Canon 1115 (1983 CIC 1138)

§ 1. The father is he whom the legal wedding says, unless the contrary is proved by evident arguments.

§ 2. Those children are presumed legitimate who were born at least six months from the day of the celebration of the marriage or within ten months from the day that conjugal life was dissolved.

Canon 1116[98] (1983 CIC 1139)

By the subsequent marriage of the parents, whether true or putative, whether newly contracted or convalidated, even if it is not consummated, children are legitimated, provided the parents were capable of contracting marriage between themselves at the time of conception, or impregnation, or birth.

Canon Law Digest
I: 550; VII: 765

Canon 1117 (1983 CIC 1140)

Children legitimated by a subsequent marriage, in what pertains to canonical effects, are in all respects equal to legitimate children, unless expressly stated otherwise.

Canon Law Digest
I: 550

---

[97] Gilbert McDevitt, "Legitimacy and Legitimation", Canon Law Studies, no. 138 (J. C. D. thesis, Catholic University of America, 1941); Almerico Cerbo, "Legitimacy, Illegitimacy, and Legitimization: A Comparative Study of the Current Law of New York and the Catholic Church" (Pontifical Lateran University, 1955).

[98] Louis Macauley, "The Effect on Illegitimate Children of the Subsequent Marriage of Their Parents in English Law, Canadian Law, and Canon Law" (Pontifical Lateran University, 1956).

Chapter 10
On the separation of spouses[99]

Article 1 — *On dissolution of the bond*

Canon 1118[100] (1983 CIC 1141)

A ratified and consummated valid marriage can be dissolved by no human power and for no cause, outside of death.

Canon Law Digest
III: 472; V: 528; VII: 765

Canon 1119[101] (1983 CIC 1142)

A non-consummated marriage between the baptized or [a marriage] between a baptized party and a non-baptized party can be dissolved by law upon solemn religious profession, or by dispensation granted by the Apostolic See for a just cause if both parties or [just] one ask for it, even if the other is unwilling.

Canon Law Digest
I: 550; II: 339–40; III: 472–74; V: 528–33;
VI: 637–41; VII: 765–70

Canon 1120[102] (1983 CIC 1143)

§ 1. Legitimate marriage between the non-baptized, even if it is consummated, is dissolved in favor of the faith by the Pauline privilege.

---

[99] James King, "The Canonical Procedure in Separation Cases", Canon Law Studies, no. 325 (J. C. D. thesis, Catholic University of America, 1952).

[100] Jeremiah Curtin, "The Indissolubility of Marriage in the Church of England: An Historical and Critical Essay in Canon Law" (MS no. 1589, Gregorian University, 1949); James Coriden, "The Indissolubility Added to Christian Marriage by Consummation" (MS no. 3194, Gregorian University, 1961; printed version, no. 1398, 1961).

[101] Aloysius Fernando, "The Dissolution of a Non-consummated Marriage by Solemn Religious Profession" (diss. no. 7, Pontifical University of St. Thomas [Rome], 1963–1964).

[102] Donald Gregory, "The Pauline Privilege", Canon Law Studies, no. 68 (J. C. D. thesis, Catholic University of America, 1931); Lewis Bennet, "The Pauline Privilege" (diss. no. 3, Pontifical University of St. Thomas [Rome], 1934–1935); Armand Pedeta, "Recent Questions concerning the Canonical Concept *In Favorem Fidei*" (Pontifical Lateran University, 1965).

§ 2. This privilege does not operate in cases of marriage between a baptized party and a non-baptized party that was entered into with a dispensation from disparity of cult.

Canon Law Digest
I: 551–52; II: 340; III: 474; IV: 344–45; V: 534–36;
VI: 641–43; VIII: 837–40

Canon 1121[103] (1983 CIC 1144)

§ 1. Before the converted and baptized spouse validly contracts a new marriage, he must, with due regard for the prescription of Canon 1125, inquire of the non-baptized party:

1.° Whether he wishes to be converted and take baptism;
2.° Whether he will at least live in peace and without contempt for the Creator.

§ 2. These inquiries must always be made, unless the Apostolic See declares otherwise.

Canon Law Digest
II: 341; III: 474–78; VI: 644

Canon 1122 (1983 CIC 1145)

§ 1. The inquiries are usually made using at least a summary and extrajudicial form under the authority of the Ordinary of the converted spouse, from which Ordinary there should be granted to the [non-converted] spouse, if he requests, time to make a decision, but warning that, if the time passes without use, the response will be presumed negative.

§ 2. Even inquiries made privately by the converted party suffice, and are even licit, if the form described above cannot be observed; but in this case, for the external forum, there must be at least two witnesses or some other legitimate manner of proof.

Canon 1123 (1983 CIC 1146)

If the inquiries have been omitted by declaration of the Apostolic See or if the [non-converted] party expressly or tacitly responds negatively, the baptized party has the right of contracting a new marriage with a Catholic

[103] Edward Woeber, "The Interpellations", Canon Law Studies, no. 172 (J. C. D. thesis, Catholic University of America, 1942); Arthur Sego, "Dispensation from the Interpellations", Canon Law Studies, no. 316 (thesis, Catholic University of America, 1951).

person, unless after baptism he gave the non-baptized party just cause for leaving.

Canon Law Digest
IV: 345–46; VI: 644–45

Canon 1124 (NA)

The [converted] spouse, even if, after taking baptism, he once again lives in marriage with the [non-converted] spouse, does not thereby lose the right of entering a new marriage with a Catholic person, and he can use this right later if the [non-converted] spouse, upon a change of will, departs without just cause or will not live in peace without contempt for the Creator.

Canon 1125[104] (1983 CIC 1148–49) Cross-Ref.: 1917 CIC 1121

Those things treating of marriage in the constitution of Paul III *Altitudo*, 1 Jun. 1537; of St. Pius V *Romani Pontificis*, 2 Aug. 1571; Gregory XIII *Populis*, 25 Jan. 1585, and whatever was written for certain regions, are extended to other regions in the same circumstances.

Canon Law Digest
I: 552–54; II: 341–43; III: 478–81; IV: 346–47; V: 536–38

Canon 1126 (NA)

The bond of the prior marriage contracted in [religious] infidelity is absolved only when the faithful spouse once again goes into a valid new marriage.

Canon Law Digest
IX: 674

Canon 1127[105] (1983 CIC 1150) Cross-Ref.: 1917 CIC 1014

In case of doubt, the privilege of the faith enjoys the favor of law.

Canon Law Digest
I: 554; II: 343; III: 481–88; IV: 347–52; V: 538–49; VI: 645–60; VII: 770–76; VIII: 840–48; IX: 674–84; X: 184–85

[104] Francis Burton, "A Commentary of Canon 1125", Canon Law Studies, no. 121 (J. C. D. thesis, Catholic University of America, 1940).

[105] Francis Kearney, "The Principles of Canon 1127", Canon Law Studies, no. 163 (J. C. D. thesis, Catholic University of America, 1942).

Article 2—*On Separation from bed, table, and dwelling*[106]

Canon 1128 (1983 CIC 1151)

Spouses must preserve the communion of conjugal life, unless a just cause excuses them.

Canon Law Digest
I: 554

Canon 1129 (1983 CIC 1152)

§ 1. Because of the adultery of a spouse, the other spouse, the bond remaining, has the right of dissolving, even in perpetuity, the communion of life, unless he consented to the crime, or gave cause for it, or otherwise expressly or tacitly condoned it, or indeed himself committed the same crime.

§ 2. Tacit condonation is considered [to have occurred] if the innocent spouse, after being made certain of the crime of adultery, freely engages in marital affection with the other spouse; but it is presumed unless, within six months, he expels or abandons the adulterous spouse, or makes a legitimate accusation against the other.

Canon 1130 (1983 CIC 1152)

The innocent spouse, whether he leaves by judicial sentence or by his own legitimate authority, is never bound by the obligation of readmitting the adulterous spouse to the consortium of life; but he may admit or recall the other, unless with his consent the other has taken up a life contrary to the married state.

Canon 1131 (1983 CIC 1153)

§ 1. If one spouse gives his name to a non-Catholic sect; if he raises the children non-Catholic; if he leads a criminal or disgraceful life; if one creates grave danger to the soul or body of the other; if by cruelty, one

[106] John Young, "Separation of Married People from the Community of Bed and Board" (diss. no. 5, Pontifical University of St. Thomas [Rome], 1934–1935); Eugene Forbes, "The Canonical Separation of Consorts: Canons 1128–1132" (doctoral diss. 16, University of Ottawa, 1947); David Wheeler, "The Obligation of Cohabitation in Marriage in Canon Law and in the Civil Law of the United States of America" (diss. no. 20, Pontifical University of St. Thomas [Rome], 1960–1961).

renders common life too difficult; these reasons and others of their sort are for the other spouse completely legitimate reasons for leaving, with the authority of the local Ordinary, or even on [the spouse's] own authority if these things appear certain and there is danger in delay.

§ 2. In all such cases, the cause of the separation ceasing, life together is to be restored; but if the separation was decided by the Ordinary for a certain or uncertain time, the innocent spouse is not bound [to return] except by decree of the Ordinary or upon the completion of the time.

Canon Law Digest
I: 554–55; II: 344–45; VIII: 848

Canon 1132 (1983 CIC 1154)

The separation having begun, the raising of the children is incumbent upon the innocent spouse or, if one of the spouses is non-Catholic, it is incumbent upon the Catholic spouse, unless in either case the Ordinary decides otherwise for the good of the children, always with due regard for their Catholic education.

Chapter 11
On the convalidation of marriage[107]

Article 1—*On simple convalidation*[108]

Canon 1133 (1983 CIC 1156)

§ 1. To convalidate a marriage invalid because of a diriment impediment, it is required that the impediment cease or be dispensed and that consent be renewed at least by the party who is conscious of the impediment.

---

[107] Patrick Sheridan, "A Historical Review of the Convalidation of Marriage and the Application of the Act of Convalidation to Non-Catholic Marriages" (thesis, Gregorian University; printed version no. 1090, 1957).

[108] James Brennan, "The Simple Convalidation of Marriage", Canon Law Studies, no. 102 (J. C. D. thesis, Catholic University of America, 1937); Leonard Bogdan, "Renewal of Consent in the Simple Validation of Marriage: An Inquiry into the Juridical Implications and the Pastoral Dimensions in the United States of America" (Pontifical Lateran University, 1979).

§ 2. This renewal is required by ecclesiastical law for validity, even if in the beginning both parties gave their consent and neither revoked it later.

Canon Law Digest
I: 555; II: 345; III: 488; VI: 660–62

Canon 1134 (1983 CIC 1157)

Renewal of consent must be a new act of the will regarding the marriage that has been shown to have been null from the beginning.

Canon Law Digest
VI: 662

Canon 1135 (1983 CIC 1158)

§ 1. If the impediment is public, consent by both parties must be renewed according to the form prescribed by law.

§ 2. If the impediment is occult and known to both parties, it is sufficient that the consent be renewed by both parties privately and in secret.

§ 3. If it is occult and one party is ignorant of it, it is sufficient that only the party who is conscious of the impediment renew consent privately and in secret, as long as the other party perseveres in the consent given earlier.

Canon Law Digest
I: 555; II: 345

Canon 1136 (1983 CIC 1159)

§ 1. A marriage invalid because of a defect of consent is convalidated if the party who did not consent now consents, provided the consent given by the other party perseveres.

§ 2. If the defect of consent was purely internal, it is sufficient that the party who did not consent consents interiorly.

§ 3. If the defect [of consent] was also external, it is necessary that the consent be exteriorly manifested, either according to the form prescribed by law, if the defect was public, or by another private and secret manner, if it was occult.

Canon Law Digest
I: 556

Canon 1137 (1983 CIC 1160)

Marriage null because of a defect of form, in order to become valid, must be contracted anew with legitimate form.

Canon Law Digest
II: 345; VI: 662–63

Article 2 — *On radical sanation*[109]

Canon 1138 (1983 CIC 1161, 1164)

§ 1. Radical sanation of marriage is its convalidation, bringing with it, in addition to a dispensation or cessation of the impediment, a dispensation from the law requiring renewal of consent and, through a fiction of the law, retroactive canonical effects to its beginning.

§ 2. Convalidation takes place from the moment the favor was granted; but its retroactivity is understood to go back to the time the marriage was entered into, unless otherwise expressly provided.

§ 3. Dispensation from the law requiring a renewal of consent can be granted even if one or both of the parties are unaware of it.

Canon Law Digest
V: 549–50; VI: 663–64; VIII: 848–49;
IX: 685; X: 185–87

Canon 1139 (1983 CIC 1163)

§ 1. Any marriage entered into with naturally sufficient consent from both parties, although juridically ineffective because of a diriment impediment of ecclesiastical law or a defect of legitimate form, can be radically sanated, provided consent perdures.

[109] Robert Harrigan, "The Radical Sanation of Invalid Marriages", Canon Law Studies, no. 116 (J. C. D. thesis, Catholic University of America, 1938); Thomas Ryan, "The Juridical Effects of the *Sanatio in Radice*", Canon Law Studies, no. 355 (thesis, Catholic University of America, 1955); John Russell, "The *Sanatio in Radice* [radical sanation] before the Council of Trent" (thesis, Gregorian University; printed version, no. 1651, 1964); Alfonse La Femina, "The Latest Ordinary Authors of Radical Sanation according to the Motu Proprio *Pastorale Minus*" (diss. no. 5, Pontifical University of St. Thomas [Rome], 1964–1965).

§ 2. The Church does not radically sanate a marriage contracted with an impediment of divine or natural law, even if the impediment later ceases, except from the moment at which the impediment ceases.

Canon Law Digest
III: 488; V: 550–52; VI: 665; X: 188–89

Canon 1140 (1983 CIC 1162)

§ 1. If there was a defect of consent in one or both parties, marriage cannot be radically sanated, whether the defect was present from the beginning or whether it was originally given and later was revoked.

§ 2. But if consent was missing from the beginning but later was given, sanation can be granted from the moment the consent was offered.

Canon 1141 (1983 CIC 1165)

Radical sanation can be granted only by the Apostolic See.

Canon Law Digest
I: 556–57; II: 345; III: 488; V: 553; VI: 665; VII: 776

Chapter 12
On second weddings[110]

Canon 1142 (NA)

Although chaste widowhood is more honorable, nevertheless, second and subsequent marriages are valid and licit, with due regard for the prescription of Canon 1069, § 2.

Canon 1143 (NA)

A woman who has once received a solemn nuptial blessing cannot accept it again in subsequent weddings.

[110] Aloisius Mehr, "The Transition from One Christian Marriage to Another" (thesis, Gregorian University; printed version, no. 754, 1952).

TITLE 8
On Sacramentals[111]

Canon 1144 (1983 CIC 1166)

Sacramentals are things or actions that the Church, in a certain imitation of the Sacraments, is wont to use to obtain, by her impetration, effects that are primarily spiritual.

Canon 1145 (1983 CIC 1167)

Only the Apostolic See can constitute new Sacramentals or authentically interpret those already received, as well as abolish or change them.

Canon 1146 (1983 CIC 1168)

The legitimate minister of Sacramentals is a cleric to whom the required power has been given by the competent ecclesiastical authority and [provided the cleric] is not prohibited from exercising it.

Canon 1147 (1983 CIC 1169)

§ 1. No one who lacks episcopal character can validly perform consecrations unless by law or apostolic indult it is permitted to him.

§ 2. Blessings can be imparted by any presbyter, excepting those that are reserved to the Roman Pontiff, to Bishops, or to others.

§ 3. A reserved blessing that is imparted by a presbyter without the necessary permission is illicit, but valid, unless the Apostolic See expressed otherwise in the reservation.

§ 4. Deacons and lectors can validly and licitly impart only those blessings that are expressly permitted to them in the law.

Canon Law Digest
III: 488–89; VI: 665; VIII: 849; IX: 685

Canon 1148 (1983 CIC 1167)

§ 1. In performing or administering Sacramentals, the rites approved by the Church are to be accurately observed.

---

[111] John Paschang, "The Sacramentals according to the Code of Canon Law", Canon Law Studies, no. 28 (J. C. D. thesis, Catholic University of America, 1925).

§ 2. Consecrations and blessings, whether constitutive or invocative, are invalid if the prescribed formulas of the Church are not followed.

Canon Law Digest
I: 557; V: 554

Canon 1149 (1983 CIC 1170)

Blessings are principally given to Catholics, but they can be given to catechumens, and indeed, unless a prohibition of the Church obstructs, even to non-Catholics in order that they might obtain the light of faith or, along with it, health of body.

Canon Law Digest
I: 557

Canon 1150 (1983 CIC 1171)

Consecrated things, or things blessed with a constitutive blessing, should be reverently treated and not applied for improper or profane use, even if they are under private control.

Canon 1151 (1983 CIC 1172)

§ 1. No one, even if endowed with the power of exorcism, can legitimately perform an exorcism over the [possessed] unless he has obtained express and specific authorization from the Ordinary.

§ 2. This authorization from the Ordinary can be granted only to priests outstanding for piety, prudence, and integrity of life; such a one shall not proceed to exorcism unless, after a diligent and prudent investigation, he finds that the one to be exorcised is actually [possessed] by a demon.

Canon 1152 (NA)

Exorcisms by legitimate ministers can be performed not only on the faithful and catechumens, but also upon non-Catholics and the excommunicated.

Canon 1153 (NA)

The ministers of the exorcisms that occur in baptism and in consecrations or blessings are those who are the legitimate ministers of those sacred rites.

SECOND PART
ON SACRED PLACES AND TIMES

SECTION 1
ON SACRED PLACES

Canon 1154 (1983 CIC 1205)

Sacred places are those that are designated for this purpose by consecration or blessing, as prescribed by the approved liturgical books, for divine cult or the burial of the faithful.

Canon Law Digest
VI: 665; VIII: 849–50; IX: 685–87

Canon 1155 (1983 CIC 1206) Cross-Refs.: 1917 CIC 1169, 1191, 1199, 1205

§ 1. The consecration of any place, even if it pertains to regulars, belongs to the Ordinary of the territory in which the site is found, provided the Ordinary is signed with episcopal character, but not to the Vicar General without a special mandate, with due regard for the right of Cardinals of the H. R. C. to consecrate a church and altar of their own title.

§ 2. The Ordinary of the territory, even though he lacks episcopal character, can give permission to any Bishop of his own rite to conduct consecrations in his own territory.

Canon 1156 (1983 CIC 1207) Cross-Refs.: 1917 CIC 1163, 1169, 1176, 1191, 1205

The right of blessing a sacred place, if it pertains to the secular clergy or to non-exempt religious, or to a lay [institute], belongs to the Ordinary of the territory in which the site is found; if [the place pertains] to exempt clerical religious, then [it belongs] to the major Superior; but either of them can delegate another priest for this.

Canon Law Digest
III: 488

Canon 1157 (NA) Cross-Ref.: 1917 CIC 239

Notwithstanding any privilege, no one can bless or consecrate a sacred place without the consent of the Ordinary.

Canon 1158 (1983 CIC 1208)

A document will be prepared on the consecration or blessing, one copy of which should be preserved in the episcopal Curia, the other in the archive of the church.

Canon 1159 (1983 CIC 1209)

§ 1. The consecration or benediction of any place, if no one suffers harm, is sufficiently proved even by one witness above all exception.

§ 2. If this is legitimately proved, neither consecration nor benediction can be repeated; in doubt, however, it is conducted as a precaution.

Canon 1160 (1983 CIC 1213)

Sacred places are exempt from the jurisdiction of civil authority and in them the legitimate authority of the Church freely exercises its jurisdiction.

TITLE 9
On churches

Canon 1161 (1983 CIC 1214)

By the name of church there is understood a sacred building dedicated to divine cult that is used as its primary end by all the Christian faithful for the public exercise of divine cult.

Canon Law Digest
III: 489

Canon 1162 (1983 CIC 1215) Cross-Ref.: 1917 CIC 497

§ 1. No church will be built without the expressed consent of the local Ordinary given in writing, which, however, the Vicar General cannot provide without a special mandate.

§ 2. The Ordinary shall not give this consent unless he prudently foresees that there will not be lacking in the future funds for the building and maintenance of the new church, the support of ministers, and other cultic [needs].

§ 3. Lest the new church cause detriment to others already existing [which detriment] is not compensated by a greater spiritual utility for the faithful, the Ordinary, before providing consent, must hear the rectors of nearby churches who have an interest, with due regard for the prescription of Canon 1676.

§ 4. Even religious members, although they have from the local Ordinary consent to establish a new house in the diocese or city, must still obtain permission from the local Ordinary before building a church or public oratory on a specific and determined site.

Canon Law Digest
III: 489

Canon 1163 (NA)

The blessing and placing of the primary stone of the church belongs to those mentioned in Canon 1156.

Canon 1164[1] (1983 CIC 1216)

§ 1. Ordinaries shall take care, even hearing, if need be, the advice of experts, that in the building or refurbishing of churches, the forms received from Christian tradition and the laws of sacred art are observed.

§ 2. In a church there shall be no entrance or window opening into the house of laity; those places under the floor of the church or above the church, if there are any, shall not be used for merely profane use.

Canon Law Digest
I: 559–60; II: 347–48; III: 489; IX: 687

Canon 1165 (1983 CIC 1217)

§ 1. Divine offices cannot be celebrated in a new church before it has been dedicated by solemn consecration or at least by blessing for divine cult.

§ 2. If it is prudently foreseen that a church is going to be converted to profane uses, the Ordinary shall not give his consent for its building, or at least, if by chance it has already been built, he will not consecrate it or bless it.

---

[1] Emmett Doyle, "The Consultation of Experts: An Historical Outline of the Legislation and Practice" (doctoral diss. 27, University of Ottawa, 1949); Arthur Fernández Santoyo, "Church Building Forms Accepted by Christian Tradition and Their Application in North America" (diss. no. 34, Pontifical University of St. Thomas [Rome], 1957–1958); Robert Seasoltz, "Directives on Sacred Art and the Building of a Church", Canon Law Studies, no. 429 (Catholic University of America, 1963).

§ 3. Cathedral churches should be dedicated by solemn consecration as should, insofar as this is possible, collegiate, conventual, and parish churches.

§ 4. Churches [made] of wood, iron, or another metal can be blessed but not consecrated.

§ 5. An altar can be consecrated even without the consecration of the church; but together with the church at least the main altar should be consecrated or a secondary altar if the main one has already been consecrated.

Canon Law Digest
III: 489–90; VIII: 850

Canon 1166[2] (NA)

§ 1. The consecration of churches, although it can be done on any day, is becomingly conducted on [Sundays] or other days of precept.

§ 2. The consecrating Bishop and those who ask that the church be consecrated should fast on the day preceding the consecration.

§ 3. When a church or altar is consecrated, the consecrating Bishop, although he lacks jurisdiction in that territory, grants an indulgence of one year to those visiting the church or altar on the day of consecration; on the anniversary day, forty days indulgence [is granted] if he is a Bishop; one hundred days [indulgence is granted] if he is an Archbishop; two hundred days if he is a Cardinal of the H. R. C.

Canon Law Digest
I: 560; V: 554–55

Canon 1167 (NA)

The feast of the consecration of a church is celebrated each year according to the norm of liturgical law.

Canon 1168 (1983 CIC 1218)

§ 1. Each consecrated or blessed church shall have its own title, which, the dedication of the church having been done, cannot be changed.

§ 2. The titular feast will also be celebrated each year according to the norms of liturgical law.

§ 3. Churches cannot be dedicated to Blesseds without an indult of the Apostolic See.

---

[2] Thaddeus Ziolkowski, "The Consecration and Blessing of Churches", Canon Law Studies, no. 187 (J. C. D. thesis, Catholic University of America, 1943).

Canon 1169 (NA)

§ 1. It is fitting that every church have bells by which the faithful are invited to divine offices and other religious acts.

§ 2. The bells of churches must also be consecrated or blessed according to the rites given in the approved liturgical books.

§ 3. The use [of the bells] belongs solely to ecclesiastical authority.

§ 4. With due regard for the conditions, [which were] approved by the Ordinary [and] attached by those who might have given the bell to the church, a blessed bell cannot be put to a profane use except for the cause of necessity or with the permission of the Ordinary or finally from legitimate custom.

§ 5. As to what pertains to the consecration or blessing of bells, the prescriptions of Canons 1155 and 1156 should be observed.

Canon Law Digest
I: 561–62; III: 490; IV: 352

Canon 1170 (1983 CIC 1212)

A church does not lose its consecration or blessing unless it is totally destroyed or the greater part of its walls collapse or it has been reduced to profane use by the local Ordinary according to the norm of Canon 1187.

Canon 1171 (1983 CIC 1219)

In a legitimately dedicated sacred building, all ecclesiastical rites can be performed with due regard for parochial rights, privileges, and legitimate customs; the Ordinary, moreover, can for a just cause establish times especially for sacred rites, provided it does not concern a church that pertains to exempt religious, with due regard for the prescription of Canon 609, § 3.

Canon Law Digest
I: 562; VI: 666

Canon 1172[3] (1983 CIC 1211) Cross-Ref.: 1917 CIC 2329

§ 1. A church is violated only by the below-listed acts, provided they are certain, notorious, and were placed inside the church:

1.° The delict of homicide;

[3] John Gulczynski, "The Desecration and Violation of the Churches", Canon Law Studies, no. 159 (thesis, Catholic University of America, 1942).

2.° An injurious and grave flow of blood;
3.° Impious and sordid use to which the church was put;
4.° Burial of an infidel or an excommunicate after a declaratory or condemnatory sentence;

§ 2. A violated church, but not the cemetery, even if it is contiguous, can be considered violated, and vice versa.

Canon 1173 (1983 CIC 1211)

§ 1. In a violated church, before it has been reconciled, it is nefarious to celebrate the divine office, to minister the Sacraments, or to bury the dead.

§ 2. If the violation occurs at the time of the divine office, these cease immediately; if [it was] before the canon of the Mass or after communion, Mass is dismissed; otherwise, the priest shall continue the Mass until communion.

Canon 1174 (NA)

§ 1. A violated church is to be reconciled as quickly as possible according to the rites described in the approved liturgical books.

§ 2. If there is doubt about whether a church has been violated, it can be reconciled as a precaution.

Canon 1175 (NA)

A church violated by the burial of an excommunicate or infidel is not to be reconciled before the cadaver is removed therefrom, if removal can be done without grave inconvenience.

Canon 1176 (NA)

§ 1. A rector, or any priest with the at least presumed consent of its rector, who can bless a church can reconcile one.

§ 2. The valid reconciliation of a violated consecrated church belongs to those who see to such things in Canon 1156.

§ 3. In case of grave and urgent necessity, however, if the Ordinary is not available, it is fundamental that rectors of consecrated churches can reconcile them, informing the Ordinary afterward.

Canon 1177 (NA)

Reconciliation of a blessed church can be done by common religious water; but reconciliation of a consecrated church is done with water blessed for this purpose according to the liturgical laws; however, not only Bishops, but also presbyters who reconcile churches can bless this water.

Canon 1178 (1983 CIC 1220) Cross-Ref.: 1917 CIC 2182

Let all those who see to such things take care that cleanliness, as befits the house of God, is observed in churches; let there be restrained from them business and transactions, even if they have a pious purpose; [as well as] generally anything that ill becomes the holiness of the place.

Canon Law Digest
III: 490

Canon 1179 (NA)

Churches enjoy the right of asylum such that pursued ones who take refuge in them shall not be removed, unless necessity urges, without the assent of the Ordinary or at least the rector of the church.

Canon 1180 (NA)

No church can be endowed with the title of basilica except by apostolic grant or immemorial custom; the privileges [of that title] are indicated by either of these sources.

Canon 1181[4] (1983 CIC 1221)

Entrance into a church for sacred rites shall be entirely free, reprobating any contrary custom whatsoever.

Canon 1182 (NA) Cross-Ref.: 1917 CIC 1183

§ 1. With due regard for the prescription of Canons 1519–28, the administration of goods that are destined for the repair or decoration of a church and the divine cult exercised therein, unless otherwise provided by special title or legitimate custom, belongs to the Bishop with the Chapter if it concerns a cathedral church; to the Chapter of the collegial church if it is a collegial church; to the rector if it is another church.

§ 2. Also, offerings made for the benefit of a parish or mission, or for a church situated within the limits of the parish or mission, are administered

---

[4] Albert Ernst, "Free Admission to the Church for Sacred Rites", Canon Law Studies, no. 380 (J. C. D. thesis, Catholic University of America, 1964).

by the pastor or missionary, unless it concerns a church having its own administration distinct from the administration of the parish or mission, or unless provided otherwise by particular law or legitimate custom.

§ 3. A pastor, missionary, or rector of a secular church, whether he is a secular or religious, must administer these types of offerings according to the norm of the sacred canons and render an accounting to the local Ordinary according to the norm of Canon 1525.

Canon 1183 (NA)

§ 1. If there are others, whether clerics or lay, who work together in the administration of the goods of some church, they constitute, together with the ecclesiastical administrator mentioned in Canon 1182 who acts as president, or the one who acts in his place, the Council of the upkeep of the church.

§ 2. Members of this Council, unless otherwise legitimately constituted, are appointed by the Ordinary or his delegate, and by him for grave cause they can be removed.

Canon 1184 (NA)

The Council of upkeep must take care of the correct administration of the goods of the church, with due regard for the prescription of Canons 1522 and 1523; but in no way shall it involve itself in those things that pertain to spiritual duties, especially:

1.° The exercise of cult in the church;

2.° The manner and time of ringing the bells and the care to be taken arranging the order of things in the church and cemetery;

3.° The manner established for collections, announcements, and other acts looking in any way to the way in which the divine cult and decoration of the church are to be done;

4.° In the disposition of altar material, the table for the distribution of the most holy Eucharist, the pulpit and what words are suggested for saying to the people, the organ, the place assigned to singers, chairs, pews, boxes for the reception of offerings, and other matters that look to the exercise of religious cult;

5.° In the admission or rejection of other sacred utensils whether destined for use, cult, or decoration of the church or sacristy;

6.° In the writing, disposition, or custody of parish books and other documents that pertain to the parish archives.

Canon Law Digest
VI: 666

Canon 1185[5] (NA)

Sacristans, singers, the moderator of the organ, choirs of children, ringer of the bells, gravediggers, and others, report only to the rector of the church, with due regard for legitimate customs and conventions and the authority of the Ordinary, and they are appointed, serve, and are dismissed by [the rector].

Canon 1186 (NA) Cross-Refs.: 1917 CIC 1297, 1469

With due regard for legitimate customs and conventions, and with the obligations that affect these things, even as constituted under civil law, remaining intact:

1.° The obligation of repairing the cathedral church falls in the order that follows:
   [a] The upkeep funds, saving that part that is necessary for the celebration of divine cult and the ordinary administration of the church;
   [b] The Bishop and canons in proportion to income, subtracting those things necessary for their honest support;
   [c] Diocesan [people], who, nevertheless, more by persuasion than by compulsion, should be led to offering up those things necessary, to the extent they are able;

2.° The duty of repairing a parish church falls in the order that follows:
   [a] The upkeep funds of the church, as above;
   [b] The patron;
   [c] Those who derive any fruits coming from the church, to be taken by tax rendered proportionally as established by the Ordinary;

[5] Brian Sparksman, "The Minister of Music in the Western Church", Canon Law Studies, no. 502 (J. C. D. thesis, Catholic University of America, 1981).

[d] Parishioners, who nevertheless, by the local Ordinary, as above, who, however, are more to be encouraged than compelled;

3.° These [rules] in due proportion are to be observed in what applies to other churches.

Canon 1187 (1983 CIC 1222, 1238) Cross-Ref.: 1917 CIC 1170

If a church in no way can be used for divine cult and its repair is entirely ruled out, it can be put to profane but not sordid use by the local Ordinary, and the duties, along with the income of the parish, if the church was parochial, are transferred by the same Ordinary to another church.

Canon Law Digest
V: 555–56; VII: 777

TITLE 10
On oratories[6]

Canon 1188 (1983 CIC 1223)

§ 1. An oratory is a place destined for divine cult, but not having as its primary end that all the faithful people use it for the public pursuit of religion.

§ 2. Thus an oratory is:

1.° *Public*, if it is principally erected for the convenience of a [group], even a private one, but nevertheless in such a way that all the faithful, at least at the time of divine offices, have the right, legitimately demonstrated, of going in;

2.° *Semi-public*, if it is erected for the convenience of a community or grouping of the faithful, to which there is not a right of free access;

3.° *Private* or *domestic*, if, in a private building, it is erected for the convenience of only one family or private person.

Canon Law Digest
III: 490; IX: 688

[6] Aloysius Feldhaus, "Oratories", Canon Law Studies, no. 42 (J. C. D. thesis, Catholic University of America, 1927); Richard Bockstie, "The Principal Oratory of Religious", Canon Law Studies, no. 368 (Catholic University of America, not published).

Canon 1189 (1983 CIC 1227)

Oratories of Cardinals of the H. R. C. and of Bishops, whether residential or titular, even though private, enjoy nevertheless all the rights and privileges that semi-public oratories enjoy.

Canon Law Digest
I: 563

Canon 1190 (NA) Cross-Refs.: 1917 CIC 1194, 1249

Little chapels erected in a cemetery by families or private persons for their burial are private oratories.

Canon Law Digest
I: 563.

Canon 1191 (NA)

§ 1. Public oratories are regulated by the same law by which churches [are regulated].

§ 2. Therefore, in a public oratory, provided it has been dedicated through blessing or consecration, by authority of the Ordinary, for the public cult of God perpetually according to the norm of Canons 1155 and 1156, all sacred functions can be celebrated, with due regard for the contrary prescription of the rubrics.

Canon 1192 (1983 CIC 1224) Cross-Refs.: 1917 CIC 1194–95

§ 1. Semi-public oratories cannot be erected without the permission of the Ordinary.

§ 2. The Ordinary is not to grant this permission unless he visits, personally or through another ecclesiastical man, the oratory and sees that it has been decently designed.

§ 3. This permission having been given, the oratory cannot be converted to profane uses without the permission of the same Ordinary.

§ 4. In colleges or residential schools of youth, high schools, lyceums, prisons, military bases, jails, and hospices, and so on, besides the principal oratory, other minor ones shall not be erected, unless in the judgment of the Ordinary, necessity or great utility so urges.

Canon Law Digest
VIII: 850

Canon 1193 (1983 CIC 1225)

In legitimately erected semi-public oratories, all divine offices and ecclesiastical functions can be celebrated, unless the rubrics or the Ordinary excepts them.

Canon Law Digest
I: 563

Canon 1194 (1983 CIC 1228)

In the little chapels of cemeteries mentioned in Canon 1190, the local Ordinary can habitually permit even the celebration of several Masses; in other domestic oratories, [he can permit] only one Mass, by individual act, in some extraordinary case, for a just and reasonable cause; the Ordinary shall not enlarge these permissions except according to the norm of Canon 1192, § 2.

Canon Law Digest
I: 563

Canon 1195 (1983 CIC 1228)

§ 1. In domestic oratories [erected] by indult of the Apostolic See, unless otherwise expressly provided by that same indult, there can be celebrated, after the Ordinary has visited and approved the oratory according to the norm of Canon 1192, § 2, one Mass, and that one read, on individual days, except on more solemn feasts; but other ecclesiastical functions shall not be done there.

§ 2. But the Ordinary, provided there are just and reasonable causes different from those for which the indult was granted, can permit by individual act the celebration of Mass even on more solemn feasts.

Canon Law Digest
III: 490

Canon 1196 (1983 CIC 1229) Cross-Ref.: 1917 CIC 822

§ 1. Domestic oratories are not to be blessed or consecrated in the manner of churches.

§ 2. Even though a domestic [or] semi-public oratory has been given a common blessing for a place or a house, or no blessing, it must nevertheless be reserved solely for divine cult and be free of all domestic use.

TITLE 11
On altars[7]

Canon 1197[8] (1983 CIC 1235)

§ 1. In the liturgical sense there are understood:

1.° By the name of *immovable* or *fixed* altar, a large table with a support consecrated together by a single act;

2.° By the name of *movable* or *portable* altar, a stone, usually small, that is consecrated alone, which is called a *portable altar* or *sacred stone*; or even a stone with a support that was nevertheless not consecrated together with it.

§ 2. In a consecrated church, at least one altar, especially the largest, must be immovable; in a church [that is] only blessed, all the altars can be movable.

Canon Law Digest
III: 490–91

Canon 1198 (1983 CIC 1236–37)

§ 1. Both the table of an altar and the sacred stone must consist of natural rock, intact and not friable.

§ 2. In an immovable altar, the top or stone table must extend along with the altar and must be suitably attached to the base; the base must also be of stone or at least the sides or columns by which the table is supported must be of stone.

§ 3. The sacred stone must be wide enough to hold the host and the greater part of the chalice.

§ 4. In both an immovable altar and a sacred stone there must be, according to the norm of liturgical law, a sepulcher containing a relic of the Saints, closed with stone.

Canon Law Digest
II: 348

---

[7] Nicholas Bliley, "Altars according to the Code of Canon Law", Canon Law Studies, no. 38 (J. C. D. thesis, Catholic University of America, 1927).

[8] Thomas Welsh, "The Use of the Portable Altar", Canon Law Studies, no. 305 (thesis, Catholic University of America, 1950); Ambrose Duffy, "The Use of the Portable Altar *extra Loca Sacra* [outside a holy place]" (diss. no. 2, Pontifical University of St. Thomas [Rome], 1950–1951).

Canon 1199 (1983 CIC 1237)

§ 1. In order that the sacrifice of the Mass can be celebrated on it, an altar must be consecrated according to the liturgical laws; that is, either the whole thing, if it concerns a immovable [altar], or only the portable altar, if it is movable.

§ 2. All Bishops can consecrate portable altars, with due regard for particular privileges; but as to what applies to immovable altars, the prescription of Canon 1155 is to be observed.

§ 3. The consecration of an immovable altar that might occur apart from the dedication of a church can be done on any day, but it is more decent that it be done on a [Sunday] or a day of precept.

Canon Law Digest
VI: 666; VIII: 851

Canon 1200 (1983 CIC 1238)

§ 1. An immovable altar loses consecration if the top or table, even for a moment of time, is separated from the base; in which case the Ordinary can permit a priest to perform again the consecration of the altar by a more brief rite and formula.

§ 2. Both an immovable altar and a sacred stone lose consecration:

1.° If they are broken enormously, whether [so considered] by reason of the quantity of the fracture or because the location [of the fracture] was anointed;

2.° If the reliquary is removed or broken or the top of the sepulcher is removed, except in the case were the Bishop himself or his delegate removed the top in order to secure it or repair it or replace it or to inspect the relics.

3.° A slight break of the top does not result in deconsecration, and any priest can repair the fissure with cement.

4.° Deconsecration of a church does not result in deconsecration of an altar, whether immovable or movable; and the reverse is true too.

Canon Law Digest
I: 563; IV: 352–53

Canon 1201 (NA)

§ 1. Just like a church, so every altar of a church, at least the immovable ones, shall have its own proper title.

§ 2. The title of the primary major altar must be the same as the title of the church.

§ 3. With the permission of the Ordinary, [the title] of a movable altar can be changed but not the title of an immovable altar.

§ 4. Without an indult from the Apostolic See, the altar of a Blessed cannot be dedicated even in churches or oratories where his office and Mass are granted.

Canon 1202 (1983 CIC 1239)

§ 1. Both an immovable and a movable altar must be reserved only for divine offices and especially the celebration of the Mass, to the exclusion of any profane use whatsoever.

§ 2. Under an altar no corpse shall be laid; corpses that by chance might be buried near an altar shall be separated from it by the space of at least one meter, otherwise it is not permitted to celebrate Mass on that altar until the corpse has been removed.

Canon Law Digest
II: 348

TITLE 12
On ecclesiastical burial[9]

Canon 1203 (1983 CIC 1176)

§ 1. The bodies of the faithful departed shall be buried, their cremation being reprobated.

§ 2. If anyone by any manner orders that his body be cremated, it is illicit to execute that desire; and if this was added to any contract or testament or any other act it is considered as not being added.

Canon Law Digest
I: 564–66; VI: 666–69; VII: 777;
VIII: 851–62; IX: 688–720

[9] John O'Reilly, "Ecclesiastical Sepulture in the New Code of Canon Law", Canon Law Studies, no. 18 (J. C. D. thesis, Catholic University of America, 1923).

Canon 1204 (NA)

Ecclesiastical burial consists in the transfer of the corpse to a church, the funeral services [that are] celebrated over it in same, and its deposition in a place legitimately deputed for laying down the faithful departed.

Chapter 1
On cemeteries

Canon 1205[10] (1983 CIC 1242)

§ 1. The corpses of the faithful are to be buried in a cemetery that, according to the rites given in the approved liturgical books, is blessed, either with a solemn blessing or a simple one given by those mentioned in Canons 1155 and 1156.

§ 2. Corpses are not to be buried in churches, unless it concerns the corpses of residential Bishops, or Abbots or Prelates *of no one*, who are to be buried in their churches, or the Roman Pontiff, or royal persons, or Cardinals of the H. R. C.

Canon Law Digest
I: 566–68; II: 348–49

Canon 1206 (1983 CIC 1240)

§ 1. The Catholic Church has the right of possessing her own cemeteries.

§ 2. Wherever this right of the Church is violated and there is no hope that the violation shall be repaired, local Ordinaries shall take care that cemeteries, in their own civil societies, are blessed, if they are so arranged that the majority [of corpses there] are of Catholics or at least, if Catholics have a space therein, that the space reserved for them is likewise blessed.

§ 3. If not even this can be obtained, individual graves shall be blessed as often as [they are used] according to the rites given in the approved liturgical books.

[10] Cornelius Power, "The Blessing of Cemeteries", Canon Law Studies, no. 185 (J. C. D. thesis, Catholic University of America, 1943).

Canon 1207 (NA) Cross-Ref.: 1917 CIC 2329

Whatever the canons prescribe concerning interdiction, violation, and reconciliation of churches is applied to cemeteries also.

Canon 1208 (1983 CIC 1241)

§ 1. Parishes shall each have their own cemeteries, unless one for several [parishes] in common has been legitimately constituted by the local Ordinary.

§ 2. Exempt religious can have their own cemetery, distinct from the common cemetery.

§ 3. Other moral persons and private families can be permitted by the local Ordinary to have a special place for burial located outside of a common cemetery and blessed in the manner of cemeteries.

Canon Law Digest
I: 568

Canon 1209 (NA)

§ 1. Both in parochial cemeteries, with the written permission of the local Ordinary or his delegate, and in the proper cemetery of another moral person, with the written permission of the Superior, the faithful can acquire for themselves a special sepulcher; this, with the consent of the same Ordinary or Superior, they can also alienate.

§ 2. The sepulcher of priests and clerics, where this can be done, should be separated from the sepulchers of laity and located in a more decent spot; moreover, where this can be done conveniently, one [location] for priests and one for ministers of the Church in lower orders should be prepared.

§ 3. The little bodies of infants, insofar as this can be done conveniently, shall have a little space special and separate from the others and be buried there.

Canon Law Digest
I: 568

Canon 1210 (NA)

Every cemetery shall be enclosed everywhere and safely locked.

Canon 1211 (NA)

Local Ordinaries, pastors, and Superiors who look to such things shall take care lest in cemeteries epitaphs, funereal praises, and ornate monuments, [and] anything [else] inconsistent with Catholic religion and piety occur.

Canon Law Digest
I: 568

Canon 1212 (NA) Cross-Ref.: 1917 CIC 1242

Besides a blessed cemetery, there should be another place, if this is possible, [also] closed and guarded, where those are buried who were not granted ecclesiastical burial.

Canon Law Digest
I: 569

Canon 1213 (NA)

No body is to be buried, especially if death was rapid, until an appropriate interval of time has run so there is removed any doubt about true death.

Canon 1214 (NA) Cross-Ref.: 1917 CIC 1242

§ 1. No corpse given perpetual ecclesiastical burial anywhere can licitly be exhumed without the permission of the Ordinary.

§ 2. The Ordinary should never grant this permission if the corpse cannot with certainty be discerned from other bodies.

Canon Law Digest
I: 569

Chapter 2
On transfer of the corpse to the church, the funeral, and burial

Canon 1215 (NA)

Unless grave cause prevents, the bodies of the faithful, before they are buried, are to be transferred from the place in which they rest to a church, where funeral rites, that is, all of the order of burial that is described in the approved liturgical books, are conducted.

Canon Law Digest
I: 569–70; II: 349–50; VII: 777

Canon 1216 (1983 CIC 1177)

Cross-Refs.: 1917 CIC 462, 1221–22, 1230

§ 1. The church to which the corpse is to be transferred by ordinary law is the proper parish church of the deceased, unless the deceased legitimately chose another church for funeral.

§ 2. If the deceased has several proper parishes, the church of the funeral is the parish church in whose territory he died.

Canon Law Digest
I: 571; II: 350; III: 491

Canon 1217 (1983 CIC 1177) Cross-Refs.: 1917 CIC 1221–22

In doubt about the right of the other church, the right of the proper parish church must always prevail.

Canon 1218 (NA) Cross-Refs.: 1917 CIC 1221–22, 1229

§ 1. Even though death occurred outside of one's own parish, the corpse nevertheless must be transferred for funeral to the church of [one of] his own parishes, [namely, the one] that is closer, if it can be conveniently reached by foot; otherwise, to the church of the parish in which the death occurred.

§ 2. Ordinaries shall designate for their own territory, having inspected special circumstances, the distance and other factors that render inconvenient the translation of the body for a funeral or place of burial; and if the parishes belong to different dioceses, the designation of the Ordinary of the diocese in which the deceased passed his last day controls.

§ 3. Although transfer to the church of funeral or burial is inconvenient, nevertheless, it is always basic that the family, heirs, or other interested persons can carry the corpse to it, having taken up the expenses of the transfer.

Canon Law Digest
I: 572; II: 350

Canon 1219 (1983 CIC 1178)

§ 1. If a Cardinal of the H. R. C. dies in the City, the body is transferred, for the sake of the funeral, to the church that the Roman Pontiff designates; if [he dies] outside the City, [then] to the more significant church in the city or place where the death occurred, unless the Cardinal chose another [church].

§ 2. Upon the death of a residential Bishop, even one signed with cardinalitial dignity, or of an Abbot or Prelate *of no one*, the body, for the sake of the funeral, must be transferred to the cathedral, abbatial, or prelature church, if this can be done conveniently; otherwise, to a more important church in the city or place, unless in either case the deceased had chosen another place.

Canon 1220 (1983 CIC 1179)

Residential beneficiaries are to be transferred to the church of their benefice, unless they have selected another church for the funeral.

Canon Law Digest
II: 350–52

Canon 1221[11] (NA) Cross-Ref.: 1917 CIC 514

§ 1. Professed religious and novices, when they are dead, are to be transferred, for the sake of the funeral, to the church oratory of their house or at least of their religious [institute], unless the novice selected another church for his funeral; but the right of carrying the corpse and of leading it there to the church of funeral always belongs to the Superior of the religious.

§ 2. If they have died a long way from the house, so that they cannot be conveniently transported to the church of their house or at least [to one] of their religious [institute], they are to be buried [from] the parish church nearest to where they died, unless the novice chose another church for the funeral, and with due regard for the rights of the Superior mentioned in Canon 1218, § 3.

§ 3. What is said about novices in §§ 1 and 2 applies also to servants actually serving and staying in a stable manner within the walls of the

[11] Thomas Kelly, "Funeral Churches for Religious" (diss. no. 11, Pontifical University of St. Thomas [Rome], 1961–1962).

house; who, however, if they die outside of the religious house, are to be buried according to the norm of Canons 1216–18.

Canon Law Digest
I: 572

Canon 1222 (NA)

As for what applies to those deceased who were in the house of regulars or a collegial [institution] as guests, or for education, or because they were infirm, and as to those who die in a hospital, Canons 1216–18 apply, unless a particular right by law or privilege can be shown; but as to what applies to those dying in a Seminary, the prescription of Canon 1368 is to be observed.

Canon Law Digest
I: 572

Canon 1223 (1983 CIC 1180)

§ 1. It is permitted to all, unless they are expressly prohibited by law, to choose the church of funeral and the cemetery of burial.

§ 2. A wife and pubescent children are entirely immune in this selection from the power of the husband and parents.

Canon Law Digest
I: 573–75; II: 352

Canon 1224 (NA)

The following are prohibited from the selection of the church of funeral or cemetery of burial:

1.° Prepubescents; but for a prepubescent son or daughter, even after death, the parents or guardian can make this choice;
2.° Professed religious in any degree or dignity; but not if they are Bishops.

Canon 1225 (NA)

In order that the choice of church be valid, it is necessary that it fall on a parochial church, or on a church of regulars, but not of nuns (unless it concerns a woman who by reason of service, education, infirmity, or as a guest was within the cloister of the monastery staying in a non-transitory manner), or on a church with the right of patronage if it concerns the patron, or on another church marked with the right of funerals.

Canon Law Digest
I: 575

Canon 1226 (NA)

§ 1. One can choose the church of funeral or the cemetery of burial either personally or through another to whom one gives a legitimate mandate; the fact of this choice and the grant of the mandate can be proven by any legitimate manner.

§ 2. If the choice was made through another, this one can fulfill his mandate even after the death of the one mandating.

Canon Law Digest
I: 576–78; III: 491

Canon 1227 (NA)

Religious and secular clerics are strictly forbidden from inducing anyone by vow, oath, or promise uttered, or in any other way, to select their own church for his funeral or their cemetery for burial or not to change a previous choice; but if they act against this the choice is null.

Canon Law Digest
I: 578

Canon 1228 (1983 CIC 1180) Cross-Ref.: 1917 CIC 1231

§ 1. If burial was chosen in a different cemetery from that of the cemetery of the parish of the deceased, the corpse will be buried in it provided there is no objection on the part of those who supervise the cemetery.

§ 2. For burial chosen in the cemetery of religious, in order that the corpse can be buried therein, the consent of the religious Superior is required and suffices according to the norm of the constitution of each religious [institute].

Canon Law Digest
I: 578

Canon 1229 (NA) Cross-Ref.: 1917 CIC 1231

§ 1. If anyone possessing a major sepulcher in any cemetery had not chosen another burial place and dies, he will be buried in it if he can be [buried there] conveniently, with due regard for the prescription of Canon 1218, § 3.

§ 2. For a wife, burial follows the husband and, if she had several [husbands], the burial of the last.

§ 3. If there are several major or husband-based sepulchers, the family of the deceased or the heirs shall select the place of burial.

Canon Law Digest
I: 578; III: 491

Canon 1230[12] (NA) Cross-Ref.: 1917 CIC 514

§ 1. The proper pastor of the deceased has not only the right but the duty, except in case of grave necessity, of guiding personally, or through another, the corpse and of committing it to his parish church where the funeral rites will be accomplished, with due regard for the prescription of Canon 1216, § 2.

§ 2. But if death occurred in a place outside the parish, and the corpse can be conveniently brought to the church of its own parish, it belongs to the proper pastor, having notified the pastor of the place, to guide thither the corpse and to commit it to his parish church where the funeral rites will be accomplished.

§ 3. If the church of funeral is a church of regulars or others exempt from the jurisdiction of the pastor, the pastor, under the cross of the funeral church, takes the corpse and leads it to the church; but the rector of the church celebrates the rites.

§ 4. But if the church of funeral is not exempt from the jurisdiction of the pastor, the celebration of the rites, with due regard for particular privileges, belongs not to the rector of the church of funeral, but to the pastor in whose territory the church is situated, provided the deceased was subject to the pastor.

§ 5. Religious women and novices who die in a religious house are brought to the limits of the cloister by other religious women; from there,

[12] Joseph Hale, "The Pastor of Burial", Canon Law Studies, no. 234 (thesis, Catholic University of America, 1949).

if it concerns religious who are not subject to the jurisidiction of the pastor, the chaplain conducts [the body] to the church or oratory of the proper house of the religious and conducts the funeral; in the case of other religious, the prescription of § 1 applies; but if it concerns a religious who dies outside of the house, the general prescriptions of the canons are observed.

§ 6. Regarding Cardinals of the H. R. C. and Bishops who die outside the City in an episcopal city, the prescription of Canon 397, n. 3 is observed.

§ 7. If the corpse is sent to a place where neither the deceased had his own parish nor any church of funeral was legitimately chosen, the right of guiding the corpse and of conducting the rites, if there are any to be performed, and of leading the corpse to burial belongs to the cathedral church in that place; but if there is none, [it belongs] to the church of the parish in which the cemetery is located, unless otherwise determined by local custom or diocesan statutes.

Canon Law Digest
I: 578–80; II: 352–54; VII: 777–78

Canon 1231 (NA)

§ 1. The funeral services having been completed in the church, the corpse is to be buried according to the norm of the liturgical books in the cemetery of the church of the funeral with due regard for the prescriptions of Canons 1228 and 1229.

§ 2. Whoever conducts the funeral services in the church has not only the right, but also the duty, except in case of grave necessity, of leading [the corpse] personally or through another priest to the place of burial.

Canon Law Digest
I: 581

Canon 1232 (NA)

§ 1. The priest who conducts [the corpse] to the church of funeral or to the place of burial can also freely cross, with the stole and even with the cross elevated, through the territory of another parish or diocese even without the permission of the pastor or Ordinary.

§ 2. If the corpse is to be buried in a cemetery to which it cannot be conveniently carried, the pastor or rector of the church of funeral cannot exercise his right of conducting it outside the limits of the city or place.

Canon Law Digest
I: 581

Canon 1233 (NA)

§ 1. A pastor cannot, without a just and grave cause approved by the Ordinary, exclude secular clerics, religious, and pious sodalities that the family or heirs wish to invite from conducting the corpse to the church of funeral and to [the place of] burial and of lending assistance in the funeral; clerics, however, belonging to the church, must be invited by the family and heirs before all others.

§ 2. Societies or insignia manifestly hostile to the Catholic religion can never be admitted.

§ 3. Those associated with the corpse are bound to conduct things concerning the funeral according to [the directions of] the pastor, with due regard for everyone's rights of precedence.

§ 4. Clerics shall not carry the corpse of laity [no matter] what was his sort or dignity.

Canon Law Digest
I: 581; II: 354; III: 491–93

Canon 1234 (1983 CIC 1181) Cross-Ref.: 1917 CIC 1507

§ 1. Local Ordinaries shall produce an index of funeral fees, that is, offerings, if one does not exist for the territory, with the advice of the cathedral Chapter and, if they think it opportune, that of the diocesan vicars forane and pastors of the episcopal city, with due attention to legitimate customs and the particular circumstances of all persons and places; and in this they shall determine with moderation in various cases the rights of everyone so that every sort of contention and occasion of scandal is removed.

§ 2. If in this index several classes [of funerals] are enumerated, [the choice] is free for those to choose a class.

Canon Law Digest
I: 582

Canon 1235 (1983 CIC 1181)

§ 1. It is strictly prohibited for anyone, for the sake of burial or funeral services or on the anniversary of death, to require anything beyond that which is established in the index of diocesan rates.

§ 2. The poor are entirely free [of the obligation of paying] and should decently receive funerals with prescribed services and burial according to liturgical laws and diocesan statutes.

Canon 1236 (NA)

§ 1. With due regard to particular law, as often as a faithful [does not receive] funeral services in his own parish church, the proper pastor of the deceased is owed the portion of the parish, except in the case where the corpse cannot be conveniently transported to the church of one's own parish.

§ 2. If anyone has several proper parishes to which the corpse can be conveniently brought, and another [is chosen for] funeral services, the portion of the parish is to be divided among all of the proper pastors.

Canon Law Digest
I: 582; II: 354–56

Canon 1237 (NA)

§ 1. The portion of the parish must be subtracted from each and every payment that is established for a funeral and interment according to the diocesan rate.

§ 2. If, for any reason, the first solemn office of funeral is not completed immediately, but within a complete month from the day of interment it is done, even though on this day there were not lacking some minor public offices, the portion of the parish nevertheless is owed even against the payments for this sort of funeral.

§ 3. The quantity of the parochial portion is determined in the diocesan rates; and if the church of the parish and the burying church belong to different dioceses, the quantity of the parochial portion is calculated according to the rate of the church of funeral.

Canon Law Digest
I: 582–83

Canon 1238 (1983 CIC 1182)

After the burial, the minister shall record the name and age of the deceased in the book of the dead, the name of the parents or spouse, the time of death, who ministered which Sacraments, and the place and time of burial.

Chapter 3

On those to whom ecclesiastical burial is to be granted or denied[13]

Canon 1239 (1983 CIC 1176, 1183)

§ 1. Those who die without baptism are not to be accorded ecclesiastical burial.

§ 2. Catechumens who through no fault of their own die without baptism are to be reckoned as baptized.

§ 3. All baptized are to be given ecclesiastical burial unless they are expressly deprived of same by law.

Canon Law Digest
I: 583

Canon 1240 (1983 CIC 1184) Cross-Refs.: 1917 CIC 2260, 2275, 2291, 2339, 2350–51

§ 1. Unless they gave before death a sign of repentance, the following are deprived of ecclesiastical burial:

1.° Notorious apostates from the Christian faith, or those who notoriously gave their name to heretical sects or schismatic or masonic sects, or other societies of this sort;
2.° Excommunicates or those under interdict after a condemnatory or declaratory sentence;
3.° Those who killed themselves by deliberate counsel;
4.° Those who died in a duel, or from wounds related thereto;
5.° Those who ordered that their body be handed over for cremation;
6.° Other public and manifest sinners.

[13] Charles Kerin, "The Privation of Christian Burial", Canon Law Studies, no. 136 (J. C. D. thesis, Catholic University of America, 1941).

§ 2. If there is any doubt about the occurrence of the above-mentioned in a case, the Ordinary is to be consulted if there is time; if doubt remains, the body should be accorded ecclesiastical burial, but in such a way that scandal is removed.

Canon Law Digest

I: 583; III: 493; IV: 353; VI: 669–70; VII: 778; VIII: 862–64

Canon 1241 (1983 CIC 1185)

One excluded from ecclesiastical burial is also to be denied any funeral Mass, even on the anniversary, as well as other public funeral offices.

Canon Law Digest

VIII: 864–66

Canon 1242 (NA)

If it can be done without grave inconvenience, the body of a banned excommunicate that, against the canonical statutes, has obtained burial in a sacred place is to be exhumed, with due regard for the prescription of Canon 1214, § 1, and replaced in a profane place mentioned in Canon 1212.

SECTION 2
ON SACRED TIMES[14]

Canon 1243 (NA)

Feast days are sacred times; to these are added days of abstinence and fast.

Canon 1244 (1983 CIC 1044)

§ 1. It is only for the supreme ecclesiastical authority to establish, transfer, or abolish feast days and days of abstinence and fast common to the whole Church.

§ 2. Local Ordinaries, by an individual act, can indicate other feasts and days of abstinence and fast for their own diocese or places.

Canon Law Digest

I: 584

[14] Henry Spencer, "Feasts and Fasts in Anglo-Saxon Church Law" (diss. no. 10, Pontifical University of St. Thomas [Rome], 1970–1971); Charles Petersen, "The Canonical Status of the Lenten Fast in the Church of England" (diss. no. 9, Pontifical University of St. Thomas [Rome], 1978–1979).

Canon 1245 (1983 CIC 1245)

§ 1. Not only local Ordinaries, but also pastors, in individual cases and for just cause, can dispense individual subjects and individual families, even outside their territory, as well as travelers in their territory, from the common law of observing a feast and likewise from observing abstinence [or] fast, or from both.

§ 2. Ordinaries, because of a particularly large gathering of people or public health, can dispense a whole diocese or place from the law of fast or abstinence or even from both by the same [act].

§ 3. In clerical exempt religious [institutes], Superiors have the same power of dispensing as do pastors in regard to those persons mentioned in Canon 514, § 1.

Canon Law Digest

I: 584–85; II: 356–57; IV: 353; V: 556–58; VI: 670

Canon 1246 (NA)

The calculation of feast days and likewise days of abstinence and fast is to be made from midnight up to midnight, with due regard for the prescription of Canon 923.

TITLE 13
On feast days

Canon 1247 (1983 CIC 1246)

§ 1. Feast days under precept in the whole Church are only: All and every [Sunday], the feast of the Nativity, Circumcision, Epiphany, Ascension, and the most holy Body of Christ, Immaculate Conception, and Assumption of Mary the Mother of God, of Saint Joseph her spouse, of the Blessed Apostles Peter and Paul, and of All the Saints.

§ 2. The feast days of Patrons do not bind by ecclesiastical precept; local Ordinaries can transfer the external solemnity to the next following [Sunday].

§ 3. If anywhere one of these named feasts has been legitimately abolished or transferred, nothing shall be innovated without consulting the Apostolic See.

Canon Law Digest

I: 585; II: 358; V: 558; VI: 670; VII: 778; VIII: 866–68; IX: 720–22

Canon 1248[15] (1983 CIC 1247)

On feast days of precept, Mass is to be heard; there is an abstinence from servile work, legal acts, and likewise, unless there is a special indult or legitimate customs provide otherwise, from public trade, shopping, and other public buying and selling.

Canon Law Digest
II: 358–60; III: 493; VI: 670–75; VII: 778–79;
VIII: 868–69; IX: 722; X: 190

Canon 1249 (1983 CIC 1248)

The law of hearing the Sacred [rites] is satisfied wherever Mass is celebrated in a Catholic rite under the sky or in any church or public or semi-public oratory and in the little building of a private cemetery mentioned in Canon 1190, but not in other private oratories, unless this privilege has been granted by the Apostolic See.

Canon Law Digest
I: 585; III: 493; IV: 354–55; V: 559

TITLE 14
On abstinence and fast[16]

Canon 1250 (NA)

The law of abstinence prohibits meat and soups made of meat but not of eggs, milks, and other condiments, even if taken from the fat of animals.

Canon Law Digest
I: 585–86; VI: 675–85; VII: 779–80; X: 190–92

---

[15] John Guiniven, "The Precept of Hearing Mass", Canon Law Studies, no. 158 (J. C. D. thesis, Catholic University of America, 1942); William Heffernan, "The Notion of Servile Work in Canon 1248" (diss. no. 6, Pontifical University of St. Thomas [Rome], 1962–1963).

[16] Nicolas of Cork, "Fast and Abstinence in Franciscan Legislation" (thesis, Gregorian University; printed version, no. 381, 1943); Jordan Sullivan, "Fast and Abstinence in the First Order of St. Francis", Canon Law Studies, no. 374 (thesis, Catholic University of America, 1957); Alfred Rodriguez, "The Spanish *Bulla Cruciatae* and the Indult on Fasting and Abstinence in the Philippines" (MS no. 2858, Gregorian University, 1958).

Canon 1251 (NA)

§ 1. The law of fast prescribes that there be only one meal a day; but it does not forbid that a little bit [of food] be taken in the morning and in the evening, observing, nevertheless, the approved custom of places concerning the quantity and the quality of the food.

§ 2. It is not forbidden to mix meat and fish in the same meal; or to exchange the evening meal with lunch.

Canon Law Digest
I: 586–87

Canon 1252 (1983 CIC 1251)

§ 1. The law of abstinence only must be observed every [Friday].

§ 2. The law of abstinence together with fast must be observed every Ash [Wednesday], every [Friday and Saturday] of Lent, each of the [Ember] Days, and the vigils of the Pentecost, the Assumption of the God-bearer into heaven, All the Saints, and the Nativity of the Lord.

§ 3. The law of fast only is to be observed on all the other days of Lent.

§ 4. On [Sundays] or feasts of precept, the law of abstinence or of abstinence and fast or a fast only ceases, except during Lent, nor is the vigil anticipated; likewise it ceases on Holy [Saturday] afternoon.

Canon Law Digest
I: 587–90; II: 360–63; III: 493–506; IV: 355–58; V: 559–65; VI: 685–86

Canon 1253 (NA)

By these canons nothing is changed concerning particular indults or the vows of any physical or moral person or the constitutions and rules of any religious [institute] or [other] approved institute, whether of men or of women, living together in common even without vows.

Canon Law Digest
I: 590–93; II: 364; III: 506

Canon 1254 (1983 CIC 1252)

§ 1. The law of abstinence binds all those who have completed seven years of age.

§ 2. All those are bound by the law of fast from the completion of the twenty-first year of age until the beginning of the sixtieth.

Canon Law Digest
I: 593; V: 565; VI: 686; VIII: 869

THIRD PART
ON DIVINE CULT

Canon 1255 (NA)

§ 1. To the most Holy Trinity and to each of its Persons, [and] to Christ the Lord, even under sacramental species, there is owed the worship of latria; to the Blessed Virgin Mary, the cult of hyperdulia [is owed]; and to the others reigning with Christ in heaven, the cult of dulia [is owed].

§ 2. Also to sacred relics and images there is a veneration and a cult owed to the respective persons to whom the images and relics refer.

Canon Law Digest
IV: 358; V: 566–72; VI: 686

Canon 1256 (1983 CIC 834)

[Worship], if it is carried on in the name of the Church by persons legitimately deputed for this and through acts instituted by the Church and given only to God, the Saints, and the Blesseds, is called *public*; anything less is *private*.

Canon 1257 (1983 CIC 838)

It belongs only to the Apostolic See to order sacred liturgy and to approve liturgical books.

Canon Law Digest
I: 595; IV: 359; V: 572–73

Canon 1258[1] (1983 CIC 844) Cross-Ref.: 1917 CIC 2316

§ 1. It is not licit for the faithful by any manner to assist actively or to have a part in the sacred [rites] of non-Catholics.

§ 2. Passive or merely material presence can be tolerated for the sake of honor or civil office, for grave reason approved by the Bishop in case of

[1] Ignatius Szal, "The Communication of Catholics with Schismatics", Canon Law Studies, no. 264 (thesis, Catholic University of America, 1947); Gerard Chidgey, "A Study of the Relationship between Catholics and Non-Catholics from Historical and Juridical Points of View" (ref. no. 18, Pontifical University Comillas [Madrid], 1945).

doubt, at the funerals, weddings, and similar solemnities of non-Catholics, provided danger of perversion and scandal is absent.

Canon Law Digest
II: 365–72; III: 506; IV: 359; VI: 687–735; VII: 780–821; VIII: 870–907; IX: 722–37; X: 192–93

Canon 1259 (1983 CIC 839)

§ 1. Prayers and pious exercises are not permitted in churches or oratories without review and express permission of the local Ordinary, who in more difficult cases will send the whole matter to the Apostolic See.

§ 2. The local Ordinary cannot approve new litanies for public recitation.

Canon Law Digest
II: 372–74; III: 506–7; IV: 359

Canon 1260 (NA)

Ministers of the Church in exercising cult must depend only on ecclesiastical Superiors.

Canon 1261 (1983 CIC 838)

§ 1. Local Ordinaries shall be vigilant that the prescriptions of the sacred canons on divine cult be scrupulously observed, and especially lest there be introduced in divine cult, whether public or private, or in the daily life of the faithful, any superstitious practice or that in any way there be admitted something alien to the faith or inconsistent with ecclesiastic tradition or anything looking like a sort of profit.

§ 2. If the local Ordinary passes laws on this for his territory, all religious, even exempt, are bound by the obligation of observing them; and the Ordinary can visit their churches or public oratories for this purpose.

Canon Law Digest
I: 595–97; II: 374–76; III: 507–12; VI: 735; VII: 821–24; VIII: 907

Canon 1262 (NA)

§ 1. It is desirable that, consistent with ancient discipline, women be separated from men in church.

§ 2. Men, in a church or outside a church, while they are assisting at sacred rites, shall be bare-headed, unless the approved mores of the people or peculiar circumstances of things determine otherwise; women, however, shall have a covered head and be modestly dressed, especially when they approach the table of the Lord.

Canon Law Digest
I: 597

Canon 1263 (NA)

§ 1. There can be a distinct place in the church for magistrates because of their dignity and grade according to the norm of liturgical law.

§ 2. Without the express consent of the local Ordinary, none of the faithful shall have a place reserved in the church for them; the Ordinary shall not give this consent unless the convenience of the other faithful is sufficiently considered.

§ 3. Whenever this grant is made there is a tacit condition that the Ordinary can, for a just cause, revoke the concession, notwithstanding whatever length of time.

Canon Law Digest
I: 597

Canon 1264 (NA)

§ 1. Music, whether of the organ or of other instruments or sung, in which there is mixed anything lascivious or impure is entirely forbidden from churches; and the liturgical laws concerning sacred music are to be observed.

§ 2. Religious women, if it is permitted to them according to the norm of their constitutions or liturgical law, and having come to the local Ordinary, can sing in their own church or public oratory, provided that they are singing from a place where they cannot be seen by the people.

Canon Law Digest
I: 597–600; II: 376; III: 512–14; IV: 359–60; V: 573–612;
VI: 735–55; VII: 824; VIII: 907; IX: 737

TITLE 15
On the custody and worship of the most holy Eucharist[2]

Canon 1265[3] (1983 CIC 934–35) Cross-Ref.: 1917 CIC 483

§ 1. The most holy Eucharist, provided there is one who has its care and a priest who regularly at least once a week celebrates Mass in a sacred place:

[2] William Cavanaugh, "The Reservation of the Blessed Sacrament", Canon Law Studies, no. 40 (J. C. D. thesis, Catholic University of America, 1927); John Danagher, "Petitions for the Indult to Reserve the Blessed Sacrament in Private Oratories" (diss. no. 1, Pontifical University of St. Thomas [Rome], 1949–1950).

[3] Daniel Cahill, "The Custody of the Holy Eucharist", Canon Law Studies, no. 292 (thesis, Catholic University of America, 1950).

1.° Must be kept in a cathedral church, in a principal church of an Abbey or Prelature *of no one*, Vicariate and Prefecture Apostolic, in any parish or quasi-parish church, and in any church connected to a house of exempt religious, whether of men or of women;

2.° Can be kept, with the permission of the local Ordinary, in a collegial church and principal oratory, whether public or semi-public, whether of a pious or religious house, or of an ecclesiastical college that is ruled by secular clerics or religious.

§ 2. In order that it be kept in other churches or oratories, an apostolic indult is necessary; the local Ordinary can grant this permission only to a church or public oratory for a just cause and by an individual act.

§ 3. It is not permitted to anyone to retain on his person or to carry on a trip the most holy Eucharist.

Canon Law Digest
I: 600; II: 376; III: 514; VIII: 907

Canon 1266 (1983 CIC 937)

Churches in which the most holy Eucharist is preserved, especially parochial ones, shall be open to the faithful every day for at least some hours.

Canon 1267 (1983 CIC 936)

Revoking any contrary privilege, the most holy Eucharist cannot be kept in a religious or pious house, except either in the church or principal oratory; and [it cannot be kept] among nuns within the choir or the walls of the monastery.

Canon Law Digest
I: 600–601; II: 376; IX: 737

Canon 1268 (1983 CIC 938)

§ 1. The most holy Eucharist cannot be kept continually or habitually, except on only one altar of the church.

§ 2. It shall be kept in the most excellent and the most noble place of the church and therefore regularly on the major altar unless it seems that the veneration and cult of such a sacrament is more convenient and decent elsewhere, observing the prescriptions of liturgical law that pertain to the final days of the great week.

§ 3. But in cathedral churches or in collegial or conventual ones in which choral functions are conducted at the main altar, lest ecclesiastical offices be impeded, it is opportune that the most holy Eucharist not regularly be kept at the major altar but in another chapel or altar.

§ 4. Let rectors of churches take care that the altar in which the most holy Sacrament is reserved be decorated above all the others so that by this appearance the faithful are moved to greater piety and devotion.

Canon Law Digest
I: 601; II: 376–77; III: 514; V: 612

Canon 1269[4] (1983 CIC 938)

§ 1. The most holy Eucharist must be preserved in an immovable tabernacle located in the center part of the altar.

§ 2. The tabernacle shall be well-constructed, closed on all sides, decently decorated according to the norm of liturgical law, empty of all foreign things, and thus carefully kept so that any sort of danger of sacrilege or profanation is excluded.

§ 3. If grave causes, approved by the local Ordinary, so persuade, it is not forbidden to preserve the most holy Eucharist at nighttime outside the altar but on a corporal in a safe and decent place with due regard for the prescription of Canon 1271.

§ 4. The key of the tabernacle in which the most holy Sacrament is preserved must be most diligently kept, gravely burdening the conscience of the priest who has care of the church or oratory.

Canon Law Digest
II: 377–89; III: 515–18; IV: 360–62; V: 612–13;
VI: 755–56; VII: 824–30; IX: 738–41

Canon 1270 (1983 CIC 939)

Small consecrated hosts that are necessary for the number of the infirm and other faithful to satisfy communion shall be perpetually conserved in a pyx [made] of decent and solid material and clean, with its lid tightly closed, and covered with a white silk veil that, insofar as possible, is decorated.

---

[4] Patrick Powell, "The Canonical Norms Referring to the Construction of Tabernacles" (diss. no. 32, Pontifical University of St. Thomas [Rome], 1958–1959).

Canon 1271 (1983 CIC 940) Cross-Ref.: 1917 CIC 1269

In the presence of the tabernacle in which the most holy Sacrament is reserved, at least one lamp shall burn continually, day and night, fed by the oil of olives or beeswax; but if true oil of the olives cannot be had, the local Ordinary can prudently permit that other oils be used, insofar as possible, vegetable [oil].

Canon Law Digest
II: 389–90; III: 518–19; V: 613–14; VIII: 908

Canon 1272 (1983 CIC 939)

Consecrated hosts, whether for the communion of the faithful or for the exposition of the most holy Sacrament, shall be recently made and frequently renewed, the old ones duly consumed, so that there is no danger of corruption, [and] the instructions that the local Ordinary gives on this matter shall be scrupulously observed.

Canon Law Digest
I: 601; II: 390

Canon 1273 (1983 CIC 898)

Those to whom the religious instruction of the faithful falls shall omit nothing that would excite piety for the most holy Eucharist in their spirits and shall especially encourage them that, not only on [Sundays] and feasts of precept, but also on regular days during the week, they assist at the sacrifice of the Mass and visit the most holy Sacrament frequently insofar as this is possible.

Canon 1274[5] (1983 CIC 941, 943)

§ 1. In churches or oratories to which it is given to preserve the most holy Eucharist, there can be private exposition, that is, with a pyx, for any just reason without the permission of the Ordinary; but public exposition, that is, with a monstrance on the feast of the Body of Christ and within the octave, can be done in all churches within solemn Mass and vespers; but at other times, it shall not [be done] unless there is just and grave cause, especially for public [exposition] and then with the permission of

[5] Francis Smyer, "Canonical Regulations regarding Exposition of the Blessed Sacrament according to Canons 1274 and 1275", Canon Law Studies, no. 366 (Catholic University of America, not published).

the local Ordinary, even though a church belongs to an exempt religious [institute].

§ 2. The minister of exposition and reposition of the most holy Sacrament is a priest or deacon; but the minister of the Eucharistic blessing is only a priest, nor can a deacon impart it, except in that case where he brings Viaticum to the infirm according to the norm of Canon 845, § 2.

Canon Law Digest
I: 602; III: 519; IV: 362; VI: 756; VII: 830–31

Canon 1275 (1983 CIC 942)

The Supplication of Forty Hours, insofar as possible, shall be conducted with solemnity every year in all parishes and other churches in which the most holy Sacrament is habitually reserved; and wherever, because of peculiar circumstances of things, it cannot be done without grave inconvenience or with the reverence due to such a sacrament, the local Ordinary shall take care that for at least some continuous hours on specified days the most holy Sacrament shall be exposed with more solemn rite.

Canon Law Digest
I: 602; III: 519

TITLE 16
On the cult of the Saints, of sacred images, and of relics[6]

Canon 1276 (1983 CIC 1186)

It is good and useful suppliantly to invoke the Servants of God reigning together with Christ and to venerate their relics and images; but before the others, all the faithful shall follow the Blessed Virgin Mary with filial devotion.

Canon Law Digest
III: 519; IV: 362–64; V: 614–16; VI: 756–59; VII: 831;
VIII: 908–12; IX: 741–44; X: 193–94

[6] Eugene Dooley, "Church Law on Sacred Relics", Canon Law Studies, no. 70 (J. C. D. thesis, Catholic University of America, 1931).

Canon 1277 (1983 CIC 1187)

§ 1. It is licit to venerate with public cult only those Servants of God who are listed by the authority of the Church among the Saints or Blesseds.

§ 2. The cult of dulia is owed [to those] canonically listed in the book of the Saints; listed Saints can [have this dulia] everywhere and by any cultic acts of this sort; but Blesseds cannot [have this] except in the place and manner that the Roman Pontiff grants.

Canon 1278 (NA)

Likewise laudably, those things being observed that ought to be observed, there should be selected Saints for nations, dioceses, provinces, confraternities, and other religious families and moral persons and places so that, with assenting confirmation of the Apostolic See, they are constituted Patrons; but not so with Blesseds without a special indult for same from the Apostolic See.

Canon Law Digest
III: 519; VII: 832; VIII: 912–16; IX: 744; X: 194

Canon 1279 (1983 CIC 1188)

§ 1. It is not permitted to anyone to place or to take care to place in a church, even an exempt one, or other holy place, any unusual image, unless it has been approved by the local Ordinary.

§ 2. The Ordinary shall not approve sacred images to be displayed for the public veneration of the faithful that are not consistent with the approved usage of the Church.

§ 3. The Ordinary shall never allow in churches or other sacred places images of false dogma to be exhibited or ones that do not offer the required decency and honesty or that present an occasion of dangerous error to the unlearned.

§ 4. If images publicly exposed for veneration are solemnly blessed, this blessing is reserved to the Ordinary, who nevertheless can commit it to any priest.

Canon Law Digest
I: 602–3; II: 390; III: 520

Canon 1280 (1983 CIC 1189)

Precious images, that is, those outstanding by virtue of age, art, or cult, exposed in churches or public oratories for the veneration of the faithful, if sometime they should require repair, shall never be restored without consent from the Ordinary given in writing, who before granting this permission shall consult wise and expert men.

Canon Law Digest
III: 520

Canon 1281 (1983 CIC 1190) Cross-Ref.: 1917 CIC 1530

§ 1. Important relics or precious images and likewise other relics or images that are honored in some church with a great veneration of the people cannot validly be alienated or perpetually transferred to another church without the permission of the Apostolic See.

§ 2. The important relics of Saints or Blesseds are the body, head, arm, forearm, heart, tongue, hand, leg, or other part of the body that suffered in a martyr, provided it is intact and is not little.

Canon Law Digest
I: 603

Canon 1282 (NA)

§ 1. Important relics of the Saints and the Blesseds cannot be preserved in buildings or private oratories without express permission of the local Ordinary.

§ 2. Non-important relics can be preserved with due honor even in private houses and carried about piously by the faithful.

Canon 1283 (NA)

§ 1. Only those relics can be honored with public cult in churches, even exempt ones, that have been shown to be genuine with an authentic document of some Cardinal of the H. R. C. or the local Ordinary or another ecclesiastical man to whom has been granted the faculty *of authenticating* by apostolic indult.

§ 2. A Vicar General cannot, without a special mandate, issue an authentication of relics.

Canon Law Digest
I: 603

Canon 1284 (NA)

Local Ordinaries shall prudently remove from public cult relics that they certainly know not to be authentic.

Canon 1285 (NA)

§ 1. Sacred relics whose documents of authenticity are lost because of civil disturbances or some other reason shall not be put out for public veneration, unless preceded by the judgment of the local Ordinary, but not of the Vicar General without a special mandate.

§ 2. Ancient relics, however, that have been up to the present in veneration are retained, unless in a particular case it is shown by certain arguments that they are false or are pretenders.

Canon Law Digest
I: 603

Canon 1286 (NA)

Local Ordinaries shall not allow, especially in sacred sermons, books, journals, or commentaries designed to foster piety, from mere conjecture, [or based] solely on probable arguments or prejudicial opinions, questions about the authenticity of sacred relics to be treated, especially in mocking terms or [ones] contemptuous of learning.

Canon 1287 (NA)

§ 1. Relics, when they are exposed, shall be closed in a reliquary or capsule and ought to be [signed as authentic].

§ 2. Relics of the most holy Cross are never exhibited for public veneration in the same reliquary with the relics of the Saints, but shall have their own separate reliquary.

§ 3. The relics of Blesseds, without a particular indult, are not carried in processions nor are they exposed in churches, except where there is a concession from the Apostolic See for the celebration of their office and Mass.

Canon 1288 (NA) Cross-Ref.: 1917 CIC 1299

Relics of the most holy Cross that the Bishop wore in his pectoral cross pass to the cathedral church upon his death [and] are to be transferred there by his successor; and if the deceased was over several dioceses, [then] they go to the cathedral church in whose territory he was on his last day, [or] if he died outside of the territory, [then] to the one from which he left.

Canon 1289 (1983 CIC 1190)

§ 1. It is nefarious to sell sacred relics; therefore local Ordinaries, vicars forane, pastors, and others having the care of souls shall take great care lest sacred relics, especially of the most holy Cross, and especially on the occasion of inheritance or the bulk alienation of goods, are sold and thus pass into the hands of non-Catholics.

§ 2. Rectors of churches, and others who look to such things, shall be sedulously careful lest sacred relics in any way be profaned, or that they be lost by negligent people, or that they are less than decently preserved.

TITLE 17
On sacred processions

Canon 1290 (NA)

§ 1. By the name of sacred processions is signified those solemn supplications that the faithful populace, led by clerics, make in [some] order from a sacred place to a sacred place, for the excitement of faithful piety, to commemorate the beneficence of God and to give him thanks, and to implore divine help.

§ 2. They are [called] *ordinary* that are made on set days during the year according to liturgical books or the custom of churches; [those are called] *extraordinary* that are indicated for public causes on other days.

Canon Law Digest
I: 603–4

Canon 1291 (1983 CIC 944) Cross-Refs.: 1917 CIC 1292–93

§ 1. Unless immemorial custom acts otherwise, or circumstances of place, in the prudent judgment of the Bishop, require otherwise, on the feast day of the Body of Christ there shall be made only one solemn procession through public streets in one place to [one of the] more worthy churches, and thereat shall be present all clerics and religious families of men, even exempt ones, and confraternities of laity, excepting only those regulars who live in strict cloister perpetually or who are more than three miles beyond the city.

§ 2. Other parishes and churches, even [those of] regulars, can, within the octave, conduct their own processions outside the limits of the church; but where there are several churches, it is for the local Ordinary [to set] the day, hours, and routes of each procession.

Canon Law Digest
I: 605

Canon 1292 (1983 CIC 944)

The local Ordinary, having heard the cathedral Chapter, can order for a public cause extraordinary processions; for which, as is true for ordinary and customary ones, all those mentioned in Canon 1291, § 1, must be present.

Canon 1293 (NA)

Even exempt religious are not to lead processions outside their churches and cloisters without the permission of the local Ordinary, with due regard for the prescription of Canon 1291, § 2.

Canon Law Digest
I: 605

Canon 1294 (NA)

§ 1. Neither a pastor nor anyone else can order new processions or transfer or abolish old ones without the permission of the local Ordinary.
§ 2. All clerics joined to a church must be present for any processions of their own church.

Canon Law Digest
I: 605

Canon 1295 (1983 CIC 944)

Ordinaries will take care that from sacred processions there be removed any bad practices, if there are any, and that they proceed in an orderly manner and with modesty and reverence observed by all, as greatly befits pious and religious acts of this sort.

Canon Law Digest
III: 520

TITLE 18
On sacred furnishings[7]

Canon 1296 (NA)

§ 1. Sacred furnishings, especially those that, according to the norm of liturgical law, must be blessed or consecrated for use in public worship, shall be cautiously stored in the church sacristy or in another safe and decent place and shall not be put to profane uses.

§ 2. According to the norm of Canon 1522, §§ 2 and 3, an inventory of all sacred furnishings shall be made and accurately preserved.

§ 3. Concerning the material and style of sacred furnishings, liturgical prescriptions are to be observed, and also ecclesiastical traditions and, to the degree it can be done for the better, also the laws of sacred art.

Canon Law Digest
I: 605; IX: 744

Canon 1297 (NA)

Unless otherwise provided, those who are bound by office to repair the church according to the norm of Canon 1186 are also bound to supply it with sacred furnishings necessary for worship.

Canon 1298 (NA) Cross-Refs.: 1917 CIC 239, 1301

§ 1. All of the sacred furnishings of a deceased Cardinal of the H. R. C. who had a domicile in the City, even though he was a suburbicarian Bishop or Abbot *of no one*, except for the ring and pectoral cross along with its sacred relics, and those other things that were destined with stability for divine cult, without regard for the quality and the nature of the income from which they arose, fall to the pontifical sacristy, unless the Cardinal donated them or by testament left [them] to some church or public oratory or pious place or to some ecclesiastical person or religious.

§ 2. It is desirable that a Cardinal who wishes to use a faculty of this sort prefer with at least some part [of his goods] those churches whose administration or title or entrustment he had.

---

[7] Erwin Sadlowski, "Sacred Furnishings of Churches", Canon Law Studies, no. 315 (thesis, Catholic University of America, 1951).

Canon 1299 (NA) Cross-Refs.: 1917 CIC 1300–1301

§ 1. The sacred furnishings of a deceased residential Bishop, even if he shined with cardinalitial dignity, fall to the cathedral church, except for the ring and pectoral cross along with its sacred relics, with due regard for the prescription of Canon 1288, and all those utensils of any sort about which it can be legitimately proven that they were acquired by the deceased Bishop from goods not pertaining to his church and it is shown that they did not pass over to church property.

§ 2. If a Bishop governed two or more successive dioceses, or he was at the same time over two or more dioceses united, or he was granted perpetual administration [of such] with each having its own distinct cathedral church, then whatever sacred utensils belonged to one diocese are returned to it; otherwise, they must be divided, in equal parts, among the individual cathedral churches, provided the diocesan income is not divided, but perpetually constitutes one episcopal table; but if the income really is divided and separate, the division shall be made between individual cathedral churches in proportion to the participation by the Bishop in the fruits and the time during which he was over them.

§ 3. A Bishop is bound by the obligation of preparing an authentic form of inventory of sacred utensils, in which he expresses the truth of the matters regarding their acquisition and describes distinctly whether they came not from the income or receipts of the church but from his own goods or from a donation made to him; otherwise, all are presumed to be purchased from the income of the church.

Canon 1300 (NA) Cross-Ref.: 1917 CIC 1301

Those things that are prescribed in Canon 1299 apply also to a cleric who obtains in any church a secular or religious benefice.

Canon 1301 (NA)

§ 1. A Cardinal of the H. R. C., a residential Bishop, and other beneficiary clerics are bound by the obligation of taking care of a testament or other instrument in a form valid by civil law so that the canonical prescriptions mentioned in Canons 1298–1300 receive due effect even in a civil forum.

§ 2. For this reason, in a timely manner and in a form valid by civil law, they shall designate a person of intact reputation according to the norm of Canon 380 who, upon the death of the former, shall proceed to send not only the sacred furnishings but also the books, documents, and other things pertaining to the church or contained in his house to whomever they are owed.

Canon 1302 (NA)

Rectors of churches and others to whom the care of sacred furnishings is accorded shall carefully see to their preservation and decorous use.

Canon 1303 (NA)

§ 1. The cathedral church must provide freely to the Bishop the sacred furnishings and other things that are necessary for the sacrifice of the Mass and other pontifical functions, even if he is celebrating privately, not only in the cathedral church but in other churches of the city or suburbs.

§ 2. If a church labors in poverty, the Ordinary can permit that from the priests who celebrate therein for their own convenience, there be required a moderate fee for the utensils and other things necessary for the sacrifice of the Mass.

§ 3. Bishops, but not the Vicar Capitulary or the Vicar General without a special mandate, can also define this stipend, and no one, even exempt religious, is permitted to ask for more than that.

§ 4. The Bishop shall define for the whole diocese this sort of stipend in the diocesan Synod, if it can be done, or outside the Synod, having heard the Chapter.

Canon 1304 (NA)

[The following] can impart a blessing on those sacred furnishings that according to the norm of liturgical law must be blessed before being put to their own proper use:

1.° Cardinals of the H. R. C. and all Bishops;
2.° Local Ordinaries, lacking episcopal character, for churches and oratories in their own territory;
3.° A pastor for churches and oratories located in the territory of his parish, and rectors of churches for their churches;
4.° Priests delegated by the local Ordinary within the limits of the delegation and the jurisdiction of the one delegating;
5.° Religious Superiors and priests delegated by those religious for their own churches and oratories and for the churches of nuns subject to them.

Canon 1305 (NA)

§ 1. Blessed or consecrated sacred furnishings lose their blessing or consecration:

1.° If they undergo such damage or change that they lose their pristine form so that they are not considered suitable any more for their use;

2.° If they have been put to an indecorous use or have been exposed to public sale.

§ 2. A chalice and paten do not lose consecration by the consumption or renovation of the gold, there remaining, however, in the first case, the grave obligation of applying the gold again.

Canon Law Digest
IX: 744–46

Canon 1306 (NA)

§ 1. Care should be taken lest a chalice, paten, or, before cleansing, purificators, palls, and corporals that were used in the sacrifice of the Mass are touched by any other than by clerics or those who have custody of these things.

§ 2. Purificators, palls, and corporals used in the sacrifice of the Mass shall not be put into the hands of laity, even religious, unless they have first been washed by a cleric constituted in major orders; and the water from this first cleansing shall be put into a sacrarium or, in its absence, into a fire.

Canon Law Digest
VI: 760

TITLE 19
On a vow and an oath

Chapter 1
On a vow

Canon 1307 (1983 CIC 1191)

§ 1. A vow, that is, a deliberate and free promise made to God about a possible and better good, must be fulfilled in [accord with] the virtue of religion.

§ 2. Unless prohibited by law, all those capable of a sufficient use of reason are capable of a vow.

§ 3. A vow given in grave and unjust fear is null by law.

Canon Law Digest
V: 616–18; VI: 760–63

Canon 1308 (1983 CIC 1192)

§ 1. A vow is *public* if it is accepted in the name of the Church by a legitimate ecclesiastical Superior; otherwise it is *private*.

§ 2. [It is] *solemn* if it is recognized by the Church as such; otherwise, it is *simple*.

§ 3. [It is] *reserved* when only the Apostolic See can grant dispensation from it.

§ 4. [It is] *personal* when an action of the one vowing is promised; *real*, when some thing is promised; *mixed* when the nature of a person and a thing participate [in it].

Canon Law Digest
I: 605; III: 520; VI: 763

Canon 1309 (NA)

The only private vow reserved to the Apostolic See is the vow of perfect and perpetual chastity and the vow of entering [a] religious [institute] of solemn vows, which are given absolutely and after the completion of eighteen years of age.

Canon 1310 (1983 CIC 1193)

§ 1. A vow does not oblige by its own reason except on the one giving it.

§ 2. The obligation of a real vow carries on to heirs and likewise the obligation of a mixed vow for that part that is real.

Canon Law Digest
II: 391–92

Canon 1311 (1983 CIC 1194)

A vow ceases with the lapse of the period of time given for the completion of its obligation, a change in the material substance of the promise, the absence of a condition upon which the vow depended, or the cessation of its purpose or final end, [as well as by] its nullification, dispensation, or commutation.

Canon Law Digest
IX: 746

Canon 1312 (1983 CIC 1195)

§ 1. Whoever legitimately exercises dominative power over the will of one vowing can nullify, and for a just cause [can do so] even licitly, the validity of the vow, so that in no case does the obligation later revive.

§ 2. Whoever has power not over the will of the one vowing but over the material of the vow can suspend the obligation of the vow for so long as the fulfillment of the vow offers a prejudice to him.

Canon 1313[8] (1983 CIC 1196) Cross-Ref.: 1917 CIC 1314

The following can dispense for a just cause a non-reserved vow, provided dispensation does not injure the acquired rights of others:

1.° The local Ordinary in what applies to all his subjects and also to travelers;
2.° The Superior of clerical exempt religious in what applies to the persons enumerated in Canon 514, § 1;
3.° Those to whom the power of dispensing has been delegated by the Apostolic See.

Canon Law Digest
I: 605; II: 392

Canon 1314 (1983 CIC 1197)

A work promised by a non-reserved vow can be commuted into a better or equal good by the very one vowing; into something less good, only by one who has the power of dispensing according to the norm of Canon 1313.

Canon 1315 (1983 CIC 1198)

Vows given out before religious profession are suspended for so long as the one vowing remains in religious [life].

[8] James Lowry, "Dispensation from Private Vows", Canon Law Studies, no. 237 (J. C. D. thesis, Catholic University of America, 1946); Maurice Walsh, "Suarez and the Decretalists: On the Dispensation of Vows and Promissory Oaths" (MS no. 1753, Gregorian University, 1951; printed version, no. 771, 1951).

Chapter 2
On an oath

Canon 1316 (1983 CIC 1199)

§ 1. An oath, that is, the invocation of the divine Name, in witness of the truth, cannot be offered except in truth, judgment, and justice.

§ 2. An oath that the canons require or admit cannot validly be offered through a procurator.

Canon 1317 (1983 CIC 1200)

§ 1. Whoever freely swears to do something is bound by a particular obligation of religion to fulfill what was affirmed in swearing.

§ 2. An oath extorted by force or grave fear is valid, but it can be relaxed by an ecclesiastical Superior.

§ 3. An oath offered without force or dolus, by which a private good or favor granted by the law itself is renounced, must be observed as long as it does not verge on the loss of eternal salvation.

Canon 1318 (1983 CIC 1201)

§ 1. A promissory oath follows the nature and conditions of the act to which it is attached.

§ 2. If an oath is attached to an act directly verging on damage to others or prejudice to the public good or eternal salvation, the act achieves no strength therefrom.

Canon 1319 (1983 CIC 1202)

The obligation of a promissory oath ceases to bind:

1.° If it is remitted by him for whose benefit the oath was given;

2.° If the sworn thing is substantially changed or, circumstances having changed, if it has become evil or entirely indifferent, or if, finally, it would impede a greater good;

3.° If the final cause ceases or the condition under which the oath might have been given [ceases];

4.° By invalidation, dispensation, commutation, according to the norm of Canon 1320.

Canon 1320 (1983 CIC 1203) Cross-Ref.: 1917 CIC 1319

Whoever can invalidate, dispense, or commute a vow has the same power concerning a promissory oath by the same reasons; but if dispensation from the oath verges on prejudice to others who refuse to remit the obligation, only the Apostolic See can dispense from the oath according to the necessity and utility of the Church.

Canon Law Digest
IX: 746

Canon 1321 (1983 CIC 1204)

An oath is strictly interpreted according to law and according to the intention of the one swearing, or, if he acted with dolus, according to the intention of the one sworn to.

Canon Law Digest
II: 392

FOURTH PART
ON ECCLESIASTICAL MAGISTERIUM

Canon 1322 (1983 CIC 747)

§ 1. Christ the Lord entrusted the deposit of faith to the Church, so that she, with the unfailing assistance of the Holy Spirit, would maintain in a holy way revealed teaching and faithfully expound it.

§ 2. The Church has the right and duty, independent of any civil power, of teaching all peoples evangelical doctrine: and thus, by divine law, all are bound to embrace the Church of God and rightly to heed her truth.

Canon Law Digest
II: 393; III: 521; IV: 364–65; V: 618; VI: 763; VII: 832;
VIII: 916–32; IX: 747–53; X: 194

Canon 1323 (1983 CIC 749–50)

§ 1. All of those things are to be believed with a divine and Catholic faith that are contained in the written word of God or in tradition and that the Church proposes as worthy of belief, as divinely revealed, whether by solemn judgment or by her ordinary and universal magisterium.

§ 2. It belongs to an Ecumenical Council or to the Roman Pontiff speaking from the chair to pronounce solemnly this sort of judgment.

§ 3. A thing is not understood as dogmatically defined or declared unless this is manifestly established.

Canon Law Digest
III: 521; VII: 832

Canon 1324 (1983 CIC 754)

It is not enough to avoid heretical depravity, but also those errors should be diligently fled that more or less approach [heresy]; therefore, all must observe the constitutions and decrees by which these sorts of depraved opinions are proscribed and prohibited by the Holy See.

Canon Law Digest
I: 607–19; II: 393–409; III: 522–30; IV: 365–78; V: 618–22;
VI: 763; VIII: 932–37; IX: 753–57

Canon 1325[1] (1983 CIC 209, 751, 755)

§ 1. The faithful of Christ are bound to profess their faith whenever their silence, evasiveness, or manner of acting encompasses an implied denial of the faith, contempt for religion, injury to God, or scandal for a neighbor.

§ 2. After the reception of baptism, if anyone, retaining the name Christian, pertinaciously denies or doubts something to be believed from the truth of divine and Catholic faith, [such a one is] a heretic; if he completely turns away from the Christian faith, [such a one is] an apostate; if

---

[1] Thomas Hanahoe, "The Catholic Church and Non-Catholics" (MS no. 1013, Gregorian University, 1942); Stephen Kelleher, "Discussions with Non-Catholics: Canonical Legislation", Canon Law Studies, no. 180 (J. C. D. thesis, Catholic University of America, 1943); Charles Cornell, "The Juridical Status of Heretics and Schismatics in Good Faith", Canon Law Studies, no. 338 (Catholic University of America, not published); Leonard Pivonka, "The Secretariat for Promoting Christian Unity: A Study of a Catholic Response to the Modern Ecumenical Movement", Canon Law Studies, no. 508 (J. C. D. thesis, Catholic University of America, 1982).

finally he refuses to be under the Supreme Pontiff or refuses communion with the members of the Church subject to him, he is a schismatic.

§ 3. Let Catholics beware lest they have debates or conferences, especially public ones, with non-Catholics without having come to the Holy See or, if the case is urgent, to the local Ordinary.

Canon Law Digest

I: 619–22; II: 409; III: 531–42; IV: 378–85; V: 622; VIII: 937

Canon 1326 (1983 CIC 753)

Bishops also, although individually and even gathered in particular Councils they do not partake of infallibility in teaching, nevertheless, for those faithful committed to their care under the authority of the Roman Pontiff, they are truly doctors and teachers.

Canon Law Digest

IV: 385–86; V: 623; VI: 764; VII: 832–33; VIII: 937–40; IX: 757–59; X: 194

TITLE 20
On preaching the divine word

Canon 1327 (1983 CIC 756–57) Cross-Ref.: 1917 CIC 336

§ 1. The responsibility of preaching the Catholic faith is committed especially to the Roman Pontiff for the universal Church [and to] Bishops for their dioceses.

§ 2. Bishops are bound by the office of personally preaching the Gospel, unless they are prohibited by a legitimate impediment; and moreover, besides pastors, they should also take help from other suitable men in pursuing the correct fulfillment of these duties in this sort of teaching.

Canon Law Digest

I: 622–30; IV: 386; V: 623–29; VI: 764; VII: 833

Canon 1328 (1983 CIC 757–59, 764–66)

No one is permitted to exercise the ministry of preaching unless he has received this mission from the legitimate Superior by a faculty specifically given or by an office conferred in which inheres the responsibility of preaching according to the sacred canons.

Canon Law Digest

I: 631

CHAPTER 1
On catechetical instruction[2]

Canon 1329 (1983 CIC 773)

A proper and most grave office, especially for pastors of souls, is to take care of the catechetical instruction of the Christian people.

Canon Law Digest
I: 631–35; II: 409–19; III: 542; IV: 386; VII: 834–39; IX: 759–60; X: 195–202

Canon 1330 (1983 CIC 777) Cross-Refs.: 1917 CIC 1331, 2182

A pastor must:

1.° At established times consisting of several days of instructions each year prepare children for the correct reception of the sacraments of penance and confirmation;
2.° And by an even more careful study especially, if nothing prevents, during Lent, so instruct children that they may approach the altar for the first holy Holy.

Canon 1331 (1983 CIC 777) Cross-Ref.: 1917 CIC 2182

Beyond the instruction of children mentioned in Canon 1330 the pastor shall not fail to instruct by a more thorough and complete catechesis those who have recently received first communion.

Canon 1332 (1983 CIC 777) Cross-Ref.: 1917 CIC 2182

On [Sundays] and other feasts of precept at those times that in their judgment are most likely to encourage attendance by the people, the pastor must also explain the catechism to adult faithful using words accommodated to their understanding.

---

[2] Raymond Jansen, "Canonical Provisions for Catechetical Instruction", Canon Law Studies, no. 107 (J. C. D. thesis, Catholic University of America, 1937); Panfilo Gianan, "The Canon Law on Catechetical Instruction" (diss. no. 6, University of St. Thomas [Manila], 1949).

Canon 1333 (1983 CIC 776)

§ 1. A pastor can, in the religious instruction of children, and indeed must if he is legitimately impeded, enlist the help of clerics present in his territory and even, if it is necessary, pious laymen, particularly those who are enrolled in a pious sodality of *Christian teaching* or something similar erected in the parish.

§ 2. Priests and other clerics who are not detained by legitimate impediment should be helpers to their pastor in this most holy work, even under penalties to be inflicted by the Ordinary.

Canon Law Digest
I: 635

Canon 1334 (1983 CIC 776, 778)

If, in the judgment of the local Ordinary, the help of religious is necessary for the catechetical instruction of the people, religious Superiors, even exempt ones, requested by the same Ordinary, are bound themselves or through their religious subjects, though without detriment to religious discipline, to provide [instruction] to the people, especially in their own churches.

Canon Law Digest
VI: 764

Canon 1335 (1983 CIC 774)

Not only parents and others who take the place of parents, but also household leaders and patrons, are strictly bound to take care that all those subject or entrusted to them are educated with catechetical instruction.

Canon Law Digest
I: 635–36; II: 419

Canon 1336 (1983 CIC 775)

It is for the local Ordinary to direct all things in his diocese that apply to the instruction of the people in Christian doctrine; and even exempt religious, as often as they teach non-exempt [persons], are bound to observe [his direction].

Canon Law Digest
II: 419

Chapter 2
On sacred sermons[3]

Canon 1337 (1983 CIC 764)

Only the local Ordinary grants to clerics, whether [they are] of the secular clergy or are non-exempt religious, the faculty of preaching in his territory.

Canon Law Digest
I: 636

Canon 1338 (1983 CIC 765)

§ 1. If the sermons are to be had only for exempt religious or others mentioned in Canon 514, § 1, the faculty of preaching in clerical religious [institutes] is given by their own Superior according to the constitutions; but in this case he can grant it also to those of the secular clergy or to those who are in other religious [institutes], provided they have been judged suitable by their own Ordinary or Superior.

§ 2. If the sermon is to be given to others, or even to nuns subject to regulars, the local Ordinary where the sermon is to be given can give the faculty even to exempt religious; the preacher, however, about to give words to exempt nuns, also requires the permission of the regular Superior.

§ 3. The local Ordinary gives the faculty for preaching among members of lay religious [institutes], even exempt ones; but the preacher cannot use this faculty without the assent of the religious Superior.

Canon Law Digest
I: 636

Canon 1339 (1983 CIC 764)

§ 1. Local Ordinaries shall not deny, except for grave cause, the faculty of preaching to religious who are presented by their own Superior or revoke [faculties] given, especially for all the priests of a religious house, with due regard for the prescription of Canon 1340.

[3] James McVann, "The Canon Law on Sermon Preaching" (MS no. 504, Gregorian University, 1938; printed version, no. 244, New York, 1938); Joseph Allgeier, "The Canonical Obligation of Preaching in Parish Churches", Canon Law Studies, no. 291 (thesis, Catholic University of America, 1950).

§ 2. In order that religious preachers may use faculties received, it is required that they also have the permission of their Superior.

Canon 1340 (1983 CIC 764) Cross-Ref.: 1917 CIC 1339

§ 1. Gravely burdened in their consciences, the local Ordinary or religious Superior shall not grant to anyone the faculty or permission for preaching, unless there is first established good morals and sufficient learning by an examination according to the norm of Canon 877, § 1.

§ 2. If, the faculty or permission having been granted, they find that necessary qualities are lacking in the preacher, they must revoke them; if [they are] in doubt about learning, they must eliminate such doubts by various arguments, and even by a new examination, if this is needed.

§ 3. Recourse is given for the revocation of the faculty or permission for preaching, but it is not suspensive.

Canon Law Digest
I: 636

Canon 1341 (1983 CIC 764)

§ 1. Extradiocesan priests, whether secular or religious, are not to be invited to preach, unless they have obtained permission of the Ordinary of the place in which the preaching will occur; but he shall not grant permission unless their suitability is shown somehow, [or] unless there is prior testimony about the doctrine, piety, and morals of the preacher from his own Ordinary; and this [latter] is burdened in conscience to respond according to the truth.

§ 2. The pastor must seek this permission at a good time if it concerns a parish church or another subject to him; the rector of a church [shall so act] if it is a church not answerable to a pastor; [likewise] by the first in dignity, with the consent of the Chapter, if it is a chapter church; [likewise] by the moderator or chaplain of a confraternity, if it concerns a church of that same confraternity.

§ 3. If a parochial church is at the same time a chapter or confraternity [church], he who performs sacred functions [there] should seek the permission.

Canon Law Digest
I: 636; III: 542

Canon 1342 (1983 CIC 764, 766)

§ 1. The faculty of preaching should be made only to priests and deacons, but not to other clerics, except for reasonable cause, in the judgment of the Ordinary, and in individual cases.

§ 2. All laity are forbidden to preach in churches, even religious.

Canon Law Digest
VIII: 941–44

Canon 1343 (1983 CIC 763)

§ 1. Local Ordinaries have the right to preach in any church in their territory, even exempt ones.

§ 2. Unless it concerns large cities, the Bishop can also prohibit lest in other churches in the same area words be said to the faithful at a time when, for a public and extraordinary reason, either he himself is preaching or he is having [preaching done] in his presence [and] to which the faithful are called.

Canon 1344 (1983 CIC 767) Cross-Ref.: 1917 CIC 2182

§ 1. On [Sundays] and other feasts of precept throughout the year, it is the personal duty of the pastor to announce the word of God to the people, in the customary homily, especially at the Mass which the greater part of the people attend.

§ 2. The pastor cannot habitually satisfy this obligation through another, except for just cause approved by the Ordinary.

§ 3. The Ordinary can permit that on certain more solemn feasts, and even, for a just cause, on [Sundays], the homily be omitted.

Canon Law Digest
I: 636; IX: 760

Canon 1345 (1983 CIC 767) Cross-Ref.: 1917 CIC 612

It is desirable that, the faithful being present, on feast days of precept that are celebrated in all churches and public oratories, there be a brief explanation of the Gospel and some part of Christian doctrine; and if the local Ordinary so orders, opportune instructions having been given, this law binds not only secular priests and clerics, but also religious, even exempt ones, in their own churches.

Canon 1346 (1983 CIC 767)

§ 1. Let Ordinaries take care that in Lent, and likewise, if it seems it can be done, during Advent, frequent sacred sermons be offered in cathedral and parish churches attended by the faithful.

§ 2. Canons and others in the Chapter are bound to attend these sermons, if they are held in their own churches immediately after choir, unless detained by a just cause; and the Ordinary can urge this [attendance] even by adding penalties.

Canon 1347 (1983 CIC 768)

§ 1. In sacred sermons there shall be set forth first of all those things that the faithful must believe and that which they ought to do for salvation.

§ 2. Preachers of the divine word shall abstain from profane or abstruse arguments exceeding the common capacity of their listeners; they shall exercise evangelical ministry, not in the persuasive words of human wisdom or in the get-up and flattery of profane emptiness and ambitious eloquence, but in a spiritual and virtuous show, preaching not themselves, but Christ crucified.

§ 3. If, far be it from here, a preacher disseminates errors or scandal, the prescription of Canon 2317 shall be observed; if he is a heretic, other things come against him according to the norm of law.

Canon Law Digest
I: 636–37

Canon 1348 (NA)

The faithful are to be diligently warned and encouraged to be present frequently for holy sermons.

Chapter 3
On sacred missions[4]

Canon 1349 (1983 CIC 770)

§ 1. Ordinaries are to be vigilant that, at least every ten years, a pastor have holy, as they call it, missions, for the flocks that are committed to their pastoral care.

[4] Howard Lavelle, "The Obligation of Holding Sacred Missions in Parishes", Canon Law Studies, no. 295 (thesis, Catholic University of America, 1949).

§ 2. A pastor, even a religious one, must stand by the mandates of the Ordinary in the matter of missions.

Canon 1350 (1983 CIC 771)

§ 1. Local Ordinaries and pastors are to consider non-Catholics living in their diocese and parishes as entrusted to them in the Lord.

§ 2. In other territories, the universal care of missions among non-Catholics is reserved solely to the Apostolic See.

Canon Law Digest
I: 637–43; II: 419–21; III: 543–44; IV: 387; V: 629; VI: 764–65;
VII: 839–61; VIII: 945–46; IX: 760–88; X: 202

Canon 1351 (1983 CIC 748)

No one unwilling is to be coerced into embracing the Catholic faith.

TITLE 21
On Seminaries[5]

Canon 1352 (1983 CIC 232)

The Church has the proper and exclusive right of instructing those who wish to devote themselves to ecclesiastical ministry.

Canon Law Digest
III: 544; VI: 765; IX: 788; X: 202

Canon 1353 (1983 CIC 233)

Priests and bishops, especially pastors are to work so that boys who give signs of an ecclesiastical vocation are kept with special care from the contagion of the world, to form piety, and from their first studies of letters are imbued with divine things that will encourage the seed of vocation in them.

Canon Law Digest
I: 643–55; II: 421; V: 629; VI: 765; VII: 861; VIII: 946–55; IX: 789–91

[5] Joseph Cox, "The Administration of Seminaries", Canon Law Studies, no. 67 (J. C. D. thesis, Catholic University of America, 1931); John Barry, "Ecclesial Norms for Priestly Formation" (doctoral diss. 65, St. Paul University [Ottawa, Canada], 1982).

Canon 1354[6] (1983 CIC 234, 237)

§ 1. In every diocese, in a convenient place chosen by the Bishop, there shall be a Seminary or college, in which, according to the manner of the faculty and the size of the diocese, a certain number of adolescents are trained for the clerical state.

§ 2. Care should be taken in larger dioceses that two Seminaries be constituted; a minor one, namely, where young boys are imbued with the knowledge of letters, and a major one for students involved in philosophy and theology.

§ 3. If a diocesan Seminary cannot be constituted or if, in a constituted Seminary, [more] convenient training, especially in philosophical and theological disciplines, is desired, the Bishop shall send students to another Seminary, unless there is an interdiocesan or regional Seminary already constituted by apostolic authority.

Canon Law Digest
I: 656–57; II: 422–25; IV: 387; V: 629–31;
VI: 765; VII: 861–68; VIII: 955

Canon 1355 (1983 CIC 264) Cross-Ref.: 1917 CIC 1505

For the constitution of the Seminary and for the support of the students, if their own income is deficient, the Bishop can:

1.° Order that pastors and rectors of other churches, even exempt ones, at stated times, take up an offering in churches for this end;
2.° Impose a tribute or *tax* in his diocese;
3.° If these are not sufficient, attribute to the Seminary some simple benefices.

Canon Law Digest
I: 657

Canon 1356 (1983 CIC 264) Cross-Ref.: 1917 CIC 1505

§ 1. Liable to the tax for the Seminary, removed from any appeal, reprobating any contrary custom and abrogating any contrary privilege, are

[6] Marcian Mathis, "The Constitution and Supreme Administration of Regional Seminaries Subject to the Sacred Congregation for the Propagation of the Faith in China", Canon Law Studies, no. 331 (thesis, Catholic University of America, 1952).

the Bishop's table, all benefices, even of regulars, and the right of patronage, parishes, and quasi-parishes, even though they have no income besides the donations of the faithful, guest houses not erected by ecclesiastical authority, canonically erected sodalities and upkeep funds of churches, if they have their own incomes, any religious house, even an exempt one, unless the members live by donations or there is in them a college of students or teachers considered by their actions to be promoting the common good of the Church.

§ 2. This tax must be general and in the same proportion for all, greater or lesser according to the needs of the Seminary, but not exceeding five percent (5%) per year of remaining income, to be diminished as the income of the Seminary increases.

§ 3. The income liable to the tax is that which, having deducted burdens and necessary expenses, remains in the year; nor will the daily distributions be calculated in this income, or, if all of the distribution fruits are shown thus, a third part of them [is not counted]; nor are the offerings of the faithful [counted], or if the whole income of the parish derives from the offerings of the faithful, then a third part of it [is not counted].

Canon Law Digest
I: 657; VIII: 955

Canon 1357 (1983 CIC 243, 259)

§ 1. It belongs to the Bishop to decide each and every thing that affects the correct governance of the diocesan Seminary, its governance, and what seems opportune for its necessary progress, and to see that these things are faithfully observed, with due regard for the prescriptions of the Holy See given for particular cases.

§ 2. The Bishop shall apply himself to the utmost in making personal visits to the Seminary, and to being carefully vigilant about how instruction is given to the students, whether in literary, scientific, or ecclesiastical [matters]; and he shall take care to make himself fully aware of the character, piety, vocation, and progress [of students], especially on the occasion of sacred ordination.

§ 3. Every Seminary shall have its own laws approved by the Bishop, in which there shall be treated what must be observed and how they, who are the hope of the Church, in the Seminary are taught, as well as [rules] for those who are striving after their education.

§ 4. The complete governance and administration of interdiocesan or regional Seminaries is governed by norms established by the Holy See.

Canon Law Digest
I: 657–60; II: 425–26; V: 631–33; VII: 868–80; IX: 792–806

Canon 1358[7] (1983 CIC 239)

Care should be taken that in every Seminary there is a rector for discipline, teachers for instruction, an econome, distinct from the rector, for taking care of household matters, at least two ordinary confessors, and a spiritual director.

Canon Law Digest
I: 660; II: 426; VI: 765; VII: 880; IX: 807

Canon 1359 (NA)

§ 1. In the diocesan Seminary there are to be constituted two committees of deputies, one for discipline, the other for the administration of temporal goods.

§ 2. Each committee of deputies shall consist of two priests, chosen by the Bishop, having heard the Chapter; excluded [from membership] are the Vicar General, householders of the Bishop, the rector of the Seminary, the econome, and ordinary confessors.

§ 3. The office of the deputies lasts for six years, nor can those selected be removed without grave cause; but they can be reappointed.

§ 4. The Bishop must seek out the committee of deputies in matters of greater importance.

Canon Law Digest
I: 660

Canon 1360 (1983 CIC 260)

§ 1. With due regard for the prescription of Canon 891, for the task of rector, spiritual director, confessors, and teachers in a Seminary, there should

[7] Frederick Sackett, "The Spiritual Director in an Ecclesiastical Seminary" (doctoral diss. 14, University of Ottawa, 1945); John Beahen, "The Seminary Rector's Ordinary Power of Jurisdiction as a Confessor" (diss. no. 12, Pontifical University of St. Thomas [Rome], 1951–1952); Casimir Peterson, "Spiritual Care in Diocesan Seminaries", Canon Law Studies, no. 342 (J. C. D. thesis, Catholic University of America, 1966).

be chosen priests outstanding not only for doctrine but also for virtue and prudence, who can form the students by word and example.

§ 2. All must yield to the rector of the Seminary in fulfilling their duties.

Canon 1361 (1983 CIC 240)

§ 1. Besides ordinary confessors, other confessors shall be designated to whom the students can have free access.

§ 2. If the confessors reside outside the Seminary and a student asks to approach one of them, the rector shall agree, in no way inquiring the reason for the request or demonstrating himself displeased; if [the confessors] live in the Seminary, the students can freely approach them with due regard for the discipline of the Seminary.

§ 3. When it concerns admitting a student to orders or expelling one from the Seminary, the vote of confessors is never sought.

Canon Law Digest
II: 426

Canon 1362 (NA)

The income from legacies for the instruction of clerics can be spent on students rightly accepted into the Seminary, whether major or minor, even though they have not received clerical tonsure, unless expressly provided otherwise in the charter of foundation.

Canon 1363 (1983 CIC 241)

§ 1. None but legitimate sons who have the characteristics and [determination] that give hope that they will perpetually bind themselves to fruitful ecclesiastical ministry should be admitted by the Ordinary to the Seminary.

§ 2. Before they are received, they must produce documents on the legitimacy of birth, of having received baptism and confirmation, and about life and morals.

§ 3. Those dismissed from other Seminaries or other [institutes] should not be admitted unless the Bishop first requests the cause of dismissal and other information from the Superior, even secretly, and [makes inquiries] about morals, character, and temperament of the dismissed and has certainly satisfied himself that there is nothing in these inconsistent with priestly status; the which information, in conformity with the truth, Superiors must supply, their consciences being gravely burdened.

Canon Law Digest

I: 661; II: 426–27; III: 544–45; IV: 387–88; V: 633–38; VI: 765–66; VII: 880; X: 202–5

Canon 1364[8] (1983 CIC 234, 249)

In the lower schools of the Seminary:

1.° Religious discipline takes first place, which will be accommodated to the temperament and age of the individuals and pursued most diligently;
2.° They will accurately pursue languages, especially latin and the national language of the students;
3.° Instruction in other disciplines will be given consistent with the general culture and status of clerics in the region where the students must exercise sacred ministry.

Canon Law Digest

I: 661–62; V: 638–81; VI: 766; VII: 880; VIII: 955; IX: 807

Canon 1365[9] (1983 CIC 250, 252, 256) Cross-Ref.: 1917 CIC 976

§ 1. The students will go through at least two complete years in rational philosophy and related disciplines.

§ 2. The theological course will contain at least four complete years and, besides dogmatic and moral theology, must especially include the study of sacred Scripture, church history, canon law, liturgy, sacred speech, and ecclesiastical chant.

§ 3. There should also be lectures on pastoral theology to which are added practical exercises especially in the manner of giving catechism to young people, hearing confessions, visiting the infirm, and assisting the dying.

Canon Law Digest

I: 662–69; II: 427; III: 545–64; V: 681–84; VI: 766–86; VII: 880–84; VIII: 955–63; IX: 807–71

---

[8] Gerard Mahoney, "The Academic Curriculum in Minor Seminaries", Canon Law Studies, no. 440 (J. C. D. thesis, Catholic University of America, 1965).

[9] Timothy Manning, "Clerical Education in Major Seminaries: Its Nature and Application" (MS no. 537, Gregorian University, 1938; printed version, no. 482, 1938); Philip Kendall, "Intellectual Formation in the Major Seminary Curriculum: Principles and Considerations", Canon Law Studies, no. 468 (Catholic University of America, 1970).

Canon 1366[10] (1983 CIC 253) Cross-Ref.: 1917 CIC 589

§ 1. With respect to the responsibility of teacher in philosophical, theological, and juridic disciplines, all things being equal, they should be preferred in the judgment of the Bishops and deputies of the Seminary who have obtained a doctoral degree in a University or Faculty recognized by the Holy See or, if it concerns religious, those who have a similar testimonial from their major Superior.

§ 2. Professors shall treat studies in rational theology and philosophy and the instruction of students in these disciplines according to the system, teaching, and principles of the Angelic Doctor and hold to them religiously.

§ 3. Care should be taken that distinct teachers are appointed at least for sacred Scripture, dogmatic theology, moral theology, and ecclesiastical history.

Canon Law Digest
I: 669–76; II: 427–34; III: 564–68; V: 684–85;
VI: 786–98; VII: 885–86; VIII: 963; IX: 871

Canon 1367 (1983 CIC 246)

Bishops should take care that Seminary students:

1.° Recite every day morning and nighttime prayers together, leaving some time for mental prayer, and assist at the sacrifice of the Mass;

2.° At least once a week approach the sacrament of penance and frequently, as is consistent with piety, take the Eucharistic bread;

3.° On [Sundays] and feast days be present for sacred Mass and solemn Vespers, serve at the altar, and exercise sacred ceremonies especially in the cathedral church if this, in the judgment of the Bishop, can be done without detriment to discipline and studies;

4.° Make time once a year for several successive days for spiritual exercises;

5.° At least once a week be present at instructions on spiritual matters that are closed with a pious exhortation.

Canon Law Digest
I: 676; II: 434; VII: 886; IX: 871–94

---

[10] George Yahn, "The Juridical Notion of the Authority of St. Thomas Aquinas" (diss. no. 26, Pontifical University of St. Thomas [Rome], 1960–1961).

Canon 1368[11] (1983 CIC 262) Cross-Ref.: 1917 CIC 1222

The Seminary shall be exempt from parochial jurisdiction and for all those who are in a Seminary, the office of pastor, except for matrimonial matters and with due regard for the prescription of Canon 891, belongs to the rector of the Seminary or his delegate, unless something else regarding a certain Seminary was constituted by the Apostolic See.

Canon Law Digest
II: 434

Canon 1369 (1983 CIC 261)

§ 1. The rector of the Seminary and all moderators under his authority shall take care that students observe most assiduously the statutes given by the Bishop and the course of studies and are imbued with a truly ecclesiastical spirit.

§ 2. The laws of true and Christian courtesy shall be given to them frequently, and they shall be encouraged to follow them by example; they are to be exhorted to observe the precepts of hygiene, cleanliness of clothes and body, and a manner of conversation marked by modesty and gravity.

§ 3. [Rectors and others] shall sedulously be vigilant that teachers rightly perform their duties.

Canon 1370 (1983 CIC 235)

Whenever students for any cause are living outside of the Seminary, the prescription of Canon 972, § 2, is to be observed.

Canon 1371 (NA)

The disruptive, incorrigible, and unruly are to be dismissed from the Seminary, as are those whose life-style and characteristics seem unsuitable for the ecclesiastical state; likewise those who are not sufficient in progress of studies and who give no hope of getting sufficient learning; and especially to be dismissed are those who offend against good morals and faith.

Canon Law Digest
I: 676

---

[11] Paul Nager, "The Exemption of the Seminary according to Canon Law, Canon 1368" (diss. no. 3, Pontifical University of St. Thomas [Rome], 1938–1939).

TITLE 22
On schools[12]

Canon 1372 (1983 CIC 793)

§ 1. All the faithful from childhood are to be instructed so that, not only is there nothing against the Catholic religion and upright life given them, but that religious and moral instruction has the principal place.

§ 2. Not only parents according to the norm of Canon 1113, but also all those who take their place, have the right and grave duty of taking care of the Christian education of children.

Canon Law Digest
I: 677–79; II: 434; III: 568–70; IV: 388; VI: 798

Canon 1373 (1983 CIC 804) Cross-Ref.: 1917 CIC 1379

§ 1. In every elementary school, children are to be given religious instruction [adapted] to their age.

§ 2. Youths who attend middle and advanced schools should be afforded a fuller religious doctrine, and local Ordinaries shall take care that this is provided by priests outstanding for their doctrine and zeal.

Canon Law Digest
I: 679; V: 686

Canon 1374 (1983 CIC 793, 797–98)

Catholic children should not frequent non-Catholic, neutral, or mixed schools, namely, those that allow non-Catholics to attend. Only local Ordinaries can make decisions in accord with instructive norms from the Apostolic See concerning circumstances of things and any necessary pre-

---

[12] Conrad Boffa, "Canonical Provisions for Catholic Schools (Elementary and Intermediate)", Canon Law Studies, no. 117 (J. C. D. thesis, Catholic University of America, 1939); William Sheridan, "The Irish National System of Primary Education" (MS no. 861, Gregorian University, 1941); John Bettridge, "Church, Parent, State, in Education: A Comparative Study in Canon Law and English and Australian Civil Practice", or "The Canonical Prohibition to Frequent Non-Catholic Schools" (MS no. 1992, Gregorian University, 1952; printed version, no. 915, 1952, 1955); Gommar De Pauw, "The Educational Rights of the Church and Elementary Schools in Belgium", Canon Law Studies, no. 336 (thesis, Catholic University of America, 1953); Wilfredo Paguio, "A Vicariate for Catholic Students in the Philippines" (diss. no. 8, Pontifical University of St. Thomas [Rome], 1976–1977).

cautions that will prevent the danger of perversion, [and] whether these things can be tolerated and such schools used.

Canon Law Digest
I: 679–80; V: 686–87; VI: 798

Canon 1375 (1983 CIC 800)

The Church has the right to found schools of any type, not only at the elementary level, but at intermediate and superior levels as well.

Canon Law Digest
I: 680; II: 434; III: 570; V: 688; VI: 798; VIII: 963; IX: 894

Canon 1376[13] (1983 CIC 816)

§ 1. The canonical constitution of any Catholic University or Faculty of studies is reserved to the Apostolic See.

§ 2. A Catholic University or Faculty, even if it is formed by a religious [institute], must have its statutes approved by the Apostolic See.

Canon Law Digest
I: 680; III: 570; V: 688; VI: 799; VII: 886; VIII: 963–81; IX: 895–97; X: 205–6

Canon 1377 (1983 CIC 817)

No one can grant academic degrees that have canonical effects in the Church except by faculty granted by the Apostolic See.

Canon Law Digest
I: 681; V: 689–90; VIII: 981–87

Canon 1378 (NA)

Those duly created as doctors have the right of wearing, outside of sacred functions, the ring along with a stone, and the doctoral biretta, with due regard for the other prescriptions of the sacred canons, [and it is established that] in the granting of offices and benefices, other things be-

[13] Alexander Sokolich, "Canonical Provisions for Universities and Colleges", Canon Law Studies, no. 373 (thesis, Catholic University of America, 1956); John Zemanick, "Canon Law and the Board of Trustees in a Catholic College", Canon Law Studies, no. 471 (Catholic University of America, not published).

ing equal in the judgment of the Ordinary, they who have obtained a [doctorate] or licentiate are to be preferred.

Canon Law Digest
I: 682

Canon 1379 (1983 CIC 800, 802, 809)

§ 1. If Catholic schools according to the norm of Canon 1373, whether elementary or middle, do not exist, care should be taken, especially by local Ordinaries, that they be founded.

§ 2. Similarly, if public Universities are not imbued with a Catholic doctrine and spirit, it is very desirable that a Catholic University be founded in the nation or region.

§ 3. The faithful shall not fail to support to the best of their ability the founding and support of Catholic schools.

Canon Law Digest
VII: 886

Canon 1380 (1983 CIC 819)

It is desirable that local Ordinaries, in accord with their own prudence, send clerics outstanding for their piety and intelligence to the classes in Universities or Faculties founded and approved by the Church, so that therein they may study especially philosophy, theology, and canon law, and earn academic degrees.

Canon 1381 (1983 CIC 803, 805–6, 810)

§ 1. The religious instruction of youth in any schools whatsoever is subject to the authority of and inspection by the Church.

§ 2. Local Ordinaries have the right and duty of being vigilant about any schools in their territory lest in them something be found or done against faith or good morals.

§ 3. In a similar way they have the right of approving teachers and books of religion; likewise, for the sake of religion or morals, they can require that either teachers or books be removed.

Canon Law Digest
I: 682–83; III: 571; V: 690–95; VII: 887–89; VIII: 987; X: 206

Canon 1382 (1983 CIC 806)

Local Ordinaries either personally or through others can visit any schools, oratories, recreation areas, patronage, and so forth, that are concerned with religious or moral instruction; from such visitation no schools or any religious are exempt, unless it concerns an internal school for professed exempt religious.

Canon Law Digest
I: 683; III: 571; IV: 388; V: 696; VI: 799

Canon 1383 (1983 CIC 985)

In the religious instruction of the students of any college, the prescription of Canon 891 is observed.

TITLE 23
On the previous censorship of books and their prohibition[14]

Canon 1384 (1983 CIC 823–24)

§ 1. The Church has the right of requiring that books that have not been recognized by her prior judgment not be published by the faithful, and that those published by anyone be prohibited for a just cause.

§ 2. Those things that are prescribed about books in this title are applicable to daily publications, periodicals, and other published writings, unless it appears otherwise.

Canon Law Digest
I: 683; II: 434; IV: 388–89; V: 696–98; VI: 799–810;
VII: 889–90; VIII: 987–91; IX: 897–900; X: 206

[14] Joseph Pernicone, "The Ecclesiastical Prohibition of Books", Canon Law Studies, no. 72 (J. C. D. thesis, Catholic University of America, 1932); Nathaniel Sonntag, "Censorship of Special Classes of Books, Canons 1387–1391", Canon Law Studies, no. 262 (thesis, Catholic University of America, 1947).

Chapter 1
On the previous censorship of books[15]

Canon 1385 (1983 CIC 824–25, 827) Cross-Ref.: 1917 CIC 1399

§ 1. Unless ecclesiastical censorship has preceded, there shall not be published, even by laity:

1.° Books of sacred Scripture or annotations on them or commentaries;

2.° Books that look to divine Scriptures, sacred theology, ecclesiastical history, canon law, natural theology, and ethics and other religious and moral disciplines of this sort; books and booklets of prayers, devotions, and teaching or religious instruction on morals, ascetics, mysticism and other [topics] of this sort, even though they seem conducive to fostering piety; and generally those writings in which there is something of special import to religion and right living;

3.° Sacred images no matter how printed, whether they are published with prayers added or without them.

§ 2. Permission for publishing books and images mentioned in § 1 can be given by the Ordinary of the place of their author, or by the Ordinary of the place in which the books or images are going to be published, or by the Ordinary of the place in which they are printed, although if one of the Ordinaries denied permission, the author cannot petition another unless he makes him aware of the denial of permission from the other.

§ 3. Religious must also obtain beforehand the permission of their major Superior.

Canon Law Digest

II: 435–36; III: 571; VI: 811; VIII: 991–96; IX: 901–7; X: 206

Canon 1386 (1983 CIC 831)

§ 1. Secular clerics are forbidden, without the consent of their Ordinaries, [and likewise] religious without the permission of their major Superiors and local Ordinaries, to edit books that treat of profane things and to write for or supervise newspapers, pamphlets, and periodical literature.

[15] Donald Wiest, "The Precensorship of Books, Canons 1384–1386, 1392–1394, 2318, "2", Canon Law Studies, no. 329 (thesis, Catholic University of America, 1953).

§ 2. Neither shall laity, unless persuaded by just and reasonable cause approved by the local Ordinary, write for newspapers, pamphlets, or periodical literature that is accustomed to attacking the Catholic religion or good morals.

Canon Law Digest
I: 683; III: 571

Canon 1387 (NA)

Whatever pertains in any way to beatification and canonization cases of the Servants of God cannot be published without the permission of the Sacred Congregation of Rites.

Canon 1388 (NA) Cross-Ref.: 1917 CIC 919

§ 1. All books, summaries, booklets, pamphlets, and so on, of indulgences, in which their grants are contained, shall not be published without the permission of the local Ordinary.

§ 2. But there is required the express permission of the Apostolic See in order that, in any language, authentic collections of prayers and pious works to which the Apostolic See has attached indulgences be published, whether it is an apostolic list of indulgences or a summary of indulgences or an earlier collection, [regardless] of whether it is approved and now for the first time has been collected from various [documents of] grant.

Canon Law Digest
I: 684

Canon 1389 (1983 CIC 828)

Collections of decrees of the Roman Congregations cannot be republished without first seeking the permission and observing the conditions prescribed by the Moderators of each Congregation.

Canon 1390 (1983 CIC 826)

In publishing liturgical books and their parts, and likewise litanies approved by the Holy See, there must be an attestation from the local Ordinary where they were published or given legal effect that they are in accordance with the approved editions.

Canon Law Digest
III: 571–72; VI: 811–14; VIII: 996–1012

Canon 1391 (1983 CIC 825, 827) Cross-Refs.: 1917 CIC 1399–1400

Versions of sacred Scripture cannot be printed in the vernacular language unless they have been approved by the Apostolic See and unless they are published under the vigilance of the Bishops, and [come] with annotations and especially excerpts from the holy Fathers of the Church and from Catholic doctors and writers.

Canon Law Digest
I: 684; II: 436; III: 572; VII: 890

Canon 1392 (1983 CIC 829)

§ 1. The approval of the original text of any work does not suffice for its translation into another language or for other editions; therefore, both translations and new editions of an approved work must be approved by a new approbation.

§ 2. Excerpts taken from periodicals are not considered new editions, nor for them is a new approval needed.

Canon 1393 (1983 CIC 830) Cross-Ref.: 1917 CIC 1406

§ 1. In every episcopal Curia, censors who examine publications shall be appointed by office.

§ 2. Examiners in undertaking their office, leaving off all consideration of persons, shall have before their eyes only the dogmas of the Church and the common Catholic doctrine that is contained in the general decrees of the Councils or constitutions of the Apostolic See or the prescriptions and the thinking of approved doctors.

§ 3. Censors shall be selected from both clergies [who are] commended by age, erudition, and prudence, and who in approving and disapproving doctrines, will follow the careful median.

§ 4. A censor must give the decision in writing. If it is favorable, the Ordinary shall supply the power of publishing, to which, however, shall be attached the judgment of the censor signed in his name. Only in extraordinary cases and hence rarely in the prudent judgment of the Ordinary can mention of the censor be omitted.

§ 5. The name of the censor shall never be given to the authors until after these have given sentence.

Canon Law Digest
II: 436; V: 698–701

Canon 1394 (1983 CIC 830)

§ 1. The permission by which the Ordinary grants the power of publication shall be granted in writing, printed in either the beginning or the end of the book or pamphlet or picture, expressly naming the grantor and the place and the time of the grant [of permission].

§ 2. But if it seems that permission is to be denied, the reasons shall be indicated to the requesting author, unless for a grave cause something else is indicated.

Chapter 2
On the prohibition of books

Canon 1395 (NA)

§ 1. The right and duty of prohibiting books for a just cause belongs not only to the supreme ecclesiastical authority for the universal Church, but for their subjects also to particular Councils and to local Ordinaries.

§ 2. From this prohibition there is given recourse to the Holy See, but it is not, however, suspensive.

§ 3. Even the Abbot of a monastery of its own right and the supreme Moderator of a clerical exempt religious [institute] with his Chapter or Council, can prohibit books for his subjects for a just cause; likewise, if there is danger in delay, other major Superiors can [act] with their own Council, notwithstanding the requirement that the matter go as quickly as possible to the supreme Moderator.

Canon Law Digest
I: 684; II: 437–38; III: 572–75; V: 702; VIII: 1012; IX: 908–9

Canon 1396 (NA)

Books condemned by the Apostolic See are considered prohibited in any place and in any language.

Canon Law Digest
I: 685; VI: 814–15

Canon 1397 (NA) Cross-Ref.: 1917 CIC 247

§ 1. It is for all the faithful, especially clerics and [those] constituted in ecclesiastical dignity and those excelling in doctrine, to send to local Ordinaries or to the Apostolic See books that they judge pernicious; this pertains by a special title to Legates of the Holy See, local Ordinaries, and Rectors of Catholic Universities.

§ 2. It is expedient that in the denunciation of depraved books, there should be indicated not only the title of the book but also, insofar as this can be done, the causes explained why the book should be considered for prohibition.

§ 3. Those to whom the denunciation is sent must religiously observe secrecy regarding the name of the one denouncing it.

§ 4. Local Ordinaries personally, or where it is necessary, through suitable priests, shall be vigilant about the books that are published in their own territory or set out for sale.

§ 5. Books that require a detailed examination or for which there seems to be required a decision of the supreme authority in order to bring about a salutary result, should be sent by Ordinaries for the judgment of the Apostolic See.

Canon Law Digest
I: 686; III: 575; VI: 815–17; X: 206–8

Canon 1398 (NA)

§ 1. The prohibition of books brings it about that the book cannot be published, read, retained, sold, translated into another language, or in any other way communicated to others without necessary permission.

§ 2. A book that in any manner is prohibited cannot once again be brought out unless, the corrections having been made, permission is given by him who prohibited the book, or by his Superior or successor.

Canon 1399[16] (NA) Cross-Ref.: 1917 CIC 1400

By the law, [the following] are prohibited:

1.° Original text editions or ancient versions of Catholic sacred Scripture, even of the Oriental Church, published by any non-Catholic; and likewise versions [of these], in any language, by these [same sort] prepared or published;

[16] James Quinn, "Censorship of Obscenity: A Comparison of Canon Law and American Constitutional Law" (Pontifical Lateran University, 1963).

2.° Books of any writers propagating heresy or schism, or attacking in any way the basis of religion;
3.° Books by design striking against religion and good morals;
4.° Books by any non-Catholics treating purposely of religion, unless it can be shown that nothing contained in them is contrary to the Catholic faith;
5.° Books mentioned in Canon 1385, § 1, n. 1, and Canon 1391; likewise all those mentioned in the cited Canon 1385, § 1, n. 2, [and] books and booklets that describe new apparitions, revelations, visions, prophecies, and miracles, or that lead to new devotions, even under the pretext of being private, if they have not been published in accord with the prescriptions of the canons;
6.° Books attacking or deriding any Catholic dogma, or protecting errors proscribed by the Holy See, or detracting from divine cult, or arguing for the avoidance of ecclesiastical discipline, or bringing about opprobrium on religion or the clerical state;
7.° Books that teach or recommend superstition in general, sorcery, divination, magic, evoking of spirits, and other things of this sort;
8.° Books that argue the liceity of dueling, suicide, or divorce, and those that in discussing masonic sects and other societies of this sort argue that they are useful and not pernicious to the Church and civil society;
9.° Books that purposely describe, teach, or treat lascivious or obscene materials;
10.° Editions of liturgical books approved by the Apostolic See in which there have been any changes so that they are not consistent with the authentic editions approved by the Holy See;
11.° Books that give out apocryphal indulgences or [ones] proscribed or revoked by the Holy See;
12.° Any images or impressions of Our Lord Jesus Christ, of the Blessed Virgin Mary, of the Angels and Saints or other Servants of God, alien to the sense and decrees of the Church.

Canon Law Digest

I: 686–92; II: 438; III: 575–76; IV: 389; VI: 817–18

Canon 1400 (NA)

The use of books mentioned in Canon 1399, n. 1, and of books published contrary to Canon 1391, is permitted only to those pursuing theological or biblical studies, provided these books have been faithfully and completely published and there is nothing in their introductions or notations that attacks dogmas of the Catholic faith.

Canon 1401 (NA)

Cardinals of the H. R. C., Bishops, even titular ones, and other Ordinaries, observing due precautions, are not restricted by the ecclesiastical prohibition of books.

Canon Law Digest
I: 692

Canon 1402 (NA)

§ 1. In what pertains to books prohibited by law or by decree of the Apostolic See, Ordinaries can grant to their subjects permission [to access them, but] only for individual books and only in urgent cases.

§ 2. But if they have obtained a general faculty from the Apostolic See of permitting their subjects to retain and read proscribed books, they shall not grant [such permission] except with care and for just and reasonable cause.

Canon Law Digest
I: 692

Canon 1403 (NA)

§ 1. Those who have been accorded the apostolic faculty of reading and retaining prohibited books cannot therefore read and retain any books proscribed by their own Ordinaries, unless this has been made express in the faculty that there is power to read and retain books no matter by whom condemned.

§ 2. Moreover they are bound by grave precept to exercise custody over the books so that they will not come into the hands of others.

Canon Law Digest
V: 702–4; VI: 818

Canon 1404 (NA)

Booksellers shall not sell, exchange, or stock books that by design treat of obscenities; nor shall they have other prohibited [books] for sale unless they have sought the required permission from the Apostolic See, nor will they sell them unless they prudently believe that they are being approached by a legitimate buyer.

Canon 1405 (NA)

§ 1. Permission obtained from anyone in no way exempts one from the prohibition in natural law against reading books that present a proximate spiritual danger to oneself.

§ 2. Local Ordinaries and others having care of souls shall opportunely advise the faithful about the danger and harm of reading depraved books, especially prohibited ones.

TITLE 24
On the profession of faith[17]

Canon 1406 (1983 CIC 833) Cross-Refs.: 1917 CIC 332, 405, 438, 461, 2403

§ 1. The following are bound by the obligation of giving a profession of faith, according to the formula approved by the Apostolic See:

1.° In the presence of the president or his delegate, one who is present at an Ecumenical or particular Council or diocesan Synod with a consultative or deliberative vote; the president, however, [does so] in the presence of the Council or the Synod;

2.° In the presence of the Dean of the Sacred College and the Cardinals first in rank in the order of presbyterate and deacons and the Chamberlain of the H. R. C., those promoted to cardinalitial dignity;

[17] Walter Canavan, "Profession of Faith", Canon Law Studies, no. 151 (J. C. D. thesis, Catholic University of America, 1942).

3.° In the presence of one delegated by the Apostolic See, one promoted to an episcopal see, even a non-residential one, or to the governance of an Abbey or Prelature *of no one*, and an Apostolic Vicariate or an Apostolic Prefecture;
4.° In the presence of the cathedral Chapter, the Vicar Capitulary;
5.° In the presence of local Ordinary or his delegate and in the presence of the Chapter, those who are promoted to a dignity or canonry;
6.° In the presence of the local Ordinary or his delegate and in the presence of the other consultors, those taking up the office of diocesan consultors;
7.° In the presence of the local Ordinary or his delegate, the Vicar General, pastors, and others to whom a benefice has been given, even a manual one, having the care of souls; the rector and professors of sacred theology, canon law, and philosophy in Seminaries, at the beginning of the school year or at least upon taking up duties; all those to be promoted to the order of subdeacon; censors of books mentioned in Canon 1393, priests destined for hearing confessions and sacred preachers before they are given faculty of exercising those responsibilities;
8.° In the presence of the Ordinary or his delegate, the Rector of a University or a Faculty; in the presence of the Rector of a University or Faculty or his delegate, all professors in a canonically erected University or Faculty, at the beginning of the school year or at least upon taking up duties; and likewise those who, having passed the test, are given academic degrees;
9.° In the presence of the Chapter or the Superior or their delegates, those who appointed the Superior in clerical religious [institutes].

§ 2. Those who, after dismissal, go on to another office or benefice or dignity, even of the same type, must again give the profession of faith according to the norm of this canon.

Canon Law Digest
I: 693; V: 704; VI: 818; VIII: 1012

Canon 1407 (1983 CIC 833) Cross-Refs.: 1917 CIC 332, 405, 438

The obligation of giving the profession of faith is not satisfied by using a procurator or by giving it in the presence of a layman.

Canon 1408 (NA) Cross-Refs.: 1917 CIC 332, 405, 438

A custom contrary to the canons of this title is reprobated.

FIFTH PART
ON BENEFICES AND OTHER NON-COLLEGIATE ECCLESIASTICAL INSTITUTES

TITLE 25
On ecclesiastical benefices[1]

Canon 1409 (NA) Cross-Ref.: 1917 CIC 146

An ecclesiastical benefice is a juridic entity constituted or erected in perpetuity by competent ecclesiastical authority consisting of a sacred office and the right of receiving income from the assets attached to that office.

Canon Law Digest
I: 695–97; II: 439; VI: 818

Canon 1410[2] (NA) Cross-Ref.: 1917 CIC 1415

The endowment of a benefice consists of property assets that belong to the juridic person itself, and of certain obligations owed from families or moral persons, whether of certain voluntary offerings from the faithful that pertain to the rector of the benefice, or of rights, as they are called, to stole fees within the limits of diocesan rates and legitimate customs, and of choir distributions, excluding a third part of them, if all of the income of the benefice consists of choral distributions.

Canon Law Digest
I: 697

---

[1] Henry Golden, "Parochial Benefices in the New Code", Canon Law Studies, no. 10 (J. C. D. thesis, Catholic University of America, 1925); Hugo McNeill, "The Parochial Benefice in England" (MS no. 592, Gregorian University, 1938; printed version, no. 196, 1939).

[2] Francis Grant, "The Income of the Benefice" (diss. no. 7, Pontifical University of St. Thomas [Rome], 1937–1938); Richard Stadfield, "Ecclesiastical Temporalities of the Parish in the United States of America" (diss. no. 40, Pontifical University of St. Thomas, 1956–1957); Dionysius Helming, "The Formation of Ecclesiastical Patrimony as Seen in the Parish" (diss. no. 25, Pontifical University of St. Thomas [Rome], 1959–1960).

Canon 1411[3] (NA) Cross-Ref.: 1917 CIC 405

Ecclesiastical benefices are called:

1.° *Consistorial* if they are usually conferred in a Consistory; the others are *non-consistorial*;
2.° *Secular* or *religious* insofar as they look only to secular clerics or only to religious clerics; but all benefices erected outside the churches or houses of religious, in doubt, are presumed to be secular;
3.° *Doubled*, that is, *residential*, or *simple*, that is, *non-residential*, insofar as, beyond the beneficial duty, there is attached or withdrawn the obligation of residence;
4.° *Manual, temporary*, that is, *removable*, or *perpetual*, that is, *irremovable*, insofar as they are conferred revocably or in perpetuity;
5.° *Curate* or *non-curate* insofar as they do or do not have attached to them the care of souls.

Canon Law Digest
I: 697–98

Canon 1412[4] (NA)

Even though they offer some similarities to benefices in law, these are nevertheless not included in the name of benefice:

1.° Parochial vicariates not erected in perpetuity;
2.° Lay chaplaincies, namely, those that were not erected by competent ecclesiastical authority;
3.° A coadjutor with or without a future of succession;
4.° Personal pensions;
5.° Temporary entrustment, that is, the grant of the proceeds of a certain church or monastery made to one so that upon one's death the income reverts to that church or monastery.

Canon Law Digest
I: 698; II: 439

[3] Dominator Ravanera, "The Parochial Benefice in the Philippine Islands" (diss. no. 7, Pontifical University of St. Thomas [Rome], 1950–1951).

[4] Sylvester Gass, "Ecclesiastical Pensions", Canon Law Studies, no. 157 (J. C. D. thesis, Catholic University of America, 1942); Richard Hill, "Ecclesiastical Pensions in the Jurisprudence of the Sacred Congregation of the Council" (MS no. 3488, Gregorian University, 1963; printed version, no. 1611, 1963).

Canon 1413 (NA)

§ 1. Unless it appears otherwise, the canons that follow must be understood [as referring to] only non-consistorial benefices properly so called.

§ 2. Canons 147–95 shall also be applied to beneficial offices or benefices.

Chapter 1

On the constitution or erection of benefices

Canon 1414 (NA)

§ 1. Only the Apostolic See erects a consistorial benefice.

§ 2. Besides the Roman Pontiff, Ordinaries in their own territory can erect a non-consistorial benefice with due regard for the prescription of Canon 394, § 2.

§ 3. Vicars General, however, cannot erect a benefice except by special mandate.

§ 4. Also, a Cardinal in his own title or diaconate can erect a non-curate benefice unless the church belongs to clerical exempt religious.

Canon Law Digest
VII: 890

Canon 1415 (NA)

§ 1. Benefices shall not be erected unless it can be shown that they have a stable and appropriate endowment from which income can be received perpetually according to the norm of Canon 1410.

§ 2. If the endowment consists of an amount of money, the Ordinary, having heard the diocesan Council of administration mentioned in Canon 1520, must take care that as soon as possible it be collected in a safe and profitable fund or investment.

§ 3. It is, nevertheless, not prohibited, where an appropriate endowment cannot be constituted, to erect parishes or quasi-parishes if it can be prudently foreseen that their necessities will be met from other contemporary sources.

Canon Law Digest
I: 698

Canon 1416 (NA)

Before the erection of a benefice, there shall be called and heard all those who have an interest, if there are any.

Canon 1417 (NA)

§ 1. Within the limits of the foundation, a founder can with the consent of the Ordinary attach conditions contrary even to common law, provided they are not repugnant to honesty and the nature of the benefice.

§ 2. Conditions once admitted cannot be validly suppressed or changed by the local Ordinary, unless it concerns a change in favor of the Church and the consent of the founder is forthcoming or, if it concerns the right of patronage, that of the patron.

Canon Law Digest
I: 698

Canon 1418 (NA)

The erection of benefices shall be made by legitimate instrument in which there will be defined the place where the benefice is erected and there will be described the endowment of the benefice and the rights and burdens of the beneficiary.

Canon Law Digest
I: 698

Chapter 2
On the union, transfer, division, dismemberment, conversion, and suppression of benefices

Canon 1419[5] (NA)

The union of benefices is:

1.° *Extinctive*, when either from the suppression of two or more benefices a single new benefice is effected, or if one or several others are united so that [they] cease to be;

[5] Thomas Mundy, "The Union of Parishes", Canon Law Studies, no. 204 (J. C. D. thesis, Catholic University of America, 1944).

2.° *Principally equal*, when united benefices remain such that neither is subjected to the other;
3.° *Minor principal*, that is, when by *subjugation* or *accession* the benefices remain, but one or several are subjected to a principal as accessories.

Canon 1420 (NA)

§ 1. In extinctive unions, the benefice that emerges or remains enjoys all the rights and duties of the extinct ones and, if they cannot be reconciled, those that are better or more favorable.

§ 2. In principally equal [unions], even though a benefice preserves its nature, rights, and duties, in view of the completed union, one title must be conferred on each cleric of the united benefices.

§ 3. In minor principal [unions], the accessory benefice follows the principal so that a cleric who obtains the principal must fulfill the duties of both that one and the accessory one.

Canon 1421[6] (NA)

The *transfer* of a benefice is had when the see of a benefice is led from one place to another; *division* [is had] when from one benefice, two or more are made; *dismemberment* [is had] when parts of the territory or goods of one benefice are withdrawn from it and assigned to another benefice or pious cause or ecclesiastical institute; *conversion* [is had] when a benefice is changed into another type; *suppression* [is had] when it is entirely extinguished.

Canon Law Digest
I: 698

Canon 1422 (NA)

The extinctive union of benefices, their suppression, or their dismemberment, which is done by withdrawing the goods from the benefice and not erecting a new benefice, is reserved to the Holy See; [as is] the equitable union or the minor principal [union] of a religious benefice with seculars and the reverse, [and] likewise any transfer, division, and dismemberment of a religious benefice.

Canon Law Digest
I: 698

[6] Edward McCaslin, "The Division of Parishes", Canon Law Studies, no. 281 (thesis, Catholic University of America, 1951).

Canon 1423 (NA) Cross-Refs.: 1917 CIC 452, 1426

§ 1. Local Ordinaries, but not a Vicar Capitulary or the Vicar General without a special mandate, can because of the necessity or the greater or evident utility of the Church unite as principally equal or minor principal any parochial churches among themselves or with non-curate benefices such that, however, in the second case, if the union is made with a minor principal, the non-curate benefice is accessory.

§ 2. They cannot unite a parish with the capitular or episcopal table [or] with monasteries, the churches of religious, or other moral persons, or with dignities or cathedral or collegial church benefices; but with a cathedral or collegial church that is situated in the territory of a parish they can unite one so that the income of the parish falls to the use of that church, leaving to the pastor or vicar an appropriate amount.

§ 3. The union of benefices cannot be done by local Ordinaries except in perpetuity.

Canon Law Digest
II: 439; IV: 389–90; VI: 819

Canon 1424 (NA)

Local Ordinaries can never unite any benefice, whether curate or non-curate, when there is detriment to those who actually obtain it over their objection; nor [may they do so] with a benefice of patronal right with [regard to] a benefice of free conferral without consent of the patrons; nor [may they do so] with a benefice of one diocese and the benefice of another diocese, even if both dioceses are principally equally united and governed by one Bishop; nor [may they do so] with exempt benefices or ones reserved to the Apostolic See with any others.

Canon 1425[7] (NA)

§ 1. If a parish is united to a religious house by the Apostolic See in what pertains *only to temporalities*, the religious house participates only in the proceeds of the parish, and the religious Superior must present to the local Ordinary a priest from the secular clergy for installment, assigning him a due proportion.

[7] Robert Dailey, "The Primary Effects of the Union *Pleno Iure* [in full law] of Parishes with Religious Communities" (thesis, Gregorian University; printed version, no. 690, 1951).

§ 2. But if it is [united] *in full right*, the parish becomes religious and the Superior can appoint a priest from his own religious [institute] to exercise the care of souls, but it is for the local Ordinary to approve and install him, and he remains under him with regard to jurisdiction, correction, and visitation [and those things] that pertain to the care of souls according to the norm of Canon 631.

Canon Law Digest
I: 699; II: 439; IX: 909–10

Canon 1426 (NA)

On account of the canonical causes mentioned in Canon 1423, § 1, Ordinaries can transfer the seat of a secular parochial benefice from one [place] to another in the same parish; but for other benefices, [they may do so] only when the church in which they were founded has collapsed and cannot be restored, and then they can transfer them to the mother churches or others in their area or vicinity, with the altars and chapels erected, if this can be done, under the same invocations and with attached all the emoluments and duties of the prior church.

Canon 1427 (NA) Cross-Ref.: 1917 CIC 476

§ 1. Ordinaries can also, for a just and canonical cause, divide any parishes over the objection of their rectors and without the consent of the people, erecting perpetual vicariates or new parishes or dismembering their territory.

§ 2. The canonical cause for the division or dismemberment of a parish can be, and only is, if either it is greatly difficult to approach the parish church or if the population is too large for the parish and it is not possible to provide for the spiritual good according to the norm of Canon 476, § 1.

§ 3. In dividing a parish, an Ordinary must assign to the perpetual vicariate or newly erected parish a decent proportion [of assets], the prescription of Canon 1500 being observed; these things, unless they can be had otherwise, must be taken from the income pertaining in any way to the mother church, provided a sufficient income remains to the same mother church.

§ 4. If a perpetual vicariate or new parish is endowed by the income of the church from which it was divided, it must defer to the honor of the mother church in a manner and end as determined by the Ordinary, who, however, is forbidden to reserve to the mother church the baptismal font.

§ 5. When a parish is divided that by law looks to another religious [institute], the perpetual vicariate or newly erected parish is not religious; similarly, if the divided parish was under the right of patronage the new parish is of free conferral.

Canon Law Digest
I: 699–701; VI: 819

Canon 1428 (NA)

§ 1. Unions, transfers, divisions, and dismemberment of benefices shall not be done by local Ordinaries except by authentic writing having heard the cathedral Chapter and those who have an interest, if there are any, especially the rectors of churches.

§ 2. A union, transfer, division, or dismemberment made without canonical cause is invalid.

§ 3. Against the decree of an Ordinary uniting, transferring, dividing, or dismembering a benefice, there is given recourse to the Holy See, but only in devolution.

Canon 1429 (NA) Cross-Refs.: 1917 CIC 1440, 1505

§ 1. Local Ordinaries cannot impose on any benefice a perpetual or temporary pension that lasts for the life of the pensioner, but they can, when conferring the benefice, for a just cause expressed in the act of conferral itself, impose temporary pensions on them that last for the life of the beneficiary, with due regard for his appropriate portion.

§ 2. They cannot impose pensions on parochial benefices except to the advantage of the pastor or vicar of that parish upon leaving office, which, nevertheless, shall not exceed a third part of the revenue of the parish, having deducted expenses and uncertain income.

§ 3. Beneficial pensions, whether imposed by the Roman Pontiff or other ones conferring such, cease upon the death of the pensioner, who, nevertheless, cannot alienate them unless this has been expressly granted.

Canon Law Digest
I: 702; II: 439–40

Canon 1430 (NA)

§ 1. Benefices with care of souls cannot be converted by the Ordinary into [benefices] without care of souls, nor religious benefices into secular [ones], nor secular [ones] into religious.

§ 2. On the other hand, simple benefices can be converted into [benefices] with care of souls by local Ordinaries, provided there are not express conditions from the founder standing in the way.

Chapter 3
On the conferral of benefices

Canon 1431 (NA)

It is the right of the Roman Pontiff to confer benefices throughout the universal Church and to reserve their conferral to himself.

Canon 1432 (NA)

§ 1. For the conferring of vacant benefices, a Cardinal in his own title or diaconal [place] and the local Ordinary in his own territory have the intention as founded in law.

§ 2. A Vicar General cannot confer a benefice without a special mandate; nor can a Vicar Capitulary [confer] vacant parishes, except according to the norm of Canon 455, § 2, n. 3, or grant by free conferral other perpetual benefices.

§ 3. If an Ordinary, within six months of having certain notice of the vacancy of a benefice, has not filled it, the conferral devolves upon the Apostolic See, with due regard for the prescription of Canon 458.

Canon Law Digest
I: 702–3; II: 440; III: 576; VII: 890

Canon 1433 (NA)

Coadjutors in benefices, with or without future succession, can be constituted only by the Apostolic See, with due regard, nevertheless, for the prescription of Canons 475 and 476.

Canon Law Digest
I: 703

Canon 1434 (NA)

Benefices reserved to the Apostolic See are invalidly conferred by inferiors.

Canon 1435[8] (NA) Cross-Refs.: 1917 CIC 403, 612

§ 1. Besides all consistorial benefices and all dignities in cathedral and collegial churches according to the norm of Canon 396, § 1, there are reserved to the Apostolic See, in whatsoever way vacant, only the benefices that are listed below:

1.° All benefices, even curacies, that have been vacated by the death, promotion, resignation, or transfer of a Cardinal of the H. R. C., Legate of the Roman Pontiff, major official of a Sacred Congregation, Tribunal, [or] Office of the Roman Curia or Family, even if only honorary, of the Supreme Pontiff at the time of the vacancy of the benefice;

2.° Those founded outside of the Roman Curia that vacate by the death of the beneficiary in the City itself;

3.° Those conferred invalidly because of the vice of simony;

4.° Finally, those benefices upon which the Roman Pontiff, himself or through another, places his hand in the ways that follow: if he has declared the election to the benefice as [being] without force, or if he has forbidden the elector to proceed; if he accepted the resignation; if he has promoted the beneficiary, transferred him, or deprived him; if he has given the benefice in entrustment.

§ 2. Manual benefices or those under the right of lay or mixed patrons are never reserved.

§ 3. In what pertains to the conferral of benefices that are established in Rome, the special laws governing them are observed.

Canon Law Digest

I: 703; II: 440–42; III: 576–79; VI: 819; VII: 890–94

Canon 1436 (NA)

An ecclesiastical benefice cannot be validly conferred on an unwilling cleric or without his express acceptance.

[8] John Haydt, "Reserved Benefices", Canon Law Studies, no. 161 (J. C. D. thesis, Catholic University of America, 1942).

Canon 1437 (NA)

No one can confer a benefice upon himself.

Canon 1438 (NA)

Secular benefices are to be conferred for the lifetime of the beneficiary, unless otherwise determined by the law of foundation, or immemorial custom, or special indult.

Canon Law Digest
I: 703

Canon 1439 (NA) Cross-Ref.: 1917 CIC 2396

§ 1. No cleric is able to accept and retain, whether in title or in perpetual commendation, several incompatible benefices, according to the norm of Canon 156.

§ 2. Not only are those two benefices incompatible when the totality of their obligations cannot be fulfilled by one person at one time, but also when two benefices are unnecessary for the decent support of the holder.

Canon 1440 (NA)

Ecclesiastical benefices are to be conferred without diminution, with due regard for the prescription of Canon 1429, §§ 1–2.

Canon Law Digest
I: 703–4

Canon 1441 (NA)

Deductions from the fruits, compensations, or payments from the cleric, in the act of making the provisions that are made to the one conferring or to patrons or others, are reprobated as simoniacal.

Canon Law Digest
I: 705; IX: 910

Canon 1442 (NA)

Secular benefices are not to be conferred except upon the clerics of the secular clergy; members of religious [institutes] should be appointed to those benefices that pertain to them.

Canon 1443[9] (NA) Cross-Refs.: 1917 CIC 405, 461

§ 1. No one shall take possession of a benefice conferred on himself, either by his own authority or without giving the profession of faith, if it concerns a benefice for which this profession of faith is prescribed.

§ 2. If it concerns a non-consistorial benefice, it belongs to the local Ordinary to put one in possession, that is, for corporeal installations, who can delegate another ecclesiastical man to do it.

Canon 1444 (NA) Cross-Refs.: 1917 CIC 405, 461, 1095

§ 1. The placing in possession of a benefice shall be done according to the manner prescribed by particular law, or by legitimate received custom, unless for a just cause the Ordinary dispenses from this manner or rite, expressly in writing; in which case, the dispensation takes the place of the reception of possession.

§ 2. The local Ordinary shall define the time within which possession of the benefice must take place; but if this time passes without effect, unless it was impeded by a just impediment, he shall declare the benefice vacant according to the norm of Canon 188, n. 2.

Canon Law Digest
I: 705; IV: 390

Canon 1445 (NA) Cross-Refs.: 1917 CIC 405, 461

Possession of a benefice can also be taken by a procurator having a special mandate.

Canon 1446 (NA)

If a cleric who possesses a benefice proves himself to have been in peaceful possession of the benefice for three whole years in good faith, even if by chance the title was invalid, provided there was no simony, he obtains the benefice by legitimate prescription.

Canon 1447 (NA)

Whoever seeks a benefice possessed by another peacefully, which he contends is vacant in a certain manner, must express in the libellus of

[9] Frederick Freking, "The Canonical Installation of Pastors", Canon Law Studies, no. 273 (thesis, Catholic University of America, 1948); Charles Garcia, "A Study on the Juridical Nature and Effects of Corporeal Institution in the Current Legislation of the Church" (MS no. 2545, Gregorian University, 1956).

supplication the name of the possessor, the time of possession, and the special reason why he asserts the possession to be null [and] his own right to the benefice; but the benefice cannot be conferred unless first the case that was submitted for litigation is resolved according to the norm of law.

Chapter 4
On the right of patronage[10]

Canon 1448 (NA)

The right of patronage is the sum of privileges along with certain duties that, by concession of the Church, are enjoyed by founders of Catholic churches, chapels, or benefices, or also by those who have a [right] from these.

Canon Law Digest
I: 705

Canon 1449 (NA)

The right of patronage is:

1.° *Real* or *personal* insofar as it attaches to a thing or directly concerns a person;

2.° *Ecclesiastical*, *lay*, or *mixed* insofar as the title in which a patron participates is ecclesiastical, lay, or mixed;

3.° *Hereditary*, *familial*, *clannish*, or *mixed* insofar as it passes to heirs or to those who are of the family or clan of the founder, or to those who are at the same time heirs and [who belong] to the family or clan of the founder.

Canon 1450 (NA)

§ 1. No right of patronage by any title can be validly constituted in the future.

§ 2. The local Ordinary can:

1.° Grant for a time or even in perpetuity spiritual suffrages to the faithful who in whole or in part build churches or fund benefices in proportion to their liberality;

[10] John Godfrey, "The Right of Patronage according to the Code of Canon Law", Canon Law Studies, no. 21 (J. C. D. thesis, Catholic University of America, 1924).

2.° Admit a foundation of a benefice to which is added a condition that the benefice be conferred the first time upon the founding cleric or another cleric designated by the founder.

Canon Law Digest
I: 705–7

Canon 1451 (NA)

§ 1. Local Ordinaries shall take care that patrons accept in place of the right of patronage that they enjoy, or at least in place of the right of presentation, spiritual suffrages for themselves, even perpetual ones.

§ 2. If patrons do not wish this, their right of patronage is governed by the canons that follow.

Canon Law Digest
I: 707; II: 442

Canon 1452 (NA)

Popular elections and presentations, even to parochial benefices wherever they are in force, can be tolerated only if the people elect a cleric from among three designated by the local Ordinary.

Canon Law Digest
I: 707–8

Canon 1453 (NA)

§ 1. The personal right of patronage cannot be validly transmitted to non-believers, public apostates, heretics, schismatics, those ascribed to secret societies condemned by the Church, or to any one excommunicated after a declaratory or condemnatory sentence.

§ 2. In order that the personal right of patronage be validly transmitted to others, the consent of the Ordinary given in writing is required, with due regard for the laws of the foundation and the prescription of Canon 1470, § 1, n. 4.

§ 3. If a thing to which a real right of patronage is attached passes to some person mentioned in § 1, the right of patronage remains suspended.

Canon Law Digest
VIII: 1012

Canon 1454 (NA)

No right of patronage is admitted unless it is evident by authentic documents or other legitimate evidence.

Canon Law Digest
I: 708

Canon 1455 (NA)

The privileges of patrons are:

1.° Presenting a cleric to a vacant church or vacant benefice;
2.° With due regard for the execution of burdens and the honest support of the beneficiary, if there is a surplus of goods obtained from equity or from the assets of the church or of the benefice, as often as the patron, through no personal fault, has been reduced to poverty, even if the patron has renounced his rights for the convenience of the Church, [for the patron] to receive a payment within the limits of the foundation, even if at the time [another payment] was reserved to the patron, if this is not sufficient to lift him out of poverty;
3.° Having, if there is a legitimate custom in the place, the clan or family coat of arms in the church of patronage and of taking precedence before other laity in processions and similar functions and [of occupying] the more dignified seat in the church, but outside the sanctuary and without a baldachin.

Canon Law Digest
I: 708

Canon 1456 (NA)

A wife may exercise the right of patronage herself, [as can] minors through parents or guardians; but if parents or guardians are not Catholic, the right of patronage in the meantime remains suspended.

Canon 1457 (NA) Cross-Ref.: 1917 CIC 1465

Presentation, no just impediment obstructing, whether it concerns lay, ecclesiastical, or mixed patronage, must be made, unless a shorter period of time has been prescribed in the law of the foundation or legitimate custom, within four months from the day on which he who has the right of institution has notified the patron about the vacancy of the benefice and about the priests who were approved by the concursus, if it concerns a benefice that must be conferred by a concursus.

Canon Law Digest
I: 708–9

Canon 1458 (NA)

§ 1. If within the prescribed time the presentation is not made, the church or benefice may be freely conferred on that occasion.

§ 2. But if a dispute should arise that cannot be settled within the useful time concerning either the right of presentation between the Ordinary and the patron or among the patrons, or concerning the rights of preference among the ones presented, the conferral is suspended until the resolution of the controversy, and in the meantime, if it is necessary, the Ordinary shall place an econome over the vacant church or benefice.

Canon 1459 (NA)

§ 1. But if several individual persons are patrons, they can bind themselves or their successors concerning an alternate [manner of] presentation.

§ 2. In order that this agreement be valid, there is required the consent of the local Ordinary given in writing, which [consent] cannot, once it is given, be validly revoked over the objections of the patrons by the Ordinary or his successors.

Canon 1460 (NA)

§ 1. If the right of patronage is exercised collegially, that one is considered presented who has obtained the major number of the votes, according to the norm of Canon 101, § 1; but if two ballots have been passed without effect, all those are considered as presented who, in the third ballot, have a majority over the others but are equal among themselves in the number of votes they have.

§ 2. If the right of patronage rests with individual persons who have not agreed among themselves for an alternate [form of] presentation, he is considered as presented who has received at least a relative majority of the number of ballots; and if these are several, all those are considered presented who have a majority in the number of ballots cast.

§ 3. Whoever obtains the right of patronage from diverse titles has as many votes in the presentation as he has titles.

§ 4. Any patron, before a presentation is accepted, can present not only one but several [candidates], either all at once or successively, within the prescribed time, in a manner that does not exclude anyone already presented.

Canon Law Digest
I: 709–10

Canon 1461 (NA)

No one can present himself or join with other patrons so that the number of votes necessary for presentation is fulfilled in his regard.

Canon 1462 (NA)

If a church or benefice must be provided through concursus, the patron, even if a layman, cannot present [a candidate] unless he is a cleric legitimately approved by concursus.

Canon Law Digest
I: 710

Canon 1463 (NA)

The person presented must be suitable, that is, on the day of presentation or at least of acceptance, [he must be] endowed with all those qualities that are required by common or particular law or the law of foundation.

Canon 1464 (NA)

§ 1. Presentation must be made to the local Ordinary who is to judge whether the presented person is suitable.

§ 2. In the formation of his judgment, the Ordinary must, according to the norm of Canon 149, diligently inquire and assess opportune information, even secret, if necessary, about the person presented.

§ 3. The Ordinary is not bound to give his reasons to the patron as to why a presented person cannot be admitted.

Canon 1465 (NA)

§ 1. If the one presented is not suitable, the patron, provided the time available for presentation has not lapsed due to his negligence, can present another within the time mentioned in Canon 1457; but if this one is not suitable either, the church or benefice shall proceed by free conferral in that case, unless the patron or the one presented shall have taken recourse from the judgment of the Ordinary to the Apostolic See within ten days of notice of the refusal; the which [recourse] pending, conferral is suspended until the matter is resolved, and in the meantime, if it is necessary, an econome for the vacant church or benefice is named by the Ordinary.

§ 2. A presentation disgraced with simony is by law invalid and renders invalid any institution that perhaps follows it.

Canon Law Digest
I: 710–11

Canon 1466 (NA)

§ 1. One legitimately presented and shown as qualified, having accepted presentation, has the right to canonical installment.

§ 2. The right of granting canonical installment belongs to the local Ordinary, but not the Vicar General without a special mandate.

§ 3. If several are presented and all are suitable, the Ordinary will select him whom he judges most suitable in the Lord.

Canon Law Digest
I: 711

Canon 1467 (NA)

Canonical installment for any benefice, even a non-curate one, must be given within two months from the time the presentation was made, there being no just impediment obstructing.

Canon 1468 (NA)

If the one presented resigns or dies before canonical installment, the patron once again has the right of presentation.

Canon 1469 (NA) Cross-Ref.: 1917 CIC 1470

§ 1. The burdens or offices of patrons are:

1.° To advise the local Ordinary if the goods of the church or benefice seem in disrepair, but without involving themselves in the administration of the goods;

2.° To build anew a collapsed church and to make those repairs to it which the Ordinary judges are necessary, if they have the right of patronage from a title of construction and unless the burden of building anew or repairing the church falls to others according to the norm of Canon 1186;

3.° To supply the income if the right of patronage comes by title of endowment when the church or benefice falters in income to the point that it is no longer possible to exercise cult decently in the church or to confer the benefice.

§ 2. If the church has collapsed or lacks necessary repairs, or if the income fails according to the norm of § 1, nn. 2 and 3, the right of patronage in the meantime halts.

§ 3. If the patron within the time given by the Ordinary, under pain of cessation of patronage, builds the church anew or restores it or supplements the income, the right of patronage revives; otherwise, by the law, and without any declaration, it ceases.

Canon 1470 (NA) Cross-Ref.: 1917 CIC 1453

§ 1. Beyond the case mentioned in Canon 1469, § 3, the right of patronage is extinguished:

1.° If the patron resigns his right; this resignation, however, can be made completely or in part, but it can never do damage to the other co-patrons, if there are any;

2.° If the Holy See revokes the right of patronage or suppresses the church or the benefice perpetually;

3.° If legitimate prescription has run against the right of patronage;

4.° If the thing in which the right of patronage inhered is destroyed or if the family, clan, or line to which it is reserved according to the documents of foundation is extinguished; in the second case the right of patronage does not become hereditary nor can the Ordinary validly permit the donation of the right of patronage to be made to another;

5.° If, with the consent of the patron, the church or benefice is united to another of free conferral or if it is made elective or [of] regulars;

6.° If the patron attempted to transfer the right of patronage simoniacally to another; or if he lapsed into apostasy, heresy, or schism; or if he usurped or detained the goods or rights of the church or benefice unjustly; if he killed or mutilated the rector or another cleric attached to the service of the church or benefice, personally or through another.

§ 2. Because of the crimes mentioned in § 1, n. 6, only the defendant patron loses the right of patronage, [but] from the delict mentioned last, the heirs also [lose the right].

§ 3. In order that patrons be considered to have lost the right of patronage because of the delicts enumerated in § 1, n. 6, a declaratory sentence is required and suffices.

§ 4. One cannot exercise the right of patronage and use its privileges for so long as a censure or infamy perdures, [which] censure or infamy of law obtains [effect herein] after a condemnatory or declaratory sentence.

Canon Law Digest
I: 711; II: 442; III: 580

Canon 1471 (NA)

If the Apostolic See has granted an indult, whether in a concordat or outside a concordat, of presentation for a vacant church or vacant benefice, the right of patronage does not arise thereby and the privilege of presentation must undergo strict interpretation from the tenor of the indult.

Canon Law Digest
I: 711; II: 442

Chapter 5
On the rights and obligations of beneficiaries

Canon 1472 (NA)

Any beneficiary, having taken legitimate possession of a benefice, derives all the fruits, whether temporal or spiritual, that are attached to the benefice.

Canon Law Digest
II: 442

Canon 1473 (NA)

Even though a beneficiary has other non-beneficiary goods, he can freely use and enjoy the fruits of the benefice that are necessary for his honest support; but he is bound by the obligation of spending the excess on the poor or for pious causes with due regard for the prescription of Canon 239, § 1, n. 19.

Canon Law Digest
I: 712

Canon 1474 (NA)

If in order to obtain a benefice, the taking of some order is required, the beneficiary must receive that order before conferral of the benefice.

Canon 1475 (NA)

§ 1. A beneficiary is bound faithfully to fulfill the special obligations attached to the benefice and, moreover, to recite the canonical hours daily.

§ 2. If, not detained by any legitimate impediment, he does not satisfy the obligation of reciting the canonical hours, he does not receive the fruits in proportion to the omission and shall hand them over for the upkeep of the church or for the diocesan Seminary or shall send them to the poor.

Canon Law Digest
I: 712–13

Canon 1476 (NA)

§ 1. A beneficiary must administer the goods pertaining to his benefice as would a guardian of the benefice according to the norm of law.

§ 2. If his negligence in any way was culpable, he must repair the harm to the benefice and shall be compelled to this compensation by the local Ordinary; and if he is a pastor he can be removed from the parish according to the norm of Canons 2147 and foll[owing].

Canon Law Digest
I: 713–14

Canon 1477 (NA)

§ 1. The ordinary expenses attached to the administration of the goods of the benefice and to participation in its fruits are to be borne by the beneficiary.

§ 2. The expenses for the extraordinary repair of the benefice house belong to those who have the burden of repairing the beneficiary church, unless the documents of foundation or legitimate contracts and customs provide otherwise.

§ 3. Minor repairs that fall on the beneficiary himself shall be performed as soon as possible, lest the necessity of major [repairs] ensues.

Canon 1478 (NA)

The local Ordinary is bound by the obligation of being vigilant, even through vicars forane, that benefice goods are preserved and rightly administered.

Canon 1479 (NA) Cross-Ref.: 1917 CIC 1541

In the rental of beneficial goods, advanced payments beyond six months are prohibited without the permission of the local Ordinary, who shall take precautions in extraordinary cases by means of appropriate prescriptions lest such a rental impose damage on a pious place or on the successor in the benefice.

Canon 1480 (NA)

The annual income of the benefice will be distributed between the successor and the predecessor or his heirs, in case of death, in proportion to the time that each was in the benefice with all of the income and burdens of the current year being calculated, unless by legitimate custom or special statutes duly approved, another manner of just calculation has been ordered.

Canon Law Digest
I: 714

Canon 1481 (NA)

With any general expenses deducted and with due regard for the prescription of Canon 472, n. 1, the fruits of a vacant benefice are divided, [with] one-half to go to the endowment of the benefice and common fund, the other half to go to the upkeep of the church or sacristy, unless there is a legitimate custom by which all the fruits are applied to the common good of the diocese.

Canon 1482 (NA)

As for what applies to the half-annates, as they are called, those things shall be retained where they are in force, and special statutes and laudable customs in force concerning these matters shall be observed in every region.

Canon 1483 (NA)

§ 1. The goods of the episcopal table shall be diligently administered by the Bishop.

§ 2. The episcopal house shall be preserved in good condition and, if necessary, shall be restored and repaired at table expense, as often as these burdens do not fall on others by special title.

§ 3. Bishops should also take care that, an accurate inventory having been made, all of the utensils and mobile goods of the episcopal house that might be added and that constitute table property are transmitted to the successor completely and securely.

Chapter 6
On termination of and changes to benefices

Canon 1484 (NA)

An Ordinary shall not admit a beneficial termination made by a cleric constituted in major orders unless he is sure that he has from other sources what is necessary for honest support and with due regard for the prescription of Canon 584.

Canon 1485 (NA)

The termination of a benefice in whose title a cleric was ordained is invalid unless express mention is made that the cleric was promoted under that title and with the consent of the Ordinary has substituted another legitimate title of ordination.

Canon 1486 (NA)

The termination of a benefice made on behalf of another or under a condition that affects the provision of that benefice or the spending of its income shall not be admitted by the Ordinary except in a case in which the benefice is in litigation and the termination was made by one of the litigants on behalf of another.

Canon Law Digest
I: 714

Canon 1487 (NA)

§ 1. The exchange of two benefices cannot be done validly except for the necessity or utility of the Church or for another just cause, with detriment to no one, and with the consent of the patron if it concerns a benefice under right of patronage and of the local Ordinary, but not the

Vicar General without a special mandate, or the Vicar Capitulary, and observing the prescription of Canon 186.

§ 2. An Ordinary shall offer or deny this consent within one month; and the exchange takes effect from the moment consent from the Ordinary is offered.

§ 3. The exchange of benefices cannot be allowed by the Ordinary if both or either benefice is reserved to the Apostolic See.

Canon 1488 (NA)

§ 1. If the benefices to be exchanged are unequal, there can be no compensation by way of reservation of the fruits or monetary offering or anything whose price can be estimated.

§ 2. An exchange cannot be made between more than two beneficiaries.

TITLE 26
On other non-collegiate ecclesiastical institutes[11]

Canon 1489[12] (NA)

§ 1. Hospitals, orphanages, and other similar institutes destined for works of religion or charity, whether spiritual or temporal, can be erected by the local Ordinary, and by his decree they are constituted juridic persons in the Church.

§ 2. The local Ordinary shall not approve these institutes unless the purpose of the foundation is truly useful and there is constituted for them an endowment that, all things considered, is sufficient or it can be prudently foreseen that such sufficiency will be secured.

§ 3. It is for rectors to administer the goods of these institutions according to the norms of the documents of the foundation; they are bound

[11] Coleman Carroll, "Charitable Institutions", Canon Law Studies, no. 189 (Catholic University of America, not published); Gerard Doyle, "The Catholic Hospitals of Canada" (doctoral diss. 47, University of Ottawa, 1964).

[12] Terrence Walsh, "The Catholic Church and the Hospitals: A Treatise on the Rights of the Church in Relation to the [Irish] National Health Service Act of 1946" (MS no. 1530, Gregorian University, 1949).

by the same obligations and enjoy the same rights as other administrators of ecclesiastical goods.

Canon Law Digest
I: 714–15; VI: 820

Canon 1490 (NA)

§ 1. In the documents of foundation, the pious founder will describe the complete constitution of the institute, its purpose, endowment, administration, and governance, the application of income, and succession of goods in case of the extinction of the institute.

§ 2. Two copies of these documents are to be made, of which one shall go into the institute archives, and the other deposited in the Curial archives.

Canon 1491 (NA)

§ 1. The local Ordinary can and must visit every institute of this sort, even if the moral person is erected and in any way exempt.

§ 2. Indeed, even if it is not erected into a moral person and is entrusted to a religious house, if it concerns a religious house of diocesan right, it is under the jurisdiction of the local Ordinary; but if the religious house is of pontifical right, it is under episcopal vigilance in those things that pertain to teaching of religion, honesty of morals, pious exercises, and administration of sacred [matters].

Canon 1492 (NA)

§ 1. Even if at the time of its foundation, a pious institute was exempt from the jurisdiction and visitation of the local Ordinary by prescription or apostolic privilege, nevertheless, the Ordinary has the right of requiring a complete accounting, reprobating any contrary custom.

§ 2. If the founder wishes administrators not to be bound to deliver an accounting to the local Ordinary, the foundation shall not be accepted.

Canon 1493 (NA)

The local Ordinary shall be vigilant that the will of pious faithful as expressed in the foundational establishment be fully observed.

Canon 1494 (NA)

Without coming to the Apostolic See, these institutes cannot be suppressed, united, or converted to another use foreign to the foundation, unless this is provided for in the records of the foundation.

SIXTH PART
ON THE TEMPORAL GOODS OF THE CHURCH

Canon 1495[1] (1983 CIC 1255)

§ 1. The Catholic Church and the Apostolic See have the native right freely and independently from any civil power of acquiring, retaining, and administering temporal goods for the pursuit of their own ends.

§ 2. Individual churches and other moral persons that have been erected into juridic personality by ecclesiastical authority have the right, according to the norm of the sacred canons, of acquiring, retaining, and administrating temporal goods.

Canon Law Digest
I: 717; II: 443; III: 580; IV: 391; VI: 820–22; VIII: 1012

Canon 1496 (1983 CIC 1260)

The Church also has the right, independently of civil power, of requiring from the faithful what is necessary for divine cult, the honest sustenance of clerics and other ministers, and for the remaining ends proper to her.

Canon 1497 (1983 CIC 1257)

§ 1. Temporal goods, whether corporeal, both immovable and movable, or incorporeal, that belong to the universal Church and to the Apostolic See or to another moral person in the Church are *ecclesiastical goods*.

§ 2. They are called *sacred* if with consecration or blessing they are destined for divine cult; [they are called] *precious* if they are of notable value by reason of art, history, or material.

Canon Law Digest
I: 717; IX: 910

[1]John Goodwine, "The Right of the Church to Acquire Temporal Goods", Canon Law Studies, no. 131 (J. C. D. thesis, Catholic University of America, 1941); James Munday, "Ecclesiastical Property in Australia and New Zealand: An Historical Synopsis and Comparative Study of the General Law of the Church, Canons 1495–1551, and the Decrees of the Fourth Plenary Council of Australia, Decrees 653–685", Canon Law Studies, no. 387 (thesis, Catholic University of America, 1957).

Canon 1498 (1983 CIC 1258)

In the canons that follow, by the name of Church is signified not only the universal Church or the Apostolic See, but also any moral person in the Church whatsoever, unless from the context of the words or nature of the matter it appears otherwise.

TITLE 27
On acquiring ecclesiastical goods[2]

Canon 1499 (1983 CIC 1256, 1259)

§ 1. The Church can acquire temporal goods by any just manner of law, whether natural or positive, that is permitted to others.

§ 2. Dominion over goods, under the supreme authority of the Apostolic See, belongs to that moral person that has legitimately acquired them.

Canon Law Digest
II: 443–45

Canon 1500[3] (1983 CIC 122) Cross-Ref.: 1917 CIC 1427

The territorial division of an ecclesiastical moral person such that one part of it is united to another moral person or a distinct moral person is to be erected from the disconnected part must be done in due proportion to goodness and equity, so that the common goods that were destined for the use of the whole territory, and the alienations that were contracted for the whole territory, [are fairly divided] by the ecclesiastical authority in charge of the division, with due regard for the intentions of donors and founders,

[2] Chester Bartlett, "The Tenure of Parochial Property in the United States of America", Canon Law Studies, no. 31 (D.C.L. thesis, Catholic University of America, 1926); William Doheny, "Church Property: Modes of Acquisition", Canon Law Studies, no. 41 (J.U.D. thesis, Catholic University of America, 1927); Michael Kremer, "Church Support in the United States", Canon Law Studies, no. 61 (J. C. D. thesis, Catholic University of America, 1930).

[3] Eugene Kohls, "An Interpretation of Canon 1500: The Division of Property and Debts in the Division of a Territorial Moral Person" (Pontifical Lateran University, 1966).

legitimate acquired rights, and particular laws by which the moral person is regulated.

Canon Law Digest
I: 717–19

Canon 1501 (NA)

Upon the extinction of an ecclesiastical moral person, its goods transfer to the ecclesiastical moral person immediately superior, always with due regard for the will of the founders or donors and legitimately acquired rights, and for special laws by which the extinct moral person was ruled.

Canon Law Digest
II: 445

Canon 1502[4] (NA)

In what pertains to the payment of tenth-parts and the first fruits, the special statutes and laudable customs in each region are observed.

Canon Law Digest
I: 719

Canon 1503[5] (1983 CIC 1265)

With due regard for the prescription of Canons 621–24, it is forbidden that private persons, whether clerics or laity, collect [donations] for any pious or ecclesiastical institute or purpose without the permission of the Apostolic See or of their own Ordinary and the Ordinary of the place [where the collection occurs], given in writing.

Canon Law Digest
I: 719; III: 580; VIII: 1013

Canon 1504 (NA)

Every church and benefice subject to the jurisdiction of a Bishop, and likewise every confraternity of laity, must, each year as a sign of subjection to the Bishop, pay a cathedraticum that is, a moderate tax, to be deter-

[4] Terrance Berntson, "Tithing and Canon 1502: The Resurgence of this Canonical Notion in the United States of America" (excerpt, Pontifical Lateran University; Rome: Catholic Book Agency, 1965).

[5] Louis Meyer, "Alms-Gathering by Religious", Canon Law Studies, no. 220 (J. C. D. thesis, Catholic University of America, 1945).

mined according to the norm of Canon 1507, § 1, unless ancient custom has already determined [otherwise].

Canon Law Digest
I: 719–20

Canon 1505[6] (1983 CIC 1263)

The local Ordinary can impose an extraordinary and moderate exaction besides the tax for the Seminary mentioned in Canons 1355 and 1356 and the benefice pension mentioned in Canon 1429 on all beneficiaries, whether secular or religious, in light of special diocesan needs.

Canon 1506 (1983 CIC 1263)

The Ordinary can only impose another tax, for the good of the diocese or for patrons of the church, on benefices and other ecclesiastical institutes that are subject to him in the act of foundation or consecration; but there can be no tax placed on Mass offerings, whether manual or foundational.

Canon Law Digest
VII: 894–95

Canon 1507[7] (1983 CIC 1264) Cross-Refs.: 1917 CIC 59, 463, 736, 1504, 2349, 2408

§ 1. With due regard for the prescription of Canon 1056 and Canon 1234, it is for the provincial Council or a convention of Bishops of the province to set fees for the whole ecclesiastical province, the taxes to be paid upon various acts of voluntary jurisdiction or for the execution of rescripts of the Apostolic See or on the occasion of the administration of the Sacraments or Sacramentals; but regulations of this sort enjoy no force unless they have first been approved by the Apostolic See.

§ 2. As for what applies to taxes for judicial acts, the prescription of Canon 1909 is observed.

Canon Law Digest
I: 720–21; II: 445–47

---

[6] Donald Fruge, "The Taxation Practices of United States Bishops in Relation to the Authority of Bishops to Tax according to the Code of Canon Law and Proposed Revisions", Canon Law Studies, no. 506 (J. C. D. thesis, Catholic University of America, 1982).

[7] William Ferry, "Stole Fees", Canon Law Studies, no. 59 (J. C. D. thesis, Catholic University of America, 1930).

Canon 1508[8] (1983 CIC 1268) Cross-Refs.: 1917 CIC 1701, 1725

Prescription, whether as a way of acquiring [assets] or for liberating oneself [from obligations], is accepted by the Church for ecclesiastical goods in the same way [that it exists] in the civil legislation of the respective nations, with due regard for the prescription of the canons that follow.

Canon Law Digest
I: 721

Canon 1509 (1983 CIC 199) Cross-Ref.: 1917 CIC 1701

[The following] are not liable to prescription:

1.° Things that are of divine law, whether natural or positive;
2.° Things that can be obtained only by apostolic privilege;
3.° Spiritual rights for which laity are not capable, if it concerns prescription to the advantage of laity;
4.° The certain and undoubted limits of ecclesiastical provinces, dioceses, parishes, vicariates apostolic, apostolic prefectures, and abbeys or prelatures *of no one*;
5.° Offerings and burdens attached to Masses;
6.° Ecclesiastical benefices without title;
7.° The right of visitation and obedience, if it [would be such] that the subjects could not be visited by any Prelate and were not under any Prelate;
8.° The cathedraticum payment.

Canon Law Digest
I: 722

Canon 1510 (1983 CIC 1269) Cross-Ref.: 1917 CIC 1701

§ 1. Sacred things that are in private ownership can be acquired by private persons by prescription, but they nevertheless cannot be put to profane use; but if they have lost their consecration or blessing, they can be acquired even for profane use, though not [for] sordid [use].

§ 2. Sacred things that are not under private ownership cannot be prescribed by private persons, but [only] by an ecclesiastical moral person against another ecclesiastical moral person.

---

[8] Thomas Martin, "Adverse Possession, Prescription and Limitation of Actions: The Canonical *Praescriptio*", Canon Law Studies, no. 202 (J. C. D. thesis, Catholic University of America, 1944).

Canon 1511 (1983 CIC 1270) Cross-Ref.: 1917 CIC 1701

§ 1. Immovable things, precious movable things, rights, and actions, whether personal or real, that pertain to the Apostolic See are prescribed by a period of one hundred years.

§ 2. Those of another ecclesiastical moral person [are prescribed] by a period of thirty years.

Canon Law Digest
I: 722–24

Canon 1512[9] (1983 CIC 198) Cross-Ref.: 1917 CIC 1701

No prescription is valid unless it is marked by good faith not only from the beginning of possession but through the entire period of possession required for prescription.

Canon Law Digest
II: 447

Canon 1513[10] (1983 CIC 1299)

§ 1. Whoever by natural and ecclesiastical law can freely dispose of his goods can relinquish goods for pious causes, whether through a living act or through a will.

§ 2. In final wills in favor of the Church, there should be observed insofar as it is possible the formalities of civil law; if these are omitted, the heirs are to be advised that they should fulfill the will of the testator.

Canon Law Digest
I: 724–25; V: 704

Canon 1514 (1983 CIC 1300) Cross-Ref.: 1917 CIC 1549

The [intentions] of the faithful [who through a gift made by] the donation or the relinquishment for pious causes, whether through a living

---

[9] Charles Struve, "Whether an Error of Law Excludes Good Faith in Prescription" (diss. no. 41, Pontifical University of St. Thomas [Rome], 1954–1955).

[10] Jerome Hannan, "The Canon Law of Wills", Canon Law Studies, no. 86 (J. C. D. thesis, Catholic University of America, 1934); William Cahill, "Destination of Property to the Pious Cause" (Pontifical Lateran University, 1952); Carl Phillip Barth, "The Formalities of Last Wills in the Code of Canon Law and in the State of New Jersey" (Pontifical Lateran University, 1960); Joseph Lucas, "Gifts *inter Vivos* [between living persons] and *Mortis Causa* [upon death] to Pious Causes in Canon Law and Ohio Law" (Pontifical Lateran University, 1962); Feliciano Palma, "A Comparative Study of Wills in Canon Law and in the Civil Code of the Philippines", Canon Law Studies, no. 448 (J. C. D. thesis, Catholic University of America, 1945).

act or through a will, are to be fulfilled most diligently, even in regard to the manner of administration and distribution of goods, with due regard for the prescription of Canon 1515, § 3.

Canon Law Digest
II: 447

Canon 1515 (1983 CIC 1301) Cross-Refs.: 1917 CIC 1514, 1516, 1549

§ 1. Ordinaries are the executors of all pious wills, whether by will or between living persons.

§ 2. Ordinaries can and must guard this right even by visitation in order that pious wills be fulfilled, and other delegated executors must render an accounting to them upon the completion of their duty.

§ 3. Clauses attached to last wills that are contrary to the right of Ordinaries are considered as if not even added.

Canon Law Digest
I: 726; II: 447

Canon 1516 (1983 CIC 1302) Cross-Ref.: 1917 CIC 1549

§ 1. A cleric or religious who accepts a trust [consisting of] goods for a pious cause, whether by a living act or by a will, must inform the Ordinary of his entrustment and indicate all of the goods, whether mobile or immobile, that have burdens attached in this regard; but if the donor expressly and entirely prohibits [this notification, the cleric] shall not accept the trust.

§ 2. An Ordinary must require that entrusted goods be safely collected together and must be vigilant about the execution of a pious will according to the norm of Canon 1515.

§ 3. In regard to goods entrusted to a religious, if the goods are attributed to a place or diocesan church or for the assistance of residents or pious causes, the Ordinary mentioned in §§ 1 and 2 is the local Ordinary; otherwise, it is the Ordinary of those religious.

Canon Law Digest
I: 726

Canon 1517 (1983 CIC 1308) Cross-Refs.: 1917 CIC 1549, 1551

§ 1. The reduction, moderation, or commutation of final wills, which must be done only for a just and necessary cause, is reserved to the Apostolic See, unless the founder has expressly granted this power to the local Ordinary.

§ 2. If, however, the execution of imposed burdens, because of insufficient income or another cause through no fault of the administrator, becomes impossible, then the Ordinary, having heard those who have an interest and observing in the best way possible the will of the founder, can diminish equitably the burdens, except for the reduction of Masses that alone belongs always to the Apostolic See.

Canon Law Digest
I: 726; III: 580; VI: 822

TITLE 28
On the administration of ecclesiastical goods[11]

Canon 1518[12] (1983 CIC 1273)

The Roman Pontiff is the supreme administrator and dispenser of all ecclesiastical goods.

Canon Law Digest
II: 447; VI: 822.

Canon 1519 (1983 CIC 1276)

§ 1. The local Ordinary shall be sedulously vigilant about the administration of all ecclesiastical goods that are in his territory and that have not been taken from his jurisdiction, with due regard for legitimate prescriptions that give him more authority.

§ 2. In light of the rights, legitimate custom, and circumstances, Ordinaries, by the publication of opportune special instructions within the limits of common law, shall take care for the complete ordering of administration of ecclesiastical goods [and] affairs.

Canon Law Digest
I: 726–27; II: 447; VIII: 1013; IX: 911

[11] Harry Byrne, "Investment of Church Funds", Canon Law Studies, no. 309 (thesis, Catholic University of America, 1951).

[12] Joseph Comyns, "Papal and Episcopal Administration of Church Property", Canon Law Studies, no. 147 (J. C. D. thesis, Catholic University of America, 1942).

Canon 1520[13] (1983 CIC 492, 1277) Cross-Ref.: 1917 CIC 1415

§ 1. In order that this responsibility be rightly undertaken, every Ordinary in his episcopal city shall institute a Council over which he who is himself the Ordinary presides and [being associated with] two or more suitable men, expert insofar as possible also in civil law and selected by the Ordinary himself, having heard the Chapter, unless by law or particular custom or other equivalent legitimate manner, he has already made provision.

§ 2. Outside of apostolic indult, they are excluded from the responsibility of administration who are related to the local Ordinary in the first or second degree of consanguinity or affinity.

§ 3. The local Ordinary shall not fail to hear in administrative actions of greater moment the Council of administration; nevertheless, these members have only a consultative vote unless common law in express special cases or the documents of foundation require consent.

§ 4. The members of this Council shall give an oath in the presence of the Ordinary to fulfill their duty well and faithfully.

Canon Law Digest
III: 580

Canon 1521 (1983 CIC 1279, 1282) Cross-Ref.: 1917 CIC 1522

§ 1. Besides this diocesan Council of administration, the local Ordinary shall associate with provident men in the administration of goods that pertain to other churches or pious places and that by law or the documents of foundation do not have their own [Council] of administration, these men to be suitable and of good repute and who, upon the elapse of three years, are replaced with others, unless the circumstances of the place suggest otherwise.

§ 2. But if laity take any part in the administration of ecclesiastical goods either by legitimate foundation or title of erection or by the will of the local Ordinary, nevertheless, they shall conduct all administration in the name of the Church and with due regard for the right of visitation by the

[13] Augustus Saldhana, "The Diocesan Board of Administration" (diss. no. 34, Pontifical University of St. Thomas [Rome], 1958–1959).

Ordinary and his requirement of accounting and of prescribing the manner of administration.

Canon Law Digest
II: 447

Canon 1522 (1983 CIC 1283) Cross-Refs.: 1917 CIC 383, 1184, 1296

Before administrators enter into their office regarding ecclesiastical goods mentioned in Canon 1521:

1.° They must offer an oath to [conduct] well and faithfully their administration in the presence of the local Ordinary or the vicar forane;

2.° They must produce an accurate and detailed inventory of all subscriptions, immovable goods, precious movable goods, and other things, with a description and their valuation; or if they take an inventory already made, they shall note which things in the meantime have been lost or acquired;

3.° One copy of this sort of inventory is to be preserved in the records of administration, another in the archive of the Curia; and in both any change should be noted that touches [negatively] the patrimony.

Canon 1523[14] (1983 CIC 1284) Cross-Refs.: 1917 CIC 383, 1184

Administrators of ecclesiastical goods are bound to fulfill their duty as would a diligent head of a household; and therefore they must:

1.° Be vigilant lest the ecclesiastical goods entrusted to their care are lost in any way or suffer detriment;

2.° Observe the prescriptions of law, both canon and civil, and those things that were imposed by a founder or donor or legitimate authority;

3.° Collect the income from goods and the proceeds accurately, and at the correct time, and preserve them in a safe place and spend them according to the mind of the founder or established laws and norms;

[14] Consult the section entitled "Temporal Goods in the United States of America" in appendix 1: "Non-assigned Dissertations".

4.° Usefully collect the money of the church that remains after expenses and apply it to the benefit of the church with the consent of the Ordinary;
5.° Have well-organized books of receipts and expenses;
6.° Correctly arrange the documents and instruments by which the rights of the church regarding goods are based, and protect them in the archive of the church or in a convenient and useful safe; where it can be conveniently done, an authentic copy of these shall be deposited in the archive or safe of the Curia.

Canon 1524[15] (1983 CIC 1286)

All of those, especially clerics, religious, and administrators of ecclesiastical affairs, must assign to workers in the work at that place an honest and just payment; they must take care that there is time for pious things at a suitable point in time; in no way should they distract them from domestic care and a thrifty life-style or impose on them works that they are not able to do because it is the wrong sort or because of age or sex.

Canon Law Digest
V: 704

Canon 1525 (1983 CIC 1207) Cross-Refs.: 1917 CIC 691, 1182, 1549

§ 1. Reprobating every contrary custom, administrators, whether ecclesiastics or laity, of any church, even the cathedral or other pious places canonically erected, or confraternities, are bound by the office of rendering to the local Ordinary an account of the administration each year.

§ 2. If, because of particular law, these are supposed to render the accounting to others, then the local Ordinary or his delegate also should be admitted to read them, [in order that] these same administrators be freed of obligations in the matter.

Canon Law Digest
IX: 911

[15] Edward Reissner, "Canonical Employer-Employee Relationship: Canon 1524", Canon Law Studies, no. 427 (J. C. D. thesis, Catholic University of America, 1964).

Canon 1526[16] (1983 CIC 1288) Cross-Ref.: 1917 CIC 1653

Administrators shall not start litigation in the name of a church or answer such unless they have obtained the permission given in writing of the local Ordinary or at least, if the matter is urgent, of the vicar forane, who shall immediately inform the Ordinary of the permission granted.

Canon 1527[17] (1983 CIC 1281)

§ 1. Unless they have first sought the faculty of the local Ordinary to be given in writing, administrators invalidly place acts that exceed the limits and manner of ordinary administration.

§ 2. The church is not bound to respond to contracts entered into by administrators without the permission of the competent Superior, unless and insofar as it is to her advantage.

Canon 1528 (1983 CIC 1289)

Even if they are not bound by title of benefice or ecclesiastical office to administration, administrators who expressly or tacitly take up a duty and put it down by their own decision in such a way that damage to the church results are bound to restitution.

TITLE 29
On contracts

Canon 1529[18] (1983 CIC 1290)

Whatever the civil law establishes in a territory concerning contracts, whether in general or in specific, whether nominate or innominate, and about resolution, is to be observed in canon law in ecclesiastical materials

[16] Thomas Kilcullen, "The Collegiate Moral Person as Party Litigant", Canon Law Studies, no. 251 (thesis, Catholic University of America, 1947).

[17] Gualtiero Mamh, "The Notion of Extraordinary Administration of Ecclesiastical Temporalities" (Pontifical Lateran University, 1954).

[18] Joseph de Vrin, "Canonical Origins of Contract Principles in Anglo-American Law" (Pontifical Lateran University, 1959).

with the same effects, unless this is contrary to divine law or canon law provides otherwise.

Canon Law Digest
I: 727; IX: 911

Canon 1530[19] (1983 CIC 1291–93) Cross-Ref.: 1917 CIC 1533

§ 1. With due regard for the prescription of Canon 1281, § 1, for the alienation of ecclesiastical goods, whether immobile or mobile, that are such that they should be preserved, there is required:

1.° An estimation of the thing by thoughtful experts done in writing;
2.° Just cause, that is, urgent necessity, or evident utility to the Church, or piety;
3.° Permission of the legitimate Superior, without which the alienation is invalid.

§ 2. Other opportune cautions to be prescribed by the Superior himself for various circumstances shall not be omitted in order that damage to the Church is avoided.

Canon Law Digest
I: 727; IX: 911

Canon 1531 (1983 CIC 1294) Cross-Refs.: 1917 CIC 534, 1533, 1541

§ 1. Property shall not be alienated for a smaller price than the one indicated in the estimate.

§ 2. Alienation shall be made by public solicitation or at least having given notice, unless circumstances suggest otherwise; and the thing should be given to him who, all things considered, pays the most.

§ 3. Money from an alienation shall be cautiously taken and carefully and usefully put to the advantage of the Church.

Canon Law Digest
I: 728; III: 580–81

[19] Joseph Cleary, "Canonical Limitations on the Alienation of Church Property", Canon Law Studies, no. 100 (J. C. D. thesis, Catholic University of America, 1936); Edward Heston, "The Alienation of Church Property in the United States", Canon Law Studies, no. 132 (J. C. D. thesis, Catholic University of America, 1941).

Canon 1532 (1983 CIC 1293) Cross-Refs.: 1917 CIC 1533, 1538, 1541–42, 1653, 2347

§ 1. The legitimate Superior mentioned in Canon 1530, § 1, n. 3 is the Apostolic See if it concerns:

1.° Precious things;

2.° Things whose value exceeds thirty thousand lira or francs.

§ 2. If it concerns things whose value does not exceed one thousand lira or francs, it is the local Ordinary, having heard the Council of administration, unless the thing is of minimal importance, and with the consent of those who are interested.

§ 3. If, finally, the price of the goods falls between one thousand lira and thirty thousand lira or francs, it is the local Ordinary, provided he has the consent either of the cathedral Chapter or of the Council of administration, and of those who are interested.

§ 4. If it concerns the alienation of divisible things, in requesting the permission or consent for alienation there must be expressed those parts alienated beforehand; otherwise the permission is invalid.

Canon Law Digest

I: 728–31; II: 447–48; III: 581; IV: 391–93; V: 704; VI: 822–23; VII: 895; IX: 911

Canon 1533[20] (1983 CIC 1295)

Formalities according to the norm of Canons 1530–32 are required not only in alienation properly so called, but also in any contract in which the condition of the Church can be made worse.

Canon Law Digest

II: 448

Canon 1534 (1983 CIC 1296)

§ 1. The Church has a personal action against him who alienates, without the required formalities, ecclesiastical goods and against his heirs; but [she has] a real [action] if the alienation was not [done correctly] against any possessor, with due regard for the rights of a buyer [in a case of] bad alienation.

[20] Joseph Stenger, "The Mortgaging of Church Property" Canon Law Studies, no. 169 (J. C. D. thesis, Catholic University of America, 1942); Eufemio de la Cruz, "The Leasing of Church Properties in the Philippines", Canon Law Studies, no. 411 (Catholic University of America, not published).

§ 2. Against an invalid alienation of ecclesiastical goods, he who alienated the goods may challenge it, [as can] his Superior and the successor of either in office, as well as any cleric assigned to that church that suffered harm.

Canon 1535 (1983 CIC 1285)

Prelates and rectors shall not presume to make donations out of the mobile goods of their churches beyond small and moderate ones according to the legitimate custom of the place, unless just cause intervenes, for the sake of remuneration or piety or Christian charity; otherwise, the donation can be revoked by his successors.

Canon 1536 (1983 CIC 1267)

§ 1. Unless the contrary is proven, it is presumed that those things given to the rectors of churches, even religious ones, are donated to the church.

§ 2. A donation made to the church cannot be refused by its rector or Superior without the permission of the Ordinary.

§ 3. An action for restitution in the entirety or indemnity is given for damages that follow from the illegitimate refusal of a gift.

§ 4. A donation made to a church and legitimately accepted by it cannot be revoked because of an ungrateful spirit on the part of the Prelate or rector.

Canon Law Digest
I: 731–32

Canon 1537 (1983 CIC 1171)

Sacred things shall not be made available for uses that are repugnant to their nature.

Canon 1538 (NA)

§ 1. If the goods of a church, upon legitimate cause, are to be obliged by pledge or loan, or if it concerns the contracting of a debt by alienation, the legitimate Superior who must give the permission according to the norm of Canon 1532 shall require beforehand that all those who are interested be heard and shall take care that, as soon as possible, the alienation debt be repaid.

§ 2. For this purpose, the annual repayment by which the debt is scheduled to be paid off shall be defined by the same Ordinary.

Canon 1539 (NA)

§ 1. In the sale or exchange of sacred things, no account of the consecration or benediction can be included in the estimate of the price.

§ 2. Administrators can exchange *titles to the bearer*, as they are called, for other titles that are more or at least the same in their degree of safety and profitability, excluding any form of commercialism or negotiating, and with the consent of the Ordinary and of the diocesan Council of administration and of others with an interest.

Canon 1540 (1983 CIC 1298)

Immovable goods of a church are not to be sold or leased to their own administrators and those related to them in the first or second degree of consanguinity or affinity without the special permission of the local Ordinary.

Canon 1541 (1983 CIC 1297)

§ 1. A contract for the lease of ecclesiastical land shall not be done except according to the norm of Canon 1531, § 2; and in these there shall always be added limitations on the boundaries [to be observed, and] regarding good cultivation, and the correct repayment of the amount due, along with opportune precautions for the fulfillment of these conditions.

§ 2. For the lease of ecclesiastical goods, the prescription of Canon 1479 is observed, [and]:

1.° If the value of the lease exceeds thirty thousand lira or francs and the lease is for more than nine years, apostolic good pleasure is required; if the lease is not for more than nine years, the prescription of Canon 1532, § 3, must be observed;

2.° If the value falls between one thousand lira and thirty thousand lira or francs and the lease is for more than nine years, the prescription of the same Canon 1532, § 3, must be observed; if the lease is not beyond nine years, the prescription of the same Canon 1532, § 2 [is observed];

3.° If the value does not exceed one thousand lira or francs and the lease is beyond nine years, the same prescription of Canon 1532, § 2, must be observed; if the lease is not for more than nine years it can be done by the legitimate administrators having informed the Ordinary.

Canon 1542 (NA)

§ 1. In the emphyteusis of ecclesiastical goods, the [lessee] cannot repay the amount due without the permission of the legitimate ecclesiastical Superior mentioned in Canon 1532; if he does repay [early], he must pay an amount of money to the church that corresponds with [the amount due].

§ 2. There shall be required from the [lessee] security for the repayment of the amount due and the fulfillment of conditions; in the document of emphyteusis agreement itself the ecclesiastical forum will be established as the arbiter to settle controversies between the parties that might arise and shall expressly declare the waiver of all improvements.

Canon Law Digest
I: 732–33

Canon 1543 (NA)

If a fungible thing is given to another so that it becomes his, and later it must be restored in the same sort, no profit can by made by reason of the contract; but in the loan of a fungible thing, it is not by itself illicit to reap a legal profit, unless it can be shown to be immoderate of itself, and even greater profit [can be made] if there is a just and proportionate title so supporting.

TITLE 30
On pious foundations

Canon 1544[21] (1983 CIC 1303)

§ 1. By the name of pious foundation there are signified those temporal goods given in any way to some moral person in the Church with the obligation, in perpetuity or for a long time, to celebrate some Masses for the proceeds, or to perform some other identified ecclesiastical functions, or to conduct pious or charitable works.

[21] Newton Miller, "Founded Masses according to the Code of Canon Law", Canon Law Studies, no. 34 (thesis, Catholic University of America, 1926).

§ 2. A foundation, legitimately accepted, by its nature parallels the contract formula: *I give that you may do.*

Canon Law Digest
III: 582

Canon 1545 (1983 CIC 1304) Cross-Ref.: 1917 CIC 1550

It is for the local Ordinary to establish norms regarding the amount of endowment below which a pious foundation cannot be accepted, and about the correct distribution of its fruits.

Canon 1546 (1983 CIC 1304) Cross-Ref.: 1917 CIC 1550

§ 1. In order that foundations of this sort be accepted by a moral person, the consent of the local Ordinary is required given in writing, [though] he shall not give it before he has legitimately shown that the moral person is able to satisfy the new obligations to be taken up along with older ones already assumed; and he shall be especially cautious that the endowment covers all of the burdens attached to it according to the usage of the diocese.

§ 2. A patron of the church has no right in the acceptance, constitution, or administration of the foundation.

Canon 1547 (1983 CIC 1305) Cross-Ref.: 1917 CIC 1550

Money and movable goods assigned to the endowment shall immediately be placed in a safe place to be designated by the same Ordinary for this purpose, and the money and precious mobile goods shall be kept there and as soon as possible applied cautiously and usefully according to the prudent judgment of the same Ordinary, having heard those who have an interest and the diocesan Council of administration, to the benefit of the foundation, with express and individual mention of the burdens.

Canon 1548 (1983 CIC 1306) Cross-Ref.: 1917 CIC 1550

§ 1. Foundations, even those made orally, are to be reduced to writing.

§ 2. One copy of the documents shall be carefully preserved in the archive of the Curia, the other in the archive of the moral person to whom the foundation looks.

Canon 1549 (1983 CIC 1307) Cross-Ref.: 1917 CIC 1550

§ 1. With due regard for the prescription of Canons 1514–17 and Canon 1525, in every church a register of the burdens that are incumbent upon a pious foundation shall be made, which will be preserved in a safe place by the rector.

§ 2. Likewise, besides the book mentioned in Canon 843, § 1, another book shall be retained and preserved by the rector in which there is noted each perpetual and temporary burden and its completion and offering so that all of these can be reported exactly to the local Ordinary.

Canon 1550 (NA)

If it concerns a pious foundation in a church, even a parish church, [belonging to] exempt religious, the rights and duties of the local Ordinary, mentioned in Canons 1545–49, belong exclusively to the major Superior.

Canon Law Digest
I: 733

Canon 1551 (1983 CIC 1308)

§ 1. The reduction of burdens that weigh on a pious foundation is reserved only to the Apostolic See, unless in the documents of foundation something else is expressly stated, and with due regard for the prescription of Canon 1517, § 2.

§ 2. An indult for reducing founded Masses is not extended to other Masses owed by the contract or to the other pious works of the foundation.

§ 3. But a general indult of reducing the burdens in a pious foundation should be understood, unless otherwise evident, in such a way that the indult prefers that works other than Masses be reduced.

Canon Law Digest
I: 734–36; III: 582; VI: 823

FOURTH BOOK
ON PROCEDURES

FIRST PART
ON TRIALS

Canon 1552 (1983 CIC 1400)

§ 1. By the term ecclesiastical trial there is understood those controversies over which the Church has the right of adjudication, in the presence of an ecclesiastical tribunal, legitimately discussed and decided.

§ 2. The objects of a trial are:

1.° The prosecution and vindication of the rights of the physical or moral persons or juridic declarations made concerning such persons; and this kind of trial is called *contentious*;

2.° Crimes duly assessed for the imposition or declaration of penalties; and this kind of trial is called *criminal*.

Canon Law Digest
I: 739; III: 585–87; VII: 899–901;
VIII: 1017–31; IX: 915

Canon 1553[1] (1983 CIC 1401)

§ 1. By proper and exclusive right the Church takes cognizance of:

1.° Cases concerning spiritual things and things connected to the spiritual;

2.° The violation of ecclesiastical law as well as all things involving sin, insofar as it applies to the definition of fault and the imposition of ecclesiastical penalties;

3.° All cases, whether contentious or criminal, that affect persons enjoying the privilege of the forum according to the norm of Canons 120, 614, and 680.

---

[1] John Bourque, "The Judicial Power of the Church–Canon 1553 § 1", Canon Law Studies, no. 337 (thesis, Catholic University of America, 1953).

§ 2. In those cases in which both the Church and the civil power are equally competent, [basically, those cases] called mixed forum, the law of prevention operates.

Canon Law Digest
I: 740; III: 587–99; VII: 901–5; VIII: 1031

Canon 1554 (NA)

A petitioner who carries off cases of mixed forum [already] presented to an ecclesiastical tribunal to a secular court for adjudication can be punished with appropriate penalties according to the norm of Canon 2222 and is deprived of the right of acting against the same persons in that matter and in related cases in an ecclesiastical forum.

Canon Law Digest
VIII: 1032

Canon 1555 (1983 CIC 1402) Cross-Ref.: 1917 CIC 1703

§ 1. The tribunal of the Congregation of the H. Office proceeds by its own usage and institutes and retains its own proper customs; lower tribunals also, in cases that concern the tribunal of the H. Office, should follow the norms given out by it.

§ 2. Other tribunals must observe the prescriptions of the canons that follow.

§ 3. In a trial about the dismissal of religious the prescriptions of Canons 654–68 are observed.

SECTION 1
ON TRIALS IN GENERAL

TITLE 1
On the competent forum[2]

Canon 1556 (1983 CIC 1404) Cross-Ref.: 1917 CIC 1558

The First See is judged by no one.

Canon Law Digest
VIII: 1032

[2] Thomas Burke, "Competence in Ecclesiastical Tribunals", Canon Law Studies, no. 14 (J. C. D. thesis, Catholic University of America, 1922).

Canon 1557 (1983 CIC 1405) Cross-Refs.: 1917 CIC 1558, 1599, 1962, 2227

§ 1. It belongs only to the Roman Pontiff to adjudicate:

1.° Those who have the supreme governing power of people, and their sons and daughters, and others who are next in the line of succession to power;

2.° Cardinal Fathers;

3.° Legates of the Apostolic See and, in criminal cases, Bishops, even titular ones.

§ 2. It is reserved to tribunals of the Apostolic See to judge:

1.° Residential Bishops in contentious cases, with due regard for the prescription of Canon 1572, § 2;

2.° Dioceses and other ecclesiastical moral persons that do not have a Superior below the Roman Pontiff, such as exempt religious, monastic Congregations, and so on.

§ 3. The Roman Pontiff may call other cases to himself to judge, and the Roman Pontiff may himself designate the judge.

Canon Law Digest
I: 740; II: 451

Canon 1558 (1983 CIC 1406)

In the cases mentioned in Canons 1556 and 1557, the incompetence of other judges is [called] *absolute.*

Canon 1559 (1983 CIC 1407)

§ 1. No one can be convened in first instance except before an ecclesiastical judge who is competent because of one of the titles determined in Canons 1560–68.

§ 2. The incompetence of the judge to whom none of these titles applies is called *relative.*

§ 3. A petitioner follows the forum of the respondent; but if the respondent has several fora, the choice is granted to the petitioner.

Canon Law Digest
I: 741

Canon 1560 (1983 CIC 1413)

There is a necessary forum over:

1.° Actions of spoliation, in the court of the Ordinary of the place where the thing is located;

2.° Cases respecting benefices, even if non-residential, in the court of the Ordinary of the place where the benefice is;

3.° Cases concerning administration, in the court of the Ordinary of the place where the administration is conducted;

4.° Cases concerning inheritance or pious legacies, in the court of the Ordinary of the place where the testator has a domicile, unless it concerns merely the execution of the legacy, in which case it is to be seen to according to the ordinary norms of competence.

Canon Law Digest
VIII: 1032

Canon 1561 (1983 CIC 1408)

§ 1. By reason of domicile or quasi-domicile, one can be convened in the court of the local Ordinary.

§ 2. An Ordinary has jurisdiction over his subjects based on domicile or quasi-domicile, even if they are absent.

Canon Law Digest
I: 741; VIII: 1033; IX: 915

Canon 1562 (NA)

§ 1. One who is traveling in the City, although there only for a short period, can be cited therein as if in his own domicile; but such a one has the right of calling upon his own domicile, that is, of asking that the case be remitted to his proper Ordinary.

§ 2. One who has been in the City for one year has the right of declining the forum of the Ordinary and insisting that he be cited in the court of the City.

Canon 1563 (1983 CIC 1409)

A vagrant has his own forum in the place where he actually is; [likewise] a religious in the place of his own house.

Canon 1564 (1983 CIC 1410)

By reason of the location of a thing, a party can be convened in the court of the Ordinary of the place where the litigated thing is located, as long as the action is directed at the thing.

Canon 1565 (1983 CIC 1411)

§ 1. By reason of contract, a party can be convened in the court of the Ordinary of the place wherein the contract was entered or where it is to be fulfilled.

§ 2. In drafting a contract, it is permitted to the contractants to choose a place in which, even if they are absent, they can be cited and convened in order to declare the obligations, or urge or fulfill the [agreement].

Canon Law Digest
I: 741

Canon 1566 (1983 CIC 1412)

§ 1. By reason of delict, a respondent is susceptible to the forum where the delict was committed.

§ 2. Even if a respondent leaves the place after the commission of the delict, the judge of the place has the right of citing him to appear and of giving sentence over him.

Canon Law Digest
I: 741

Canon 1567 (1983 CIC 1414)

By reason of connection or contents, cases connected among themselves should be heard by the same judge, unless a prescription of law obstructs.

Canon 1568 (1983 CIC 1415)

By reason of prevention, when two or more judges are equally competent, the right of hearing the case goes to the one who first cited the respondent.

Canon Law Digest
II: 451

TITLE 2
On the various grades and types of tribunals

Canon 1569 (1983 CIC 1417) Cross-Ref.: 1917 CIC 1597

§ 1. Because of the primacy of the Roman Pontiff, it is fundamental to every member of the faithful throughout the Catholic world that they have the right of sending any case, criminal or contentious, in any level of trial and at any stage of the proceeding, to the Holy See for adjudication and of introducing it there.

§ 2. Recourse interposed to the Apostolic See, however, does not suspend the exercise of jurisdiction by the judge who has already begun to judge it, except in cases of appeal; therefore the [first] judge can continue to pursue the case even to definitive sentence unless the Apostolic See calls the case to itself.

Canon Law Digest
VIII: 1033–34

Canon 1570[3] (1983 CIC 1418) Cross-Ref.: 1917 CIC 1770

§ 1. Except for those cases reserved to the Apostolic See or called to it, all others are treated by various tribunals as discussed in Canons 1572 and foll[owing].

§ 2. Nevertheless, any tribunal, in what pertains to the examination or citation of parties or witnesses, or inspection of documents of controverted things, and the intimation of decrees about these, has the right of calling for help from another tribunal, in which case the prescribed norms for individual juridic acts are to be followed.

Canon Law Digest
I: 741; VII: 905–29; VIII: 1034–36; IX: 916–18

Canon 1571 (1983 CIC 1447)

Whoever acts in a case in one grade of judgment cannot judge the same case in another [grade].

Canon Law Digest
VII: 929

---

[3] Marion Reinhardt, "The Rogatory Commission", Canon Law Studies, no. 288 (thesis, Catholic University of America, 1949); James Searson, "The Forum of Prorogation" (MS no. 2200, Gregorian University, 1954; printed version, no. 869, 1954).

Chapter 1

On the ordinary tribunal of first instance[4]

Article 1 — *On the Judge*

Canon 1572 (1983 CIC 1419) Cross-Refs.: 1917 CIC 274, 1557, 1578

§ 1. In every diocese and for every case not expressly excepted by law, the local Ordinary is the judge of first instance, who can exercise judicial power himself or through others, according to the canons that follow.

§ 2. But if it concerns the rights or temporal goods of Bishops or diocesan or Curial [assets], for resolution the matter shall be referred either, with the Bishop's consent, to the collegial diocesan tribunal, which consists of the [judicial vicar] and the two most senior synodal judges, or to the judge immediately superior.

Canon Law Digest
II: 451–52; VIII: 1037–39; X: 211–14

Canon 1573 (1983 CIC 1420, 1422)

§ 1. Every bishop is bound to choose an officialis with the ordinary power of judging, distinct from the Vicar General, unless the smallness of the diocese or the paucity of cases persuades that this office should be committed to the Vicar General.

§ 2. The officialis constitutes one tribunal with the Bishop of the place; but he cannot judge cases that the Bishop reserves to himself.

§ 3. The officialis can be given assistants, who have the name vice-officialis.

§ 4. Both the officialis and vice-officialis must be priests, of intact reputation, doctors or otherwise expert in canon law, and not be less than thirty years of age.

§ 5. They are removable at the discretion of the Bishop; when the see is vacant, they do not cease from office, nor can they be removed by the Vicar Capitulary; but upon arrival of the new Bishop, they need confirmation.

---

[4] Henry Dugan, "The Judiciary Department of the Diocesan Curia", Canon Law Studies, no. 26 (J. C. D. thesis, Catholic University of America, 1925); William Vaughan, "Constitutions for Diocesan Courts", Canon Law Studies, no. 210 (J. C. D. thesis, Catholic University of America, 1944).

§ 6. When the same person is both Vicar General and officialis, during the vacancy of the see, [he] ceases office as Vicar [General], but not as officialis.

§ 7. If the officialis is elected Vicar Capitulary, he chooses a new officialis.

Canon Law Digest
I: 742; II: 452; VII: 929–30; VIII: 1039; X: 214–16

Canon 1574[5] (1983 CIC 1421–22)

§ 1. In each diocese, presbyters of proven life and expert in canon law, even from outside the diocese, though not more than twelve, are to be chosen, so that they can take part in the judicial power delegated by the Bishop in adjudicating cases; these are known by the name of *synodal judge* or *pro-synodal* [*judge*], if they were constituted outside the Synod.

§ 2. As for what applies to their election, substitution, cessation, or removal from duty, the prescriptions of Canons 385–88 are to be observed.

§ 3. Under the name of synodal judge there are, in the law, also included the pro-synodal judges.

Canon Law Digest
I: 742; VII: 930; VIII: 1039–40

Canon 1575 (1983 CIC 1424)

A single judge can add to himself two consulting assessors in any trial; these must be selected from among the synodal judges.

Canon Law Digest
I: 742; VII: 930

Canon 1576 (1983 CIC 1425) Cross-Refs.: 1917 CIC 1892, 1966

§ 1. Reprobating contrary custom and revoking any contrary privilege of any sort:

1.° Contentious cases about the bond of sacred ordination and marriage, or the rights and temporal goods of cathedral churches; and likewise criminal cases in which the defendant is subject to privation of an irremovable benefice or the imposition or declaration of excommunication are reserved to a collegial tribunal of three judges;

[5] George Graham, "Synodal and Pro-synodal Judges", Canon Law Studies, no. 452 (Catholic University of America, 1967).

2.° But cases that concern delicts for which deposition, perpetual privation of ecclesiastical habit, or the penalty of degradation [could be imposed] are reserved to a collegial tribunal of five judges.

§ 2. The local Ordinary can commit other cases to adjudication by a collegial tribunal of three or five judges and he ought to do so especially whenever it concerns cases that, in light of the times, places, or condition of persons and matters to be judged, seem more difficult or of greater importance.

§ 3. The Ordinary shall select, unless in his own prudence he considers it opportune otherwise, by turn among the synodal judges, two or four judges who, together with the president, constitute a tribunal.

Canon Law Digest
I: 742; II: 452; VII: 930–31; X: 217–18

Canon 1577[6] (1983 CIC 1426)

§ 1. A collegial tribunal must proceed collegially and pass sentence according to the greater part of the votes.

§ 2. It is for the same officialis or vice-officialis to preside over and direct the process and to decide those things that are necessary for the administration of justice in the case.

Canon Law Digest
VIII: 1040

Canon 1578 (NA)

Except for the cases mentioned in Canon 1572, § 2, the Bishop can always preside over the tribunal himself; but it is greatly expedient that he leave the judging of cases, especially criminal and contentious ones of great moment, to the ordinary tribunal, over which the officialis or vice-officialis presides.

Canon Law Digest
II: 453

[6] Avitus Lyons, "The Collegiate Tribunal of First Instance", Canon Law Studies, no. 78 (J. C. D. thesis, Catholic University of America, 1932).

Canon 1579 (1983 CIC 1427) Cross-Refs.: 1917 CIC 1594, 1658

§ 1. If the controversy is between exempt religious or between the same clerical religious [institute], the judge of first instance, unless provided otherwise in the constitutions, is the provincial Superior or, if it is a monastery of its own right, the local Abbot.

§ 2. With due regard for the prescription of the constitution, if it concerns a contentious matter between two provinces, the supreme Moderator of the religious [institute] will judge personally or through a delegate; if it is between two monasteries, the supreme Moderator of the monastic Congregation [judges].

§ 3. If, finally, controversy emerges between physical or moral religious persons of diverse religious [institutes], or between religious of the same non-exempt [religious institute] or laity, or between a secular or religious cleric and a layman, the judge of first instance is the local Ordinary.

Canon Law Digest
I: 743

Article 2—*On Auditors and Reporters*

Canon 1580 (1983 CIC 1428)

§ 1. The Ordinary can constitute one or several auditors, that is, instructors of the case, whether with stability or for a certain specific case.

§ 2. The judge can select an auditor only for a case he is hearing, unless the Ordinary provides otherwise.

Canon Law Digest
II: 453

Canon 1581 (1983 CIC 1428)

Auditors for the diocesan tribunal, insofar as possible, are to be taken from the synodal judges; but for the tribunal of religious, they must always be members of the religious [institute] according to the norm of the constitutions.

Canon Law Digest
I: 743

Canon 1582 (1983 CIC 1428)

They can cite and hear witnesses, and instruct other judicial acts according to the tenor of their mandate, but they cannot pass definitive sentence.

Canon 1583 (NA)

An auditor can be removed from office at any stage of the trial by the one who appointed him, for a just cause, and without prejudice to the parties.

Canon 1584[7] (1983 CIC 1429) Cross-Ref.: 1917 CIC 1872

The president of a collegial tribunal must designate one of the collegial judges to be the ponens or relator who presents matters in committee [discussions] about the case and who reduces to writing the sentences; and the same president can substitute another [ponens] for a just cause.

Canon Law Digest
II: 453

Article 3—*On the Notary, Promoter of justice, and Defender of the bond*

Canon 1585[8] (1983 CIC 1437)

§ 1. There shall be a notary involved in every process who acts in the office of actuary; consequently, those acts are considered null that were not produced by the hand of the notary, or at least were not signed by him.

§ 2. Wherefore the judge, before taking cognizance of a case, must select an actuary from among the notaries legitimately constituted, unless the Ordinary himself has already designated one for a case.

Canon Law Digest
I: 743; II: 453

---

[7] John Metz, "The Recording Judge in the Ecclesiastical Collegiate Tribunal", Canon Law Studies, no. 287 (thesis, Catholic University of America, 1949).

[8] Harry Trower, "The Actuary in Ecclesiastical Judicial Procedure" (University of Laval, 1947); Charles Duerr, "The Judicial Notary", Canon Law Studies, no. 312 (thesis, Catholic University of America, 1951).

Canon 1586[9] (1983 CIC 1430,1432) Cross-Ref.: 1917 CIC 1967

There shall be constituted in a diocese a *promoter of justice* and a *defender of the bond*; the former [acts] in cases, whether contentious in which the public good, in the judgment of the Ordinary, can be called into question, or in criminal cases; the latter [acts] in cases in which the bond of sacred ordination or matrimony is concerned.

Canon Law Digest
I: 743–44; VIII: 1040–43

Canon 1587 (1983 CIC 1433) Cross-Ref.: 1917 CIC 2010

§ 1. In cases in which his presence is required, [if] the promoter of justice or the defender of the bond is not cited, the acts are invalid unless he, even though not cited, actually participated.

§ 2. If, [although] legitimately cited, they do not participate in certain acts, the acts are still valid, although they must be subjected to their careful examination and they must be allowed, either orally or in writing, to make observations and to propose anything that they judge to be necessary or opportune.

Canon Law Digest
I: 744; II: 453; VII: 931–32

Canon 1588 (1983 CIC 1436)

§ 1. The same person can hold the office of promoter of justice and defender of the bond unless from a multiplicity of affairs and cases this is prohibited.

§ 2. The promoter and the defender can be constituted both for a universe of cases and for individual cases.

Canon Law Digest
II: 453

---

[9] Philip Pocock, "The Defender of the Matrimonial Bond" (diss. no. 1, Pontifical University of St. Thomas [Rome], 1933–1934); John Dolan, "The *Defensor Vinculi* [defender of the bond], His Rights and Duties", Canon Law Studies, no. 85 (J. C. D. thesis, Catholic University of America, 1934); John Glynn, "The Promoter of Justice, His Rights and Duties", Canon Law Studies, no. 101 (J. C. D. thesis, Catholic University of America, 1936); John Meszaros, "The Present and Possible Functions of the Promoter of Justice in Administrative Procedures of the Church" (diss. no. 5, Pontifical University of St. Thomas [Rome], 1977–1978).

Canon 1589 (1983 CIC 1435) Cross-Ref.: 1917 CIC 655

§ 1. It is for the Ordinary to select the promoter of justice and defender of the bond; [these] shall be priests of intact reputation, doctors of canon law or otherwise expert, and proven for prudence and zeal for justice.

§ 2. In the tribunal of a religious [institute], the promoter of justice must also be a member of the religious [institute].

Canon Law Digest

I: 744; VII: 932; VIII: 1043–47; IX: 918–19

Canon 1590 (1983 CIC 1436)

§ 1. The promoter of justice and the defender of the bond appointed for a universe of cases do not cease from responsibility upon the vacancy of the see, nor can they be removed by a Vicar Capitulary; the new Prelate arriving, however, they need confirmation.

§ 2. A just cause interceding, however, the Bishop can remove them.

Article 4—*On Couriers and Messengers*

Canon 1591 (NA)

§ 1. For the communication of judicial acts, unless there is another approved custom in the tribunal, couriers shall be constituted, whether for all cases or for particular cases; likewise, messengers [shall be constituted] for the required execution of the sentences and judicial decrees committed to them.

§ 2. The same person can function in both offices.

Canon 1592 (NA)

They shall be laity, unless prudence in some case suggests that the responsibility should be assumed by an ecclesiastic; but as for what pertains to their appointment, suspension, and revocation, the same rules established for notaries in Canon 373 shall be observed.

Canon 1593 (NA)

The acts that they prepare are worthy of public trust.

Chapter 2
On the ordinary tribunal of second instance

Canon 1594 (1983 CIC 1438) Cross-Refs.: 1917 CIC 274, 501

§ 1. From the tribunal of a Suffragan Bishop there is appeal to the Metropolitan.

§ 2. From a case conducted in first instance in the tribunal of the Metropolitan, there is appeal to the local Ordinary whom that Metropolitan, with the approval of the Apostolic See, has designated once for all.

§ 3. For causes first treated in the tribunal of an Archbishop who lacks Suffragans, [and] for the tribunal of a local Ordinary immediately subject to the Apostolic See, there is appeal to the Metropolitan mentioned in Canon 285.

§ 4. Among exempt religious, for all cases [treated] in the tribunal of the provincial Superior, the tribunal of second instance is [that of] the supreme Moderator; for cases [treated] in the tribunal of a local Abbot, it is [that of] the supreme Moderator of the monastic Congregation; but for cases mentioned in Canon 1579, § 3, the prescription of §§ 1, 2, 3 of this canon is observed.

Canon Law Digest
I: 744; III: 599; IV: 397–98; V: 707;
VI: 827; VII: 932; X: 218–19

Canon 1595 (1983 CIC 1441)

The tribunal of appeal must be constituted in the same manner as the tribunal of first instance; and the same rules, accommodated to the matter, are to be observed in the discussion of the case.

Canon Law Digest
VIII: 1047–48

Canon 1596 (1983 CIC 1441)

If a case was treated collegially in first instance, it shall also [be treated] collegially in the appellate grade, nor must it be decided by a smaller number of judges.

CHAPTER 3
On the ordinary tribunals of the Apostolic See

Canon 1597 (1983 CIC 1442)

The Roman Pontiff is the supreme judge for the whole Catholic world according to the norm of Canon 1569, [and] he pronounces law personally through himself, or through tribunals constituted by him, or through judges delegated by him.

Canon Law Digest
VIII: 1048–54

Article 1—*On the Sacred Roman Rota*

Canon 1598 (1983 CIC 1443)

§ 1. The ordinary tribunal constituted by the Holy See for receiving appeals is the Sacred Roman Rota, which is a collegial tribunal containing a certain number of Auditors over whom presides a Dean, who is a first among equals.

§ 2. These priests must have doctoral degrees at least in both [canon and civil] law.

§ 3. The selection of Auditors is reserved to the Roman Pontiff.

§ 4. The Sacred Rota works justice either through individual groups of three Auditors or in the presence of all [Auditors], unless the Supreme Pontiff constitutes otherwise for some case.

Canon Law Digest
II: 453–58; III: 599–603; V: 707; VI: 827; VII: 933;
VIII: 1055–79; IX: 920–48; X: 219–48

Canon 1599 (1983 CIC 1444)

§ 1. The Sacred Rota judges:

1.° In second instance, cases that have come from the tribunals of any Ordinaries in the first grade and were sent hither by legitimate appeal to the Holy See;

2.° In the final instance, cases already treated by the same Sacred Rota and by other tribunals in the second or last instance, [but] that have not become adjudicated matters.

§ 2. This tribunal judges also in first instance [cases] mentioned in Canon 1557, § 2, and others that the Roman Pontiff, either on his own or at the request of a party, calls to his tribunal and commits to the Sacred Rota; and these, unless otherwise provided in the rescript of commission, the Sacred Rota judges also in the second and third instance by turns that succeed each other.

Canon Law Digest
I: 744–46; II: 459–60; IV: 398–99; VII: 933–35; VIII: 1079–89; X: 249–51

Canon 1600 (NA)

Major cases are entirely excluded from the ambit of competence of this tribunal.

Canon 1601[10] (1983 CIC 1400, 1445)

Against the decrees of Ordinaries there is given no appeal or recourse to the Sacred Rota; but the Sacred Congregations exclusively see to these kinds of recourse.

Canon Law Digest
I: 746–47

Article 2—*On the Apostolic Signatura*

Canon 1602 (NA)

The Supreme Tribunal of the Apostolic Signatura consists of some Cardinals of the H. R. C., one of whom functions in the capacity of Prefect.

Canon 1603 (1983 CIC 1445) Cross-Refs.: 1917 CIC 1604, 1614

§ 1. The Apostolic Signatura, by ordinary power, sees to [cases involving]:

1.° The violation of secrets by Auditors of the Sacred Rota, and damages that they caused by null or unjust acts;

[10] Justin McClunn, "Administrative Recourse", Canon Law Studies, no. 240 (J. C. D. thesis, Catholic University of America, 1946); Leonardo Medroso, "Protection of Subjective Rights against the Administrative Acts of the Ordinary of the Place" (diss. no. 21, University of St. Thomas [Manila], 1974); Joseph Serrano, "The Juridical Remedies against Administrative Acts in the Church" (diss. no. 9, Pontifical University of St. Thomas [Rome], 1976–1977); Thomas Molloy, "The Document of the National Conference of Catholic Bishops of the United States on Due Process" (thesis, Gregorian University, 1977; printed version, no. 2907, Rome: Catholic Book Agency, 1980).

2.° The exception of suspicion against any Auditor of the Sacred Rota;
3.° The complaint of nullity against a rotal sentence;
4.° The demand for restoration in the entirety against a rotal sentence that has become an adjudicated matter;
5.° Recourse against rotal sentences in marriage cases that the Sacred Rota refuses to admit to a new examination;
6.° Conflicts of competence that happen to arise between inferior tribunals, according to the norm of Canon 1612, § 2.

§ 2. By delegated power, it sees to petitions by supplicational libelli sent to the Most Holy One in order to obtain the commission of a case before the Sacred Rota.

Canon Law Digest
I: 747–48; II: 460; VIII: 1090; IX: 949–50; X: 252–55

Canon 1604 (NA)

§ 1. In criminal cases mentioned in Canon 1603, §1, n. 1, if there is perhaps place for a judicial appeal, this is [heard within] the same Supreme Tribunal.

§ 2. In a case of suspicion, the Apostolic Signatura decides whether or not there is a basis for recusing an Auditor; the which being decided, [the case] is sent back to the Sacred Rota in order that it may proceed according to its regular methods, with the Auditor against whom a motion of exception was placed either staying or being excluded from his group.

§ 3. In a case of a complaint of nullity, or restitution in the entirety, or the recourse mentioned in Canon 1603, §1, nn. 3, 4, 5, the only thing it decides is whether the rotal sentence is null or whether there is a basis for restitution, or [whether] recourse should be admitted; and the nullity declared or restitution granted or recourse admitted, it sends the case back to the Sacred Rota unless the Most Holy One provides otherwise.

§ 4. In examining the supplication libellus, the Signatura, having opportune notice and hearing those whose interest is involved, decides whether the request is to be allowed or not.

Canon 1605 (NA) Cross-Ref.: 1917 CIC 1894

§ 1. The sentences of the Supreme Tribunal of the Signatura have force even though they do not contain reasons in law or fact.

§ 2. Nevertheless, either at the request of a party, or by office, if the matter suggests it, the Supreme Tribunal can order that the aforesaid reasons be expounded according to the proper rules of the Tribunal.

Chapter 4
On the delegated tribunal[11]

Canon 1606 (NA)

Delegated judges are bound by the rules established in Canons 199–207 and 209.

Canon 1607 (NA)

§ 1. A judge delegated by the Holy See can use those ministers constituted in the Curia of the diocese in which he must judge; but he can also select and assume those whom he wants, unless in the rescript of delegation something else is provided.

§ 2. But judges delegated by local Ordinaries must use the ministers of the diocesan Curia, unless the Bishop, in a certain case [and] for grave cause, decided to constitute his own extraordinary ministers.

Canon Law Digest
I: 748

TITLE 3
On the discipline to be observed in tribunals

Chapter 1
On the office of judge and tribunal ministers

Canon 1608 (NA)

A competent judge shall not recuse his ministry to a party so requesting, with due regard for the prescription of Canon 1625, § 1.

Canon Law Digest
I: 748; X: 255

[11] George Pavloff, "Papal Judge Delegates at the Time of the *Corpus Juris Canonici*", Canon Law Studies, no. 426 (J. C. D. thesis, Catholic University of America, 1963).

Canon 1609 (NA)

§ 1. A judge, before he [allows] something to be brought before his tribunal and he sits down to adjudicate it, shall see whether or not he himself is competent.

§ 2. And in the same way, before he admits anything to be treated before him, he is bound to decide whether such things can by law be treated in a trial.

§ 3. It is not necessary, however, to refer to these things in the acts.

Canon 1610 (1983 CIC 1460)

§ 1. If an exception is proposed against the competence of the judge, the judge himself must see to the matter.

§ 2. In the case of an exception [based on] relative incompetence, if the judge pronounces himself competent, his decision admits of no appeal.

§ 3. But if the judge declares himself incompetent, the party that considers itself injured [thereby] can, within the space of ten days, place an appeal before the superior tribunal.

Canon Law Digest
I: 748; II: 460

Canon 1611 (1983 CIC 1461)

A judge at any stage of the case who becomes aware of his absolute incompetence is bound to declare his incompetence.

Canon 1612 (1983 CIC 1416) Cross-Ref.: 1917 CIC 1603

§ 1. If between two or more judges a controversy arises as to which of them is competent to conduct the matter, the issue is to be decided by the tribunal immediately superior.

§ 2. But if the judges between whom there exists the conflict of competence are under different superior tribunals, the resolution of the controversy is reserved to the superior tribunal in whose court that case was first brought; [but] if they do not have superior tribunals, the conflict is settled either by a Legate of the Holy See, if there is one, or by the Apostolic Signatura.

Canon Law Digest
VIII: 1090–91

Canon 1613 (1983 CIC 1448)

§ 1. A judge should not take up hearing a case in which, by reason of consanguinity or affinity in any degree of the direct line and in the first or second degree of the collateral line, or in which, by reason of guardianship or care or intimate custom of life, or great animosity, or the possibility of making a profit or of avoiding damages, or anything else, he has an interest, or in which in any way he [earlier] acted as an advocate or procurator.

§ 2. Under the same circumstances of things, the promoter of justice and defender of the bond must abstain from their office.

Canon Law Digest
I: 749

Canon 1614[12] (1983 CIC 1449)

§ 1. When a judge, even if competent, is [opposed] by a party as suspect, this exception, if it is posed against the only delegated judge in the case or against the college or the majority part of the delegated judges, is to be decided by the one delegating; if [the exception is lodged] against one or another [judge] among several delegated judges or even the president of a College, [the matter is decided] by the other delegated and non-suspect judges; and if it is [lodged] against an Auditor of the Sacred Rota, [it is decided] by the Apostolic Signatura according to the norm of Canon 1603, §1, n. 2; and if [the exception] is against another official, [it is decided] by the Bishop; if [the exception] is against an auditor, [it is decided] by the principal judge.

§ 2. If the Ordinary is himself the judge and against him an exception of suspicion is raised, he should either abstain from judging or commit the deciding of the question of suspicion to the judge immediately superior.

§ 3. If the exception of suspicion is raised against the promoter of justice, the defender of the bond, or other administrators of the tribunal, the president of the collegial tribunal or the judge himself, if he sits alone, will see to this exception.

Canon Law Digest
I: 749; II: 460; VIII: 1091–92

---

[12] Harold Darcy, "The Concept of Prejudice in the Procedural Law of Contentious Cases in Ecclesiastical Courts" (thesis, Gregorian University; printed version, no. 1328, 1960).

Canon 1615 (1983 CIC 1450) Cross-Refs.: 1917 CIC 1855, 1896

§ 1. If one judge or another or even all the judges who constitute a collegial tribunal are declared suspect, the persons must be changed, but not the grade of the trial.

§ 2. It is for the Ordinary in the place of the trial where the judges have been declared suspect to absolve them of suspicion.

§ 3. But if the Ordinary himself has been declared suspect, the judge immediately superior acts.

Canon Law Digest
I: 749; II: 460

Canon 1616 (1983 CIC 1451)

The exception of suspicion is to be decided most expeditiously, hearing the parties [and] the promoter of justice and the defender of the bond, if they are present, unless suspicion falls on them.

Canon 1617 (NA)

As to what applies to the time in which exceptions of incompetence and suspicion must be proposed, the prescription of Canon 1628 is to be observed.

Canon 1618 (1983 CIC 1452) Cross-Ref.: 1917 CIC 2355

In matters that involve only private interests, a judge can proceed only upon the request of a party; but for delicts and in those things that affect the public good of the Church and the salvation of souls, [he can proceed] by office.

Canon 1619 (1983 CIC 1452)

§ 1. If a petitioner is able to offer evidence for himself, [but] he does not offer it, or if a respondent does not oppose [the petitioner with] those exceptions for which he is eligible, the judge shall not supply them.

§ 2. But if it concerns the public good or the salvation of souls, he can and must provide them.

Canon Law Digest
II: 460

Canon 1620 (1983 CIC 1453)

Judges and tribunals are to take care that as soon as possible, with due regard for justice, all cases are terminated, and that in first instance they not be protracted beyond two years, and in second instance not beyond one year.

Canon Law Digest
I: 749

Canon 1621[13] (1983 CIC 1454) Cross-Ref.: 1917 CIC 1941

§ 1. Except for a Bishop who exercises judicial power personally, all those who constitute a tribunal or perform tasks therein are bound to offer an oath to fulfill their office correctly and faithfully, in the presence of the Ordinary, or in the presence of the judge by whom they were selected, or in the presence of an ecclesiastical man delegated by either; and this [oath they shall offer] upon taking up their office, if they are stable [appointees], or before treating the case, if they were constituted only for some particular case.

§ 2. Even a judge delegated by the Apostolic See or an ordinary judge in a clerical exempt religious [institute] is bound to offer the same oath when the tribunal is first constituted, there being present a notary of the same tribunal who will record in the acts the presentation of the oath.

Canon Law Digest
II: 461

Canon 1622[14] (NA) Cross-Ref.: 1917 CIC 1941

§ 1. Whenever the oath is offered, whether by judges, tribunal administrators, or by parties, witnesses, or experts, it must always be given with a prior invocation of the divine Name and with priests also covering their hearts and by other faithful touching a book of the Gospels.

§ 2. A judge receiving an oath from a party, witness, or expert shall regularly communicate to them the sanctity of the act and about what a

[13] Eugene Moriarty, "Oaths in Ecclesiastical Courts", Canon Law Studies, no. 110 (J. C. D. thesis, Catholic University of America, 1937).

[14] Vincent McDevitt, "Perjury", Canon Law Studies, no. 201 (Catholic University of America, not published).

grave delict it is to violate an oath, and about those penalties to which those who affirm by oath a falsehood in a trial are liable.

§ 3. The oath must be presented according to a formula approved by the judge in the presence of the same judge or his delegate, and in the presence of either or both parties who wish to be present for the presentation of the oath.

Canon 1623 (1983 CIC 1455) Cross-Refs.: 1917 CIC 1769, 1941

§ 1. Judges and tribunal assistants are bound to secrecy of office always in a criminal trial and in a contentious [trial] whenever the revelation of a procedural act might bring prejudice to the parties.

§ 2. They are also bound to preserve inviolate the secrecy concerning the discussion that is conducted in a collegiate tribunal before passing sentence, and also about the various votes and opinions given therein.

§ 3. Indeed, whenever the nature of the case or of the evidence is such that, from the divulgence of the acts or the evidence, anyone's reputation is at risk or there can be had an opportunity for dissension or scandal or any other sort of inconvenience that might arise, the judge can bind witnesses, experts, and parties and their advocates or procurators with an oath to preserve secrecy.

Canon Law Digest
II: 461

Canon 1624 (1983 CIC 1456) Cross-Refs.: 1917 CIC 1071, 1941

The judge and all tribunal ministers are prohibited from accepting any sort of gift upon the occasion of conducting the trial.

Canon 1625 (1983 CIC 1457) Cross-Ref.: 1917 CIC 1608

§ 1. Judges who are certainly and obviously competent [but] who recuse themselves from [doing] justice or who rashly declare themselves competent, or who, from culpable negligence or dolus, posit a null or unjust act with [resulting] harm to others, or who bring some damage upon the litigants are bound [to compensate] for the damages and can be punished by the local Ordinary or, if it concerns a Bishop, by the Apostolic See with appropriate penalties for the gravity of the fault, not excluding privation of office at the request of a party or even by office.

§ 2. Judges who violate the law of secrecy or who presume to communicate in any way secret acts to others shall be punished with a monetary fine and other penalties not excluding privation of office according to the diverse gravity of the deed with due regard for particular statutes by which even more grave penalties are prescribed.

§ 3. The same sanctions apply to tribunal officials and assistants if they act as above in their office, [and] all of these can be punished by the judge.

Canon 1626 (NA)

Whenever a judge foresees that a petitioner will probably spurn the ecclesiastical sentence if by chance it is contrary to him, and the rights of the respondent cannot sufficiently be safeguarded, he can impose on the petitioner, at the request of the respondent or even by office, the delivery of an appropriate bond for the observance of the ecclesiastical sentence.

Chapter 2
On the order of treatment

Canon 1627 (1983 CIC 1458)

Judges and tribunals are bound to hear cases sent to them in the order in which they were proposed, unless something requires the speedier treatment [of one case] before the others, which indeed will be established by special decree of the judge or tribunal.

Canon 1628 (1983 CIC 1459) Cross-Ref.: 1917 CIC 1617

§ 1. Dilatory exceptions, especially those that respect persons and the manner of trial, are to be proposed and heard before the joinder of issues, unless the matter emerged only after the joinder or the parties affirmed by oath that they only just now became aware of them.

§ 2. An exception of absolute incompetence of the judge, however, can be raised by the parties at any stage or grade of the case.

§ 3. Likewise, the exception of excommunication can be raised at any stage or grade of the trial, provided it is before definitive sentence; indeed, if it concerns a banned excommunicate or a tolerated [excommunicate] after a condemnatory or declaratory sentence was laid down, these must always be excluded by office.

Canon Law Digest
II: 461

Canon 1629 (1983 CIC 1462)

§ 1. Preemptory exceptions that are called *litigation-ending*, such as an exception of an adjudicated matter, settlement, and so on, must be proposed and heard before the joinder of issues; whoever raises them at a later point, though they should not be rejected, will be held for the [resulting] expenses, unless he proves that the presentation was not maliciously delayed.

§ 2. Other preemptory exceptions must be raised after the joinder of issues and are to be treated in their own time according to the rules on incidental questions.

Canon Law Digest
I: 749–50

Canon 1630 (1983 CIC 1463)

§ 1. Counterclaims can be raised sufficiently immediately after the joinder of issues [and], practically speaking, at any moment in the trial though before sentence.

§ 2. They are to be heard together with the basic subject of the action and in the same grade with it, unless the judge thinks it opportune or necessary to treat them separately.

Canon 1631 (1983 CIC 1464)

Questions about a bond to be given for judicial expenses or about the free grant of legal assistance that is to be presented immediately from the outset and other things of this sort should normally be examined before the joinder of issues.

Canon 1632 (NA)

Whenever, the principal controversy having been set forth, a prejudicial question arises and the solution of the principal question depends on the resolution of the [prejudicial] question, it shall be heard before anything in the trial.

Canon 1633[15] (NA)

§ 1. If incidental questions are created from the principal controversy, they should be heard first whose solution prepares the way for the solution of the other [matters].

§ 2. But if there is no logical connection coordinating them among themselves, those that were first presented by one or the other party shall be settled before the others.

§ 3. If a question of spoliation occurs, this is to be decided before everything.

Chapter 3
On time limits and deadlines

Canon 1634 (1983 CIC 1465) Cross-Ref.: 1917 CIC 2021

§ 1. Those things are called *legal deadlines* that bring about the termination of rights constituted by law [and] they cannot be extended.

§ 2. Judicial or agreed-upon limits, before they lapse, can be extended for a just cause by the judge, having heard or upon the petition of the parties.

§ 3. The judge will nevertheless take care lest the delays in the trial become too much because of extensions.

Canon 1635 (1983 CIC 1467)

If the day indicated in the judicial acts is a holiday and nothing in the decree of the judge expressly states that the vacationing tribunal will nevertheless hear the case, then it is understood that the deadline is delayed until the first day following that is not a holiday.

Chapter 4
On the time and place of trial

Canon 1636 (1983 CIC 1468)

Although the Bishop has the right to erect a tribunal anywhere in his diocese that is not exempt, nevertheless, he shall establish within the hall

[15] Kevin Conners, "Incidental Causes in Judicial Procedure", Canon Law Studies, no. 479 (Catholic University of America, 1971).

of his see that place that will ordinarily be for trials: and there shall be prominent there an image of the Crucifixion and a book of the Evangelists.

Canon 1637 (1983 CIC 1469) Cross-Ref.: 1917 CIC 201

A judge out of his territory in virtue of expulsion or impeded from exercising jurisdiction there, can exercise his jurisdiction and pass sentence outside of the territory, nevertheless, making the local Ordinary aware of this fact.

Canon 1638 (1983 CIC 1468)

§ 1. In every diocese the Bishop will take care to establish by public decree the days and hours that are convenient, given the place and circumstances of time, on which the tribunal can regularly be approached and [on which] the administration of justice can be requested from it.

§ 2. For a just cause, however, whenever there is danger in delay, it is fundamental that the faithful can invoke at any time the ministry of a judge for the protection of their rights or the public good.

Canon 1639 (NA)

§ 1. Feast days of precept and the last three days of holy week are considered holidays; and it is forbidden to send citations, have audiences, examine the parties and witnesses, take evidence, issue decrees and sentences, or to announce or execute these, unless necessity or Christian charity or the public good indicate otherwise.

§ 2. It is for the judge to establish and announce in individual cases whether and which acts must be fulfilled on the above-mentioned days.

Chapter 5

On persons to be admitted to judicial discussion and on the manner of producing and preserving the acts

Canon 1640 (1983 CIC 1470)

§ 1. While cases are being treated in the presence of the tribunal, outsiders shall be prohibited from the hall and only those should be present whom the judge determines are necessary for the completion of the case.

§ 2. All those assisting at trial who gravely impair the required reverence and tribunal obedience can be corrected immediately with censures and other appropriate penalties by the judge, without waiting if they offend in the presence of the tribunal so seated, and advocates and procurators may also be deprived of the right of handling other cases before the ecclesiastical tribunal.

Canon Law Digest
II: 461

Canon 1641 (1983 CIC 1471)

If a person ignorant of the language of the place [becomes involved in a case by] some procedural act and the judges and the parties do not understand the language of this person, a sworn interpreter shall be used designated by the judge against whom neither party proposes legitimate exception.

Canon 1642 (1983 CIC 1472) Cross-Ref.: 1917 CIC 1644

§ 1. Judicial acts, whether they look to the merit of the question, that is, *the acts of the case*, for example, the sentence and general sorts of evidence, or whether they pertain to the form of proceeding, that is, *acts of procedure*, for example, citations, communications, and so on, must be reduced to writing.

§ 2. Unless a just cause persuades otherwise, the latin language is to be used insofar as it is possible; but questions to and answers from witnesses and other similar [things] must be done in the vernacular language.

Canon Law Digest
I: 750

Canon 1643 (1983 CIC 1472–73) Cross-Ref.: 1917 CIC 1644

§ 1. The individual pages of the process are to be numbered; and the signature of the actuary with the seal of the tribunal are to be attached to each page.

§ 2. Each of the complete acts or the interrupted ones, that is, ones put off to another session, shall have the signature of the actuary and of the judge or of the one presiding over the tribunal.

§ 3. As often as the signature of the parties or witnesses is required in judicial acts, if the party or witness fails to or does not wish to give this, it will be noted in the acts and the judge or actuary shall certify that the act was read word-for-word to the party or to the witness, and the party or the witness could not or would not sign.

Canon 1644 (1983 CIC 1474) Cross-Ref.: 1917 CIC 1890

§ 1. In case of appeal, a copy of the acts [drawn up] according to the norm of Canons 1642 and 1643, signed and bound in a packet, with an index of all the acts and documents and a verification by the actuary [or] chancellor about their faithful and complete transcription, shall be sent to the superior tribunal; if a copy cannot be produced without grave inconvenience, the original acts themselves shall be sent with due precautions.

§ 2. If they are being sent to where the vernacular language is not known, the acts themselves will be translated into the latin language, taking precaution that it be a faithful translation.

§ 3. If acts cannot be produced in the required form and character, they can be rejected by the superior judge: in that case, those to whom the fault is attributable shall produce the acts at their own expense once again and are bound to send them.

Canon Law Digest
I: 750; II: 461

Canon 1645 (1983 CIC 1475)

§ 1. The trial being completed, the documents must be restored to the parties, unless in a criminal case, the public good so requiring, the judge decides to retain some.

§ 2. All documents that remain with the tribunal shall be deposited in the archive of the Curia, whether public or secret, insofar as their nature requires.

§ 3. Notaries, actuaries, and the chancellor are prohibited, without a mandate of the judge, from giving copies of judicial acts or documents that were acquired in the process.

§ 4. Anonymous letters that contributed nothing to the case, as well as those that were signed [but that] were certainly calumnious, shall be destroyed.

TITLE 4
On the parties in the case

CHAPTER 1
On the petitioner and the convened respondent[16]

Canon 1646 (1983 CIC 1476)

Anyone can act in a trial, unless he is prohibited by the sacred canons; a respondent legitimately convened must respond.

Canon Law Digest
VI: 827–28; VII: 935–38; VIII: 1092–93; IX: 950

Canon 1647 (1983 CIC 1477)

Even though a petitioner or respondent has constituted a procurator or advocate, nevertheless, he is always bound to be present himself in court according to the prescription of law or the judge.

Canon 1648[17] (1983 CIC 1478)

§ 1. Parents or guardians are bound to act and respond for their minor [charges] and those who are deprived of the use of reason.

§ 2. If a judge thinks their rights to be in conflict with the rights of parents or guardians, or they are such a long distance from parents or guardians so that these can scarcely or only with difficulty act, then they will stand trial through a guardian given by the judge.

§ 3. But in spiritual cases and those connected with the spiritual, if minors have reached the use of reason, they may act and respond without

---

[16] John Krol, "The Defendant in Contentious Trials, Exclusive of Vincular Cases", Canon Law Studies, no. 146 (J. C. D. thesis, Catholic University of America, 1942); Maurice Dingman, "The Plaintiff in Contentious Trials", Canon Law Studies, no. 230 (Catholic University of America, not published).

[17] Gennaro Sesto, "Guardians of the Mentally Ill in Ecclesiastical Trials", Canon Law Studies, no. 358 (thesis, Catholic University of America, 1956); Justin Rigali, "The Law of Tutela" (MS no. 3617, Gregorian University, 1964; printed version, no. 1695, 1964).

the consent of parents or guardians; and indeed, if they have completed the age of fourteen years they can even [act and respond] themselves; otherwise, they [act and respond] through a guardian given by the Ordinary or even through a procurator constituted by themselves with the Ordinary's authorization.

Canon Law Digest
VI: 828–32

Canon 1649 (1983 CIC 1480)

In the name of those mentioned in Canon 100, § 3, the rector or administrator stands trial with due regard for the prescription of Canon 1653; but if there is a conflict between their rights and the rights of the rector or administrator, a procurator [is] designated by the Ordinary.

Canon 1650 (1983 CIC 1478)

Those who are forbidden [the use] of goods and those who are of a weak mental state can stand trial for themselves only in order to respond for their own delicts or at the prescription of the judge; in other [matters], they must act and respond through their guardians.

Canon 1651 (1983 CIC 1479)

§ 1. In order that a guardian given to someone by the civil authorities be admitted into an ecclesiastical trial, there must precede the consent of his own Ordinary given to him.

§ 2. The Ordinary can also constitute another guardian for the ecclesiastical forum if, having maturely weighed everything, he thinks it prudent to establish one.

Canon Law Digest
II: 461; III: 603

Canon 1652 (NA)

Religious, without the consent of their Superiors, have no personal standing in a trial, except in the cases that follow:

1.° If [the case] is concerned with the vindication of rights against the religious [institute] that were acquired by one's profession;
2.° If they are legitimately staying outside the cloister and the protection of their rights so urges;
3.° If they wish to institute a denunciation against the Superior.

Canon 1653 (1983 CIC 1480) Cross-Ref.: 1917 CIC 1649

§ 1. Local Ordinaries can stand trial in the name of the cathedral church or the episcopal table; but in order to act licitly, they must hear the cathedral Chapter or Council of administration and have their consent or advice whenever the amount of money at issue would require their consent or advice for alienation according to the norm of Canon 1532, §§ 2 and 3.

§ 2. All beneficiaries can act or respond in trial in the name of the benefice; but in order that they do so licitly, the prescription of Canon 1526 must be observed.

§ 3. Prelates and Superiors of Chapters, sodalities, and any sort of college cannot stand trial in the name of the community without its consent according to the norm of the statutes.

§ 4. Against those mentioned in §§ 1–3 who stand trial without the required consent or advice, the pious cause or community has a right to pursue damages.

§ 5. But in case of a lack of or negligence in [due care by] those who fill the office of administrator, the local Ordinary, himself or through another, can stand trial in the name of a moral person who is subject to his jurisdiction.

§ 6. Religious Superiors cannot stand trial in the name of their community except according to the norm of the constitution.

Canon 1654 (NA) Cross-Ref.: 1917 CIC 2263

§ 1. A banned excommunicate or a tolerated [excommunicate] after a declaratory or condemnatory sentence is permitted to act personally only to impugn the justice or legitimacy of his excommunication; [such a one can act] through a procurator in order to avoid prejudice to his own soul; in other things he is repelled from acting.

§ 2. Other excommunicates generally can stand trial.

Chapter 2
On procurators for litigation and advocates[18]

Canon 1655 (1983 CIC 1481)

§ 1. In a criminal trial the defendant must always have an advocate chosen by himself or given by the judge.

§ 2. Even in a contentious trial, if it concerns minors or if the trial affects the public good, the judge can assign by office a defender to a party lacking one or, if there is need, add another to a party already having [one].

§ 3. Beyond these cases, a party can freely constitute an advocate or procurator, but he can also act and respond personally in the trial, unless the judge thinks the service of a procurator or advocate is necessary.

§ 4. But a Bishop, whenever he is in a case, shall constitute another for his person who will act as a procurator in name.

Canon Law Digest
II: 461; VII: 938–39

Canon 1656 (1983 CIC 1482)

§ 1. Anyone can select one procurator who cannot substitute another for himself unless this express faculty has been given him.

§ 2. But if, a just cause so persuading, several [procurators] have been deputed by one, these shall be so constituted that the operation of prevention applies between them.

§ 3. Several advocates can be constituted together.

§ 4. The same person can exercise both responsibilities [namely, that of] procurator and advocate, even in the same case and for the same client.

Canon 1657 (1983 CIC 1483)

§ 1. The procurator and advocate must be Catholic, of majority age, and of good reputation; a non-Catholic is not to be admitted unless by exception and in necessity.

---

[18] James Hogan, "Judicial Advocates and Procurators", Canon Law Studies, no. 133 (J. C. D. thesis, Catholic University of America, 1941); Charles Connors, "Extra-Judicial Procurators in the Code of Canon Law", Canon Law Studies, no. 192 (J. C. D. thesis, Catholic University of America, 1944).

§ 2. The advocate must also be a doctor or otherwise at least truly expert in canon law.

§ 3. A religious can be admitted, unless provided otherwise in the constitutions, only in those cases in which there is usefulness for his religious [institute], albeit with the permission of the Superior.

Canon Law Digest
I: 750–51; II: 461; V: 707–8; IX: 951–52

Canon 1658 (1983 CIC 1483)

§ 1. Anyone, by the free choice of a party, can be selected and deputed a procurator, provided he is suitable according to the preceding canons, and it is not necessary that the approval of the Ordinary be obtained.

§ 2. An advocate, however, in order to be admitted to service, requires the approval of the Ordinary, which shall be either general for all cases or special for a certain case.

§ 3. In a trial before one delegated by the Holy See, the one delegated must approve and admit that advocate that the party indicates he wishes to use.

§ 4. The procurator and advocate in cases that are treated in a regional tribunal according to the norm of Canon 1579, §§ 1 and 2, are to be selected from the same religious [institute] and, before taking up service, be approved by him who takes the part of judge in the case; but in cases that are treated according to the norm of § 3 of the same canon, an outsider to the religious [institute] can also be admitted before the tribunal of the local Ordinary.

Canon Law Digest
I: 751; II: 461

Canon 1659 (1983 CIC 1484) Cross-Ref.: 1917 CIC 2006

§ 1. A procurator shall not be admitted by a judge before he deposits in the tribunal a special written mandate for litigation, even [if placed] at the foot of the citation itself, bearing the signature of the mandator and referring to the place, day, month, and year.

§ 2. But if the one mandating does not know how to write, this must be shown in writing, and the pastor or notary of the Curia or two witnesses in the place of the one mandating shall sign the mandate.

Canon Law Digest
II: 461

Canon 1660 (1983 CIC 1484)

The mandate of the procurator must be reserved in the acts of the case.

Canon 1661 (1983 CIC 1484)

An advocate, in order to take up the service of a case, must have a commission from the party or from a judge along the lines of a mandate for a procurator, which must be preserved in the acts.

Canon 1662 (1983 CIC 1485)

Unless he has a special mandate, a procurator cannot renounce an action, an instance, or a judicial act, or settle, make peace with, or commit to arbitration an offer, or take an oath [as evidence or in resolution of a case], or generally do those things for which the law requires a special mandate.

Canon 1663 (1983 CIC 1487)

Both a procurator and an advocate can be removed from service by a judge, having given a decree, whether by office or at the request of a party, albeit for just cause.

Canon Law Digest
II: 462

Canon 1664 (1983 CIC 1486)

§ 1. Advocates and procurators can be removed by the one who constituted them, with due regard for the obligation of paying the fees that are owed to them; but in order that this removal take effect, it is necessary that it be communicated to them and, if the litigation has already been undertaken, the judge and the opposing party must be informed of the removal.

§ 2. Definitive sentence having been given, the right and duty of appealing, if the one mandating has not refused [it], remains with the procurator.

Canon 1665 (1983 CIC 1488)

§ 1. It is forbidden for either [advocates or procurators] to buy the litigation or to seek immoderate payments or to strike a deal for part of the proceeds of the matter under litigation.

§ 2. If they do this, the agreement is null and they can be penalized with monetary fines by the judge or by the Ordinary; an advocate moreover can be suspended from office and even, if there is recidivism, be stripped and deprived of title [for acting].

Canon Law Digest
I: 751; II: 462; IV: 399

Canon 1666 (1983 CIC 1489)

Advocates and procurators who for gifts or promises or in any other manner shirk their duty shall be repelled from office and, besides being liable for damages, can be struck with monetary fines or other appropriate penalties.

TITLE 5
On actions and exceptions[19]

Canon 1667 (1983 CIC 1491–92)

Any right is protected not only by an action but also by an exception, unless something else is expressly provided that is always available and, by its nature, is perpetual.

Canon 1668 (NA)

§ 1. Whoever wishes to vindicate a thing to himself or who acts in a trial in pursuit of his right under a title authorized by law, fights in an action that is called *petitionary*.

§ 2. But if one postulates possession of a thing or a right of quasi-possession, that action is called *possessory*.

Canon 1669 (1983 CIC 1493)

§ 1. A petitioner can act against a respondent by several actions together that nevertheless do not conflict among themselves either with regard to the same thing or with regard to different things if they do not overstep the competence of the tribunal.

§ 2. A respondent is not prohibited from using several exceptions, even contrary [ones].

[19] Paul Coyle, "Judicial Exceptions", Canon Law Studies, no. 193 (J. C. D. thesis, Catholic University of America, 1944).

Canon 1670 (NA)

§ 1. A petitioner can combine in one instance possessory and petitionary actions unless the exception of spoliation has been raised by the adversary.

§ 2. It is likewise fundamental that the respondent in a petitionary [action] can counter-sue the petitioner in a possessory [action], and the reverse is true, unless it is a matter of spoliation.

Canon 1671 (NA)

§ 1. It is likewise fundamental that the petitioner, before the conclusion of the case, may go from a petitionary action in the trial to a possessory [action] in order to acquire or retake something.

§ 2. Indeed, for a just cause, the judge can even permit this switch after the conclusion of the case but before definitive sentence.

§ 3. It is for the judge, attentive to the allegations of the parties, to define in a single sentence the whole group of questions or to satisfy them one after another, insofar as it seems to him the better to expedite the speedy and full protection of rights.

Chapter 1
On sequestration of things and restraints on the exercise of rights

Canon 1672 (1983 CIC 1496) Cross-Ref.: 1917 CIC 1854

§ 1. Whoever can show that there is imminent danger to himself because something to which he has a right is detained by another, unless the thing is handed over for custody, has the right of obtaining from the judge the sequestration of the thing [on his behalf].

§ 2. In similar circumstances of things, he can obtain [an order] whereby the exercise of rights by another is restricted.

§ 3. The sequestration of a thing and restraint on the exercise of rights can be ordered by the judge by office, especially at the request of the promoter of justice or defender of the bond, whenever this seems indicated by the public good.

Canon Law Digest
II: 462

Canon 1673 (1983 CIC 1497) Cross-Ref.: 1917 CIC 1854

§ 1. Sequestration of a thing is also admitted for the security of a creditor, provided the right of the creditor is clearly shown and observing the norms mentioned in Canon 1923, § 1.

§ 2. Sequestration is extended also to the goods of a debtor that, for the sake of deposit or by some other title, have been taken by other persons.

Canon 1674 (1983 CIC 1498)

The sequestration of a thing and suspension of the exercise of a right can in no way be ordered if the damage that is feared can be otherwise repaired and a suitable bond has been offered for its repair.

Canon 1675 (NA)

§ 1. For the custody of a thing subject to sequestration, a suitable person proposed by the parties shall be designated by the judge who is called the sequestror; if the parties disagree among themselves, the judge will appoint a sequestror by office.

§ 2. A sequestror must apply in the custody, care, and preservation of the thing no less diligence than he would apply for his own goods, and afterward he is bound to return [the thing] wih all its effects to whomever the judge orders.

§ 3. The judge can order an appropriate payment to the sequestror if he asks for it.

Chapter 2
On actions to prevent new operations and threatened damages

Canon 1676 (NA) Cross-Refs.: 1917 CIC 1162, 1677

§ 1. Whoever fears that damages from some new work might come to his situation in the future can denounce it to the judge in order to interrupt the work until the rights of both parties, by sentence of the judge, can be defined.

§ 2. One to whom the prohibition has been communicated must cease from continuing the work but, provided there is suitable precaution regarding a flawless restitution of all things if he loses by the decision of the judge, he can seek from the judge [permission] for its continuation.

§ 3. Those denouncing a new work are allowed two months to demonstrate their rights; for a just and necessary cause, having heard the other party, the judge can extend or reduce this [period].

Canon 1677 (NA)

If an old work is being changed in greater part, the same right that applies to a new work in Canon 1676 is established.

Canon 1678 (NA)

Whoever finds himself at imminent risk of grave damage to his property from some building that is verging on ruin or from a tree or from any other thing has an action *for the prevention of impending harm* in order to obtain the removal of the danger or [to obtain] a bond for damages in avoidance or compensation if by chance it happens.

Chapter 3
On actions [arising] from the nullity of acts[20]

Canon 1679 (NA)

If an act or a contract is null by the law there is given to him who has an interest in it an action to obtain a declaration of nullity from the judge.

Canon Law Digest
I: 751–52

Canon 1680 (1983 CIC 124)

§ 1. The nullity of an act is considered present only when there are lacking in it those things that essentially constitute it or there are missing the formalities or conditions required by the sacred canons under pain of nullity.

---

[20] John Noone, "Nullity in Judicial Acts", Canon Law Studies, no. 297 (thesis, Catholic University of America, 1950); William Curtin, "The Plaint of Nullity against the Sentence", Canon Law Studies, no. 360 (J. C. D. thesis, Catholic University of America, 1956).

§ 2. The nullity of an act does not imply the nullity of acts that preceded or that followed and are not dependent on the act.

Canon Law Digest
I: 752

Canon 1681 (1983 CIC 128)

Whoever posited an act infected with the vice of nullity is bound [to make good] the damages and expenses of those wounded thereby.

Canon 1682 (NA)

An act cannot be declared null by a judge by office, unless it affects the public or it concerns the poor or minors or others who are considered minors in law.

Canon 1683 (1983 CIC 1405)

A lower judge cannot examine the confirmation added to an act or instrument by the Roman Pontiff unless a mandate of the Apostolic See precedes.

Canon Law Digest
I: 752

Chapter 4
On rescissory actions and on restitution in the entirety

Canon 1684 (NA)

§ 1. If anyone, moved by unjustly incurred grave fear or confused by dolus, has placed an act or entered a contract that is not null by the law, he can, having proved the fear or fraud, obtain a rescission of the act or contract by an action that is called *rescissory*.

§ 2. The same action can be used within two years by someone who has suffered grave injury exceeding one-half of a contract by suffering an error.

Canon 1685 (NA)

This action can be instituted:

1.° Against him who imposed the fear or who perpetrated the fraud even though he did it not for his own interest but for the convenience of another;

2.° Against anyone who possesses in bad faith, or even in good faith, the goods that were extorted by fear or fraud, with due regard for the right of having recourse against anyone who was himself the author of the fear or fraud.

Canon 1686 (NA)

If one who imposed fear or perpetrated fraud urges the execution of the act or contract, the wounded party or the one deceived can utilize the exception of fear or fraud.

Canon 1687 (NA) Cross-Ref.: 1917 CIC 1905

§ 1. The extraordinary remedy of restitution in the entirety assists minors or those acting like minors in law who are gravely injured and their heirs and successors for the repair of injuries from a transaction or action that [though] valid is rescindable, besides the other ordinary remedies [that they have].

§ 2. This benefit is also granted to those of majority [status in law] who lack a rescissory action or other ordinary remedy, provided there is just cause and they can prove that the injury is not imputable to themselves.

Canon 1688 (NA) Cross-Ref.: 1917 CIC 1905

§ 1. Restitution in the entirety can be petitioned from the ordinary judge who was competent with respect to him against whom it is sought, within four years from attaining their majority if it concerns minors, [and otherwise four years] from the day the injury was done or the cessation of the impediment if it concerns one with majority [rights] or a moral person.

§ 2. Restitution [in the entirety] can be granted to minors or to those who act [in law] like minors by the judge, even by office, having heard or at the request of the promoter of justice.

Canon 1689 (NA)

Restitution in the entirety has the effect of recalling all things flawlessly, that is, they are restored to the state in which they were before the injury, with due regard for the rights of others who in good faith acquired [something] before the restitution petition.

Chapter 5
On mutual petitions or counter-suits

Canon 1690 (1983 CIC 1494)

§ 1. An action that a respondent files against a petitioner in the presence of the same judge and in the same trial for the defeat or diminishment of the claim [of the petitioner] is called a *counter-suit.*

§ 2. Counter-suing a counter-suit is not admitted.

Canon 1691 (NA)

A counter-suit has a place in all contentious cases except for cases of spoliation; but in criminal [cases], it is not allowed except according to the norm of Canon 2218, § 3.

Canon 1692 (1983 CIC 1495)

It shall be proposed to the judge in whose presence the principal action was filed even though he was delegated for only one case or he is otherwise incompetent, unless the incompetence is absolute.

Chapter 6
On actions or possessory remedies

Canon 1693 (1983 CIC 1500)

Anyone who can pursue possession of something or who wants to obtain the exercise of some right that he enjoys by legitimate title can ask that he be placed in possession of the thing or [enabled to] exercise the right.

Canon 1694 (1983 CIC 1500)

Not only possession but even simple detention offers an action or possessory exception according to the norm of the canons that follow.

Canon 1695 (1983 CIC 1500)

§ 1. Whoever has been in possession of a thing or in quasi-possession of a right for one full year, if he suffers any molestation that threatens retention of his possession or quasi-possession, has an action *for retaining possession*.

§ 2. This action is not admitted except within one year from the onset of molestation, [and] against the author of the molestation in order that he cease from molestation.

Canon 1696 (1983 CIC 1500)

§ 1. Even one who possesses by force, stealth, or precariously can use an action *for retaining possession* against whoever disturbs him: but not against the person from whom the thing was taken by force or stealth or who brought about the precarious [possession].

§ 2. In cases that look to the public good, the promoter of justice has the right to raise vitiated possession against him who possesses by force, stealth, or precariously.

Canon 1697 (1983 CIC 1500) Cross-Ref.: 1917 CIC 1869

§ 1. If a controversy arises between two [parties] over which one of them is in possession, the possession shall be decided with preference to him who within the [last] year exercised more frequent and more influential acts of possession.

§ 2. In doubt, the judge shall attribute possession to both parties indivisibly.

§ 3. But if the character of the thing or the right, or the danger of disputes or quarrels, will not suffer that undivided possession be attributed to the litigants, in the meantime the judge can have the thing deposited with a sequestror or order the suspension of the right of quasi-possession until the completion of the petitory trial.

Canon 1698 (1983 CIC 1500)

§ 1. Whoever has been ejected by force or stealth in any way from possession of a thing or quasi-possession of a right has an action *for recov-*

ering possession against any author of the spoliation or detainer of the thing, or [he has an action] of spoliation and the exception of spoliation.

§ 2. This action is not admitted after the lapse of one year from having notice that the spoliation of the thing has been suffered; an exception, on the other hand, is perpetual.

Canon 1699 (1983 CIC 1500)

§ 1. The one despoiled, taking exception against the spoliator and proving spoliation, is not bound to respond unless he is first restored to his possession.

§ 2. The one despoiled, in order to be restored to possession, need prove nothing besides the fact of spoliation.

§ 3. But if in the restitution of a thing or the exercise of a right there arises some danger (for example, savagery when a man seeks restitution of conjugal relations from his wife), the judge, at the request of the party of the promoter of justice, can decide in light of the diversity of cases and persons, either to suspend restitution or to have a sequestrator take possession of the object or person until the case of the petitioner is resolved.

Canon 1700 (1983 CIC 1500)

Possessory trials are concluded with only the adverse party who is retaining or recovering cited for trial; but all those who have an interest are cited in a trial of acquisition.

Chapter 7
On the extinction of actions[21]

Canon 1701 (1983 CIC 1492)

In contentious actions, whether real or personal, [the process] is extinguished by prescription according to the norm of Canons 1508–12; but actions on the status of persons are never extinguished.

[21] Henry Byrne, "The Extinction of Criminal Actions and of Penalties in the Code of Canon Law" (MS no. 883, Gregorian University, 1941); William Kettron, "The Extinguishment of Action in Criminal Causes: A Study of the Exclusion of Criminal Action by Reason of Beneficial Time" (MS no. 3490, Gregorian University, 1963; printed version, no. 1584, 1963).

Canon 1702 (NA)

Every criminal action is ended by the death of the respondent, or by condonation by legitimate power, or the lapse of useful time to pursue a criminal action.

Canon Law Digest
VIII: 1093

Canon 1703 (1983 CIC 1362) Cross-Ref.: 1917 CIC 2240

With due regard for the prescription of Canon 1555, § 1, concerning delicts reserved to the Sacred Congregation of the H. Office, the useful time for pursuing a criminal action is three years, unless it concerns:

1.° An action for injuries, which is ended after one year;
2.° An action from a qualified delict against the sixth or seventh divine precept, which is ended in five years;
3.° An action for simony or homicide, against which the criminal action lasts for ten years.

Canon 1704 (NA)

[Even though] a criminal action is prevented by prescription:

1.° There is not, because of that fact, a prevention of a contentious action that might perhaps arise from the delict in order to seek damages;
2.° [And] the Ordinary can still use the remedies established in Canon 2222, § 2.

Canon 1705 (1983 CIC 1363)

§ 1. Prescription in a contentious [case] runs from when the action could first be proposed in law; in criminal [cases, it runs] from the day of the committed delict.

§ 2. If the delict has, as they say, a successive course, prescription does not run until the day on which the delict ceases its course.

§ 3. In a habitual or continual delict, prescription does not run until after the final act; and a respondent [prosecuted] for some criminal act not prescribed is bound for the older ones if they are connected in the same act, even if taken individually they would be excluded by prescription.

TITLE 6
On the introduction of the case

Chapter 1
On the libellus introducing the litigation[22]

Canon 1706 (1983 CIC 1502)

Whoever wishes to convene another must show a libellus to the competent judge in which the object of the controversy is set forth and which requests the ministry of the judge to pursue the asserted rights.

Canon Law Digest
II: 462

Canon 1707 (1983 CIC 1503) Cross-Ref.: 1917 CIC 1882

§ 1. Whoever does not know how to write or who is legitimately impeded from giving a libellus can propose his petition orally in the presence of the tribunal.

§ 2. Likewise in cases that are easier to investigate and of small importance and therefore can be completed quickly, it is left to the decision of the judge to admit a petition made to him orally.

§ 3. In either case, nevertheless, the judge will order the notary to reduce to writing the acts that are to be read by the petitioner and proved by him.

Canon Law Digest
II: 463

Canon 1708 (1983 CIC 1504)

The libellus by which litigation is introduced must:

1.° Express in the presence of which judge the cause is introduced, what is being asked, and from whom it is sought;

[22] John Kealy, "The Introductory Libellus in Church Court Procedure", Canon Law Studies, no. 108 (J. C. D. thesis, Catholic University of America, 1937).

2.° Indicate at least generally by what right the petitioner undertakes [the action] and what things are alleged and asserted by way of proof;

3.° Be signed by the petitioner or his procurator giving that day, month, and year, as well as the place in which the petitioner or procurator lives, or another location for the sake of receiving the acts [there].

Canon Law Digest
II: 463

Canon 1709 (1983 CIC 1505) Cross-Refs.: 1917 CIC 1710, 1882

§ 1. The judge or the tribunal, after it sees both that the thing is within its competence and that the petitioner has legitimate personal standing in the trial, must promptly admit or reject the libellus, adding in the second case the cause for rejection.

§ 2. If the libellus was rejected by decree of the judge because of flaws that can be amended, the petitioner can produce a new libellus correctly drawn before the same judge once again; but if the judge rejects the amended libellus, he must explain his reasons for the new rejection.

§ 3. Against the rejection of a libellus it is always integral that the party can interpose to the superior tribunal recourse within the time of ten useful days: by whom, having heard the party and the promoter of justice and the defender of the bond, the question of rejection is to be settled most expeditiously.

Canon Law Digest
I: 752; II: 463; III: 603; IV: 400–401; IX: 952–53

Canon 1710 (1983 CIC 1506)

If the judge, for a continual month from the presentation of the libellus, does not give a decree by which he admits or rejects the libellus according to the norm of Canon 1709, the interested party can insist that the judge perform his duty; but if, nevertheless, the judge is silent and fifteen days have lapsed from the insistence, [the party] can interpose recourse to the local Ordinary, if he is not the judge himself, or to the superior tribunal, in order either that the judge be compelled to accept the case or that it be subrogated to another place.

Chapter 2

On the citation and the communication of judicial acts[23]

Canon 1711 (1983 CIC 1507)

§ 1. A libellus or oral petition being admitted, the calling before justice, that is, citation, of the other party is in order.

§ 2. But if the litigating parties freely present themselves in the presence of the judge to treat of the case, citation is not necessary, but the actuary shall signify that the parties were freely at trial.

Canon 1712 (1983 CIC 1508)

§ 1. Citation having been made by the judge, the libellus for introducing the litigation shall be signed or attached.

§ 2. [It] shall be communicated to the respondent and, if they are several, to each individual.

§ 3. Moreover the petitioner must be notified that on an established day and hour he shall also be present before the judge.

Canon Law Digest
II: 463; III: 603–4; VIII: 1093

Canon 1713 (1983 CIC 1508)

If litigation is moved in regard to him who does not have the free administration of things that are at issue, the citation must be communicated to him who is bound to respond in court in the name of that one according to the norm of Canons 1648–54.

Canon 1714 (NA)

Any citation is preemptory; nor need it be repeated, except in the case mentioned in Canon 1845, § 2.

Canon Law Digest
II: 463

Canon 1715 (1983 CIC 1508) Cross-Ref.: 1917 CIC 1723

§ 1. The citation must be communicated through a summons that expresses the precept of the [tribunal] to the convened party that is issued for

[23] Victor Goertz, "The Judicial Summons", Canon Law Studies, no. 362 (thesis, Catholic University of America, 1957).

his appearance, that is, before which judge, and using words that at least generally indicate the cause and by what petitioner [it is introduced], and [indicating] the respondent by name and surname as [being] rightly designated and convened; along with the place and the time, that is, with the year, the month, the day, and the hour, established for appearance clearly indicated.

§ 2. Citation with the seal of the tribunal attached shall be signed by the judge or by his auditor and a notary.

Canon Law Digest
I: 752; VII: 939–43; VIII: 1093–1100

Canon 1716 (NA)

Two copies of the citation will be produced, one of which is sent to the convened respondent, the other preserved in the acts.

Canon Law Digest
I: 752

Canon 1717 (NA)

§ 1. The document of citation if possible will be carried by a courier of the Curia to the one convened wherever he is found.

§ 2. For this the courier can enter the boundaries even of another diocese if the judge thinks this expedient and has so ordered the courier.

§ 3. If the courier does not find the person in the place where he stays, he can leave the citation document with his family or householders if they are prepared to accept it and answer that they will deliver the accepted document to the convened respondent as soon as possible; this lacking, he shall refer the matter to the judge in order that it be transmitted according to the norm of Canons 1719 and 1720.

Canon 1718 (1983 CIC 1510)

A respondent who refuses to receive the citation document is considered legitimately cited.

Canon 1719 (1983 CIC 1509) Cross-Refs.: 1917 CIC 1717, 1877, 2143

If because of distance or some other cause it is difficult to deliver the document of citation to the convened respondent by courier, it can be transmitted by order of the judge through public postal system and securing a signed document of its receipt, or through another way that according to the laws and conditions of the place is safest.

Canon Law Digest
I: 753

Canon 1720 (NA) Cross-Ref.: 1917 CIC 1717

§ 1. Whenever, despite diligent inquiry, the whereabouts of the respondent remain unknown, citation by edict is in order.

§ 2. This shall be done by affixing to the entrance of the Curia the document of citation by the courier in a manner to be determined by edict and for a time set by the prudent decision of the judge, and it will also be inserted in some public periodical; but if neither of these [ways] can be done, some other way suffices.

Canon Law Digest
I: 753; II: 463

Canon 1721 (NA)

§ 1. The courier, when he has left the summons of citation in the hands of the convened respondent, must sign it, noting the day and hour that it was given to the respondent.

§ 2. He will do likewise if he leaves it in the hands of some family or householders of the convened respondent, adding moreover the name of the person to whom he gave the summons.

§ 3. If citation was made by edict, the courier will sign at the foot of the edict what day and hour the edict was affixed to the entrance of the Curia and how long it stayed affixed there.

§ 4. If the respondent refuses to receive the summons the courier will return the summons signed by himself, adding the day and hour of refusal.

Canon Law Digest
II: 463

Canon 1722 (1983 CIC 1509)

§ 1. The courier will record for the judge in a writing signed by his own hand what he did, which document will be preserved in the acts.

§ 2. If citation was delivered by postal services, the official record thereof will be preserved in the acts.

Canon 1723 (1983 CIC 1511)

If the summons of citation does not include those things prescribed by Canon 1715 or was not legitimately communicated, the citation and acts of the process are of no account.

Canon 1724 (1983 CIC 1509)

The rules established above for the citation of the respondent are to be accommodated and applied to other judicial acts, though in accord with their different natures, such as decrees and sentences of denunciations and other things of this sort.

Canon 1725 (1983 CIC 1512)

When citation has been legitimately done or the parties have come freely before the judge:

1.° The matter ceases to be an integral thing;

2.° The case becomes proper before the judge or tribunal in whose presence the action was instituted;

3.° The jurisdiction of a delegated judge is rendered firm so that it does not expire upon the loss of authority of the one delegating;

4.° Prescription is interrupted unless otherwise provided according to the norm of Canon 1508;

5.° The litigation gets underway; and therefore immediately the principle applies: *while litigation is pending nothing is to be innovated.*

Canon Law Digest
I: 753; II: 463

TITLE 7
On the joinder of issues[24]

Canon 1726 (1983 CIC 1513)

The object, that is, material of a trial is constituted by the joinder of issues, that is, the formal denial by the respondent to the action of the

[24] Edward Steichen, "The Joinder of Issues and the Ecclesiastical Contentious Procedure, Its Nature and Necessity" (diss. no. 7, Pontifical University of St. Thomas [Rome], 1959–1960).

petitioner made with the intention of litigating in the presence of the judge.

Canon 1727 (1983 CIC 1513)

For the joinder of issues, no formality is necessary but it suffices that, with the parties appearing together in the presence of the judge or his delegate, the petition of the petitioner and the denial by the respondent are inserted into the acts whereby it is shown what the case concerns or what is the scope of the controversy.

Canon 1728 (1983 CIC 1513)

In complex cases, however, in which the petition of the petitioner is not clear or simple, or the denial of the respondent is blurred with difficulties, the judge by office or at the request of the petitioner or respondent shall cite the parties in order to establish correctly the articles of the controversy, that is, when the *questions* of the case, as they say, *are agreed upon*.

Canon 1729 (1983 CIC 1513–14)

§ 1. If on the day designated for agreement on the questions, a party who is called before justice neither appears nor presents a just excuse for absence, he shall be declared contumacious and the formulation of questions established by office upon the request of the party who is present. Notice shall be delivered, however, immediately to the contumacious party by office so that if he wishes to propose exceptions against the formulation of questions or the articles and to purge himself of contumacy, [he may do so] within a time that seems appropriate to the judge.

§ 2. With the parties being present and in agreement with the formulation of questions or articles, and the judge in what applies to him thinks there is nothing objectionable [about it], he shall express the matter in his decree by which the formulation is settled upon.

§ 3. But if the parties disagree or their conclusions do not seem sufficient to the judge, the judge himself will resolve the controversy by decree.

§ 4. Once the formulation of questions or the articles is set, it cannot be changed except by a new decree and for grave cause at the request of a party or a promoter of justice or the defender of the bond and having heard both [parties] or the other party and having weighed their reasons.

Canon Law Digest
II: 463; VII: 943

Canon 1730 (1983 CIC 1529)

Before the joinder of issues takes place, the judge shall not proceed to receive evidence or testimony, except in the case of contumacy or unless the deposition of the witnesses must be received lest it cannot be received later, or [would be only] received with difficulty, because of the probable death of the witness or his leaving the area or some other just cause.

Canon 1731 (1983 CIC 1514–16)

The issue having been joined:

1.° It is not licit that the petitioner change the libellus, unless with the respondent consenting, the judge thinks the change ought to be allowed for a just cause, always with due regard for the compensation of damages to and expenses for the respondent if these are owed. The libellus is not considered to have been changed if the manner of proof is restricted or changed; [or] if the petition or accessory petition is reduced; [or] if the facts adduced in the libellus are later shown or completed or emended in such a way that the object of the controversy remains the same; [or] if, instead of the thing, an award is sought, or interest or something equivalent;

2.° The judge shall present the parties with an appropriate time to propose and complete the evidence; the which time, upon the request of the parties, [the judge] can in his own judgment extend, provided the litigation is not protracted beyond what is equitable;

3.° The possessor of an alienated thing ceases to be in good faith; and therefore he must restore the thing if convicted, and not only the thing itself, but also the proceeds of the thing, during the time since the joinder of issues, [and] he is required to restore and he must make up for any damages that have also followed.

TITLE 8
On the instance of the litigation[25]

Canon 1732 (1983 CIC 1517)

The beginning of the instance is the joinder of issues; it can end in any way in which a trial is terminated, but it can also be interrupted before, and it can even be finished by abatement or renunciation.

Canon 1733 (1983 CIC 1518) Cross-Ref.: 1917 CIC 1885

Should a litigating party die or change status or cease from the office by which account he acts:

1.° If the case is not yet concluded, the instance is interrupted until the heirs of the deceased one or the successor [in office] takes up the suit;

2.° If the case is concluded, the instance is not interrupted but the judge must proceed further, having cited the procurator, if there is one, otherwise the heirs of the deceased one or his successor [in office must act].

Canon Law Digest
IV: 402–3; VIII: 1100–1108

Canon 1734 (NA)

If there is a controversy between litigating clerics about the right to a benefice and one of them dies while the case is pending or resigns the benefice, the instance is not interrupted but the promoter of justice prosecutes it against the survivor on behalf of the liberty of the benefice or the church, unless the benefice was of free conferral by the Ordinary and he prefers to award the case to the survivor as if he won.

Canon 1735 (1983 CIC 1519)

Upon a procurator or a guardian ceasing from duty, the instance remains interrupted until a party or those to whom it pertains appoints a new procurator or guardian or indicates that he wishes to act in the future for himself.

---

[25] Albert Olkovikas, "The Instantia of the Lawsuit", Canon Law Studies, no. 371 (thesis, Catholic University of America, 1957).

Canon 1736 (1983 CIC 1520)

If no procedural act, even though no impediment obstructs, has been placed in the tribunal of first instance for two years or in the appellate grade for one year, the instance is terminated and in the second case the sentence impugned by appeal becomes an adjudicated matter.

Canon Law Digest
II: 463

Canon 1737 (1983 CIC 1521)

Abatement is obtained by the law against all those including minors and those who are equivalent to minors and must also [be raised] by way of exception by office with due regard for the right of regress for indemnity against guardians, administrators, and procurators who cannot prove themselves to be without fault.

Canon 1738 (1983 CIC 1522)

Abatement extinguishes the acts of the process but not the acts of the case; indeed, these retain their force even in another instance provided it is between the same people and is used in the same matter; but as for what pertains to outsiders, it has no other force except documentary.

Canon 1739 (1983 CIC 1523)

In a case of abatement, whatever things were incurred by the litigants, each carries as the expense of the abated trial.

Canon 1740 (1983 CIC 1524)

§ 1. In any stage or grade of trial a petitioner can renounce the instance; likewise both the petitioner and the respondent can renounce the acts of the process, whether completely or only in part.

§ 2. In order that the renunciation be valid, it must be done in writing and must be signed by the party or his procurator, provided he has a special mandate for this, and must be communicated to the other party and accepted by him, or at least not impugned, and admitted by the judge.

Canon 1741 (1983 CIC 1525)

Once admitted, renunciation has the same effect over those acts as does abatement of the instance: and the one renouncing is obliged to cover the expenses of the action that he has renounced.

TITLE 9
On the interrogation of the parties to be made in trial

Canon 1742 (1983 CIC 1530)

§ 1. The judge must interrogate the parties in order to elucidate the truth of those facts that the public interest [demands] be established beyond doubt.

§ 2. In other cases, he can interrogate one of the contenders not only at the request of the other party but also by office as often as it concerns the illustration of evidence adduced.

§ 3. The interrogation of the parties can be made by the judge at any stage of the trial prior to the conclusion of the case; after the conclusion of the case, the prescription of Canon 1861 is observed.

Canon Law Digest
II: 463

Canon 1743[26] (1983 CIC 1531) Cross-Refs.: 1917 CIC 1755, 1794

§ 1. Parties legitimately interrogated by the judge are bound to respond and to offer the truth, unless it concerns a crime committed by them.

§ 2. If the party legitimately interrogated refuses to respond, it is for the judge to decide what should be made of this refusal, whether it is just or whether or not it is equivalent to a confession.

§ 3. A party who must respond, if he illegitimately refuses to respond or after he responded was shown to be lying, shall be punished at a time to be defined by the judge in light of circumstances and removed from legitimate ecclesiastical acts; and if before response he gave an oath to speak the truth, a layman [will be punished with] personal interdict and a cleric will be struck with suspension.

Canon Law Digest
I: 753; II: 464

[26] Donald Diederich, "The Right of an Accused in a Criminal Trial to Refuse to Testify against Himself according to the Norms of Canon Law and the Federal Law of the United States" (MS no. 3333, Gregorian University, 1962; printed version, no. 1607, 1963).

Canon 1744 (1983 CIC 1532, 1728)

The judge cannot offer an accused an oath to speak the truth in a criminal case; in contentious [cases], as often as the public good is at issue, he must require [an oath] from the parties; in other [cases] he can do so in accord with his prudence.

Canon 1745 (1983 CIC 1533–34)

§ 1. Both the petitioner and the respondent in turn, and even the promoter of justice and defender of the bond, can exhibit to the judge articles, that is, desires, upon which the parties can be questioned and which are commonly called *positions*.

§ 2. In treating of positions and the rules of admitting and proposing them to the parties, the regulations that are established in Canons 1773–81 are observed in proportion.

Canon 1746 (NA)

Parties must personally assist in the presence of the judge in giving their oath and in responding to questions, excepting those cases mentioned in Canon 1770, § 2, nn. 1–2.

TITLE 10
On evidence[27]

Canon 1747 (1983 CIC 1526)

Requiring no evidence are:

1.° Notorious facts, according to the norm of Canon 2197, nn. 2 and 3;
2.° Those things that are presumed by law;
3.° Facts asserted by one claiming it and admitted by the other, unless evidence is nevertheless required by law or by the judge.

Canon Law Digest
VII: 943

[27] Martin McManus, "Presentation of Evidence in Canon Law and American Trials" (Pontifical Lateran University, 1965; Rome: Catholic Book Agency, 1965).

Canon 1748 (1983 CIC 1526)

§ 1. The burden of proving [something] falls on the one who asserts [it].

§ 2. If the petitioner does not prove [the case], the respondent is absolved.

Canon 1749 (NA)

Evidence that seems to tend to the delay of the trial, or [that requires] the examination of witnesses from afar, or of whose domicile it is not certain, or knowledge of documents that the cited party cannot have should not be admitted by the judge, unless this evidence seems necessary because other matters are missing or are insufficient.

Canon Law Digest
II: 464

Chapter 1
On confession of the parties

Canon 1750 (1983 CIC 1535) Cross-Refs.: 1917 CIC 1752, 2197

The assertion of any fact in writing or orally by one party against himself and in favor of the adversary in the presence of the judge, whether freely offered or upon interrogation of the judge, is called a judicial confession.

Canon 1751 (1983 CIC 1536)

If it concerns some private matter and the case does not involve the public good, the judicial confession of one party, provided it was made freely and with awareness, relieves the other of the burden of proof.

Canon 1752 (1983 CIC 1538)

A party who has confessed something in trial cannot oppose his confession, unless this is done promptly or [if he] shows that the confession either lacked the expressed condition [described] in Canon 1750 or was owed to error of fact.

Canon 1753 (1983 CIC 1537)

A confession, whether in writing or orally, that is made outside the trial to the adversary himself or to others is called extrajudicial: it is for the judge, having admitted it to the trial and weighing the circumstances of all things, to decide what is to be made of it.

Canon Law Digest
VI: 832–36

Chapter 2
On witnesses and attestations[28]

Canon 1754 (1983 CIC 1547)

Evidence through witnesses can be admitted in any case to be moderated, however, by the judge according to the manner defined in the canons that follow.

Canon 1755 (1983 CIC 1548) Cross-Ref.: 1917 CIC 1823

§ 1. Witnesses legitimately interrogated by the judge must respond and offer the truth.

§ 2. With due regard for the prescription of Canon 1757, § 3, n. 2, [the following] are exempted from this obligation:

1.° Pastors and other priests in what concerns things manifested to them by reason of sacred ministry outside of sacramental confession; civil magistrates, doctors, obstetricians, lawyers, notaries, and others who are bound to secrecy of office or even by reason of advice they offered in what pertains to those matters liable to this secret;

2.° Whoever as a result of testimony fears infamy, dangerous vexations, or other great evils arising to himself or blood-relatives or affines in any degree of the direct line and in the first degree of the collateral line.

§ 3. Witnesses knowingly affirming falsehoods when legitimately interrogated by the judge or hiding the truth shall be punished according to the norm of Canon 1743, § 3; likewise all those should be struck with a

[28] John Manning, "The Admission and Evaluation of Testimonial Evidence in the Ancient Ecclesiastical Law" (diss. no. 37, Pontifical University of St. Thomas [Rome], 1956–1957); Simon Chin, "Proof by Witnesses in Canon Law from the Beginning to the Council of Trent" (thesis, Gregorian University; printed version, no. 2307, Taipei, 1971).

penalty who dare to induce witnesses or experts by gifts, solicitations, or in any other way to give false testimony or to hide the truth.

Canon Law Digest
I: 753

Article 1 — *Who can be a witness*

Canon 1756 (1983 CIC 1549)

Anyone can be a witness unless expressly repudiated by law in whole or in part.

Canon 1757 (1983 CIC 1550) Cross-Refs.: 1917 CIC 1755, 1795, 1974, 2027

§ 1. Rejected as unsuitable from giving testimony are children and the mentally disabled.

§ 2. [Rejected] as suspect:

1.° Excommunicates, perjurers, [and] the infamous, after a condemnatory or declaratory sentence;

2.° Those who have abandoned morals such that they are not considered worthy of trust;

3.° The public and grave enemies of the parties.

§ 3. [Rejected] as incapable:

1.° Those who are parties in the case or who act in the place of parties, such as a guardian in the case of a ward, a Superior or administrator in the case of his community or pious cause in whose name the trial was instituted, the judge and his assistants, the advocates and others who assist or aid the parties in this case;

2.° Priests in what pertains to all things that they know from sacramental confession, even if they are absolved of the bond of the seal; indeed, what was heard in any way or in any manner upon the occasion of confession cannot be received even as an indication of the truth;

3.° One spouse in the case of [the other] spouse or blood-relatives or affines in a case of the blood-relatives or affines in any grade of the direct line and in the first grade of the collateral, unless it concerns a case that looks to the civil status of religious persons of whom no other information can be had and the public good requires that it be made available.

Canon Law Digest
I: 753; II: 464

Canon 1758 (NA) Cross-Refs.: 1917 CIC 1764, 1767

Unsuitable and suspect [witnesses] can be heard by decree of the judge that declares this expedient; but their testimony contributes only as an indication in a small way to the evidence and generally it should be heard unsworn.

Article 2—*By whom, and how, and how many witnesses can be introduced, and who can be excluded*

Canon 1759 (1983 CIC 1551) Cross-Ref.: 1917 CIC 1975

§ 1. Witnesses are introduced by the parties.

§ 2. They can also be introduced by the promoter of justice and the defender of the bond, if they are involved in the case.

§ 3. But the judge himself, whenever it concerns minors or those who are equivalent to minors, and generally whenever the public good requires it, can introduce witnesses by office.

§ 4. A party who introduced a witness can renounce his examination; but the adversary can postulate that, nothwithstanding the renunciation, he be subjected to examination.

Canon Law Digest
II: 464

Canon 1760 (NA) Cross-Ref.: 1917 CIC 1752

§ 1. If anyone spontaneously presents himself for the sake of giving testimony, it is for the judge to admit or reject such testimony as he feels expedient.

§ 2. But he must reject any witness, offering himself spontaneously, who he feels appeared only for the sake of delaying the trial or in any manner offending justice or truth.

Canon Law Digest
II: 464

Canon 1761 (1983 CIC 1552)

§ 1. When evidence through witnesses is proposed, their names and domicile shall be indicated to the tribunal; moreover the positions or articles of argument upon which the witnesses are to be interrogated shall be disclosed.

§ 2. If, within a certain preemptory period established by the judge, [things] have passed without effect, the request is considered abandoned.

Canon Law Digest
I: 754

Canon 1762 (1983 CIC 1553)

The judge has the right and obligation of preventing too great a number of witnesses.

Canon Law Digest
II: 464

Canon 1763 (1983 CIC 1554) Cross-Ref.: 1917 CIC 1767

The parties must make the names of witnesses known to each other before their examination begins or, if in the prudent estimation of the judge this cannot be done without grave difficulty, at least before the publication of the testimony.

Canon Law Digest
II: 464; VIII: 1108

Canon 1764 (1983 CIC 1555) Cross-Refs.: 1917 CIC 1758, 1783

§ 1. Witnesses must be excluded by office if it is clearly shown to the judge that they are prohibited from offering testimony with due regard for the prescription of Canon 1758.

§ 2. And also, on the request of an adversary, he can exclude witnesses if a just cause for exclusion is demonstrated, which exclusion is called *reprobation of personal witnesses.*

§ 3. A party cannot reprobate a personal witness whom he introduced himself unless a new cause for reprobation occurs, although he can reprobate statements of the witness.

§ 4. The reprobation of a witness must be done within three days from when the name of the witness was communicated to the party, nor can it be accepted later unless it is demonstrated by the party, or at least affirmed by oath, that the defect of the witness was not known to him before.

§ 5. The judge will reserve discussion of reprobation until the end of the litigation, unless there is a presumption of law against his testimony, or if the defect is notorious or at least can be immediately and easily proven, or it cannot be proven later.

Canon Law Digest
II: 464

Canon 1765 (1983 CIC 1556)

The citation of witnesses will be done by ministry of the judge using a decree, and witnesses are to be contacted according to the norm of Canons 1715–23.

Canon 1766 (1983 CIC 1557)

§ 1. One correctly cited must appear or inform the judge of the reason for the absence.

§ 2. An uncooperative witness, namely, one who does not appear without legitimate cause or, even if he appears, refuses to respond or to give an oath or to sign the attestations, can be coerced by the judge with appropriate penalties, and moreover he can be fined in proportion to the damages that occurred to the parties from the lack of cooperation.

Article 3—*On the oath of witnesses*

Canon 1767 (1983 CIC 1562)

§ 1. A witness before giving testimony must present an oath to say all and only the truth, with due regard for the prescription of Canon 1758.

§ 2. Parties or their procurators can be present for the presentation of the oath of witnesses, with due regard for the prescription of Canon 1763.

§ 3. Witnesses can be excused from the oath with both parties consenting if it concerns the merely private rights of parties.

§ 4. But even when an oath is not required from a witness, the judge is under a grave obligation to make sure that a witness knows that he is always bound to speak the truth.

Canon 1768 (NA)

Witnesses, even though they have given an oath to speak the truth, can, nevertheless, in the prudent judgment of the judge upon completion of their examination, be compelled to swear *about the truth of the utterances*, whether concerning all of the articles of the position or about only some of them, whenever the gravity of the matter and the circumstances of the giving of the testimony seem to suggest it.

Canon 1769 (NA)

Witnesses can also be required to swear to observe secrecy concerning the questions posed and the answers given to the questions until the acts and the allegations are given public effect; it can even be perpetual according to the norm of Canon 1623, § 3.

Canon Law Digest
II: 464

Article 4—*On the examination of witnesses*[29]

Canon 1770 (1983 CIC 1558) Cross-Ref.: 1917 CIC 1746

§ 1. Witnesses are subject to examination in the seat of the tribunal.

§ 2. From this general rule are excepted:

1.° Cardinals of the H. R. C., Bishops, and illustrious persons who are exempted by their civil law from the obligation of appearing in the presence of the judge for the sake of testifying: all of these can choose for themselves the place where they will testify and must inform the judge about it;

2.° Those who are ill in body or who are impeded in spirit or by condition of life, such as nuns, from going to the seat of the tribunal; these are to be heard in their houses;

3.° Those present outside the diocese who cannot return to the diocese and approach the seat of the tribunal without grave in-

[29] Robert Clune, "The Judicial Interrogation of the Parties", Canon Law Studies, no. 269 (thesis, Catholic University of America, 1948).

convenience; these are to be heard in the tribunal of the place in which they are present according to the norm of Canon 1570, § 2, according to the questions and instructions sent by the judge of the case;

4.° Those who are indeed present in the diocese but in some place so far from the seat of the tribunal that they cannot without grave expenses go to the judge nor the judge to them. In this case the judge must depute a dignified and suitable priest from nearby so that with the assistance of someone who can act as actuary, he can perform the examination of these witnesses according to interrogatories also sent to him, along with opportune instructions given.

Canon Law Digest
I: 754; II: 465

Canon 1771 (1983 CIC 1559)

The parties cannot assist at the examination of witnesses unless the judge thinks that they ought to be admitted.

Canon 1772 (1983 CIC 1560)

§ 1. Witnesses are to be examined individually.

§ 2. It is left to the prudent decision of the judge whether, after having given their testimony, the witnesses are to be conferenced among themselves or with a party, that is, as commonly put, *to confront* them.

§ 3. This can be done if all of these things occur together, namely:

1.° If the witnesses disagree among themselves or with a party in a grave matter that affects a substantial [aspect] of the case;

2.° If there is no other easier way available for the easier detection of the truth;

3.° If there is no danger of scandal or divisiveness from the mixing of these persons together.

Canon Law Digest
I: 754; II: 465

Canon 1773 (1983 CIC 1561)

§ 1. Examination shall be conducted by the judge or by his delegate or auditor, and a notary must assist.

§ 2. In the examination, the questions must be presented to the witnesses by no one other than the judge or one who holds the place of judge. Therefore, if the parties or promoter of justice or defender of the bond are present for the examination and have new questions to be given to the witnesses, they must suggest them to the judge or to the one holding his place, but not to the witnesses, in order that he may present [the questions] to [the witnesses].

Canon Law Digest
I: 754

Canon 1774 (1983 CIC 1563) Cross-Ref.: 1917 CIC 2050

Witnesses must first of all be interrogated not only about general things concerning their person, such as name, surname, origin, age, religion, condition, domicile, but also about their connection with the parties in the case; hence questions are to be presented that look to the case and help it, and from where and in what manner the witness has knowledge about the things asserted.

Canon Law Digest
I: 755; II: 465

Canon 1775 (1983 CIC 1564)

Questions shall be brief and not complicated with many things, and not misleading, not tricky, not suggestive of a response, removed from all sorts of offense, and pertinent to the case with which they are concerned.

Canon Law Digest
I: 755; II: 465

Canon 1776 (1983 CIC 1565)

§ 1. The questions are not to be communicated to the witnesses beforehand.

§ 2. Nevertheless, if they are to testify about things remote from memory so that it could not be recalled earlier and affirmed certainly, the judge can advise the witness [about them] in part if he thinks this can be done without danger.

Canon Law Digest
I: 755

Canon 1777 (1983 CIC 1566)

Witnesses shall give their testimony orally and shall not read any writing, unless it concerns a calculation or an accounting; and then they can consult their notes that they brought with them.

Canon Law Digest
I: 755

Canon 1778 (1983 CIC 1567)

A response is to be reduced to writing without delay by the actuary, not only in what pertains to its substance, but also using the words given in the testimony, unless the judge, attentive to the exigencies of the case, thinks it sufficient to record just the substance of the deposition.

Canon Law Digest
I: 755; II: 465

Canon 1779 (1983 CIC 1568)

The actuary shall make mention in the acts about the giving, or omission, or refusal of the oath, about the presence of the parties or others, about questions added by office, and generally about all those things worthy of recalling that might have happened when the witnesses were examined.

Canon Law Digest
I: 755

Canon 1780 (1983 CIC 1569)

§ 1. Witnesses, before they leave the witness stand, must have read to them what the actuary reduced to writing about the things they testified to in living voice, giving them the ability to add, suppress, correct, or modify [it].

§ 2. Finally, the judge and the notary must sign the acts of the witness.

Canon Law Digest
I: 756; II: 465

Canon 1781 (1983 CIC 1570) Cross-Ref.: 1917 CIC 1983

Witnesses, even though they have already been excused, can be called for a new examination at the request of a party or by office before their acts or testimonies have become official, if the judge thinks it necessary or useful, provided that every danger of collusion or corruption is removed.

Canon Law Digest
I: 756; II: 465

Article 5 — *On the disclosure and the rejection of testimony*[30]

Canon 1782 (NA)

§ 1. When the parties or their procurators were not present for the examination, testimony can be released immediately upon the completion of the examination of all the witnesses by decree of the judge.

§ 2. But the judge can defer the release of testimony until a time when other matters of proof have been completed if he thinks it correct to do so.

Canon 1783 (NA)

After the release of testimony:

1.° The personal faculty of rejecting witnesses ceases except for the case mentioned in Canon 1764, § 4;

2.° But there remains the right of rejecting witnesses, whether in regard to the manner of examination, which namely can be an objection [asserting] that a rule of law was neglected in conducting their examination, or whether it pertains to the testimony itself when namely the testimony is attacked as false or various or contradictory or obscure or [as being offered despite] a lack of knowledge and similar things.

Canon 1784 (NA)

The judge shall reject this reprobation by his decree if he believes that it rests on a useless basis or was made to delay the trial.

[30] Thomas Gallagher, "The Rejection of Judicial Witnesses and Testimony", Canon Law Studies, no. 308 (Catholic University of America, not published); Henri Larroque, "The Rejection of Judicial Witnesses and Their Testimony", Canon Law Studies, no. 457 (J. C. D. thesis, Catholic University of America, 1967).

Canon 1785 (NA)

If the judge admits the reprobation, the judge shall establish a brief period for the requesting party to prove the reprobation, and from there it shall proceed as [would] other incidental issues.

Canon 1786 (NA) Cross-Refs.: 1917 CIC 1891, 1983

After giving testimony, witnesses already heard shall not be interrogated once again on the same articles, nor shall new witnesses be admitted, except cautiously and for grave reason, in cases that never become an adjudicated matter; in other [cases, this shall be done] only for the gravest reason, and in any case avoiding every sort of fraud and with danger of subornation removed, and the other party being heard, and having requested the opinion of the promoter of justice or defender of the bond, if they are involved in the trial; all of these things the judge decides by his decree.

Canon Law Digest
I: 756; II: 465

Article 6—*On the indemnification of witnesses*[31]

Canon 1787 (1983 CIC 1571)

§ 1. A witness has the right to request compensation for expenses that he incurred by reason of travel or staying in a place for the trial and to [receive] an appropriate indemnification for the interruption of his business or work.

§ 2. It is for the judge, having heard the party and the witness, and if necessary also experts, to award indemnification and to cover the expenses of the witness.

Canon Law Digest
II: 465

Canon 1788 (NA)

If, within a preemptory period defined by the judge, the one who wanted to call the witness has not deposited an appropriate amount of money

[31] Francis Kelleher, "Judicial Expenses", Canon Law Studies, no. 375 (Catholic University of America, not published).

mentioned in Canon 1909, § 2, he is considered to have renounced the examination of the witness.

Article 7—*On the trustworthiness of witnesses*

Canon 1789 (1983 CIC 1572)

In considering testimony, the judge shall keep before his eyes:

1.° The condition of the person and whether the witness enjoys an honest [reputation] and any dignity;

2.° Whether he testifies from personal knowledge, especially as an eyewitness or from personal hearing, or from credulity or from reputation or about what has been heard from others;

3.° Whether the witness is constant and firmly consistent with himself; or whether [the testimony] is varied, uncertain, or vacillating;

4.° And finally whether there are co-witnesses for the testimony, or if it is isolated.

Canon Law Digest
II: 465–66; III: 604

Canon 1790 (NA)

If the witnesses disagree among themselves, the judge shall decide whether the testimony given by them is adverse to that of others or whether it is only different or circumstantial.

Canon 1791 (1983 CIC 1573)

§ 1. The deposition of one witness cannot result in full proof, unless it is a qualified witness who testifies about matters conducted by office.

§ 2. But if two or three persons sworn to trustworthiness and above all exception, being firmly consistent with each other, testify from their own knowledge about some matter or fact in a trial, it is considered sufficiently proven; unless in a certain case the judge, because of the great gravity of the affair or from indications that suggest some doubt about the truth of the matter asserted, thinks it necessary to augment the evidence.

Canon Law Digest
I: 756; II: 466; III: 604–5

CHAPTER 3
On experts[32]

Canon 1792 (1983 CIC 1574)

The work of experts shall be used whenever their examination and vote is required by law or by prescription of the judge to prove some fact or to discern the true nature of some matter.

Canon Law Digest
II: 466

Canon 1793 (1983 CIC 1575)

§ 1. It is for the judge to select and designate experts.

§ 2. The judge can make this designation in merely private cases upon the request of both parties or even one, though with the other [party] consenting; but in cases that look to the public good, the promoter of justice and defender of the bond shall be heard.

§ 3. It is left to the prudent judgment of the judge to select one or more experts according to the nature of the case and the difficulty of the thing, unless the law itself sets a number of experts.

Canon Law Digest
II: 466

Canon 1794 (NA)

It is for experts to apply their expertise according to the laws of truth and justice and not falsely to affirm or hide the truth; if they offend in this, they shall be punished according to the norm of Canon 1743, § 3.

Canon 1795 (NA)

§ 1. All things being equal, they are to be chosen for the office of expert who have been shown to be suitable by the authority of a competent body.

§ 2. Whoever is excluded from offering testimony according to the norm of Canon 1757 cannot assume the office of expert either.

---

[32] Lawrence Lover, "The Juridical Value of Peritial Proof" (diss. no. 18, Pontifical University of St. Thomas [Rome], 1954–1955); Raymond Wahl, "The Use of Experts in Canon Law" (thesis, Gregorian University; printed version, no. 1073, 1957); William Pickard, "Judicial Experts: A Source of Evidence in Ecclesiastical Trials", Canon Law Studies, no. 389 (thesis, Catholic University of America, 1958).

Canon 1796 (1983 CIC 1576)

§ 1. Experts can be recused for the same reasons as witnesses.

§ 2. The judge shall decide by his decree whether the recusal should be admitted or not, and if recusal is admitted, another can fill the place of the recused expert.

Canon Law Digest
II: 466

Canon 1797 (NA)

§ 1. Experts are considered to have accepted the assigned duty by the offering of an oath to fulfill faithfully the duty.

§ 2. The parties can be present not only for the presentation of the oath but also for the execution of the required duties by the expert, unless something else is required by the nature of the thing or by uprightness or the law or the judge orders [otherwise].

Canon 1798 (NA)

After the presentation of the oath, if the expert does not appear within a time set by the mandate or, without just cause, puts off its completion, he is bound for the damages.

Canon 1799 (1983 CIC 1577)

§ 1. The judge, attentive to those things that might be brought up by the litigants, shall define in his decree each and every issue concerning which the task of the expert must be focused.

§ 2. The time within which the examination is to be done and the opinion presented, if it seems necessary or opportune to the judge, can be set by the same judge and even, having heard the parties, extended.

Canon Law Digest
II: 466

Canon 1800 (NA)

§ 1. If there is doubt about who wrote something, the judge shall assign to experts not only the writing that is liable to question but also, at the request of the parties, other writings with which it must be compared and [contrasted].

§ 2. If the parties disagree about the writings that are to be compared among themselves, the judge will select for the sake of comparison those others that the parties themselves recognize or those that the author accused of the controversial writings wrote as a public person and that are stored in archives or other public repositories; or [resort can be had to] his writings that have been notarized or that were produced in the presence of public persons.

§ 3. But if the writings designated by the parties and by the judge for comparison are not sufficient for investigation in the judgment of experts, and if the one to whom the controversial writing is attributed is alive, the judge at the request of a party and also by office shall cite him and in his own hand in the presence of the judge or his delegate will write whatever the experts or the judge himself or his delegate might dictate.

§ 4. The refusal of writing, if no legitimate cause for refusal is proven, is considered as a confession of the genuineness of the controversial writing to the prejudice of the one refusing.

Canon 1801 (1983 CIC 1578)

§ 1. Experts shall offer their opinion in writing or orally in the presence of the judge, but if it is offered orally, it shall immediately be reduced to writing and signed by the notary and by the expert.

§ 2. An expert, especially if his decision is offered in writing, can be approached by the judge in order to supply explanations that seem additionally necessary.

§ 3. Experts must indicate clearly by what route and manner they proceeded in fulfilling the duty given to them and upon what leading arguments the decision given by them is based.

Canon Law Digest
I: 756

Canon 1802 (1983 CIC 1578)

Each expert will prepare a report distinct from the others unless, the law not forbidding, the judge orders that one [report] shall be made to be signed by the individuals; if this is done, disagreements in the decision, if there are any, shall be diligently noted.

Canon Law Digest
II: 466

Canon 1803 (NA)

§ 1. If the experts disagree among themselves, it is permitted for the judge to ask for a vote on the reports given by the first experts from a greater expert or to use entirely new experts.

§ 2. The judge has the same authority whenever the experts after their selection fall under suspicion or are shown to be unequal to or not suitable for their duties.

Canon 1804 (1983 CIC 1579)

§ 1. The judge shall attentively weigh not only the conclusions of the experts, even if they are in agreement, but also the other circumstances of the case.

§ 2. When he gives his reason for decision, he must express how he was moved by argument to admit or reject the conclusions of the experts.

Canon Law Digest
II: 466; III: 605

Canon 1805 (1983 CIC 1580)

The expenses and fees of the experts are decided by the judge having before his eyes the received custom of each place and goodness and equity with due regard for the right of recourse according to the norm of Canon 1913, § 1.

Chapter 4
On judicial access and examination

Canon 1806 (1983 CIC 1582)

If the judge thinks it necessary to go to the place of controversy and to inspect the matter under debate, he issues a decree to that effect in which he describes in summary form, having heard the parties, what will be done in the visit.

Canon 1807 (NA)

The judge can conduct the examination himself or through an auditor or delegated judge.

Canon 1808 (NA)

§ 1. The judge, in examining the object or place, can use experts if their efforts seem necessary or useful.

§ 2. If experts are used there shall be observed, insofar as possible, those things prescribed in Canons 1793–1805.

Canon 1809 (NA)

If the judge foresees a danger of fights or confusion attached to the visit, he can prohibit the parties or their judicial advocates from being present for the examination.

Canon 1810 (NA)

The judge can subject the witnesses to be present either by office or [at the request of] the parties before the examination rightly conducted if it would seem to expedite fuller evidence or the removal of doubts about which the examination is being conducted.

Canon 1811 (1983 CIC 1583)

§ 1. A notary shall take care diligently to record in the acts what day and hour the examination was made, which persons were there, and what during the examination was said or done or decreed by the judge.

§ 2. The instruments of the conducted examination must be signed by the judge and the notary.

Chapter 5
On evidence through instruments[33]

Article 1—*On the nature and trustworthiness of instruments*

Canon 1812 (1983 CIC 1539)

In every sort of trial, evidence from public and private documents can be admitted.

Canon Law Digest
VIII: 1108

Canon 1813 (1983 CIC 1540)

§ 1. The primary public ecclesiastical documents are:

1.° The acts of the Supreme Pontiff and of the Roman Curia and of Ordinaries compiled in authentic form in the exercise of their duties with authentic attestations about these acts given by them or their notaries;

2.° Instruments produced by ecclesiastical notaries;

3.° Ecclesiastical judicial acts;

4.° Inscriptions of baptism, confirmation, ordination, religious profession, marriage, and death that are contained in the registers of the Curia or parish or religious [institute], and written attestations about them taken from pastors or Ordinaries or produced by ecclesiastical notaries and authentic copies of these.

§ 2. Public civil documents are those that are considered so in law, according to the laws of each place.

§ 3. Letters, contracts, wills, and writings of any sort produced by private [persons] are counted among private documents.

Canon Law Digest
II: 466

[33] Robert Willett, "The Probative Value of Documents in Ecclesiastical Trials", Canon Law Studies, no. 171 (J. C. D. thesis, Catholic University of America, 1942).

Canon 1814 (NA)

Public documents, whether ecclesiastical or civil, are presumed genuine until the contrary is evinced by evident arguments.

Canon Law Digest
II: 467

Canon 1815 (NA)

Recognition or impugning of writing can be proposed in trial both incidentally or in the manner of a principal case.

Canon Law Digest
VIII: 1108

Canon 1816 (1983 CIC 1541)

Public documents are to be given faith in those matters that are directly and principally affirmed in them.

Canon Law Digest
II: 467

Canon 1817 (1983 CIC 1542)

Private documents, whether admitted by the parties or recognized by the judge, are evidence against the authors and signatories [thereto] and the cases of those [that are] based on them, and are like an extrajudicial confession; by themselves they do not have force of proof against outsiders.

Canon Law Digest
VI: 836–38

Canon 1818 (1983 CIC 1543)

If there are demonstrated erasures, corrections, additions, or other anomalies affecting documents, it is for the judge to decide whether and in what way such documents were made.

Canon Law Digest
I: 756–57

Article 2—*On the production of documents and action for exhibition*

Canon 1819 (1983 CIC 1544)

Documents do not have force of proof in trial unless they are originals or are shown [to be] authentic copies deposited within the chancery of the tribunal, except for those documents that are of public effect, such as laws duly promulgated.

Canon Law Digest
II: 467

Canon 1820 (1983 CIC 1544)

Documents are to be exhibited in their authentic form and deposited in the trial so that they can be examined by the judge and by the adversary.

Canon 1821 (NA)

§ 1. If doubt is raised about whether a writing is a faithful sample or not, the judge can decide at the request of a party or even by office that the document itself shall be shown whence the copy was taken.

§ 2. If this cannot be done at all or [done only] with great difficulty, the judge can delegate an auditor or the local Ordinary to inquire regarding an examination and comparison of the document prescribing those points and how the comparison must be done; both parties may assist at the comparison.

Canon 1822 (1983 CIC 1545)

Common documents or those that treat of a common affair, such as wills and instruments that look to succession, the division of goods, contracts, and other [documents] of this sort that are at issue between the parties, can by any of the litigants be postulated for exhibit in trial by the party who is said to possess them.

Canon 1823 (1983 CIC 1546)

§ 1. No one, however, is bound to exhibit a document, even a common one, that cannot be communicated without danger of harm according to the norm of Canon 1755, § 2, n. 2, or without danger of violating a secret to be preserved.

§ 2. Nevertheless, if even a part of the document that is at issue can be copied and shown in a sample without the [above-]mentioned inconveniences, the judge can decide that this [part] be shown.

Canon 1824 (NA)

§ 1. If a party refuses to show a document that ought to be produced at trial and that it seems he possesses, the judge upon the request of the other party, and having heard if necessary the promoter of justice or defender of the bond, shall issue an interlocutory sentence as to whether and how the exhibition of this document is to be done.

§ 2. Should the party refuse to produce it, it is for the judge to decide how much should be made of this refusal.

§ 3. But if a party denies having the document, the judge can submit him to an examination and impose the taking of an oath on the matter.

Canon Law Digest
I: 757

Chapter 6
On presumptions

Canon 1825[34] (1983 CIC 1584)

§ 1. A presumption is a probable conjecture about an uncertain matter; it can be of law when it is established in the law; or [it can be] of man that is formed by the judge.

§ 2. A presumption of law can be simply of law or [it can be] of law and by law.

Canon 1826 (NA)

Against a simple presumption of law there can be admitted both direct and indirect evidence; but against a presumption of law and by law, only indirect [evidence can be admitted] that is against the fact upon which the presumption is based.

---

[34] John Toomey, "The Nature of *Fictio Juris* [presumption] and Its Use in Canon Law" (thesis, Gregorian University; printed version, no. 1070, 1957).

Canon 1827 (1983 CIC 1585)

Whoever has a presumption regarding his rights is freed from the burden of proving [them], which then redounds to the opposing party; if it cannot be overcome, sentence must be given in favor of the party who stands with the presumption.

Canon 1828 (1983 CIC 1586)

Presumptions that are not established in the law shall not be formed by the judge except from certain and determinate facts that are directly consistent with the matter about which there is controversy.

Chapter 7
On the oath of the parties

Canon 1829[35] (NA)

If there is available only semi-full proof and there is no other additional proof available, the judge can order or admit an oath to supplement the evidence, this oath being called *supplementary*.

Canon Law Digest
II: 467

Canon 1830 (NA)

§ 1. This oath is especially appropriate in circumstances where the civil or religious status of a person is at issue and cannot be proven otherwise.

§ 2. But the judge shall abstain from it both in criminal cases and in contentious [cases] if [so required] by law, or if it concerns an object of great price, or [if it is] about a fact of little importance, or if the right thing or deed is not proper to the person to whom the oath would be offered.

§ 3. But he can offer this oath either by office or at the request of the other party or the promoter of justice or the defender of the bond, if they are present at the trial.

§ 4. It should usually be offered to those who have the fuller evidence.

---

[35] Kodwo Mensah-Brown, *The Supplementary Law in Canonical Jurisprudence: A Doctoral Dissertation in Canon Law* (Obuasi, Ghana: Ashanti Times Press, 1965).

§ 5. But it is for the judge to define by decree whether and what circumstances must come together and why he must offer a supplementary oath.

Canon Law Digest
II: 467

Canon 1831 (NA)

§ 1. The party to whom the supplemental oath is offered in matters that do not pertain to his civil or religious state can refuse it for a just cause or refer it to his adversary.

§ 2. It is for the judge to evaluate what should be made of this refusal, whether it is just, and whether it is equivalent to confession.

§ 3. A supplemental oath given by one party can be impugned by the other.

Canon 1832 (NA)

If reparation for damages has been established at law but it is not possible to estimate the quantity of the damages with certainty, the judge can give an oath to the party who suffered the damages that is called *estimative*.

Canon 1833 (NA)

In giving an estimative oath:

1.° The judge asks the party who suffered the damage to designate by a holy oath those things lost to himself or that perished [as a result of the respondent's] dolus, and to express their price or value according to his probable estimation;

2.° If the amount seems too much to the judge, he can reduce it for equity, having before his eyes all those indications and arguments used for demonstration and using, if he thinks it necessary, experts, the better to advance truth and justice.

Canon 1834 (NA)

§ 1. The parties can agree not only before the start of litigation that the controversy can be settled by an oath to be offered by the other, but also during the litigation, and at any time or stage this other party can, with the approval of the judge, offer the oath to the other [party] with the condition that the question, whether principal or incidental, will be considered decided according to the oath.

§ 2. An oath of this sort is called *decisive*.

Canon 1835 (NA)

The decisive oath cannot be offered unless:

1.° It concerns a thing in which cession or settlement is admitted and that in regard to the litigating persons is of small importance or price;
2.° It would come from one who is able to cede or make a settlement;
3.° [It comes from] those who are able to cede or make a settlement and they do not have full evidence in their favor;
4.° It concerns mere notice of facts or a deed that is proper to them to whom the oath is to be offered.

Canon Law Digest
II: 467

Canon 1836 (NA)

§ 1. This oath can be recalled by the party who demanded it if it has not yet been given, and it can be accepted and given by the other party, or not, or returned to the adversary.

§ 2. The oath having been given, the question is solved according to the sworn formula, and from there the cession or judicial settlement must proceed.

§ 3. If the oath is refused and not returned to the adversary, it is for the judge to consider what should be made of this refusal, whether there was a just cause for so acting, or whether it should be considered equivalent to a confession.

§ 4. If it is returned to the adversary, this one must present it, otherwise the case falls.

§ 5. In order that the oath be returned to the adversary, it is necessary that those conditions appear together that were required for it to be offered and that there intercedes again the ministry of the judge.

TITLE 11
On incidental cases

Canon 1837 (1983 CIC 1587)

It is considered an incidental case whenever, a trial having started at least by citation, a question is proposed by one of the parties or by the promoter of justice or defender of the bond, if they are in the trial, that, even though it is not expressly contained in the libellus by which the litigation is introduced, nevertheless pertains to the case and must be resolved for the most part before the principal question.

Canon Law Digest
I: 757; II: 467; V: 708

Canon 1838 (1983 CIC 1588)

An incidental case is proposed either orally or in the libellus, indicating the connection that exists between it and the principal cause and observing insofar as this can be done the rules established in Canons 1706–25.

Canon 1839 (1983 CIC 1589)

A judge having received a libellus or verbal petition, and having heard the parties and if necessary the promoter of justice or defender of the bond, will decide with them whether the proposed incidental question is pointless and has been raised only to delay the principal trial; and likewise whether the incidental cause is of such a nature and applies with such relevance to the principal cause that it must be resolved before it. If it is considered such, he shall admit the libellus or instance; otherwise, he rejects it by his decree.

Canon Law Digest
II: 467

Canon 1840 (1983 CIC 1589–90) Cross-Ref.: 1917 CIC 1878

§ 1. The question of whether the incidental [issues] that are raised should be resolved in a form observed at trial or merely by decree is for the judge to consider, being attentive to the quality and gravity of the matter.

§ 2. If an incidental cause is to be judicially defined, the rules insofar as possible are to be observed that apply to ordinary trials; nevertheless, the judge will take care that the delay of things be as brief as possible.

§ 3. The judge in a decree that, [although] not observing judicial forms, will either reject or resolve the incidental question, will indicate the reasons behind it and briefly explain [them] in law and in fact.

Canon Law Digest
I: 757; II: 467; VIII: 1108

Canon 1841 (1983 CIC 1591)

Before the principal cause is finished, the judge can correct or revoke an interlocutory sentence, just cause intervening, either on his own having heard the parties or at the request of one party having heard the other party, and inquiring always the opinion of the promoter of justice or defender of the bond, if they are involved.

Canon Law Digest
I: 757

Chapter 1
On contumacy[36]

Canon 1842 (1983 CIC 1592)

A respondent cited who without just cause does not appear either personally or through a procurator can be declared contumacious.

Canon 1843 (1983 CIC 1592)

§ 1. A judge is not to declare a respondent contumacious unless it is first shown:

1.° That a citation legitimately made came to the notice of the respondent within a useful time or at least should have come to him;

2.° The respondent fails to offer an excuse for the absence or presents an unjust one.

§ 2. These things can be proved either by a new citation made to the respondent in order for him to excuse, if he can, his contumacy, or in some other way.

Canon Law Digest
I: 757

[36] Alphonse Kress, "Contumacy in Ecclesiastical Trials", Canon Law Studies, no. 279 (Catholic University of America, not published).

Canon 1844 (1983 CIC 1592)

§ 1. At the request of a party or promoter of justice or defender of the bond, if they are involved in the trial, a judge can declare the contumacy of a respondent and, [contumacy] being declared, can proceed, those things being observed that ought to be observed, even to definitive sentence and its execution.

§ 2. If things proceed to definitive sentence without the litigation being argued, the sentence must concern itself only with what is petitioned in the libellus; if the litigation is contested [then it concerns itself] with the object of that contest.

Canon 1845 (NA) Cross-Ref.: 1917 CIC 1714

§ 1. In order to break the contumacy of a respondent, the judge can also impart ecclesiastical penalties.

§ 2. But in order to do this, the citation of the respondent must be repeated with an indication of the penalties; nor is it yet permitted to declare contumacy or, it being declared, to impose penalties unless it is proven that even this second citation lacked all effect.

Canon Law Digest
II: 467

Canon 1846 (1983 CIC 1593)

A respondent receding from contumacy and being present at trial before the resolution of the case must be allowed to submit conclusions and evidence if he offers any; but the judge shall take care lest the trial be protracted by unnecessary delays and lengthened by bad faith.

Canon 1847 (1983 CIC 1593)

But after the sentence has been laid down, a contumacious one can seek the benefit of restitution in the entirety through appeal from the judge who laid down the sentence, but not beyond three months from communication of the sentence, unless it concerns a case that does not pass into an adjudicated matter.

Canon 1848 (NA)

The rules given above also have a place when the respondent, even if cooperating with the first citation, nevertheless later in the progress of the trial becomes contumacious.

Canon 1849 (1983 CIC 1594)

If, on the day and hour at which a respondent according to the prescription of the citation is first to present himself in the presence of the judge, the petitioner is not present and offers no or an insufficient excuse for his absence, the judge shall cite him again at the request of the convened respondent; and if the petitioner does not obey the new citation or later starts the trial or, it having started, fails to pursue it, at the request of the convened respondent or the promoter of justice or the defender of the bond, he shall be declared contumacious by the judge, observing the same rules that were given above regarding contumacy of the respondent.

Canon Law Digest
II: 468

Canon 1850 (NA)

§ 1. A contumacious petitioner, declared such by the judge, loses his right to pursue his action in that instance.

§ 2. It is permitted, nevertheless, for the promoter of justice or defender of the bond to pursue the instance on his own as often as this seems warranted by the public good.

§ 3. A respondent, however, after this, has the right of petitioning that either he be allowed to leave the trial freely or that all of the actions taken be regarded as null or that he be definitively absolved from the petition of the petitioner, or that the trial, given the absence of the petitioner, be led to its end.

Canon Law Digest
I: 758; II: 468

Canon 1851 (1983 CIC 1595)

§ 1. One who is declared contumacious and who does not purge his contumacy, whether petitioner or respondent, is condemned both to the expenses of the litigation that have resulted from his contumacy and also if necessary to offering indemnity to the other party.

§ 2. But if both the petitioner and the respondent are contumacious, they are bound to the expenses together.

CHAPTER 2
On the intervention of third parties in a case

Canon 1852 (1983 CIC 1596)

§ 1. One who has an interest can be admitted to intervene in a case at any instance of the litigation.

§ 2. But to be admitted, he must show to the judge a libellus before the conclusion of the case in which he explains briefly his right of intervention.

§ 3. Whoever intervenes in a case is to be admitted in that stage in which the case is found, having been assigned a brief and peremptory period to produce his evidence if the case has come to the time for evidence.

Canon 1853 (1983 CIC 1597)

If the intervention of a third party appears necessary, the judge at the request of a party or even by office must order intervention in a case.

CHAPTER 3
On attempts while litigation is pending[37]

Canon 1854 (NA)

An attempt is anything that, while the litigation is pending, either one party against the other party or the judge against either or both parties innovates over the party's objection and to his prejudice; [this includes] whether the innovation regards the material of the trial with due regard for the prescription of Canons 1672 and 1673, or whether it regards the [time] limits assigned to the parties either by law or by the judge in order to place certain judicial acts.

---

[37] Peter Goncalvez, "Attempt Pending the Trial" (MS no. 1738, Gregorian University, 1950); John Dunnivan, "Prejudicial Attempts in Pending Litigation", Canon Law Studies, no. 379 (J. C. D. thesis, Catholic University of America, 1960).

Canon 1855 (NA)

§ 1. Attempts are null by the law.

§ 2. Therefore a party wounded by an attempt may pursue an action to obtain a declaration of nullity.

§ 3. This action must be instituted in the presence of the judge of the principal case; but if the wounded party suspects the judge of the attempt, he can raise the exception of suspicion that is pursued according to the norm of Canon 1615.

Canon 1856 (NA)

§ 1. The question of attempt having been raised, the course of the principal case is normally suspended, but if it seems opportune to the judge, the question of attempt can be treated and resolved together with the principal case.

§ 2. Questions of attempt are to be treated most expeditiously and resolved by decree of the judge having heard the parties and the promoter of justice and the defender of the bond, if these are involved in the trial.

Canon 1857 (NA)

§ 1. Attempt having been demonstrated, the judge must order its revocation or purging.

§ 2. But if an attempt has been perpetrated by force or dolus, the one who committed it is also bound regarding the damages to the party thus wounded.

TITLE 12
On the publication of the process, on the conclusion of the case, and on the discussion of the case

Canon 1858 (1983 CIC 1598)

Before the discussion of the case and sentence, all the evidence that is in the acts and that till then has remained secret must be published.

Canon Law Digest
II: 468

Canon 1859 (1983 CIC 1598)

If the faculty has been granted to the parties and their advocates to inspect the procedural acts or to petition a copy of them, it is understood that publication of the process has been done.

Canon 1860 (1983 CIC 1599)

§ 1. All those things being completed that pertain to the production of evidence, one arrives *at the conclusion of the case.*

§ 2. This conclusion is considered [to have arrived] whenever the parties interrogated by the judge declare that they have nothing else to submit, or when the useful time established by the judge for the proposing of evidence has run, or the judge declares that he considers the case sufficiently instructed.

§ 3. Upon the conclusion of the case, in whatsoever manner it occurred, the judge shall issue a decree.

Canon Law Digest
II: 468

Canon 1861 (1983 CIC 1600) Cross-Refs.: 1917 CIC 1742, 1891

§ 1. After the conclusion of the case, new evidence is prohibited unless it concerns a case that never passes into an adjudicated matter, or documents that have just been found, or witnesses who were not able to be included during the useful time because of legitimate impediment.

§ 2. If he considers that new evidence should be admitted, the judge will decide this, having heard the other party, to whom he will grant an appropriate time to study the new evidence and to defend himself [in its regard]; otherwise, the trial is considered of no moment.

Canon Law Digest
II: 468

Canon 1862 (1983 CIC 1601)

§ 1. The conclusion of the case being done, the judge in his prudent judgment will give the parties an appropriate period of time to produce their defenses or allegations either personally or through an advocate.

§ 2. This period can be extended by the judge at the request of a party, having heard the other [party]; or it can even be shortened with the consent of the other [party].

Canon Law Digest
II: 468

Canon 1863 (1983 CIC 1602) Cross-Ref.: 1917 CIC 1865

§ 1. The defense shall be made in writing and normally there shall be prepared as many copies as there are judges so that each individual judge can receive a copy.

§ 2. A copy must also be given to the promoter of justice and the defender of the bond, if they are present in the trial; the parties must also exchange copies between themselves.

§ 3. The president of the tribunal, as often as he thinks it necessary in his prudent judgment, and if he finds that it would not be too grave a burden on the parties, shall order that the defenses be printed in type together with the principal documents and bound together as a fascicle that contains a summary of the acts and the documents.

§ 4. In this case, he shall order that it not be printed [until] the manuscript has been shown to him and permission has been obtained for its publication; moreover, secrecy shall be sedulously observed, if it is a case where [secrecy] is required.

Canon 1864 (1983 CIC 1602) Cross-Ref.: 1917 CIC 1865

It is for the judge [or] for the president in a collegiate tribunal to moderate [things] according to his prudence lest the defense extend too long, unless there is a provision on this in the special law of the tribunal.

Canon Law Digest
II: 468

Canon 1865 (1983 CIC 1603)

§ 1. Once the parties have exchanged between themselves a written defense, it is permitted to each party to give a response within a brief time set by the judge and observing the rules and precautions mentioned in Canons 1863 and 1864.

§ 2. This right is granted to the parties only once unless it seems to the judge that for grave causes it ought to be granted again; but once the concession is made to one party it is considered made to the other.

Canon 1866 (1983 CIC 1604–5)

§ 1. *Oral*, as they are called, *informations*, namely those by which the advocates attempt to instruct the judge about circumstances respecting the law and facts of the case, are prohibited.

§ 2. A moderate discussion can be admitted, however, in the presence of the judge sitting for the tribunal in order to illustrate something if, at the request of either or both parties, the judge thinks it useful and admits it.

§ 3. In order to obtain this discussion, the parties must produce in writing the headings of the questions to be discussed with the other party expressed in few words; but it is for the judge then to communicate this to the parties and to assign a day and an hour for the discussion and to moderate the discussion.

§ 4. One of the tribunal notaries shall assist at the discussion in order that, if the judge orders or a party requests and the judge consents, he be able to put into writing the discussion, confessions, or conclusions in order to achieve justice by the contents.

Canon Law Digest
II: 468

Canon 1867 (1983 CIC 1606)

In contentious cases, if the parties fail to appear before the useful time for defense or leave [the matter] to the knowledge and conscience of the judge, the judge, if he has from the acts and the evidence, a full perspective on the matter, can immediately pronounce sentence.

TITLE 13
On the sentence[38]

Canon 1868 (1983 CIC 1607, 1617)

§ 1. A sentence is a legitimate pronouncement by which the judge resolves the case proposed by the litigants and treated in a judicial manner:

[38] Delisle Lemieux, "The Sentence in Ecclesiastical Procedure", Canon Law Studies, no. 87 (J. C. D. thesis, Catholic University of America, 1934).

these are called *interlocutory* if they answer an incidental case; [they are called] *definitive* if [they answer] the principal case.

§ 2. The other pronouncements of the judge are called *decrees*.

Canon 1869[39] (1983 CIC 1608)

§ 1. For the pronouncement of any sentence the judge is required to achieve moral certitude concerning the matter to be settled in the sentence.

§ 2. The judge must reach this certitude from the acts and the evidence.

§ 3. The judge must evaluate the evidence according to his conscience, unless the law expressly established something about the effects of some [types of] evidence.

§ 4. A judge who is not able to form this certitude himself shall pronounce that the right of the petitioner is not proven and shall dismiss the respondent, unless it concerns a case of favor, in which case it shall be pronounced [in benefit of] the favor and with due regard for the prescription of Canon 1697, § 2.

Canon Law Digest
III: 605–11

Canon 1870 (NA)

Sentence must be given by the judge upon the completion of the discussion of the case; but if the case is more complicated and has been made more difficult by contention or documentation, he can set aside an appropriate interval of time.

Canon Law Digest
II: 468

Canon 1871 (1983 CIC 1609)

§ 1. The president of the college shall set on what day and hour the judges will meet for deliberation in a collegiate tribunal; and unless some aspect of the case suggests otherwise, the meeting should be held in the seat of that tribunal.

---

[39] Paul Simms, "The Motivation of the Ecclesiastical Judicial Sentence" (diss. no. 18, Pontifical University of St. Thomas [Rome], 1953–1954).

§ 2. On the day assigned for the meeting, the individual judges will offer their written conclusions on the merits of the case and the reasons, whether in fact or in law, by which they came to their conclusion: which conclusions shall be added to the acts of the case, observing secrecy.

§ 3. Being given in an order according to precedence, it shall nevertheless always be that the ponens or reporter in the case begin things, [and after] conclusions on individual issues, there will be held a moderate discussion under the leadership of the president of the tribunal, especially in order to establish what shall be set forth in the dispositive part of the sentence.

§ 4. In the discussion, it is fundamental that each [judge] may withdraw from his earlier conclusions.

§ 5. But if the judges in the first discussion do not wish or are not able to arrive at this sentence, the discussion can be put off to a new meeting; which, however, must not be adjourned beyond one week.

Canon 1872 (1983 CIC 1610)

If the judge sits alone, only he drafts the sentence; but in a collegiate tribunal the prescription of Canon 1584 is observed.

Canon 1873 (1983 CIC 1610–11)

§ 1. A sentence must:

1.° Settle the controversy treated in the presence of the tribunal; that is, absolve the respondent or condemn him in what pertains to the petitions or accusations leveled against him, giving to each question or article of controversy an appropriate response;

2.° Determine (at least insofar as it is fundamental [to the matter] and the subject allows) what the condemned party must give or do or offer or allow or from what he must abstain, likewise in what manner, place, or time the obligation is to be fulfilled;

3.° Contain reasons, that is, *motives*, as they are called, whether in fact or in law, on which the definitive part of the sentence is based;

4.° Assign the expenses for litigation.

§ 2. In a collegiate tribunal, the motives are taken by the referee from those things that the individual judges put in the discussion unless the majority part of the judges has established what motives are to be offered.

Canon 1874 (1983 CIC 1612)

§ 1. A sentence must always be given with the invocation of the divine Name from the beginning.

§ 2. From there it must express, in order, who the judge was or the tribunal; who was the petitioner, respondent, and procurator, correctly designated by name and domicile, and the promoter of justice and defender of the bond, if they had any part in the trial.

§ 3. It must then briefly present an account of the facts together with the conclusions of the parties.

§ 4. There then follows the dispositive part of the sentence, especially the reasons upon which it is based.

§ 5. It concludes with an indication of the day and place in which it was drafted and with the signature of the judge or of all the judges, if there were several, and of the notary.

Canon Law Digest
I: 758; VIII: 1109–11; IX: 953

Canon 1875 (1983 CIC 1613)

The rules given above are applicable especially in giving a definitive sentence; but they are also to be applied when the difference of subject matter allows it in giving interlocutory [decisions].

Canon Law Digest
VIII: 1111

Canon 1876 (1983 CIC 1614)

A sentence produced in this manner shall be published as soon as possible.

Canon 1877 (1983 CIC 1509, 1615)

Publication of the sentence can be made in three ways, either by citing the parties to hear a reading of the sentence, solemnly done, by the judge sitting in the tribunal; or by informing the parties that the sentence is within the chancery of the tribunal and giving to them the faculty of reading it and of requesting a copy; or finally, where the practice exists, by sending a copy of the sentence to the parties by public post according to the norm of Canon 1719.

Canon Law Digest
III: 611; X: 255–56

TITLE 14
On the remedies at law against a sentence

Canon 1878 (1983 CIC 1616)

§ 1. If it concerns a material error that occurred in transcribing the dispositive part of the sentence or in relating the facts or in the petition of the parties or in calculating [the amount] to be paid, the judge himself is able to correct the error.

§ 2. The judge shall go about this correction by giving a decree at the request of the party, unless the other party objects.

§ 3. If the other party objects, [it is considered] an incidental question to be resolved by decree according to the norm of Canon 1840, § 3; and the decree shall be attached at the foot of the corrected sentence.

Canon Law Digest
II: 468

Chapter 1
On appeal[40]

Canon 1879 (1983 CIC 1628)

A party who considers himself injured by a sentence, and likewise the promoter of justice and defender of the bond in cases in which they participate, have the right of appealing a sentence, that is, of going from the inferior judge who passes the sentence to a superior [judge], with due regard for the prescription of Canon 1880.

Canon Law Digest
I: 758; II: 469; VIII: 1111–21

Canon 1880 (1983 CIC 1629) Cross-Refs.: 1917 CIC 1879, 1902

Appeal has no place:

1.° From a sentence of the Supreme Pontiff himself or from the Apostolic Signatura;

[40] Thomas Connolly, "Appeals", Canon Law Studies, no. 79 (J. C. D. thesis, Catholic University of America, 1932).

2.° From a sentence of a judge who has been delegated by the Holy See to conduct a case with the clause *"removed from appeal"*;
3.° From a sentence vitiated by a defect of nullity;
4.° From a sentence that has passed into an adjudicated matter;
5.° From a sentence that was based on a decisive oath in litigation;
6.° From a decree of a judge or from an interlocutory sentence that does not have definitive force unless it is combined with an appeal from a definitive sentence;
7.° From a sentence in a case that the law requires to be resolved most expeditiously;
8.° From a sentence against one contumacious who has not purged himself of contumacy;
9.° From a sentence given against him who expressly in writing claimed to renounce appeal.

Canon Law Digest
II: 469

Canon 1881 (1983 CIC 1630)

Appeal must be interposed in the presence of the judge *from whom* the sentence was given within ten days of notice of the publication of the sentence.

Canon Law Digest
II: 469

Canon 1882 (1983 CIC 1630)

§ 1. Appeal can be made orally in the presence of the judge sitting in the tribunal if the sentence is publicly read, and [the appeal] shall be immediately reduced to writing by the actuary.

§ 2. Otherwise it is to be done in writing, with due regard for the case mentioned in Canon 1707.

Canon 1883 (1983 CIC 1663)

Appeal to be prosecuted in the presence of the judge *to whom* shall be directed [there] within one month from its interposition unless the judge *from whom* has established a longer time for its prosecution for the party.

Canon 1884 (1983 CIC 1634)

§ 1. For the prosecution of appeal, there is required and it suffices that a party invoke the ministry of a superior judge for the amendment of an impugned sentence, having attached a copy of the sentence and the libellus of appeal that was presented to the inferior judge.

§ 2. But if the party cannot obtain a copy of the impugned sentence within the useful time from the tribunal *from which*, the time limits do not run in the meantime, and this impediment is to be signified to the appellate judge, who shall instruct by precept the judge *from whom* to satisfy his duty as soon as possible.

Canon Law Digest
V: 708–10

Canon 1885 (NA)

§ 1. If the case mentioned in Canon 1733 occurs within the useful period for appeal and before the appeal is placed, the sentence must be communicated to those who have an interest; it is understood that to them there is granted the time limits established by law to be calculated from the day of this communication.

§ 2. If [the above scenario] occurs after appeal, the interposed appeal is communicated to them in whose favor [the law applies], and from the day of this communication there begins to run a new useful period to prosecute the appeal.

Canon 1886 (1983 CIC 1635)

If the deadline for appeal has passed without use, whether in the presence of the judge *from whom* or in the presence of the judge *to whom*, the appeal is considered deserted.

Canon Law Digest
II: 469; VI: 838; VIII: 1122–33

Canon 1887 (1983 CIC 1637)

§ 1. Appeal made by the petitioner applies to the respondent, and the opposite is true.

§ 2. If [appeal] is interposed by one party upon a certain heading of the sentence, the adverse party, even if the deadline for appeal has run, can appeal other headings incidentally; he can do this even under condition of receding if the first party recedes from the instance.

§ 3. If the sentence contains several headings and the one appealing impugns only a certain heading, the other headings are considered excluded; but if he chooses no heading, the appeal is presumed to be made against all the headings.

Canon 1888 (1983 CIC 1637)

If one of the several co-respondents or co-petitioners impugns the sentence, it is considered as made by all of them as often as the object sought is individual or the obligation applies to all; but the judicial expenses must be sustained only by him who appeals if the judge of appeal confirms the first sentence.

Canon 1889 (1983 CIC 1638)

§ 1. Suspensive appeal suspends the execution of the appealed sentence and therefore the principle remains in force: "*while litigation is pending nothing is to be innovated*"; but appeal in devolution only does not suspend the execution of the sentence even though litigation is still pending concerning the merits of the case.

§ 2. All appeal is suspensive, unless something else is expressly provided in the law with due regard for the prescription of Canon 1917, § 2.

Canon Law Digest
VIII: 1133–34

Canon 1890 (1983 CIC 1634)

Appeal being interposed, the tribunal *from which* must send an authentic copy of the acts of the case or the original acts of the case themselves to the judge *to whom*, according to the norm of Canon 1644.

Canon Law Digest
II: 469; IV: 403–4

Canon 1891 (1983 CIC 1639)

§ 1. In the appellate grade, a new cause of petition cannot be admitted, not even by way of a useful *accumulation*; and therefore the joinder of issues must be concerned only with whether the prior sentence should be confirmed or reformed, whether in whole or in part.

§ 2. But the cause can be instructed with new exhibits of documents or new evidence observing the rules given in Canons 1786 and 1861.

Canon Law Digest
IV: 403–4

CHAPTER 2
On the complaint of nullity against the sentence

Canon 1892 (1983 CIC 1620) Cross-Ref.: 1917 CIC 1893

A sentence labors under the weakness of irremediable nullity when:

1.° It was given by a judge who is absolutely incompetent or by a collegiate tribunal without the legitimate number of judges against the prescription of Canon 1576, § 1.
2.° It was given between parties at least one of whom did not have personal standing in the trial;
3.° One acted in the name of another without a legitimate mandate.

Canon Law Digest
I: 758; II: 469; III: 611; IV: 404–5; VI: 839

Canon 1893 (1983 CIC 1621)

The nullity mentioned in Canon 1892 can be raised by way of exception in perpetuity or by way of an action in the presence of the judge who issued the sentence within thirty years from the day of publication of the sentence.

Canon 1894 (1983 CIC 1622) Cross-Ref.: 1917 CIC 1895

A sentence labors under the weakness of remediable nullity when:

1.° Legitimate citation was lacking;
2.° The motives or reasons for deciding [the case] were missing, with due regard for the prescription of Canon 1605;
3.° It lacks the signatures required by law;
4.° It gives no indication of the year, month, day, and place in which it was given.

Canon Law Digest
I: 758; III: 611; VIII: 1134–37

Canon 1895 (1983 CIC 1623–25)

A complaint of nullity in the cases mentioned in Canon 1894 can be proposed either with the appeal within ten days or on its own merits and alone through a complaint within three months from the day of publication of the sentence in the presence of the judge who issued the sentence.

Canon Law Digest
II: 469; V: 710–12

Canon 1896 (1983 CIC 1624)

If a party is concerned that the judge who issued the sentence that is being impugned by a complaint of nullity has a prejudiced attitude and therefore is rightly considered as suspect, he can ask that another judge, albeit in the same tribunal, be substituted in his place according to the norm of Canon 1615.

Canon Law Digest
II: 469

Canon 1897 (1983 CIC 1626)

§ 1. A complaint of nullity can be interposed not only by the parties, if they think themselves injured, but also by the promoter of justice or defender of the bond, whenever they took part in the trial.

§ 2. Indeed, the judge himself by office can retract a null sentence given by him and amend it within the period for acting established above.

Chapter 3
On the opposition of a third [party]

Canon 1898 (NA)

If a prescription of a definitive sentence injures the rights of others, these have the extraordinary remedy that is called *opposition of a third [party]*, in virtue of which those who fear injury to their rights by the sentence can impugn that sentence before its execution and oppose themselves to it.

Canon 1899 (NA)

§ 1. This opposition can be made at the choice of the one opposing it either by proposing a revision of the sentence by the same judge who issued it or by appealing to a superior judge.

§ 2. In either case the opposer must prove that his rights are truly injured or that they probably will be injured.

§ 3. This injury must arise from the sentence itself insofar as it was the cause of injury or, if its execution is mandated, that it will affect with grave prejudice the one opposing.

§ 4. If neither is proven, the judge notwithstanding the objection of the third [party] must order the execution of the sentence.

Canon 1900 (NA)

If the instance is admitted [and] if the opposer wishes to act in the appellate grade, he is bound by the laws established for appeal; if [he acts] in the presence of the judge who issued the sentence, the rules given for incidental cases are to be observed.

Canon 1901 (NA)

If the case is won by the opposer, the sentence given earlier by the judge must be changed according to the request of the opposer.

TITLE 15
On an adjudicated matter and restitution in the entirety[41]

Canon 1902 (1983 CIC 1641)

A matter is considered adjudicated [when]:

1.° [There are] two conforming sentences;

2.° A sentence is not appealed within the useful time; or if, even though appealed in the presence of the judge *from whom*, it was deserted in the presence of the judge *to whom*;

3.° There is a sole definitive sentence from which there is given no appeal, according to the norm of Canon 1880.

Canon Law Digest

I: 759; IV: 405–6; VI: 839–42; VII: 943–45; VIII: 1138

[41] Thomas Feeney, "*Restitutio in Integrum* [restitution in the entirety]", Canon Law Studies, no. 129 (thesis, Catholic University of America, 1941); William Stetson, "Treatise on the Application, Extension, and Effects of *Res Judicata* [an adjudicated matter]" (diss. no. 23, Pontifical University of St. Thomas [Rome], 1958–1959); Martin Mangan, "*Res Judicata* [an adjudicated matter]: An Historico-Juridical Study" (MS no. 3205, Gregorian University, 1961; printed version, no. 1514, 1962).

Canon 1903 (1983 CIC 1643–44) Cross-Ref.: 1917 CIC 1989

Cases on the status of persons never pass into an adjudicated matter; but if there occurs in these cases two conforming sentences, a later proposition must not be admitted unless there are offered new and grave arguments or documents.

Canon Law Digest
I: 759–61; II: 470; III: 611; IV: 406–8; VI: 843; IX: 953–57

Canon 1904 (1983 CIC 1642)

§ 1. An adjudicated matter has the presumption of law and by law of being true and just and cannot be directly impugned.

§ 2. It effects justice between the parties and gives an exception for impeding the new introduction of the same case.

Canon 1905 (1983 CIC 1645)

§ 1. Against a sentence against which [in turn] there is no ordinary remedy of appeal or complaint of nullity, there is given the extraordinary remedy of restitution in the entirety within the limits of Canons 1687 and 1688, provided the injustice of the adjudicated matter is shown to be manifestly evident.

§ 2. The injustice is not considered to have been proven manifest unless:

1.° The documents upon which the sentence is based were later shown to be false;
2.° There were later found documents that prove new facts and require a preemptory contrary decision;
3.° The sentence was pronounced because of the dolus of one party to the damage of another;
4.° A prescription of law was evidently neglected.

Canon Law Digest
I: 761–62; VIII: 1138–44; IX: 957–63

Canon 1906 (1983 CIC 1646)

That judge who gave the sentence is competent to grant restitution in the entirety, unless it is petitioned because the judge neglected a prescription of law; in which case the appellate tribunal grants it.

Canon 1907 (1983 CIC 1647)

§ 1. Petition for restitution in the entirety suspends the execution of a sentence that has not yet started.

§ 2. If, however, there is suspicion arising from probable indicators that the petition was made in order to delay the execution [of the sentence], the judge can decide that the sentence be executed as demanded, assigning, however, to the one seeking restitution a suitable bond to indemnify him if restitution in the entirety [is granted].

TITLE 16
On judicial expenses and gratuitous service

Chapter 1
On judicial expenses

Canon 1908 (1983 CIC 1649)

In contentious cases the parties can be required to make payment under the title of judicial expenses, unless they are exempted from this burden according to the norm of Canons 1914–16.

Canon Law Digest
I: 762; II: 470

Canon 1909 (1983 CIC 1649) Cross-Refs.: 1917 CIC 1507, 1788

§ 1. It is for a provincial council or meeting of the Bishops to establish the regular and customary fees in which will be established what the parties pay for judicial expenses; [likewise to set] what will be paid by the parties for the work of advocates and procurators; [similarly] the cost for translations and transcriptions; [similarly the cost] for examinations and granting public trust [to documents]; and likewise for the copying of archival documents.

§ 2. It is for the judge in his prudent judgment to require that money for judicial expenses, indemnification of witnesses, and the fees for experts be paid by the party who uses these or, if the judge acts by office, by the petitioner, [and that] these be deposited beforehand in the chancery of the tribunal or at least that an appropriate bond be offered from which amount these can be paid.

Canon Law Digest
II: 470; VII: 945–50

Canon 1910 (1983 CIC 1649)

§ 1. The one who loses is normally bound to pay judicial expenses to the winner both for principal cases and for incidental [cases].

§ 2. If the petitioner or the respondent litigated frivolously, they can also be condemned to repayment of the damages.

Canon Law Digest
I: 762

Canon 1911 (1983 CIC 1649)

If the [case of the] petitioner or respondent was only partially overcome, or if the litigation was conducted between blood-relatives or affines, or if it was a very difficult case to try, or there were any other just and grave causes, the judge can, according to his prudent judgment, apportion the expenses in whole or in part among the litigants; this he must decide in the tenor of the sentence itself.

Canon 1912 (1983 CIC 1649)

If there are several [persons] in a case who deserve condemnation for the expenses, the judge shall impose [it] on them as a group if it concerns the obligations of a group; otherwise, [he shall do so] in proportion.

Canon 1913 (1983 CIC 1649) Cross-Ref.: 1917 CIC 1805

§ 1. From the pronouncement concerning expenses there is given no distinct appeal; but a party who considers himself injured can offer opposition within ten days in the presence of the same judge, who can then take up the matter again and amend or moderate the imposition.

§ 2. Appeal from a sentence concerning the principal case carries with it appeal from the assignment of expenses.

Canon Law Digest
II: 470

Chapter 2
On free service and the reduction of judicial expenses

Canon 1914 (1983 CIC 1649) Cross-Ref.: 1917 CIC 1908

The poor who are entirely impaired from incurring judicial expenses have the right to free patronage; if [they are impaired] only in part, [they have the right] to a diminution of expenses.

Canon Law Digest
I: 762

Canon 1915 (1983 CIC 1649) Cross-Ref.: 1917 CIC 1908

§ 1. Whoever wishes to obtain an exemption from expenses or their diminution must seek it from the judge providing a supplemental libellus or other documents by which the condition of the one requesting or of his personal possessions is demonstrated; he must also prove that he does not conduct futile or frivolous cases.

§ 2. The judge shall not admit or reject the request until he has received, if it is necessary, information even secretly by which the status of the personal goods of the one requesting can be proven and having heard the promoter of justice; moreover, he can revoke a concession if in the course of the process he receives evidence that the asserted poverty was not actually so.

Canon Law Digest
II: 470

Canon 1916 (1983 CIC 1649) Cross-Ref.: 1917 CIC 1908

§ 1. For gratuitous service to the poor, the judge shall select in individual cases one of the advocates approved for his forum, who shall not seek to avoid fulfilling this responsibility except for a cause approved by the judge; otherwise he can be struck by the judge with an appropriate penalty, even suspension from office.

§ 2. In case of a lack of advocates, the judge shall ask the local Ordinary to designate another suitable person, if possible, to take up the service of the poor.

Canon Law Digest
II: 470

TITLE 17
On the execution of the sentence

Canon 1917 (1983 CIC 1650) Cross-Ref.: 1917 CIC 1889

§ 1. Sentences that have passed into an adjudicated matter can be the subject of execution.

§ 2. The judge, however, can order the provisional execution of a sentence that has not yet passed into an adjudicated matter:

1.° If it concerns provisions or presentations necessary for the support [of a party];
2.° If other grave necessity urges but in such a way that if provisional execution is granted there be sufficient provision for the indemnity of the other party by bonds, bail, or security in case the execution is revoked.

Canon 1918 (1983 CIC 1651)

Execution shall not take place before a decree of execution is issued by the judge by which, namely, the execution of the sentence itself must be ordered; this decree, according to the diverse nature of cases, shall be included in the text of the sentence itself or issued separately.

Canon Law Digest
II: 470

Canon 1919 (1983 CIC 1652)

If the execution of a sentence requires the rendering of accounts, this shall be considered an incidental case to be decided by the same judge, those things being observed in law that ought to be observed, who issued the sentence to be ordered for execution.

Canon 1920 (1983 CIC 1653)

§ 1. The Ordinary of the place where the sentence was given in the first grade, himself or through another, must order the execution of a sentence.

§ 2. But if this one refuses or fails, then the execution looks to the judge of appeal upon the request of an interested party or even [can proceed] by office.

§ 3. The execution of a sentence among religious looks to the Superior who gave the definitive sentence or who delegated the judge.

Canon 1921 (1983 CIC 1654)

§ 1. An executor must execute the sentence according to the obvious meaning of the words, unless there was permission to use his judgment in the text of the sentence itself.

§ 2. It is permitted to him to consider exceptions concerning the manner and force of execution, but not the merits of the case; but if he considers it somehow shown that the sentence is manifestly unjust, he shall abstain from execution and remit [the case] to the party who committed the execution to him.

Canon 1922 (1983 CIC 1655)

§ 1. In what pertains to real actions in which something is adjudicated to the petitioner, this is to be given to the petitioner immediately upon the matter becoming adjudicated.

§ 2. But in what pertains to personal actions, when the respondent is condemned to present a moveable thing or to pay money or to give or do something, four months are granted for the fulfillment of the obligation.

§ 3. The judge can reduce or extend the prescribed period, but he shall not reduce it below two months or exceed six months.

Canon 1923 (NA) Cross-Refs.: 1917 CIC 474, 1673

§ 1. In performing the execution, the executor shall take care that [the respondent] is not harmed, and for this reason he shall begin execution by taking those things that are minimally necessary to him, always with due regard for those things that preserve sustenance and labor; and if it concerns a cleric, [he shall act] with due regard for his honest upkeep according to the norm of Canon 122.

§ 2. The judge shall not proceed to the execution of a privation of a benefice against a cleric who has gone to the Holy See; but if it concerns a benefice to which is attached care of souls, the Ordinary shall provide [for this] by the designation of a vicar substitute.

Canon 1924 (NA)

An executor shall use first admonitions and precepts against a reluctant one; he shall not go to spiritual penalties and to censures except from necessity and gradually.

SECTION 2
ON PARTICULAR NORMS TO BE OBSERVED IN CERTAIN TYPES OF TRIALS

TITLE 18
On methods for avoiding a contentious trial

Chapter 1
On settlement

Canon 1925 (1983 CIC 1446, 1713)

§ 1. Because it is greatly to be desired that litigation among the faithful be avoided, the judge shall apply exhortations such that, whenever some controversial contention respecting the goods of private persons has been brought to trial for resolution, a settlement, if there is hope of agreement apparent, might resolve the litigation.

§ 2. This duty the judge can satisfy whether before the parties are called to trial or when they first stand for trial or finally whenever he thinks it might be tried with effect and opportuneness.

§ 3. It is, nevertheless, consistent with judicial dignity that, as a rule, [the judge] not take up this sort of business personally, but that he commit it to some priest, especially one of the synodal judges.

Canon 1926 (1983 CIC 1714) Cross-Ref.: 1917 CIC 1930

In a settlement there are to be observed the norms established by civil law in the place in which the settlement is undertaken, unless by divine or ecclesiastical law there is some opposition, and with due regard for the prescriptions of the canons that follow.

Canon 1927 (1983 CIC 1715) Cross-Ref.: 1917 CIC 1930

§ 1. A settlement can never be done validly, whether in a criminal case or in a contentious [case], in which is concerned either the dissolving of marriage, or a beneficial matter when the title to the benefice itself is in dispute, unless legitimate authority approves, or in spiritual matters whenever the resolution of a temporal matter intervenes.

§ 2. But if the question concerns ecclesiastical temporal goods and those goods that, even though connected to the spiritual, nevertheless cannot be considered spiritual in themselves, settlement can be made, observing, however, if the matter so requires, the formalities established by law for the alienation of ecclesiastical things.

Canon Law Digest
II: 470

Canon 1928 (NA)

§ 1. The effect of a settlement brought to a happy conclusion is called *composition* or *concord.*

§ 2. Each party resolves its own expenses that are incurred in the settlement, unless otherwise expressly provided.

Chapter 2
On compromise by arbitration

Canon 1929 (1983 CIC 1713)

In order to avoid judicial contention, the parties can also enter into an agreement by which the controversy is committed to one or several judges who would, according to norms of law, determine the matter, or [who would] treat and resolve the matter according to goodness and equity; these former are known as *arbiters*, [and the latter] are known by the name of *arbitrators*.

Canon 1930 (1983 CIC 1714–15)

The prescriptions of Canons 1926 and 1927 are to be observed in compromise by arbitration.

Canon Law Digest
II: 470

Canon 1931 (NA)

Laity are prohibited from validly fulfilling the role of arbiter in the cases of ecclesiastics, [as are] excommunicates and the infamous after declaratory or condemnatory sentence; religious, moreover, shall not take up the role of arbiter without the permission of the Superior.

Canon 1932 (NA)

If the parties do not wish to consent either in a settlement or in a compromise by arbiters or arbitrators, the controversy is to be decided by formal trial according to the norms of the First Section.

TITLE 19
On the criminal trial[42]

Canon 1933 (1983 CIC 1342, 1720)

§ 1. Delicts that fall under criminal trials are public delicts.

§ 2. Delicts that are punished under the penal sanctions mentioned in Canons 2168–94 are excepted.

§ 3. In delicts of mixed forum, Ordinaries should not normally proceed if the accused is a layman and the civil magistrate seeing to the matter is acting in accord with the public good.

§ 4. Penances, penal remedies, excommunication, suspension, [and] interdict, provided the delict is certain, can be imposed even by means of extrajudicial precept.

Canon Law Digest
III: 612; VIII: 1144–54

CHAPTER 1
On accusatory action and denunciation

Canon 1934 (1983 CIC 1721)

Criminal action or accusation is reserved only to the promoter of justice, to the exclusion of all others.

Canon 1935 (NA)

§ 1. Any member of the faithful, however, can always denounce the delict of another in order to seek satisfaction or to recover damages that

[42] Francis Kelly, "A Comparative Study of the Rights of a Person Accused of Crime in Roman Law, Canon Law, and English Law" (MS no. 2995, Gregorian University, 1952; printed version, no. 1503, Sydney, 1962).

have affected them, or even for the sake of justice and for the repair of scandal or harm.

§ 2. Indeed, the obligation of denunciation binds anyone to whom such things apply under law or particular precept, or by natural law itself [they are bound] when there is danger to faith or religion or some other imminent public evil [is present].

Canon 1936 (NA)

Denunciation, in writing signed by the denouncer or orally, must be made to the local Ordinary or the chancellor of the Curia and the vicar forane or a pastor, who however, if it was done by a living voice, shall reduce it to writing and immediately refer it to the Ordinary.

Canon 1937 (NA)

Whoever denounces a delict to the promoter of justice must supply the assistance necessary for the proof of the delict.

Canon 1938[43] (NA) Cross-Ref.: 1917 CIC 2355

§ 1. In a case of injury or defamation, in order that a criminal action be instituted, there is required a previous denunciation or request from the injured party.

§ 2. But if it concerns a grave injury or defamation done to a cleric or religious, especially one constituted in a dignity, or where a cleric or religious attacked another, criminal action can be instituted even by office.

Chapter 2
On the investigation[44]

Canon 1939 (1983 CIC 1717)

§ 1. If a delict is neither notorious nor entirely certain, but is known by rumor or public story, whether by denunciation or from a request for damages, or by general investigation done by the Ordinary, even for any

[43] Edward Surges, "Defamation and Insult in Rotal Jurisprudence and Canonical Doctrine" (MS no. 3463, Gregorian University, 1963; printed version, no. 1585, 1963).

[44] Gary Schumacher, "The Procedural Regulations of the Pre-trial Special Inquiry in Criminal Cases according to the Norms of Canon Law and United States Federal Law" (MS no. 3169, Gregorian University, 1961; printed version, no. 1388, 1961).

reason, and before one is cited to answer for the delict, a special investigation is to be done in order that it can be shown whether and on what basis imputability can be based.

§ 2. This [investigation] is in place whether it concerns the imposition of a vindicative penalty or censure, or whether it concerns the passing of a declaratory sentence of a penalty or censure into which one has fallen.

Canon 1940 (1983 CIC 1717)

The investigation, although it can be conducted by the Ordinary, as a general rule is to be committed to one of the synodal judges, unless the same Ordinary for special reasons sees that it should be committed to another.

Canon 1941 (1983 CIC 1717)

§ 1. An investigator is delegated, not for a universe of cases, but as often as necessary for one case.

§ 2. The investigator is bound by the same obligations as ordinary judges and especially must take an oath of observing secrecy and faithfully fulfilling the office and to abstain from accepting duties according to the norm of Canons 1621–24.

§ 3. The investigator cannot act as judge in the same case.

Canon 1942 (1983 CIC 1718)

§ 1. It is left to the prudent judgment of the Ordinary to determine whether those things presented as arguments are sufficient to institute an investigation.

§ 2. Nothing is to be done with denunciations from obvious enemies or that come from vile or unworthy persons, or anonymous ones lacking those circumstances or elements that might tend to give the accusation support.

Canon 1943 (1983 CIC 1717)

The investigation must always be secret and be most cautiously conducted lest rumor of the delict get out or anyone's good name be called into question.

Canon 1944 (NA)

§ 1. In the pursuit of his purpose the investigator can call others who he feels are knowledgeable about the matter and interrogate them under oath of saying the truth and of preserving secrecy.

§ 2. In his examination the investigator will, insofar as possible and the nature of the investigation allows, observe the regulations established in Canons 1770–81

Canon 1945 (NA)

The investigator, before he closes the investigation, can require the advice of the promoter of justice as often as he encounters difficulties and can communicate the acts to him.

Canon 1946 (1983 CIC 1718–19)

§ 1. At the conclusion of the investigation, the investigator, adding his own opinion, refers everything to the Ordinary.

§ 2. The Ordinary or an official with his special mandate decides whether:

1.° If it appears that the denunciation lacks sufficient foundation, this is to be declared in the acts and the acts themselves deposited in the secret archive of the Curia;

2.° If there are indications of crime, but not sufficient to institute a criminal action, the acts are to be preserved in the same archives and in the meantime the behavior of the suspected one shall be observed and who, in the prudent judgment of the Ordinary, shall be opportunely heard about the matter and, if there is cause, warned according to the norm of Canon 2307;

3.° If finally there are certain or at least probable and sufficient arguments available to institute an accusation, the respondent shall be cited to appear and [the matter] shall progress according to the norm of the canons that follow.

Chapter 3
On correction of the delinquent

Canon 1947 (NA) Cross-Ref.: 1917 CIC 1950

If a respondent interrogated confesses the delict, the Ordinary, in place of a criminal trial, shall use judicial correction if it seems in order.

Canon 1948 (NA) Cross-Ref.: 1917 CIC 1950

Judicial correction has no place:

1.° In delicts that include the penalty of excommunication specially or most specially reserved to the Apostolic See, or [that include] the privation of a benefice, infamy, deposition, or degradation;
2.° When it concerns the imposition of a declaratory sentence of a vindicative penalty or censure into which one has fallen;
3.° When the Ordinary thinks that it would not be sufficient for the repair of scandal or the restitution of justice.

Canon 1949 (NA)

§ 1. Correction can take place once, and then twice, but not three times with the same defendant.

§ 2. Therefore, if after the second correction the same defendant commits a delict, a criminal trial is to be instructed, or if it is begun, it must be continued according to the norm of Canons 1954 and foll[owing].

Canon 1950 (NA)

Within the limits of Canons 1947 and 1948, correction can be applied by the Ordinary not only at any stage prior to the trial, but even once it has started and before the conclusion of the case; and in that case the trial is suspended unless it nevertheless has to be continued because the correction has fallen into uselessness.

Canon 1951 (NA)

§ 1. Correction can be used even when a suit for damages because of a delict has been introduced.

§ 2. In this case, the Ordinary, [with an eye for] goodness and equity, and the parties consenting, shall see to and decide the question of damages.

§ 3. But if he thinks that the question of damages is going to be difficult to assess in light of goodness and equity, he can remit to the ordinary judicial process the solution of this question and proceed with correction for the repair of scandal and the reform of the delinquent.

Canon 1952 (NA)

§ 1. Judicial correction, besides [consisting of] a salutary admonition, must usually be joined with certain opportune remedies, or [be joined with] a prescribed penance or pious work, which suffices for the public repair of injured justice and scandal.

§ 2. Salutary remedies, penances, and pious works prescribed for the defendant ought to be mitigated or lighter than those that in a criminal trial could and ought to be imposed by condemnatory sentence.

Canon 1953 (NA)

Correction is considered to be uselessly applied if the defendant does not accept it or does not execute the remedies, penances, and pious works prescribed for him.

Chapter 4

On the instruction of the criminal process and the [arraignment] of the defendant

Canon 1954 (1983 CIC 1721) Cross-Ref.: 1917 CIC 1949

If judicial correction is insufficient for the repair of scandal and the restitution of justice, or if it cannot be applied because the defendant denies the delict, or if it was applied without result, the Bishop, or officialis with his special mandate, will see to it that the acts of the investigation are handed over to the promoter of justice.

Canon 1955 (NA)

The promoter of justice will immediately produce a libellus of accusation and present it to the judge according to the norms established in the First Section.

Canon 1956 (1983 CIC 1722) Cross-Ref.: 1917 CIC 1958

In more serious delicts, if the Ordinary thinks that, with offense to the faithful, the [accused] would minister sacred things or perform some spiritual office or ecclesiastical or pious function or approach publicly the sacred Synax, he can, having heard the promoter of justice, prohibit him from sacred ministry, or the exercise of his office, or even from the public participation in the sacred Synax according to the norm of Canon 2222, § 2.

Canon 1957 (1983 CIC 1722) Cross-Ref.: 1917 CIC 1958

Likewise, if the judge thinks that the accused will impose fear on witnesses or suborn them, or by some other manner impede the course of justice, he can, having heard the promoter of justice, decree by his mandate that he leave a town or parish for a time, or even that he go to a definite location where he can [be kept under] special vigilance.

Canon 1958 (1983 CIC 1722)

The decrees in Canons 1956 and 1957 cannot be issued unless the defendant is cited and he appears or is contumacious, either after his first hearing or after his [arraignment], or late in the course of the process; and against them there is not given a remedy of law.

Canon 1959[45] (1983 CIC 1728)

For remaining [matters], the rules given in the First Section of this Book are followed, [as well as] those given in the Fifth Book regarding the infliction of penal sanctions.

---

[45] James Hughes, "Witnesses in Criminal Trials of Clerics", Canon Law Studies, no. 106 (J. C. D. thesis, Catholic University of America, 1937).

TITLE 20
On marriage cases[46]

Chapter 1
On the competent forum

Canon 1960 (1983 CIC 1671)

Matrimonial cases between the baptized pertain to ecclesiastical judgment by proper and exclusive right.

Canon Law Digest
I: 762–63; II: 471–540 & 583–84; III: 612–37; IV: 408–16; V: 712–13; VII: 950–75; VIII: 1155–77; IX: 963–94; X: 256–62

Canon 1961 (1983 CIC 1672)

Cases that concern merely the civil effects of marriage, if these are the principal matters, belong to the civil magistrates according to the norm of Canon 1016; but if these matters are raised only incidentally and as accessory [concerns], they can also be treated by the ecclesiastical judge as part of his power to adjudicate and decide.

Canon 1962 (1983 CIC 1698)

That Sacred Congregation or Tribunal or special Commission, as often as the Supreme Pontiff delegates it, takes exclusive cognizance of marriage cases involving those mentioned in Canon 1557, § 1, n. 1; cases of dispensation from a ratified [but] non-consummated marriage [look to] the Sacred Congregation for the discipline of Sacraments; but cases that are

[46] Thomas Kay, "Competence in Matrimonial Procedure", Canon Law Studies, no. 53 (D. C. L. thesis, Catholic University of America, 1929); Ernest Unterkoefler, "The Presiding Judge in Matrimonial Causes of First Instance", Canon Law Studies, no. 321 (Catholic University of America, not published); Archibald Bottoms, "The Discretionary Authority of the Ecclesiastical Judge in Matrimonial Trials of the First Instance", Canon Law Studies, no. 349 (thesis, Catholic University of America, 1955); Clara Henning, "Court Procedure for Marriage Cases of Nullity and the Renewal of Pope Benedict XIV", Canon Law Studies, no. 474 (Catholic University of America, not published); Robert Sanson, "A Preliminary Investigation in Marriage Nullity Trials" (doctoral diss. 57, St. Paul University [Ottawa, Canada], 1976); Anthony Diacetis, "The Judgment of Formal Matrimonial Cases: Historical Reflections, Contemporary Developments, and Future Possibilities", Canon Law Studies, no. 492 (J. C. D. thesis, Catholic University of America, 1977).

governed by the Pauline privilege [look to] the Sacred Congregation of the H. Office.

Canon Law Digest
I: 763; II: 540; VI: 843–44; VIII: 1177–88;
IX: 995–96; X: 262–63

Canon 1963[47] (1983 CIC 1681, 1699)

§ 1. Therefore, no inferior judge can instruct a process in a case of dispensation on a ratified [marriage] unless the Apostolic See has given him this faculty.

§ 2. If, however, a competent judge, on his own authority, was conducting a trial of marriage nullity under the heading of impotence and in it found evidence not of impotence but of the non-consummation of the marriage, all the acts shall be sent to the Sacred Congregation [of the discipline of the Sacraments], which may use them for passing sentence on the ratified non-consummated [marriage].

Canon Law Digest
I: 764–96; II: 540–41; III: 638; V: 713; VI: 844–45;
VII: 975–97; VIII: 1188; X: 263

Canon 1964 (1983 CIC 1673)

In other matrimonial cases the competent judge is the judge of the place in which the marriage was celebrated or in which the convened party, or if this one is not Catholic, [where] the Catholic [party], has domicile or quasi-domicile.

Canon Law Digest
I: 796–806; II: 541; VI: 845–46; VII: 997–98;
VIII: 1188–97; X: 263–66

Canon 1965 (1983 CIC 1676)

If marriage is accused from a defect of consent, the judge shall take care before everything to induce by opportune admonitions the party whose consent cannot be affirmed to renew consent; if [the case concerns] a defect of substantial form or a diriment impediment that can be and usu-

---

[47] Peter Flood, "Non-consummation as a Ground for Annulment or Dissolution of Marriage: A Study of English Civil and Church Law Compared with Canon Law" (thesis no. 183, Pontifical Lateran University, 1961).

ally is dispensed, he shall try to induce the parties to renew consent in legitimate form or to seek a dispensation.

Chapter 2
On the constitution of the tribunal

Canon 1966 (1983 CIC 1700)

With due regard for the prescription of Canon 1576, § 1, n. 1, there is only one judge instructor in the investigation for dispensation from a ratified [but] non-consummated marriage.

Canon 1967 (1983 CIC 1701)

If it concerns the nullity of marriage or with proving non-consummation and cases for dispensation from a ratified [marriage], the defender of the matrimonial bond must be cited according to the norm of Canon 1586.

Canon 1968[48] (1983 CIC 1432, 1678)

It is for defenders of the bond:

1.° To be present at the examination of parties, witnesses, and experts; to present judicial interrogatories, sealed and signed, to be opened by the judge in the act of examination [and then] to be proposed to the parties and witnesses; and to suggest to the judge new interrogatories emerging from this examination;

2.° To consider the articles proposed by the parties and insofar as possible to contradict them; to review the documents exhibited by the parties;

3.° To compose and allege observations against the nullity of marriage and [to assert] evidence in favor of the validity or the consummation of the marriage, and to produce all those things that they think are useful to uphold the marriage.

Canon Law Digest
I: 806; II: 541–42

[48] Eugene Frein, "The Discretionary Power of the Defender of the Matrimonial Bond", Canon Law Studies, no. 318 (Catholic University of America, not published).

Canon 1969 (1983 CIC 1678)

The defender of the bond has the right:

1.° Always and at every moment of the case to inspect the acts of the process even if they are not yet published; to request new deadlines for the completion of his writing, which can be extended in the prudent judgment of the judge;

2.° To be informed of all the evidence and allegations so that he is able to produce counterarguments;

3.° To ask that other witnesses be called and [to ask] that they be subjected to another examination, even though the process is completed or published, and to issue new observations;

4.° To require that other acts that he himself suggests be produced, unless the tribunal by unanimous vote disagrees.

Canon Law Digest
I: 806–7

Chapter 3

On the right to accuse marriage and to request a dispensation from a ratified [marriage]

Canon 1970[49] (NA)

A collegial tribunal can hear and decide no matrimonial case unless it is preceded by a regular accusation or by a petition legally made.

Canon Law Digest
I: 807

Canon 1971[50] (1983 CIC 1674)

§ 1. [The following] are capable of accusing [marriage]:

1.° The spouses in all cases of separation and nullity unless they themselves were the cause of the impediment;

[49] Lawrence Berger, "Rejection of the Introductory Libellus in Matrimonial Causes with Special Reference to the Ecclesiastical Tribunals of the United States of America" (MS no. 3513, Gregorian University, 1963; printed version, no. 1669, 1964).

[50] John Marquardt, "A Treatise on the Final Clause of Canon 1971 § 1" (Pontifical Lateran University, 1948); Ralph Asplan, "The Impugning of Marriage by the Promoter of Justice as Governed by the Demands of the Common Welfare" (diss. no. 10, Pontifical University of St. Thomas [Rome], 1949–1950); Vincent Foy, "The Right of the Consorts to Attack the Mar-

2.° The promoter of justice in [cases involving] impediments [that are] public by their nature.

§ 2. All others, even relatives, have no right to accuse marriage, but only [the right] to denounce the nullity of marriage to an Ordinary or promoter of justice.

Canon Law Digest
I: 807–8; II: 542–48; III: 638–43; IV: 417–19; V: 713–14

Canon 1972 (1983 CIC 1675)

A marriage that, while both spouses were alive, had not been accused is presumed to have been valid after the death of either or both spouses, and against this presumption no evidence is admitted except when the question arises incidentally.

Canon Law Digest
II: 548; VIII: 1197

Canon 1973 (1983 CIC 1697)

Only the spouses have the right of petitioning for a dispensation from a ratified but non-consummated marriage.

Canon Law Digest
I: 809

Chapter 4
On evidence[51]

Article 1—*On witnesses*[52]

Canon 1974 (NA)

Blood-relatives and affines mentioned in Canon 1757, § 3, n. 3, are considered capable witnesses in the cases of their close ones.

riage Bond" (University of Laval, 1954); Arthur Nace, "The Right to Accuse a Marriage of Invalidity", Canon Law Studies, no. 418 (J. C. D. thesis, Catholic University of America, 1961).

[51] Francis Wanenmacher, "Canonical Evidence in Marriage Cases", Canon Law Studies, no. 9 (J. C. D. thesis, Catholic University of America, 1935).

[52] Donald Whalen, "The Value of Testimonial Evidence in Matrimonial Procedure", Canon Law Studies, no. 99 (J. C. D. thesis, Catholic University of America, 1935).

Canon 1975[53] (NA)

§ 1. In cases of impotence or non-consummation, unless the impotence or non-consummation is otherwise certain, both spouses must introduce witnesses who [are known as] seven-hand witnesses, [being] related by blood or affinity to them, although neighbors of good reputation [are acceptable], as are others knowledgeable about these things who are able to swear about the probity of the spouses and especially about their truthfulness concerning the matter under controversy; to which the judge according to the norm of Canon 1759, § 3, can add other witnesses by office.

§ 2. Seven-hand testimony is an argument about credibility that adds strength to the deposition of the spouses; but it does not obtain full force of evidence unless it is enhanced by other aspects and arguments.

Canon Law Digest
I: 809; VI: 846

Article 2—*On the inspection of the body*

Canon 1976 (1983 CIC 1680)

An inspection of the body of either or both spouses to be conducted by experts is required in cases of impotence or non-consummation, unless this appears evidently useless under the circumstances.

Canon Law Digest
I: 809; II: 548; V: 714–15; VI: 846

Canon 1977 (NA)

In the selection of experts, besides the norms given in Canons 1792–1805, the prescriptions of the canons that follow are observed.

Canon 1978 (NA)

There shall not be admitted to the duty of expert those who have privately inspected the spouses concerning the fact that led to the petition for

[53] Timothy McNicholas, "The *Septimae Manus* Witness", Canon Law Studies, no. 255 (thesis, Catholic University of America, 1949).

the declaration of nullity or non-consummation; but these can be introduced as witnesses.

Canon Law Digest
I: 809; II: 548

Canon 1979 (NA)

§ 1. Regarding the inspection of the man, two medical experts must be deputed by office.

§ 2. But regarding the inspection of the woman, two midwives who have legitimate evidence of [their] expertise must be designated by office; unless the woman wanted to be inspected by two physicians also designated by office or if the ordinary considered it necessary.

§ 3. The inspection of the woman's body must be made fully observing the dictates of Christian modesty and always in the presence of an upright matron designated by office.

Canon Law Digest
I: 809; II: 549–51

Canon 1980 (NA)

§ 1. The midwives or experts must conduct the inspection of the woman individually.

§ 2. Individual physicians or obstetricians shall produce individual reports within the time limit defined by the judge for them to be offered.

§ 3. The judge can subject the reports made by the midwives to the examination of other medical experts if he thinks it opportune.

Canon 1981 (NA)

The report having been completed, the experts, the midwives, and the matron, individually, will be interrogated by the judge and respond according to the articles developed beforehand by the defender of the bond, and all of these [statements are] under oath.

Canon 1982 (1983 CIC 1680)

Also in cases of defect of consent from amentia, there is required the vote of experts who, if there is cause, shall examine the infirm one, according to the precepts of the art, [as well as] the actions that led to the suspicion of amentia; moreover, the experts must hear as witnesses those who visited the infirm one before.

Canon Law Digest
II: 551

Chapter 5
On the publication of the process, the conclusion of the case, and the sentence

Canon 1983 (NA)

§ 1. The process being published, it is fundamental that the parties can introduce new witnesses according to the norm of Canon 1786 on various articles.

§ 2. But if the witnesses have already been queried on the articles proposed before [and now] are to be heard anew, the prescription of Canon 1781 is observed, the right of the defender of the bond remaining intact to propose opportune exceptions.

Canon 1984 (NA)

§ 1. The defender of the bond has the right of being heard last in the allegations, requests, and responses both in writing and in oral defense.

§ 2. Wherefore the tribunal shall not come to a definitive sentence unless first the defender of the bond is asked to declare that there is nothing else to be inquired upon or studied by himself.

§ 3. But if [by] the day defined by the judge for judgment the defender has produced nothing, it is presumed that he has nothing [to add] to what was already deduced.

Canon Law Digest
I: 809; II: 551

Canon 1985 (1983 CIC 1703–5)

In cases that look to dispensation from a ratified but non-consummated marriage, the judge instructor will not come to the publication of the process or to a sentence upon the non-consummation or cause of dispensation, but [instead] will transmit to the Apostolic See all of the acts of the case along with the written opinion of the Bishop and of the defender of the bond.

Canon Law Digest
I: 809–10

Chapter 6
On appeals[54]

Canon 1986 (1983 CIC 1682) Cross-Ref.: 1917 CIC 1998

From the first sentence that has declared the nullity of marriage, the defender of the bond, within the legitimate time, must [take the case] to the superior tribunal, and if he neglects to fulfill his office, he shall be compelled by judicial authority.

Canon Law Digest
II: 551; VII: 998–1001

Canon 1987 (1983 CIC 1684) Cross-Ref.: 1917 CIC 1998

After the second sentence that confirms the nullity of the marriage, if the defender of the bond in the appellate grade does not believe in his conscience it ought to be appealed to a [higher tribunal], the parties have the right, after ten days have elapsed from intimation of the sentence, to contract a new wedding.

Canon Law Digest
I: 810; II: 551–52; III: 644

Canon 1988 (1983 CIC 1685) Cross-Ref.: 1917 CIC 1998

The nullity of the marriage being decreed, the local Ordinary shall take care that mention be made of this in the baptismal and matrimonial registers where the marriage took place and where [the celebration of the marriage] can be found recorded.

---

[54] Loras Lane, "Matrimonial Procedure in the Ordinary Courts of Second Instance", Canon Law Studies, no. 253 (thesis, Catholic University of America, 1947); Edward Egan, "The Introduction of a New 'Chapter of Nullity' in Matrimonial Courts of Appeal: A Study of Legislation in the Code of Canon Law and Instruction *Provida Mater Ecclesia*" (thesis, Gregorian University; printed version, no. 1944, Rome: Officium Libri Catholici, 1967).

Canon 1989 (NA) Cross-Ref.: 1917 CIC 1998

Because a sentence in a matrimonial case never passes into an adjudicated matter, these cases can always be reheard if new arguments are presented, with due regard for the prescription of Canon 1903.

Canon Law Digest
I: 810; II: 552

Chapter 7
On cases excepted from rules given to this point[55]

Canon 1990[56] (1983 CIC 1686) Cross-Refs.: 1917 CIC 1991–92

When from a certain and authentic document that is susceptible to no contradiction or exception there can be proven the existence of an impediment of disparity of cult, orders, solemn vow of chastity, prior bond, consanguinity, affinity, or spiritual relationship, and it is also apparent with equal certitude that no dispensation was granted from the impediment[s], in these cases, omitting the heretofore recited formalities, the Ordinary, having cited the parties, can declare the nullity of the marriage, with, however, the intervention of the defender of the bond.

Canon Law Digest
I: 810–12; II: 552–53; III: 644–46; V: 715–16; VI: 846–48;
VII: 1001–2; VIII: 1198–99

Canon 1991 (1983 CIC 1687)

Against this declaration, the defender of the bond, if he prudently thinks the impediment mentioned in Canon 1990 was not certain or that dis-

[55] Edwin Kennedy, "The Special Matrimonial Process in Cases of Evident Nullity", Canon Law Studies, no. 93 (J. C. D. thesis, Catholic University of America, 1935); Thomas Dupre, "The Summary Process of Canons 1990–1992", Canon Law Studies, no. 451 (Catholic University of America, 1967).

[56] Adolph Marx, "The Declaration of Nullity of Marriages Contracted outside the Church", Canon Law Studies, no. 182 (J. C. D. thesis, Catholic University of America, 1943); William Genuario, "The 1990 Process: The Essential Distinction between the Exceptional Case and the Matrimonial Cause" (MS no. 3458, Gregorian University, 1963; printed version, no. 1579, 1963).

pensation from it was probably obtained, is bound to take the matter to the judge of second instance, to whom the acts are to be transmitted and who is to be advised in writing that this treats of an exception case.

Canon 1992 (1983 CIC 1688)

The judge of the second instance, with only the intervention of the defender of the bond, shall decide in the same manner mentioned in Canon 1990 whether the sentence shall be confirmed or whether the case needs to be treated in a judicial manner; in which case he sends it back to the tribunal of first instance.

Canon Law Digest
II: 553

TITLE 21
On cases against sacred ordination

Canon 1993 (1983 CIC 1709–10)

§ 1. In cases in which the obligations contracted from sacred ordination are impugned, or the validity of sacred ordination itself [is impugned], the libellus must be sent to the Sacred Congregation for the discipline of Sacraments, or if the ordination is impugned due to substantial defect of sacred rite, [to] the Sacred Congregation of the H. Office; and [either] Sacred Congregation decides whether the case will be treated in the judicial order or heard as a disciplinary case.

§ 2. If the first [route is chosen], the Sacred Congregation sends the case to the diocesan tribunal where the cleric was [incardinated] at the time of ordination, or, if ordination is impugned due to a substantial defect of sacred rite, [then to] the tribunal of the diocese in which the ordination was done; as for grades of appeal, the prescriptions of Canons 1594–1601 stand.

§ 3. If the second [route is chosen], the Sacred Congregation itself decides the matter, the prior fact-finding process having been done by the competent [diocesan] tribunal of the Curia.

Canon Law Digest
I: 812–33; II: 554–56; VII: 1002–15; VIII: 1199

Canon 1994 (1983 CIC 1708)

§ 1. A cleric can attack the validity of sacred ordination, as can the Ordinary to whom the cleric [accounts] or in whose diocese he was ordained.

§ 2. Only a cleric who thinks he has not contracted the obligations attached to ordination from sacred ordination can seek the declaration of the nullity of the burdens.

Canon Law Digest
I: 833

Canon 1995 (1983 CIC 1710)

All of those things whether they are in the First Section of this Part or are said in a particular title on the process in matrimonial cases must also be observed, due adaptation being made, in cases against sacred ordination.

Canon Law Digest
I: 833

Canon 1996 (1983 CIC 1711)

The defender of the bond of sacred ordination enjoys the same rights and is bound by the same duties as is the defender of the bond of marriage.

Canon 1997 (1983 CIC 1709)

Even though an action was instituted not on the nullity of sacred ordination itself but only on the obligations that flow from that sacred ordination, nevertheless, a cleric is prohibited from the exercise of orders as a precaution.

Canon 1998 (1983 CIC 1712)

§ 1. In order that a cleric be free from the obligations that remain from the bond of ordination, there are required two conforming sentences.

§ 2. As for what pertains to appeal in these cases, the prescriptions of Canons 1986–89 on marriage cases are observed.

SECOND PART
ON CAUSES FOR BEATIFICATION OF THE SERVANTS OF GOD AND ON THE CANONIZATION OF THE BLESSED

Canon 1999 (1983 CIC 1403)

§ 1. Causes for the beatification of the Servants of God and for canonization of the Blesseds are reserved solely to the judgment of the Holy See.

§ 2. According to the norm of Canon 253, § 3, only the Congregation of Sacred Rites is competent in these causes.

§ 3. Local Ordinaries by proper law can do only those things that in the canons that follow are expressly asked of them.

Canon Law Digest
I: 835; VII: 1015–19; X: 266–82

Canon 2000[1] (NA)

§ 1. Causes of this sort can proceed in two ways, namely, the ordinary non-cult or the extraordinary case of exception, that is, of cult.

§ 2. The ordinary way is followed when, before there is any discussion of the virtues, it is understood that there can be shown no public cult for the Servant of God already in place or, if there was an abuse, that it has been put aside; the extraordinary [way] is used when it can be shown that a certain Servant of God is already in possession of a public and ecclesiastical cult.

Canon 2001 (NA)

§ 1. The causes of martyrs, whether they proceed in the ordinary way or the extraordinary, are not cumulative, but are treated each individually, unless it concerns martyrs who suffered in the same persecution and the same place.

§ 2. This also must be extended to the distinct processes and discussions that in these causes must be prescribed from the introduction of the cause to its end.

[1] Damian Blaher, "The Ordinary Processes in Causes of Beatification and Canonization", Canon Law Studies, no. 268 (thesis, Catholic University of America, 1949).

Canon 2002 (NA)

In the canons that follow, by the name of Ordinary is not understood a Vicar General unless he has a special mandate.

TITLE 22
On some persons who have a part in this process

Chapter 1
On the Petitioner and the Postulator

Canon 2003 (NA)

§ 1. Any member of the faithful or legitimate committee of Christian faithful has the right of petitioning that a cause be instructed before a competent tribunal.

§ 2. If a petition has been admitted by a legitimate and competent authority of the Church, the petitioner has the right of promoting the cause legitimately and of pursuing it to completion.

§ 3. The local Ordinary can instruct [a beatification cause] either by office or upon request.

Canon Law Digest
VIII: 1199–1203

Canon 2004 (NA)

§ 1. An actor can act personally or through a procurator legitimately constituted for this; women [cannot act] except through a procurator.

§ 2. Whoever is competent to conduct a cause before the competent tribunal is called a postulator.

§ 3. A postulator, whether he acts on his own or in the name of another, must be either a secular or religious priest having a fixed see in the City.

Canon Law Digest
II: 557

Canon 2005 (NA)

Individual postulators are admitted for individual causes: and not others, [though] the postulator of a cause has the right of substituting for himself by legitimate mandate others who are called vice-postulators.

Canon 2006 (NA)

§ 1. Both a postulator and vice-postulators, if they treat of the cause by another's mandate, must show the mandate to the tribunal before they are admitted to the exercise of their office.

§ 2. The mandate of the postulator shall be prepared according to the norm of Canon 1659, nor is it considered legitimate unless it has been admitted by the Sacred Congregation and inscribed in the acts; but a mandate of a vice-postulator must be recognized and admitted by the tribunal in which they exercise their duties.

Canon 2007 (NA)

To the office of postulator it belongs:

1.° To treat the cause before competent judges;

2.° To pay necessary expenses; but money collected from the faithful for the expenses of the cause must be administered according to the norm of instructions of the Apostolic See;

3.° To present the names of witnesses and documents to the tribunal;

4.° To prepare and present articles to the promoter of faith on which witnesses in the process must be interrogated.

Canon 2008 (NA)

The mandate of a postulator, if the postulator acts in the name of another, has its termination for the same reasons by which, in accord with the norm of law, the mandate of other procurators is extinguished.

Chapter 2

On the Cardinal Reporter, Promoters of faith, and Sub-promoters

Canon 2009 (NA)

§ 1. In causes that are treated before the Sacred Congregation, the reporter or secretary who acts shall be one of the Cardinal Fathers attached to the same Congregation designated by the Roman Pontiff.

§ 2. His office demands special attention to the cause committed to him, and he shall record everything in the plenary or ordinary meetings, whether these seem in favor of the cause or work against it.

Canon 2010 (NA)

§ 1. A *promoter of faith* must take part by a protected right in any process [and] must always be cited according to the norm of Canon 1587.

§ 2. The promoter of faith before the Sacred Congregation is called the *Promoter general of faith*, and the Assessor of the Sacred Congregation who assists him is called the *Sub-promoter general of faith*.

Canon 2011 (NA)

§ 1. A promoter of faith outside the Sacred Congregation can be constituted either for all causes or for a certain particular cause.

§ 2. The Promoter general of faith and the Sub-promoter general are selected by the Roman Pontiff; a promoter of faith before a tribunal of Ordinaries, if indeed it concerns an apostolic process, is appointed by the Promoter general and then takes the name sub-promoter; otherwise, he is appointed by the Ordinary before the edict mentioned in Canon 2043.

Canon 2012 (NA)

§ 1. It is for the promoter of faith to prepare straightforward interrogatories [that are] merely historical [and] that do not look to elicit a given certain response from those interrogated, but which are suitable for eliciting the truth on those articles proposed by the postulator and that are shown to the judge, who is bound by secrecy.

§ 2. It is, moreover, for the same promoter to ensure that witnesses by office are cited and to raise opportune exceptions; but the judge can by office seek witnesses even without a request by the promoter of faith or over his objection, although [the promoter] must be so informed.

Chapter 3
On the notary, chancellor, and advocates

Canon 2013 (NA)

§ 1. A notary or actuary must assist in the instruction of processes, whether apostolic or under the authority of a local Ordinary.

§ 2. The notary must be among the participating number of Protonotaries before the Sacred Congregation.

Canon 2014 (NA)

Religious cannot validly perform the office of notary except by necessity; they are always excluded from causes of their own religious [institute].

Canon 2015 (NA)

In processes to be instructed by a local Ordinary outside the City, a notary of the Curia itself must perform the function of a notary; in the City, a Protonotary of the Sacred Congregation performs the function of notary, and in his absence a notary of the Vicariate of the City [so acts].

Canon 2016 (NA)

A notary can be given an assistant or, as they say, an *adjunct*, who renders him help in comparing copies with the original acts and in transcribing copies of documents written out in libraries, archives, and so on.

Canon 2017 (NA)

The adjunct notary and chancellor of the Sacred Congregation must be priests of intact reputation and above all exception; but the chancellor must also be possessed of a degree in canon law.

Canon 2018 (NA)

Advocates and procurators in causes of beatification and canonization before the Sacred Congregation must be endowed with degrees in canon law and at least a licentiate in sacred theology, and they must have passed an internship with some of the advocates of the same Sacred Congregation or with the Sub-promoter general of faith; for advocates, moreover, there is required the legitimate title of rotal advocate.

TITLE 23
On the evidence to be used in these processes

Chapter 1
On evidence generally

Canon 2019 (NA) Cross-Ref.: 1917 CIC 2050

In these causes the evidence must be in every way complete; nor shall other [sorts of evidence] be admitted except that which is derived from witnesses and from documents.

Canon Law Digest
VII: 1019–22; VIII: 1203–4; IX: 997

Canon 2020 (NA) Cross-Ref.: 1917 CIC 2050

§ 1. To prove that there was no cult of a Servant of God outstanding, at least four witnesses are necessary.

§ 2. To prove the reputation for virtue, martyrdom, and miracles, at least eight witnesses are required who can be singular [witnesses] for that singularity that, as they say, is circumstantial; moreover, at least two witnesses will be called by office.

§ 3. To prove virtues or martyrdom, there are required eyewitnesses and co-witnesses: historical documents provide only circumstantial support.

§ 4. If in the apostolic process there are witnesses who heard things from eyewitnesses and eyewitnesses with information, all of these can be added along in the line of evidence.

§ 5. But if there are eyewitnesses with information and, in the apostolic [process], witnesses who only heard [things], these have circumstantial force either more or less weighty according to the prudent estimation of the judge; and then [the matter] can proceed to the final [phase], namely, the discussion of the miracles, when, from the combination of all the evidence of this sort, there could be had the probability that a prudent man weighing grave things could reach confidence about their trustworthiness and accuracy.

§ 6. In ancient causes, however, proceeding by the non-cult way, in which visual witnesses are lacking [as are] those who heard things from eyewitnesses, and in causes proceeding by the exceptional-case way, virtues and martyrdom can be proven by witnesses who heard about the public reputation, as they say, that proves the tradition by hearing, and through contemporaneous documents and records recognized as authentic.

§ 7. Finally, miracles can always be proven by eyewitnesses and co-witnesses.

Canon Law Digest
II: 557–59

Canon 2021 (NA)

An immemorial cult is proven by authentic records that antedate by a period of a hundred years the constitution of [Pope] Urban [VIII] promulgated in the year 1634 or that perdured for a century at publication, provided they contain facts that [it lasted] for at least a hundred years before, together with a popular tradition that was never interrupted.

Canon Law Digest
IX: 997

Canon 2022 (NA)

A cult permitted by the Apostolic See of the longest time is proven by contemporaneous documents.

Chapter 2
On witnesses and experts

Canon 2023 (NA) Cross-Refs.: 1917 CIC 2025, 2043, 2051

In the process of beatification, all the Christian faithful, with due regard for the prescription of Canon 2027, § 2, n. 1, are bound, even though they are not called, to bring to the attention of the Church whatever seems to work against the virtue or miracles or martyrdom of the Servant of God.

Canon 2024 (NA) Cross-Refs.: 1917 CIC 2025, 2043, 2051

Among the witnesses to be called first by the promoter of faith, even if not listed by the postulator, are all those who had familiarity or extended experience with the Servant of God.

Canon 2025 (NA) Cross-Refs.: 1917 CIC 2011, 2043, 2051

§ 1. All of those mentioned in Canons 2023 and 2024, unless they know they are going to be called as witnesses, must give letters to their own Ordinary by which they either briefly explain the extended experience they had with the Servant of God or describe some other peculiar fact that they know and that ought to be noted; the Ordinary shall take care that these letters are transmitted to the promoter of faith.

§ 2. Religious men or religious women shall transmit letters of this sort, closed with a seal, immediately and directly to the Ordinary or promoter of faith or hand them to a confessor who shall take care to forward them as soon as possible to the Ordinary or promoter of faith.

§ 3. Illiterates shall explain the matter to the pastor, who will refer it to the Ordinary or promoter of faith.

Canon 2026 (NA)

Religious Superiors are bound by the grave obligation of taking care that all their subjects who ought to go to deposition [do so], which testimony, however, neither directly nor indirectly, shall they compel in one direction more than another.

Canon 2027 (NA) Cross-Ref.: 1917 CIC 2023

§ 1. Blood-relatives, affines, householders, heretics, and also infidels are admissible as witnesses.

§ 2. [The following] cannot be admitted:

1.° The confessor according to the norm of Canon 1757, § 3, n. 2;

2.° The postulator, advocate, or procurator in the cause for the duration of their duty; but if they are dismissed from their duty they can be admitted, but only to provide circumstantial [information];

3.° Whoever serves as judge at any point in the cause.

Canon 2028 (NA)

§ 1. Physicians attending the cure, if there were any, should it concern a miracle, are to be included as witnesses.

§ 2. But if they refuse to assist the tribunal, the judge will take care that at least a signed sworn report about the illness be produced for the process and be included in the acts, or that their opinion be prepared by a person who shall be subject to examination.

Canon 2029 (NA)

Witnesses must give testimony from their own knowledge [and explain] the reasons why they assert the things [they do]; otherwise, nothing is to be done with their testimony.

Canon 2030 (NA)

To prove the reputation for sanctity or martyrdom of a Servant of God who belonged to a certain religious [institute], at least one-half of the witnesses must be [from] outside [the religious institute].

Canon 2031 (NA)

When the work of experts is necessary:

1.° There shall be at least two experts, one of whom is unknown to the other with due regard for the prescription of n. 4;
2.° They shall be deputed by the tribunal through a majority part of the votes, having heard the promoter of faith or, if they will present their work within the Sacred Congregation, by the Cardinal Reporter, having heard the Promoter general of faith; but those who perform any responsibility in the cause as a witness must always be excluded;
3.° The postulator shall not be informed at all about who has been designated an expert; and the experts themselves must observe secrecy about their designation;
4.° The experts will go about their investigation as individuals unless for a just cause the judge with the agreement of the promoter of faith permits that they undertake their [investigation] together;
5.° The experts will give individual written reports made by themselves; but they can be interrogated individually even if they conducted their investigation together.

Chapter 3

On documents to be included in the process

Canon 2032 (NA)

§ 1. The documents on which the postulator relies must be exhibited integrally to the tribunal.

§ 2. But the tribunal can require also other documents from the postulator that seem to the same tribunal to assist in the detection of truth.

Canon 2033 (NA)

§ 1. Extrajudicial testimony shall be consigned to writing either by those interrogated by the postulator in the process concerning the virtues and martyrdom of the Servant of God or by those whom the postulator proposes to interrogate even if outside the process, although they cannot be included among the documents that have probative force in the trial about the sanctity or martyrdom of the Servant of God.

§ 2. Nor do funeral eulogies or necrologies written or published immediately after the death of the Servant of God constitute legitimate proof.

§ 3. Much less do the testimonies of men, however illustrious, concerning the virtues and works of the Servant of God if they were written, not spontaneously, but at the request of friends while [the Servant of God] was yet living.

Canon 2034 (NA)

Whoever exhibits documents must declare them to be original and authentic.

Canon 2035 (NA)

§ 1. Histories do not have the force of documents unless they are founded in documents exhibited in the process.

§ 2. If some men of great authority have shown these documents to be used, their testimony must be offered only to confirm the authenticity and authority of the documents.

Canon 2036 (NA) Cross-Ref.: 1917 CIC 2045

§ 1. Historical documents, whether written by hand or printed in type, by which the postulator intends to prove the virtues of the Servant of God or that his cult has gone on since ancient days continuously without interruption shall be inserted in the process and transmitted with it to the Sacred Congregation and will be examined by expert men.

§ 2. But if these are preserved in a library or tabulary whence they cannot be removed, a written or photographic copy made thereof can be exhibited with written testimony given by the notary of the tribunal about its authenticity.

§ 3. But if even this cannot be done, the matter shall be referred to the Sacred Congregation, which shall designate experts in order to examine them where they are reserved.

TITLE 24
On the process of beatification of Servants of God by the non-cult way

Canon 2037[2] (NA)

§ 1. The persons who have a part in the process, whether under the authority of the local Ordinaries or under the instruction of delegates of the Apostolic See, namely judges, the promoter of faith and sub-promoters, notary, and assistants must from the beginning of each process, according to a formula prescribed by the Sacred Congregation, give an oath to fulfill faithfully their office to maintain secrecy until the publication of the process and not to accept gifts of any sort.

§ 2. The Ordinary, even if he does not act the part of judge, is nevertheless bound to give an oath to maintain secrecy.

§ 3. Beyond that of observing secrecy, the witnesses, none of them being exempt or dispensed, must also swear, before they are interrogated, to speak the truth and, after their interrogation, to have said the truth; experts, interpreters, reviewers, and scribes [must take an oath] on fulfilling well their duties before [performing their duties], converting from one language to another, reviewing, and producing the transcript, and [they will take an oath] about having fulfilled their duties well after the [investigation], translation, transcription, and review. Also the courier or messenger will take an oath of faithfully fulfilling his office.

§ 4. Postulators and vice-postulators must give an oath of *calumny*, that is, where they swear that they will say the truth throughout the whole of the process and in no way defraud others.

§ 5. Within the Sacred Congregation, as to what applies to oaths, its proper law is observed.

---

[2] B. Lopez, "The Oath *de Calumnia* in Decretal Law" (MS no. 2542, Gregorian University, 1955).

Chapter 1
On the process to be instructed by the local Ordinary under his own authority

Canon 2038 (NA)

§ 1. In order to obtain from the Apostolic See the introduction of a cause for the beatification of a Servant of God, it must first be proven in law [that there exists] purity of doctrine in his writings and likewise the reputation of his sanctity, virtues, and miracles or martyrdom and the absence of any obstacle that would seem to be preemptory [to the cause], and that no public cult is being offered him presently.

§ 2. Therefore, at the request of the postulator, the Ordinary, if he thinks the petition should be admitted, must:

1.° Examine the writings of the Servant of God;
2.° Instruct the informative process on the reputation for sanctity, virtues in general, or martyrdom, and the cause of martyrdom and miracles;
3.° And instruct the process on non-cult.

Canon 2039 (NA) Cross-Ref.: 1917 CIC 2051

§ 1. For this the competent Ordinary is the [one of the] place in which the Servant of God died on his last day or in which miracles have occurred; who, however, must not instruct the cause himself if he is [related to] the Servant of God.

§ 2. If an ancient process exists on the reputation for sanctity or martyrdom done thirty years before, but the cause before it obtained legitimate introduction by the Apostolic See for any reason was interrupted, it pertains to those same Ordinaries or their successors to conduct the informative process on the continuation of the reputation for sanctity or martyrdom.

Canon Law Digest
I: 835

Canon 2040 (NA)

§ 1. The tribunal must consist of a president who is the Ordinary himself, personally or through a priest delegated for this, and in this latter case two other judges are to be selected by the same Ordinary [from] among the synodal judges.

§ 2. The Ordinary will designate the president of the tribunal by decree whether he reserves this role to himself or appoints a delegate with two other judges; in the same decree he will appoint the promoter of faith and a notary.

Canon 2041 (NA)

§ 1. The tribunal sessions for taking the oath and the examination of witnesses shall be held during the daytime insofar as possible and in a sacred place.

§ 2. After each session the acts of the cause must be closed and sealed with the seal of the judge and are not to be opened except in the following session after the judge recognizes the seal to be integral and intact; if the seal is not found integral and intact, the judge shall refer the matter to the Sacred Congregation.

Article 1—*On the review of the writings of the Servant of God*

Canon 2042 (NA)

By the name of writings come not only non-published works of the Servant of God but also those that were already printed in type; such as sermons, letters, diaries, autobiographies, and whatever remains, whether written by his own self or through another hand.

Canon 2043 (NA) Cross-Ref.: 1917 CIC 2011

§ 1. The Ordinary shall direct through a public decree set out, if it can be done, in each parish or by some other opportune way that the writings of the Servant of God that exist shall be brought to the tribunal by everyone, and calling to mind and urging the prescriptions of Canons 2023–25.

§ 2. But if it concerns a cause of a Servant of God belonging to some religious [institute], the edict must also be published in every individual house of the same religious [institute]; and Superiors are bound by the grave obligation of taking care that this publication be done, having made express mention of the prescription of Canon 2025, § 2, that likewise all their subjects who have writings forward them.

§ 3. It is the responsibility of the promoter of faith to insist that the edict also be published in other places where there might be a hope that some might be found who have some writings.

Canon 2044 (NA)

§ 1. The Ordinary shall diligently examine the writings of the Servant of God not only at the request of the postulator but also by office.

§ 2. Whenever writings are found in another diocese, the judge will ask the Ordinary of that diocese that he examine them himself according to the norm of law and transmit them to himself together with the acts.

Canon 2045 (NA)

§ 1. If anyone wishes to keep autograph [documents] in their possession, the notary himself shall take care to make an authentic depiction of them for transmittal together with the process to the Sacred Congregation.

§ 2. As to what applies to writings preserved in libraries or tabularies, the prescription of Canon 2036, §§ 2 and 3, stands.

Canon 2046 (NA)

The notary shall diligently describe both the number and quality of writings and all of the acts of their review; these acts must also be signed by the Ordinary or by his delegate and the promoter of faith and sealed with the seal of the Ordinary.

Canon 2047 (NA)

§ 1. The postulator will give an oath in the presence of the Ordinary about the review of the writings to be diligently done by him and afterward [give an oath] that he has diligently done this.

§ 2. If it concerns a [female] Servant of God who belongs to some religious [institute], the supreme Moderatrix of the religious [institute] or Superioress of the monastery will also give an oath about diligence in reviewing the writings, [and] that all the writings of the [female] Servant of God that are possessed will be handed over, and that she cannot show that any of her subjects or other persons have retained till then the writings of the same [female] Servant of God.

Canon 2048 (NA)

If it concerns the cause of some martyr, the examination of writings can also be done by a commission assigned for the introduction of the cause at the Sacred Congregation according to instructions to be given about it by the Promoter general of faith.

Article 2—*On the informative process*

Canon 2049 (NA)

The informative process is instructed through Ordinaries, and if it has not been started within thirty years of the death of the Servant of God, in order that it progress further, it must be proven that there was no fraud in the case or dolus or culpable negligence.

Canon 2050 (NA) Cross-Ref.: 1917 CIC 2090

§ 1. In the examination of witnesses on the reputation of sanctity, martyrdom, and miracles, the prescriptions of Canons 2019 and 2020 are observed.

§ 2. It is not necessary that there be shown specifics on virtues, martyrdom, or miracles, but it suffices that there be evidence of reputation in general, spontaneous [in nature], not developed by art or human diligence, arising among honest and grave persons, [active] from the days of the individual, and continuing in the present among the greater part of the population.

§ 3. The general questions according to the norm of Canon 1774 having preceded, the question to be put by the judge to the witnesses first deals with how they came into notice of the life, virtues, miracles, or martyrdom of the Servant of God, and how they learned these things and whether they knew about them from public reputation, and then they are to be interrogated according to the questions made by the promoter of faith and on the articles presented by the postulator.

Canon 2051 (NA)

The informative process cannot be completed unless first the promoter of faith examines all those letters sent to him mentioned in Canon 2025 and shows those [persons] to have been examined as mentioned in Canons 2023–25.

Canon 2052 (NA)

When the tribunal judges that all of the evidence, whether through examination of witnesses or through exhibition of documents, has been collected and all the writings of the Servant of God that can be had are in the acts, and having heard the promoter of faith, it shall advise the postulator that, if he has others he must offer them within a certain period of time, the which [period] having elapsed, the end of the process can be imposed.

Canon 2053 (NA)

The judge so ordering and the promoter of faith not objecting, the notary shall publish the process; which will be given for transcription to scribes designated by the tribunal.

Canon 2054 (NA) Cross-Ref.: 1917 CIC 2097

A copy of the process, or, as they say, a *transcript*, like an archetype of the acts, shall be transcribed by hand.

Canon Law Digest
VI: 848; VII: 1022

Canon 2055 (NA) Cross-Ref.: 1917 CIC 2097

The official transcript being completed, its collation with the original shall be done by the notary and by his assistant in the presence of one of the judges and the promoter of faith; when the collation is completed, in order to prove the authenticity of the official transcript, both the notary and the judge and the promoter of faith shall confirm it by their signature and set their seal on the transcript.

Canon Law Digest
VI: 848

Canon 2056 (NA) Cross-Ref.: 1917 CIC 2097

§ 1. The collation being completed, the original is closed and marked with a seal and will be preserved diligently in the archive of the Curia and will never be opened without coming to the Apostolic See.

§ 2. The [copied] transcript will be closed and marked with the seal of the Ordinary, and the notary will prepare a duplicate instrument about this, sending one to Rome and keeping the other in the archive of the Curia.

Article 3—*On the process of non-cult*

Canon 2057 (NA)

The tribunal will produce two witnesses by office besides those introduced by the postulator and will question all of them whether there was ever given any public cult to the Servant of God.

Canon 2058 (NA)

The tribunal shall also go and diligently inspect the tomb of the Servant of God, the room in which he lived or died, and any other places that might exist where signs of cult could rightly be suspected of being present.

Canon 2059 (NA)

If in the course of the process there are found not insignificant indications that a cult for the Servant of God arose in the meantime, it is the duty of the promoter of faith to insist that additional inquiries be conducted on this.

Canon 2060 (NA)

The tribunal must give sentence as to whether or not a cult of the Servant of God did arise.

Article 4—*On the process of transmitting the writings of the Servant of God, the informative process, and the non-cult [process] to the Sacred Congregation*

Canon 2061 (NA) Cross-Ref.: 1917 CIC 2128

The Ordinary shall immediately complete the review of writings and send them to Rome with a *manifest of diligence*, that is, with a juridical report on the diligence that was used in examining the writings.

Canon 2062 (NA) Cross-Ref.: 1917 CIC 2128

If after the examination of the writings of the Servant of God other [writings] are discovered in the course of the cause, these shall be immediately transmitted to the Sacred Congregation, nor is it possible to proceed further until [these] have been reviewed.

Canon 2063 (NA) Cross-Refs.: 1917 CIC 2097, 2128

§ 1. The Ordinary shall give to the postulator for transmittal to the Sacred Congregation the record of the informative process.

§ 2. Together with this record, he shall also send letters both from the judge to the Sacred Congregation and from the promoter of faith to the Promoter general of faith in order to inform the Sacred Congregation both of the trustworthiness of the witnesses and of the completion of all legitimate acts.

§ 3. The Ordinary shall also transmit a description of the form of the seal with which the record has been sealed and a copy of the same seal.

Canon Law Digest
VI: 848

Canon 2064 (NA)

Likewise the Ordinary shall transmit the completed process on non-cult to the Sacred Congregation through the postulator.

CHAPTER 2
On the introduction of the cause before the Sacred Congregation

---

Article 1—*On the review of writings*

Canon 2065 (NA)

As soon as the writings of the Servant of God are transmitted to Rome they shall be subjected to examination; but the Sacred Congregation must opportunely investigate whether, besides those exhibited, other writings of the Servant of God also exist, whether in private custody or consigned to public archives.

Canon Law Digest
IV: 419–20

Canon 2066 (NA) Cross-Ref.: 1917 CIC 2069

§ 1. Reviewers of writings in individual causes will be selected by the Cardinal Reporter having heard the Promoter general of faith; their appointment must remain secret.

§ 2. To this responsibility shall be assigned priests who have at least a doctorate in theology or, if they are religious, who have been given an equivalent title.

Canon 2067 (NA)

§ 1. The writings of the Servant of God are given by the secretary to the reviewers assigned to this responsibility in order that each of the writings be examined by two reviewers who shall remain unknown to each other.

§ 2. If the number of the writings of the Servant of God are too many, nothing prevents that they be divided into parts to be treated by distinct groups of reviewers.

Canon 2068 (NA)

§ 1. The judgment of the reviewers must indicate whether in the writings there is anything adverse to faith or good morals and explain generally by what manner certain characteristics or habits of virtue or defects seem to apply to the Servant of God in the writings.

§ 2. The reviewers shall give this judgment in writing, supported by arguments and reasons.

Canon 2069 (NA)

If the opinions of the reviewers disagree, a third reviewer shall be designated according to the norm of Canon 2066 who shall complete his responsibility in the same way.

Canon 2070 (NA)

The Promoter general of faith shall propose for discussion by the Cardinal Fathers any objections, if he has any, taken from the writings of the Servant of God and the judgment of the reviewers.

Canon 2071 (NA)

If it has been certainly demonstrated that there is contained in the writings of the Servant of God something not entirely consistent with the faith or that there is anything else that at present might give offense to the faithful, the Roman Pontiff, having heard the opinion of the Cardinal Fathers and weighing all the circumstances of the case, will decide whether it is possible to proceed further.

Canon 2072 (NA)

The favorable judgment of the Roman Pontiff does not bring with it approval of the writings, nor does it in any way impede the Promoter general of faith and the consultors from being able and required to propose objections in the discussion of the virtues taken from the writings of the Servant of God.

Article 2—*On the discussion of the informative process*

Canon 2073 (NA) Cross-Ref.: 1917 CIC 2097

The informative process produced by the Ordinary is transmitted to Rome and is then [subjected to] an inspection regarding the integrity of the seals by the Protonotary of the Sacred Congregation, and if nothing obstructs, upon a special decree coming from the Roman Pontiff, it shall be opened in the presence of the Cardinal Prefect of the Sacred Congregation, who commits [the contents] to the chancellor for transcribing.

Canon 2074 (NA) Cross-Ref.: 1917 CIC 2097

The Cardinal Reporter shall take care that if necessary a version of the process be produced in the City by an approved interpreter that later will be subjected to the examination of a reviewer.

Canon 2075 (NA) Cross-Ref.: 1917 CIC 2097

The transcript of the process sent by the Ordinary shall be preserved in the tabulary of the Sacred Congregation; a copy of it, recognized by prescription of law, will be given to the postulator.

Canon 2076 (NA)

§ 1. The advocate and procurator shall produce a summary of the transcript, of all the transcripts if there are several, and attach a brief that summarizes the information.

§ 2. To the summary there must be attached an assurance by the Subpromoter general of faith that the summary of the witnesses is in accord with those exhibited acts of the Sacred Congregation.

Canon 2077 (NA)

Letters of petition from significant persons constituted in ecclesiastical or civil dignities or from moral persons proposing to the Supreme Pontiff that a cause for beatification of a certain Servant of God be taken in hand are usefully exhibited, provided they were given spontaneously and [were based on] their own knowledge.

Canon Law Digest
II: 559–61

Canon 2078 (NA)

If, having considered the writings, [there comes] a decree that it is possible to proceed further, the Promoter general of faith shall express his objections against the introduction of the cause to which the advocate of the cause will respond.

Canon 2079 (NA) Cross-Ref.: 1917 CIC 2016

§ 1. The Promoter general of faith will preface his objections raised to the introduction of the cause [with] a sober and perceptive synopsis that presents the life of the Servant of God.

§ 2. In drafting this synopsis he may use not only those documents referred to in the summary, but also others, if there are any, [that he thinks] it opportune to consult.

Canon 2080 (NA) Cross-Ref.: 1917 CIC 2099

The objections and responses shall be arranged briefly and perceptively in a scholastic manner according to the age-old customs of the Sacred Congregation.

Canon 2081 (NA)

Oral debates are prohibited not only before the judges but also before all those who must cast a vote whether in this phase or in others that will follow.

Canon 2082 (NA)

Judgment concerning the value of the informative process instructed by the Ordinary [and] concerning the reputation of sanctity and of martyrdom and concerning the absence of any preemptory obstacles shall be offered by the Cardinal Fathers in the ordinary committee, the Cardinal Reporter supervising, and the question proposed [as follows]: *whether a commission for the introduction of the cause shall be assigned in this cause and to what purpose it works.*

Canon Law Digest
II: 561–63

Canon 2083 (NA)

§ 1. If the judgment of the Cardinal Fathers is favorable, it shall be proposed to the Most Holy One for him to sign, if he pleases, *the commission of the introduction of the cause.*

§ 2. If the Most Holy One signs the commission, the Secretary of the Sacred Congregation shall produce a decree about this and give it public effect.

Canon 2084 (NA)

§ 1. The decree on the introduction of the cause having been given, the Ordinaries can do nothing else concerning [the cause] without the express permission of the Sacred Congregation.

§ 2. The Servant of God whose cause is only introduced cannot be decorated with the title *venerable*, and postulators shall take care lest on the occasion of the introduction of the cause anything be done that suggests public cult in honor of the Servant of God.

Article 3—*On the discussion of the process on non-cult*

Canon 2085 (NA)

The commission for the introduction of the cause having been assigned, there is subject to discussion by the Cardinal Fathers in the ordinary particular committee the question as to whether the sentence on non-cult given by the Ordinary shall be confirmed. If the decision of the Cardinal Fathers indicates that cult has been given, [it is left to] the decision of those Fathers, being attentive to all of the circumstances, [whether] the cause shall be suspended while all the signs of the forbidden cult are removed, and this [decision shall] be obeyed for a certain time to be established by those same Fathers.

Canon 2086 (NA)

§ 1. If the Ordinary has not yet completed the process on non-cult before the introduction of the cause, the process will be undertaken by apostolic authority.

§ 2. For this purpose the Promoter general of faith shall produce interrogatories that, together with remissorial letters mentioned in Canons 2087 and foll[owing], shall be sent by the Sacred Congregation to the judges designated by it.

§ 3. When it concerns martyrdom in the cause of which the Ordinary omitted to instruct the process on non-cult before the introduction of the cause, a commission for the collection of evidence on non-cult shall be added to the remissorial letters for the production of the process on martyrdom and the cause of martyrdom together with particular interrogatories proposed by the Promoter general of faith.

Chapter 3
On the apostolic process

Article 1—*On instructing the apostolic process*

Canon 2087 (NA)

§ 1. The decree on non-cult having been issued, remissorial letters are sought from the Supreme Pontiff and sent to the Cardinal Prefect that call for the instruction of the apostolic process both on the reputation for sanctity, miracles, or martyrdom, and on the virtues and specific miracles or on the martyrdom and its cause.

§ 2. These two processes should be done distinctly; but the first can be omitted if it does not seem necessary or opportune to the Cardinal Prefect and Promoter general of faith to inquire again about the continuation of the reputation.

§ 3. The commission having been assigned, but the decree of non-cult not yet having been issued, if there is a danger that some of the eyewitnesses in the meantime might be lost, remissorial letters can be granted immediately for the instruction of the apostolic process on virtues and specific miracles and on martyrdom and its cause *lest the evidence disappear.*

Canon 2088 (NA)

§ 1. Remissorial letters are to be given to at least five judges constituted, if possible, in ecclesiastical dignity.

§ 2. If an Ordinary was counted among the judges, he acts as president; otherwise the president shall be designated by the same Sacred Congregation; it is expedient that at least the president not be the same one who [presided] over the informative process.

§ 3. If it concerns a process on miracles, at least one expert shall also be appointed who is present at tribunal sessions and who can ask the judge to propose necessary interrogatories to the witnesses in order to achieve greater clarity of words and subjects.

Canon 2089 (NA)

Special letters of the Promoter general of faith shall be added to the remissorial letters by which he designates two sub-promoters who take part in the process in his name.

Canon 2090 (NA)

Interrogatories shall be produced by the Promoter general of faith on the objections raised at the introduction of the cause and on the testimonies received in the informative process according to the norm of Canon 2050, likewise on the extrajudicial information that he thinks ought to be required, including the work of the expert if it concerns a miracle.

Canon 2091 (NA)

§ 1. The remissorial letters are given to the postulator of the cause, who shall take care that they are transmitted to the delegated president of the tribunal.

§ 2. At the same time, interrogatories upon which the witnesses included are to be interrogated are sent to one of the sub-promoters, sealed, and not to be opened except in the acts of examination.

Canon 2092 (NA)

Delegated judges, before they undertake the fulfillment of their duties, shall show letters of delegation to the Ordinary, who must render them the assistance of his authority.

Canon 2093 (NA)

§ 1. Having received the remissorial letters, the president of the tribunal shall take care to convoke the tribunal quickly and never to defer its convocation beyond three months unless a just impediment intervenes about which, nevertheless, he shall not fail to advise the Sacred Congregation within the same time.

§ 2. The tribunal in its first session will select a notary and his assistant, an expert, and if there is reason, a courier, and about these selections the notary of the Curia shall give guarantees.

Canon 2094 (NA)

Although all of those to whom remissorial letters were sent can be present at individual sessions of the apostolic process, for validity it nevertheless suffices that the president be present with two judges or, with him agreeing and being absent, three other judges, and likewise one of the sub-promoters of faith and the notary or the assistant.

Canon 2095 (NA)

The process shall be completed within [at most] two years calculated from the day of opening the letters; the which two-year [period] having elapsed, the process cannot be continued without coming to the Apostolic See, [and] the Sacred Congregation shall be advised about the impediments that prevented the apostolic mandate from being brought to conclusion.

Canon 2096 (NA)

Before the apostolic process is concluded on the specific virtues, a juridical review shall be done by the tribunal on the remains of the Servant of God according to the prescription of the remissorial letters.

Canon 2097 (NA)

§ 1. In the transcription, comparison, and transmittal to Rome of the original copy of the acts, there shall be observed what is prescribed above in Canons 2054–56 and 2063 for the informative process.

§ 2. The process shall be shown, opened, and transcribed at the Sacred Congregation according to the norm of Canons 2073–75.

Canon Law Digest
VI: 848

Article 2—*On the discussion of the validity of the apostolic process*

Canon 2098 (NA)

The apostolic process having been sent to the Sacred Congregation, it must first of all be shown whether this process is valid, and at the same time the validity of the informative process shall be recalled for examination.

Canon 2099 (NA)

Therefore before discussion, a position is prepared by the advocate of the cause in which is shown:

1.° Information that in the production of documents contained in the process and necessary for this, it can be shown that all the things therein were done according to the norm of law;

2.° The animadversions of the Promoter general of faith against [their] validity with the responses of the advocate, both of which are prepared according to the norm of Canon 2080.

Canon 2100 (NA)

§ 1. A congregation shall be held for the discussion of the validity of the process in the presence of the Cardinal Prefect of the Sacred Congregation, the Cardinal Reporter, and three other Cardinals of the same Sacred Congregation chosen by the Roman Pontiff, as well as the Secretary Protonotary Apostolic, the Promoter general of faith, and the Sub-promoter.

§ 2. In the congregation chaired by the Cardinal Reporter, the above-mentioned prelates shall offer their opinions; and the Promoter general of faith shall propose objections if he has any.

§ 3. All these things having been discussed, the Cardinal Fathers shall come to a decision that, if it is favorable and confirmed by the Supreme Pontiff, shall result in a decree on the validity of the process.

Article 3—*On the judgment on heroicity of virtues in specific or on martyrdom and its cause*

Canon 2101 (NA)

The discussion of virtues shall not be undertaken before fifty years [have passed] from the death of the Servant of God.

Canon Law Digest
I: 835

Canon 2102 (NA)

The heroicity of virtue of the Servant of God or of his martyrdom and its cause shall be discussed by three congregations; namely, in an antepreparatory, preparatory, and general [congregation].

Canon 2103 (NA)

§ 1. Official prelates and consultors shall offer their votes in writing in every congregation.

§ 2. After all of the prelates and consultors have given their votes both in the antepreparatory congregation and in the preparatory [congregation], they can declare once again as individuals before the congregation is dissolved that they wish to revoke a vote already given.

§ 3. The conclusions of the individual votes shall be reduced to writing by the Secretary and preserved secretly; but the written votes shall be handed over to the Promoter general of faith.

Canon 2104 (NA)

In the causes of confessors the [following] question must be discussed: *whether there is proven the theological virtues of Faith, Hope, Charity both toward God and toward neighbor as well as the cardinal [virtues] of Prudence, Justice, Temperance, and Fortitude, and that these [exist] in a heroic degree in the cause and to what effect they worked*; but in causes of martyrs [the question is]: *whether the martyrdom and its cause have been shown and what signs, that is, miracles, [exist] in the cause and to what effect they worked.*

Canon 2105 (NA)

The antepreparatory congregation shall be held in the presence of the Cardinal Reporter together with official prelates and consultors.

Canon 2106 (NA)

For the antepreparatory congregation a position paper shall be prepared that shows:

1.° A summary taken from the original process, and that it was produced so that the testimonies and documents have been produced integrally;

2.° A writing of the advocate in which, briefly, there are illustrated from the materials in the summary the life and heroicity of virtue of the Servant of God or his martyrdom and its cause, and all those distinct items most diligently [presented] that are offered as arguments for proof and those things that are added more as circumstances and aids to proof;

3.° A synopsis by the Promoter general of faith mentioned in Canon 2079;

4.° The animadversions of the Promoter general of faith and the responses of the advocate;
5.° The opinions that have been produced by the reviewers on the writings of the Servant of God.

Canon 2107 (NA)

When two out of three of those present have given a negative vote, [the process] shall not advance from the antepreparatory congregation to the preparatory [congregation] unless, the matter having been turned over to the Roman Pontiff by the Cardinal Prefect, [the Roman Pontiff] decides something else shall be done.

Canon 2108 (NA)

The preparatory congregation is held by all Cardinal Fathers of the Sacred Congregation with official prelates and consultants present.

Canon 2109 (NA) Cross-Refs.: 1917 CIC 2113, 2122

A position paper shall be produced for the preparatory congregation [concerning]:

1.° The difficulties [raised by] the Promoter general of faith;
2.° The difficulties that have been proposed by the consultors in their votes if they do not seem negligible to the Promoter general;
3.° The responses of the advocate;
4.° Documents recently discovered, whether for the cause or against the cause, with additional summaries, whether to impugn [them] or to defend [them].

Canon 2110 (NA)

§ 1. In the preparatory congregation, the Cardinal Fathers, having heard the consultors, decide whether it is possible to proceed further.

§ 2. The Secretary and Promoter general of faith, even if they were not asked, can always interject [things] by which the issues might be more clarified and facts better illustrated.

Canon 2111 (NA)

After the discussion, the matter is referred to the Supreme Pontiff by the Cardinal Prefect, who shall inform the Most Holy One not only about the result of the discussion, but also about particular arguments that were raised therein.

Canon 2112 (NA)

The general congregation is held in the presence of the Most Holy One with the Cardinal Fathers of the Sacred Congregation being present, [along with] official prelates and consultors.

Canon 2113 (NA) Cross-Ref.: 1917 CIC 2123

For the general congregation there will be prepared the most recent position according to the norm of Canon 2109 to which shall be added a brief report made by office of all those things that have occurred in the cause, actually, a basic concordance of the facts.

Canon 2114 (NA) Cross-Ref.: 1917 CIC 2123

In the general congregation, the judgment as to whether the heroicity of virtue of the Servant of God or his martyrdom and its cause is reserved to the Supreme Pontiff, but consultors, official prelates, and Cardinal Fathers place only a consultative vote.

Canon 2115 (NA)

§ 1. At the command of the Most Holy One, a decree shall be issued by the Secretary of the Sacred Congregation by which, in the name of the Supreme Pontiff, all of the virtues of the Servant of God are authentically declared to be of heroic grade or the martyrdom well proven: which decree will be published at a time and in a manner prescribed by the Most Holy One.

§ 2. This decree being published, the Servant of God may be named *venerable*; but this title, however, brings with it no permission for public cult.

Article 4—*On the trial on the miracles of the Servant of God in specific*

Canon 2116 (NA)

§ 1. Besides heroicity of virtue or martyrdom, miracles are required for the beatification of the Servant of God wrought through his intercession.

§ 2. If, however, it concerns a martyr, and the martyrdom and the cause of the martyrdom have been clearly shown in both their material and formal aspects, but miracles are lacking, it is for the Sacred Congregation to decide whether the signs in the cause are sufficient and, these lacking, whether to approach the Most Holy One for a dispensation from signs in the cause.

Canon 2117 (NA)

For the beatification of Servants of God, there are required only two miracles, if eyewitnesses in either the informative or apostolic process can provide proof of virtues or if the witnesses examined in the apostolic process at least [testify] concerning what they heard from eyewitnesses; three [miracles are required] if the eyewitnesses [were questioned] in the informative process about what they heard from others who were heard in the apostolic process; four [miracles are required] if the virtues were proven in either process only through witnesses who testified from tradition or [who have their knowledge through] documents.

Canon 2118 (NA)

§ 1. To prove miracles, two experts are to be included by office at the beginning of the discussion; and if both are in agreement in rejecting a miracle, [the cause] cannot proceed further.

§ 2. Because most frequently the discussion of miracles concerns a cure from some type of disease, the experts must be well known in medical or surgical fields, indeed, where this can be done, they ought to be selected who are outstanding experts in the diagnosis and cure of the disease with which the proposed miracle is involved.

Canon 2119 (NA)

The opinion of the experts, though brief, shall be written with clear bases in fact and contain these two [items], namely:

1.° Whether, if it concerns a cure, the one in whom it occurred must truly be considered healed;

2.° Whether or not the fact proposed as a miracle can be explained by the laws of nature.

Canon 2120 (NA)

Miracles must be discussed in three congregations in just the way established above concerning heroicity of virtues; but for each discussion in the same congregation, except for the general [discussion] in the presence of the Most Holy One, there shall never be more than two miracles submitted.

Canon 2121 (NA)

The antepreparatory document for the congregation must include:

1.° Information written by the advocate;
2.° A summary of the testimony of the witnesses;
3.° The two opinions written by the experts regarding the truth of each miracle;
4.° The objections of the Promoter general of faith;
5.° The responses of the advocate.

Canon 2122 (NA)

§ 1. For the preparatory congregation, a position [paper] shall be developed as was established in Canon 2109, to which is added the opinion of the experts according to the norm of § 2.

§ 2. If in the antepreparatory congregation the two experts were in agreement in affirming the miracle, then only one expert is designated for the preparatory congregation; but if only one expert stood for the miracle, then two new experts must be appointed by office.

§ 3. The Cardinal Fathers of the Sacred Congregation always have the right to designate more experts than are required if they think this is necessary in a cause.

§ 4. Even though an advocate in the cause can have the assistance of an expert in producing his responses, [the expert] has no vote, as they say, *upon that opportunity*.

Canon 2123 (NA)

For the general congregation, the prescriptions of Canons 2113–14 are observed.

Canon 2124 (NA)

§ 1. After the decree of approval of the miracles, there must be conducted a new discussion in the presence of the Supreme Pontiff on the question: *Whether it is safe to proceed to the beatification of the Servant of God.*

§ 2. About this, having heard the thoughts of the consultors and the Cardinal Fathers, the Pontiff shall decide [the matter] and, if he wishes, can order that a decree about this be drawn up and promulgated.

TITLE 25
On the process of beatification of Servants of God by the way of cult, that is, an exceptional case

Canon 2125 (NA)

§ 1. For those Servants of God who, after the pontificate of Alexander III and before the time established by the constitution of [Pope] Urban, had a cult by tolerance, the positive approval of the Roman Pontiff can be petitioned.

§ 2. For this there is required a process according to the norm of the canons that follow.

Canon 2126 (NA)

The Ordinary competent to instruct this process is the Ordinary of the place where the cult is active or where the documents of the cult are stored, with due regard for the right of prevention if there are several Ordinaries of this sort.

Canon 2127 (NA)

At the request of the postulator the Ordinary must:

1.° Examine the writings of the Servant of God;

2.° Instruct a process on the reputation of holiness of life, virtues, or martyrdom and miracles that shall respond to the questions: *whether there is in the place a constant and common reputation and conviction about the holiness of the Servant of God in the place of his life or of his martyrdom and about the cause of the martyrdom, as well as about miracles performed at his intercession; and whether at present there is an active cult for this Servant of God in that area and by what marks the Servant of God is honored.*

Canon 2128 (NA)

With all of these things sent to the Sacred Congregation according to the norm of Canons 2061–63, the question: *Whether a commission shall be assigned for the introduction of the cause* shall be subjected to a discussion by the Cardinal Fathers in an ordinary congregation moderated by the Cardinal Reporter.

Canon 2129 (NA)

The commission having been assigned, remissorial letters shall be sent to those men designated by the Sacred Congregation so that the apostolic process to be conducted in law can be instructed on the exceptional case and a decision passed by the delegated judge.

Canon 2130 (NA)

From this process, there must be proved both the beginning of the cult and its uninterrupted continuation up to the sentence of the delegated judge.

Canon 2131 (NA)

The process having been transmitted to the Sacred Congregation and opened, and with a position [paper] prepared by the advocate of the cause, along with the observations of the Promoter general of faith, and [with] the responses of the patrons, the question to be proposed in the ordinary congregation [is]: *Whether the sentence of the delegated judge should be confirmed [and] therefore whether it has been shown that [the matter] can proceed as an exceptional case further on.*

Canon 2132 (NA)

Confirmation of the sentence of the delegated judge on the part of the Roman Pontiff has as its only effect the proving of the fact that the cult of the Servant of God has been immemorial and has lasted until the sentence.

Canon 2133 (NA)

If the sentence of the exceptional case was favorable and approved by the Supreme Pontiff, remissorial letters shall be sent to undertake the process on the virtues or on the martyrdom and its cause according to the diversity of causes; and the prescriptions of Canons 2087–2115 are observed.

Canon 2134 (NA)

The decree on the fact of the immemorial cult and on the heroicity of virtues or of martyrdom having been given, the Servant of God is considered equivalently beatified if confirmation of his cult has come by decree of the Roman Pontiff.

Canon 2135 (NA)

A Servant of God equivalently beatified can be granted the same acts of public cult with which those formally beatified are typically honored.

TITLE 26
On the canonization of the Blesseds

Canon 2136 (NA)

No one can seek from the Sacred Congregation the canonization of anyone or request that anyone be honored with a certain cultic act unless it is first shown that the Servant of God with whom it is concerned has been formally or equivalently listed among the Blesseds.

Canon 2137 (NA)

§ 1. In order that the formal or equivalent beatification be shown in a cause, an authentic document must be presented to the Sacred Congregation.

§ 2. If a document of this sort cannot be had, a legitimate process is to be instituted to prove the fact of positive permission for the cult on the part of the Roman Pontiff.

§ 3. The process having been completed, there shall be given in ordinary congregation a sentence of approval to be submitted to the Roman Pontiff.

Canon 2138 (NA)

§ 1. For the canonization of Blesseds who were formally beatified, the approval of two miracles is required that occurred after formal beatification.

§ 2. But for the canonization of those Blesseds who were beatified equivalently, the approval of three miracles is required that have been worked after the equivalent beatification.

Canon 2139 (NA)

§ 1. When some miracle is said to be worked by the intercession of some Blessed, the Sacred Congregation issues at the request of the postulator a decree, if it is pleasing to the Most Holy One, about resuming the cause and of instructing a new process according to the norms given in the above canons.

§ 2. The validity of the process being proved, the discussion of the new miracles is guided by those same laws that were established above in Canons 2116–24.

Canon 2140 (NA)

After all these things, the Roman Pontiff, having heard the opinion of the Cardinal Fathers and the consultors, if and when he judges it opportune, issues a decree by which he decides that it is possible safely to proceed to the solemn canonization of the Blessed.

Canon 2141 (NA)

The solemn canonization of the Blessed, after it is decreed in the Consistory, is done according to the received rites and formalities of the Roman Curia.

Canon Law Digest
III: 646

THIRD PART
ON THE MANNER OF PROCEEDING IN RESOLVING CERTAIN MATTERS OR IN APPLYING PENAL SANCTIONS[1]

Canon 2142 (NA)

In the procedures discussed below, a notary shall always be used, who will put into writing the acts that must be signed by all and that must be preserved in the archive.

Canon 2143 (NA)

§ 1. As often as warnings are required, these must be done either orally in the presence of the chancellor or other official of the Curia or two witnesses, or by letter according to the norm of Canon 1719.

§ 2. The fact of the warnings and their tenor must be preserved by authentic document in the acts.

[1] Thomas Ronchetti, "On the Administrative Removal of Parish-Priests" (MS no. 712, Gregorian University, 1939; printed version, no. 555, 1939).

§ 3. Whoever impedes a warning in any way from reaching himself is considered as warned.

Canon Law Digest
I: 837

Canon 2144 (NA)

§ 1. Examiners and consultors, as well as the notary, by an oath interposed at the beginning of the process, must observe secrecy concerning everything that they know by reason of their office and especially concerning occult documents, discussions held in committee, and the number of and motives for votes.

§ 2. If this prescription is not adequately observed, not only must they be removed from duty, but they can be struck with other deserved penalties by the Ordinary, those things being observed that ought to be observed; and moreover for any damages that might have flowed therefrom, they are bound to make good.

Canon 2145[2] (NA) Cross-Ref.: 1917 CIC 2153

§ 1. In these matters the summary process is observed; but two or three witnesses, whether called by office or brought by the party to be heard, are not prohibited, unless the Ordinary, having heard the pastor consultors or examiners, believes the parties are calling them just to delay things.

§ 2. Witnesses and experts, unless sworn, are not admitted.

Canon 2146 (1983 CIC 1747, 1752)

§ 1. From a definitive decree, the only remedy of law that is given is recourse to the Apostolic See.

§ 2. In which case, all the acts of the process are to be transmitted to the Holy See.

§ 3. Pending recourse, the Ordinary cannot validly confer the parish or benefice of which the cleric has been deprived to another on a stable basis.

Canon Law Digest
I: 837; VII: 1023

---

[2] Maurice Connor, "The Administrative Removal of Pastors", Canon Law Studies, no. 104 (J. C. D. thesis, Catholic University of America, 1937).

TITLE 27
On the manner of proceeding in the removal of irremovable pastors

Canon 2147 (1983 CIC 1740–41) Cross-Refs.: 1917 CIC 389, 2148, 2157, 2293

§ 1. An irremovable pastor can be removed from his parish for cause whereby his ministry, even through no grave fault of his own, has been rendered noxious or at least ineffective.

§ 2. The causes of this are especially the following:

1.° If inexpertness or permanent infirmity of mind or body impairs the pastor from rightly fulfilling his duties in the judgment of the Ordinary and an adjutant vicar cannot provide for the good of souls according to the norm of Canon 475;

2.° Hatred [arising from] the people, even though it is unjust and not universal, provided it is such that it will impede the useful ministry of the pastor and is not foreseen as ceasing in a brief time;

3.° The loss of good estimation among prudent and grave men, whether this has arisen from the levity of the life-style of the pastor or from old crimes that have recently been detected, even though already prescribed from penalty, or from the behavior of familiars and blood-relatives with whom the pastor lives, unless the good reputation of the pastor can be sufficiently provided for by their leaving;

4.° From a probable occult crime imputed to the pastor that the Ordinary prudently foresees might arise later to the great offense of the faithful;

5.° From the poor administration of temporal affairs along with grave damage to the church or benefice, as often as this evil cannot be averted either by restricting the administration of the pastor or in some other way, even though in other regards the pastor is exercising a useful spiritual ministry.

Canon Law Digest
VI: 848; VIII: 1204–5; IX: 997

Canon 2148 (1983 CIC 1742) Cross-Ref.: 1917 CIC 2152

§ 1. As often in the prudent judgment of the Ordinary a pastor seems to have fallen into one of the situations mentioned in Canon 2147, the

Ordinary himself having heard the two examiners and having discussed the truth and gravity of the matter with them, shall invite the pastor in writing or orally to resign the parish within a certain time, unless it concerns a pastor laboring under mental problems.

§ 2. The invitation, in order that the acts be valid, must contain the cause that moves the Ordinary and the arguments that have convinced him of same.

Canon Law Digest
I: 838–39; VII: 1023

Canon 2149 (1983 CIC 1744) Cross-Refs.: 1917 CIC 2159, 2169

§ 1. If the pastor within the allotted days neither resigns nor asks for a delay nor opposes the reasons adduced for removal, the Ordinary, after he has proven that an invitation for resignation rightly done was communicated to the pastor and he still did not respond [to it, even though] he was not legitimately impeded, shall immediately remove him from the parish without being bound by the prescription of Canon 2154.

§ 2. But if he has not proven the above-indicated two circumstances, the Ordinary shall opportunely provide either for a repetition of the invitation to resign or for a delay in the useful time for response.

Canon 2150 (1983 CIC 1743)

§ 1. If the pastor resigns the parish, the Ordinary shall declare the parish vacant by resignation.

§ 2. But the pastor, in place of the causes given by the Ordinary, can offer another [basis for] resignation less bothersome and less grave to himself, provided it is true and honest, such as, for example, that he is being compliant with the desires of the Ordinary.

§ 3. Resignation can be made not only purely and simply but also under condition, provided it can be legitimately accepted by the Ordinary and actually is accepted, and with due regard for the prescription of Canon 186.

Canon Law Digest
I: 839

Canon 2151 (1983 CIC 1745)

A pastor, if he wishes to oppose the reason adduced in the invitation, can ask for a delay to order to gather evidence that the Ordinary in his prudent judgment can grant provided it does not work harm to souls.

Canon 2152 (1983 CIC 1745)

§ 1. In order to act validly, the Ordinary must weigh and approve or reject the reasons presented against the invitation by the pastor, having heard these with the examiners mentioned in Canon 2148, § 1.

§ 2. The decision, whether affirmative or negative, must be communicated by decree to the pastor.

Canon 2153 (1983 CIC 1745)

§ 1. Against a decree of removal a pastor can interpose recourse within ten days before the same Ordinary, who, lest he act invalidly, must examine and approve or reject the new allegations from the same pastor, [who in turn must have] produced them within ten days of having interposed recourse, and having heard the two pastor consultors, together with the reasons first presented.

§ 2. A pastor can introduce witnesses according to the norm of Canon 2145, § 1, if he is able to prove that he was not able to introduce them the first time.

§ 3. The decision must be made known to the pastor by decree.

Canon Law Digest
I: 839; VII: 1023–24; VIII: 1205

Canon 2154 (1983 CIC 1746) Cross-Refs.: 1917 CIC 2149, 2161

§ 1. The pastor being removed, the Ordinary with the examiners or pastor consultors who took part in deciding about the removal shall carefully discuss with their advice whether transfer to another parish or assignment to another office or benefice, if he is suitable for this, or a pension [should be pursued], insofar as there is cause and circumstances permit.

§ 2. All things being equal, in this provision one resigning is more favored than one removed.

Canon Law Digest
I: 839

Canon 2155 (NA) Cross-Ref.: 1917 CIC 2161

The Ordinary can expedite the business of new provision for the removed pastor either in the decree of removal itself or afterward, but in any event as soon as possible.

Canon 2156 (1983 CIC 1747) Cross-Ref.: 1917 CIC 2161

§ 1. A priest removed from a parish must relinquish as soon as possible the parish house, and all those things that pertain to the parish he shall hand over to the new pastor or to the administrator appointed by the Ordinary in the meantime.

§ 2. If, however, it concerns an infirm [priest] who cannot be transferred from one parish house to another without inconvenience, the Ordinary shall allow him the use, even exclusive use, [of the house] for so long as necessity exists.

TITLE 28
On the manner of proceeding in the removal of removable pastors

Canon 2157 (1983 CIC 1740, 1742)

§ 1. A removable pastor can be removed from his parish for a just and grave cause according to the norm of Canon 2147.

§ 2. As for what applies to religious pastors, the prescription of Canon 454, § 5, is observed.

Canon Law Digest
VI: 849

Canon 2158 (1983 CIC 1742)

If the Ordinary believes that any of these causes are present, he shall paternally advise the pastor and encourage him to resign the parish, indicating the reasons that have rendered his parochial ministry harmful to the faithful or at least ineffective.

Canon 2159 (1983 CIC 1745)

With due regard for the prescription of Canon 2149, if the pastor refuses, he shall give reasons in writing that the Ordinary, in order to proceed validly, must evaluate together with two examiners.

Canon 2160 (NA)

If the Ordinary, having heard the examiners, does not consider the proffered reasons sufficient, he shall repeat the paternal exhortations to the pastor, mentioning removal, if within an appropriate time [the pastor] does not give up his parish on his own.

Canon 2161 (1983 CIC 1744–47)

§ 1. The defined time having run, the which he can extend according to his prudence, the Ordinary shall issue a decree of removal.

§ 2. [The Ordinary] is bound to provide for a removed or resigning pastor according to the norm of Canons 2154–56.

TITLE 29[3]
On the manner of proceeding in the transfer of pastors

Canon 2162 (1983 CIC 1748)

If the good of souls suggests that a pastor should be removed from his parish, [even] one that he has governed well, to another parish, the Ordinary shall propose it to him and persuade him to consent to it for the love of God and souls.

Canon Law Digest
I: 840; VI: 849

Canon 2163 (NA)

§ 1. The Ordinary cannot transfer an unwilling irremovable pastor unless he obtains special faculties from the Apostolic See.

§ 2. But a removable pastor, if the parish *to which* [he is being transferred] is not greatly beneath his rank, can be transferred even over his objection, with due regard for the prescription of the canons that follow.

Canon 2164 (1983 CIC 1749)

If the pastor does not yield to the advice and persuasions of the Ordinary, he shall explain his reasons in writing.

Canon 2165 (1983 CIC 1750)

If the Ordinary, notwithstanding the proffered reasons, decides in the case not to reconsider, he must, in order to act validly, hear two pastor consultors on the case and with them weigh the circumstances of both the parish *from which* and the parish *to which* and the reasons why the transfer seems useful and necessary.

[3] William Galvin, "The Administrative Transfer of Pastors", Canon Law Studies, no. 232 (J. C. D. thesis, Catholic University of America, 1946).

Canon 2166 (1983 CIC 1750)

If, having heard the pastors, the Ordinary decides to go ahead with the transfer, he should repeat his paternal exhortations in order that the pastor will perform willingly the will of the Superior.

Canon 2167 (1983 CIC 1751)

§ 1. These things being done, if the pastor still refuses and the Ordinary still thinks the transfer should be done, he shall order the pastor that within a certain time he take himself to his new parish, signifying this in writing, [and] with the elapse of the established time, the parish that he presently holds will be automatically vacant.

§ 2. This time having run without result, he shall declare the parish vacant.

TITLE 30
On the manner of proceeding against non-resident clerics

Canon 2168 (NA)

§ 1. The Ordinary shall warn a pastor, canon, or other cleric who, being bound by the law of residence by reason of the benefice he holds, neglects [that law] and, in the meantime, if it concerns a pastor, make his own provision lest the welfare of souls suffer harm.

§ 2. In the warning, the Ordinary shall recall the penalties that non-residential clerics incur and the prescription of Canon 188, n. 8, and indicate to the cleric that within an appropriate time defined by the Ordinary he resume residence.

Canon Law Digest
I: 840

Canon 2169 (NA)

If within the limit of the pre-established time the cleric does not resume residence or offer a cause for the absence, the Ordinary, observing the prescription of Canon 2149, shall declare the parish or other benefice vacant.

Canon 2170 (NA)

If the cleric resumes residence, the Ordinary nevertheless must, if the absence was illegitimate, inflict a privation of the fruits [of the post] for the time of the absence, described in Canon 2381, and can also, if there is cause, punish [the cleric] appropriately for the gravity of the fault.

Canon 2171 (NA) Cross-Ref.: 1917 CIC 2174

If the cleric does not resume residence, but offers a cause for the absence, the Ordinary, having summoned and briefed two examiners, if it can be done, by means of an opportune investigation, must see whether the cause is legitimate.

Canon 2172 (NA)

If, having heard the examiners, the Ordinary feels that the proffered reasons are not legitimate, he must again give the cleric a time limit within which he must go back, with due regard for the privation of fruits for the time of the absence.

Canon 2173 (NA) Cross-Ref.: 1917 CIC 2174

If a removable pastor does not return within the prescribed time, the Ordinary can immediately proceed to a privation of the parish; if he does return, the Ordinary shall give him a precept of not leaving again without written permission under penalty of privation of the parish to be incurred by that fact.

Canon 2174 (NA)

§ 1. If a cleric who has obtained an irremovable benefice does not take residence, but gives new reasons, the Ordinary with the same examiners shall reexamine these according to the norm of Canon 2171.

§ 2. After deducing these other things, if these are not found to be legitimate, the Ordinary shall order the cleric, within the prescribed time or a time again to be prescribed, to return under penalty of privation of the benefice to be incurred by that fact.

§ 3. If he does not return, the Ordinary shall declare him to be deprived of the benefice; if he returns, the Ordinary shall give him the same precept mentioned in Canon 2173.

Canon 2175 (NA)

In neither case will the Ordinary declare the benefice vacant until after he has weighed with the examiners the reasons that the departed cleric might have offered and has established that the same permission could have been asked of the Ordinary.

TITLE 31
On the manner of proceeding against concubinious clerics

Canon 2176 (NA)

An Ordinary shall warn a cleric who, against the prescription of Canon 133, has a suspicious woman with him or in any manner keeps company with her, that he should dismiss her or abstain from being with her, mentioning the penalties established in Canon 2359 for concubinious clerics.

Canon 2177 (NA) Cross-Refs.: 1917 CIC 2180–81

If a cleric neither respects the precept nor responds to it, the Ordinary, after he has proven to himself that the cleric could have responded:

1.° Shall suspend him from divine [things];
2.° Deprive a pastor, moreover, of his parish immediately;
3.° But if a cleric has a benefice without the care of souls, two months having passed since suspension, if he has not amended himself, [the Ordinary] shall deprive him of a half-part of the fruits of the benefice; but after another three months, [he shall deprive him] of all the parts of the benefice; and after three more months, [he shall deprive him] of the benefice itself.

Canon 2178 (NA) Cross-Ref.: 1917 CIC 2180

If the cleric does not obey but adduces reasons by way of excuse, the Ordinary must hear these with two examiners.

Canon 2179 (NA)

If having heard the examiners the Ordinary considers that the reasons given are not legitimate, he shall convey this to the cleric as soon as possible and shall give him a formal precept that, within a brief time to be defined by [the Ordinary], he shall [correct himself].

Canon 2180 (NA)

An Ordinary can immediately coerce a disobedient, removable pastor according to the norm of Canon 2177; but if it concerns a cleric who, holding an irremovable benefice, does not [correct himself] but alleges new rationales, the Ordinary shall put them to an examination according to the norm of Canon 2178.

Canon 2181 (NA)

But if these are also judged not to be legitimate the Ordinary shall order the cleric again that, within a decent time, he comply with the mandate; which time having passed without effect, he shall proceed according to the norm of Canon 2177.

TITLE 32
On the manner of proceeding against a pastor who is negligent in fulfilling parochial duties[4]

Canon 2182 (NA) Cross-Ref.: 1917 CIC 2382

A Bishop shall warn a pastor who gravely neglects or violates parochial duties mentioned in Canons 467, § 1, 468, § 1, 1178, 1330–32, and 1344, recalling to his mind both the strict obligation that weighs on his conscience and the penalties established for this delict in law.

Canon Law Digest
II: [565]

Canon 2183 (NA) Cross-Refs.: 1917 CIC 2184, 2382

If a pastor does not amend himself, the Bishop shall administer formal correction to him and shall punish him with other appropriate penalties for the gravity of the fault, [consequent to] having heard the two examiners, and having offered the pastor the opportunity of defending himself, and having proof that the aforesaid parochial duties are then, and that these have been for a notable period of time, in matters of moment, omitted or violated, and there is no just cause excusing their omissions or violations.

Canon 2184 (NA) Cross-Ref.: 1917 CIC 2382

If both formal correction and punishment go without effect the Ordinary, having proved according to the norm of Canon 2183 the persistent and culpable omission or violation of parochial duties in grave things, can immediately deprive a removable pastor of his parish; but in regard to an irremovable pastor, he shall deprive him of the fruits of the benefice, [which

[4] Carl Meier, "Penal Administrative Procedure against Negligent Pastors", Canon Law Studies, no. 140 (J. C. D. thesis, Catholic University of America, 1941).

are then] to be distributed to the poor by the Ordinary, in whole or in part according to the gravity of the fault.

Canon 2185 (NA) Cross-Ref.: 1917 CIC 2382

Bad will being persistent and proven, as above, the Ordinary can remove from his parish even an irremovable pastor.

TITLE 33
On the manner of proceeding in inflicting suspension from an informed conscience[5]

Canon 2186 (NA)

§ 1. It is permitted for Ordinaries in virtue of an informed conscience to suspend from office, whether in part or in whole, clerics under their authority.

§ 2. This extraordinary remedy may not be applied if the Ordinary can, without grave inconvenience, proceed against the subject according to the norms of law.

Canon 2187 (NA)

In imposing this suspension, neither judicial forms nor canonical admonitions are required; it is sufficient that the Ordinary, following the prescriptions of the canons that follow, declares by simple decree the suspension to have occurred.

Canon 2188 (NA)

A decree of this sort should be given in writing, unless circumstances require otherwise, denoting the day, month, and year; and in it:

1.° It should be expressly said that suspension has been carried out from an informed conscience, that is, for causes known to the Ordinary;

2.° There shall be indicated the time the penalty lasts; the Ordinary shall abstain from imposing this in perpetuity. But it can be

[5] Edwin Murphy, "Suspension *Ex Informata Conscientia*", Canon Law Studies, no. 76 (J. C. D. thesis, Catholic University of America, 1932).

imposed in the manner of a censure, such that it affects a cleric as long as does the cause for which it was imposed;

3.° There should be a clear indication of the acts that are prohibited, if the suspension was not given in whole but in part.

Canon 2189 (NA)

§ 1. If a cleric is suspended from an office in which another has been substituted for him, such as, for example, an econome in [a benefice with] the care of souls, the one who was substituted can continue to draw the fruits of the benefice to be determined according to the prudent judgment of the Ordinary.

§ 2. A suspended cleric, if he feels himself injured, can ask a reduction in the pension from the immediate Superior, who, in a judicial case, would be the appellate judge.

Canon 2190 (NA)

An Ordinary who conducts suspension from an informed conscience must, through a conducted investigation, have gathered such proofs as to make him certain that a cleric has truly perpetrated a delict and that it is so grave that he ought to be coerced by this sort of penalty.

Canon 2191 (NA)

§ 1. Suspension from an informed conscience is used justly and legitimately against an occult delict according to the norm of Canon 2197, n. 4.

§ 2. Suspension from an informed conscience can never be carried out for a notorious delict.

§ 3. In order that a public delict be punished with suspension from an informed conscience, it is necessary that there occur one of the circumstances that follow:

1.° If there are trustworthy and serious witnesses to a delict before the Ordinary, but by no means can they be induced to provide this testimony in a trial, and there is no other way to adduce other evidence about the delict in a judicial process;

2.° If the cleric himself, by threats or by other means, impedes a judicial process from being started or, once started, completed;

3.° If the conduct of the judicial process or the passing of sentence is impeded for reasons arising from adverse civil law or the danger of grave scandal.

Canon 2192 (NA)

Suspension from an informed conscience can be applied if out of several delicts only one of them was occult.

Canon 2193 (NA) Cross-Ref.: 1917 CIC 2225

It is left to the prudent judgment of the Ordinary whether to disclose or retain the cause or crime that led to the suspension of the cleric, applying, of course, pastoral solicitude and charity, so that, if he decides to inform the cleric of the cause, the penalty, which he will impose through a paternal warning, not only works to expunge the guilt, but also serves to reform the offender and toward the elimination of the occasion of sin.

Canon 2194 (NA)

If a cleric places recourse from a suspension imposed upon him, the Ordinary must send to the Apostolic See the evidence by which he showed a clerical delict really to have been committed [and] that could be punished by this extraordinary penalty.

FIFTH BOOK
ON DELICTS AND PENALTIES

FIRST PART
ON DELICTS

TITLE 1
On the nature of delicts and their division

Canon 2195 (1983 CIC 1321)

§ 1. By the term delict in ecclesiastical law is understood an external and morally imputable violation of a law to which a canonical sanction, at least an indeterminate one, is attached.

§ 2. Unless it appears otherwise from the circumstances, what is said about delicts also applies to the violation of precepts to which a canonical penalty is attached.

Canon Law Digest
VIII: 1209; IX: 1001

Canon 2196 (NA)

The quality of a delict is determined by the object of the law; but the quantity is measured not only by the various levels of gravity attached to the violated law, but also by the greater or lesser imputability [of the act], or by the damage inflicted.

Canon 2197[1] (NA) Cross-Refs.: 1917 CIC 1747, 2191

A delict is:

1.° *Public*, if it is already known or is in such circumstances that it can be and must be prudently judged that it will easily become known;

[1] Cecil Parres, "The Concept of the Division of Crimes into Public, Notorious, and Occult according to the Code of Canon Law" (diss. no. 2, Pontifical University of St. Thomas [Rome], 1952–1953).

2.° *Notorious by notoriety of law*, [if it is] after a sentence by a competent judge that renders the matter an adjudicated thing, or after confession by the offender made in court in accord with Canon 1750;

3.° *Notorious by notoriety of fact*, if it is publicly known and was committed under such circumstances that no clever evasion is possible and no legal opinion could excuse [the act];

4.° *Occult*, if it is not public; *materially occult*, if the delict is hidden; *formally occult*, if imputability [is not known].

Canon 2198 (NA)

A delict that violates only a law of the Church can, by its nature, be pursued only by ecclesiastical authority, which authority can call upon the arms of civil authority when it judges it opportune and necessary; a delict that violates only laws of civil authority by proper law, according to the prescription of Canon 120, is punishable by civil authority, although the Church retains competence by reason of sin; a delict that violates the laws of both societies can be punished by both powers.

TITLE 2
On the imputability of a delict, and on the causes that increase or diminish it, and on the juridic effects of a delict[2]

Canon 2199[3] (1983 CIC 1321)

Imputability of a delict depends on the dolus of the offender or on his fault in ignorance of the violation of law or failure with regard to due diligence; therefore all causes that can increase, decrease, or remove dolus or culpability likewise increase, decrease, or remove imputability of the delict.

[2] Victor de Gabriele, "Uniting the Juristic Effects of Crime" (MS no. 2012, Gregorian University, 1952; printed version, no. 1660, Malta, 1964).

[3] John McGrath, "A Comparative Study of Crime and Its Imputability in Ecclesiastical Criminal Law and in American Criminal Law", Canon Law Studies, no. 385 (thesis, Catholic University of America, 1957).

Canon 2200[4] (1983 CIC 1321)

§ 1. Here, dolus is the deliberate will to violate a law and is countered on the part of the intellect by a lack of knowledge and on the part of the will by a lack of freedom.

§ 2. Positing an external violation of the law, dolus in the external forum is presumed until the contrary is proven.

Canon Law Digest
I: 843

Canon 2201 (1983 CIC 1322–25)

§ 1. Those who actually lack the use of reason are incapable of a delict.

§ 2. Those who are habitually out of their minds, even though they sometimes have lucid intervals, [and despite the fact that] at the time [in question] they seemed to be acting with a certain rationality, are nevertheless presumed incapable of a delict.

§ 3. A delict committed in voluntary drunkenness does not remove imputability, but it is less than the same delict committed with full use of the mind, unless, however, the drunkenness was sought to commit or excuse the delict; but a violation of the law during involuntary drunkenness excludes imputability completely if the drunkenness deprived one of the use of reason completely; it diminishes it if it was only in part. The same is said for other similar mental perturbations.

§ 4. Mental debility diminishes imputability of a delict, but does not remove it entirely.

Canon 2202[5] (1983 CIC 1323–24)

§ 1. Violation of a law in ignorance is imputed to no one, if the ignorance was not culpable; otherwise it is imputable more or less according to the culpability of the ignorance.

§ 2. Ignorance only of the penalty does not toll the imputability of the delict, but decreases it in part.

---

[4] Randolf Brown, "The Presumption of Innocence: An Historical Investigation concerning the Existence of the Presumption in Favor of the Accused in the Criminal Law of the Church" (MS no. 3456, Gregorian University, 1962).

[5] Innocent Swoboda, "Ignorance in Relation to the Imputability of Delicts", Canon Law Studies, no. 143 (J. C. D. thesis, Catholic University of America, 1941).

§ 3. Whatever is established for ignorance applies also to inadvertence and error.

Canon 2203 (1983 CIC 1323, 1326)

§ 1. If someone violates a law through the omission of due diligence, imputability is diminished in a manner to be determined by the prudence of the judge under the circumstances; but if he could foresee the matter, and nevertheless failed to take the precautions for its avoidance that a diligent person would have taken, fault is approximate to dolus.

§ 2. Fortuitous cause that cannot be foreseen, or that [seen, still] cannot be prevented from occurring, leaves off any sort of imputability.

Canon 2204 (1983 CIC 1323)

Minor age, unless otherwise established, reduces imputability for a delict as one approaches closer to childhood.

Canon 2205[6] (1983 CIC 1323–24)

§ 1. Physical force that prevents all faculty of action entirely excludes a delict.

§ 2. Additionally, grave fear, even if it is only relative, necessity, and even grave inconvenience for the most part thoroughly toll a delict, if it concerned a merely ecclesiastical law.

§ 3. But if the act was intrinsically evil or verged on contempt for the faith or ecclesiastical authority or harm to souls, the causes that [were outlined] in § 2 indeed diminish imputability, but do not eliminate it.

§ 4. [Force] for the sake of legitimate protection against unjust aggression, if due moderation is observed, eliminates a delict completely; otherwise it only diminishes imputability according to the cause of the provocation.

Canon 2206 (1983 CIC 1324)

Passion, if it is voluntarily and deliberately excited or fed, actually increases imputability; otherwise it diminishes it more or less according to the different degrees of passion; it entirely tolls it if all deliberation of mind and consent of the will disappears and impedes [responsibility].

---

[6] Alan McCoy, "Force and Fear in Relation to Delictual Imputability and Penal Responsibility", Canon Law Studies, no. 200 (J. C. D. thesis, Catholic University of America, 1944).

Canon 2207 (1983 CIC 1326)

Besides other aggravating circumstances, a delict is increased by:

1.° The higher dignity of the person who commits the delict or who was offended by the delict;

2.° An abuse of authority or office for the perpetration of the delict.

Canon 2208 (1983 CIC 1326)

§ 1. A recidivist in the legal sense is one who, after a condemnatory sentence, commits again a crime of the same sort under such circumstances, particularly of time, so that pertinacity in bad will can be prudently identified.

§ 2. Whoever commits several [delicts] of different sorts adds to his culpability.

Canon 2209[7] (1983 CIC 1329) Cross-Refs.: 1917 CIC 2211, 2230–31

§ 1. Whoever, by common counsel of offending, concurs together physically in the delict, they are all considered as defendants in that matter, unless from the circumstances of the matter, something increases or diminishes culpability.

§ 2. In a delict that by its nature postulates an accomplice, each one is equal in the manner of culpability, unless it appears otherwise from circumstances.

§ 3. Not only the one commanding is [considered] the principal author of the delict, but also whoever induces the consummation of the delict or who concurs in it in any way contracts no less imputability, all things being equal, than does the one who executed the delict, if the delict would not have been committed without the assistance of the other.

§ 4. But if the assistance of one only rendered the delict easier, but it would have been committed without that one's concurrence, less imputability is involved.

§ 5. But if one opportunely and fully pulls away from being involved in the perpetration of the delict, he is freed of all imputability, even if the executor of the delict for his own reasons nevertheless commits [the delict]; but if withdrawal is not complete, the retraction diminishes but does not wipe out culpability.

---

[7] Louis Eltz, "Cooperation in Crime", Canon Law Studies, no. 156 (J. C. D. thesis, Catholic University of America, 1942).

§ 6. Whoever concurs in a delict simply by failing in office is bound by imputability in proportion to the obligation by which they were required by office to prevent the delict.

§ 7. Praise for the commission of a delict, participation in its fruits, hiding the delinquent, and performance of other things regarding a delict [that] has already been fully committed constitute a new delict if indeed [such deeds] are struck with a penalty in law; but, unless they were present to the delinquent before the delict was done, they do not occasion imputability for the committed crime.

Canon Law Digest
III: 649

Canon 2210 (NA)

§ 1. From a delict there arises:

1.° A penal action for the declaration or infliction of a penalty and for seeking satisfaction;

2.° A civil action for the repair of damages, if someone was damaged by the delict.

§ 2. In either case the action is addressed according to the norm of Canons 1552–1959; and the same judge in the criminal trial can, at the request of the injured party, convoke and decide the treatment of the civil action.

Canon 2211 (NA)

All those who concur in a delict according to the norm of Canon 2209, §[§] 1–3, are bound by the obligation as a group to make good the damages and expenses that have arisen from the delict of each individual, even though the judge has assessed proportionate damages.

TITLE 3
On the attempted delict

Canon 2212 (1983 CIC 1328)

§ 1. Whoever places or omits an act that, by its nature is conducive to the execution of a delict, but who does not consummate the delict, whether because he gave up the plan, or because the delict could not be completed because of insufficient or inept methods, commits an *attempted delict.*

§ 2. When all the acts that, by their nature, are conducive to the execution of a delict have been placed or omitted, and they are sufficient to bring about the delict, [but then] for some other cause, besides the will of the agent, the effect does not occur, this attempted delict is known by its proper name of *frustrated* delict.

§ 3. The action of one who tried to get another to commit a delict, but without success, approaches attempted delict.

§ 4. If an attempted delict is scored in law by special penalty, it constitutes a true delict.

Canon 2213 (1983 CIC 1328) Cross-Ref.: 1917 CIC 2235

§ 1. An attempt of a delict has its own imputability and is greater the more it approaches consummation, although it is less than for a consummated delict, with due regard for the prescription of § 3.

§ 2. A frustrated delict involves greater culpability than does a simple attempt at a delict.

§ 3. One who spontaneously ceases from starting the execution of a delict is freed from all imputability, unless some harm from the attempt or scandal has arisen.

SECOND PART
ON PENALTIES

SECTION 1
ON PENALTIES IN GENERAL

Canon 2214 (1983 CIC 1311)

§ 1. The Church has the native and proper right, independent of any human authority, of coercing delinquents subject to her by penalties, both spiritual and also temporal.

§ 2. She shall always have before her eyes the advice of the Coun. of Tr., sess. 13, *on ref.*, chap. 1: "Let Bishops and other Ordinaries bear in mind that they are pastors and not prosecutors and that they ought so to preside over those subject to them so as not to lord it over them, but to love them as children and brethren and to strive by exhortation and admonition to deter them from what is unlawful, that they may not be obliged, should [their subjects] transgress, to coerce them by due punishments. In regard to those, however, who should happen to sin through frailty, that command of the Apostle is to be observed, [namely] that they reprove, entreat, and rebuke them in all kindness and patience, since benevolence toward those to be corrected often effects more than severity, exhortation more than threat, and charity more than force. But if on account of the gravity of the offense there is need of the rod, then is rigor to be tempered with gentleness, judgment with mercy, and severity with clemency, that discipline, so salutary and necessary for the people, may be preserved without harshness and they who are chastised may be corrected, or, if they are unwilling to repent, that others may, by the wholesome example of their punishment, be deterred from vices."

TITLE 4
On the notion, types, interpretation, and application of penalties

Canon 2215 (NA)

An ecclesiastical penalty is the privation of some good [and is] inflicted by the legitimate authority for the correction of a delinquent or the punishment of a delict.

Canon Law Digest
IX: 1001

Canon 2216 (1983 CIC 1312)

In the Church delinquents are punished by:

1.° Medicinal penalties, that is, censures;
2.° Vindicative penalties;
3.° Penal remedies and penances.

Canon 2217[1] (1983 CIC 1314–15)

§ 1. A penalty is called:

1.° *Determinate* if it is taxatively established in the law itself or a precept; *indeterminate* if it is left to the prudent judgment of the

[1] Edward Adams, "The Automatic Penalty" (diss. no. 3, Pontifical University of St. Thomas [Rome], 1974–1975).

judge or of the Superior, whether [it is expressed in] preceptive or facultative words;

2.° *Automatic* if a determinate penalty is added to the law or precept such that it is incurred upon the fact of the delict being committed; *formal* if it must be inflicted by a judge or Superior;

3.° *Of law* if a determinate penalty is established in the law itself, whether automatic or formal; *of man* if it is imposed by means of a special precept or by condemnatory judicial sentence, even though it is established in the law; wherefore a formal penalty added to the law before a condemnatory sentence is *only of law*, afterward [it is] both *of law* and *of man*, but it is considered only *of man*.

§ 2. A penalty is always considered formal, unless it is expressly said to be *automatically* contracted or *upon the fact* or *by the law*, or unless other similar words are used.

Canon 2218 (NA) Cross-Ref.: 1917 CIC 1691

§1. In applying penalties, equitable proportion must be observed with the delict, taking into consideration imputability, scandal, and harm; wherefore there must be considered not only the object and gravity of the law but also the age, knowledge, training, sex, condition, and mental state of the delinquent, the dignity of the person who was offended by the delict, or who committed the delict, the intended purpose, the place and time wherein the delict was committed, whether the delinquent was moved by passion or acted with great fear, and whether he repented of the delict and tried himself to prevent its evil effects, and other similar things.

§ 2. Not only those things that excuse from all imputability, but also those things [that excuse] from grave [imputability], equally excuse from any penalty, whether automatic or formal, even in the external forum if the excuse was brought in the external forum.

§ 3. Mutual injuries are [self-]compensated, unless one party must be [held liable] because of the greater degree of injury caused by him, [and] the penalty is diminished if there is cause for doing so.

Canon Law Digest
II: 569–70

Canon 2219 (NA)

§ 1. In penalties, the more benign interpretation is to be followed.

§ 2. But if there is doubt whether a penalty inflicted by the competent Superior is just or not, the penalty is to be observed in both forums, except in the case of suspensive appeal.

§ 3. It is not permitted to take a penalty from person to person or from case to case, even though there is an equal basis, and indeed even more [basis for doing so], with due regard, however, for the prescription of Canon 2231.

TITLE 5
On the Superior having coercive power[2]

Canon 2220 (NA)

§ 1. Whoever has the power of imposing laws or precepts can also attach penalties to a law or precept, but one who only [has] judicial [power] can only apply penalties legitimately established according to the norm of law.

§ 2. A Vicar General without a special mandate does not have the power to inflict penalties.

Canon 2221 (1983 CIC 1315)

Those having legislative power can, within the limits of their jurisdiction, enhance with an appropriate penalty not only a law laid down personally or by a predecessor, but also, because of the special circumstance of things, divine law, as well as ecclesiastical [law] laid down by a superior power that is in force in that territory, or [they can] enhance a penalty established by law.

Canon Law Digest
VIII: 1209

[2] Anthony Esswein, "The Extrajudicial Coercive Powers of Ecclesiastical Superiors", Canon Law Studies, no. 127 (thesis, Catholic University of America, 1941).

Canon 2222[3] (1983 CIC 1399) Cross-Refs.: 1917 CIC 1554, 1704, 1956

§ 1. Even though a law has no sanction attached to it, the legitimate Superior may nevertheless punish its transgression by a just penalty, even without a previous mentioning of the penalty if scandal perhaps was given or the special gravity of the transgression makes it necessary; otherwise a defendant cannot be punished unless he was first warned with mention of the penalty, [whether] automatic or formal, in case of transgression, and nevertheless violated the law.

§ 2. Likewise the legitimate Superior, even though it is only probable that a delict has been committed or a penal action for a certainly committed delict has been prescribed, has not only the right but also the duty of not promoting a cleric of whose suitability he is not sure and, in order to avoid scandal, of prohibiting the cleric from the exercise of sacred ministry, and even of removing him from office according to the norm of law; and all these things in this case do not have the nature of a penalty.

Canon Law Digest
I: 845; II: 570

Canon 2223 (1983 CIC 1343–45, 1348–49) Cross-Ref.: 1917 CIC 2232

§ 1. In applying a penalty a judge cannot increase a determinate penalty, unless it is required because of extraordinary aggravating circumstances.

§ 2. If a law in establishing a formal penalty makes use of facultative words, it is committed to the prudence and conscience of the judge to inflict it or, if the penalty was determinate, to temper it.

§ 3. But if the law uses preceptive words, the penalty is ordinarily to be imposed; but it is left to the conscience and prudence of the judge or Superior:

1.° To put off the application of the penalty to a more opportune time if from the punishment of the defendant it is foreseen that greater evils will arise;

2.° To abstain from inflicting the penalty if the defendant is completely amended and has repaired scandal or has been sufficiently punished, or it is foreseen that he will be punished with penalties by the civil authorities;

[3] James Casey, "A Study of Canon 2222 § 1", Canon Law Studies, no. 290 (thesis, Catholic University of America, 1949).

3.° To temper a determinate penalty or to apply some penal remedy in its place if there are some circumstances notably reducing imputability or if it is considered that the amendment of the defendant [was achieved by] castigation by infliction [of a penalty] by civil authority, even though the judge or Superior concludes it appropriate to add some punishment, increasing it somewhat.

4.° Generally the declaring of an automatic penalty is committed to the prudence of the Superior; but a declaratory sentence must be given either at the request of an interested party or when so required by the common good.

Canon Law Digest
VIII: 1209

Canon 2224 (1983 CIC 1346)

§ 1. Ordinarily there are as many penalties as there are delicts.

§ 2. If, however, because of the number of delicts, there would be too great a number of penalties to be inflicted, it is left to the prudent judgment of the judge either to inflict the gravest of all the penalties, adding, if the matter calls for it, some penance or penal remedy, or to moderate the penalty within equitable bounds, taking into consideration the number and gravity of the delicts.

§ 3. If a penalty is constituted both for an attempt at the delict and for the consummation of the delict [then], this being admitted, the penalty must only be inflicted that is established for the consummated delict.

Canon 2225[4] (NA)

If a penalty is declared or inflicted by judicial sentence, the prescriptions of the canons concerning pronouncement of judicial sentences must be observed; but if an automatic or formal penalty is inflicted in the manner of a particular precept, it ordinarily should be declared or imposed in writing or in the presence of two witnesses, indicating the cause of the penalty with due regard for the prescription of Canon 2193.

---

[4] Hugh Quinn, "The Particular Penal Precept", Canon Law Studies, no. 303 (thesis, Catholic University of America, 1953).

TITLE 6
On the subject liable to coercive power

Canon 2226 (1983 CIC 1313, 1351)

§ 1. That one is liable to the penalty attached to a law or precept who is bound by the law or precept, unless expressly exempted.

§ 2. Even though a later penal law abrogates an earlier, if a delict was already committed when the later law was laid down, the law that is more favorable is to be applied.

§ 3. But if the later law removes the law or only the penalty, [the penalty] ceases immediately, unless it concerns a censure already contracted.

§ 4. A penalty binds a defendant everywhere in the world, even upon the end of the authority of the Superior, unless expressly provided otherwise.

Canon Law Digest
I: 845

Canon 2227 (NA)

§ 1. A penalty cannot be imposed or declared against those mentioned in Canon 1557, § 1, except by the Roman Pontiff.

§ 2. Unless expressly named, Cardinals of the H. R. C. are not included under penal law, nor are Bishops [liable] to the penalty of automatic suspension and interdict.

Canon 2228 (NA)

A penalty established in law is not incurred unless a delict of its sort was completed according to the proper words of the law.

Canon 2229 (NA)

§ 1. From no automatic penalty does affected ignorance, whether of the law or only of the penalty, excuse, even though the law contains the words mentioned in § 2.

§ 2. If the law has the words: *presumes*, *dares*, *knowingly*, *deliberately*, *recklessly*, *acting advisedly*, and other similar [phrases] that convey full knowledge and deliberation, any diminishment either on the part of the mind or on the part of the will brings about a diminishment of imputability [regarding] an automatic penalty.

§ 3. If the law does not have those words:

1.° Ignorance of the law, or even of only the penalty if it was crass or supine, does not excuse an automatic penalty: if it was not crass or supine, it excuses from medicinal but not from vindicative automatic penalties;

2.° Drunkenness, omission of due diligence, mental debility, or impulse of passion, if the action was not gravely culpable, does not excuse from an automatic penalty notwithstanding the diminution of imputability;

3.° Grave fear, if the delict verges on contempt of the faith or ecclesiastical authority or public harm to souls, does not excuse at all from an automatic penalty.

§ 4. Even though a defendant is not bound by the automatic censures according to the norm of § 3, n. 1, that does not, if the matter calls for it, prevent him from being treated with another appropriate penalty or penance.

Canon Law Digest
II: 570–71; III: 649

Canon 2230 (1983 CIC 1323)

Children are excused from automatic penalties, and they should be corrected with educational punishment rather than censures or more grave vindicative penalties; but those who lead children into violating the law or who concur with them in the delict according to the norm of Canon 2209, §§ 1–3, incur themselves the penalty established in law.

Canon 2231 (NA) Cross-Ref.: 1917 CIC 2219

If several [persons] concur in the perpetration of a delict, even though only one of them is named in the law, they too, [as] mentioned in Canon 2209, §§ 1–3, are bound by the same penalty, unless the law expressly determines otherwise; but the others are not to be punished with the same penalty, but [rather with] another just penalty in the prudent judgment of the Superior, unless the law established a particular penalty for them.

Canon 2232 (1983 CIC 1352)

§ 1. An automatic penalty, whether medicinal or vindicative, binds upon that fact a delinquent who is conscious of having committed a delict, in both fora; but a delinquent is excused, however, from observing a penalty before sentence or declaration, as often as he cannot observe it without infamy, and in the external forum no one can coerce him to the observance of the penalty, unless the delict is notorious, with due regard for the prescription of Canon 2223, § 4.

§ 2. A declaratory sentence makes the penalty retroactive to the moment of committing the delict.

Canon Law Digest
I: 845

Canon 2233 (1983 CIC 1347) Cross-Ref.: 1917 CIC 2242

§ 1. No penalty can be imposed unless it is certain that the delict was committed and that it is not legitimately prescribed.

§ 2. Although this has been legitimately shown, if it concerns the infliction of a censure, the defendant is to be addressed and warned to recede from contumacy according to the norm of Canon 2242, § 3, and given, if in the prudent judgment of the judge or the Superior it ought to be done, a decent period to return to sensibility; contumacy persisting, the censure can be imposed.

Canon Law Digest
I: 845–46

Canon 2234 (NA)

Whoever commits several delicts can not only be punished more gravely, but can also, in the prudent judgment of the judge, if it comes to that, be subjected to vigilance or another penal remedy.

Canon 2235 (1983 CIC 1328)

A frustrated delict or an attempted delict, unless punished as a distinct delict by law, can be punished with an appropriate penalty according to its gravity, with due regard for the prescription of Canon 2213, § 3.

Canon Law Digest
I: 846

TITLE 7
On the remission of penalties

Canon 2236 (1983 CIC 1354–56) Cross-Ref.: 1917 CIC 2289

§ 1. Remission of penalty, whether by absolution, if it concerns a censure, or by dispensation, if it was a vindicative penalty, can be granted only by him who imposed the penalty, or by the competent Superior or successor, or by him to whom this power has been granted.

§ 2. Whoever can exempt from a law can also remit a penalty attached to it.

§ 3. A judge who applies a penalty constituted by a Superior by office cannot remit it once applied.

Canon Law Digest
II: 571

Canon 2237 (1983 CIC 1355–56)

§ 1. In particular cases, the Ordinary can remit automatic penalties established by common law, except for:

1.° Cases taken to the forum of contention;
2.° Censures reserved to the Apostolic See;
3.° Penalties incapacitating one for benefice, office, dignity, duties in the Church, privation of active or passive voice, perpetual suspension, infamy of law, privation of the right of patronage, or privileges or favors, granted by the Apostolic See.

§ 2. But in occult cases, with due regard for the prescription of Canons 2254 and 2290, the Ordinary can remit automatic penalties established by common law, personally or through another, except for censures reserved specially or most specially to the Apostolic See.

Canon 2238 (1983 CIC 1360)

The remission of a penalty extorted by force or grave fear is invalid by law.

Canon 2239 (1983 CIC 1361)

§ 1. A penalty can be remitted for one present or absent, absolutely or under condition, in the external forum or only in the internal.

§ 2. Although a penalty can be remitted orally if it was inflicted in writing, it is better that its remission be granted in writing.

Canon 2240 (1983 CIC 1362)

As for what pertains to the prescription of a penal action, the disposition of Canon 1703 is observed.

SECTION 2
ON PENALTIES IN SPECIFIC

TITLE 8
On medicinal penalties or censures

Chapter 1
On censures in general

Canon 2241 (1983 CIC 1318, 1358)

§ 1. A censure is a penalty by which a delinquent and contumacious baptized man is deprived of a spiritual good [or] some thing connected with the spiritual,until,receding from contumacy,he is absolved.

§ 2. Censures,especially automatic ones,and especially excommunication,are not to be imposed except soberly and with great circumspection.

Canon 2242[5] (1983 CIC 1347, 1358) Cross-Refs.: 1917 CIC 2233, 2248

§ 1. Only a delict that is external, grave, consummated, and joined with contumacy is punished with a censure; a censure can be placed also on unknown delinquents.

§ 2. If it concerns censures formally imposed, one is contumacious who, notwithstanding the admonitions mentioned in Canon 2233, § 2, has not desisted from the delict or performed the penance for the delict and who has avoided the reparation owed for damages and scandal; in order to incur an automatic censure, it suffices that there be a transgression of the law or precept to which is attached an automatic penalty, unless a legitimate cause excused the accused from this.

§ 3. One is said to have withdrawn from contumacy when one truly repents of the delict committed and at the same time gives appropriate satisfaction for the damages or scandal or at least sincerely promises this; the judgment about whether or not the penitence is true, and satisfaction

[5] Terence Cunningham, "Contumacy for Censures" (D.C.L. thesis, Librarian's Office 703, Maynooth [Ireland], 1951).

is sufficient, or the promise concerning these is sincere belongs to him from whom absolution of the censure is requested.

Canon Law Digest
II: 571

Canon 2243 (1983 CIC 1353)

§ 1. Censures inflicted by judicial sentence go into execution as soon as they are laid down, nor is there given an appeal from them except in devolution; likewise, recourse is given for censures inflicted in the manner of a precept, but only in devolution.

§ 2. But appeal or recourse from a judicial sentence or precept threatening censures, even if they have not been contracted automatically, suspends neither the sentence or precept nor the censures, if it concerns a subject in which the law does not admit appeal or recourse coupled with suspensive effect; otherwise the censures are suspended with due regard, however, for the obligation of observing what the sentence or precept commanded, unless the defendant interposed appeal or recourse not only from the penalty but also from the sentence or precept itself.

Canon Law Digest
I: 846

Canon 2244 (NA)

§ 1. Not only those of diverse sorts, but also censures of the same species can be multiplied on the same subject.

§ 2. Automatic censures are multiplied:

1.° If different delicts, each encompassing an individual censure, are committed by one or different acts;

2.° If one delict punished by a censure is repeated several times, so that there are several distinct delicts;

3.° If a delict punished by diverse censures and by distinct Superiors is committed once or several times.

§ 3. Censures of man are multiplied if several precepts or several sentences, or if several distinct parts of the same precept or sentence, have each imposed their own censure.

Canon 2245[6] (NA) Cross-Ref.: 1917 CIC 2253

§ 1. Some censures are *reserved* and others are *non-reserved.*

§ 2. A censure *from man* is reserved to him who inflicted the censure or passed the sentence, or to the competent Superior or his successor or delegate; but among censures reserved *by law*, some are reserved to the *Ordinary*, others to the *Apostolic See.*

§ 3. Among those reserved to the Apostolic See some are *reserved simply*, others *specially*, and others *most specially.*

§ 4. Automatic censures are not reserved unless this is expressly stated in the law or precept; in doubt about law or fact, reservation does not apply.

Canon Law Digest
I: 846; III: 649–50

Canon 2246 (1983 CIC 1354) Cross-Ref.: 1917 CIC 893

§ 1. A censure should not be reserved except in response to especially grave delicts and [in light of] the necessity of better providing for ecclesiastical discipline and improving the consciences of the faithful.

§ 2. Reservation receives a strict interpretation.

§ 3. The reservation of a censure impeding the reception of the Sacraments brings about the reservation of the sin to which the censure is attached; but if anyone is excused from the censure or has been absolved of it, the reservation of the sin wholly ceases.

Canon 2247 (NA) Cross-Ref.: 1917 CIC 893

§ 1. If a censure is reserved to the Apostolic See, an Ordinary cannot impose another censure reserved to himself for the same delict.

§ 2. The reservation of a censure in a particular territory does not have force outside the limits of that territory, even if the one censured left the territory in order to obtain absolution; but a censure of man is reserved everywhere so that the one censured cannot be absolved anywhere without the required faculty.

---

[6] Edward Dargin, "Reserved Cases according to the Code of Canon Law", Canon Law Studies, no. 20 (J. C. D. thesis, Catholic University of America, 1924); Casimir Stadalnikas, "Reservation of Censures", Canon Law Studies, no. 208 (J. C. D. thesis, Catholic University of America, 1944); Abelard Navata, "The Difference between the Reservation of Sins *Ratione Sui* and the Reservation of Sins *Ratione Censurae*" (diss. no. 14, Pontifical University of St. Thomas [Rome], 1961–1962).

§ 3. If a confessor, ignorant of the reservation, absolves the penitent from the censure and the sin, the absolution of the censure is valid provided it was not a censure of man or a censure most specially reserved to the Apostolic See.

Canon 2248 (1983 CIC 1358)

§ 1. Any censure, once contracted, is lifted only by legitimate absolution.

§ 2. Absolution cannot be denied once a delinquent withdraws from contumacy according to the norm of Canon 2242, § 3; one absolving from a censure can, if the matter requires it, impose an appropriate vindicative penalty or penance for the committed delict.

§ 3. A censure, removed by a delivered absolution, does not revive, except in the case where a burden imposed under pain of reincidence has not been fulfilled.

Canon 2249 (1983 CIC 1359)

§ 1. If anyone is detained by several censures, he can be absolved of one while the others are not absolved.

§ 2. One seeking absolution must indicate all the cases, otherwise the absolution is valid only for the expressed case[s]; but if the absolution, even though the petition was made in regard to particulars, was general [in scope], it is valid also for those withheld in good faith, except for censures most specially reserved to the Apostolic See, [but] not for those withheld in bad faith.

Canon 2250 (NA)

§ 1. If it concerns a censure that does not impede the reception of the Sacraments, one censured, rightly disposed and withdrawing from contumacy, can be absolved from sins, the censure remaining.

§ 2. But if it concerns a censure that impedes the reception of the Sacraments, one censured cannot be absolved from sins unless [one is] first absolved from the censure.

§ 3. Absolution of a censure in the sacramental forum is contained in the usual form for absolution of sins prescribed in the ritual books; in the non-sacramental forum, any method may be followed, but it is preferable that the regular form for absolution from excommunication given in these same books be applied.

Canon 2251 (NA)

If absolution of a censure is given in the external forum, it applies in the other forum; if [it is given] in the internal [forum], the one absolved, avoiding scandal, may conduct himself in this way, even for actions of the external forum; but, unless the grant of absolution can be proved or at least legitimately presumed in the external forum, a Superior of the external forum to whom the defendant owed compliance can enforce the censure until absolution in that forum can be had.

Canon Law Digest
I: 846

Canon 2252[7] (1983 CIC 1357) Cross-Refs.: 1917 CIC 882, 2161

Those constituted in danger of death can receive from a priest, without special faculties, absolution from any censure of man or from a censure most specially reserved to the Apostolic See, [but] are bound after recovering by the obligation of taking recourse under pain of reincidence to him who passed the censure, if it concerned a censure of man; [similarly] to the S. Penitentiary or to a Bishop or another endowed with the faculty according to the norm of Canon 2254, § 1, if it was a censure of law; and they must obey his mandates.

Canon Law Digest
I: 846–47; II: 571

Canon 2253 (1983 CIC 1355)

Outside of danger of death, [the following] can absolve from:

1.° A non-reserved censure in the sacramental forum, any confessor; outside the sacramental forum, whoever has jurisdiction over the defendant in the external forum;
2.° A censure *of man*, he to whom the censure is reserved according to the norm of Canon 2245, § 2; and he can grant absolution even if the defendant has gone off to another domicile or quasi-domicile;
3.° A censure *reserved in law*, he who constituted the censure or to whom it was reserved, [as well as] his successors or competent Superiors or delegates. Therefore from a censure reserved to a

[7] James Donahue, "Absolution from Sins and Censures of Persons in Danger of Death" (MS no. 574, Gregorian University, 1938).

Bishop or *Ordinary*, any Ordinary can absolve his subjects, and a local Ordinary [can absolve] travelers also; from one reserved to the *Apostolic See*, [besides it,] those who have sought from it the power of absolving, whether generally if the censure is *simply reserved*, or specially if it is *specially reserved*, or finally most specially if it is *most specially reserved*, with due regard for the prescription of Canon 2254.

Canon Law Digest
II: 571–72; VI: 853; IX: 1001

Canon 2254[8] (1983 CIC 1357) Cross-Refs.: 1917 CIC 2237, 2252–53, 2290

§ 1. In more urgent cases, namely if the automatic censure cannot be observed exteriorly without danger of grave scandal or infamy, or if it is hard on the penitent to remain in a state of grave sin for the time necessary for the competent Superior to provide, then any confessor in the sacramental forum can absolve from these, no matter how reserved, [and he will enjoin] the burden of having recourse, under pain of reincidence, within a month at [most] by letter and through the confessor, if this can be done without grave inconvenience, withholding the name, to the S. Penitentiary or to a Bishop or other Superior endowed with the faculty [of absolving], and standing by his mandates.

§ 2. Nothing prevents, however, a penitent, even after acceptance of absolution as above, and having taken recourse to the Superior, from going to another confessor endowed with the faculty [of absolving], and from him, having repeated the confession at least about the delict with the censure, securing absolution; the which obtained, he shall accept instructions from him and later is not bound to stand by [any] other mandates from a supervening Superior.

§ 3. But if in some extraordinary case this recourse is morally impossible, then the confessor himself, except in a case that concerns the absolution of a censure mentioned in Canon 2367, can grant absolution without the burden [mentioned] above, but with the injunctions of law nevertheless enjoined, and imposing an appropriate penance and satisfaction for the censure, such that, unless the penitent within an appropriate time de-

[8] Francis Moriarty, "The Extraordinary Absolution from Censures", Canon Law Studies, no. 113 (J. C. D. thesis, Catholic University of America, 1938).

termined by the confessor performs the penance and gives the satisfaction, he reincurs the censure.

Canon Law Digest
I: 847; II: 572; VII: 1027

Chapter 2
On censures in specific

Canon 2255[9] (NA) Cross-Ref.: 1917 CIC 2261

§ 1. Censures are:
1.° Excommunication;
2.° Interdict;
3.° Suspension.

§ 2. Excommunication can affect only physical persons, and therefore, if they are imposed on moral persons, they are understood to apply only to those individuals who concurred in the delict; interdict and suspension [can affect] even a community, such as a moral person; excommunication and interdict [can affect] even laity; suspension [affects] only clerics; interdict [can affect] also a place; excommunication is always a censure; interdict and suspension can be both a censure and a vindicative penalty; but in doubt they are presumed censures.

Canon 2256[10] (NA)

In the canons that follow:
1.° By the name of divine offices are understood those functions of the powers of orders that, by institution of Christ or the Church, are ordered to divine cult and need to be performed only by clerics;
2.° By the name of legitimate ecclesiastical acts are signified: to conduct the responsibility of the administration of ecclesiastical goods; to act the part of judge, auditor, relator, defender of the bond, promoter of justice and faith, notary and chancellor, courier

[9] Kevin Mullen, "The Ecclesiastical Censures of the Irish Confederacy" (diss. no. 2, Pontifical University of St. Thomas [Rome], 1969–1970).

[10] William Tierney, "Authorized Ecclesiastical Acts", Canon Law Studies, no. 414 (J. C. D. thesis, Catholic University of America, 1961).

and messenger, advocate and procurator in ecclesiastical cases; to perform the responsibility of sponsor in the sacraments of baptism and confirmation, to cast a vote in ecclesiastical elections, and to exercise the right of patronage.

Article 1—*On excommunication*[11]

Canon 2257 (1983 CIC 1331)

§ 1. Excommunication is a censure by which one is excluded from the communion of the faithful with the effects that are enumerated in the canons that follow and that cannot be separated.

§ 2. Moreover, it is called *anathema* especially when it is inflicted with the formalities that are described in the Roman Pontifical.

Canon Law Digest
IV: 423

Canon 2258 (NA)

§ 1. Some excommunicates are *banned*, others *tolerated*.

§ 2. No one is banned unless so named as an excommunicate by the Apostolic See, the excommunication is publicly announced, and it is expressly stated in the decree or sentence that he must be avoided with due regard for the prescription of Canon 2343, § 1, n. 1.

Canon Law Digest
II: 572–73; III: 650

Canon 2259 (1983 CIC 1331, 1335)

§ 1. Any one excommunicated lacks the right of assisting at divine offices, but not of [attending the] preaching of the word of God.

§ 2. If a tolerated [excommunicate] passively assists [at these], it is not necessary that he be expelled; if [he is] banned, he should be expelled or if he does not wish to be expelled, there should be a cessation of the [divine] offices, provided this can be done without grave inconvenience; but from active assistance that includes any participation in the celebration

[11] Francis Hyland, "Excommunication, Its Nature, Historical Development and Effects", Canon Law Studies, no. 49 (D.C.L. thesis, Catholic University of America, 1928); Joseph Williger, "The Significance of Excommunication in the Pre-Nicean Church" (MS no. 2845, Gregorian University, 1958).

of divine offices, not only should one banned be repelled, but [so should] any [one excommunicated] after a declared or condemnatory sentence or who is otherwise notoriously excommunicated.

Canon 2260 (1983 CIC 1331, 1335) Cross-Ref.: 1917 CIC 2275

§ 1. Nor can one excommunicated receive the Sacraments; or, indeed, after a declaratory or condemnatory sentence, the Sacramentals.

§ 2. In what applies to ecclesiastical burial, the prescription of Canon 1240, § 1, n. 2, is observed.

Canon 2261 (1983 CIC 1331, 1335) Cross-Refs.: 1917 CIC 2264, 2275, 2284

§ 1. One excommunicated is prohibited from confecting and administering licitly the Sacraments and Sacramentals, except for the exceptions that follow.

§ 2. The faithful, with due regard for the prescription of § 3, can for any just cause seek the Sacraments and Sacramentals from one excommunicated, especially if other ministers are lacking, and then the one who is excommunicate and approached can administer these and is under no obligation of inquiring the reasons from the one requesting.

§ 3. But from a banned excommunicate and from others excommunicated after a condemnatory or declaratory sentence has come, only the faithful in danger of death can ask for sacramental absolution according to the norm of Canons 882 and 2252 and even, if other ministers are lacking, other Sacraments and Sacramentals.

Canon Law Digest
III: 650

Canon 2262 (1983 CIC 1331, 1335) Cross-Ref.: 1917 CIC 809

§ 1. One excommunicated is not able to participate in the indulgences, suffrages, and public prayers of the Church.

§ 2. Nevertheless, it is not prohibited:

1.° For the faithful to pray privately for him;

2.° For priests privately and avoiding scandal to apply Mass for him; but, if he is banned, only for his conversion.

Canon Law Digest
VIII: 1210

Canon 2263 (1983 CIC 1331, 1335)

One excommunicated is removed from legitimate ecclesiastical acts within his limits and in the places defined by law; nor can he act in ecclesiastical cases, except according to the norm of Canon 1654; he is prohibited from conducting ecclesiastical offices or responsibilities, and from enjoying earlier concessions and privileges from the Church.

Canon 2264 (1983 CIC 1331, 1335) Cross-Ref.: 1917 CIC 208

Acts of jurisdiction, whether for the external forum or the internal forum, placed by one excommunicated are illicit; and if a condemnatory or declaratory sentence has been laid down, they are also invalid with due regard for the prescription of Canon 2261, § 3; otherwise, they are valid and, indeed, are even licit if they are sought by a member of the faithful according to the norm of the mentioned Canon 2261, § 2.

Canon 2265 (1983 CIC 1331, 1335) Cross-Refs.: 1917 CIC 36, 2275, 2283

§ 1. Anyone excommunicated:

1.° Is prohibited from the right of electing, presenting, or appointing;

2.° Cannot obtain dignities, offices, benefices, ecclesiastical pensions, or other duties in the Church;

3.° Cannot be promoted to orders.

§ 2. An act posited contrary to the prescription of § 1, nn. 1 and 2, however, is not null, unless it was posited by a banned excommunicate or by another excommunicate after a condemnatory or declaratory sentence; but if this sentence has been given, the one excommunicated cannot validly pursue any pontifical favor, unless in the pontifical rescript mention is made of the excommunication.

Canon 2266 (1983 CIC 1331, 1335)

After a condemnatory or declaratory sentence, one excommunicated remains deprived of the fruits of dignity, office, benefice, pension, and duty if he had one in the Church; and a banned [excommunicate is deprived] of the dignity, office, benefice, pension, and duty itself.

Canon 2267 (1983 CIC 1331, 1335)

The faithful must avoid association in profane things with a banned excommunicate, unless it concerns a spouse, parents, children, householders, subjects, and so on, unless reasonable cause excuses.

Article 2—*On interdict*[12]

Canon 2268 (1983 CIC 1332)

§ 1. Interdict is a censure by which the faithful, remaining in the communion of the Church, are prohibited those sacred things that are enumerated in the canons that follow.

§ 2. The prohibition can be either direct through a personal interdict when persons themselves are interdicted from the use of things; or indirect through a local interdict when the dispensation of or participation in such things is prohibited in certain places.

Canon Law Digest
II: 573; VII: 1027

Canon 2269 (NA)

§ 1. A general interdict, whether local over a diocesan territory or a republic, or personal over the people of a diocese or republic, can be issued only by the Apostolic See or by its mandate; but a general interdict over a parish or the people of a parish and a particular interdict, whether local or personal, can also be imposed by the Bishop.

§ 2. Personal interdict follows persons everywhere; a local [interdict] does not apply outside the place of the interdict, but all those in the place of an interdict, even externs and exempt [ones] outside of special privilege, are bound to observe it.

Canon 2270 (NA)

§ 1. A local interdict, whether general or particular, does not forbid the administration of the Sacraments and Sacramentals to the dying, those things being observed that ought to be observed, but it does prohibit in that place any divine office or sacred rites, with due regard for the exceptions in § 2 of this canon and in Canons 2271 and 2272.

[12] Edward Conran, "The Interdict", Canon Law Studies, no. 56 (thesis, Catholic University of America, 1930).

§ 2. On the day of the birth of the Lord, Easter, Pentecost, most holy Body of Christ, and the assumption into heaven of the Blessed Virgin Mary, a local interdict is suspended and there is prohibited only the conferral of orders and the solemn blessing of weddings.

Canon 2271 (NA) Cross-Refs.: 1917 CIC 2270, 2272

If there is a general local interdict and the decree of the interdict does not expressly provide otherwise:

1.° Clerics are permitted, provided they are not personally interdicted, to perform privately all divine offices and sacred rites in whatever church or oratory, with the doors locked in quiet voice and with the bells not being struck;

2.° But in a cathedral church or parish churches or a church that is the only one in town, and in these only, the celebration of one Mass is permitted, [as is] the reservation of the most holy Sacrament, the administration of baptism, Eucharist, penance, assistance at marriage [though] excluding the wedding blessing, rites for the dead, avoiding, however, any solemnity, the blessing of baptismal water and of sacred oils, and the preaching of the word of God; but in these sacred functions, singing is prohibited as well as pomp in sacred furnishings and the sounding of bells, organs, and other musical instruments; and sacred Viaticum will be brought to the infirm privately.

Canon 2272 (NA) Cross-Ref.: 1917 CIC 2270

§ 1. In a particular local interdict, if the interdict was on an altar or chapel of a church, no sacred office or sacred rite can be celebrated therein.

§ 2. If a cemetery was interdicted, the corpses of the faithful can indeed be buried therein, but without any ecclesiastical rite.

§ 3. If [the interdict] was placed on a certain church or oratory:

1.° If it is a chapter church, and the Chapter is not interdicted, the prescription of Canon 2271, n. 1 applies, unless the decree of the interdict ordered that the conventual Mass be celebrated and canonical hours be recited in another church or oratory;

2.° If it was a parish [church], the prescription of the above-cited Canon 2271, n. 2, is observed, unless the decree of the interdict substituted another church for it during the time of the interdict.

Canon 2273 (NA)

A city being interdicted, the interdict also affects accessory places, even exempt ones, and the cathedral church itself; if a church is interdicted, likewise interdicted are attached chapels, but not the cemetery; if a chapel is interdicted, the main church is not interdicted nor, if a cemetery is interdicted, is a church attached to it interdicted, but all oratories erected in the cemetery are interdicted.

Canon 2274 (NA)

§ 1. If a community or a college of clerics commits a delict, interdict can be imposed either on individual delinquent persons, or on the community, or on delinquent persons and the community.

§ 2. In the first case, the prescriptions of Canon 2275 are observed.

§ 3. In the second case, the community or college cannot exercise any spiritual rights that belong to them.

§ 4. In the third case, the effects are combined.

Canon 2275 (1983 CIC 1332) Cross-Refs.: 1917 CIC 36, 2274

Those personally interdicted:

1.° Cannot celebrate divine offices or, except for the preaching of the word of God, assist at them; but if they are passively assisting, it is not necessary to expel them; but if they are actively assisting, which involves some participation in the celebration of divine offices, those interdicted after the laying down of a condemnatory or declaratory sentence are to be repelled, [likewise if] they are notoriously interdicted;

2.° Are prohibited from ministering, confecting, and receiving Sacraments and Sacramentals, according to the norm of Canons 2260, § 1, and 2261;

3.° Are bound also by the prescription of Canon 2265;

4.° Lack ecclesiastical burial according to the norm of Canon 1240, § 1, n. 2.

Canon 2276 (NA)

Whoever is under a local interdict or a community or collegial interdict, [but] without giving cause for it, and who is not bound by another censure, can, if rightly disposed, receive the Sacraments, according to the norm of the preceding canon, without absolution or otherwise satisfying the interdict.

Canon 2277 (NA)

Interdiction from entering church carries with it prohibition from celebration of divine offices in the church and assisting at them or having ecclesiastical burial; but if one does assist, it is not necessary to expel him, nor, if he is buried, must the body be removed.

Canon Law Digest
V: 719

Article 3—*On suspension*[13]

Canon 2278 (1983 CIC 1333)

§ 1. Suspension is a censure by which a cleric is prohibited from office or benefice or both.

§ 2. The effects of suspension can be separated; but, unless otherwise provided, *suspension* generally imposed includes all the effects that are enumerated in the canons of this article; otherwise, suspension *from office* or *from benefice* contains only the effects specified in either.

Canon 2279 (1983 CIC 1333)

§ 1. Simple suspension *from office*, with no limitations being added, forbids every act, whether of the power of orders and jurisdiction, or even merely of administration, of the involved office, except for the administration of the goods of one's own benefice.

§ 2. Suspension:

1.° *From jurisdiction* generally forbids every act of jurisdictional power in both fora, whether ordinary or delegated;

2.° *From divine things* [restricts one] from every act of the power of orders, whether one has obtained it from ordination or through privilege;

3.° *From orders* [restricts one] from every act of the power of orders received from ordination;

[13] Eligius Rainer, "Suspension of Clerics", Canon Law Studies, no. 111 (J. C. D. thesis, Catholic University of America, 1937).

4.° *From sacred orders* [restricts one] from every act of the power of orders received from sacred ordination;
5.° *From the exercise of a certain and definite order* [restricts one] from every act of the designated order; one suspended is also prohibited from conferring that order and from receiving a higher order and from exercising one received after suspension;
6.° *From the conferral of a certain and definite order* [restricts one] from conferring that order, but not from conferring an inferior or superior one;
7.° *From a certain and definite ministry*, for example, hearing confessions, or *office*, for example, one with care of souls, [restricts one] from every act of that ministry or office;
8.° *From pontifical orders* [restricts one] from every act of the power of episcopal orders;
9.° *From pontificals* [restricts one] from the exercise of pontifical acts according to the norm of Canon 337, § 2.

Canon Law Digest
VII: 1027; VIII: 1210

Canon 2280 (1983 CIC 1333)

§ 1. Suspension *from benefice* deprives [one] of the fruits of the benefice, except for dwelling in the benefice building, but not of the right of administering the goods of the benefice, unless the sentence of decree of suspension expressly takes from the one suspended the power of administration and gives it to another.

§ 2. If, even though a censure obstructs, a beneficiary receives the fruits [of the benefice], he must restore the fruits, and to this restitution he can be coerced even, if necessary, by canonical sanctions.

Canon 2281 (1983 CIC 1333)

Suspension generally laid down or suspension *from office* or *from benefice* affects all offices and benefices that the cleric had in the diocese of the suspending Superior, unless it appears otherwise.

Canon 2282 (1983 CIC 1333)

The local Ordinary cannot suspend a cleric from a determined office or benefice that is located in another diocese; but an automatic suspension, imposed by common law, affects all offices or benefices in whatever diocese they are possessed.

Canon 2283 (NA) Cross-Ref.: 1917 CIC 36

Those things established for excommunication in Canon 2265 apply also to suspension.

Canon 2284 (1983 CIC 1335) Cross-Ref.: 1917 CIC 208

If the censure of suspension is incurred that forbids the administration of Sacraments and Sacramentals, the prescription of Canon 2261 is observed; if the censure of suspension prohibits an act of jurisdiction in the internal or external forum, the act is invalid, for example, sacramental absolution, if a condemnatory or declaratory sentence has been laid down, or if the Superior expressly declares this power of jurisdiction to be revoked; otherwise, it is only illicit, unless it is sought by a member of the faithful according to the norm of the above-mentioned Canon 2261, § 2.

Canon 2285 (NA)

§ 1. If a community or a college of clerics commits a delict, suspension can be imposed either on individual delinquent persons, or on the community, or even on delinquent persons and the community.

§ 2. In the first case, the canons of this article are observed.

§ 3. In the second case, the community is prohibited from the exercise of spiritual rights that they as a community exercise.

§ 4. In the third case, the effects are combined.

TITLE 9
On vindicative penalties

Canon 2286 (NA)

Vindicative penalties are those that directly tend to the expiation of a delict such that their remission does not depend on the cessation of contumacy in the delinquent.

Canon 2287 (1983 CIC 1353)

From the infliction of a vindicative penalty, suspensive appeal or recourse is given, unless otherwise expressly provided in law.

Canon 2288 (1983 CIC 1344)

Except for the penalty of degradation, deposition, [or] privation of office or benefice, and unless the necessity of repairing scandal urges [otherwise], it is left to the prudence of the judge, if the defendant has offended for the first time after a life conducted laudably, to suspend the execution of ordinary penalties inflicted by a condemnatory sentence, with, however, the condition that, if the defendant commits the same delict or one of another sort within the next three years, the penalty for both delicts applies.

Canon 2289[14] (NA)

A vindicative penalty is finished by its expiation or by dispensation granted by him who has the legitimate power of dispensation according to the norm of Canon 2236.

Canon 2290 (1983 CIC 1352) Cross-Ref.: 1917 CIC 2237

§ 1. In more urgent occult cases, if from the observance of an automatic vindicative penalty the defendant will undergo infamy and scandal, any confessor can suspend the obligation of observing the penalty in the sacramental forum, imposing the obligation of taking recourse at [most] within a month by letter, or through the confessor, if this can be done without grave inconvenience, withholding the name, to the S. Penitentiary or to the Bishop endowed with the faculty [of acting] and of standing by its [or his] orders.

§ 2. And if, in some extraordinary case, this recourse is impossible, then the confessor himself can grant dispensation according to the norm of Canon 2254, § 3.

Canon Law Digest
I: 848; II: 573

Chapter 1
On common vindicative penalties

Canon 2291 (1983 CIC 1336)

In the Church, vindicative penalties that can affect all members of the faithful according to the gravity of the delicts are especially:

[14] Joseph Christ, "Dispensation from Vindicative Penalties", Canon Law Studies, no. 174 (J. C. D. thesis, Catholic University of America, 1943).

1.° Local interdict and interdict of a community or a college, in perpetuity or for a predetermined time or at the good pleasure of the Superior;
2.° Interdict from entering a church, in perpetuity or for a predetermined time or at the good pleasure of the Superior;
3.° The penal transfer or suppression of an episcopal see or parish;
4.° Infamy of law;
5.° Privation of ecclesiastical burial according to the norm of Canon 1240, § 1;
6.° Privation of the Sacramentals;
7.° Privation or suspension for a time of a pension that is funded by the Church or [that comes] out of the goods of the Church, or of another right or ecclesiastical privilege;
8.° Removal from exercising legitimate ecclesiastical acts;
9.° Incapacity for ecclesiastical favors or functions in the Church that do not require the clerical state, or for academic degrees pursued by ecclesiastical authority;
10.° Privation or suspension for a time from responsibilities, faculties, or favors already obtained;
11.° Privation of the right of precedence, or of active and passive voice, or of the right of bestowing honorary titles, vestments, [or] insignia that the Church has granted;
12.° Monetary fines.

Canon 2292 (NA)

Penal suppression or transfer of an episcopal see is reserved to the Roman Pontiff; but for a parochial see, local Ordinaries cannot make this determination except with the advice of the Chapter.

Canon 2293[15] (NA)

§ 1. Infamy is either of law or of fact.

§ 2. Infamy of law is that which is expressly established for cases in common law.

[15] Thomas Connolly, "Infamy of Law" (Pontifical Lateran University, 1952); Frank Rodimer, "The Canonical Effects of Infamy of Fact", Canon Law Studies, no. 353 (thesis, Catholic University of America, 1954); Vincent Tatarczuk, "Infamy of Law", Canon Law Studies, no. 357 (thesis, Catholic University of America, 1954).

§ 3. Infamy of fact is contracted when someone, because of the perpetration of a delict or from depraved morals, has lost the good estimation of the thoughtful and grave members of the faithful, which determination looks to the Ordinary.

§ 4. Neither affects the blood-relatives or affines of the delinquent, with due regard for the prescription of Canon 2147, § 2, n. 3.

Canon 2294 (NA)

§ 1. Whoever labors under infamy of law not only is irregular according to the norm of Canon 984, n. 5, but moreover is incapable of obtaining benefices, pensions, offices and ecclesiastical dignities, and of conducting legitimate ecclesiastical acts, of exercising rights and ecclesiastical responsibilities, and even must be prevented from exercising ministry in sacred functions.

§ 2. Whoever labors under infamy of fact must be repelled from the reception of orders according to the norm of Canon 987, n. 7, [and] dignities, benefices and ecclesiastical offices, and from exercising sacred ministry and from legitimate ecclesiastical acts.

Canon 2295 (NA)

Infamy of law ceases only with the grant of dispensation by the Apostolic See; infamy of fact [ceases] upon a good estimation among the prudent and grave members of the faithful with all circumstances being weighed, and especially long-lasting reform of the defendant who has recovered in the prudent judgment of the Ordinary.

Canon 2296 (NA)

§ 1. If it concerns things involved with capacity for acquiring as commonly established by law, the penalty of incapacity can be imposed only by the Apostolic See.

§ 2. Rights already acquired are not lost by supervening incapacity, unless there was added this penalty of privation.

Canon 2297 (NA)

Regarding monetary fines inflicted in common law, when their imposition is not defined in that law or other statutes or provisions of particular law, local Ordinaries must impose [them] for a pious use, but not for the convenience of the episcopal or chapter table.

Chapter 2

On vindicative penalties special to clerics

Canon 2298[16] (1983 CIC 1336)

Vindicative penalties that are applied only to clerics are:

1.° The prohibition of exercising sacred ministry outside a certain church;
2.° Suspension in perpetuity or for a predetermined time or for the good pleasure of the Superior;
3.° A penal transferal from an obtained office or benefice to an inferior [one];
4.° The privation of some right joined to a benefice or office;
5.° Incapacity for all or for some dignities, offices, benefices, or other responsibilities proper to clerics;
6.° Penal privation of a benefice or office with or without a pension;
7.° A prohibition against staying in a certain place or territory;
8.° A prescription for staying in a certain place or territory;
9.° Privation for a time of ecclesiastical habit;
10.° Deposition;
11.° Perpetual privation of ecclesiastical habit;
12.° Degradation.

Canon Law Digest
I: 848

Canon 2299 (1983 CIC 1350)

§ 1. If a cleric obtains an irremovable benefice, he can be deprived of same by penalty only in cases expressed in law; if [the benefice is] removable, [he can be removed] also for any other reasonable cause.

§ 2. Clerics obtaining benefices, offices, and dignities can be prohibited for a certain time from exercising any or only the ministry attached to them, for example, the ministry of preaching, of hearing confessions, and so on.

§ 3. A cleric cannot be deprived of a benefice or pension regarding the title to which he was ordained, unless his decent sustenance is provided by

[16] Joseph Shields, "Deprivation of the Clerical Garb", Canon Law Studies, no. 334 (thesis, Catholic University of America, 1958).

some other way, with due regard for the prescription of Canons 2303 and 2304.

Canon 2300 (NA)

If a cleric gives grave scandal and does not respect a warning, and the scandal cannot otherwise be removed, he can, in the meantime, be deprived of the right of wearing ecclesiastical habit; that privation, for as long as it lasts, includes the prohibition of exercising any ecclesiastical ministry and the privation of clerical privileges.

Canon Law Digest
V: 720; IX: 1001–2

Canon 2301 (1983 CIC 1337)

An Ordinary cannot order a cleric to live in a certain place outside the limits of the diocese unless the consent of the Ordinary in that place gives consent, or unless it concerns a house of penance or correction for clerics, but not [for just local] diocesan [clerics]; but even if it is reserved for outsiders or is an exempt religious house, the consent of the Superior [is required].

Canon 2302 (NA)

A command or a prohibition about living in a certain place or a relocation to a house of penance or a religious house, especially if it is imposed without term, shall be done only for grave cases in which, in the prudent judgment of the Ordinary, the penalty is truly necessary for the reform of the cleric or the repair of scandal.

Canon 2303 (1983 CIC 1350) Cross-Refs.: 1917 CIC 2299, 2304

§ 1. Deposition, with due regard for the obligations taken up in ordination and clerical privileges, includes both suspension from office and incapacity for any office, dignity, benefice, pension, or duties in the Church, and even the privation of those things that the defendant has, although they were the title of the one ordained.

§ 2. But in this last case, if the cleric is truly indigent, the Ordinary in his charity, by whatever manner is best, shall take care of him and not let him go around begging in a state indecorous for clerics.

§ 3. The penalty of deposition cannot be inflicted except for those cases expressed in law.

Canon 2304 (NA) Cross-Refs.: 1917 CIC 123, 2299

§ 1. If a deposed cleric gives no sign of reform, and especially if he continues to give scandal and does not respect warnings, the Ordinary can deprive him perpetually of the right of wearing ecclesiastical habit.

§ 2. This privation carries with it the privation of clerical privileges and the cessation of the prescription of Canon 2303, § 2.

Canon 2305 (NA)

§ 1. Degradation contains within itself deposition, the perpetual privation of ecclesiastical habit, and the reduction of the cleric to the lay state.

§ 2. This penalty can only be carried out for a delict expressed in law, or if it is a cleric who is already deposed and deprived of ecclesiastical habit, if he continues to give out grave scandal for a year.

§ 3. One form is *verbal*, that is, *by edict*, which can only be imposed by sentence so that all of its juridic effects take place immediately without execution; the other form is *real*, if the solemn prescripts in the Roman Pontifical are observed.

Canon Law Digest
I: 848

TITLE 10
On penal remedies and penances

CHAPTER 1
On penal remedies[17]

Canon 2306 (NA)

Penal remedies are:

1.° Admonition;
2.° Correction;
3.° Precept;
4.° Vigilance.

[17] Paul Love, "The Penal Remedies of the Code of Canon Law", Canon Law Studies, no. 404 (J. C. D. thesis, Catholic University of America, 1960).

Canon 2307 (1983 CIC 1339) Cross-Ref.: 1917 CIC 1946

An Ordinary, personally or through someone interposed, can warn one who is found in the proximate occasion of committing a delict or upon whom, as a result of a performed inquiry, grave suspicion regarding a committed delict falls.

Canon 2308 (1983 CIC 1339)

If, from one's way of life, scandal or grave disturbance of order arises, correction is in order, [coming] from the Ordinary himself or with another intervening, even done by letter, accommodated to the particular circumstances of the person and facts with which it is concerned.

Canon Law Digest
I: 848

Canon 2309 (1983 CIC 1339)

§ 1. Both admonition and correction can be public or secret.

§ 2. Correction or public admonition shall be done in the presence of a notary or two witnesses, or by letter so that its reception and the tenor of the letter are shown by some document.

§ 3. Public correction can only be done against a defendant who has confessed or who has been convicted of the delict; and it is judicial if it is done by a judge sitting in a tribunal or by the Ordinary before the criminal process.

§ 4. Judicial correction can take the place of a penalty or be used to increase a penalty, especially if it concerns a recidivist.

§ 5. There must be preserved in the secret archive of the Curia some document about the correction or admonishment, even if it was done secretly.

§ 6. Both correction and admonishment can be done once or several times, according to the judgment and prudence of the Superior.

Canon Law Digest
I: 848

Canon 2310 (NA)

Admonitions or formal correction having been applied without effect, or if there seems no hope that an effect will come of it, a precept should be given, in which there is accurately indicated what the one prevented must do or avoid, with a statement of the penalty in case of transgression.

Canon Law Digest
I: 848; VIII: 1210

Canon 2311 (NA)

§ 1. If the case is grave and especially if it concerns one regarding whom there is danger of relapse into the same crime, the Ordinary shall submit him to vigilance.

§ 2. Vigilance can also be precepted in order to increase a penalty, especially against recidivists.

Chapter 2
On penances

Canon 2312 (1983 CIC 1340)

§ 1. Penances are imposed in the external forum in order that a delinquent might avoid a penalty or, the penalty already being contracted, so he might receive absolution or dispensation.

§ 2. For an occult delict or transgression, a public penance is never imposed.

§ 3. Penances are measured, not according to the quantity of the delict, but rather according to the contrition of the penitent, considering qualities of the person and circumstances of the delicts.

Canon 2313 (1983 CIC 1340)

§ 1. The chief penances ordered are:

1.° Recitation of determined prayers;
2.° Performing a pious pilgrimage or other work of piety;
3.° Observing a special fast;
4.° Putting alms to pious uses;
5.° Performing spiritual exercises in a pious or religious house for a certain number of days.

§ 2. The Ordinary, according to his prudence, can add penances to the penal remedy of admonition and correction.

Canon Law Digest
II: 573–75

THIRD PART
ON PENALTIES FOR INDIVIDUAL DELICTS

TITLE 11
On delicts against the faith and unity of the Church

Canon 2314[1] (1983 CIC 1364)

§ 1. All apostates from the Christian faith and each and every heretic or schismatic:

1.° Incur by that fact excommunication;

2.° Unless they respect warnings, they are deprived of benefice, dignity, pension, office, or other duty that they have in the Church, they are declared infamous, and [if] clerics, with the warning being repeated, [they are] are deposed;

3.° If they give their names to non-Catholic sects or publicly adhere [to them], they are by that fact infamous, and with due regard for the prescription of Canon 188, n. 4, clerics, the previous warnings having been useless, are degraded.

§ 2. Absolution from the excommunication mentioned in § 1, sought in the forum of conscience, is specially reserved to the Apostolic See. But if, however, the delict of apostasy, heresy, or schism has been brought in any manner to the external forum of the local Ordinary, even by voluntary confession, that same Ordinary, but not the Vicar General without a special mandate, can by his own ordinary power absolve one duly recovered in the external forum, the prior abjuration being conducted juridically and observing those other things that in law ought to be observed; and one thus absolved can thereupon be absolved from sin by any confessor in the forum of conscience. Abjuration is considered juridically done if it happens in the presence of the same local Ordinary or his delegate and at least two witnesses.

Canon Law Digest
I: 849–53; II: 577; III: 650–60; IV: 423; VI: 853–54;
VII: 1027; VIII: 1210

[1] Eric MacKenzie, "The Delict of Heresy in Its Commission, Penalization, Absolution", Canon Law Studies, no. 77 (J. C. D. thesis, Catholic University of America, 1932); Joseph Goodwine, "The Reception of Converts", Canon Law Studies, no. 198 (J. C. D. thesis, Catholic University of America, 1944).

Canon 2315 (NA)

One suspected of heresy who, having been warned, does not remove the cause of suspicion is prohibited from legitimate acts; if he is a cleric, moreover, the warning having been repeated without effect, he is suspended from things divine; but if within six months from contracting the penalty, the one suspected of heresy does not completely amend himself, let him be considered as a heretic and liable to the penalties for heretics.

Canon Law Digest
IV: 423–24; V: 720–21

Canon 2316 (1983 CIC 1365)

Whoever in any manner willingly and knowingly helps in the promulgation of heresy, or who communicates in things divine with heretics against the prescription of Canon 1258, is suspected of heresy.

Canon Law Digest
III: 660–61; IV: 424

Canon 2317 (1983 CIC 1371) Cross-Ref.: 1917 CIC 1347

Those pertinaciously teaching and defending, whether publicly or privately, doctrines that have been condemned by the Apostolic See or a General Council, but not formally defined as heretical, are prevented from the ministry of preaching the word of God and [from the ministry] of hearing sacramental confessions and from any office of teaching, with due regard for other penalties that a sentence of condemnation might establish or that an Ordinary, after a warning, concludes were necessary to repair scandal.

Canon 2318 (NA)

§ 1. Publishers of the books of apostates, heretics, and schismatics that propagate apostasy, heresy, and schism incur by that fact excommunication specially reserved to the Apostolic See upon the publication being re leased, and likewise those defending these books or others prohibited by name in apostolic letters, [as do those who] knowingly and without required permission read and retain them.

§ 2. Authors and publishers who, without the required permission, run off printings of the books of sacred Scripture and notations and commentaries thereon incur by that fact excommunication reserved to no one.

Canon Law Digest
I: 853; VI: 854

Canon 2319 (1983 CIC 1366)

§ 1. Those Catholics fall under automatic excommunication reserved to the Ordinary who:

1.° Enter marriage in the presence of a non-Catholic minister against the prescription of Canon 1063, § 1;

2.° Enter marriage with the explicit or implicit agreement that all or any of the children will be educated outside of the Catholic Church;

3.° Knowingly presume to offer their children to non-Catholic ministers for baptism;

4.° Being parents or holding the place of parents, knowingly hand their charges over for non-Catholic education or formation.

§ 2. Those in § 1, nn. 2–4, are also suspected of heresy.

Canon Law Digest
I: 853–54; IV: 424–25; VI: 854; VII: 1027

TITLE 12
On delicts against religion

Canon 2320 (1983 CIC 1367)

Whoever throws away the consecrated species or who takes or retains them for an evil purpose is suspected of heresy; such a one incurs automatic excommunication reserved most specially to the Apostolic See; such a one is by that fact infamous, and a cleric, moreover, is to be deposed.

Canon Law Digest
I: 854; II: 577–78

Canon 2321 (NA)

Priests who, against the prescriptions of Canons 806, § 1, and 808, presume to offer Mass twice on the same day or who fail to fast [before] celebrating are suspended from the celebration of Mass for a time to be established by the Ordinary according to the various circumstances of the case.

Canon 2322 (1983 CIC 1378–79)

Regarding those not promoted to sacerdotal orders:

1.° If they simulate the celebration of Mass or the hearing of confessions, they incur upon that fact excommunication specially reserved to the Apostolic See; if such a one is, moreover, a layman, he is deprived of any pension or responsibility that he might have in the Church and is to be punished with other penalties according to the gravity of the fault; a cleric is deposed;

2.° If such a one usurps another sacerdotal responsibility, he is to be punished by the Ordinary according to the gravity of the fault.

Canon 2323 (1983 CIC 1368–69)

Whoever blasphemes or commits perjury outside of a trial is to be punished according to the prudent judgment of the Ordinary, especially [if the offender] is a cleric.

Canon 2324 (1983 CIC 1385)

Whoever offends against the prescription of Canons 827, 828, and 840, § 1, is to be punished by the Ordinary according to the gravity of the fault, not excluding, if the matter calls for it, suspension or deprivation of a benefice or ecclesiastical office or, if it concerns a layman, excommunication.

Canon 2325 (NA)

Whoever excites superstition or perpetrates a sacrilege is to be punished by the Ordinary according to the gravity of the fault, with due regard for the penalties established by law against such superstitious or sacrilegious acts.

Canon 2326 (NA)

Whoever concocts false relics or who knowingly sells them or distributes or puts them up for the public veneration of the faithful incurs upon that fact excommunication reserved to the Ordinary.

Canon 2327 (NA)

Whoever profits from indulgences is, upon that fact, struck with excommunication simply reserved to the Apostolic See.

Canon 2328 (NA)

Whoever violates a body or burial place of the dead for theft or another evil end is punished with a personal interdict, is upon that fact infamous, and, [if a] cleric, is moreover deposed.

Canon 2329 (NA)

Violators of churches or cemeteries described in Canons 1172 and 1207 are interdicted from entering a church and are punished with other appropriate penalties according to the gravity of the delict by the Ordinary.

TITLE 13

On delicts against ecclesiastical authorities, persons, and things

Canon 2330 (NA)

As to what applies to penalties established against delicts that can be committed in electing the Supreme Pontiff, consult the const. of [Pope] Pius X, *Vacante Sede Apostolica*, of 25 Dec. 1904.

Canon Law Digest
VIII: 1210

Canon 2331[2] (1983 CIC 1371, 1373)

§ 1. Whoever pertinaciously does not obey the Roman Pontiff or a proper Ordinary or another [competent authority] legitimately precepting or prohibiting shall be punished with appropriate penalties, not excluding censures, according to the gravity of the fault.

§ 2. But those conspiring against the authority of the Roman Pontiff or his Legates or a proper Ordinary or against their legitimate mandates, and likewise those provoking their subjects to disobedience regarding same, are to be coerced with censures and other penalties; and if they are clerics, [they are deprived of] dignities, benefices, and other duties; [and they are deprived of] active and passive voice and office, if they are religious.

Canon Law Digest
III: 661; IV: 425–26

Canon 2332 (1983 CIC 1372)

Each and every one of whatever status, grade, or condition, even if he is regal, episcopal, or cardinalitial, appealing from the laws, decrees, or

[2] Marion Mazgaj, "The Communist Government of Poland as Affecting the Rights of the Church from 1944 to 1960", Canon Law Studies, no. 472 (Catholic University of America, 1970).

mandates of the Roman Pontiff existing at that time to a Universal Council, is suspected of heresy and by that fact incurs excommunication specially reserved to the Apostolic See; but Universities, Colleges, Chapters, and other moral persons, by whatever name they are called, incur interdict equally specially reserved to the Apostolic See.

Canon 2333 (1983 CIC 1375)

Those having recourse to lay power or impeding letters or any acts of the Apostolic See or made by its Legates, prohibiting directly or indirectly their promulgation or execution, or injuring or intimidating on their account those to whom such letters or acts pertain or others, fall by that fact under excommunication specially reserved to the Apostolic See.

Canon 2334 (1983 CIC 1375) Cross-Ref.: 1917 CIC 2336

They are struck with an automatic excommunication specially reserved to the Apostolic See, who:

1.° Issue laws, mandates, or decrees contrary to the liberty or rights of the Church;

2.° Impede directly or indirectly the exercise of ecclesiastical jurisdiction, whether in the internal or external forum, having recourse in this to any lay power.

Canon Law Digest
I: 854; III: 661–62; IV: 426

Canon 2335[3] (1983 CIC 1374) Cross-Ref.: 1917 CIC 2336

Those giving their name to masonic sects or other associations of this sort that machinate against the Church or legitimate civil powers contract by that fact excommunication simply reserved to the Apostolic See.

Canon Law Digest
I: 854–55; V: 721; VI: 854; VIII: 1210–13;
IX: 1002–6; X: 285

Canon 2336 (NA)

§ 1. If a cleric commits the delict mentioned in Canons 2334 and 2335, besides the penalties established in those referenced canons, he can be struck

[3] Joseph Quigley, "Condemned Societies", Canon Law Studies, no. 46 (D.C.L. thesis, Catholic University of America, 1927); Richard Murphy, "The Canonico-Juridical Status of a Communist", Canon Law Studies, no. 400 (J. C. D. thesis, Catholic University of America, 1959).

with penal suspension or with privation of benefices, offices, dignities, pensions, and responsibilities, if by chance he has any in the Church; religious likewise [suffer] the loss of office, of active and passive voice, and other penalties according to the norms of the constitutions.

§ 2. Moreover, clerics and religious giving their names to masonic sects and other similar associations must be denounced to the Sacred Congregation of the H. Office.

Canon Law Digest
VI: 855

Canon 2337 (1983 CIC 1375)

§ 1. If a pastor, in order to impede the exercise of ecclesiastical jurisdiction, dares to incite a crowd or to promote public subscriptions for himself or to excite the people by sermons or writings or similar things shall be punished for the gravity of the fault according to the prudent judgment of the Ordinary, not excluding, if the matter deserves it, suspension.

§ 2. In the same manner an Ordinary shall punish a priest who excites in any way a crowd in order to impede the entrance into a parish of a priest legitimately appointed pastor or econome.

Canon 2338 (NA)

§ 1. Those presuming to absolve, without the required faculty, from automatic excommunication specially or most specially reserved to the Apostolic See incur upon that fact excommunication simply reserved to the Apostolic See.

§ 2. Those offering any sort of help or favor to a banned excommunicate in the delict for which he was excommunicated, and likewise clerics who knowingly and freely communicate in divine things with same and receive [the offender] in divine offices, incur upon that fact excommunication simply reserved to the Apostolic See.

§ 3. Those knowingly celebrating or facilitating the celebration of divine things in interdicted places or admitting to the celebration of divine offices censured clerics banned by excommunication, those interdicted, [and] those suspended after a declaratory or condemnatory sentence contract by law an interdict from entering churches until, in the judgment of him whose sentence they spurned, they have made satisfactory amends.

§ 4. Whoever gave cause for a local interdict or for a community or college interdict is by that fact personally interdicted.

Canon 2339 (NA)

Whoever dares to order or force the ecclesiastical burial of infidels, apostates from the faith, or heretics, schismatics, or others, whether excommunicated or interdicted, against the prescription of Canon 1240, § 1, contracts automatic excommunication reserved to no one; but those giving them burial on their own [contract] interdict from entering churches reserved to the Ordinary.

Canon Law Digest
II: 578

Canon 2340 (NA)

§ 1. If anyone from an obdurate spirit stays for a year under the censure of excommunication, he is suspected of heresy.

§ 2. If a cleric stays for six months under the censure of suspension, he shall be gravely warned; and if, a month from the warning having passed, he has not withdrawn from contumacy, he shall be deprived of benefices and offices that he might have had in the Church.

Canon 2341 (NA)

If anyone dares, against the prescription of Canon 120, to drag before a lay judge a Cardinal of the H. R. C. or a Legate of the Apostolic See or a major Official of the Roman Curia for matters pertaining to their duties, or their own Ordinary, he contracts upon that fact excommunication specially reserved to the Apostolic See; if [it concerns] another Bishop, even merely titular, or an Abbot or Prelate *of no one* or another supreme Superior of a religious [institute] of pontifical right, [he contracts] automatic excommunication simply reserved to the Apostolic See; and finally, if not having obtained permission from the local Ordinary, [one does likewise] with another person enjoying the privilege of the forum, [then, if] a cleric, he incurs upon that fact suspension from office reserved to the Ordinary, while a layman shall be punished with an appropriate penalty for the gravity of the fault by his own Ordinary.

Canon Law Digest
I: 855; III: 662–65; V: 721

Canon 2342[4] (NA)

They are, upon that fact, struck by excommunication simply reserved to the Apostolic See:

1.° Who violate the cloister of nuns of whatever sort or condition or sex they might be, entering into their monastery without legitimate permission, and likewise those introducing or admitting them; but if they are clerics, they are moreover suspended for a time to be defined by the Ordinary for the gravity of the fault;

2.° Women violating the cloister of religious men and other Superiors, whoever they may be, introducing or admitting them of whatever age; and moreover religious introducing or admitting [them] are deprived of office, if they have one, and of active and passive voice;

3.° Nuns illegitimately leaving the cloister against the prescription of Canon 601.

Canon Law Digest
I: 855; VII: 1027

Canon 2343 (1983 CIC 1370) Cross-Ref.: 1917 CIC 2258

§ 1. Whoever lays violent hands on the person of the Roman Pontiff:

1.° Contracts automatic excommunication most specially reserved to the Apostolic See; and is by that fact banned;

2.° Is infamous by the law;

3.° [If] a cleric, he shall be degraded.

§ 2. Whoever [does likewise] to the person of a Cardinal of the H. R. C. or Legate of the Roman Pontiff:

1.° Incurs automatic excommunication specially reserved to the Apostolic See;

2.° Is by the law infamous;

3.° Is deprived of benefices, offices, dignities, pensions, and any sort of responsibility if he had one in the Church.

§ 3. Whoever [does likewise] to the person of a Patriarch, Archbishop, Bishop, even if only a titular one, incurs automatic excommunication specially reserved to the Apostolic See.

[4] Garrett Barry, "Violation of the Cloister", Canon Law Studies, no. 148 (J.C.D. thesis, Catholic University of America, 1942).

§ 4. Whoever [does likewise] to the person of other clerics or to religious of either sex is upon that fact subjected to excommunication reserved to his own Ordinary, who shall punish such a one with other penalties, if the matter requires it, according to his prudent judgment.

Canon Law Digest

I: 855; II: 578; III: 665–68; IV: 426; V: 721

Canon 2344 (1983 CIC 1369, 1373)

Whoever gives injury to the Roman Pontiff, a Cardinal of the H. R. C., a Legate of the Roman Pontiff, to Sacred Roman Congregations, Tribunals of the Apostolic See, and their major Officials, and their own Ordinary by public journals, sermons, or pamphlets, whether directly or indirectly, or who excites animosity or odium against their acts, decrees, decisions, or sentences shall be punished by an Ordinary not only at the request of a party but even by office with censures and, in order to accomplish satisfaction, other appropriate penalties and penances for the gravity of the fault and the repair of scandal.

Canon 2345 (1983 CIC 1375)

Those usurping or detaining, themselves or through others, goods or rights pertaining to the Roman Church are subjected to automatic excommunication specially reserved to the Apostolic See; and if they are clerics, they shall be deprived moreover of dignities, benefices, offices, and pensions and declared incapable of them.

Canon 2346[5] (1983 CIC 1375–76)

If anyone dares to convert or usurp for his own use ecclesiastical goods of any sort, whether mobile or immobile, whether corporeal or incorporeal, whether personally or through others, or to impede those to whom they pertain by law [from] participating in the fruits or incomes of these, he is subject to excommunication for as long as it takes to restore the goods completely and to remove the aforesaid impediment and finally to seek absolution from the Apostolic See; but if it was a patron of the Church or of the goods, he is also considered by that [fact] deprived of the right of patronage; and if it is a cleric committing the delict or consenting in it,

[5] Edward Barrett, "The Abuses of Ecclesiastical Property Contemplated in Canon 2346" (diss. no. 2, Pontifical University of St. Thomas [Rome], 1959–1960).

he shall be deprived of any benefice whatsoever and shall be rendered incapable for any, and shall be suspended from the execution of his [sacred] orders until a complete satisfaction and absolution [is performed] in the judgment of his Ordinary.

Canon Law Digest
III: 668

Canon 2347 (1983 CIC 1377)

Notwithstanding the nullity of the act and the obligation to restore goods illegitimately acquired and to repair damages perhaps caused, [these] even to be urged by censure, whoever dares to alienate ecclesiastical goods or gives consent for their alienation against the prescription of Canon 534, § 1, and Canon 1532:

1.° If it concerns an object whose price did not exceed one thousand lira, he shall be punished with an appropriate penalty by the legitimate ecclesiastical Superior;
2.° If it concerns an object whose price is above one thousand but below thirty thousand lira, a patron is deprived of the right of patronage; an administrator [is deprived] of the duty of administration; a Superior or religious econome [is deprived] of his office and the capacity for other offices, besides other appropriate penalties to be inflicted by the Superiors; but an Ordinary and other clerics obtaining [thereby an] office, benefice, dignity, or duty in the Church owe double the amount to the church or wounded pious cause; other clerics are suspended for a time to be determined by the Ordinary;
3.° But if the apostolic good pleasure required in the above-mentioned canons was knowingly omitted, all of those who in any manner either gave or received things without the required consent remain moreover in an automatic excommunication reserved to no one.

Canon Law Digest
VII: 1027

Canon 2348 (NA)

Whoever obtains a legacy or donation for a pious cause either from the living or by will, even in trust, and fails to fulfill it shall be coerced to it, even by censures, by the Ordinary.

Canon 2349 (NA)

Those refusing the fees legitimately required according to the norm of Canons 463, § 1, and 1507 shall be punished in accord with the prudent judgment of the Ordinary until they satisfy it.

TITLE 14
On delicts against life, liberty, property, good reputation, and good morals

Canon 2350[6] (1983 CIC 1398)

§ 1. Procurers of abortion, the mother not excepted, incur, upon the effect being secured, automatic excommunication reserved to the Ordinary, and if they are clerics, they are also deposed.

§ 2. Those who [attempt to] kill themselves by their own hand, if indeed death follows, are deprived of ecclesiastical burial according to the norm of Canon 1240, § 1, n. 3; otherwise, they are prevented from legitimate ecclesiastical acts and, if they are clerics, they are suspended for a time to be determined by the Ordinary and are removed from having benefices and offices to which the care of souls is attached in the internal or external forum.

Canon Law Digest
III: 669–70; VIII: 1213; IX: 1006

Canon 2351 (NA)

§ 1. With due regard for the prescription of Canon 1240, § 1, n. 4, those perpetrating a duel, or simply provoking or accepting one, and any one offering help or encouragement for one, including those on-lookers whose efforts permitted or at least did not prohibit it, of whatever dignity they might be in, are by that fact excommunicated, simply reserved to the Apostolic See.

[6] Roger Huser, "The Crime of Abortion in Canon Law", Canon Law Studies, no. 162 (J. C. D. thesis, Catholic University of America, 1942); Bruno Arcenas, "Viability and the Crime of Abortion" (diss. no. 20, University of St. Thomas [Manila], 1964); Martin Lavin, "Ecclesiastical Legislation concerning Abortion: Its History and Its Present Relationship to the Civil Legislation of the United States" (diss. no. 1, Pontifical University of St. Thomas [Rome], 1971–1972).

§ 2. The duelers and those who are called [seconds] are also by that fact infamous.

Canon Law Digest
I: 856–57; III: 670

Canon 2352 (NA)

An excommunication reserved to no one strikes all those, of whatever dignity they might be graced, who by any manner coerce either a man to embrace the clerical state or a man or a woman to enter into religious [life] and to give a religious profession, whether solemn or simple, or perpetual or temporary.

Canon Law Digest
I: 857

Canon 2353 (1983 CIC 1397)

One intending marriage or who, for sake of satisfying lust, carries off an unwilling woman by force or fraud, or even a consenting woman of minor age, but without consent of her parents or guardians, or without their knowledge, is considered by that fact excluded from legitimate ecclesiastical acts and moreover can be punished by other penalties for the gravity of the fault.

Canon 2354 (1983 CIC 1397)

§ 1. A layman who was legitimately convicted of the delict of homicide, abduction of a youth of the opposite sex, sale of humans into servitude or other evil end, usury, robbery, qualified theft, or non-qualified [theft] in the case of very notable items, arson, or the malicious and very wanton destruction of notable things, or grave mutilation or wounding or violence is by the law itself considered as excluded from legitimate ecclesiastical acts and from any responsibility, if he had any in the Church, with the obligation of repairing the damage that remains.

§ 2. But if a cleric commits one of the delicts mentioned in § 1, he shall be punished by an ecclesiastical tribunal, according to the varying gravity of the fault, with penances, censures, privation of office and dignity, and, if it seems necessary, also with deposition; but a defendant culpable of homicide is to be degraded.

Canon 2355 (1983 CIC 1390)

If someone, not by [physical acts] but by words or writings, or in any other way, imposes injuries on another and wounds his good reputation, not only can he be coerced according to the norm of Canons 1618 and 1938 to offer satisfaction for the repair of the damage, but he can also be punished by suitable penalties, not excluding, if the case involves clerics, suspension or removal from office or benefice.

Canon 2356 (NA)

Bigamists, that is, those who, notwithstanding a conjugal bond, attempt to enter another marriage, even a civil one as they say, are by that fact infamous; and if, spurning the admonition of the Ordinary, they stay in the illicit relationship, they are to be excommunicated according to the gravity of the deed or struck with personal interdict.

Canon Law Digest
VIII: 1213–14

Canon 2357 (NA) Cross-Ref.: 1917 CIC 2358

§ 1. Laity legitimately convicted of a delict against the sixth [commandment of the Decalogue] with a minor below the age of sixteen, or of debauchery, sodomy, incest, or pandering, are by that fact infamous, besides other penalties that the Ordinary decides should be inflicted.

§ 2. Whoever publicly commits the delict of adultery, or publicly lives in concubinage, or who has been legitimately convicted of another delict against the sixth precept of the Decalogue is excluded from legitimate ecclesiastical acts until he gives a sign of returning to his senses.

Canon 2358 (NA)

A cleric constituted in minor orders [who is] a respondent in some delict against the sixth precept of the Decalogue shall be punished for the gravity of the fault even with dismissal from the clerical state, if the circumstances of the delicts so persuade, besides [suffering] those penalties mentioned in Canon 2357, if these are in order.

Canon 2359 (1983 CIC 1395) Cross-Ref.: 1917 CIC 2176

§ 1. Concubinious clerics in sacred [orders], whether secular or religious, previous warnings not being heeded, are to be coerced into giving up their illicit relationship and to repair scandal by [being] suspended from divine things [and by suffering] the loss of the benefits of office, benefices, and dignities, the prescriptions of Canons 2176–81 being observed.

§ 2. If they engage in a delict against the sixth precept of the Decalogue with a minor below the age of sixteen, or engage in adultery, debauchery, bestiality, sodomy, pandering, incest with blood-relatives or affines in the first degree, they are suspended, declared infamous, and are deprived of any office, benefice, dignity, responsibility, if they have such, whatsoever, and in more serious cases, they are to be deposed.

§ 3. If they otherwise sin against the sixth commandment of the Decalogue, let them be coerced with appropriate penalties according to the gravity of the case, not excepting deprivation of office or benefice, especially if they have care of souls.

TITLE 15
On the crime of falsehood

Canon 2360 (1983 CIC 1391)

§ 1. All fabricators or falsifiers of letters, decrees, or rescripts of the Apostolic See, or those knowingly using such letters, decrees, or rescripts, incur by that fact excommunication specially reserved to the Apostolic See.

§ 2. Clerics committing the delict in § 1 can be coerced by other penalties, which can be extended even to privation of a benefice, office, dignity, and ecclesiastical pension; religious moreover are deprived of all offices that they have in the religious [institute], and of active and passive voice, besides other penalties established in the constitutions of each [institute].

Canon 2361 (1983 CIC 1391)

Whoever, in a request seeking a rescript from the Apostolic See or from a local Ordinary, fraudulently or with dolus withholds the truth or expresses a falsehood can be punished by his Ordinary for the gravity of the fault, with due regard for the prescription of Canons 45 and 1054.

Canon 2362 (1983 CIC 1391)

Fabricators or falsifiers of letters or ecclesiastical acts, whether public or private, or those knowingly using documents of this sort, are to be coerced according to the gravity of the delict, with due regard for the prescription of Canon 2406, § 1.

Canon Law Digest
I: 857

Canon 2363[7] (1983 CIC 1390)

Whoever personally or through others falsely denounces to Superiors a confessor of the crime of solicitation by that fact incurs excommunication reserved specially to the Apostolic See, from which case he cannot be absolved until the false denunciation is retracted formally and the damages that might have flowed therefrom are repaired to the best of one's ability, and grave and long-lasting penances are also imposed, with due regard for the prescription of Canon 894.

Canon Law Digest
I: 857

TITLE 16
On delicts in the administration or the reception of orders and the other Sacraments[8]

Canon 2364 (NA)

A minister who dares to administer Sacraments to those who, by either divine or ecclesiastical law, are prohibited from receiving same is suspended from the administration of the Sacraments for a time to be defined by the prudent judgment of the Ordinary and shall be punished with other penalties for the gravity of the fault, with due regard for penalties established in law for other delicts of this sort.

Canon 2365 (NA)

A presbyter who does not have, either by law or by concession of the Roman Pontiff, faculty to administer the sacrament of confirmation [but] who dares to administer [it] is suspended; but if he presumes to exceed the limited faculties made for him, he is considered by that [fact] to be deprived of that faculty.

---

[7] Herbert Linenberger, "The False Denunciation of an Innocent Confessor", Canon Law Studies, no. 236 (thesis, Catholic University of America, 1949).

[8] George Murphy, "Delinquencies and Penalties in the Administration and Reception of the Sacraments", Canon Law Studies, no. 17 (J. C. D. thesis, Catholic University of America, 1923).

Canon 2366 (1983 CIC 1378)

A priest who, without necessary jurisdiction, presumes to hear sacramental confessions is by that fact suspended from divine things; but one who absolves from reserved sins is by that fact suspended from hearing confessions.

Canon 2367 (1983 CIC 1378) Cross-Ref.: 1917 CIC 2254

§ 1. One absolving or pretending to absolve an accomplice in a sin of turpitude incurs by that fact excommunication most specially reserved to the Apostolic See; likewise, [he incurs this penalty] even [acting] in danger of death, if there is another priest, even though not approved for confessions, who could, without grave danger or infamy or scandal arising, hear the confession of the dying one, except in the case where the one dying refuses to be confessed by the other.

§ 2. One does not escape the same excommunication who, absolving or pretending to absolve an accomplice who is implicated in [the crime of the priest], but who is not yet absolved [because he has not confessed the crime], but rather has so acted because the implicated confessor directly or indirectly induced him [to confess].

Canon Law Digest
I: 858–59; II: 578

Canon 2368 (1983 CIC 1387) Cross-Ref.: 1917 CIC 2369

§ 1. Whoever commits the crime of solicitation mentioned in Canon 904 is suspended from the celebration of Mass and from hearing sacramental confessions and even, for the gravity of the delict, is declared incapable of receiving them, is deprived of all benefices, dignities, active and passive voice, and is for all of these declared incapable, and in more serious cases is also subject to degradation.

§ 2. But the faithful who knowingly omit to denounce him by whom they were solicited within one month against the prescription of Canon 904 incur automatic excommunication reserved to no one, and shall not be absolved until after satisfying the obligation or seriously promising to satisfy it.

Canon 2369 (1983 CIC 1388)

§ 1. A confessor who presumes to violate directly the sacramental seal remains in an excommunication most specially reserved the Apostolic See;

but one who only indirectly [violates the seal] is liable to the penalties mentioned in Canon 2368, § 1.

§ 2. Whoever accidentally violates the prescription of Canon 889, § 2, is struck with a salutary penalty for the gravity of the deed, which can even be excommunication.

Canon Law Digest
I: 859; II: 578; VIII: 1214–16

Canon 2370 (1983 CIC 1382)

A Bishop consecrating another Bishop, and the assistant Bishops or, in the place of Bishops, priests, and those who receive consecration without an apostolic mandate against the prescription of Canon 953 are by the law suspended until the Apostolic See dispenses them.

Canon Law Digest
III: 670; VIII: 1216–17; X: 285–87

Canon 2371 (1983 CIC 1380)

All, even those signed with episcopal dignity, who knowingly promote or who were promoted through simony to orders or [who similarly] minister or receive other Sacraments are suspected of heresy; clerics, moreover, incur suspension reserved to the Apostolic See.

Canon 2372 (NA)

They incur upon the fact a suspension from divine things, reserved to the Apostolic See, who presume to receive orders from one excommunicated or suspended or interdicted after a declaratory or condemnatory sentence, or from a notorious apostate, heretic, or schismatic; but whoever in good faith was ordained by such a one as these lacks the exercise of the orders thus received until he is dispensed.

Canon 2373 (1983 CIC 1383)

[The following] incur upon the fact suspension from the conferral of orders for one year reserved to the Apostolic See:

1.° Those who contrary to the prescription of Canon 955 ordain another's subject without dimissorial letters from his own Ordinary;
2.° Those who contrary to the prescriptions of Canons 993, n. 4, and 994 ordain their own subject who spent enough time somewhere to be able to incur a canonical impediment;

3.° Those who contrary to the prescription of Canon 974, § 1, n. 7, promote someone to major orders without a canonical title;

4.° Those who, outside of cases of legitimate privilege, promote a religious belonging to a [religious] family that is outside of the territory of the one ordaining, even if they have dimissorial letters from their own Superiors, unless there is legitimate proof that this has happened for one of the reasons mentioned in Canon 966.

Canon Law Digest
VIII: 1218

Canon 2374 (1983 CIC 1383)

Whoever approaches orders without dimissorial letters or with false ones, or before the canonical age, or at least in some evil way, is by that fact suspended from the order received; and if [one does so] without testimonial letters or while detained by a censure, irregularity, or other impediment, he is to be punished with grave penalties according to the circumstances of things.

Canon Law Digest
VIII: 1218

Canon 2375 (NA)

Catholics who dare to go into a mixed marriage without dispensation from the Church, even if it is valid, are by that fact excluded from legitimate ecclesiastical acts and Sacramentals, until they obtain a dispensation from the Ordinary.

TITLE 17
On delicts against the obligations proper to the clerical state or religious [life]

Canon 2376 (NA)

A priest who, not being dispensed by the Ordinary or detained by legitimate impediment, refuses to undergo the examination described in Canon 130 is to be compelled to it by the Ordinary by appropriate penalties.

Canon 2377 (NA)

Priests who are contumacious against the prescription of Canon 131, § 1, should be punished by the Ordinary in accord with his own prudent judgment; if they are religious confessors not having care of souls, he can suspend them from hearing secular confessions.

Canon 2378 (NA)

Major clerics who gravely neglect in their sacred ministry the rites and ceremonies prescribed by the Church, having been warned, and failing to reform themselves, are suspended according to the varying gravity of the thing.

Canon 2379 (NA)

Clerics who, against the prescription of Canon 136, do not wear ecclesiastical habit and clerical tonsure are to be gravely warned; but if a month passes from the warning without result, [then] as to minor clerics the prescription of the same Canon 136, § 3, is observed; but major clerics, with due regard for the prescription of Canon 188, n. 7, are suspended from the orders received, and if they notoriously go to a sort of life alien to the clerical state, [then] unless, once again being warned, they recover their senses, after three months from the final warning they are deposed.

Canon Law Digest
I: 860

Canon 2380 (1983 CIC 1392)

Clerics or religious who carry on trade or business themselves or through others against the prescription of Canon 142 are to be coerced by the Ordinary with penalties appropriate to the gravity of the fault.

Canon Law Digest
III: 670

Canon 2381 (1983 CIC 1396) Cross-Ref.: 1917 CIC 2170

Whoever obtains an office, benefice, or dignity with the obligation of residence, if he is illegitimately absent:

1.° By that [fact] is deprived of all the fruits of his benefice or office for as long as he is illegitimately absent, and these he must turn over to the Ordinary, who will distribute them to a church or other pious place or to the poor;

2.° Is deprived of the office, benefice, or dignity according to the norm of Canons 2168–75.

Canon Law Digest
I: 860; II: 579

Canon 2382 (NA)

If a pastor gravely neglects the administration of the Sacraments, assistance to the infirm, instruction of children and people, proper attention to [Sundays] and other feasts, care of the parochial church or of the most holy Eucharist or of the sacred oils can be coerced by the Ordinary according to the norm of Canons 2182–85.

Canon 2383 (NA)

A pastor who does not diligently keep and preserve the parish books according to the norm of law shall be punished by his own Ordinary in accord with the gravity of the fault.

Canon Law Digest
II: 579

Canon 2384 (NA)

A canon theologian or penitentiary negligent in undertaking his duties will be gradually compelled by the Bishop with warnings, mentioning penalties and subtracting a portion of the fruits assigned to him [in favor of] others who take his place; and if this negligence lasts for another year after a warning, he shall be struck with suspension from the benefice; and if this negligence is stretched out over another half year, he shall be deprived of the benefice.

Canon 2385 (NA)

With due regard for the prescription of Canon 646, a religious abandoning religious life incurs by the law itself excommunication reserved to his own major Superior or, if it is a non-exempt lay religious, to the Ordinary of the place where he is, is excluded from legitimate ecclesiastical acts, and is deprived of all the privileges of his religious [institute]; and if he leaves again, he perpetually lacks active and passive voice and must be punished by the Superiors with other penalties for the gravity of the fault according to the norm of the constitutions.

Canon Law Digest
I: 860; VII: 1028

Canon 2386 (NA)

A fugitive religious, by that fact, incurs privation of office, if he had any in the religious [institute], and [falls under] suspension reserved to his own major Superior if he is in sacred [orders]; if he flees again, he shall be punished according to the constitutions and, if the constitutions provide nothing concerning this, the major Superior will inflict penalties according to the gravity of the fault.

Canon Law Digest
I: 860

Canon 2387 (NA)

A religious cleric whose admission was declared null by the fact of dolus in the profession, if he was constituted in minor orders, is cast out of the clerical state; if in major [orders], he remains by that fact suspended until the [matter] is otherwise seen to by the Apostolic See.

Canon Law Digest
I: 860

Canon 2388 (1983 CIC 1394)

§ 1. Clerics constituted in sacred [orders] or regulars, or nuns after a solemn vow of chastity, and likewise all those who presume to contract even a civil marriage with any of the aforesaid persons incur automatic excommunication simply reserved to the Apostolic See; clerics moreover, having been warned, if they do not come back to their senses within a time defined by the Ordinary according to the diversity of circumstances, will be degraded, with due regard for the prescription of Canon 188, n. 5.

§ 2. But for those professed of simple perpetual vows, whether to an Ordinary or to a religious Congregation, all of them, as above, receive excommunication automatically reserved to the Ordinary.

Canon Law Digest
I: 860; II: 579–81

Canon 2389 (NA)

Religious violating in a notable way the law of common life prescribed in the constitutions shall be gravely warned, and if amendment does not follow, they shall be punished even with privation of active and passive voice, and if they are Superiors, also of office.

Canon Law Digest
I: 860

TITLE 18
On delicts in the conferral, acceptance, and dismissal from dignities, offices, and ecclesiastical benefices

Canon 2390 (1983 CIC 1375)

§ 1. All those impeding the liberty of ecclesiastical elections, by any means, either personally or through others, or the electors or those elected, the canonical election being completed, shall be punished according to the manner of the fault for whatever manner of harm they caused.

§ 2. But if [in] an election conducted by a college of clerics or of religious, laity or secular powers illegitimately presume to involve themselves against canonical liberty, the electors who sought such involvement, or who chose to admit it, are by that fact deprived for that time of the right of voting; but if some [one] knowingly consented to being elected this way, he is by that fact incapable of the office or benefice that it concerned.

Canon 2391 (NA)

§ 1. A college that knowingly elects an unworthy person is by that fact deprived for that time of the right of proceeding to a new election.

§ 2. Individual electors who knowingly violate the substantial form of the election can be punished by the Ordinary for the gravity of the fault.

§ 3. Clerics or laity who knowingly present or appoint an unworthy person by that fact lack the right of presenting or appointing for that time.

Canon 2392 (NA)

With due regard for the prescription of Canon 729, perpetrators of the delict of simony in any office, benefice, or ecclesiastical dignity:

1.° Incur automatic excommunication simply reserved to the Apostolic See;
2.° Are by that fact deprived in perpetuity of the right of electing, presenting, or appointing, if they had such [rights];
3.° If they are clerics, they are also suspended.

Canon 2393 (NA)

All those who, legitimately enjoying the right of electing, presenting, or appointing, presume to confer an office, benefice, or ecclesiastical dignity while neglecting the authority of the one who is competent for confirmation or institution are deprived by that fact of their rights for the time it happens.

Canon 2394 (1983 CIC 1381)

Whoever occupies on his own authority a benefice, office, or ecclesiastical dignity, or having been elected, presented, or appointed to such, [and] becomes involved in their possession or governance or administration before taking the necessary letters of confirmation or institution and showing them to those to whom by law he needs to show them:
1.° Is by law incapable of [the post] and, moreover, shall be punished by the Ordinary according to the gravity of the fault;
2.° Shall be coerced to recede immediately from the occupation of the benefice, office, dignity, or its governance or administration, having been warned, by suspension [or] privation of an earlier benefice, office, or dignity, if there was one;
3.° But the Chapter, convention, or others who see to such things, allowing this sort of one to be elected, presented, or appointed before exhibition of the letters, by that fact remains suspended from the right of electing, appointing, or presenting for the good pleasure of the Apostolic See.

Canon Law Digest
III: 670–71

Canon 2395 (NA)

Whoever knowingly accepts the conferral of an office, benefice, or dignity that is not vacant by law and who allows himself to be put in possession of it is by that fact incapable of later acquiring it and should be punished with other penalties according to the manner of culpability.

Canon 2396 (NA)

A cleric who goes into quiet possession of an office or benefice that is incompatible with a prior, and he presumes to retain the earlier against the prescription of Canons 156 and 1439, is considered by the law to be deprived of both.

Canon 2397 (NA)

If one promoted to the dignity of the cardinalate refuses to tender the oath described in Canon 234, he is by that fact deprived of the cardinalitial dignity and remains perpetually deprived.

Canon 2398 (NA)

If one promoted to the episcopate, against the prescription of Canon 333, neglects to take up consecration within three months, he enjoys no fruits [from the appointment], which [instead] are turned over for the upkeep of the cathedral church; and if thereafter he persists in this negligence for [three more] months, he is by law deprived of the episcopate.

Canon 2399 (NA)

Major clerics who, with a task committed to them by their Ordinary, and without the permission of the Ordinary, presume to desert it are suspended from divine things for a time determined by the Ordinary according to the diversity of the case.

Canon 2400 (NA)

Clerics who presume to resign a benefice or ecclesiastical dignity into the hands of lay officials by that fact incur suspension from divine things.

Canon 2401 (1983 CIC 1381)

Whoever persists in detaining an office, benefice, or dignity, notwithstanding legitimate privation and removal, or lest he lose it engages in illegitimate delays, having been warned, can be coerced to leave it by suspension from divine things and other penalties, not excluding deposition, if the case warrants.

Canon 2402 (NA)

An Abbot or Prelate *of no one* who, against the prescription of Canon 322, § 2, does not receive the blessing is by that fact suspended from jurisdiction.

Canon 2403 (NA)

Whoever, against the prescription of Canon 1406, neglects without just impediment to give the profession of faith shall be warned, with an appropriate predetermined time limit; the which having run, the contumacious one shall be punished by privation of the office, benefice, dignity, or post; nor in the meantime shall he make his own the fruits of the benefice, office, dignity, or duty.

TITLE 19
On the abuse of ecclesiastical power and office

Canon 2404 (1983 CIC 1389)

Abuse of ecclesiastical power, in the prudent judgment of the legitimate Superior, shall be punished according to the gravity of the fault, with due regard for the prescriptions of those canons that establish certain penalties for various abuses.

Canon 2405 (NA)

A Vicar Capitulary or any others, whether within the Chapter or outside of it, who carry off, destroy, hide, or substantially mutilate any document pertaining to the episcopal Curia, either personally or through another, incur automatic excommunication simply reserved to the Apostolic See and can also be struck by the Ordinary with deprivation of office or benefice.

Canon 2406 (1983 CIC 1391) Cross-Ref.: 1917 CIC 2362

§ 1. Whoever is bound by office to produce, inscribe, or preserve acts, whether documents or books of ecclesiastical Curias or parish books, [yet] dares to falsify, adulterate, destroy, or hide them is deprived of office and shall be punished with other grave penalties by the Ordinary according to the manner of fault.

§ 2. Anyone who withholds legitimately sought acts, documents, or books, or who with dolus refuses to copy, transmit, or display them, or who in any other way harms his duties, can be punished by privation of office or suspension from same and by fines left to the decision of the Ordinary according to the gravity of the case.

Canon 2407[9] (1983 CIC 1386)

Those giving gifts or inducements to Curial officials or administrators of any ecclesiastical sort, [or] judges, advocates, or procurators, in order to tempt them to action or omission contrary to their office, shall be struck with congruent penalties and will be compelled to repair the damages, if there are any.

Canon 2408 (NA)

Those increasing the usual taxes legitimately approved according to the norm of Canon 1507, or requiring anything above them, are to be coerced with grave monetary fines, and recidivists are suspended from office or removed according to the gravity of the fault, besides [being bound by] the obligation of restoring whatever was unjustly received.

Canon 2409 (NA)

A Vicar Capitulary granting dimissorial letters for ordination against the prescription of Canon 958, § 1, n. 3, by that fact lies under a suspension from divine things.

Canon 2410 (NA)

Religious Superiors who, against the prescription of Canons 965–67, presume to send their subjects to other Bishops for their ordination by that fact are suspended for a month from the celebration of Mass.

Canon Law Digest
I: 861

Canon 2411 (NA)

Religious Superiors who receive into the novitiate unsuitable candidates against the prescription of Canon 542 or without the required testimonial letters against the prescription of Canon 544, or who admit [unsuitable candidates] to profession against the prescription of Canon 571, § 2, are to be punished in accord with the gravity of the fault, not excluding deprivation of office.

Canon Law Digest
I: 861

[9] Donald Zimmermann, "The Crime of Collusion in Ecclesiastical Trials" (MS no. 2782, Gregorian University, 1958; printed version, no. 1156, 1958).

Canon 2412 (NA)

A Superioress, even of exempt religious [women], is to be punished by the local Ordinary according to the gravity of the fault, not excluding, if deserved, privation of office, [if she]:

1.° Against the prescription of Canon 549, presumes to spend the dowry of received girls in any way, always with due regard for the obligation mentioned in Canon 551;
2.° Against the prescription of Canon 552, fails to notify the local Ordinary about the coming admission of anyone to the novitiate or to profession.

Canon 2413 (NA)

§ 1. A Superioress who, after an indicated visit, and without the consent of the Visitator, transfers a religious to another house, and likewise all those religious, whether Superioress or subject, who personally or through another, directly or indirectly, induce religious to be quiet when questioned by a Visitator or in any way to conceal the truth or not sincerely explain [things] or, because of an answer given to the Visitator, molest them or under any pretext attack [them] are incapable of pursuing any office that encompasses the governance of others and are to be deprived of the office that they hold, and the Superioress is to be so declared by the Visitator.

§ 2. Those things prescribed in the above paragraph also apply to religious men.

Canon Law Digest
I: 861

Canon 2414 (NA)

A Superioress who acts against the prescriptions of Canons 521, § 3, 522, and 523 is to be warned by the local Ordinary; if she offends again, she is to be punished by the same person with deprivation of office, with immediate notice sent to the Sacred Congregation for Religious.

[To the Greater Glory of God]

End

DOCUMENTS

DOCUMENT 6

From the Constitution *Altitudo*, Pope Paul III, 1 June 1537

Since, as We have learned with great joy, many inhabitants of West and South India, ignorant though they are of divine law, through the enlightenment of the Holy Spirit have utterly rejected from their minds and hearts the errors to which they have hitherto been subject, and having embraced the truth of the Catholic Faith and the unity of Holy Church, desire and intend to live according to the manner of the Roman Church . . . , We decree that this is to be observed in the matter of their marriages: that those who before their conversion had, according to their customs, several wives and are unable to recall whom they married first shall, on their conversion, take from among them the one whom they wish and contract marriage with her, wording the contract in the present tense, as is the custom; those, however, who do remember whom they married first shall retain her and dismiss the others. To them We also grant that until the Holy See decides otherwise they shall not be excluded from marriage, even though they be related in the third degree whether of consanguinity or affinity.

DOCUMENT 7

Constitution *Romani Pontificis*, Pope St. Pius V, 2 August 1571

It has been the custom for the Roman Pontiff, in his equitable and circumspect providence, to see to it by declarations and other opportune means that hesitation or doubt does not impede the working out of measures that must be provided for the salutary guidance of the Indians newly converted to the Faith. Therefore since, as We have learned, infidel Indians are permitted to have several wives whom they repudiate for the least reason, it has resulted that they are permitted after their conversion to remain with that wife who received baptism at the same time as her husband; and since very often it happens that because she is not the first wife both priests and Bishops are torn by grave doubts that that is not a true marriage; but because it is most severe to separate them from the wives with whom they received baptism, especially because it is most difficult to find the first wife, We, desiring in Our paternal affection to consult the best interests of the Indians themselves and to free the Bishops and priests from their anxiety, on Our own initiative and with certain knowledge and the fullness of Our apostolic power, by these presents declare in virtue of Our apostolic authority that Indians both baptized and to be baptized may remain with the wife who has been or will be baptized with them, and affirm that such a marriage between them is legitimate and must be so pronounced by all judges and commissioners of whatever authority they may be, there being removed from them singly and collectively all authority and right of deciding otherwise; and We declare null and void whatever decision may have been knowingly or in ignorance made by anyone whatsoever in virtue of any authority whatsoever, notwithstanding any general or special Constitution or Ordination, whether it be of Apostolic origin or given by provincial or synodal decree or any other decision to the contrary.

Given at Rome at St. Peter's, under the ring of the Fisherman, 2 August 1571.

DOCUMENT 8

Constitution *Populis*, Pope Gregory XIII, 25 January 1585

It is advisable to be lenient, in the matter of freedom to contract marriage, toward the peoples and nations recently converted from paganism to the Catholic Faith, lest men, unaccustomed to continence, might less willingly persevere in the Faith and deter others from receiving it by their example. Now, since it often happens that many infidels of both sexes, especially men, who have contracted marriage in pagan rites have been captured and taken from Angola, Ethiopia, Brazil and other countries of the Indies and exiled in distant lands far from their own country and their spouses, so that both they and those who remain captive in their own country cannot, as is required when they are converted, ask their infidel spouses, who are separated from them by such wide expanses of land, whether they are willing to cohabit with them without insult to the Creator, either because sometimes access even by messenger to hostile and barbarous regions is impossible, or because they do not know whither they have been transported, or because the length of journey presents great difficulties; therefore, aware that marriages of this kind contracted among infidels, although they are true marriages, are not so [ratified] that they cannot be dissolved in cases of necessity, and [showing compassion] in Our paternal love [for] the weakness of these peoples, We by Our Apostolic authority, by these presents grant to each and every Ordinary and to pastors of these regions, and to the priests of the Society of Jesus approved for hearing confessions by the superiors of that Society and sent for a time to the aforesaid regions or admitted therein, full faculty of dispensing the Christian inhabitants, of both sexes, natives of the aforesaid lands who have in serious mind embraced the Faith and have contracted marriage before their baptism, so that all of them, despite the survival of the infidel spouse and without asking his or her consent or awaiting his or her reply, may licitly contract marriage with any Christian even of another rite, and solemnize it before the Church, and after its consummation remain in it as long as they live: provided that it be evident even from a summary and extrajudicial investigation that the aforesaid absent spouse cannot be admonished according to law, or has not, within the time fixed in the monition, signified his or her intention; moreover, these marriages are never to be rescinded even though it become known afterwards that the infidel was prevented by just cause from declaring his or her intention and had even become a convert at the time of the second marriage, but in virtue of Our decree shall remain valid and firm, and the offspring shall be legitimate. All Apostolic constitutions and decrees and those emanating even from general Councils and all else to the contrary notwithstanding. And because it would be difficult for this letter to be shown and published in every place where it will have effect, We will that the same credence be placed in its printed copies, when signed by the hand of a Notary Public or the Secretary of the aforesaid Society and stamped by the seal of an ecclesiastical dignitary or of the Superior General of the said Society then in office, as would be placed in this letter itself if it could be exhibited and shown.

Granted at Rome at St. Peter's, under the ring of the Fisherman, the 25th day of January, 1585, in the thirteenth year of Our pontificate.

APPENDIX 1

NON-ASSIGNED DISSERTATIONS

Eastern Canon Law

Joseph Marbach, "Marriage Legislation for the Catholics of the Oriental Rites in the United States and Canada", Canon Law Studies, no. 243 (J. C. D. thesis, Catholic University of America, 1946); Varkey Vithayathil, "The Origin and Progress of the Syro-Malabar Hierarchy" (diss. no. 4, Pontifical University of St. Thomas [Rome], 1958–1959); Thomas Puthiakunnel, "General Obligations of the Syro-Malabar Clergy" (MS no. 3309, Gregorian University, 1964; printed version, no. 1742, 1964); Thomas Asariparampil, "The Malabar Church and Her Legislation with Particular Reference to the Clergy" (Pontifical Lateran University, 1962); Raymond Misulich, "The Foundation and Juridic Status of the Eparchies of Pittsburgh and Passaic", Canon Law Studies, no. 469 (Catholic University of America, 1968); Cyril Malancharuvil, "The Syro-Malankara Church: Its Juridical Status" (Gregorian University; printed version, no. 2534, Alwaye, India, 1974); Walter Paska, "Sources of Particular Law for the Ukrainian Catholic Church in the United States", Canon Law Studies, no. 485 (J. C. D. thesis, Catholic University of America, 1975); John Myers, "The Trullan Controversy: Implications for the Status of the Orthodox Churches in Roman Catholic Canon Law", Canon Law Studies, no. 491 (J. C. D. thesis, Catholic University of America, 1977).

History of Canon Law

Severinus de Jong, "The Hierarchical Order in Holland at the Time of the Reformation" (Gregorian University; printed version, no. 121, 1938); Francis Gossman, "Pope Urban II and Canon Law", Canon Law Studies, no. 403 (J. C. D. thesis, Catholic University of America, 1960); John Buckley, "The Use of the Writings of St. Augustine as Sources of Canon Law", Canon Law Studies, no. 445 (J. C. D. thesis, Catholic University of America, 1965); Donald Brown, "The Origins of the Grades in the Society of Jesus, 1540 to 1550" (Gregorian University; printed version, no. 2276, 1971); Gerardo Ty Veloso, "*Usque ad mortem in Monasterio Perseverantes* (*Regula Benedicti*, pr. 50): The Obligation of Monks to Persevere and to Reside in Their Monastery ... The Discipline in the West from the

4th to the 7th Century, Mainly on Monastic Rules, Conciliar Canons, Papal Decretals, and Imperial Constitutions" (Gregorian University; printed version, no. 2471, Manila, 1973); William Kelly, "Pope Gregory II on Divorce and Remarriage: A Canonical-Historical Investigation of the Letter *Desiderabilem mihi*, with Special Reference to the Response *Quod proposuisti*", Analecta Gregoriana, no. 203 (Gregorian University, 1976); Clarence Gallagher, "Canon Law and the Christian Community: The Role of Law in the Church according to the *Summa Aurae* of Cardinal Hostiensis", Analecta Gregoriana, no. 208 (Gregorian University, 1978).

Philosophy of Canon Law

Francis Reh, "The Rules of Law and Canon Law" (Gregorian University; printed version, no. 191, 1939); Raymond Bégin, "Natural Law and Positive Law", Canon Law Studies, no. 393 (J. C. D. thesis, Catholic University of America, 1959); Constancio Mesiona, "A Comparative Study on the Immutability of the Natural Law in Amor Ruibal and in the Traditional Scholastic Doctrine" (rev. no. 42, Pontifical University Comillas [Madrid], 1959); Thaddeus Oblak, "Marriage Law in Japan and Its Relation to Natural Law" (MS no. 3404, Gregorian University, 1962); Henry Lacerte, "The Nature of Canon Law according to Suarez" (doctoral diss. 46, University of Ottawa [Canada], 1963); G. Garthoeffner, "A Critical Analysis of the Theory of *Jus Publicum* [public law] in the Writings of James Warren Doyle, Bishop of Kildare and Leighlin, 1819–1934" (Pontifical Lateran University, 1964); Joseph Tinoko, "Church and Law (A Critical Study of the Different Methodological Approaches to the Question of the Existence of the Juridical Factor in the Church)" (diss. no. 4, Pontifical University of St. Thomas [Rome], 1972–1973); Thomas Doran, "Canon Law in the Twelfth Century: The Views of Bernold of Constance, Ivo of Chartres, and Alger of Liège" (Gregorian University; printed version, no. 2830, 1979); Elizabeth McDonough, "Canon Law in Pastoral Perspective: Principles for the Application of Law according to Antoninus of Florence", Canon Law Studies, no. 504 (J. C. D. thesis, Catholic University of America, 1982).

Procedural Law

Joseph Windle, "A Study of Regional Tribunals in Canada for Cases of Nullity of Marriage" (Pontifical Lateran University, 1953); Anthony Bevilacqua, "Procedure in the Ecclesiastical Courts of the Church of England with Its Historical Antecedents in Roman and Decretal Law" (MS no. 2497, Gregorian University, 1956; printed version, no. 995, 1956); James Hayes, "The Powers of the Moderator of the Regional Tribunal in Canada" (diss. no. 8, Pontifical University of

St. Thomas [Rome], 1956–1957); William LaDue, "Papal Rescripts of Justice and English Royal Procedural Writs 1150–1250" (Pontifical Lateran University, 1960); James Pieper, "The Danger of Scandal and Matrimonial Procedure" (diss. no. 6, Pontifical University of St. Thomas [Rome], 1964–1965).

Secular Legal Philosophers

James St. Leger, "Natural Law and International Law in the *De jure belli ac pacis libri tres* of Hugo Grotius" (diss. no. 24, Pontifical University of St. Thomas [Rome], 1960–1961); John Sullivan, "The Relevance of Three Common-Law Jurists [Hart, Pound, & Cardozo] for a Theory of Interpretation in Canon Law" (Pontifical Lateran University, 1966); Joseph Pepe, "H.L.A. Hart: An Examination of His Common Sense Principle" (diss. no. 1, Pontifical University of St. Thomas [Rome], 1975–1976); Donald Walker, "The Jurisprudence of Oliver Wendell Holmes" (diss. no. 8, Pontifical University of St. Thomas [Rome], 1977–1978).

Christianity and Politics

Alexander Olalia, "A Comparative Study of the Christian Constitution of States and the Constitution of the Philippine Commonwealth", Canon Law Studies, no. 206 (thesis, Catholic University of America, 1944); Clayton O'Donoghue, "Educational System of Ontario, Canada, and the Code of Canon Law" (Pontifical Lateran University, 1952); Giacomo Booth, "Church Educational Problems in the State of California" (Pontifical Lateran University, 1952); Antonio Hulme, "The Education Act of 1944 *Iuventutis Institutio* in Anglia" (Pontifical Lateran University, 1953); Michael Richards, "The Teaching of the Church and the Universities in England" (diss. no. 16, Pontifical University of St. Thomas [Rome], 1959–1960); Hugh Whelan, "The Problem of State Aid to Catholic Schools in the United States: A Comparative Study of Canon Law and American Constitutional Law in the Field of Education" (thesis no. 158, Pontifical Lateran University, 1960); Richard Carney, "The Evolution of the Concept of Sovereignty" (Pontifical Lateran University, 1961); Grato Falzon, "Contemporary Church-State Problems in the Light of the Teaching of Pope Pius XII" (Pontifical Lateran University, 1963); Richard Campbell, "The Social Damages of Crime" (diss. no. 8, Pontifical University of St. Thomas [Rome], 1963–1964); Paul Hansen, "Church-State Relations in Canadian Higher Education: A New Trend" (diss. no. 12, Pontifical University of St. Thomas [Rome], 1964–1965); Thomas Donovan, "The Status of the Church in American Civil Law and Canon Law", Canon Law Studies, no. 446 (J. C. D. thesis, Catholic University of America, 1966); Jeremy Prabhu, "Subjective Element or Causes Originating from the Operation of the Intellect and Will; Considered to Apply to General Exception to Criminal

Responsibility of a Delinquent to the Indian Penal Code" (Pontifical Lateran University, 1966); Anthony Boylan, "Religious Liberty and the Church of England" (diss. no. 1, Pontifical University of St. Thomas [Rome], 1969–1970); Denise Doyle, "Religious Freedom in Canada" (D.C.L. thesis no. 66, St. Paul University [Ottawa, Canada], 1982).

Inter-Religious Studies

Gerard Dolan, "Legislation for Religious in Anglican Institutes and the Code of Canon Law" (Gregorian University; printed version, no. 1066, Heythrop, England, 1956); Constantine Kurisinkal, "The Concept of the State of Perfection in the Code of Manu and in the Code of Canon Law (in Hinduism and in Catholicism)" (diss. no. 10, Pontifical University of St. Thomas [Rome], 1963–1964); Ivan Zuzek, "Kormcaja Kniga: Studies on the Chief Code of Russian Canon Law", Orientalia Christiana Analecta, no. 168 (Gregorian University; published by the Pont. Institutum Orientalium Studiorum, 1964); Michael Quinlan, "Kindred and Affinity in the Church of England" (D.C.L. thesis, Librarian's Office 702, Maynooth [Ireland], 1969); Joseph Thyil, "Mahatma Gandhi's Theory and Practice on *Ahimsa* (non violence) and *Satyagrha* (holding on truth)" (diss. no. 7, Pontifical University of St. Thomas [Rome], 1980–1981); Leslie Sachs, "Thomas Cranmer's *Reformatio Legum Ecclesiasticarum* of 1553 in the Context of English Church Law from the Later Middle Ages to the Canons of 1603", Canon Law Studies, no. 509 (J. C. D. thesis, Catholic University of America, 1982).

Marriage, Postconciliar Issues

Alexander Stenson, "Marriage Today and the Question of Due Discretion" (diss. no. 2, Pontifical University of St. Thomas [Rome], 1971–1972); Colin Correa, "Intrapersonal and Interpersonal Integration in Marital Consent: Evolution of the Concept of Defect of Consent in Cases of Nullity according to Jurisprudence" (diss. no. 1, Pontifical University of St. Thomas [Rome], 1977–1978); Charles Guarino, "The Effect of Personality Disorders on the Validity of Marriage" (diss. no. 2, Pontifical University of St. Thomas [Rome], 1977–1978); David Fellhauer, "The *Consortium Omnis Vitae* [Partnership of the whole of life] as a Juridical Element of Marriage" (Ph.D. diss. no. 60, St. Paul University [Ottawa, Canada], 1978); James Graham, "Transsexualism and the Nullity of Marriage" (Gregorian University; printed version, no. 2881, 1979); John Renken, "The Contemporary Understanding of Marriage: An Historico-Critical Study of *Gaudium et Spes* 47–52 and Its Influence on the Revision of the *Codex Iuris Canonici*" (diss. no. 2, Pontifical University of St. Thomas [Rome], 1980–1981).

Marriage Issues, Inter-Religious

Charles Taylor, "Mormon Marriage and Its Canonical Consequences" (Pontifical Lateran University, 1959); Thomas Candreva, "Protestant Episcopal and Roman Catholic Canon Law on the Indissolubility of Marriage" (diss. no. 1, Pontifical University of St. Thomas [Rome], 1970–1971); Patrick McManus, "Divorce and Remarriage: A Comparative Study of the Teaching and Practice of the Church of England and the Roman Catholic Church" (diss. no. 10, Pontifical University of St. Thomas [Rome], 1971–1972); John Mulackal, "Dissolution of the Marriage Tie in the Canonical and Hindu Legislations" (diss. no. 2, Pontifical University of St. Thomas [Rome], 1978–1979); Jerome Listecki, "Indissolubility and the United Methodist Church" (diss. no. 1, Pontifical University of St. Thomas [Rome], 1980–1981).

Marriage Issues, Church and State

Robert Dillon, "Common Law Marriage", Canon Law Studies, no. 153 (J. C. D. thesis, Catholic University of America, 1942); John Jorna, "The Concept of Marriage and Divorce according to the Code of Canon Law and Current Scandinavian Law" (Pontifical Lateran University, 1946); Donald Duffie, "Comparative Marriage Law in the Catholic Church and the Provinces of Canada (Quebec Excepted)" (University of Laval [Quebec, Canada], 1948); Leo Hinz, "The Celebration of Marriage in Canada: A Comparative Study of Civil and Canon Law outside of the Province of Quebec" (doctoral diss. no. 38, University of Ottawa [Canada], 1953); Samuel Wiley, "A Comparative Study of the Validity of Marriage in Canon Law in the Civil Code of the Republic of the Philippines" (MS no. 2071, Gregorian University, 1953; printed version, no. 808, 1953); Michael Green, "A Comparison of the Civil Matrimonial Legislation of the State of Michigan with Canonical Matrimonial Legislation" (Pontifical Lateran University, 1954); Peter Quinn, "A Comparative Study of Western Australian Marriage Law and Canon Law" (Pontifical Lateran University, 1954); Cormac Burke, "The Legal Value of the Antenuptial Agreement in the Civil Law of England, Ireland, and the United States of America" (diss. no. 12, Pontifical University of St. Thomas [Rome], 1954–1955); Thomas Sharkey, "A Comparison of the Nature, Impediments, and Form of the Civil Matrimonial Legislation of the State of New Jersey with Canonical Legislation" (Pontifical Lateran University, 1955); Thomas Heneghan, "The Annulment and Invalidity of Marriage in the State of New York" (MS no. 2338, Gregorian University, 1955); Vincent Tracy, "A Comparative Study of the Divorce and Separation Laws of the State of Wisconsin and Canon Law" (Pontifical Lateran University, 1955); Francis Karwoski, "A Comparison of the Matrimonial Impediments of the State of Ohio and the Code of Canon Law"

(Pontifical Lateran University, 1955); Stanislaus Swierzowski, "The Catholic Parties in Civil Divorce and Separation", Canon Law Studies, no. 434 (Catholic University of America, not published); Patrick Daly, "A Survey of the Civil Laws regarding Christian Marriage in Comparison with Canon Law" (Pontifical Lateran University, 1960); Thomas Faulkner, "A Comparison of the Marriage Legislation of the Catholic Church and State of South Dakota" (Pontifical Lateran University, 1961); Charles O'Hern, "The Matrimonial Impediments of the State of Arizona and the Code of Canon Law" (Pontifical Lateran University, 1961); Terentio Monihan, "A Comparative Study of Marriage Legislation of the Catholic Church and the State of Pennsylvania" (Pontifical Lateran University, 1963); Thomas Gumbleton, "Separation and Divorce: A Comparative Study of the Canon Law of the Catholic Church and the Civil Law of the State of Michigan" (Pontifical Lateran University, 1964); James Connor, "The Invalidity of Marriage in the Roman Catholic Church and in the Civil Laws in the United States: A Comparative Study", Canon Law Studies, no. 456 (J. C. D. thesis, Catholic University of America, 1968); Glenn Gardiner, "Divorce in the United States" (diss. no. 2, Pontifical University of St. Thomas [Rome], 1976–1977).

Temporal Goods in the United States of America

Urban Wiggins, "Property Laws of the State of Ohio Affecting the Church", Canon Law Studies, no. 367 (thesis, Catholic University of America, 1956); Joseph Murphy, "The Laws of the State of New York Affecting Church Property", Canon Law Studies, no. 388 (thesis, Catholic University of America, 1957); Manuel Rodriguez, "The Laws of the State of New Mexico Affecting Church Property", Canon Law Studies, no. 406 (thesis, Catholic University of America, 1959); Donald McLeaish, "The Laws of the State of Texas Affecting Church Property", Canon Law Studies, no. 405 (J. C. D. thesis, Catholic University of America, 1960); Raymond Klaas, "The Laws of the State of Wisconsin Affecting Church Property" (thesis no. 151, Pontifical Lateran University, 1960); Maurice Welsh, "The Laws of the State of Nevada Affecting Church Property", Canon Law Studies, no. 409 (thesis, Catholic University of America, 1962); James McGough, "The Laws of the State of Mississippi Affecting Church Property", Canon Law Studies, no. 417 (J. C. D. thesis, Catholic University of America, 1962); Paul Schierse, "Laws of the State of Delaware Affecting Church Property", Canon Law Studies, no. 428 (J. C. D. thesis, Catholic University of America, 1963); John Goeke, "The Laws of the State of Kentucky Affecting Church Property", Canon Law Studies, no. 433 (J. C. D. thesis, Catholic University of America, 1963); John Catoir, "The Laws of the State of New Jersey Affecting Church Property", Canon Law Studies, no. 436 (J. C. D. thesis, Catholic University of America, 1964); Peter Fleming, "The Laws of the State of Minnesota Affecting Church Property", Canon Law

Studies, no. 438 (J. C. D. thesis, Catholic University of America, 1964); William Sullivan, "The Laws of the State of Illinois Affecting Church Property", Canon Law Studies, no. 444 (J. C. D. thesis, Catholic University of America, 1964); Ambrose De Pauli, "Property Law of the State of Florida Affecting the Church" (Pontifical Lateran University, 1964).

Postconciliar Canonical Structures and Institutes

Daniel Foley, "The Synod of Bishops: Its Canonical Structure and Procedures", Canon Law Studies, no. 481 (Catholic University of America, 1973); Peter Smith, "General Sacramental Absolution" (diss. no. 5, Pontifical University of St. Thomas [Rome], 1976–1977); Sydney Marceaux, "The Pastoral Council" (diss. no. 1, Pontifical University of St. Thomas [Rome], 1979–1980); Stanley Teixeira, "Personnel Policies: A Canonical Commentary on Selected Current Clergy Personnel Policies in the United States of America", Canon Law Studies, no. 503 (J. C. D. thesis, Catholic University of America, 1981).

APPENDIX 2

MULTIPLE EXPRESS REFERENCES WITHIN CANONS

Canons **124–42**	are expressly referenced in	Canon 592.
Canons **147–95**	are expressly referenced in	Canon 1413.
Canons **160–82**	are expressly referenced in	Canons 433, 507, 697.
Canons **183–91**	are expressly referenced in	Canon 371.
Canons **199–207**	are expressly referenced in	Canon 1606.
Canons **275–80**	are expressly referenced in	Canon 273.
Canons **281–91**	are expressly referenced in	Canon 304.
Canons **339 ff.**	are expressly referenced in	Canon 306.
Canons **356–62**	are expressly referenced in	Canon 304.
Canons **366–71**	are expressly referenced in	Canon 323.
Canons **423–28**	are expressly referenced in	Canon 326.
Canons **429 ff.**	are expressly referenced in	Canon 317.
Canons **432 ff.**	are expressly referenced in	Canon 327.
Canons **472–76**	are expressly referenced in	Canons 455, 477.
Canons **487–681**	are expressly referenced in	Canon 685.
Canons **499–530**	are expressly referenced in	Canon 675.
Canons **520–27**	are expressly referenced in	Canon 566.
Canons **532–37**	are expressly referenced in	Canon 676.
Canons **595–612**	are expressly referenced in	Canon 679.
Canons **646–72**	are expressly referenced in	Canon 681.
Canons **654–68**	are expressly referenced in	Canon 1555.
Canons **656–62**	are expressly referenced in	Canon 649.
Canons **663–68**	are expressly referenced in	Canon 667.
Canons **993–1000**	are expressly referenced in	Canon 960.
Canons **1337–42**	are expressly referenced in	Canons 484, 698.
Canons **1448–71**	are expressly referenced in	Canon 148.
Canons **1519–28**	are expressly referenced in	Canon 1182.
Canons **1552–1959**	are expressly referenced in	Canon 2210.
Canons **1560–68**	are expressly referenced in	Canon 1559.
Canons **1572 ff.**	are expressly referenced in	Canon 1570.
Canons **1573–93**	are expressly referenced in	Canon 365.
Canons **1594–1601**	are expressly referenced in	Canon 1993.
Canons **1598–1605**	are expressly referenced in	Canon 259.
Canons **1648–54**	are expressly referenced in	Canon 1713.

Canons **1684–89**	are expressly referenced in	Canon 103.
Canons **1706–25**	are expressly referenced in	Canon 1838.
Canons **1715–23**	are expressly referenced in	Canon 1765.
Canons **1773–81**	are expressly referenced in	Canon 1745.
Canons **1770–81**	are expressly referenced in	Canon 1944.
Canons **1792–1805**	are expressly referenced in	Canon 1977.
Canons **1793–1805**	are expressly referenced in	Canon 1808.
Canons **1939 ff.**	are expressly referenced in	Canon 658.
Canons **1954 ff.**	are expressly referenced in	Canon 1949.
Canons **1993–98**	are expressly referenced in	Canon 214.
Canons **1999 ff.**	are expressly referenced in	Canon 420.
Canons **2087 ff.**	are expressly referenced in	Canon 2086.
Canons **2087–2115**	are expressly referenced in	Canon 2133.
Canons **2116–24**	are expressly referenced in	Canon 2139.
Canons **2147 ff.**	are expressly referenced in	Canons 389, 475, and 1476.
Canons **2162–67**	are expressly referenced in	Canon 193.
Canons **2168–75**	are expressly referenced in	Canon 2381.
Canons **2168–94**	are expressly referenced in	Canon 1933.
Canons **2176–81**	are expressly referenced in	Canon 2359.

ABOUT THE CURATOR

Edward N. Peters was born in St. Louis, Missouri, on July 13, 1957. He attended Chaminade College Preparatory (1975) and St. Louis University (BA, 1979) and obtained his civil law degree from the University of Missouri at Columbia in 1982, being thereafter admitted to the Missouri Bar Association. In 1984 he married Angela Marie Morelli, and in 1985 he began course work in canon law at the Catholic University of America, being sponsored to studies by Bishop Robert Brom of the Diocese of Duluth. He obtained his licentiate degree in canon law in 1988, was named a Quasten Fellow for doctoral studies, and successfully defended his dissertation in August of 1991.

For two years he served as Chancellor and Defender of the Bond in the Diocese of Duluth under Bishop Roger Schweitz, O.M.I., and in 1992, he joined the staff of the Diocese of San Diego under Bishop Brom, where he served as Director of the Office for Canonical Affairs and as a collegial judge in marriage nullity cases in the diocesan and appellate tribunals for nine years. He currently teaches canon law for the Institute for Pastoral Theology at Ave Maria University in Michigan. His articles and reviews have appeared in a wide variety of scholarly and popular journals, and he is a frequent guest on Catholic media apostolates. He is the author of *100 Answers to Your Questions on Annulments* (1997) and the compilator of the *Tabulae congruentiarum inter Codicem iuris canonici et versiones anteriores canonum* (2000). He and Angela are home-schooling their six children.